CW00547090

# 'Parterres Bright with Flowers'

A history of the walled gardens at Alnwick Castle as revealed through excavations and standing building survey

The quote 'Parterres Bright with flowers' comes from a description of the garden published in the last decade of the nineteenth century:

*'There are terraces sloping up one above another, parterres bright with flowers arranged with geometric precision, parterres green with convolutions of Box and Ivy without flowers, leafy screens of Linden trees, squared edges of Yew and Privet almost as compact as masonry, banks with festoons of foliage on them, wide walks bordered on either side with wide flower-beds all the more brilliant for the contrast with their smooth grass bordering and on three sides of the goodly acres thus treated, stands a high red-brick wall covered with fruit trees....'*

(*The Gardeners' Chronicle* 1891)

Published by Pre-Construct Archaeology Limited

Copyright © Pre-Construct Archaeology Limited 2018

All rights reserved. No part of this publication may be reproduced, stored in a retrieval system or transmitted, in any form or by any means, electronic, mechanical, photocopying, recording or otherwise, without prior permission of the copyright owner.

ISBN 978-1-9996155-0-5

Edited by Victoria Ridgeway

Typeset by Cate Davies

**Printed by Henry Ling Ltd, The Dorset Press**

Cover image: The Garden as it may have appeared in the 1860s, looking south from the central conservatory

Inside cover images

Front: Illustration of convolvulus, or morning glory, from a notebook of 1796 portraying Chinese imports to Calcutta (DP/D2/1/182/15)

Back: Illustration of unidentified flower and fruit from a notebook of 1796 portraying Chinese imports to Calcutta (DP/D2/I/182/4)

# 'Parterres Bright with Flowers'

A history of the walled gardens at Alnwick Castle as revealed through excavations and standing building survey

By Victoria Ridgeway and Jennifer Proctor

*"The Public have still much to learn on the subject of Hothouses."*

(Banks 1811)

# PCA Monographs

# Contributors

| | |
|---|---|
| Principal authors | Victoria Ridgeway and Jennifer Proctor |
| Publication manager | Victoria Ridgeway |
| Academic advisers | Harry Beamish and Fiona Green |
| Project manager | Robin Taylor-Wilson |
| Post-excavation manager | Frank Meddens |
| Graphics | Josephine Brown and Cate Davies |
| Animal bone | Kevin Rielly |
| Reconstructions and modelling | Chris Mitchell |

# Contents

# Figures

# Summary

The walled garden at Alnwick lies some 300m east of Alnwick Castle, within the castle grounds. Extensive excavations and building recording carried out over two seasons, in 2000 and 2004, have revealed details of the garden's development from its initial origin as a kitchen garden in the mid-eighteenth century through various expansions, up until the eve of its transformation into its current incarnation as The Alnwick Garden. Indeed, the later stages of fieldwork were undertaken during construction work for the new garden; the cascade was already in place when the remains of a conservatory located against the north wall of the garden were being recorded in 2004.

The fieldwork, in conjunction with archival research, has established that the gardens underwent a series of modifications (and extensions) through time, which reflect both prevailing trends in garden and glasshouse technology and the interests of the various dukes and duchesses of Northumberland. The establishment of a chronological sequence of garden development can be hard to pin down; gardens, by their very nature, are subject to frequent change and modification and would vary seasonally as well as over the years. Nevertheless, it has been possible to identify some major changes in garden design, buildings and layout through time, as well as modifications to the technologies employed to maintain the various hothouses which occupied the garden. The text has been structured to reflect these major transformations, with successive dukes' alterations reflected in a series of garden designs, numbered Garden 1 to Garden 6; the evidence for these is presented in Chapters 2 to 7 of this book. Within this scheme the current Alnwick Garden forms Garden 7.

The construction of the first garden was thus overseen by the first Duke of Northumberland. Initially constructed in the 1760s or early 1770s, it covered approximately 1.5 hectares and was a kitchen garden, primarily intended to supply the castle household (and retinue) with fruit. But this garden also fulfilled another function, as a nursery for the cultivation of young trees which were used in planting up the surrounding landscape, to designs influenced by Capability Brown. Below-ground archaeological remains of the early garden were slight, amounting to evidence for a central pond. Three sides of the original brick and stone external walls of the earliest hothouse survived (Hothouse 1), constructed against the northern wall of the garden These were identified incorporated into the basement of a much later conservatory (Hothouse 6), illustrating how garden buildings were frequently modified and adapted through time to reflect changing fashions and requirements.

During the late eighteenth and early nineteenth centuries the second duke similarly made significant changes to the surrounding parkland, but also invested considerably in improvements within the walled garden. Forcing frames, hothouses and conservatories were built to assist in the cultivation of exotic fruit. Remains of a heated forcing frame were identified, as was one of the hothouses constructed during this period (Hothouse 2), incorporated into a later structure.

The most radical, and enduring, changes to the buildings within the garden were made c. 1830, in Garden 3. New construction, combined with modifications to existing buildings, created houses for the cultivation of peaches, grapes and pineapples, extensive remains of which survived until the time of the fieldwork. A central conservatory, with a domed cupola reflecting that which still survives at Syon today, no doubt involved extensive investment, but was a short-lived building, swept away in the 1860s during the most radical changes to the garden seen so far.

Led by the fourth duke and inspired by prevailing trends and the popularity of the 'Grand Tour', the new garden was extended to the south, and its size more than doubled. The new garden was Italianate in design, with strong architectural lines, a large ornamental pond and fountain, parterre borders, and sweeping vistas. Whilst the pinery, peach house and vinery of the third duke's garden remained, the redesign of the garden involved landscaping on such a vast scale that the backhouses of the original hothouse, constructed against the garden's north wall, were reduced to cellars, serving a newly-constructed grand conservatory above. Even though the fortunes of the castle and hence the garden declined during the twentieth century, many of the changes instigated by the fourth duke remained visible when fieldwork commenced in 2000.

Combining the results of excavation within the gardens and building recording work on the standing structures with an examination of hothouse technology and archival research, this book charts the first 200 years of the evolution of this remarkable walled garden.

# Acknowledgements

Pre-Construct Archaeology would like to thank The Alnwick Garden and Northumberland Estates for generously funding the archaeological project herein described.

For the 2000 season of work, the liaison role of W.A. Fairhurst and Partners during the early stage of the project is acknowledged. The curatorial role of Northumberland County Council Conservation Team, particularly Sara Rushton, Mike Collins, Karen Derham and Nick Best, is acknowledged.

The roles of Iain Ramage of Summers Inman, Peter Mouncey of Hopkins Architects and Aidan Harrison of Sir Robert McAlpine Limited are acknowledged for their assistance with the 2004 season as is Karen Derham, Northumberland County Council Conservation Team.

The 2000 season of excavations and building recording work were supervised by Robin Taylor-Wilson, assisted by Adrian Bailey, Jaki Benton, Zoe Coughlan, Andy Crabb, Julie Dilcock, Heather Hirons, Darren Lankstead, Jennifer Lowe, Scott MacDonald, Natasha Mulder, Rachel Nowakowski, Jennifer Proctor, Mark Randerson, William Ravenscroft, Steve Sampson, Pia Tohveri, Sean Wallis, Andy Willis and Don Wilson. The recording of the pavilion, remains of the conservatory and subsequent watching brief were undertaken by Adrian Bailey, assisted by Victoria Ridgeway, Emma Allen, Paul Morrison and Julie Parker. Victoria Ridgeway produced the post-excavation assessments for both phases of work and would like to thank Frank Meddens for his help and support during the writing of these reports.

The authors are indebted to Harry Beamish, for advice on the workings of hothouses and for showing them around the site at Auckland Castle, shortly following excavation. We are also grateful to Tim Maxwell for allowing access to Felton Park glasshouse and finally to Harry Beamish and Fiona Green for commenting on versions of this text. The archive research contained within this volume would not have been possible without the assistance, dedication and unfailing enthusiasm of Christopher Hunwick, Alnwick Castle archivist.

Many of the photographs within this volume were taken during the fieldwork, others were supplied by Robin Kent from survey work undertaken in 1998 (marked RK 1998) or by Victoria Ridgeway between 2015 and 2017 (shown with the initials VR and the date). The authors are grateful to Darryn Wade for permission to use his beautiful contemporary photographs of the garden and castle. Chris Mitchell produced the reconstruction images for this publication working with us to produce models of the gardens at two specific points in time. We are not only grateful for the excellent models of the garden he has created, but would also like to thank him for his enthusiasm for the project, his patience and his insightful questions concerning particular aspects of the buildings and landscape which have in turn enhanced our own awareness and understanding of these gardens.

We are indebted to Josephine Brown and Cate Davies for their enduring patience over endless revisions to the graphics. This publication is very much the result of a collaborative effort between the principal authors and the graphics staff.

*Dedicated to the memories of Valerie Proctor and David Ridgeway, both of whom inspired an enduring love of archaeology and gardens in their respective daughters.*

# Chapter 1

## Introduction

*'Alnwick Castle, Alnwick; Duke of Northumberland. A most extensive castellated pile, with curious ornaments : the grounds of great extent, watered by the river Alne, and well wooded. The kitchen-garden lately much improved by a range of hot-houses erected from the designs of J. Hay, Edinburgh.'*
(Loudon 1825, 1080)

Archaeological investigations were undertaken by Pre-Construct Archaeology Limited (PCA) at Alnwick Castle Gardens, Alnwick Castle, Northumberland in 2000 and 2004 in advance of re-development of the historic walled gardens known today as The Alnwick Garden. The work was commissioned by The Northumberland Estates, although since the completion of the fieldwork an independent trust, The Alnwick Garden, has been created to manage the re-development project.

Standing structures and below ground archaeological remains of successive gardens of the dukes of Northumberland, dating from *c.* 1772 onwards, were recorded during the archaeological project. Many of the dukes of Northumberland were promoters of gardening excellence, as reflected in the changes to the layout of the gardens through time. The hothouses, constructed as part of the original walled garden and modified and adapted as technologies progressed, bear witness to the dukes' reputations as men at the forefront of design and technological innovation and reputed collectors of exotic specimens.

Many of the developments and innovations introduced at Alnwick may have been first implemented at the conservatory gardens of Syon House, the London home of the dukes of Northumberland.

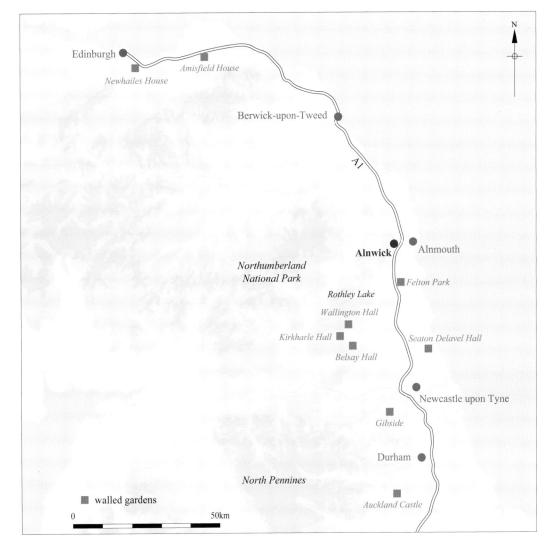

**Fig. 1.1** The site location, showing contemporary walled gardens in the vicinty (scale 1:1,250,000 )

## 1.1 Site Description and Setting

Alnwick Gardens form part of the extensive lands of Alnwick Castle, the second largest inhabited castle in England (the first being Windsor Castle), sometimes called the 'Windsor of the North', located on the north-eastern edge of the market town of Alnwick in north Northumberland. The town is situated on the River Aln *c.* 8 km west of the coast, and 12 km by river from Alnmouth where the river enters the sea (Fig. 1.1). The border town of Berwick-upon-Tweed lies approximately 46km to the north and Newcastle upon Tyne 59km to the south.

The town of Alnwick occupies a terrace of land overlooking the River Aln, to the north, with the castle constructed on a natural promontory. The first walled garden was constructed *c.* 300m

to the south-east of the castle towards the northern edge of this terrace just before the point where the land drops steeply down towards the river (Fig. 1.2). The 48m contour runs around the top of the castle ramparts in the south-east and along the northern and north-eastern edges of the walled garden, beyond which the ground slopes steeply away to the River Aln, which, *c.* 200m to the north of the walled garden, follows the 25m contour (Fig. 1.3). The walled garden lies on ground that slopes down from south-west to north-east. The underlying solid geology of the area is sedimentary bedrock of the Scremerston Coal Member; sandstones, siltstones and mudstone formed in the Carboniferous Period (British Geological Survey 1975). In the vicinity of the site the superficial deposits overlying bedrock are glaciofluvial sand and gravel deposits of Devensian origin.

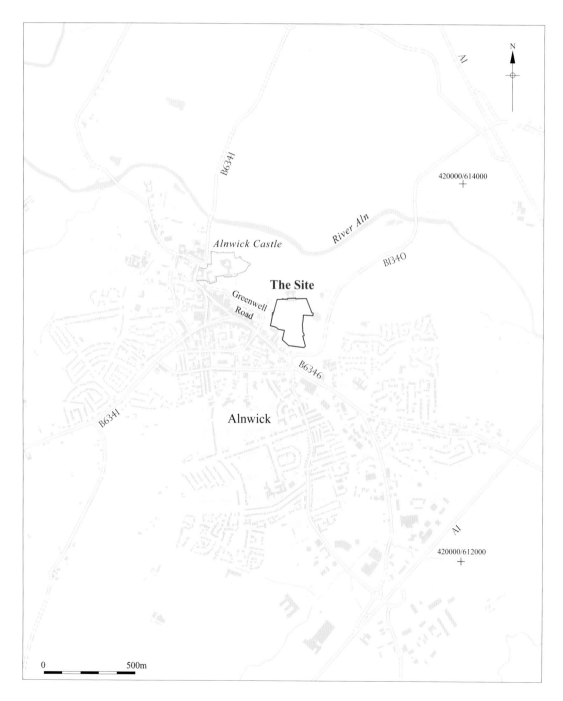

**Fig. 1.2** Alnwick Castle and Gardens in their modern setting, in relation to the town of Alnwick (scale 1:20,000)

In 2000 the gardens were surrounded on all but the south-eastern side by a perimeter wall, stretches of which date from various periods of the garden's history, which encompassed an irregular-shaped hexagonal walled garden at the southern end. In total, the walled garden comprised an irregular-shaped area covering *c.* 3.8 hectares with a maximum distance from wall to wall of 255m north–south and 225m east–west (Fig. 1.4). The perimeter wall stood up to 5.10m high externally and 4.20m internally above ground level, ground level inside the garden having been raised substantially over the centuries of use, and in some areas was in a state of disrepair. Access to the gardens was through a gate in the north-western corner, which had been widened at some date, via Greenwell Road off Bondgate. There had been a maximum of nine gates in total through the garden walls although at the time of the fieldwork only three were in use, the gate in the north-west corner of the garden (Entrance 1), a second one adjacent to the northern pavilion (Hothouse 1/Hothouse 6; Entrance 4), and one adjacent to the Gardener's House (Entrance 2). Several dilapidated stone structures in varying states of disrepair stood in the garden at the time of the fieldwork; these represent the remains of backhouses which once contained the heating infrastructure for long-since demolished glasshouses attached to the front.

Over the course of the last 250 years, these gardens have been variously termed the 'kitchen gardens', 'walled gardens', 'old gardens' and 'conservatory gardens'. Prior to their redevelopment, their function changed from kitchen garden to more decorative gardens for display, eventually being used as a nursery for the cultivation of young trees, ironically echoing

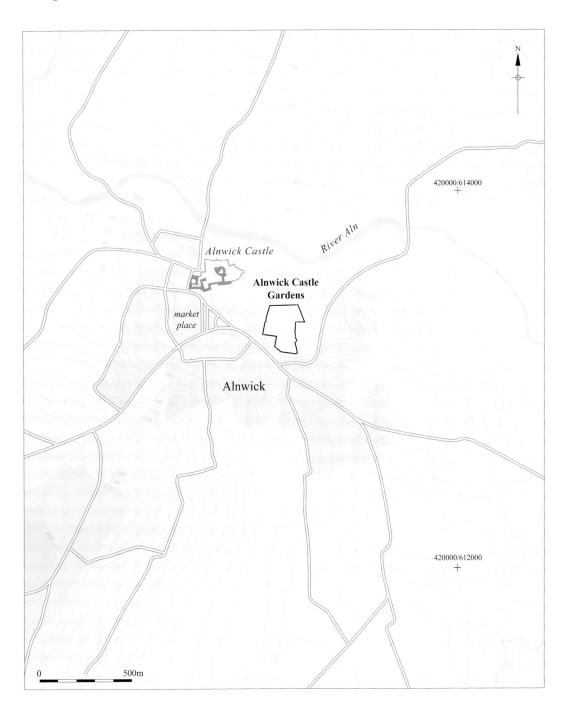

**Fig. 1.3** Alnwick Castle and Gardens in relation to their nineteenth-century setting showing the natural topography, road layout and extent of the town, *c.* 1860 (scale 1:20,000)

their first use (see section 10.3 below); to avoid confusion with the modern Alnwick Garden, within this publication, the gardens subject to archaeological study will be termed the Alnwick Walled Garden.

Their history begins with Hugh, the first Duke of Northumberland (1750–1786), who embarked on a major programme of reorganisation of both the castle and its extensive grounds. The walled 'kitchen gardens' were created *c.* 1772,

set *c.* 300m to the south-east of the castle. Modifications and enlargements to this garden were carried out by the second (1786–1817), third (1817–1847), and fourth (1847–1865) dukes of Northumberland. The garden's fortunes began to decline during the First World War and it was turned over to productive use during the Second World War as allotments for vegetable growing. The present project, The Alnwick Garden, began in 1996, was instigated by the current Duchess of Northumberland,

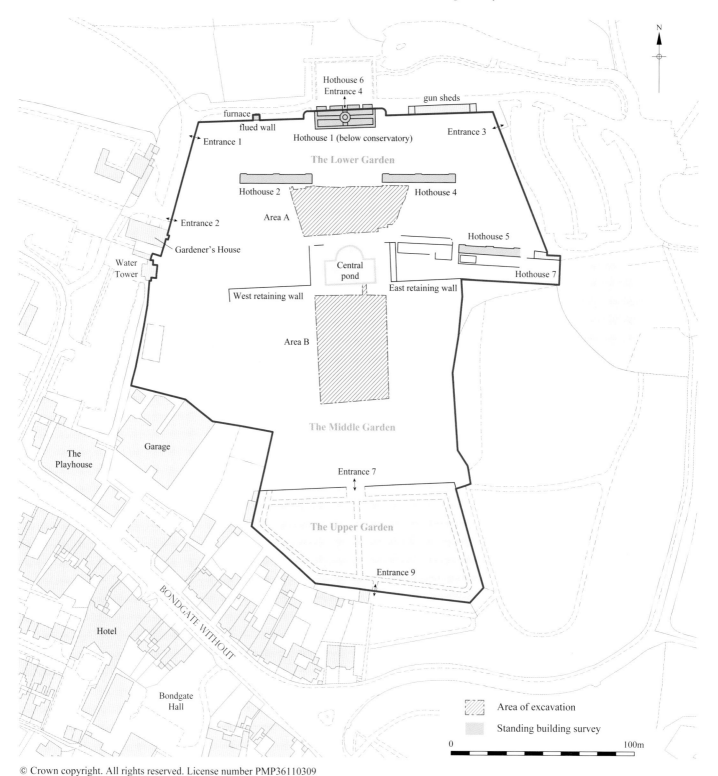

© Crown copyright. All rights reserved. License number PMP36110309

**Fig. 1.4** The lower, middle and upper gardens showing areas of archaeological investigation and standing building survey (scale 1:1250)

Jane Percy, whose vision was to transform the derelict walled gardens into a 'Garden for the 21st Century', thereby re-creating the former splendour of the site through an innovative and ambitious design. These remodelling works provided the impetus for the archaeological and building recording works recorded here.

## The Gardens at the time of the 2000 fieldwork

Three distinct areas within the Alnwick Walled Garden are associated with the chronological expansion of the gardens. The northernmost lower original walled kitchen garden, set out *c.* 1772 by the first duke, comprised a trapezoidal area of *c.* 1.5 hectares sloping away gently to the east, which measured *c.* 210m east–west by *c.* 70m north–south (see Fig. 1.4). In 2000 the lower garden was surrounded on three sides by the garden boundary wall, most of the southern wall having been demolished in the mid-nineteenth century when the garden was expanded by the fourth duke. Adjacent and external to the central part of the northern boundary wall was a cellar which, prior to external landscaping, formed the backhouses for the hothouse constructed here *c.* 1772 (Hothouse 1). This had subsequently been substantially modified and incorporated into a new conservatory (Hothouse 6). The north-west perimeter wall was originally constructed as a flued wall, heated by an external furnace located towards the centre of this segment of wall. Two gates along the west wall (Entrance 1 and Entrance 2) appear to be contemporary with the earliest garden.

The dilapidated ruins of a large stone hothouse built by the second Duke of Northumberland (1786–1817) were situated in the western part of the lower garden (Fig. 1.4, Hothouse 2). This had been significantly modified by the third duke (1817–1847) and, at the same time, further hothouses constructed of which two (Hothouse 4 and Hothouse 5) survived in a similarly ruinous condition. Of these buildings Hothouses 1, 2, 4, 5 and 6 were to be demolished and all were subject to detailed standing building recording. Open area excavation, designated 'Area A', was carried out in the central area of this lower garden, which partially revealed remains of a large conservatory (Hothouse 3) and other structural remains. At the time of the fieldwork the

**Fig. 1.5** Aerial photograph of the walled garden before excavation showing the standing remains of hothouses, the pond and the northern conservatory (compare Fig. 1.4). Seen from the north-west the southern extents of the garden extend beyond this photograph and are largely obscured by trees

remainder of the eastern side of the lower garden was covered with saplings and dirt access tracks, the central part was covered in waste grassland and the western part was covered with rough grassed areas, waste ground and an area of tarmac in the north-west corner (Fig. 1.5). In the south-eastern corner of the original lower garden were the remains of a small hothouse which had subsequently been converted into a toilet block, dilapidated in 2000 (Hothouse 7); remains of this structure, which was not subject to standing building recording, still survive in this part of the garden.

The 'middle' garden, to the south of the lower garden, largely dates from modifications carried out by the fourth duke, *c.* 1860, although the western side was incorporated at an earlier date by the second duke who created a walled kitchen garden adjoining the original lower garden to the south-west. A house external to the west wall was built by the second duke between 1808 and 1811 for his head gardener; this has been renovated and is now used as offices for The Alnwick Garden. A sandstone water tower with castellated walls was constructed to the south of this house by the third duke. At the time of the fieldwork this was largely intact, though dilapidated, and has now been renovated. A gate through the garden wall was situated between the tower and the house.

The middle garden comprised a roughly rectangular area of *c.* 1.7 hectares sloping down steeply to the north. This measured a maximum of 220m east–west by 130m north–south. Historic features surviving in the middle garden at the time of the fieldwork largely dated from the re-design of the garden in the 1860s by the fourth duke. Towards the northern end of the middle garden were two substantial east–west aligned stone ashlar retaining walls situated to either side of the central axis of the garden. Between the retaining walls was a central pond, rectangular with an apse on the northern side; by 2000 it no longer contained water. Ashlar cross-terrace retaining walls were situated to the east and west of the central pond, elements of which remain and have been incorporated into the modern garden. An avenue of hornbeams ran to the south of the east retaining wall but by 2000 only the southern side of the corresponding avenue adjacent to the west retaining wall survived. A central mound at the southern end of the middle garden was flanked on both sides by symmetrical curving earthworks. The areas to the east and west of these earthworks were covered by plantations of mixed mature trees while to the north of the central mound was a rectangular area planted with conifer saplings. Open area excavation, designated 'Area B', was carried across the sloping ground to the south of the pond.

On higher, level ground to the south, was the 'upper' garden, also dating from *c.* 1860, comprising an irregular hexagonal walled

kitchen garden of *c.* 0.6 hectares and a maximum of 120m east–west by 60m north–south, surrounded by a brick wall. Access from the middle garden was via steps leading up to a central triple-arched gateway in the northern boundary wall. This was part of two pairs of sixteenth-century Venetian gates bought by the fourth duke; three of these gates now hang in the entrance to the upper garden with a fourth in the main entrance into the garden. An ornamental iron gate hung in the central opening with plain iron gates of more recent origin to each side. At the time of the archaeological fieldwork in 2000 this garden was largely occupied by a larch plantation with an overgrown tennis court in the eastern side. A path ran around the perimeter of the upper garden and another bisected the area north–south leading from the gate in the northern wall.

Standing structures dating from the time of the fourth duke also survived in the lower garden. Adjacent to the central part of the northern boundary wall was a structure known at the time of excavation as 'the pavilion' which comprised a paved terrace with a small central pond and surrounding stone balustrade; this represents the demolished remains of a conservatory built in 1862 (Hothouse 6) and constructed over the foundations of the earliest glasshouse (Hothouse 1). Part of the original northern garden wall had been demolished to accommodate this conservatory and the perimeter wall surviving in this area in 2000 stepped back to the north to encompass the structure with curved walls to either side adjoining the original perimeter wall. A gate led through the garden wall from the centre of the pavilion on the north–south axis which ran through the garden from the upper garden in the south. In 2000 one of the Venetian gates hung in this gateway through the northern wall.

Attached to the external side of the north-eastern boundary wall in the lower garden were single-storey external buildings known as the gun sheds built by the sixth duke (1867–1899). These were used for site offices and tool storage by the archaeologists during the fieldwork and subsequently refurbished as visitors' toilet blocks and offices as part of the new Alnwick Garden. These were not subject to excavation or standing building survey as part of this project.

At the time of the investigations present ground level at the southern boundary of excavation lay at *c.* 66.80m OD and at the northern boundary of the walled gardens lay at *c.* 51.60m OD, a drop of 15.20m over 240m. The lowest part of the gardens at the time of the excavation was adjacent to the boundary wall in the north-east corner where ground level lay at 48.50m OD. A series of raised banks and mounds in the central part of the garden represent landscaping associated with the *c.* 1860 re-design of the garden and it was evident that substantial landscaping activity had taken place within the gardens.

# 1.2 Planning Background

The archaeological investigations were undertaken in advance of the re-development of the historic walled garden at Alnwick Castle as a new garden. Even at an early stage, and with just conceptual designs available, it was evident that the proposed scheme would almost certainly lead to the loss of components of earlier designs of the garden, as well as demolition of buildings included within the curtilage. Prior to the archaeological investigations, an assessment of historic buildings and structures at the site had been commissioned by The Northumberland Estates (Kent 1998), as was a desk-based study outlining the historical development of the garden (Green 1998). Structural reports on the condition of the perimeter walls of the garden and associated buildings and all structures within the gardens were also commissioned by The Northumberland Estates (Fairhurst and Partners 1998a; 1998b; 1998c).

Northumberland County Council Conservation Team (NCCCT) recommended an archaeological field evaluation of the site prior to determination of the planning application for the re-development scheme. Two archaeological trial trenching evaluations were undertaken in 1998 (Young 1998; McMaster 1998) the conclusions of which were outlined in an 'Archaeological Recording Action Brief', prepared by English Heritage in 1999, to advise Alnwick District Council (Dix 1999). The findings of the evaluations suggested that the condition of buried archaeological remains would vary between different parts of the site. The Alnwick Garden was to be developed in stages, with the main component of Phase 1 being the creation of a spectacular water feature, 'The Grand Cascade', within the sloping central portion of the old 'middle garden'. Underlain by vast holding tanks, it was evident that any archaeological remains within that area would be destroyed by the development. The removal of the central ornamental pond, retaining walls of the cross-terrace and three ruined hothouses was also proposed. In addition, there was to be significant ground reduction in the central portion of the original 'lower' garden, immediately to the north of the central pond. The brief prepared by English Heritage outlined the necessity for open area excavation, earthwork survey and standing building recording, to record important archaeological and structural remains at the site prior to their destruction.

## Archaeological methodology

The Project Design for the archaeological investigations was prepared by PCA following discussions with The Northumberland Estates, Fairhurst and Partners, NCCT and the English Heritage Regional Advisor on Archaeological Science (Taylor-Wilson 2000). This document contains details of all the methodologies employed during excavation and post-excavation phases of work. There were three elements to the fieldwork: earthwork survey; standing building recording; and open area excavation.

## Earthwork survey

Earthworks derived from the mid nineteenth century re-design of the garden still dominated the rising ground to the south of the central pond. An analytical survey of these remains was undertaken to record 'soft' detail (essentially the earthwork remains themselves, where the points to be measured were a matter of subjective judgement). An overall site survey was also undertaken, primarily to record 'hard' detail, and a contour plan of the site was produced from the electronic data, although this proved to be of little use in terms of illustrating any detail of the earthworks.

## Standing building recording

The structural remains within the garden comprised the following: the brick garden boundary walls and inner garden cross walls; a central pond and its ashlar terrace retaining wall; the ashlar cross-terrace retaining walls, to the east and west of the central pond; three hothouses; the 'pavilion' (terrace with small central pond, representing the structural remains of a former conservatory) with underlying cellar adjacent to the northern boundary wall. Gun sheds on the northern boundary wall, the water tower on the western boundary wall and the toilet block at the south-eastern corner of the gardens were standing at the time of the survey, but were not recorded as part of these works.

The design proposals involved demolition of the central pond and its southern terrace retaining wall, the cross-terrace retaining walls and the three hothouses. A full archive record of these structures (a Level 3 survey) was required, as defined by the Royal Commission on the Historical Monuments of England (RCHME 1991). The remainder of the standing structures were to be incorporated into the development scheme.

Rectified photography supplemented by field recording was employed to record elevations of all three hothouses, the interior of the pond and its retaining wall and the cross-terrace retaining walls. Additional recording included hand drawn plans, elevations and sections at scales of 1:100, 1:20 or 1:10. A full detailed photographic record was also compiled of the structures using 35mm SLR cameras, employing monochrome print and colour slide formats.

Structural recording within the three hothouses was limited by Health and Safety considerations. The condition of the western and south-eastern hothouses allowed the interiors of these buildings to be investigated within the main phase of fieldwork at the site, between 28th February and 1st April 2000. As partial demolition

**Fig. 1.6** The site during excavation in spring 2000, looking north; the 'pavilion', which constitutes the remains of the original northern conservatory, Hothouse 6, can be seen in the distance

**Fig. 1.7** The site, during recording work on the northern conservatory, Hothouse 6, in spring 2004; looking north, this is the same view as that shown in Fig. 1.6, illustrating the construction of the Cascade in Alnwick Garden in the intervening period

**Fig. 1.8** The Alnwick Garden in 2015, looking north, following construction of the Pavilion Café

of the eastern hothouse had to be undertaken before its interior could be investigated, structural recording took place during a later phase of fieldwork between the 4th and the 11th July 2000. Where possible, archaeological excavation was undertaken within the hothouses in order to identify features associated with earlier structural phases. Archaeological recording within the structures followed the methodology set out below.

Recording of the 'old pavilion' or former conservatory and underlying cellar (the backhouse of Hothouse 1) took place in May 2004. The terrace of the pavilion, was surveyed using a Total Station (TST) EDM and located with respect to the Ordnance Survey grid established during the 2000 investigations. It was drawn in plan (1:50) and the full southern elevation of the surrounding balustrade was drawn (1:10). A photographic record was compiled. Recording of the cellar was undertaken prior to removal of its vaulted roof and the terrace above. Artificial lighting was used to illuminate the cellar whilst all recording work was undertaken. The interior of the cellar was cleaned by the archaeological team prior to the photographic record being compiled, since the floor was covered with *c.* 50mm of soil and the ruined furnace was almost completely buried by *c.* 1m of material. Due to the restricted working area, rectified photography could not be undertaken within the cellar prior to demolition. The entire floor of the cellar, along with the surviving elements of the furnaces at either end, was drawn in plan (1:20). The entire northern elevation was drawn (1:10) and the southern elevation was drawn (1:10), to illustrate different builds (including representative samples of brickwork), with detail of pipework added. Two perpendicular cross-sections across the structure were based on existing architect's drawings.

A watching brief was undertaken during groundworks in the vicinity of the cellar. However, it proved impossible to record in any detail archaeological deposits within this area due to Health and Safety considerations; the considerable depth of the excavated area along with the unstable nature of deposits meant that it was not safe to enter the trench, although it was possible to observe archaeological features in some areas.

**Open area excavation**

Open area excavation was undertaken within two areas (Areas A and B) between 1 March and 21 April 2000 (see Fig. 1.4). Area A, situated in the central part of the lower garden, comprised a trapezoidal area covering a total area of 1,406m² which measured 26m north–south by a maximum of 66m east–west in the north. Area B occupied the sloping ground located to the south of the pond in the centre of the middle garden. It measured 38m east–west by 57m north–south covering a total area of 2,188m².Topsoil and any modern overburden in Areas A and B was removed

using a 20–ton 360° tracked excavator. Following an initial phase of archaeological recording in part of Area A, further ground reduction took place by mechanical excavator to expose underlying archaeological deposits of significance. Thereafter, all cleaning, excavation and recording was undertaken by hand; a team of up to 20 field archaeologists was employed to undertake the investigations in Areas A and B. Post-excavation assessment reports described the archaeological methodologies employed during the work, included descriptions and illustrations of the archaeological remains and quantified the written, graphic and photographic elements of the project archives and contained specialist assessments of all the artefactual and palaeoenvironmental evidence. (Ridgeway 2004; 2005). Northumberland Historic Environment Record (HER) holds a copy of the assessment reports. The completed archives comprising written, drawn and photographic records and artefactual material recovered will be deposited at the Great North Museum, Newcastle upon Tyne under the site code ACG00 for the first phase of fieldwork and ACG04 for the recording of the pavilion and cellar.

## 1.3 The Historical Background

Following the Norman Conquest, the site of Alnwick Castle was given to the Norman Lord, Gilbert de Tesson, William the Conqueror's standard-bearer at the Battle of Hastings. At this time there are no records of a castle, though it is possible that a simple motte-and-bailey was constructed. Around 1096 the land fell to Yves de Vescy, who built the first recorded castle, described as 'very strongly fortified' in the 1130s. Frequently besieged by Scottish Kings, the castle was substantially rebuilt and by 1157 most of the structure now visible had been constructed. It had a circular keep composed of a series of towers surrounding a courtyard, with two outer keeps or baileys and was perhaps one of the first Norman castles of this form. The castle continued to feature sporadically in conflicts between Scotland and England. In 1314, the direct male line of the de Vescy family died out with the death in battle of the final (and illegitimate) heir, William de Vescy. It appears, however, that his father (also William) had already given the manors of Alnwick to Anthony Beck, Bishop of Durham, who sold the castle and Barony of Alnwick to Henry de Percy in November 1309.

Henry, the first Lord Percy of Alnwick, was a descendant of William de Percy, who had accompanied William the Conqueror in 1066, and already possessed lands in Yorkshire, Lincolnshire and Sussex. By the time the Percy family acquired Alnwick Castle they were already one of the most powerful and influential families in England. Maintaining the general form and design of the castle, Henry began a process of restoration. The history of the castle and the Percy family remained tumultuous, bound

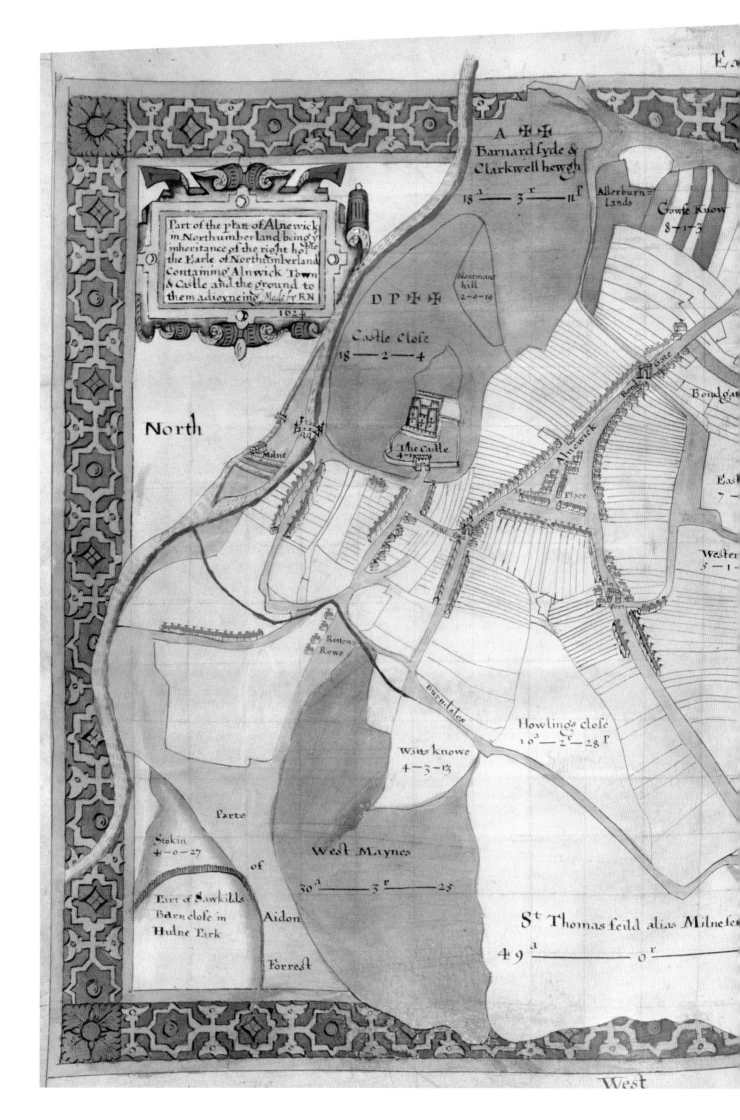

10

North

West

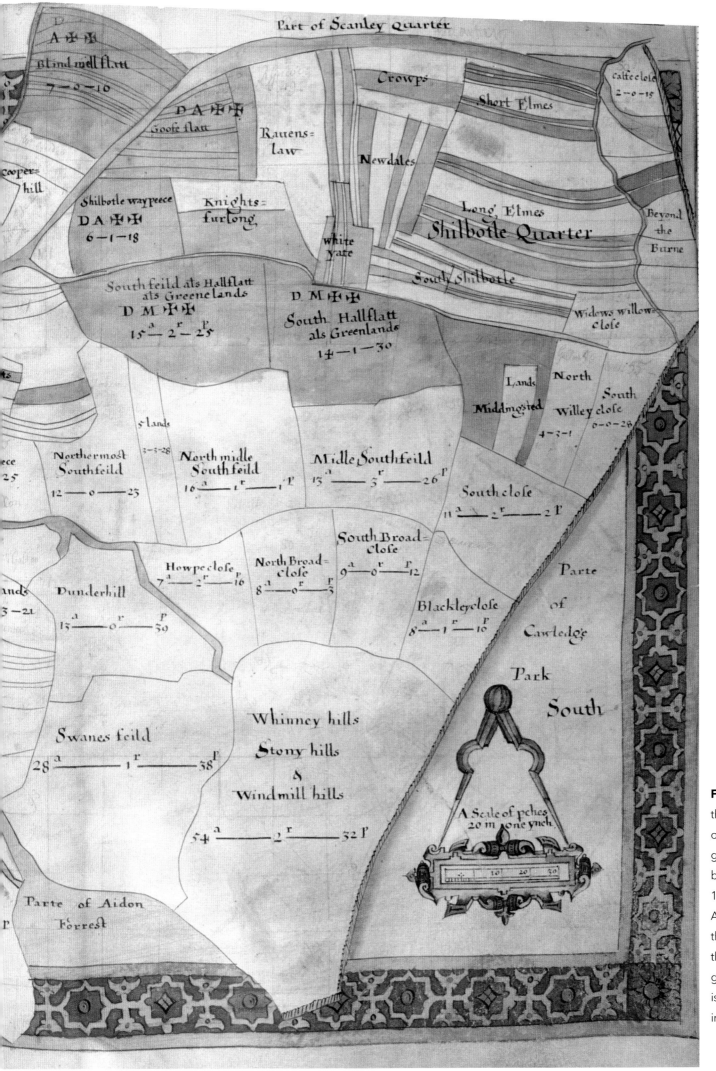

**Fig. 1.9** 'A platt of the town and castle of Alnwick and the grounds adjoining', by Robert Norton, 1624, showing Alnwick before the creation of the walled kitchen garden NB north is to the left of the image (AC O/I/1b)

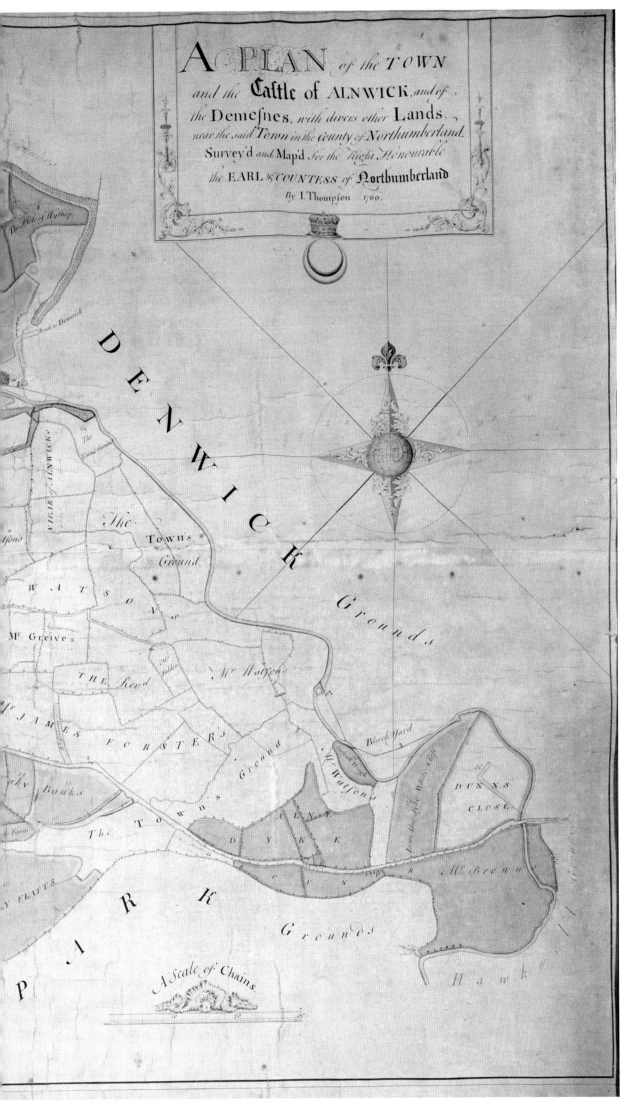

**Fig. 1.10** 'Plan of the Town and Castle of Alnwick', by I. Thompson, 1760; the castle grounds appear to have been extended since Norton's map (Fig. 1.9) was produced, but the garden has not yet been enclosed (AC O/I/7)

up in Border conflict and the Wars of the Roses, and by the early seventeenth century the Earls of Northumberland had ceased to live at Alnwick and their influence in the north declined. Over the next hundred years or so the fortunes of Alnwick deteriorated and the castle fell into a state of disrepair. In 1677 it was only partly habitable and by 1691 part of it was in use as a school. The last Earl of Northumberland, Josceline, died in 1670 and was succeeded by a daughter, Elizabeth, Baroness Percy, Duchess of Somerset who was widowed twice before marrying Charles Seymour, the sixth Duke of Somerset in 1682. He restored part of Alnwick Castle for his son, Algernon. The duke and duchess were also at this time in possession of Syon House in the county of Middlesex and the property remains with the Percy family today. Algernon, who succeeded the duke and duchess in 1748, acquired the title of Earl of Northumberland following a distinguished career in the army. He was the first member of the family to live in the castle in over a hundred years. Algernon was succeeded by a daughter, Elizabeth, who married Sir Hugh Smithson, a Yorkshire baronet in 1740.

It is with Sir Hugh Smithson, who became the Earl of Northumberland in 1750 and the first Duke of Northumberland in 1766 when the earldom was raised to a dukedom, that the history of the walled gardens at Alnwick Castle begins. Sir Hugh embarked on a major programme of reorganisation of both the castle and its extensive grounds. He modernised farming of his lands and reorganised the administration and management of the estate. He employed the celebrated Robert Adam as architect for the renovation of the castle, which was restored, inside and out, in a Gothic style. The bank extending from the ramparts of the castle down to the River Aln was landscaped and the area planted with trees, creating a 'picturesque' setting for the castle under the direction of Lancelot 'Capability' Brown, who had been taken on to transform the gardens and parkland around the castle, and bring them up to the forefront of contemporary design. As part of these transforming works, the walled 'kitchen gardens' at Alnwick Castle were first created, set at a distance of approximately 300m to the south-east of the castle.

The area where the walled garden was to be constructed is shown as a close called 'Barniside' on a 1760 'Plan of the Town and Castle of Alnwick,' with open fields to the south and the river to the north (Thompson Fig. 1.10). By 1772, a sub-rectangular enclosure labelled 'Garden' had been constructed with a structure shown towards the centre of the northern wall (Thomas Wilkin, see Fig. 8.1). This is presumably a representation of the garden as initially laid out by the first Duke of Northumberland. The first duke died in 1786, although a 1788 map probably largely reflects the first duke's works (Sauthier, see Fig. 8.2). This shows the garden divided into a series of regular rectangular plots or beds with a central pond and a

hothouse spanning the centre of the north perimeter wall, hinting at the beginnings of the duchy's horticultural preoccupations. A contemporary account of the first duke's walled garden by one of his gardeners, Peter Wadell, describes how it contained espaliered fruit trees and a vinery and was also used as a nursery to grow trees for planting in the parks and pleasure grounds designed by Capability Brown (Acc 163; see section 10.3 below).

The second duke (1786–1817), also named Hugh after his father, was a military man who fought in the Seven Years' War with Germany, the American War of Independence and the Napoleonic campaigns. Despite his impressive military career, the duke still found time for his garden, promoting the cultivation of exotic fruits and investing in new hothouses, a fruiting pine stove, two vineries and a mushroom house between 1808 and 1811 (Shrimpton 2006, 58).

The third duke (1817–1847), again named Hugh, was a keen collector of exotic plants and varieties from around the world were brought to Alnwick to be cultivated (Shrimpton 2006, 64). The third duchess, Charlotte Florentia, a painter and plantswoman, built fashionable rockeries and stocked the garden with exotic flowers; the interest in the gardens was such that in 1842 they were opened to the local gentry one day a week (August 2006, 104). Both the second and third dukes extended the gardens, constructing additional walled kitchen gardens adjacent to the original eighteenth-century garden.

Algernon, the fourth duke (1847–1865), implemented a radical programme of improvements to the estate and significant alterations to the original garden were undertaken. He travelled extensively and became fascinated with Renaissance Italy; Anthony Salvin was commissioned to remodel the castle in an Italian High Renaissance style, work on which commenced in 1854 but was not finished in either his, or his successor's lifetime (August 2006, 104). The acquisition by Algernon of land to the north of Bondgate Within, the Goose Knows hillside field to the south of the original gardens, almost doubled the size of the walled garden and William Andrews Nesfield was commissioned to draw up plans for a new Italianate garden (Shrimpton 2006, 64). The duke's plans for the walled garden were monumental and reflected the increasing trend away from the 'picturesque' and the naturalistic landscaping of Capability Brown towards a much more formal Italianate style. Although Nesfield's design was never implemented, an Italianate garden was created with parterres, pond, walkways and a sunken area in the shape of a Maltese cross (August 2006, 105). This garden was in the process of being constructed at the time of the fourth duke's death in 1865 (Shrimpton 2006, 64). The fourth duke was a great benefactor, creating endowments for sailors and building schools, churches, farmhouses and cottages on the estates; Hulne Park, the parkland surrounding the castle, was opened to the public on Sundays and Thursdays.

Successive dukes continued to maintain the gardens at Alnwick over the next fifty years. Following a short dukedom, George, the fifth duke (1865–1867), died at the age of 87. Algernon the sixth duke (1867–1899) and Henry seventh duke (1899–1918) oversaw the flourishing success of the gardens. By the 1880s there were 20 acres (*c.* 8 hectares) of flower garden and 7 acres (*c.* 2.8 hectares) of kitchen gardens and Alnwick Castle Gardens were the subject of much attention from regional amateur gardening societies as well as national gardening press (Shrimpton 2006, 73). By 1900, 21 staff were employed in the gardens, including six gardeners to care for the exotics in the Conservatory and to maintain the Palm House, Vineries, peach house and pine-stoves (*ibid.*; see section 10.2 below).

The decline of the Castle Gardens began with the First World War. The glasshouse element of the south-eastern vinery, Hothouse 7, was pulled down in 1935; the building's backhouse remains standing and represents the only surviving structural remains of the hothouses which once stood in the garden. The garden was turned over to intense vegetable growing during the Second World War, as part of the 'Dig for Victory' campaign and produce from the garden was sold locally. The financial success of this enterprise came to an end when food shortages in the years after the war abated; the remaining glasshouses were dismantled in 1953 and the walled garden given over to the Woods Department to be used as a conifer nursery, seeing the use of the gardens turn full circle (Shrimpton 2006, 73).

## 1.4 The Garden Reconstructions

From an early stage we were determined that one of the best ways to illustrate the gardens at Alnwick was through artist's reconstructions. As well as recreating an artistic impression of a particular period and location, undertaking such an exercise usually raises, and ultimately helps to answer, important questions about the remains encountered and Alnwick Castle Gardens were no exception. Our initial publication outline provided for some three-dimensional modelling, which was intended to bring the results of archaeological excavation, standing building recording and topographic survey together.

**Fig. 1.11** The third duke's garden as it may have appeared in the mid-1830s, based on standing building recording, archaeological excavation and cartographic evidence, viewed from the south-east; planting beds for which no evidence survives are deliberately left blank, reconstruction by Chris Mitchell (c.mitchell02@btinternet.com)

**Fig. 1.12** The fourth duke's garden as it may have appeared around 1870, based on standing building recording, archaeological excavation and cartographic evidence, viewed from the south; planting beds for which no evidence survives are deliberately left blank, reconstruction by Chris Mitchell (c.mitchell02@btinternet.com)

We had also allowed for two reconstruction images, the principal aim of which was to show how the hothouses and other buildings appeared in their garden settings. Following consultation with reconstruction artist Chris Mitchell it was decided to create three-dimensional models of the garden, using 'Sketchup' software and to use these as the basis for producing the resulting reconstruction images. Taking this approach meant that rather than creating still views from two fixed viewpoints, we were able to view the garden from whatever vantage point we chose. Rather than concentrating efforts on a 'finished image' this has resulted in a series of somewhat schematic and impressionistic views, which it is hoped will assist with visualising what it may have been like to experience these gardens.

There were some constraints on what we were able to illustrate. The gardens, as this monograph demonstrates, were fluid and subject to constant change, both to their appearance, and in the technologies employed through time as well as by season. The first decision to be made was what period(s) to show; resources would not allow for full reconstructions of all gardens at all periods, and therefore two distinct time periods were chosen.

The ensuing decision to illustrate the gardens *c.* 1830 and *c.* 1870 was determined by the evidence available and the perceived value of the resulting images. For Gardens 1 and 2 it was decided that there was too little available information to produce meaningful reconstructions, the garden was relatively empty at both periods, furthermore the extent of these gardens, presence and appearance of Hothouse 1 would be indicated by the reconstruction of Garden 3. A further consideration was the geographic extent of coverage. Being enclosed by high walls, the garden would have been viewed as a discrete entity (see section 10.3 below) and thus reconstruction ends at the perimeter to the gardens, albeit with some indications of tree cover beyond. The resulting models are described below.

The first model, illustrating Garden 3 around 4pm on an October afternoon in the mid-1830s, is based on standing building recording and excavation supplemented by information from Barnfather's map of 1829. It does not include modelling of additional kitchen gardens to the south and east as indicated on this mapping, which fell beyond the limits of excavation. It shows the garden following the construction of curvilinear hothouses, Hothouse 2, Hothouse 4, Hothouse 5 (see Chapter 4), the backhouses of which were recorded during excavation. Their appearance from the north is based on the surviving rear wall of Hothouse 4. The presence of curvilinear glass frontages to these structures is implied by the 'Bailey Bill' of 1836, their extent in plan and presence of internal subdivisions has been determined by excavation and surviving documentation and the form of the superstructures has been based on a roughly contemporary and relatively local example at Felton Park, Northumberland (see sections 5.4 below, 9.3 below). No archaeological evidence was found for the frontage of Hothouse 1, although its dimensions in plan could be determined by the excavation of the backhouses to this structure in conjunction with Barnfather's plan of 1829; a reconstruction in the form of a simple lean-to glasshouse frontage to this vinery is presented here. Reconstruction of the central conservatory, Hothouse 3, was more problematic as only a small section of the foundations of this building's curving frontage was observed archaeologically. The reconstruction of this structure is based on records of the late 1820s, which state that the builders of the magnificent conservatory which still survives at Syon Park, were '*now engaged in erecting a most extensive range of the same kind at Alnwick Castle*', and evidence presented on Barnfather's map of 1829, which indicates a dome to the rear of the structure and a curved frontage flanking by two wings (see section 10.3 below). Indications of a decorative parterre, enclosing hedging, pond and pergola in front of this hothouse are again based on Barnfather. Within this model the planting beds that flank these structures are deliberately left blank (shown green). No evidence for such planting was encountered and this would, in any case, change with the seasons. The beds may have been occupied by annual vegetables and flowers, as well as more permanent planting, perhaps in the form of fruit trees, espaliered along path edges.

The second model depicts the newly expanded Fourth Garden in the late afternoon or early evening in August, at some time in the early 1870s. The massive expansion brought about by the inclusion of Goose Knows field into the garden's perimeter and attendant landscaping is clearly demonstrated here. More evidence survives for this garden than for earlier manifestations, in terms of plans, documentary evidence, standing building recording and archaeology; additionally, a few photographs survive from the early twentieth century (see Chapters 4 and 8). In this reconstruction, the central conservatory (Hothouse 3) has been swept away, Hothouse 1 has been demolished and the area levelled. The northern garden wall has been slightly extended to accommodate a large and imposing conservatory (Hothouse 6), for which sufficient archaeological and documentary evidence survives to enable a faithful reconstruction of the form of this building. Hothouses 2, 4 and 5 were retained with little external

modification, other than changes to the external ground surfaces surrounding these buildings. A new building, Hothouse 7 (elements of which survive), was constructed in the south-east corner of the garden. The large, ornamental, central pond survived to be recorded, while details of its central, red granite fountain were found within the castle archives. The triple-arched entranceway to the garden from the south, which would have provided access to the gardens for the public, still survives at the time of writing, as do the Gardener's House and water tower to the west of the garden. Excavated evidence combined with original designs held in the archive, enabled the parterres to be indicated. As with the reconstruction of Garden 3, the planting beds that flank the central beds and hothouse structures, for which no evidence survives, have been deliberately left blank.

Details of the particular views chosen for representation in this publication will be commented on below, where appropriate. Obviously, these reconstructions are somewhat schematic, but it is hoped they will lead the viewer to a better comprehension of the size, appearance and scale of these impressive gardens and the massive transformations they underwent, often over short periods of time.

## 1.5 Contemporary Walled Gardens in the Region

Alnwick is only one among many contemporary gardens across Northumberland, East Lothian, and Durham which are comparable in date and which have been referenced in this publication as comparanda for the Alnwick Walled Garden (see Fig. 1.1). It was until recently perhaps unique in the region in terms of the extensive excavation and survey work which has been carried out, although recent investigations at Auckland Castle have revealed extensive remains of structures within its southern walled garden (Beamish 2014).

The walled garden at Gibside, County Durham, is being restored by the National Trust. This garden, built 1734–36, was provided with a heated wall in 1771 and pineapple house in 1772. Essential repairs to a hot-wall at Belsay, constructed *c.* 1833, enabled the detailed recording of this structure (Green 2000). Excavations at Amisfield, East Lothian revealed remains of a central glasshouse on the north wall and revealed stonework from a 1783 building containing both a tile hypocaust system and later cast-iron pipe heating system. Raised beds and walkways related to the original use as a pineapple house (pinery-vinery) built by the Wemyss Estate, while at Newhailes House, also in East Lothian, a collapsed 18th-century heated wall has been recorded (Connolly *et al.* 2012). At Auckland Castle excavation and building recording have revealed details of two pinery-vineries set close to the northern wall of an extensive walled garden, terraced into a steep slope. Several peach houses and other heated garden structures were also revealed (*ibid.*). Examination of the excavated heating apparatus, particularly the evidence for hot-air flues, has been extremely informative in helping to reconstruct the systems in use at Alnwick (Beamish 2014). Restoration work has recently been carried out on a curvilinear glasshouse and heated garden wall at Felton Park, Northumberland. The date and construction details of this structure are closely comparable to those of the vinery and probably also the peach house at Alnwick (Beamish 2016).

## 1.6 The Report Structure

The focus of this publication is on the mid-eighteenth to early twentieth century Castle Gardens, their organisation, expansion, use, appearance and the changing technological developments which were employed in the heating systems of the various glasshouses. Very little evidence was found pre-dating the establishment of the walled garden in the mid-17th century. The evidence that was found reflects the natural topography of the site and medieval and early post-medieval horticultural and agricultural use and this is detailed below as a precursor to the description of the Castle Gardens.

The archaeological investigations have resulted in the identification of five main phases of garden development (Gardens 1–5) that can broadly be equated to the tenure of various dukes. Garden 6 refers to the use of the garden during the 20th century; the original walled garden was given over to food production during World War II and was subject to a lengthy period of decline in the post-war years. Garden 7 refers to the present Alnwick Garden, construction of which began in the early years of the 21st century. Documentary and cartographic evidence has revealed the broad timescale during which construction of the garden schemes of the various dukes began (see Fig. 1.13); in some cases, modifications and additions to these schemes continued after the death of a particular duke. This diagram also illustrates the principal structures constructed during each phase of garden; the excavation, standing building survey and documentary and cartographic research has revealed that many of these structures were long-lived, with some being constructed in the earliest phases of the garden and subsequently modified. The function of individual structures therefore

changed over time, but in this publication they are referred to as Hothouses 1–6. Historically attested hothouses, for which no archaeological or standing building evidence was found, are not numbered. In this text individual context/feature numbers appear in square brackets [100].

Within this volume Chapters 2–7 present the evidence for each of the gardens as outlined above. Each of these chapters begins with a brief introduction, putting the garden into its historic setting, before the archaeology and standing buildings for that garden are described. Chapter 8 presents a detailed chronological summary of the gardens, based on the foregoing chapters, surviving documentary evidence and contemporary mapping. Chapter 9 presents a review of technological developments of the period, primarily in relation to hothouse construction and heating, concluding with a consideration of the hothouses identified at Alnwick and their specific functions. Chapter 10 discusses the experience of being in the garden, the plants grown, the people who worked there and the appearance of the garden in its landscape setting.

## Terminology

The term 'hothouse' here refers to any structure with a heated glass frontage in which the plants are grown, and backhouses to the rear which contain heating mechanisms and which might be used for a range of additional functions. Initially termed 'stove', because of the method of heating used in the earliest structures, 'hothouse' is a term which implies a heated structure constructed and maintained for the cultivation of tropical and subtropical plants, in contrast with a conservatory or greenhouse, which would tend to be cooler (Grant 2013, 17). Heating would have been supplied to the frontage of a hothouse via one of several mechanisms (detailed in section 9.2 below): from furnaces within backhouses to the rear via a central hot wall, via flues along the wall or beneath the floors, or by pipes carrying hot water. Individual furnaces and boilers gave way to more centralised systems over time, particularly in larger establishments like Alnwick. Various technologies were employed at Alnwick, including the provision of steam heating from a central boiler, and these are described below in due course. The land-use diagram presents a model of the development of the garden, including the use and modification of garden structures and the numerous elements of the garden identified by excavation (Fig. 1.13).

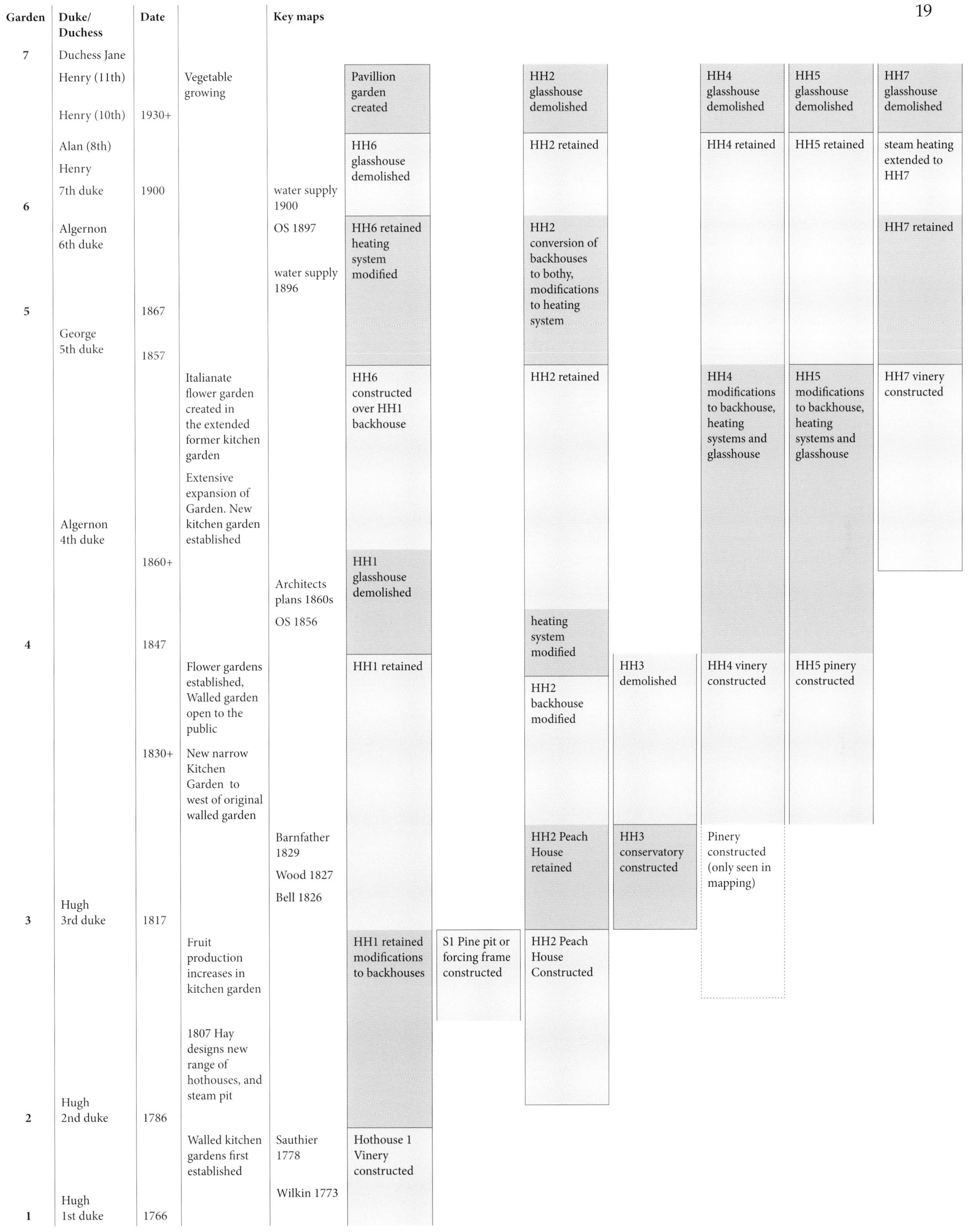
Garden
Duke/ Duchess
Date
Key maps
7
Duchess Jane
Henry (11th)
Vegetable growing
Henry (10th)
1930+
Alan (8th)
Henry
7th duke
1900
water supply 1900
6
Algernon 6th duke
OS 1897
water supply 1896
5
1867
George 5th duke
1857
Italianate flower garden created in the extended former kitchen garden
Extensive expansion of Garden. New kitchen garden established
Algernon 4th duke
1860+
Architects plans 1860s
OS 1856
4
1847
Flower gardens established, Walled garden open to the public
1830+
New narrow Kitchen Garden to west of original walled garden
Barnfather 1829
Wood 1827
Bell 1826
Hugh 3rd duke
3
1817
Fruit production increases in kitchen garden
1807 Hay designs new range of hothouses, and steam pit
Hugh 2nd duke
2
1786
Walled kitchen gardens first established
Sauthier 1778
Wilkin 1773
Hugh 1st duke
1
1766
Pavillion garden created
HH6 glasshouse demolished
HH6 retained heating system modified
HH6 constructed over HH1 backhouse
HH1 glasshouse demolished
HH1 retained
HH1 retained modifications to backhouses
Hothouse 1 Vinery constructed
S1 Pine pit or forcing frame constructed
HH2 glasshouse demolished
HH2 retained
HH2 conversion of backhouses to bothy, modifications to heating system
HH2 retained
heating system modified
HH2 backhouse modified
HH2 Peach House retained
HH2 Peach House Constructed
HH3 demolished
HH3 conservatory constructed
HH4 glasshouse demolished
HH4 retained
HH4 modifications to backhouse, heating systems and glasshouse
HH4 vinery constructed
Pinery constructed (only seen in mapping)
HH5 glasshouse demolished
HH5 retained
HH5 modifications to backhouse, heating systems and glasshouse
HH5 pinery constructed
HH7 glasshouse demolished
steam heating extended to HH7
HH7 retained
HH7 vinery constructed

**Fig. 1.13** The chronology of construction and changes in garden design at Alnwick

**Glossary of terms used in this report**

*Alnwick Walled Garden*   The area of walled garden covered by this publication (see Fig. 1.4), this term is used to distinguish this from other areas of kitchen garden.

*Backhouse*   The masonry element of a hothouse, usually forming the northern half of the structure, which contains back sheds, furnaces or other heating apparatus.

*Basement*   Element of a building below ground floor level. Used in this report to describe elements of the hothouses which had floors below ground floor level but shared the same roof height as adjoining spaces. Generally, the term is used in reference to furnace rooms. These are technically semi-basements, but the term *basement* is used here (particularly for brevity in illustrations) to distinguish such spaces from *cellars* with roofs at ground floor height and rooms above.

*Cellar*   Room below ground floor level, with a roof at ground floor height and rooms above.

*Conservatory*   Similar to a hothouse, a conservatory, in common with a greenhouse, is often, but need not necessarily be, artificially heated.  Usually attached to a building, a conservatory may also be placed against a wall or may be freestanding. Throughout the 18th century the terms 'conservatory' and 'greenhouse' were interchangeable, but in the 19th century the meanings diverged; the greenhouse was used for the overwintering and propagation of evergreen plants, whilst the conservatory would be used for the cultivation of both temporary and more permanent plants and was frequently linked to a large house as an 'outdoor room'.

*Curvilinear*   In relation to glasshouses, the term 'curvilinear' is applied extensively in contemporary literature and refers to a building in which the glazed elements are curved, in whatever plane.

*Glasshouse*   The glazed element of a hothouse, in which plants are grown, usually the southern part of the structure.

*Hothouse*   Any artificially heated and glazed structure, greenhouse or glasshouse, in which delicate plants, needing protection from cold weather, can be grown, overwintered or forced. In this publication it refers to those structures which comprise a backhouse and glasshouse element.

*Spine wall*   Commonly termed the 'back wall' in contemporary literature, the term 'spine wall' has been extensively used here to refer to the central wall between glasshouse and backhouse and to avoid any confusion that the term 'back wall' might introduce in relation to the overall hothouse structure.

*The Alnwick Garden*   The Duchess of Northumberland's newly created garden within the area of the Alnwick Walled Garden.

# Chapter 2

## Garden 1, the Garden of the First Duke (1766–1786)

*'..if the place where you intend to make the Kitchen garden should not be level, but high in one part and low in another, I would by no means advise the levelling it; for by this situation you will have advantage which could not be obtained on a perfect level, which is, the having one part dry ground for early crops, and the low part for late crops, whereby the kitchen might be better supplied throughout the season with the various sorts of herbs, roots, &c.'*

(Miller 1754)

To appreciate the landscape setting of the earliest walled garden at Alnwick Castle, and to understand the process of land acquisition that led to the garden being established where it was, it is necessary to consider archaeological deposits which preceded garden construction.

Natural glaciofluvial deposits revealed wherever excavations were sufficiently deep in the lower garden (Area A) varied in colour and composition, but were identified by their lack of inclusions and clean and locally consistent nature. The level of the natural sub-stratum displayed a marked slope from south down to north across this area, with a gentler incline from west to east. The highest recorded height in the far south-west was 51.57m OD, encountered at a depth of *c.* 0.60m below ground level at the time of the 2000 fieldwork. A minimum (untruncated) height of 49.26m OD was recorded at the eastern limit of excavation at a depth of *c.* 1m below the 2000 ground level.

To the south, attempts were made to reach natural sub-stratum in the middle garden (Area B) by machine excavation, but the major scheme of landscaping associated with Garden 4 in this area had buried the original ground level under deep ground-raising deposits. Only at the far north of the middle garden, adjacent to the southern edge of the pond, were deposits encountered which can reasonably be interpreted as being of natural origin. At this location, natural sub-stratum was encountered at a level of 51.40m OD at a depth of *c.* 1.80m below the 2000 ground level. The height of the natural sub-stratum therefore dropped over 2m across *c.* 50m.

There is no evidence for any occupation of the land prior to the medieval period. Traces of the agricultural use identified by excavation in Area A included a shallow, curvilinear drainage gully up to 0.20m deep extending for 2.40m, the primary clay fill of which may represent a deliberate lining to facilitate drainage (see Fig. 4.5). This would have lain within a medieval or later field system. The gully was overlain by a 0.40m-thick developed soil which produced seven sherds of medieval pottery This was probably re-worked into a plough soil since it bore evidence of a plough scar on its upper surface. Elsewhere across the site, other traces of medieval activity appeared to have been obscured by later reworking of the deposits.

In the early seventeenth century, the land where the walled garden was to be constructed lay within an area of agricultural fields located to the east of Alnwick Castle and to the north of the town, with the river Aln lying beyond to the north (see Fig. 1.9). This area is shown on a 1758 as a close named 'Barniside' (see Fig. 1.10).

At the northern end of the middle garden, layers of colluvium cut by deep plough scars up to 0.10m wide and 0.30m deep, were filled and sealed with plough soil. This deposit was over 0.70m thick and although no dating evidence was recovered, such a depth of accumulation suggests development within an open field over a relatively long period of time,

The garden was thus constructed on a high terrace overlooking the River Aln, also occupied by Alnwick Castle to the west, approximately 200m beyond which the ground slopes steeply down to the river. Natural deposits and horizons indicative of previous agricultural use were generally deeply buried below contemporary ground level, due to the deposition and accumulation of soils caused by centuries of gardening, as well as deliberate landscaping events. The landscaping in the middle garden was particularly prominent, with substantial quantities of imported sand across the excavated area. It is possible that some of this material derived from contemporary excavation of the central pond and the associated terrace construction, although the quantities involved suggest that material would also have been imported from elsewhere (see section 5.2 below).

## 2.1 The Construction of the First Walled Garden at Alnwick

Following his marriage to Elizabeth Seymour in 1740, Sir Hugh Smithson was to inherit the Percy Estates of Alnwick Castle and Syon House in London in 1750 and become the first Duke of Northumberland in 1766. Already a keen gardener, having improved the parklands of his estate at Stanwick, North Yorkshire, he set about redesigning the landscape at Syon. Lancelot 'Capability' Brown was commissioned for this work and swept away the formal landscape to the south and west of Syon House, replacing it with the open views characteristic of the English Landscape movement. The history of the gardens at Syon and Alnwick are inextricably linked and many of the innovations in garden and hothouse technology within Syon's walled kitchen garden were paralleled at Alnwick. Sir Hugh brought his head gardener from Stanwick, Thomas Call, to Alnwick to begin transforming the Alnwick landscape and in 1751 Call produced a plan for the redesign of the parklands into pleasure grounds (Shrimpton 2006, 37). By the late 1760s, Capability Brown also became involved with the first duke's parklands' scheme at Alnwick (*ibid.*)

The precise date of construction of the walled garden is unknown, but cartographic evidence demonstrates that it was built between 1760 and 1772. The earliest known plan depicting the walled garden is Thomas Wilkin's (1772), which shows a sub-rectangular enclosure labelled 'Garden' located *c.* 300m to the south-east of the castle on the terrace of land which overlooks the River Aln (Fig. 8.1). A structure is depicted against the northern wall with four backhouses extending beyond the line of the wall, although this plan is assumed to be rather schematic as a subsequent 1788 map shows the layout of the Garden 1 in greater detail and the hothouse is shown with three backhouses (Fig. 8.2).

Large stretches of the original boundary wall survive along three sides of the garden with an external furnace on the north-west wall which was a heated wall for growing fruit. Standing building recording of a cellar situated adjacent to the central north wall revealed elements of the now below-ground remains of the original backhouses of the Garden 1 hothouse attached to the north wall. Sauthier's plan (1788) plan shows the garden divided into a series of regular rectangular plots or beds with a central pond. Whilst this may be a schematic convention used by the artist to represent any large garden (Green 1998), elements of a central pond and associated path deposits revealed during the archaeological investigations in roughly this location suggest that the plan reflects, at least, an approximation of the layout of the first duke's garden.

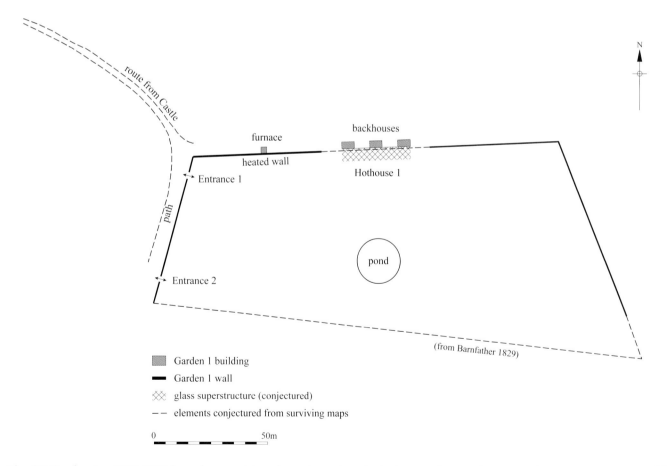

**Fig. 2.1** Garden 1, *c.* 1760-1772, based on surviving elements, archaeological excavation, conjecture and contemporary map evidence (scale 1:1600)

## 2.2 Excavated Remains of Garden 1

### Garden soils

Predominantly silty and sandy soils varying in thickness from 0.25m to 0.80m, and with a combined maximum thickness of *c.* 1.25m were recorded towards the central part of Garden 1 (Area A). These soils presumably represent use of the garden over some length of time, with little formal structure or construction taking place. Where untruncated, these deposits reflected the topography of the area, sloping down from south-west to north-east. Towards their lower interfaces, the soils typically became progressively cleaner, with indistinct interfaces with underlying deposits suggesting working-in of natural material. In places, dumps of crushed sandstone had been used to raise levels or facilitate drainage. These deposits are broadly interpreted as representing garden soils, but probably largely incorporated earlier plough soils. A small quantity of medieval pottery, seventeenth-century clay pipe fragments and some eighteenth-century pottery were recovered from the garden soils.

### Central pond and encircling path

A few surviving elements of a central ornamental pond with brick and sandstone surround represents the earliest evidence for development of the land as a formal garden. Waterlain deposits representing the silting of the pond and a segment of enclosing wall together formed elements of a pond, correlating with the large central circular pond shown on Sauthier's 1788 map, with a projected internal diameter of 18m. The construction cut for the base of the pond [1517] was traced for 4.20m east–west, with a gently sloping side, and a more pronounced drop to a level base at a maximum depth of 0.30m. The pond was filled with waterlain silts and clays from which three sherds of late eighteenth- or possible nineteenth-century pottery, an iron buckle, probably for a horse, and a strip of leather were recovered. Waterlain deposits were observed extending for a distance of at least 14.50m north–south.

The only recorded evidence for the pond wall was on its eastern side were a 0.60m-wide and 0.19m-deep linear construction cut exposed for a length of 2.50m, containing the remains of a partially robbed-out red brick and sandstone wall. The bricks were handmade and slop-moulded and broadly datable to the eighteenth to nineteenth century, presumably manufactured at the earlier end of this range.

To the north of the pond, the remains of a path comprising a 0.15m-thick crushed yellow sandstone surface overlying a 0.40m-thick silty sand levelling/make-up deposit were recorded at the limit of excavation. To the east, two deposits incorporating significant quantities of coal, ash and cinder may have provided well-draining path surfaces. The location of these surfaces correlates with a path encircling the pond on the 1788 plan.

## 2.3 Structural Remains of Garden 1

### Hothouse 1

Cartographic evidence demonstrates that the earliest hothouse in the garden (Hothouse 1), located at the centre of the northern boundary wall, was built by 1772 at the latest. Wilkin's (1772) plan depicts a long rectangular structure with four projecting

Location of section

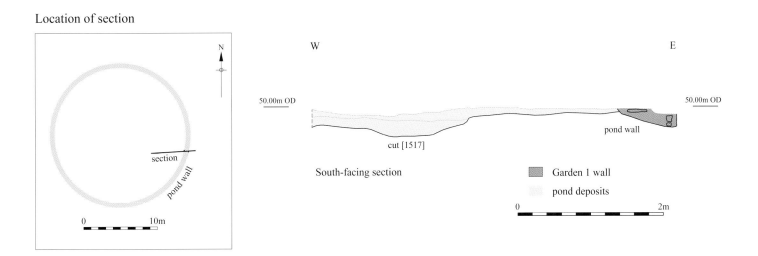

**Fig. 2.2** Section through the pond in the central part of Area A (scale 1:50)

elements along the northern side, external to the garden wall (see Fig. 8.1). The building is probably more accurately shown by Sauthier (1788) who depicts a building in the same location with three backhouses (see Fig. 8.2); this corresponds more closely to the excavated evidence. By 1826 (Garden 3) the structure had been modified with the original three backhouse rooms amalgamated into one long rectangular structure (see Fig. 8.3). Subsequent rebuilding (Garden 4) associated with the construction of a conservatory (Hothouse 6) and a major change in external ground levels, resulted in the structure changing from what was originally a semi-basemented backhouse to a fully below-ground cellar (Garden 4). The conservatory was demolished in the twentieth century, and the base converted into an ornamental garden with central pond and surrounding balustrading, formed of the lower part of the original walls of Hothouse 6, known as the 'old pavilion' (Garden 6).

The cellar, as surviving in 2004, comprised a rectangular sunken structure, *c.* 30m long east–west by *c.* 2.30m wide, with a vaulted brick roof up to *c.* 2.40m high and a stone flagged floor throughout. The recording work and subsequent analysis identified three major phases of construction and heating modifications within the cellar, the earliest of which represents the few surviving elements of the original backhouses of Hothouse 1, constructed before 1772. Parts of the eastern and western furnace rooms with a few internal features and the spine wall which formed the northern wall of the glass-fronted element and the southern walls of the backhouses were identified.

Several factors suggest that parts of the 'cellar' and associated features are likely to date to the original construction of the hothouse before 1772. Numerous modifications to the structure through time suggest that the cellar was in existence over a long period and different construction techniques, building materials and mortars were apparent. Various heating technologies were employed within the structure, again indicating use over a considerable time span. The foundations of the earliest phase of building appear to have been reused and modified throughout the building's use. Cartographic evidence suggests that the overall east–west dimensions of the structure did not change through time and therefore it seems probable that the earliest elements of building identified through the survey equate to the earliest structure constructed on site.

The spine wall, which measured 29.38m east–west, had been subject to substantial modifications and a later brick duct and other structural features built in front of it all but obscured the original build. However, the two courses of the original spine wall [4001] could be seen above and behind a brick duct for a maximum height of 0.38m. This was constructed with randomly coursed, squared sandstone blocks, bonded with pale creamy

mortar. This wall, which was contiguous with the garden's north wall, would have continued to a higher level; the brick-vaulted ceiling being a later modification to the building (see Fig. 2.8, Fig. 5.24).

The east and west walls of the structure and elements of the north wall at each end represented surviving elements of the original backhouses at either end of the building; the eastern and western furnace rooms (Rooms 1 and 3). As with the visible part of the southern wall, these were all constructed with randomly coursed, squared sandstone blocks, bonded with pale creamy mortar.

Room 1, the western furnace room, was 2.20m wide internally and the 1.95m-high wall defining its northern side survived for a length of 4.80m with the west end of the room defined by wall [4028]. A 1.05m-wide and 1.85m-high door provided access into the backhouse from the north, external to the Garden 1 perimeter wall. A small area of original flagstone floor [4038] visible internally had a *c.* 0.60m-high brick structure [4032] constructed on top of it. Subsequent modifications had largely disguised its original form, but it is assumed to have been the base of a furnace or a platform for such representing the earliest heating system for the glasshouse to the south (Fig. 2.3). The surviving elements comprised two projecting east–west aligned side walls in the east with a gap of 0.35m between and a platform in the west. A brick-lined heating duct [4033] which exited through the south-western corner of the building at an angle, seems likely (on the basis of construction techniques and location) to have been associated with the earliest phase of use of this structure.

The eastern furnace room was similarly constructed with a doorway in the north; the east wall survived along with part of the north wall (Fig. 2.7). A brick-lined heating duct [4020] in the north wall in the corner of the room, mirroring that in the western room, was the only surviving evidence for the original heating system. Part of the original flagstone floor [4014] also survived, at a height of 49.32m OD. Holes in two of the flagstones set 0.40m apart hint at the presence of a removed fitting in this area. Two test pits excavated through the floor of each room during the evaluation phase of work revealed natural clay sub-stratum overlain by make-up deposits up to *c.* 0.25m thick for the floor of the building, although in both excavated areas the surviving floor represented a later replacement.

The furnace rooms or firehouses would have been built as subterranean rooms so that the fireplaces could be constructed at a suitable height for optimum performance of the hot air system used to heat the glasshouse.

Sauthier (1788) depicts a third, central backhouse which may also have contained a furnace. The presence of later walls and

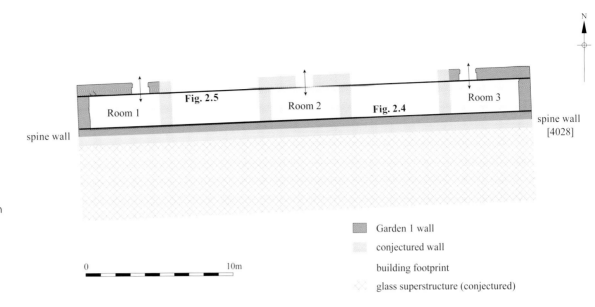

**Fig. 2.3** Hothouse 1, Garden 1, plan of backhouses and conjectured glasshouse frontage (scale 1:250)

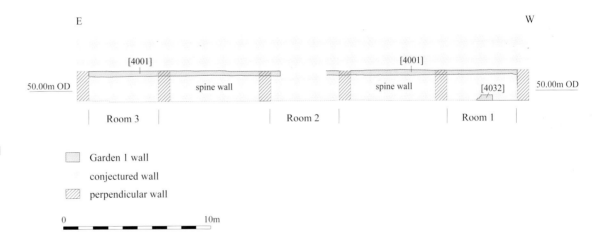

**Fig. 2.4** Hothouse 1, internal north facing elevation of the spine wall showing Garden 1 elements (scale 1:250)

**Fig. 2.5** Hothouse 1, internal south facing elevation of the three backhouse walls showing Garden 1 elements (scale 1:250)

**Fig. 2.6** Hothouse 1, western backhouse room (Room 1), showing brick-lined heating duct [4033] exiting the south-western corner of the building (scale 0.5m)

**Fig. 2.7** Hothouse 1, eastern backhouse room (Room 3) showing the eastern and northern walls with later nineteenth-century brick floor [4015] on top of original flagstones [4014] (scale 1m)

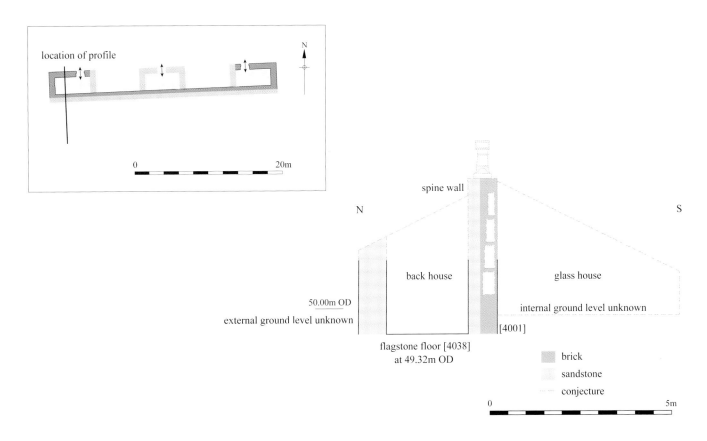

**Fig. 2.8** Hothouse 1, Garden 1, profile showing recorded elements and the conjectured superstructure (scale 1:100)

a water tank (Garden 5) obscured any elements of the original build which may have survived in this area, although this arrangement remains plausible. This third, central furnace room (Room 2) has been conjectured (Fig. 2.3, Fig. 2.4). Wilkin (1772) depicts four furnace houses; whether this is an inaccuracy in mapping or a depiction of an early arrangement cannot be established on the surviving evidence, although the former seems more likely.

A 0.68m-wide and 0.70m-high brick-lined vent [4009] extended out of the north wall in the corner of the backhouse and ran westwards and upwards out of the room. This was also probably associated with the earliest heating system. A similar feature was identified at the eastern end of the southern wall of the building. The latter appeared, at the time of the field survey, to have been recently blocked up. The phasing of these vents was not established although they appear integral with the original build. It seems unlikely, given their position in the northern wall, that they were intended to convey heat to the glasshouse element of the structure and may have been associated with drawing fresh air into the backhouse to aid the efficient functioning of the furnaces.

The earliest heating system thus identified was presumably a simple furnace fuelled by coal in each of the backhouses. The hot air produced by the furnace would have been directed through ducts in the corner of the rooms into internal flues through the south wall of the structure to heat the glasshouse to the south. Given the early date of these furnace rooms and the presence of a heated garden wall to the east, it is considered most likely that this element of the building was provided with a heated wall (see section 9.1 below). The garden wall in this location had been demolished at the time of the survey and replaced by a new wall line set back to the north from the original (compare Wood 1827 and Ordnance Survey 1856; Fig. 8.4, Fig. 8.10).

The precise level of the associated external ground surfaces could not be established with any certainty. At the time of the survey, external ground surface lay at around 52m OD, but watching brief observations determined that this had been raised considerably by the deposition of layers of sand. The internal level on which the furnaces were constructed lay at around 49.33m OD. The presence of flues forming part of the original build and leading out of the southern wall of the backhouse in Room 1 provide an indication of the possible level of the internal floor of the glasshouse element of this building, which would have been at about 50.50m OD. We might reasonably assume that this equates (more or less) to the internal ground level in the original garden; north of the garden wall the ground may have sloped away.

## Boundary wall

Large sections of the original boundary wall constructed between 1760 and 1772 survive, as suggested by cartographic evidence and the size of the bricks used in its construction (Kent 1998, 6–9). The external faces of the garden wall were built in stone, a much more durable fabric than brick, with the internal faces brick built, a material more suited to cultivation of fruit trees. The southern wall of Garden 1 was demolished ahead of the substantial expansion of the garden by the fourth duke (Garden 4).

The east wall, aligned approximately north-west to south-east, extends for 81m and is 5.10m high externally at the north end and 4m high internally; the wall was heightened after 1860 (Chapter 5; Fig. 2.1; Kent 1988). The wall is 0.60m wide and the inside face is built in a rough facing bond brick and the external face with regular coursed sandstone rubble. The west wall, aligned approximately north-east to south-west, extends for 60m and is 0.60m wide and 3.40m high, topped with sandstone slab coping stones; this segment of wall does not appear to have been heightened. At the time of the survey the original lime mortar survived.

Two entrances through the west wall, in the north-west (Entrance 1) and south-west (Entrance 2) corner of the garden are contemporary with Garden 1 (Fig. 2.1); Sauthier's 1788 plan indicates entrances at these locations with a path leading to them from the castle (Fig. 8.2). Entrance 2 survives in its original form as a gateway with a gothic arch (Fig. 2.9; Fig. 2.10) but Entrance 1 has been widened and modified at some stage (Fig. 2.11). The location of the gates is typical for gardens of the period as the entrance would be situated along the shortest wall in order to provide the longest view of the garden (Campbell 2005, 45). The north-west gate at Alnwick is likely to have been the principal entrance as it was the first gate along the route from the castle; Entrance 2 in the south-west corner may perhaps have been for staff. This is supported by a contemporary description of the garden (Acc 163) which describes refuse being transported out of the garden and manure brought in via the southern entrance (see section 10.3 below).

The northern wall is now divided into two segments (Fig. 2.1) but would have originally extended for a distance of *c.* 160m; the central part of this wall would have formed the back wall of Hothouse 1. A *c.* 45m-long central stretch of this wall was demolished in the 1860s to accommodate a conservatory built by the fourth duke with a new stretch of boundary wall stepped back to the north (Garden 4). Although this would have formed one contiguous wall, the two elements either side of the central section were of differening construction and so are described separately here. The north-east wall survives for a length of 58m and is 0.58m wide and 4m high; this is of the same construction as the east wall and has also been heightened.

**Fig. 2.9**  Garden 1, Entrance 2 in south-west corner of original walled garden, internal view, looking west to the outside of the garden (VR 2015)

**Fig. 2.10**  Garden 1, Entrance 2 in south-west corner of original walled garden, external view, looking east to the inside of the garden (VR 2015)

**Fig. 2.11**  Garden 1, Entrance 1 in the north-west corner of the garden (RK 1998)

## Heated wall and external furnace

The north-west wall, which also survives for a length of 58m (demonstrating the symmetry of the garden), was a heated wall with internal horizontal flues; several flue access doors or cleaning holes, all at the same level, survive on the external side of the wall. The internal face is built in facing bond brickwork and the external face is built in regular coursed sandstone rubble. The original Garden 1 wall survives to a height of 2.80m high wall, raised to 4m (Garden 4). Espalier frames which survived on the internal face in 2000 are a later modification, but as this wall was constructed as a heated wall for growing fruit, supports for fruit cultivation would have been integral to its function.

An external furnace is located towards the central part of the heated wall of wall, *c.* 30m from the north-west corner of the garden (Fig. 2.1). The 1788 map shows that the furnace had been built by this date (see Fig. 8.2). The furnace is square in plan and was constructed with sandstone ashlar; the upper part and battlements are a later build (Fig. 2.13). A pointed arched door situated on the sheltered east side would have prevented excessive draughts aggravating the problem of overheating which was inherent in heated walls (Kent 1988, 8). The structure is semi-basemented and flue connections with the heated wall survive internally. Built within the north wall is a Maltese Cross loop window which is now extremely eroded.

**Fig. 2.12** Internal (south-facing) element of Garden 1 heated wall; this brick elevation is the southern side of the wall shown in Fig. 2.14 (VR 2015)

**Fig. 2.13** External furnace for Garden 1 heated wall showing the eroded Maltese Cross loop window, looking south-west, as seen before renovation works (RK 1998)

**Fig. 2.14** External furnace for Garden 1 heated wall, the same structure as shown in Fig. 2.13 after conservation (VR 2015)

# Chapter 3

## Garden 2, The Garden of the Second Duke (1786–1817)

*'The Nursery Grounds are divided into two parts surrounded by high Walls well furnished with Peach, Nectarine, Plum, and other Wall Fruit Trees: Within these Walls are also large Pineries, Grape Houses, Melon Frames etc. And in the Borders are great numbers of Currant, Goose berries etc. – but the Beds are occupied by Firs of various kinds, Oaks, Ash, Beach [sic], and a great Variety of other young Forest Trees.'*
(Wadell 1785; Acc 163)

The second Duke of Northumberland (1786–1817), also named Hugh, was keen on promoting the cultivation of exotic fruits for the table at Alnwick and Northumberland House and invested in new hothouses designed by John Hay of Edinburgh, including a fruiting pine stove for pineapples, a mushroom house and two vineries (Shrimpton 2006, 58). New pine pits and a peach house were also constructed (Shrimpton 2006, 58). The pine stove and two new hothouses were built between 1808 and 1811 by local masons Nesbitt and Shepherd (Shrimpton 1997, 10). The second duke created two new walled kitchen gardens to the south-west and east of the original walled garden and also built a house for the head gardener adjacent to the west wall of the garden (Fig. 3.1).

Bell's 1826 and Barnfather's 1829 maps, although later, largely reflect the layout of Garden 2 (if not all of the structures within it). These show that the layout of paths and borders within the walled garden, which again enclosed a series of rectangular beds, was apparently not significantly modified by the second duke (see Fig. 8.3; Fig. 8.6).

Elements of the perimeter wall of the new kitchen garden to the south-west of Garden 1 are extant. The Gardener's House survives and is currently in use as the offices of The Alnwick Garden. Parts of the westernmost of the three buildings shown on Bell's 1826 map survived much modified and in a ruinous condition at the time of the 2000 fieldwork, and was subject to standing building recording (as Hothouse 2). Elements of a heated structure with an associated furnace were excavated in the central part of the garden; these do not appear on any map of the garden discovered to date and may represent the earliest structure in this area. To the east, beyond a central conservatory (Hothouse 3, see below) Barnfather's plan of 1829 shows a 3–bay glasshouse, in front of a much shorter backhouse. This depiction appears to show that the glasshouse element of the structure was constructed with three bays. No structural elements of this building were identified during the fieldwork. Other archaeological remains of Garden 2 included paths, culverts, wells, levelling deposits and garden soils.

## 3.1 Excavated Remains of Garden 2

### Levelling and landscaping

With the establishment of a new kitchen garden to the south-west (Fig. 3.1; see Fig. 8.3; Fig. 8.6), substantial modifications occurred within the original walled garden. Numerous levelling and ground-raising dumps, recorded across the central part of the garden (Area A), were laid down as preparation for the construction of the new garden. To the west a series of dumps containing fragmented ash, cinder and coal overlay the infilled pond in the centre of the garden. These deposits had a combined maximum thickness of *c.* 0.35m and raised the ground level to 50.54m OD.

### Drainage and garden paths

The archaeological excavation of the central part of the garden revealed elements of a regular series of culverts and drains installed before paths were laid down. These may have acted as drains and/or supplied water and their frequency within the excavated area indicates that water control, supply and drainage was an important issue, unsurprisingly given the sloping topography of the area. The archaeological remains indicate the division of this part of the garden into three rectangular areas (Plots 1–3, from west to east) (Fig. 3.2). Only the full width of the central Plot (2) was revealed within the excavation area. Map evidence (Sauthier 1788; Bell 1826) demonstrates that the paths identified archaeologically formed part of a larger network of north–south and east–west aligned paths which changed little over a 40–year period, although the number of plots was subject to some change, presumably following the removal of the central pond. Bell (1826) shows the area of excavation to be a garden with three buildings along the east–west axis, each situated at the northern end of a plot (see Fig. 8.3) and this layout of paths correspond most closely to the archaeological evidence.

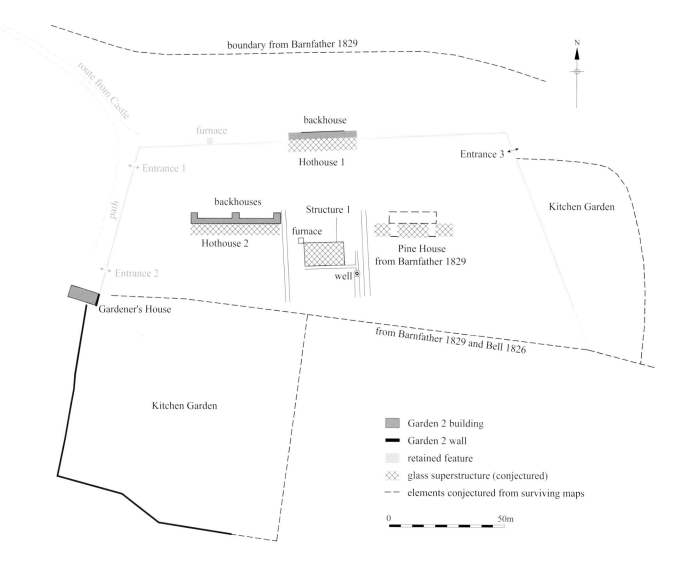

**Fig. 3.1** Garden 2, 1786–1817, based on surviving elements, archaeological excavation, conjecture and contemporary map evidence (scale 1:1600)

Between Plots 1 and 2, a 0.80m-wide north-west to south-east aligned sandstone slab culvert was exposed for a distance of 1.40m (Fig. 3.2), overlain by a 1.90m-wide north–south aligned pea grit path [917] which formed the border between the plots. At its south-eastern extent the culvert connected with a similar 0.85m-wide culvert which ran adjacent to the eastern edge of the path. A section of north–south path to the east defined the boundary between Plots 2 and 3 (Fig. 3.2). This was built within a substantial construction cut 2.60m wide and 0.35m deep, which contained a sequence of fills culminating in a gravel path surface [317] surviving to a maximum width of 1.80m, although the east–west dimension of the construction cut is probably a better indicator of the original width of the path. Plot 2, delineated by paths [317] and [917], thus measured 33m east–west and historic maps indicate a similar north–south dimension creating a roughly square area flanked on all sides by paths with a central building located in the north (see Fig. 8.3).

A smaller north–south aligned gravel path [415] located inside Plot 2, 2.50m to the west of the boundary path [317], ran for 14m apparently accessing a well. The southern element of the path at *c.* 2m wide was wider than that to the north. Between paths [317] and [415] a series of thin mixed deposits represent levelling and garden use. A mixed 60mm-thick garden soil was overlain by the eastern edge of path [415]; this indicates that there was no formal edging to define the path. To the west a 0.40m-wide and 0.28m-high brick culvert was capped with sandstone blocks.

A fall in recorded heights of the paths from west to east observed across Plot 2 reflects the sloping underlying natural topography; from 51.65m OD on the western path [917], to 50.64m OD on the internal path [415] to 50.23m OD on the eastern path [317]. The paths and associated deposits produced a small quantity of pottery. Most of this material points towards an eighteenth-century date, with a deposit associated with internal path [415] producing 23 sherds and being the most securely dated context. Seventeen sherds of flower pot were, perhaps unsurprisingly, recovered from path construction deposits.

## Structure 1: heated forcing frame or pine pit and associated furnace

A series of robbed-out walls within Plot 2 represent the remains of a heated building with an associated brick furnace located externally to its north-west corner. Brick-lined flues led from the furnace and entered the structure in the west, heating the building internally. The foundations of the building revealed a structure of notably different plan to the hothouses, and this structure may have functioned as a heated pine pit for the cultivation of pineapples (see Chapter 9).

Five east–west aligned robber trenches which varied in width between 0.70m and 1.20m, being more substantial in the south-east, defined a building measuring *c.* 11m wide and over 19m east–west (Fig. 3.2). The eastern extent of the building was not identified within the confines of the excavation, although internal

Plot 2 path [415] indicates a point beyond which the building did not extend. This path may have provided access to the building in the east, indicating that the overall east–west dimensions of the building would have been between 19 and 22m. A clinker path also ran along the southern side of the building; this was recorded for a distance of 6m and was at least 1.20m wide.

Fragmentary surviving traces of the walls at the south-east end of the structure comprised roughly hewn blocks of yellow sandstone with more regular, dressed blocks on the wall faces, bonded with hard grey sandy mortar. Internally the building was divided into three areas (Cells 1–3), which measured 2m, 1.50m and 2m wide with a 1m-wide clinker path running along the length of the building between Cells 2 and 3. An indication of robbing of masonry at the west end of the path could have been part of a threshold, indicating the location of a door providing access into the west end of the building. In the south-east part of Cell 3, drainage was provided by a brick culvert running adjacent and parallel to the southernmost wall of the building and constructed with handmade, slop-moulded bricks of broadly eighteenth- to nineteenth-century date (Fig. 3.2). Cells 1 to 3 contained elements of hardstanding which may have provided

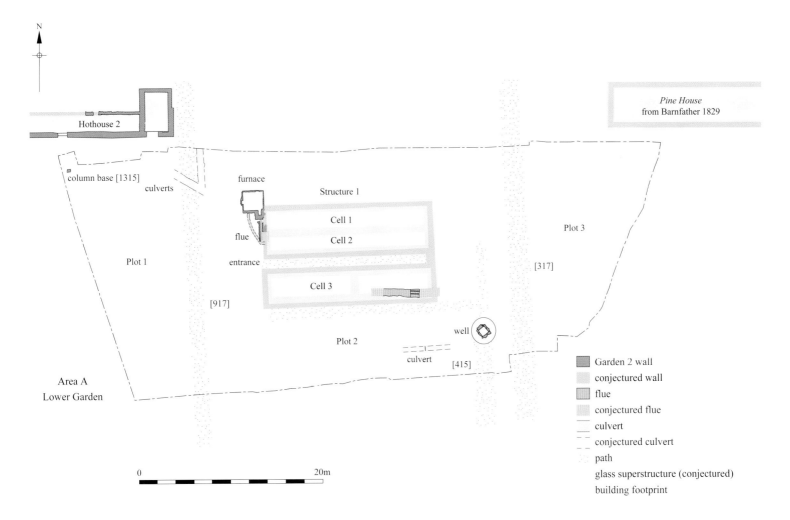

**Fig. 3.2** Garden 2, excavated remains as seen in Area A, shown in relation to recorded elements of Hothouse 2 (scale 1:400)

free-draining surfaces on which to set plants, or above which plants were set on raised platforms or in raised beds. The wide variety of materials used to construct these all would have provided good drainage; clinker; crushed sandstone, fragments of sandstone, mortar, pantiles and cobbles. One of these deposits produced two sherds of eighteenth-century pot and another produced five sherds of possible nineteenth-century pottery. A robber cut running across the width of Cell 3 may have removed an internal wall or fitting.

The heights of the walls and of the building itself remain unknown, although it is assumed that the external walls supported glass superstructures, the internal divisions perhaps indicating planting beds. The deposits in Cells 1–3 survived to a level of 50.42m in the north and 50.23m in the south, with the internal path slightly higher at 50.58m OD; the external path to the south also stood at this height. Perhaps unsurprisingly these levels are not significantly different from that of an external surface associated with the furnace, which stood at 50.56m OD, reflecting the level of truncation of the building.

The remains of a brick and stone furnace survived at the north-western corner of the heated structure (Fig. 3.2; Fig. 3.3; Fig. 3.4). The walls survived to a height of 0.76m with the highest recorded level being 50.66m OD; the lowest floor level at 49.84m OD demonstrated that this was a sunken room set *c.* 0.70m below the contemporary ground level of the paths surrounding the heated building. The structure comprised two main elements; a brick and stone furnace room and parts of two linear brick-lined flues extending from its southern side. The furnace room had internal dimensions of 2.20m east–west by 1.80m north–south and was built with red unfrogged bricks, some of which were vitrified, surviving to a maximum of 13 courses, although demolished to only two bricks high in the north. The room was floored with flagstones except for a roughly square area in the north-eastern corner which was surrounded by a low brick wall and may represent the position of a robbed-out stairwell (Fig. 3.5), providing access to the furnace. Excavation in this area revealed the structure to be founded on a thick layer of brick rubble. The floor stepped down slightly in the east, from a level of 49.90m OD to 49.84m OD, and though slight, this step appeared deliberate. In the centre of the western side was a steeply-sloping coal chute. On the floor of the structure along its western side was a deposit of black ash clinker and charcoal up to 0.32m thick, presumably material deriving from the raking-out of fires; fragments of flower pot were recovered from this deposit, suggesting that at least in part the material represented dumped waste.

In the south-east corner of the room, a 1.50m-wide brick-lined 'niche' extended 2.50m to the south, also floored with sandstone with one large slab extending beneath the walls. The area surrounding this part of the structure and the soil to the south was

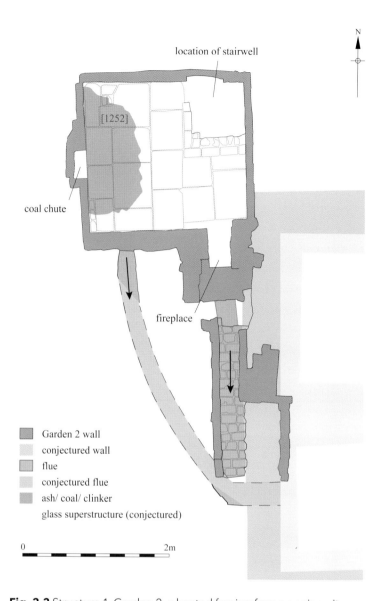

**Fig. 3.3** Structure 1, Garden 2, a heated forcing frame or pine pit; detailed plan of excavated furnace (scale 1:50)

**Fig. 3.4** Structure 1, Garden 2, furnace room and flue for heated building, looking south (scale 1m)

heavily reddened and the brick walls were vitrified. Concentrated against the south wall of this part of the structure was a 100mm-thick deposit of clinker, coal and ash. This evidence suggests that a fire was set within this niche. The extra thickness of the walls at this point may suggest a more substantial superstructure than elsewhere, perhaps a chimney. Extending south from this fire chamber, at a higher level, was the surviving part of a north–south aligned brick-lined flue. This was 2.50m long, although the eastern wall only survived for 1m. This part of the structure is interpreted as a flue or heating duct which supplied hot air to the structure to the east. The flue had an internal width of 0.22m, with walls surviving to a height of 0.22m. It had been truncated in the south-east, and its western wall curved to the south-east at its southern extent, presumably where the flue turned to feed into the building to the east. Other potentially associated brickwork survived to the east and the maximum width at this point was 0.80m. A gap between the north end of the flue and the furnace room may be due to robbing of the brick, or to the presence of an internal feature, subsequently robbed. The base of the flue sloped gently up from a level of 50.35m OD in the north to 50.48m OD in the south.

To the west of the flue were the fragmentary remains of a largely robbed out narrow linear feature which appeared to be beginning to curve round to the south-east at its southern extent. This may represent the partial remains of a vent drawing air through the building system, or alternatively a second flue. Reddening of the deposits around the southern end of this part

of the building suggest that it was subject to extreme heat. It is plausible that this represents an earlier flue, which had been replaced by the better-surviving example to the east, the latter conceivably being constructed from robbed-out fabric of the original flue.

Since the structural elements of the building associated with this furnace had been systematically and thoroughly robbed, the exact functioning of the building is hard to elucidate. It seems likely that that at least some of the robbed-out areas of walling may have incorporated heated flues, whether running around the whole of the building, or concentrated in the central portion, is hard to determine, but the dimensions of the robbed-out features certainly allow for such an interpretation, whilst the survival of a flue, rising to serve the building, suggests that it is likely. The heated structure may have served as a forcing frame or propagating pit for the drawing on of plants, or alternatively as a pine pit, for the cultivation of pineapples (see section 9.5 below).

The heated structure had been systematically dismantled to ground level or below and much of the masonry robbed out, presumably for use elsewhere in the garden and perhaps to assist cultivation once this area was given over to planting. The building does not appear on any known plans of the garden; in Garden 1 this part of the walled garden was occupied by the central pond and by the time of Bell's 1826 map, the heated building had evidently been demolished and a structure built within Plot 2 farther to the north (see Fig. 8.3).

**Fig. 3.5** Structure 1, Garden 2, furnace showing robbed-out stairwell in north-east corner and coal chute on western wall, looking east (scale 1m)

## Hothouse 2: a peach house

Archaeological excavation revealed two main phases of glasshouse construction south-east of Hothouse 2 backhouse, the earliest of which was represented by a large robber cut (which preceded the construction of a later glass frontage, see Garden 3) and a single column base [1315]. This provided the only evidence of the glasshouse superstructure of the building (Fig. 3.2) the robber cut, extending approximately 6.4m from the spine wall, indicated the maximum width of the Garden 2 glass frontage.

## Stone-lined well

A well within the south-eastern part of the Plot 2 comprised a circular construction cut measuring at least 2.92m by 3.28m with a sub-rectangular sandstone lining [327] (Fig. 4.3; Fig. 3.6). The well does not appear on any maps or plans of the garden. and dating its initial construction is problematic. The well construction cut backfill produced fragments of flower pot, three sherds of probable eighteenth-century pottery and fragments of flower pot along with medieval pottery were recovered from silting deposits within the well, suggesting eighteenth-century, or earlier, construction. The well was excavated to a depth of over 1.70m, although its base was not reached and thus the date of any primary deposits remains unknown. The construction cut for the well appeared to truncate the earliest paths in this area, but this was presumably in use over a considerable period of time and this

**Fig. 3.6** Garden 2, the sandstone well in the central plot (scale 1m)

truncation is likely to have been the result of later modifications to the upper structural elements or excessive erosion of surfaces around the well associated with its use. Paths and surfaces surrounding the well would have provided an area of associated hardstanding and there was clear evidence that these had been repaired more frequently than path surfaces elsewhere. Provision of a well would have been essential, prior to the introduction of piped water to the gardens in 1829 (see section 8.3 below), and it is considered likely that it remained in position throughout successive phases of redesign and use of the gardens, only being infilled when the garden was significantly redesigned in the 1860s (Garden 4).

## Open ground and the development or introduction of garden soils

A dark brown silty sand deposit up to 0.75m thick in the south-west of the central part of the garden represents a developed and worked garden soil which extended for over 20.80m north–south. Its substantial depth implies the perpetuation of a garden bed in the same location over a considerable period, with new material being incorporated and worked into the soil. This deposit sloped down from a maximum height of 51.46m OD in the south to 50.48m OD in the north; across the site the underlying slope of the natural topography was still apparent. Extensive deposits of garden soil up to 1m thick were also recorded in section against the central southern limit of excavation and in the south-eastern part of Area A. Cartographic evidence demonstrates that this part of the garden in the southern parts of Plots 1–3 remained clear of garden structures and were therefore occupied by garden beds for a considerable length of time. The gardens soils represent the development and lengthy use of these beds.

Garden soil up to 0.43m thick was also recorded in section towards the northern end of Plot 2 overlain by a substantial levelling deposit. A short distance to the east, ground-raising dumps interleaved with and overlain by garden soils raised the contemporary ground surface to a height similar to that of Structure 1 and surrounding paths, at 50.69m OD. The basal deposits contained rubble and crushed sandstone, perhaps incorporated for drainage purposes (Fig. 3.2). The dumps incorporated building material; thin lenses of crushed sandstone, mortar and rubble were apparent throughout these deposits and it would appear that this area was open and subjected to trampling and the discard of waste from building during the soil development.

## 3.2 Structural Remains of Garden 2

### Hothouse 1: amalgamation of three backhouses into one backhouse

Evidence for the amalgamation of the three small backhouses to the north of Hothouse 1 into one long structure could be observed in the south-facing elevation of the northern wall. The lower part of the two segments of wall to either side of the later central tank, which had divided the basement into two separate elements, were of notably different construction to the upper part, comprising four rough courses of irregular-shaped sandstone blocks, surviving to 0.60m high. Wall [4039] is interpreted as representing a wall built to join the eastern and western backhouse rooms to the central room, thus creating one long backhouse (Fig. 3.7, Fig. 3.8, Fig. 3.9).

This modification to the backhouses of Hothouse 1 may well have been associated with the construction of one of the hothouses designed by John Hay of Edinburgh and built between 1808 and 1811 by local masons Nesbitt and Shepherd (Shrimpton 1997, 10). The earliest map to show this hothouse with one long backhouse is Bell's map of 1826 (see Fig. 8.3) which shows one long backhouse,

located external to the garden boundary wall, with a glasshouse to the south inside the garden. The structure is labelled for the first time on Barnfather's map (1829; see Fig. 4.3) as a vinery, indicating that it may have been one of the two vineries designed by Hay for the second duke.

### Hothouse 2: a peach house

The surviving above ground elements of Hothouse 2 comprised four ruinous external walls defining a structure 39m in length by 5.30m wide and surviving to a maximum height of *c.* 4.50m above ground. The spine wall, which would have formed the south wall of the glasshouse and the north walls of the backhouses, was the best preserved. The west wall was largely intact, but the east wall had been destroyed towards the north. The northern wall was badly damaged and had almost entirely collapsed. This hothouse had been subject to various modifications since its original creation, with at least three phases of construction and use identified within the backhouse element, but it had evidently been initially constructed as a glasshouse with three small backhouses to the north. The later modifications and additions are described below with the

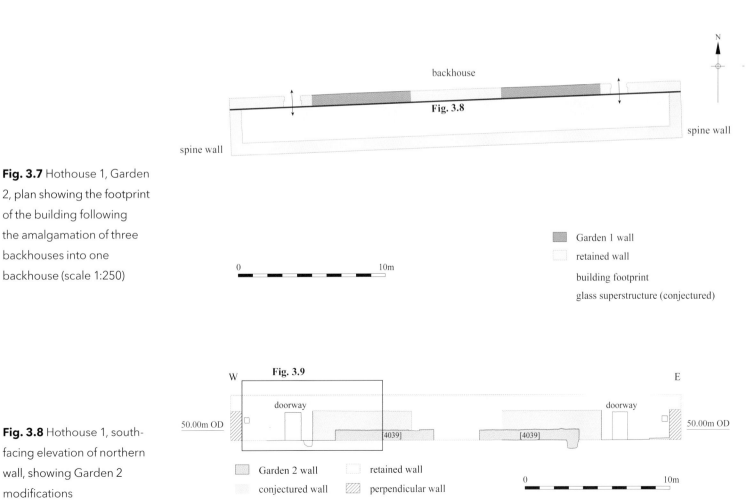

**Fig. 3.7** Hothouse 1, Garden 2, plan showing the footprint of the building following the amalgamation of three backhouses into one backhouse (scale 1:250)

**Fig. 3.8** Hothouse 1, south-facing elevation of northern wall, showing Garden 2 modifications (scale 1:250)

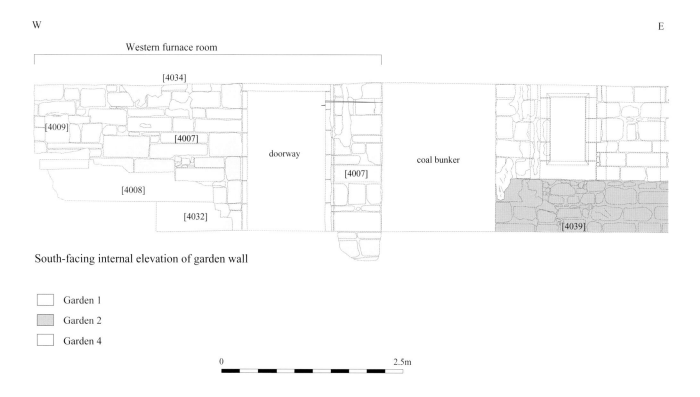

W                                                                                                      E

Western furnace room

[4034]

[4009]

[4007]

doorway

coal bunker

[4007]

[4008]

[4039]

[4032]

South-facing internal elevation of garden wall

Garden 1
Garden 2
Garden 4

0                                                    2.5m

**Fig. 3.9** Hothouse 1, phased detail of elevation of southern wall, illustrating the differing builds of Garden 1 and Garden 2; Garden 4 modifications replaced the original upper courses of the infilled elements of wall with new stonework, incorporating window openings (scale 1:50)

relevant garden phase. Archaeological excavation to the south of the structure had revealed that the associated glasshouse element, represented by a robber cut and a column base only (Fig. 3.2; see section 3.1 above) was originally *c.* 6.4m wide.

In its earliest phase of construction, Hothouse 2 comprised three small, semi-basemented backhouses to the north of a spine wall; these would have contained the furnaces to heat the glasshouse element to the south (Fig. 3.10). All three backhouses measured 5m north–south externally and the west and east rooms measured 3.40m and 3.70m wide externally, respectively. The central backhouse would have been at least 3.50m wide; its north wall was truncated at either end, so the full width was not seen. The east and west backhouses were semi-basemented and surviving elements demonstrate that they were originally built as furnace rooms for the glasshouse to the south; flues (F1 and F3) led from fireplaces in the east and west furnace rooms into the glasshouse. Later modifications meant that few details of the original form of the central backhouse were identified. The Hothouse 2 backhouses had evidently been built as subterranean

rooms so that the fireplaces could be constructed at a suitable height for optimum performance of the hot air system used to heat the glasshouse. Little survived of the original spine wall of Hothouse 2; this wall had evidently been largely rebuilt during later phases of use. Parts of the north walls of the original furnace rooms comprising roughly coursed sandstone masonry could be seen at either end of the structure.

The western furnace room, Room 1, measured 2.40m east–west by 4m north–south internally with the south wall of the furnace room formed by the hothouse spine wall and was *c.* 1.40m deep from contemporary ground level in the east, as indicated by the top of a flight of steps leading into the room. The west and north walls of the room were built in squared regular courses (Fig. 3.13). The north wall was the least well-preserved and had largely collapsed to just above the original floor level. Internally the original roof line in the west wall could be seen, sloping down to the north (Fig. 3.14). The projected roof pitch would have finished at the level suggested by ceiling joists integral to the spine wall.

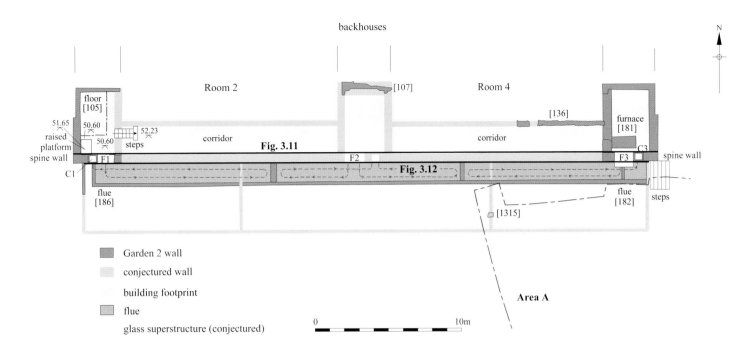

**Fig. 3.10** Hothouse 2, Garden 2, plan of backhouses and conjectured glasshouse frontage (scale 1:250)

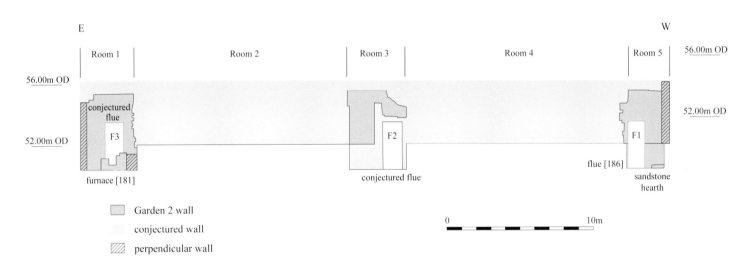

**Fig. 3.11** Hothouse 2, Garden 2, north-facing elevation of the spine wall within the backhouse (scale 1:250)

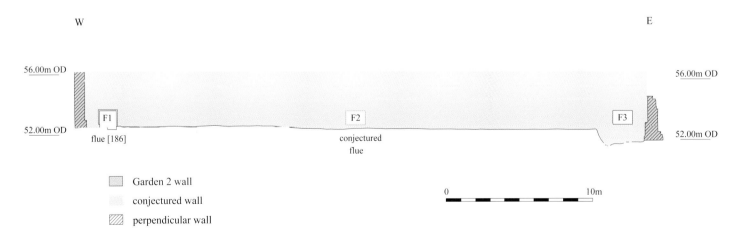

**Fig. 3.12** Hothouse 2, Garden 2, south-facing elevation of spine wall, within the glasshouse (scale 1:250)

Only below-ground elements of the east wall of Room 1 survived, the above-ground element having been demolished and capped by a stone floor when the rooms were amalgamated into one long backhouse (Garden 3). The west–facing internal elevation, which was 1.39m high from the floor of the furnace room, was visible. A flight of seven steps set within the east wall would have originally led into the furnace room from a level of 52.23m OD in the east. On either side of the steps were supporting walls up to the height of the later stone floor. The variety of techniques used in the finish of the sandstone blocks in these walls, sawn, pecked and chiselled, implies reuse of materials from elsewhere.

Sample excavation of rubble backfill along the eastern and southern sides of the room revealed a pink and yellow flagstone floor at a level of 50.77m OD. A drainage channel was cut into the flagstones in the north-east and in this corner of the room a short section of wall had been constructed around a ceramic drainpipe, presumably extending through the external wall. These features indicate the necessity of draining water from this sunken room. The floor level in the south-east corner of the room, adjacent to the spine wall, was over 1m higher than flagstone floor [105], at 51.65m OD, extending for 0.80m east–west and 1m into the room, providing a raised platform. In front of these higher areas were apertures in the back wall which marked the position of hearths. An area of fireproof flagstones in the south-east corner of the room, some worn and cracked, formed a surface in front of one of the hearths. A 1.50m-wide hearth capped with flagstones [153] at a height of 0.77mm (Fig. 3.12) was integral to the original structure. Set 0.80m above this infilled hearth, a 1.20m wide and 1.40m high aperture [186] in the spine wall represents the original flue (F1: blocked up with later brickwork at the time of recording), which would have carried the hot air into the glasshouse. In the south face of the spine wall, internal to the glasshouse, this aperture was surrounded by an iron frame (Fig. 3.12).

Room 3 measured 2.70m by 4m internally. Its east and north walls were less well-preserved than the walls of Room 3 and the west wall had been damaged by the insertion of later east–west brick floor joists. Only the subterranean element of the west wall survived, the upstanding elements having been demolished during later conversion into a single long backhouse (Fig. 3.10). Extending 6m westwards from the west wall, and assumed to be contemporary with it, a 0.32m-wide sandstone block wall [136] survived below contemporary ground level; traces of mortar at its top edge indicate an original continuation above this point (Fig. 3.16). This wall would presumably have formed a narrow 1.80m-wide corridor adjacent to the glasshouse. Barnfather's 1829 plan shows two such narrow corridors linking the eastern, central and western backhouses (see Fig. 4.3). No traces of the western corridor wall were revealed as a later stone floor in that part of the structure remained unexcavated.

Excavation revealed that, like Room 1, Room 3 had originally been semi-basemented, its floor at approximately 50.60m OD. Indications of a staircase leading down into the cellar from the west were provided by a construction cut and mortar foundation for a step. A flue (F3: blocked up with later brickwork and plastered over at the time of recording) led through the spine wall. On the opposite side, internal to the glasshouse, the flue was 1.23m wide and 1.53m high, mirroring the opening in the western furnace room. A soot-stained brick structure [181] in two parts with a sandstone slab on top presumably formed part of the heating system.

A segment of earlier wall in the central north wall of the building [107], equidistant between the eastern and western furnace rooms (Fig. 3.10), presumably represents part of the north wall of a central backhouse room, Room 2, as shown on historic maps of the garden (see Fig. 8.3). No traces of the east or west walls were recorded and it was not possible to elucidate any details about this furnace room as various modifications associated with the later use of the building obscured any original features.

Little of the original build of the central backhouse could be seen amongst the numerous modifications which had taken place over time in this part of the structure. As originally built the spine wall stood at least *c.* 3m high above contemporary ground level; the upper 1m of walling, which resulted in the full recorded height of *c.* 4m, represents a later build associated with Garden 3. A flue (F2, subsequently blocked) would have heated the element of glasshouse to the south; an associated chimney is assumed on the basis of the interpretation of this room as a furnace.

## Heating apparatus

The mechanisms behind heating the hothouses are discussed in detail below (see Chapter 9). These were subject to continued change and modification and the following sets out the evidence for the initial layout and arrangement of furnace and flues, which, it is concluded, supplied heat by means of hot air, vented through flues (Fig. 4.6). The flue heating system within the glasshouse was identified during excavation as parallel walls, heavily truncated and comprising both brick and stone elements (Fig. 4.16). The flues, constructed within the glasshouse element of the hothouse, adjacent to the spine wall, would have carried hot air from the furnaces to warm the internal area of the glasshouse, before venting via the chimneys. There was little evidence for the furnaces which supplied the heat to the flue system and the method of heating has been conjectured based on the surviving flues (represented by badly-truncated walls on the southern side of the spine wall), sunken furnace rooms and chimneys, in tandem with examination of surviving evidence from Hothouse 4, similar systems elsewhere and contemporary accounts (see Chapter 9).

**Fig. 3.13** Hothouse 2, Garden 2, western furnace room (Room 1) showing the original surviving element of furnace room wall, the later partially rebuilt spine wall with ceiling joist voids, and the western wall with later clasping buttress, looking south (scales 2m and 1m)

**Fig. 3.14** Hothouse 2, Garden 2, the western furnace room of Hothouse 2 showing the original west wall and roof line, looking west (scale 1m)

**Fig. 3.15** Hothouse 2, Garden 2, the eastern furnace room (Room 5) showing external walls with later clasping buttress, looking south (scale 1m)

**Fig. 3.16** Hothouse 2, Garden 2, the eastern furnace room (Room 5) showing the wall foundation [136] of possible corridor between the furnaces, looking east (scale 2 x 1m)

**Fig. 3.17** Entrance 3 at the northern end of the east wall of the garden, looking north-east (VR 2015)

The recorded evidence is supported by historic maps of the garden and demonstrates that when originally constructed Hothouse 2 comprised three semi-basemented backhouses, which contained the furnaces to heat the glasshouse to the south via a system of hot air flues. Each flue would have been associated with an adjacent chimney. The furnace houses were linked by two narrow corridors. Cartographic and documentary evidence demonstrates that Hothouse 2 was used a peach house (see section 9.5 below); it first appears on Bell's map of 1826 and on Barnfather's plan of 1829 it is labelled as a 'Peach House' (see Fig. 8.3 and Fig. 4.3). The second duke's peach house has been described elsewhere as being of four compartments (Shrimpton 2006, 58), although the source of this quote remains unknown and it is difficult to reconcile this description with either cartographic or excavated evidence.

## New kitchen gardens and Gardener's House

An entrance (Entrance 3) was created through the northern end of the Garden 1 west wall which led into a new adjoining walled garden attached to the east of the original walled garden; paths are shown leading to this entrance on Wood's 1827 map (see Fig. 8.4). This square-headed doorway with sandstone dressings is extant (Fig. 3.17).

Historic maps show that a new walled kitchen garden was also added to the south-east of Garden 1 (see Fig. 8.3; Fig. 8.4). The western wall of this new kitchen garden survives, aligned north-north-east to south-south-west it measures 58m by 0.50m wide and 2.10m high on its internal face, and higher externally. The inside face of the wall is constructed with regular coursed sandstone rubble and the coping comprises sandstone saddle backs. A stretch of the south wall of the new kitchen garden also survives; this is of the same construction as the west wall and measures 30m in length, 0.50m wide, and 2m high.

The Gardener's House, originally built between 1808 and 1811 for a new Head Gardener, George Robson, previously in charge at Seaton Delaval in Northumberland (Green 1998), was located at the north-west corner of the new kitchen garden, adjacent to Entrance 2. This Grade II listed building has recently been renovated for use as offices for the present Alnwick Garden. The east wall, facing the garden, is built in facing bond brick and is contiguous with the Garden 1 wall. Brick coursing and tooth joints in this elevation demonstrate that the original house was extended to the north (Kent 1998, 16). The date of this extension is unknown, but would have been before 1826 when the extended structure is depicted on Bell's map (see Fig. 8.3).

**Fig. 3.18** The east elevation of the Gardener's House, built in facing bond brick and contiguous with the garden wall, photographed from inside the garden; the left half of this elevation forms part of the original build (1808–1811), whilst the right half forms a later extension (constructed between 1811 and 1826) (RK 1998)

**Fig. 3.19** The recently-renovated Gardener's House, originally built 1808–1811 at the south-west entrance (Entrance 2) into the garden; this north-facing elevation shows a later extension to the original build as illustrated in Fig. 3.18 (VR 2015)

# Chapter 4

## Garden 3, The Garden of the Third Duke (1817–1847)

*'Where the range of hot-houses is situated in the middle of the garden, great care must be taken, that it present nothing offensive, and that the sheds behind neither resemble a row of workshops, alms-houses, brickmakers' sheds, or cattlehovels'*
(Loudon 1825)

The third duke began redevelopment of the gardens in 1817; some of the impetus for change may have been provided by the duchess Charlotte Florentia, who had an enthusiasm for flower gardens. Under the control of the third duke more land was devoted to productive gardens, and another kitchen garden was added between 1827 and 1829 to the western side of the south-west kitchen garden (Fig. 4.1; see Fig. 8.6) and west of the Gardener's House, which had been extended northwards, doubling its original footprint, by this date (Kent 1998, 16). The role of the original walled garden seems to have broadened and as well as producing fruits, the garden provided a place of entertainment for the family. A new central conservatory (identified archaeologically as Hothouse 3), with parterre gardens in front, containing a central decorative pond, formed the focal point for Garden 3 by 1829 (see Fig. 8.6). The gardens were opened to the public by 1828 and pineapples and fruits produced in the hothouses were used at the Alnwick table and sent to the duke's properties in London as well as to Dublin and Paris (Shrimpton 2006, 64). The third duke was a keen plant collector and exotic varieties were brought to Alnwick from around the world. Considerable changes took place within the original walled garden, with the construction of new hothouses or conservatories and the modification of some of the existing hothouses. The excavated remains and standing building surveys, supported by cartographic and documentary evidence, demonstrate that new hothouses were built and others modified between the late 1820s and mid-1830s. The third duke's changes to the garden, spanning a period of some 30 years, are reflected in piecemeal, rather than sweeping, changes. Illustrating the layout of the garden at any one period therefore entails producing a snapshot in time of the overall layout. The duke inherited Hothouse 1 and Hothouse 2 described above; he went on to construct an impressive conservatory, Hothouse 3, which was ultimately short-lived. Changes to Hothouse 1 and Hothouse 2 as well as the construction of new buildings, Hothouse 4 and Hothouse 5 eventually resulted in a more unified appearance to the garden structures.

The three blocks of land in the central part of the garden were maintained in Garden 3 with structures located at the northern end of each in a line of three. Standing building recording revealed that Hothouse 2 was substantially modified to create the new western structure. The three-celled backhouse was converted into one long building, although its original form was in part preserved in the new building, with projections to the north in the centre and at each end. The spine wall was partially rebuilt and the glass frontage was rebuilt. A new eastern hothouse (Hothouse 4) was constructed to mirror Hothouse 2 with a central projection to the north and one at each end, reflecting the original three furnace rooms of the western structure. Elements of the foundations of the glass frontage of this hothouse were also excavated.

The robbed-out south wall of a new conservatory (Hothouse 3) was recorded; this has been equated to a documented structure built in 1827 by Richards and Jones of Cheapside, Birmingham (Loudon 1827, 108). Substantial stone-lined culverts to the south of the glasshouses provided drainage and may also have supplied a pond within the conservatory with rain water.

A fifth hothouse constructed in the south-east corner of the garden (Hothouse 5) survived as a standing structure; archaeological excavation revealed structural elements of the glass frontage. This was apparently also designed to reflect Hothouse 2 and Hothouse 4, although it was slightly smaller, with three projecting bays echoing the earlier furnace rooms.

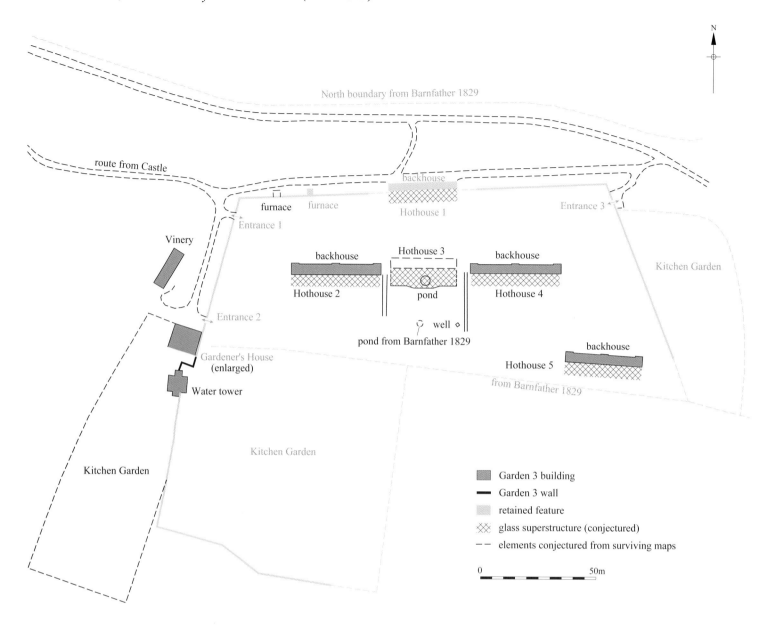

**Fig. 4.1** Garden 3, *c.* 1830, based on surviving elements, archaeological excavation, conjecture and contemporary map evidence and showing retained elements of Garden 1 and Garden 2 (scale 1:1250)

## 4.1 Excavated Remains of Garden 3

### Demolition and clearance of Garden 2 structures

Features interpreted as being associated with roughly contemporary robbing, demolition and levelling events represent a phase of deliberate clearance of existing structures which presumably took place as part of a planned reorganisation of the layout of the garden by the third duke. Most of the structural fabric of the Garden 2 heated forcing frame in the central part of the garden was removed leaving a rectilinear series of 'robber' trenches. These have been illustrated with Garden 2 as they indicate the location and plan of the demolished

features which formed part of this phase of use (see Fig. 3.1). These trenches were backfilled with mixed demolition debris such as crushed and fragmented sandstone and mortar and the area was subsequently levelled. The furnace to the west of the heated building was partially demolished with some elements of internal walling on the northern side of the brick furnace and the western flue removed. Mixed demolition debris incorporating quantities of brick rubble, charcoal, mortar and clinker was dumped into the flue and the furnace room; any internal fittings had presumably been removed by this stage. Excavated elements of the glasshouses of Hothouse 2, Hothouse 4 and Hothouse 5 are described with the standing buildings to which they belong (see Section 4.2 below).

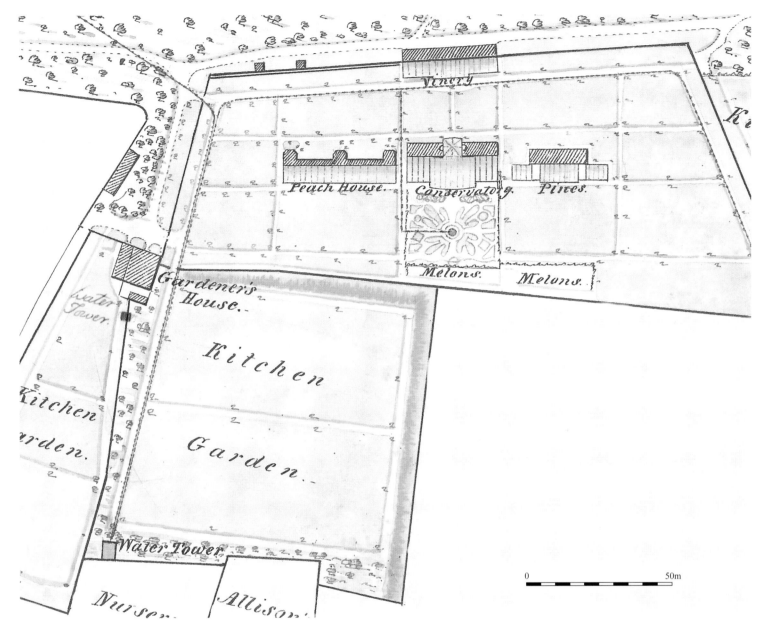

**Fig. 4.2** Extract from a plan of 1829 showing the vinery (Hothouse 1), peach house (Hothouse 2, in its earliest phase), conservatory (Hothouse 3) and a pinery; the water supply (shown dashed and leading from the water tower in the south-west) can be seen supplying the hothouses and a central pond to the south of the conservatory (Barnfather 1829) NB this depicts the garden at an earlier stage of development than the figure opposite (scale approx 1:1250)

## Hothouse 3: a conservatory

A robber trench [932] situated towards the northern end of Plot 2 extended east–west from the western limit of excavation then curved south-eastwards, closely following the alignment of a stone-lined culvert [946] (see below). It was recorded for a total distance of *c.* 15.50m (see Fig. 4.3). In the west, the vertical-sided trench was 0.60m wide and at least 0.50m deep and had been backfilled with mixed deposits incorporating much mortar and crushed yellow sandstone. To the east it was up to 1m deep. This feature clearly represents the robbing of a large masonry-founded building. Archaeologically, there were few clues as to the nature of this building, however, it seems

most likely to have been a large conservatory, which lay at the centre of the garden and can be seen on Barnfather's 1829 plan. The latter shows the conservatory as 100 feet- (*c.* 30.50m) long with a bow front and cupola with 16 ribs along the width of the building, although the actual number of ribs is considered more likely to be schematic than accurate (Fig. 4.2; see Fig. 8.6). A brick-lined heating duct recorded in section at the northern limit of excavation may have been associated with this structure. Loudon reported that in 1827 a large conservatory was in the process of being constructed at Alnwick by Richards and Jones of Cheapside, Birmingham, who had constructed a range of hothouses at Syon over 400 feet long (Loudon 1827, 108; see section 10.3 below).

The conservatory, Hothouse 3, as shown on Barnfather's plan was flanked to the west by a peach house (identified archaeologically as Hothouse 2) and a pinery, of which no archaeological remains were found. Hothouse 2 was to be substantially rebuilt and a new structure (Hothouse 4) built in place of the pinery (see 4.2 below). The exact date of construction of these remains unknown, but is likely to have taken place in the early to mid-1830s, shortly following the construction of Hothouse 3 (see 8.3 below).

The date of demolition of Hothouse 3 was not established, however it was clearly destroyed before 1856, as the Ordnance survey map of this date shows the central plot occupied by only a small pond or large fountain (see Fig. 8.20). The pond had possibly been originally sited within this conservatory.

## Garden paths

The three plots of land defined by north–south aligned paths continued to define the layout of the central part of the Garden 3 walled garden. Deposits associated with the re-surfacing and maintenance of paths indicate that once established this layout was modified and maintained over time. There is evidence that, especially towards the periphery of the excavations, paths 'migrated' as they were resurfaced. In some places, the paths sealed drainage culverts and loose material was used beneath paths and over culverts, facilitating drainage through path surfaces.

Plot 2 was defined to east and west by paths, creating an area that measured *c.* 33m east–west. The excavated evidence suggested that Plot 3 south of Hothouse 4 may have been sub-divided by a north–south aligned hedge. Such features, subdividing gardens into a series of parterres, would be a common feature of ornate gardens of the period. It is likely that more of these were present than have survived into the archaeological record, the garden soils having been extensively reworked in the intervening period. The overall layout of this garden suggests that symmetry was an important factor in design and it is likely that this feature would have been mirrored in Plot 1. The full extent of the eastern and western plots was not revealed within the excavated area, but historic maps indicate that each measured *c.* 38m east–west.

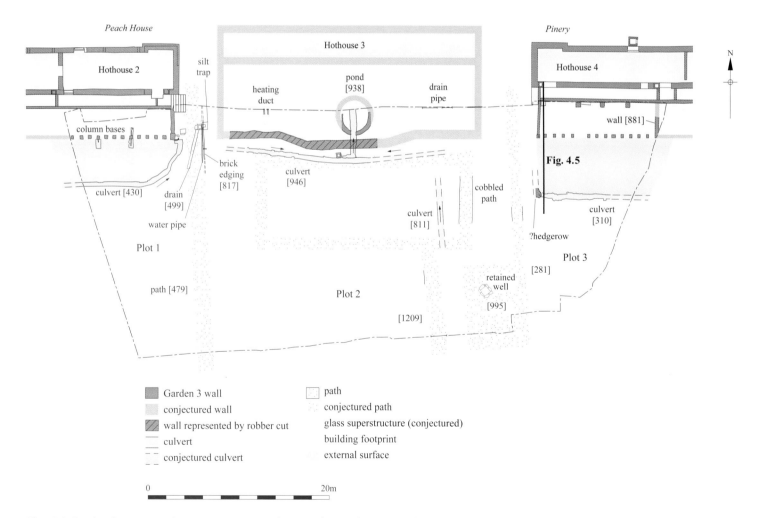

**Fig. 4.3** Garden 3, excavated remains in Area A, showing the garden at a slightly later date than Barnfather's map, and in relation to the rebuilt Hothouse 2 and new Hothouse 3 and Hothouse 4 (scale 1:400)

The western side of Plot 2 was defined by a north–south path [479] at least 2m wide (its western edge truncated), edged in the east with a single row of red, unfrogged bricks [817]. Running parallel to the edging bricks, just beneath the path surface, was a cast iron water pipe; Barnfather's 1829 plan for the proposed water supply to the gardens shows a pipe branching from the main east–west supply running to the north of the hothouses and then southwards down this path, turning at right angles to feed an ornamental pond in the central plot in front of the conservatory (Fig. 4.2; see Fig. 8.6). A ceramic drain [499] ran north-east to south-west under the path; the pond was not identified archaeologically and probably lay beyond the southern limit of excavation. Deposits associated with the north–south aligned eastern path demonstrated that it respected the line of the earlier Garden 2 path [317], although was narrower at only 1.20m wide. Use of the path was evidenced by two resurfacing episodes, both employing similar techniques of coarser grained sediments overlain by fine surface deposits, culminating in a gravel surface [281]. Robber trenches to either side had removed masonry or brick walls lining this path (Fig. 4.3). The excavated evidence therefore demonstrates that in Garden 3 paths were constructed with formal edges in contrast to the earlier gardens.

Towards the southern end of Plot 2, developed garden soils were overlain by a series of paths and associated make-up deposits and probable small drainage features culminating in a path surface [995] extending more than 3.20m east–west. This formed either a north–south path, widening out in the south, or a surface that presumably extended beyond limits of excavation; it seems likely that the surface was constructed to allow access to the well area (see above, Garden 2). Extending beyond the southern limit of excavation was a 1.70m-wide north–south aligned gravel path [1209], presumably an internal path within the south-eastern part of the plot.

Elements of an east–west aligned path and construction deposits crossed the centre of Plot 2, overlying a sandstone culvert. Along the northern edge of the uppermost path surface run-off deposits had accumulated, presumably due to the south–north slope of the site, and here the path had been resurfaced.

A substantial cobbled path was recorded in plan and section in the north-east part of Plot 2 and this appeared to form three sides of a rectangular path, possibly surrounding a central garden feature (Fig. 4.3). The north–south element of the path was built within a vertical-sided and flat-based linear construction trench, 1.40m wide and 0.38m deep, and extended for at least 5m in length. The path was composed of large cobbles and incorporated 16 sherds of eighteenth-century pottery. An east–west aligned element of path on the northern side of the rectangular feature comprised a 1.80m-wide and 0.30m-deep construction cut with the cobble path

subsequently resurfaced with crushed sandstone and truncated along its northern edge by a drainage ditch immediately overlying an extensive east–west sandstone culvert [946] (Fig. 4.3). It seems probable that the drainage ditch was cut to facilitate drainage from the path through the capping stones of the culvert. The path was resurfaced with heavily compacted gravel which partly overlay the infilled drainage ditch. Immediately to the north of the path a substantial 1.60m-wide east–west aligned construction cut containing fragments of masonry represents a heavily robbed stone wall which presumably formed a northern boundary to the path.

## Culverts and terraces to south of the hothouses

Elements of substantial stone-lined culverts were recorded to the south of the hothouses and conservatory. It is considered likely that these were designed and sited specifically to channel water away from the buildings, necessitated by the sloping topography, and were therefore integral to the layout of the Garden 3 structures. The culverts were all similarly constructed with sandstone walls and sandstone slab capping and appeared to incorporate reused materials (Fig. 4.4). Within Plot 1, sandstone culvert [430] ran *c*.

**Fig. 4.4** Garden 3, north-south aligned stone culvert [811] in Plot 2, looking south (scale 1m)

4.50m to the south of the glasshouse foundations of Hothouse 2 running parallel to the structure and then gradually curving to run in a north-easterly direction to the south-east corner of the glasshouse where it drained into a silt trap. Numerous silt traps and drains identified at the corner of Hothouse 2 apparently represented an associated drainage system, presumably collecting rainwater from downpipes as well as water from drains within the structure, and associated land drainage. It is likely that this represents a system established and modified over time, with downpipes and drains added as buildings were constructed and modified.

A 40mm-thick spread of mortar survived in patches between the southern edge of the Hothouse 2 glasshouse and the culvert, in some places partially overlying the drain. This may represent the remnants of a surface, or a bedding for a more substantially constructed surface, forming a 4.50m-wide terrace in front of the glasshouse at height of 51.37m OD. The surface was partially overlain to the south by extensive deposits of silty sands and clays interpreted as garden soil, up to 0.70m thick and extending in total at least 18m north–south and 10m east–west, indicating that the area south of the hothouse remained as open gardens, any sub-divisions being of a temporary nature (i.e. planting).

This arrangement was mirrored to the east with Hothouse 4, where culvert [310] ran *c.* 6m to the south of the glasshouse foundations, curving round in the west to run towards the south-west corner of this glasshouse. Sooty deposits were found in this feature, but there were no signs of burning and it is considered unlikely to have functioned as a flue; rather the soot elements

of the fill may have washed in and settled in the base of the feature. Between the culvert and the excavated foundations of the glasshouse (see below) and overlying earlier path surfaces, was a 5.80m-wide well-surfaced terrace which comprised a deposit of rubble and rounded cobblestones [312] at a height of 49.40m OD. The difference in level of *c.* 1m over *c.* 40m between the terraces in front of the western and eastern hothouses reflects the natural topography and this persisted throughout the life of the garden (see Fig. 5.6).

Two silty clayey organic deposits represent use of the surface in front of the glasshouse, the uppermost deposit in particular contained a great deal of organic matter, perhaps indicative of compost or manure usage in the garden. Bulk sediment samples taken from this deposit for palaeoenvironmental assessment produced seeds of bramble, elder, thistle, nightshade, and grape. Five sherds of pottery from 'trample' deposit [311] appeared nineteenth century in date.

Within Plot 2, a 0.80m-wide east–west aligned sandstone culvert [946] was recorded for a distance of over *c.* 19.50m. A drop of 0.30m along the base of the feature across its length in the western part of the plot demonstrates that water flowed from west to east. A smaller part of an eastern counterpart to this drain demonstrated a slope to the west. The capstones were covered by a *c.* 20mm-thick layer of river pebbles, presumably to facilitate drainage. This was overlain by crushed sandstone and clinker, apparently forming a path. The culvert construction incorporated a large proportion of reused stones which may have derived from one of the recently demolished buildings, as described above.

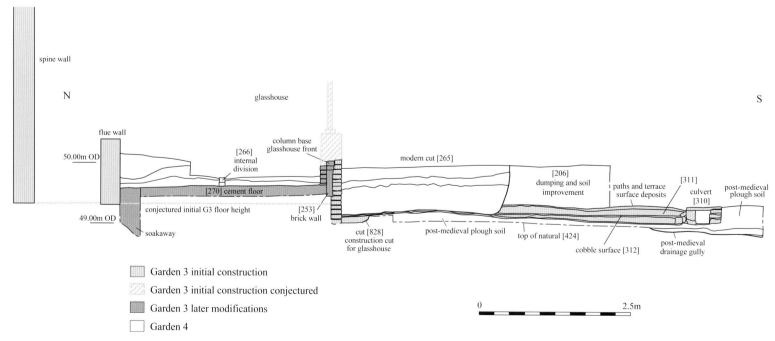

**Fig. 4.5** West-facing section through glasshouse frontage of Hothouse 4 and gravel terrace to south, showing conjectured elements of the glasshouse superstructure (scale 1:50)

A north–south aligned culvert drained northwards from east–west culvert [946]. Features recorded in plan and section represent the robbing of a curvilinear wall [938] defining a circular structure with an internal diameter of *c.* 3m. This is interpreted as the robbed out remains of a pond (Fig. 4.3); demolition rubble infilling the feature suggests that it was of sandstone construction. The north–south aligned culvert which drained into the centre of the pond was of similar construction, with a sandstone base, and was traced for *c.* 5m, continuing to the north beyond the limit of excavation. This is presumed to be associated with the pond, presumably supplying water collected in the various culverts and drains identified.

A further 2.50m length of sandstone culvert [811] which drained from south to north was exposed towards the eastern side of Plot 2; this may have joined with the drainage system identified *c.* 4m to the north (Fig. 4.3; Fig. 4.4). This culvert also incorporated reused stone, evidenced by tool marks on some of the blocks. A small rectangular brick-built drain for a down-pipe was a later addition on the northern side of the culvert. The bricks were handmade and slop-moulded and of broadly eighteenth- to nineteenth-century date.

Stratigraphic relationships suggest that the system of culverts, and the terraces identified, were associated with the construction of Hothouse 3. They were probably associated with modifications to Hothouse 2 and the construction of Hothouse 4, although it was not possible to determine the order of construction; it seems likely that these drainage measures preceded construction work on the western and eastern hothouses. They would have continued to operate, running beneath the paths of the garden, over time, with additions (in the form of downpipes and soakaways) feeding into the system. The pond, on the basis of observed stratigraphic relationships, seems most likely to have been an integral part of the original Hothouse 3. Map evidence suggests that it survived the demolition of this conservatory, as a circular feature is shown between Hothouse 2 and Hothouse 4 on Thomas Bell's map (*c.* 1849; see Fig. 8.9) and the Ordnance Survey map of 1856 (see Fig. 8.10).

The evidence for mortar spreads immediately to the south of Hothouse 2 and gravel surfacing immediately south of Hothouse 4 suggests hardstanding in front of the glasshouses. Subsequent use of this area in front of the glasshouses has been obscured by later truncations. Planting, particularly of vines into Hothouse 4's glasshouse, may have been inserted through this surfacing. Alternatively, and perhaps less plausibly, the vine roots may have been planted within the hothouse, although this was not common procedure.

## 4.2 Standing Structures of Garden 3

Between 1829 and 1849, the central part of Garden 3 contained three structures. Standing building recording revealed that Garden 2 Hothouse 2 was substantially modified to create a structure of dramatically different appearance, albeit incorporating elements of the original. The three furnace rooms were amalgamated into one long backhouse, large parts of the spine wall were rebuilt, and a new glasshouse was constructed to the south. The original three furnace rooms were still evident in the north side of the modified structure as three projections incorporating the original north walls of the furnaces. A new hothouse (Hothouse 4) constructed in the eastern plot was evidently designed to mirror the plan of the western example with three projections also in the north wall. Between the two hothouses a grand, though short-lived, conservatory was erected, the only evidence for this being the excavated remains of the robbed out south wall described above.

### Hothouse 1: a vinery

There is little structural evidence for modification of Hothouse 1 in the period 1817 to 1847. Barnfather's (1829) plan of the garden (see Fig. 8.6) labels the structure as a vinery. Historic mapping suggests some modifications to both the backhouse and the glasshouse at different times. On Bell's 1826 plan (Fig. 8.3) the glasshouse is rectangular, but is shown on Wood's 1827 plan (Fig. 8.4) and subsequent plans with the central section projecting; this may be a modification associated with new hothouses designed by John Hay of Edinburgh. No evidence of the glasshouse was identified archaeologically, due to it being obscured by the foundations of the fourth duke's conservatory, Hothouse 6. The backhouse also appears to have been modified; a central projection on the northern side on Bell's map of *c.* 1849 (see Fig. 8.9) can also be seen on the more detailed Ordnance Survey plan of 1856 (Fig. 8.10). This may relate to steps into the structure from the north. No evidence of this was seen in the standing building record, possibly due to the insertion of a later water tank.

### Hothouse 2: a peach house

The amalgamation of the three original Hothouse 2 furnace rooms created a backhouse with three slightly projecting bays. Little survived of the northern wall which was at best just three courses high, however the available evidence suggests a form of construction very similar to that of the northern wall of Hothouse 4 to the east, which was in a better state of preservation and with which it can be compared. The earlier form of Hothouse 2, with three furnace rooms, appears to have partly dictated the subsequent appearance of both buildings. The two, although differing slightly in dimensions and minor detail, would have presented a symmetrical and unified whole when viewed from the north. No windows were present within the northern wall of Hothouse 4, and Hothouse 2 is assumed to have been the same. One of the principal functions of the building, to provide heat to the glasshouse element to the front, would presumably not require external light and any light illuminating the building would have entered through open doors. This room was almost certainly a mushroom house given its similarity in layout to contemporary designs for such structures (see Fig. 9.36). A dark and warm environment would be required for mushroom cultivation (and for the forcing of other crops such as asparagus and sea kale) making windows unnecessary. On a later plan of the garden, a room in this position in Hothouse 4 is labelled as a '*Mushroom House*' (see Fig. 9.13).

These changes appear to represent modifications to the rear of the backhouses and were probably undertaken whilst the glasshouse frontage remained. A later phase of modification occurred when the original glasshouse frontage was replaced with an iron and glass curvilinear frame. Archaeologically this was attested in excavation to the south of Hothouse 2, which revealed a large robber cut [433] (see 3.2 above), at least 0.36m deep, infilled with a heavily compacted deposit of clean yellow clay. This had removed earlier glasshouse elements and preceded the construction of a later glass frontage, as documented in a bill of 1836 (DP/D3/I/43).

## Modifications to external structure of Hothouse 2 backhouses

The amalgamation of the three furnace rooms involved the construction of two clasping buttresses around the north-west and north-east corners of the structure which encompassed the northern half of the furnace rooms, thus creating bays which projected *c.* 0.30m north at each end of the building and were 4m wide externally (Fig. 4.6). In the central part of the hothouse a stretch of east–west wall constructed around the original north wall of the central furnace room created a third projecting bay which was joined to the bays at each end by long walls set back slightly to the south. The backhouse thus created measured *c.* 40m by 5.30m wide externally and 38.80m by 4m internally. This method of amalgamating the furnace rooms differed from that used in Hothouse 1 where new stretches of wall had been built flush with the original three furnace rooms. The clasping buttresses around the corners of Hothouse 2 were constructed in well-faced ashlar, with chamfered quoins, perhaps indicating a greater concern with architectural detail than previously

apparent, as well as a need to strengthen and consolidate the structure (Fig. 4.9). Unlike Hothouse 1, the north face of this building could be seen from within the garden and thus its external appearance may have been an important factor in its design (see below). Comparison with Hothouse 4 indicates that the north wall of the peach house would have been of well-built ashlar construction to its full height; the two doorways are also likely to have had Tudor-style moulded sandstone arches.

It is not possible to be certain whether the slope of the roof (shown on Fig. 3.14) reflects the original roof pitch of the Garden 2 backhouse, or a later addition, although both internal and external elevations demonstrate rebuilding above this height (Fig. 3.13, Fig. 3.14). However, this would appear to reflect the slope of the roof in the newly remodelled building, and this slope was apparently hidden from the north by parapets; such disguising of a lean to roof was recommended by Loudon (1825, 323):

'*Where the range of hot-houses is situated in the middle of the garden, great care must be taken, that it present nothing offensive, and that the sheds behind neither resemble a row of workshops, alms-houses, brickmakers' sheds, or cattlehovels. An effectual way of preventing this, is by carrying up the walls of the sheds as high as the other walls, thus completely concealing their roofs*'

The central buttress was poorly preserved, particularly towards its western end. The two sections of 0.50m-wide north wall which connected the three projecting elements appeared of uniform and contemporary build to this buttressing; where the north face survived this was of ashlar build. Air vents *c.* 0.20m-wide were constructed through the width of the north wall along its length.

## Modifications to Hothouse 2 spine wall

A large part of the spine wall was rebuilt or refaced when the three furnaces rooms were amalgamated into one; this was evident in the northern face as long stretches of well-constructed ashlar wall joining three segments of the original spine wall at each end and in the centre of the building (Fig. 4.6; Fig. 4.7; Fig. 4.8). The well-faced ashlar blocks utilised in this construction contrast with the less well-finished elements of building at either end and in the central section, suggesting that these elements represent later modifications, though whether only to the northern face of the original wall, in a similar manner to the clasping buttresses identified, or as part of an entire rebuild remains uncertain. The former hypothesis would allow rebuilding to be contemporaneous with the modifications noted above, as suggested by the similarity of construction techniques. Complete rebuilding of this wall seems less plausible and would presumably entail remodelling of the glasshouse frontage. Later plaster

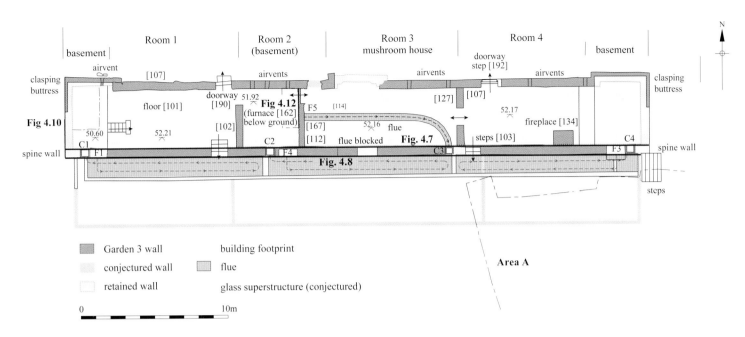

**Fig. 4.6** Hothouse 2, Garden 3, modified backhouse and retained glasshouse frontage (scale 1:250)

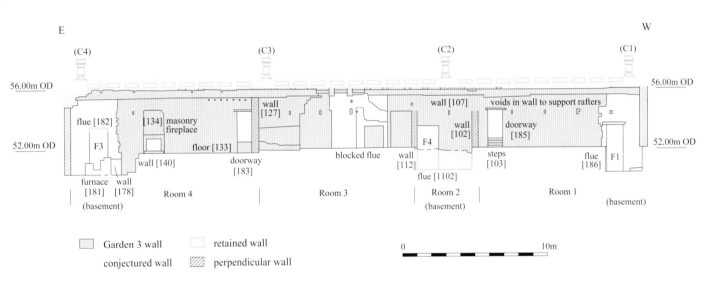

**Fig. 4.7** Hothouse 2, Garden 3, north-facing elevation of the spine wall, internal to the backhouse, showing Garden 3 modifications (scale 1:250)

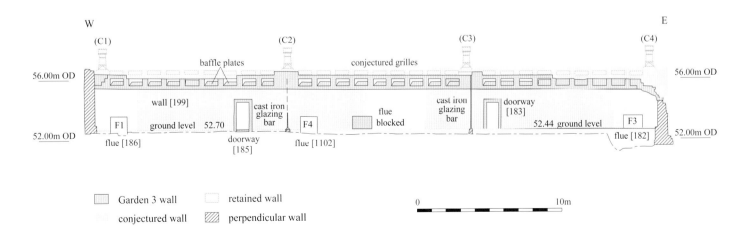

**Fig. 4.8** Hothouse 2, Garden 3, south-facing elevation of spine wall, internal to the glasshouse, showing Garden 3 modifications (scale 1:250)

**Fig. 4.9** Hothouse 2, external west wall showing the original wall of western furnace room, the later clasping buttress to north and heightened back wall to the south, looking east (scale 1m)

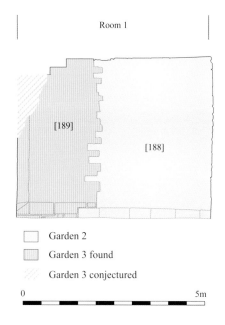

**Fig. 4.10** Hothouse 2, the west facing elevation of the west wall (scale 1: 100)

**Fig. 4.11** Internal view of the backhouse to Felton Park hothouse, showing the arrangement of supporting roof trusses; a similar arrangement would have been used in the backhouse of Hothouse 2 (VR 2017)

rendering on the southern side of the spine wall, internal to the glasshouse, obscured much of this face and therefore made it impossible to record most phases of construction.

Two *c.* 1m-wide doorways, the eastern one of which was subsequently blocked, would have allowed access from each end of the backhouse into the glasshouse to the south. Two stone steps [103] led up to the threshold from the north from the level of the flagstone floor, which was a later modification, inside the backhouse, demonstrating that the floor of the backhouse was at a higher level than the glasshouse. Substantial wear on the steps and threshold support suggest that they were part of the original build. As the flagstones remained unexcavated, it was not possible to identify the height of the original floor surface in the backhouse nor to determine if the steps exposed represent the original full flight.

Voids in the north face of the wall, 0.10m wide and 0.25m high at a height of 2.10m above floor level, would have been to accommodate the tie beams that supported the rafters of the roof trusses inside the backhouse (Fig. 4.7; Fig. 4.11).

**Hothouse 2 backhouse rooms (Rooms 1–4)**

The newly-built segments of north wall created one long backhouse for Hothouse 2 which was divided internally into four rooms (Rooms 1–4 from west to east).

Room 1 contained the original semi-basemented furnace room at its western end, the east wall of which was demolished to just below the new floor level and topped with pink and yellow sandstone slabs which formed the floor of Room 1 at a height of 52.20m OD. The eastern side of Room 1 was defined by a new 0.50m-wide north–south sandstone wall [102], creating a room 11m in length (Fig. 4.6). The stairs which had provided access down into the furnace room from the corridor of the Garden 2 structure were reused as access into the lower furnace room element of Room 1, with its floor at a level of 50.60m OD.

A 1.10m-wide doorway [190] in the north wall allowed external access into the backhouse; almost directly opposite this a door in the rebuilt section of spine wall provided access into the glasshouse. A 1.10m-wide doorway allowed access between Rooms 1 and 2, although this had been infilled during the latest modifications to the building (see section 6.2 below).

Room 2 measured *c.* 4m square internally, defined to the east by a brick wall which only survived to ground level. Excavation of infilling deposits in a sondage in the north-eastern corner of the room revealed that in its earliest phase Room 2 was semi-basemented; its eastern wall extended to a depth of 1.60m below the floor level in Room 1 and Room 3 and contained a furnace for heating a flue which ran under the floor of Room 3. At the base of the sondage was the mortar setting at a level of 50.65m OD for what had evidently been a brick-tiled floor, represented by pavior brick in the demolition debris infilling the room.

A blocked-up opening [102] in the spine wall in the south-east corner of Room 2, at 1.20m wide by *c.* 1m high and with an iron surround, was very similar to those in the western and eastern furnace rooms (Rooms 1 and 4). This suggests that it may originally have been associated with this building phase, forming a flue (F4) which would have provided hot air to flues identified south of the wall. Deposits which infilled the room were not excavated in the south side of Room 2 and no traces of the postulated furnace were revealed.

The eastern wall of Room 2 comprised three sections; well-faced ashlar block walls at each end with an inset brick furnace between (F5). The full extent of the northern element of stone wall was exposed, this was 1.10m wide and 1.17m high; only a small stretch of the southern wall was exposed within the excavated area (Fig. 4.12). The 1.10m-wide brick furnace [162] had two square openings in front, a stokehole and ash pit set one above the other (Fig. 4.13). Iron surrounds and hinges demonstrated that both had originally had iron doors. A substantial iron grate was set between the two. Beyond the stokehole extending to the east was a recess with an arched roof, to the rear of which was a flue built with brick

walls and an arched roof for added strength, *c.* 0.25m high. The flue continued east beneath the floor of Room 3. Over the top of the brick furnace and ashlar walls was a roughly coursed sandstone wall [160] upon which the brick wall [112] which divided Rooms 2 and 3 was constructed. A 1m-wide doorway in this wall in the north-east corner of the room, blocked-up during a later period of use, allowed access between Rooms 2 and 3.

Room 3 measured 10.40m by a maximum of 4.20m wide; part of the room encompassed the northern wall of the earlier central firehouse and therefore stepped out to the north by 0.30m for a length of 4m. The flue (F5) leading from the furnace in the dividing wall between Rooms 2 and 3 ran along the length of Room 3 beneath its floor, exiting into the glasshouse in the south-east corner of the room, providing under-floor heating to the room. There were no windows in this room which is interpreted as a mushroom house. The dark and warm environment would have been ideal for mushroom cultivation, blanching winter salads, preserving cauliflowers and broccoli and for forcing crops such as sea kale and asparagus (see Section 9.5). A later plan of 1900 shows that a similar room with flue in Hothouse 4 was used as a mushroom house, though by this date Rooms 1–3 in Hothouse 2 had been amalgamated into one long potting shed (see Fig. 9.13).

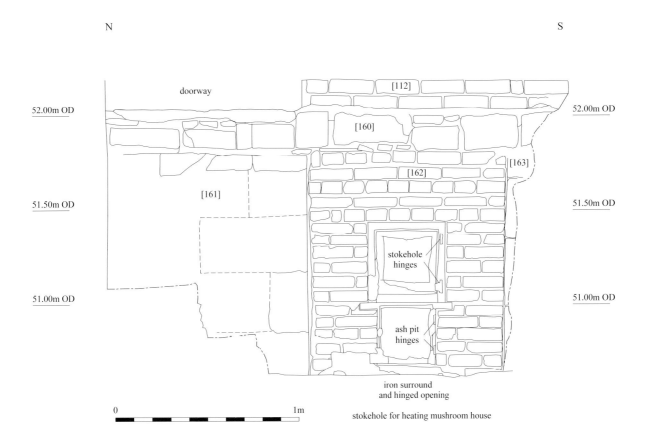

**Fig. 4.12** Hothouse 2, the east wall of Room 3, west facing elevation with mushroom house furnace (scale 1:20)

**Fig. 4.13** Hothouse 2, east wall of Room 2 showing mushroom house furnace in wall [162], looking east (scale 1m)

**Fig. 4.14** Hothouse 2, fireplace [134] on the south wall of Room 4, looking south (scale 1m)

The flue, exposed in the eastern end of Room 3 where the floor surface did not survive, comprised two parallel sandstone walls curving from the centre of the room towards its south-eastern corner and into the spine wall, from where a chimney (C3) led up through the thickness of the wall, venting the flue. This structure formed a housing for a brick-lined duct and presumably provided structural support. Slates at the top of the surviving wall were indicative of a levelling layer for a sandstone slab roof to the structure. It was ultimately infilled with sooted sandstone fragments, presumably from the collapsed roof of the structure. In the west, where the heating duct emerged from beneath the surviving floor, was an element of brick supporting wall, [167], which probably formerly supported a sandstone threshold. To either side of the duct, infilling and levelling deposits would have supported the floor in this area.

The eastern side of Room 3 was formed by a 0.50m-wide wall [127] of rough sandstone construction. A 1.10m-wide doorway with stone lintel set in the middle of this wall allowed access between Rooms 3 and 4, but had subsequently been blocked. The floor of Room 3 comprised sandstone, shale, brick and cement set on loose orange bedding sand and was at a height of *c.* 52.18m OD. This floor was well-worn, cracked in places and had evidently been repaired numerous times. The surviving eastern extent of the floor was of similar construction and also worn, but less patched; this area of flooring was contained within what were to become two small antechambers in a later use of the building, which may account for the lesser wear in these areas.

In a mirror image of Room 1, Room 4 encompassed the original eastern semi-basemented furnace room at its eastern extent. The western external wall of the original firehouse had been demolished to ground level to form the new larger room, 12m in length. As with Room 1, access through to the glasshouse was provided by a door through the rebuilt section of spine wall. Room 4 was provided with external access into the backhouse though a doorway in the northern wall. A 1m-wide doorway and step with a sandstone and cement threshold and 0.52m surviving of the stone jamb, had inset sockets in the corner of the jamb indicating the position of the doorframe. Markings on the floor of the room indicate the position of a former stairwell, demonstrating that the doorway was accessed via wooden steps in the south-west corner of the room. The floor surface only survived at the western end of Room 4, encompassing the area of what was to become a small room (Room 6) within the latest phase of the building. This was a regularly laid floor of predominantly pink, with some yellow, sandstone flags, the same as in Room 1, at a height of 52.17m OD. Access between Rooms 3 and 4 was via a 1.10m-wide doorway in the centre of the internal wall.

Set against the southern wall of the room, offset slightly to the east, was a sandstone chimney and fire surround [134]. Unlike later fireplaces in the backhouse, this did not abut the southern wall but was of free standing construction with four walls, set adjacent to the southern wall of the building. The outer faces of the sandstone blocks were pecked, perhaps to help adhesion of plaster rendering. There were indications of a former mantel and iron façade. The form of this chimney and use of massive ashlar blocks suggests contemporaneity with the buttressing of the corners of the building, construction of the northern wall and rebuilding of part of the spine wall. This interpretation is not without problems; the chimney associated with this fireplace would have appeared odd, given the otherwise perfectly symmetrical external appearance of this building and it is therefore quite possible that this represents a later addition or modification. At a later date the fireplace was infilled with brick to make a smaller aperture and a cast iron grate/surround was inserted.

## Heating apparatus

It is assumed that the hot flue heating system employed in the earlier glasshouse adjacent to the southern face of the spine wall was initially retained and incorporated into the new structure. The newly remodelled building incorporated three semi-basemented furnaces, one at each end of the structure (at the western and eastern extents of Rooms 1 and 4 respectively) and one off-set to the centre west (Room 2). Levels indicated that these were some 1.60m or so below the ground level through the rest of the backhouse. The eastern and western furnaces supplied hot air through vents in the wall and along flues (F1 and F3) situated to the south of the spine wall, within the glasshouse element of the building, and thence back to the spine wall where the smoke would have vented through chimneys (C1 and C4). Room 2 is assumed (on the basis of flues through the spine wall) to have incorporated a fireplace adjacent to the southern wall. This remained unexcavated but would have similarly supplied hot air to a system of flues (F4) in the central section of the southern backhouse and vented via a chimney (C2). A second fire, within Room 2 in its eastern wall, and incorporated beneath the floor at the western end of Room 3, supplied hot air via an underfloor flue (F5) and vented through a chimney (C3). With the exception of the furnace in the eastern side of Room 2 (Fig. 4.12, Fig. 4.13) none of the original furnaces were seen.

The upper part of the spine wall incorporated a ventilation system for the glasshouses; the surviving part comprised a 1m high ashlar wall with 27 openings in regularly spaced in three groups of nine, reflecting the three sections of the glasshouse (see Fig. 4.8). These openings measured 1m long x 0.50m high and were

**Fig. 4.15** Sole surviving trellised cast-iron plate above the ventilators, on the south face of spine wall, internal to glasshouse of Hothouse 2, looking north (RK 1998)

provided with metal shutters, to vent the glasshouse element of the building. When the 1998 survey of the gardens was carried out these openings contained cast hopper ventilators with very heavy cast iron frames and most still had brass pulleys and iron chain controls for the cast iron baffle plates (Kent 1998, 26). One rectangular pierced cast iron plate survived above the level of ventilators (Fig. 4.15). A curvilinear glasshouse dating from 1830 which has recently been restored at Felton Park, Morpeth, has very similar ventilators at the top of the spine wall, internal to the glasshouse with mechanisms for opening the ventilator plates (see Fig. 9.11). Along the top of the back wall of that structure, above the ventilators and external to the glasshouse, was a stone wall with pierced cast iron plates very similar to the single surviving example in Hothouse 2 (see Fig. 9.10).

## Hothouse 2: modifications to the Garden 3 peach house

The hothouse in this form, with reused hot air flues, presumably retained the original structure of the glasshouse, which would have been timber framed. Cartographic and documentary evidence demonstrates that the glasshouse in this form was short-lived. Barnfather's map indicates that the backhouse elements of the structure were rebuilt after 1829, but the associated glasshouse, as well as the original heating system in this hothouse, did not survive for long, as demonstrated by a bill of 1836 (DP/D3/I/43), which documents the replacement of the glass frontage of the building as well as the insertion of hot water boilers into the structure. Between 1829 and 1836 therefore the hothouse had been rebuilt, utilising an existing heating system, and then modified to accommodate technological developments.

**Fig. 4.16** Foundations of Hothouse 2 glasshouse and culvert in excavation Area A, looking north (scale 2 x 1m)

**Fig. 4.17** Detail of foundations of Hothouse 2 glasshouse in excavation Area A, looking south-west (scale 2 x 1m)

## Hothouse 2: rebuild of glass frontage

A rebuild of the glass frontage revealed within the excavation area to the south-east of Hothouse 2 is considered likely to be associated with the insertion of hot water boilers and construction of a new curvilinear iron frontage as documented on a bill of 1836 (DP/D3/I/43). A line of twelve brick column bases extended for a distance of over 10m, continuing to the west beyond the limits of excavation (Fig. 4.16; Fig. 4.17; Fig. 4.18). These represent the eastern end of the southern wall of the glass element of Hothouse 2 which had been built in a continuous linear trench, 1.20m wide. The area around the column base foundations was then backfilled with brick rubble, cobbles and sandstone fragments. Pottery of probable nineteenth-century date was recovered from this backfill.

The westernmost exposed column base comprised a sandstone block *c.* 0.48m square and 0.12m thick, on top of which five courses of brick, 0.34m by 0.32m, survived. The tops of the other bases were of identical construction. The east wall of the glasshouse was represented by a 0.48m wide north–south aligned sandstone block wall foundation [864], recorded for a distance of 2.90m. The glasshouse element would have been 4.80m wide and 38m long.

Extending to the north and south of one column base was a large, roughly hewn sandstone slab which measured 2.10m by 0.44m, into which was set a horizontal iron bar. To the west, a similar slab with horizontal bar, extended south from another column base. These bars, only seen at foundation level, may have formed an integral part of the cast iron superstructure. They resemble the 'long standards' seen on an architect's drawing (for Hothouse 4) dated 1830 (see

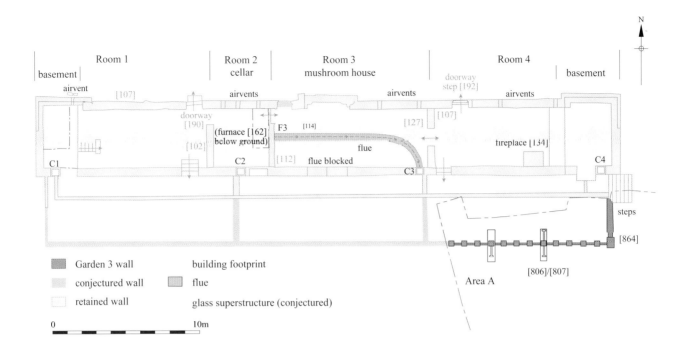

**Fig. 4.18** Hothouse 2, Garden 3 the backhouse and glasshouse following remodelling, including the construction of a new glass frontage and modifications to the heating system (scale 1:250)

**Fig. 4.19** Interior view of Felton Park glasshouse, showing the glazed panels which separate the different glasshouse elements; this is probably a similar arrangement to Hothouse 2, following the remodelling of the front of the structure (VR 2016)

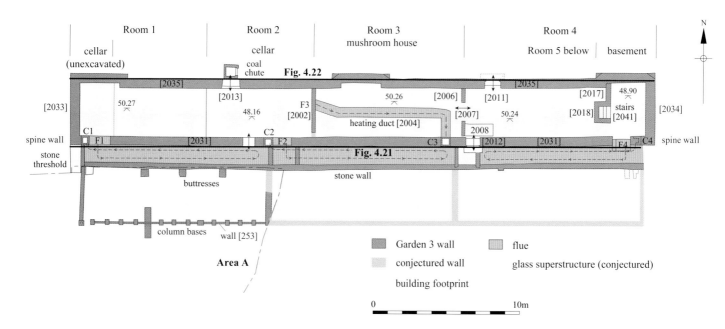

**Fig. 4.20** Hothouse 4, Garden 3, plan of the backhouse and glasshouse frontage (scale 1:250)

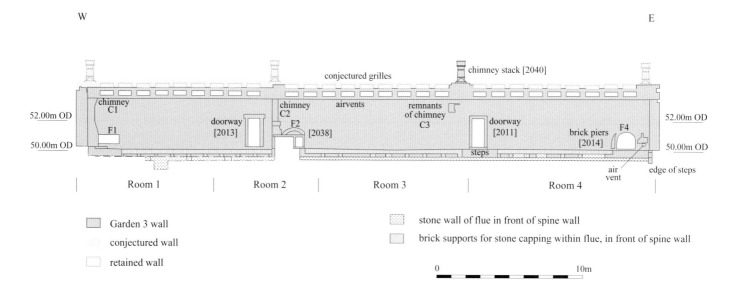

**Fig. 4.21** Hothouse 4, Garden 3, south facing elevation of the spine wall, the internal face of the glasshouse (scale 1:250)

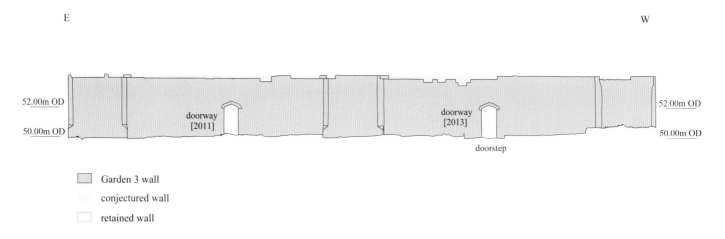

**Fig. 4.22** Hothouse 4, north facing elevation of north wall, the external face of backhouse (scale 1: 250)

Fig. 9.31) and presumably supported structural elements, carried up through the dwarf wall of the glasshouse.

Evidence for the division of the glasshouse into three separate rooms was seen in the survival of iron glazing bars on the spine wall of the structure (see Fig. 4.8). These demonstrate that the glasshouse element of the structure would have been subdivided by glazed panels, a detail which can be seen in the contemporary glasshouse at Felton Park (Fig. 4.19).

## Hothouse 2: modifications to heating system

Documented modifications to the hothouse, contemporary with the construction of the new curvilinear frontage, comprise the insertion of three new boilers to serve the three glasshouse elements of this structure. Little remained of these, except the occasional presence of cast iron pipes. The furnace which served the mushroom house apparently remained, heating the above-ground structure via a hot air flue.

The basement in Room 1 continued to provide heat to the corresponding glasshouse element to the south, but with the hot air flue system replaced by hot water pipes heated by a boiler in this room. The flagstones immediately in front of the original hearth contained two shallow sockets, 0.44m apart, which had residual iron encrustations and appear to be anchor holes for the boiler. There are indications that this may have continued south into the original hearth. To the west was a hearthstone, covered in black ash, with a 0.84m wide and 0.82m high opening in the back wall above this; this hearth may have been associated with the new boiler. The 1896 water supply plan shows pipes leading into Hothouse 4 from the main supply north of the building and running east–west adjacent to the spine wall, internal to the backhouse (see Fig. 6.11). The plan shows that the upper floor level of Room 1 [101] extended over the cellar to the south of the stairs, adjacent to the spine wall. On top of the floor was a square tank into which the western end of the water pipe fed and this presumably supplied the boiler underneath in the cellar. To the immediate south of the backhouse, internal to the glasshouse, a small stretch of north–south aligned pipework was observed, it is presumed that most of the hot water pipes had been removed, as had the boiler, for recycling or reuse elsewhere when the heating system was replaced by steam heating in the 1890s.

An opening [1102] in the back wall in the south-east corner of Room 2, at 1.20m wide by *c.* 1m high with an iron surround, was very similar to those in the western and eastern backhouses (see Fig. 4.7). The 1896 plan of the water supply shows a pipe leading through this opening, and it is possible that a water tank here may have fed a boiler in the Room 2 basement. Deposits which infilled the room were not excavated in the south side of Room 2 and no traces of a boiler were revealed.

## Hothouse 4: a vinery

The backhouse of Hothouse 4, the eastern hothouse, was presumably planned to mirror the western backhouse as this structure, despite the fact that it did not incorporate an earlier three-celled building, also had three external projections, in the centre and at each end, so that viewed from the north both buildings would have presented a unified and symmetrical appearance (Fig. 4.25). The structure measured 39.80m east–west, and up to 4.80m wide. The backhouse was 0.20m shorter than the western hothouse and 0.50m narrower. The four upstanding walls survived to a maximum height of *c.* 5m and, as the upper portions of these walls were in a state of partial collapse, investigation of the interior of the backhouse was not possible. The exterior was recorded and, following demolition to ground level, the surviving elements were recorded during a second phase of work at the site. The eastern hothouse is first labelled as a 'Vinery' on a plan of the gardens dated 1860 (see Fig. 8.11; Fig. 8.12). An architect's drawing in the castle archives dated 1830 shows some construction details of the vinery (see Chapter 9, Fig. 9.9; Fig. 9.29; Fig. 9.30; Fig. 9.31).

## Hothouse 4 spine wall

The spine wall of Hothouse 4 comprised a foundation course of large pink sandstone ashlar blocks above which were laid roughly hewn blocks in random bond to a height of 3.50m topped with a row of iron ventilators (Fig. 4.20; Fig. 4.21; Fig. 4.23). At the eastern end of the building the spine wall was exposed for a maximum height of *c.* 4m. The 1830 architect's drawing of the back wall for the vinery range shows a height of *c.* 4.65m from floor level to the top of the wall (12 feet 9 inches for the main wall topped with 1–foot high ventilators and 18–inch stone wall and gratings; see Fig. 9.9). The main upstanding element of the spine wall was *c.* 0.60m wide, which corresponds to the 2 feet wide wall shown on the drawing. At its base, elements of stone and brick walling extended to a maximum width of 2.10m in the south. These elements represent the remains of flues that would have heated the glasshouse (as in Hothouse 2); a drop in floor levels between the backhouse and glasshouse elements of the building was noted.

The heating operations appear to have been similar to the hot air vent system recorded in Hothouse 2. One chimney pot survived; this was an octagonal gothic chimney (Fig. 4.24), but there was evidence that the hothouse originally had four, one at each end, and the others spaced evenly between (Fig. 4.21). Four regularly-spaced chimneys were noted in the thickness of the walls in positions which corresponded to higher elements of the surviving stonework. These presumably vented hot air from the

**Fig. 4.23** Hothouse 4, rectified photograph of the southern face of back wall internal to the glasshouse, looking north

three flues which heated the glasshouse elements, with chimney C3 venting the heating duct which ran under the mushroom house in the backhouse and through the spine wall (see Room 3 below; Fig. 4.20; Fig. 4.21; Fig. 4.23).

The top of the vinery spine wall was capped with fine sandstone ashlar blocks which incorporated 27 rectangular air vents, symmetrically arranged between chimney stacks, in three groups of nine, a very similar arrangement to the spine wall in Hothouse 2. The air vents measured 1m wide and 0.30m high and the groups of nine reflected the three sections of the glasshouse. The 1830 drawing shows that the upper part of the back wall was of hollow construction with 1–foot-high iron ventilators (*c.* 0.30m) internal to the glasshouse topped with a 9–inch-high stone wall, incorporating ventilation grilles.

The spine wall was partially plaster-rendered on the southern side, internal to the glasshouse (Fig. 4.23); it was not possible to record the northern side as it was not safe to enter the building before demolition. Two doorways through the wall, each set 11m from the ends of the building, would have led through the backhouse into the glasshouse; the western one was blocked with brick at the time of recording (Fig. 4.21; Fig. 4.23). Traces of brickwork were evident in the spine wall to the immediate east of the western blocked-in doorway (Fig. 4.21; Fig. 4.23) and to the west of the eastern doorway. These appear integral to the original wall construction and extended to the chimney stacks, suggesting that the chimneys, which were integral to the wall structure, were built wholly in brick, presumably to better withstand heat. This detail was also observed and recorded in plan at the base of the wall, following the demolition of the structure. The 1896 plan of the gardens shows that, like the western hothouse, this glasshouse was divided into three elements. The western internal

wall was apparently demolished prior to the insertion of a rectangular sandstone structure into the wall, this remodelling was probably contemporary with the blocking-in of the doorway.

Traces of three arched brick apertures which had subsequently been blocked were also observed in the spine wall; these presumably represent wall flues which would have provided heat into each of the three elements of the glasshouse from furnaces in the backhouse. The easternmost flue was 1.20m wide and 1.10m high, largely blocked and with a water tank later inserted. A blocked-in arched flue was visible in the plaster rendering at the western end of the spine wall.

To the west of the centre of the building, east of the door between the glasshouse and the backhouse, was a brick arch for a flue (F2; later infilled with the insertion of a rectangular structure containing a water tank). Two stubs of north–south brick walls which protruded from the base of the spine wall on either side of the flue may represent the remains of the brick flue leading into the glasshouse. The water tanks were presumably inserted into two of the wall flues when the heating system was modified to hot water pipes.

## Heating apparatus

Based on evidence for flues, chimneys and hot air vents, and by direct comparison with Hothouse 2, it is suggested that Hothouse 4 had a similar heating system of hot air moving through flues adjacent to the northern wall of the glasshouse (see section 9.5, below). The brick and stone work which made up the glasshouse elements of this were clearly visible, although these had been subject to later modifications when later heating systems were introduced. At the time of recording the central furnace room

(Room 2) was exposed to its original floor level and two brick bases within this structure appear to have formed the supports for later boilers. However, traces of the original flues associated with the hot air heating system were visible, in the eastern and southern walls of Room 2 (Fig. 4.27).

## Hothouse 4 backhouse north wall

The northern (external) backhouse wall, which survived to a height of 4m, was constructed with well-faced pink and yellow sandstone ashlar blocks and had three projecting bays to the north, one at each end and one centrally placed, each 4m wide and projecting 0.30m (Fig. 4.20). The elevation of this wall (the only external backhouse wall to survive) is useful in terms of providing an idea of how Hothouses 2, 4 and 5 would have looked when viewed from the north. The plan of the building was evidently designed to mirror Hothouse 2, with the projecting bays of that building reflecting the integration of three furnace rooms from the earliest hothouse at that location. The western and eastern walls of the building [2033] and [2034] were of well-faced ashlar construction with chamfered quoins to the north; these reflected the quoins at the corners of Hothouse 2, although in the case of Hothouse 4 the quoins did not act as buttresses around the earlier furnace rooms. Evidence of the wall's rubble core was present to the east, west and centrally, visible above the height of surviving walls (Fig. 4.25).

Two 1m-wide doorways through the north wall were symmetrically placed between the bays, with Tudor-style moulded sandstone arches over (Fig. 4.22; Fig. 4.25). No windows were present in any wall of the building, a fact that presumably reflected the function of some elements of the building; the mushroom house would need to be dark as would any rooms used to store fruit.

**Fig. 4.24** Hothouse 4, octagonal chimney, looking north (RK 1998)

**Fig. 4.25** Hothouse 4, rectified photograph of the north wall looking south; showing the external face of backhouse, which was extant at the time of the standing building recording

## Hothouse 4 backhouse Rooms 1–4

Internally, four distinct rooms were identified, although only the remains of one upstanding internal division survived, between Rooms 3 and 4. Elsewhere, divisions between rooms were marked by changes in floor height. A brick wall [2002] between Rooms 2 and 3 showed no evidence for a doorway and appeared to have originally continued straight up to ceiling height from the cellar, although had been demolished to floor level at the time of recording. The building would thus have been in two parts, each with separate entrances to the north and south.

Room 1, at the western end of Hothouse 4, measured *c.* 9m by 3.50m at its widest point, where it formed the projecting western end of the building, narrowing to *c.* 3.20m (Fig. 4.20; Fig. 4.26). There are indications of a stub wall between Rooms 1 and 2 beyond which the eastern *c.* 2m of the room extended over Room 2, which was a cellar, the vaulted ceiling of which, and thus the floor at the eastern end of Room 1, had largely collapsed. The western wall of the cellar extended to the floor height of Room 1. Beyond, to the east, were indications of a brick-vaulted ceiling to the cellar, above which it is presumed the flagstone floor of Room 1 would have extended; this would have enabled entry into the room from door [2013] in the north wall. The doorway thus led into the building at ground level, with the floor, at a height of 50.27m OD, supported in this area by vaulting over the cellar. At the time of excavation this entrance was approached externally by a cobbled square floor surface incorporating a coal chute (which must originally been covered by a hatch); these external features presumably date to after a substantial phase of levelling (Garden 4 below). However, evidence for the coal chute in the northern wall of the cellar suggests that from the outset coal would have been supplied through an external chute into a cellar (Room 2) below.

In the south-western corner of Room 1 a bricked-up archway led through the wall and was visible in the plaster rendering on the south face of the spine wall. This would indicate that the room originally contained a furnace, which would have provided heat to the glasshouse via a flue (F1). Slumping of the flagstones within the western end of the room indicates the presence of an underlying infilled semi-basement or cellar, with the floor surface in this area representing a later modification after the cellar had been infilled.

Room 2, a 2m-deep cellar beneath the floor of Room 1, measured *c.* 7m east–west by *c.* 3.20m north–south. The western wall of the cellar comprised well-faced sandstone with evidence of brick capping for a brick barrel-vaulted ceiling. Although little of this vaulting remained, it was possible to determine that the ceiling to the cellar was formed of a single span vault running in an east–west direction. The provision of stone steps into the cellar adjacent to the spine wall appears to have been a later addition, as the doorway which entered the glasshouse through the spine wall (later blocked) lay adjacent to these steps; the doorway was presumably blocked by the time the stairs were inserted. This addition was probably contemporary with the construction of a boiler base for a hot-water heating system (Chapter 5). The barrel-vaulted element of the cellar appears contemporary with the building of the main structure and thus it is unlikely that the overall size of the cellar changed. It is suggested, therefore, that the original staircase took a different form; possibly timber or iron steps leading down into the cellar.

An arched flue through the spine wall in the south-east corner of the cellar indicated the location of a furnace to heat the central part of the glasshouse via flue F2. The 1896 plan of the garden water supply shows a '*drain from vinery stokehole*' exiting the cellar providing further evidence for the presence of a furnace in the original construction of Hothouse 4. Another furnace represented by a blocked-in aperture in wall [2002], the east wall of the cellar, would have fed the underfloor heating duct F3 which ran along the centre of the adjoining Room 3. This was very similar to

the arrangement in the western hothouse, which still contained the furnace and stokehole for the heating duct; it was evidently constructed as a mushroom house (Fig. 4.27; see section 9.5 below).

The lowest element of the cellar was floored with sandstone flags at a height of 48.16m OD. The coal chute entered the room from the north at this point, below doorway [2013], demonstrating that this area was used as a coal cellar, to supply fuel to the furnaces and presumably the later boiler in the cellar.

The form and layout of Room 3, which had a central underfloor heating duct, indicated that this was a mushroom house of very similar layout to that in Hothouse 2; a 1900 plan of the garden labels this room as such (see Fig. 9.13). The room measured *c.* 10m by 3.20m, with a projecting bay, west of centre in the north, extending the room width to 3.50m; this was built to mirror the central projection of the western hothouse. Room 2 was divided from Room 3 by brick wall [2002]. It seems unlikely that there was ever any doorway linking these rooms (which would, in any case, have emerged directly above a furnace) and thus the two elements were physically separate. Room 3 would have been accessed via Room 4, from which it was separated by a brick partition wall [2006], via a centrally placed doorway [2007] with sandstone threshold; sockets for the doorframe were apparent in the floor. The room was floored with pink and yellow sandstone flags and was divided centrally by the capping of the underfloor heating duct [2004] visible running along the length of the room. The floor was at the same level, 50.26m OD, as Room 1.

The floor was badly damaged in the north-east, but two lines of roughly hexagonal cuts visible in the stones either side of heating duct, at regular intervals (2m apart east–west and 1.50m apart north–south) presumably held the timber superstructure for the stacked mushroom beds. The surviving evidence suggests that this staging ran the length of the northern and southern walls in line with the 1800 design for a mushroom house (see Fig. 9.36).

The underfloor heating duct comprised a brick lining [2004] largely composed of broken bricks and comparable to elements of the heating duct in Room 3 of Hothouse 2 (Fig. 4.20). The duct was capped with sandstone slabs [2005] one slab (0.60m) wide, running for at least 8.50m (Fig. 4.28). In the west, the northern edge followed a diagonal line to the north-west, but the corresponding edge in the south was not so clear; the duct may have maintained the same width and turned north-west, or may have opened out towards the heat source. The course of the duct was also less clear towards the east, but the evidence of occasional bricks and cement repairs suggests that it turned to the south to vent via chimney stack C3 (Fig. 4.21). The sandstone capping may indicate a removeable cover to the flue.

Room 4 measured *c.* 9.50m in length and was entered from the north via a doorway represented by threshold [2011]. Another doorway, slightly offset to the west of the threshold led into the glasshouse to the south; a single stone step survived along with foundations for further steps (Fig. 4.20). Just inside the southern doorway, within the backhouse, a slate tiled area [2008] perhaps represented a repair to a worn area of floor in the vicinity of the entrance. Elsewhere the floor was formed by flagstones at a level 50.24m OD incorporating a large patch of cement repair, again indicative of heavy wear. The floor only survived in patches and a sandy, clayey bedding deposit with sandstone fragments was exposed in some areas. The floor extended *c.* 7m east–west and finished at a good, well-faced edge, perhaps suggesting an internal division (possibly of timber) of which nothing remained.

The cellar, Room 5, measured *c.* 2.30m by 3.50m internally. The western extent of the room was formed by a sandstone block north–south wall [2017] incorporating steps. There was no indication as to whether the wall continued above the height of ground level, although it is assumed that it did not. The cellar was reached from Room 4 by a flight of at least three steps [2041];

**Fig. 4.26** Hothouse 4, Room 1 with Room 2 (cellar) beyond, looking east (scale 1m)

**Fig. 4.27** Hothouse 4, Room 2, showing the wall [2002] between the cellar and mushroom house, looking east. The blocked-in aperture below the mushroom house heating duct presumably originally allowed heat to be supplied to the house; photograph taken before excavation of deposits overlying the cellar floor (scale 2m)

**Fig. 4.28** Hothouse 4, Room 3, the mushroom house with its central flagstone-capped underfloor heating duct, looking east (scale 1m)

mortar with a very rough finish probably represents the base for sandstone steps which had been removed. The steps descended at least 0.82m but the floor of the cellar was not seen as the material backfilling the room was not fully excavated.

An arched opening in the spine wall, F4 (subsequently blocked in with brickwork [2014]) represents a wall flue; a furnace in the cellar would have provided the heat source for the glasshouse (Fig. 4.21; Fig. 4.23).

### Hothouse 4 glass frontage

Elements of the foundations for the western end of what is considered most likely to be the original glasshouse of Hothouse 4 were revealed during excavation. Twelve column bases were exposed for a distance of 11m east–west set at regular intervals of *c.* 1m (see Fig. 3.2). Sample excavation revealed a shallow rectilinear construction cut [828] (see Fig. 4.5) and it is assumed that a single construction cut extended for the length of the structure. Fourteen courses of red unfrogged bricks, surviving to a height of 1.04m, represent one of the column bases; the rest were not excavated (Fig. 4.20). The column bases were apparently founded from a level of *c.* 49.20m OD, but the relative height of the corresponding internal floor area was not observed due to subsequent resurfacing. Adjacent to the eastern limit of excavation a north–south aligned sandstone wall [881] 0.40m wide extended for at least 2.2m but remained unexcavated. It is possible that the sandstone wall adjacent to the eastern limit of excavation represents a structural element of the westernmost bay. Immediately south of the structure, a thin (100mm thick) deposit of purplish-brown gravel overlain by an extensive layer of crushed sandstone up to 0.12m thick and extending 5.80m north–south, formed a broad, well-surfaced path or terrace extending along the front of the hothouse, at a height of 49.23m OD.

Part of an irregular feature located 5m to the south of Hothouse 4 ran on the same alignment as its western wall (see Fig. 4.3). Evidence of heavy root action visible at its base suggests that this represents the position of a hedgerow representing a planting division.

Modifications to the front wall of Hothouse 4 were recorded in plan along its exposed length. A series of construction cuts were made between earlier existing column bases into which were built lengths of east–west wall, utilising orange-pink frogged brick. An excavated example one brick thick survived to a height of six courses ([253] see Fig. 4.5). These walls were presumably built to strengthen and prepare the existing structure for the erection of a new curvilinear glass frontage. At the easternmost exposed end of the column bases, a 0.40m-wide north–south aligned sandstone wall was recorded for a distance of 2.20m. This may represent an internal partition which divided the glasshouse into three segments; detailed drawings of the garden from 1896 show this arrangement (see Fig. 9.12). A stone wall [292] on the same alignment to the west between column bases [210] and [211] supported an iron girder and may represent part of an internal fitting. A glasshouse floor, comprising a 0.15m thick layer of cement[270], may represent the associated internal surface, or the bedding for a stone or tile floor, since removed.

A drawing in the castle archives (dated 1859) of a cross section of the garden (PB 236) shows the western gable end of Hothouse 4 as a curvilinear glasshouse attached to the backhouse (see Fig. 9.7). The frame of the glasshouse is resting on a low wall; prefabricated cast-iron glasshouses frames would be ordered from the manufacturers and erected on stone walls (or in the case of the front of this glasshouse, brick supports, presumably with a stone lintel above) built to a specification supplied by the ironmongers. The date of the installation of the curvilinear frontage to this glasshouse is unknown, other than that it had been constructed

**Fig. 4.29** Hothouse 5, Garden 3, Room 3 showing the upstanding spine wall with all other walls of the backhouse reduced to floor level, looking south (scale 2 x1m)

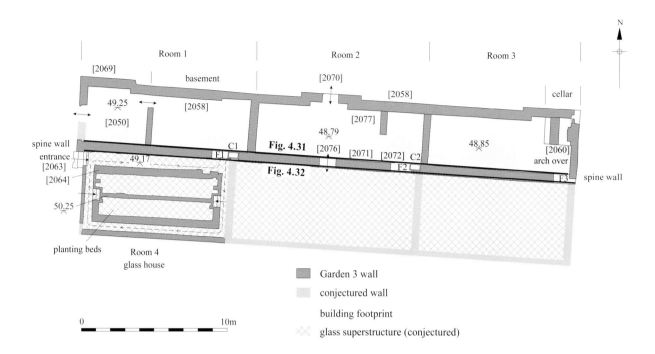

**Fig. 4.30** Hothouse 5, Garden 3, plan of backhouse, excavated element of glasshouse and conjectured glasshouse frontage (scale 1:250)

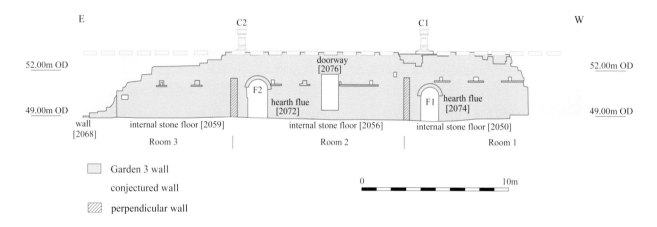

**Fig. 4.31** Hothouse 5, Garden 3, north-facing elevation of the spine wall, the internal face of the backhouse (scale 1:250)

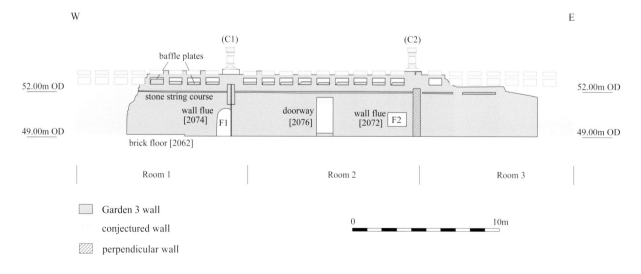

**Fig. 4.32** Hothouse 5, Garden 3, south-facing elevation of the spine wall, the internal face of the glasshouse (scale 1:250)

before 1854. Logic dictates that it is likely to have been added at the same time as that on Hothouse 2, but whether it was initially constructed as a curvilinear-fronted building, or with a pent roof is unknown. The Bailey Bill of 1836 (DP/D3/I/43) suggests that the installation of curvilinear frontages was closely connected with the installation of hot water boilers, the two technologies being complementary, however Hothouse 4 was obviously originally constructed with flues running along the back wall, and thus is seems most probable that water-heating was a later introduction.

## Hothouse 5: a pinery

The backhouse element of Hothouse 5, located in the south-eastern corner of the original walled garden, was less well preserved than that of Hothouse 2 or Hothouse 4 with only the spine wall surviving above contemporary ground level (Fig. 4.29). In contrast, approximately one third of the glasshouse beds and external walls were exposed in the south-west, although only limited investigation of these glasshouse elements was possible due to health and safety issues. No excavation was carried out, beyond clearance and cleaning of the existing structure.

The backhouse was a three-bayed building, constructed to reflect Hothouse 2 and Hothouse 4, although this hothouse was substantially shorter at 34.50m. The backhouse was divided into three distinct elements, with some internal sub-divisions (Fig. 4.30). As with the other hothouses, each bay of the building initially contained a furnace, represented by flues through the spine wall, subsequently blocked, which would have fed into heating ducts in the glasshouse.

This hothouse is shown on a plan of the garden from the 1860s as a '*Pinery*' (see Fig. 8.14), on the 1900 water supply plan as a 'Forcing House' with sheds at the back (see Fig. 9.13) and on a plan of the gardens from 1928 as for 'Pears, Figs and Plums' (Kent 1998). The original use of this building, as a pinery, is reflected in the distinctive construction technique of the glasshouse element of the buiding.

### Hothouse 5 external structure

Hothouse 5 measured 34.50m east–west with a 5m-wide backhouse and 5.50m-wide glasshouse, giving an overall external width of 10.50m for the structure. The northern wall of the building [2058] had collapsed almost down to ground level when recorded. Three projecting bays were evident, one at each end of the building and one centrally placed, to mirror the two hothouses to the north. The bays were *c.* 4m wide, though with slight variations, and protruded 0.30m to the north of the line of the northern wall. The surviving north-western corner of the building

[2069] was of sandstone ashlar construction.

The spine wall, which was constructed in dressed ashlar blocks with rubble and cement infill, was 0.60m wide and survived to a height of 4.20m. It was plaster rendered on its southern face, internal to the glasshouse, to a height of around 2m; the upper and lower parts of the wall were not rendered. At the top of the plaster rendering was a thin flagstone string course, partially jutting out, forming a stone shelf and above this 5–6 courses of ashlar blocks were visible for a height of 1.20m (Fig. 4.32; Fig. 4.33).

The top part of the wall comprised groups of rectangular openings through the wall (1m wide by 0.40m high) which contained cast iron hopper ventilators. The upper courses of the wall did not survive at the eastern and western ends of the building and only one and four vents survived at these ends of the building, respectively (Fig. 4.33). The central group of nine vents survived intact, giving an indication of the arrangement of vents along the length of the spine wall; this would have been similar to the arrangement in Hothouse 2 and 4.

Excavation of the deposits infilling the glasshouse revealed the lower part of the spine wall at the western end of the building, below the level of the plaster rendering. Three openings through the spine wall, which had subsequently been bricked up, represent wall flues through the spine wall leading from furnaces in the backhouse suggesting that the building was originally heated via hot-air flues, as with Hothouse 2 and Hothouse 4, and a single central doorway provided access between backhouse and glasshouse. The northern face of the spine wall contained a series of holes up to 0.30m square which would have housed the timber beams for the rafters of the roof trusses.

### Hothouse 5 backhouse Rooms 1–3

The backhouse was divided into three parts by internal walls. Unlike Hothouse 2 and Hothouse 4, the north wall contained just one centrally placed doorway, allowing access into Room 2. The western third, Room 1 was accessed via a wide doorway in the west wall of the building and incorporated a basement at its eastern end. Room 3 had incorporated a cellar at its eastern end in the original build. Survival of the east wall of the structure was limited so it was not possible to determine if access into this part of the backhouse was via a door in the east wall, although this seems probable. As with Hothouse 2 and Hothouse 4, the glasshouse element of Hothouse 5 was divided into three sections and, in its original build, three furnaces in the backhouse would have heated these parts of the glasshouse via the three flues in the spine wall.

Room 1 measured 4.10m by a maximum of 3.60m internally, narrowing to 3.40m wide in the east where the projecting bay ended. An unusually wide doorway (2.20m at its narrowest point)

**Fig. 4.33** Hothouse 5, rectified photograph of the southern face of the spine wall, looking north, the internal face of the glasshouse

**Fig. 4.34** Hothouse 5, rectified photograph of the northern face of the spine wall, looking south, the internal face of the backhouse

allowed access from the west end of the building (Fig. 4.35). A rebate in the stone threshold to the north of the entrance and bricks set against the sandstone surround, creating a rebate in the south formed sockets for the doorframe. The internal east wall of the room was brick, two courses wide, with a doorway at the northern end leading into Room 2. The floor of Room 1 in the west, at 49.25mOD, was *c.* 0.50m higher than Rooms 2 and 3 and was paved with predominantly yellow, with some pink, sandstone flags.

The basemented area of the room measured 6.70m by 3.30m internally with the eastern extent formed by a sandstone wall. As there were no signs of any doorway through the wall, the building was apparently divided at this point. In the south-east corner of the room a semi-circular brick arch [2074] in the spine wall, 1.10m wide and 2.10m high, had been infilled with brickwork (Fig. 5.32). Only the upper half of this arch was visible above the floor level of the glasshouse to the south (Fig. 5.33). A furnace within the basement, which would have provided heat to flues within the glasshouse, would have been housed within this arched opening. This was very similar to the arrangement observed in the furnace rooms of Hothouse 4, with the base of the furnaces being built

below the level of the bottom of the flue thus creating a strong through-draught for optimal performance. It was not possible to fully excavate the rubble and demolition debris which infilled the cellar and its full depth was not ascertained.

Room 2 measured 11.30m by 3.60m internally at its widest point. A sandstone wall which divided Rooms 2 and 3 only survived to foundation level so it was not possible to ascertain whether a doorway provided internal access into Room 3. The room was entered externally via the central doorway in the northern wall which was predominantly apparent as a single sandstone block threshold, well worn at the centre. This entrance was positioned directly opposite the door [2076] through the spine wall and into the glasshouse; this had a stressed quoin surround to the north and dressed sandstone jambs and lintel to the south, defining the door against the rendered and limewashed southern face of the spine wall. The door emerged at contemporary ground level in the glasshouse to the south, but was *c.* 0.70m above the floor level of 48.76mOD in the backhouse and thus would have been accessed via steps (Fig. 5.34); the floor level of the backhouse was lower than that in the glasshouse. The floor of Room 2 was

also of predominantly yellow, with some pink, sandstone flags, bedded on pale yellow sand. Occasional square recesses visible in the floor, set adjacent to and *c.* 1m away from the southern wall, presumably housed elements of timber staging.

In the south-eastern corner of Room 2, a semi-circular brick arch [2072] through the spine wall, 0.90m wide and 2.50m high, also presumably represents the remains of a furnace for the original heating system (F2). To the east of the external doorway [2070] a north–south stub wall [2077] against the northern wall of the building only survived to foundation level; this was probably a short partition to sub-divide the room, perhaps separating the furnace area from the rest.

Room 3 had maximum dimensions of 7.80m by 3.60m, wider at the eastern end where it incorporated part of the projecting bay. The floor was predominantly yellow sandstone flags with occasional regularly spaced recesses representing elements of internal fittings. In the north-eastern corner of the room the floor had slumped above barrel vaulting [2060] over a cellar covered (where surviving) with mortar infill. There were indications of a former flagstone floor above. In the south-eastern corner of the room, brick infilling

was apparent in the spine wall, though this had largely collapsed when recorded. This represents the location of a furnace, set within the cellar. In the north-east corner at ground floor level a stone-lined aperture (with later stone slab on top) was presumably a coal chute into the cellar providing fuel for the furnace below (Fig. 4.36). It is possible that there was a door in the east wall of the building providing access into this part of the backhouse, but due to the extent of collapse this could not be determined.

## Hothouse 5 glasshouse

The western third of Hothouse 5 glasshouse, which represents one of three separate glasshouse elements, measured 9.70m internally. Sandstone ashlar block wall foundations formed the southern and western extents, respectively, of the *c.* 5m-wide glasshouse; these would have supported a superstructure, of which nothing remained. The glasshouse was accessed from the north-west corner via steps [2063] comprising two sandstone slabs forming a threshold, beyond which brick steps led up to the east.

Inside the glasshouse a rectangular structure [2064] comprised

**Fig. 4.35** Hothouse 5, Room 1, looking east with Hothouse 7 and the garden boundary wall in the background (scale 1m)

four narrow walls with a longitudinal central division. A *c.* 0.50m-wide gap between the external walls of the glasshouse provided access along the outside edges of this room, which were plaster rendered on their external faces. The northern side survived to a height of 0.63m at 49.80m OD and comprised a brick and sandstone wall set on brick plinths set at roughly 0.80m intervals, extending north from a stretcher laid wall, with a brick base. Between this and the spine wall was a 1m-wide brick surface at a level of 49.17m OD. It is possible that a suspended ironwork floor above this surface may have been inserted at a later date over pipework when hot water boilers were introduced, as suggested by the lack of rendering to the lower part of the wall (see Chapter 6 below); such heating systems have been observed elsewhere. However, this suggestion remains speculative. The flues which would have extended around all four sides of the raised planting bed were not excavated (see section 9.5 below).

The walls defined a rectangular area that measured 8.80m east–west by 3.70m north–south externally with a central east–west division. This formed two planting beds, the northern set at a higher level than the southern one, probably to maximise sunlight (Fig. 4.37). In the southern bed, the internal sandstone element of the wall sloped up to the north in the east and west, suggesting that planting within this part was set on a slope. Steps at either end provided access to the higher, northern, bed. The central internal wall of the planting bed, set 1.50m to the south of the north wall, was seven courses high and two wide, on sandstone foundations. The wall widened at either end where the brickwork extended around sandstone steps two courses high. Externally the southern wall was of brick and internally was formed of large, dressed sandstone blocks, infilled with cobbles and cement.

**Fig. 4.36** Hothouse 5, eastern end, showing Room 3 with a stone-lined coal chute (and later stone capping) in the north-west corner and covered cellar, looking west (scale 2 x 1m)

**Fig. 4.37** Hothouse 5, foundations of the glasshouse with internal planting beds at western end, looking east (scale 1m)

## The water tower

Barnfather's 1829 plan shows the proposed plan for a water supply for the gardens which was undertaken by the third duke and includes a plan and elevation of the water tower which provided this supply (see Fig. 4.38). The need for a reliable water supply may have been dictated by the construction of the large lily pond to the south of the central conservatory and was to become even more essential with the introduction of hot water heating to some of the hothouses. The water tower was originally intended to be sited adjacent to the southern wall of the eastern kitchen garden extension (see Fig. 8.6) but was ultimately built just to the south of the Gardener's House, straddling the west wall of the new kitchen garden, as shown on the 1856 Ordnance Survey plan (Fig. 8.10). A pencil note on Barnfather's plan indicates this new location (see Fig. 4.2).

The water tower is extant and has been repaired as part of the new Alnwick Garden (Fig. 4.39). The tower is of roughly similar design to that proposed in 1829, comprising a crenellated tower square in plan with wings to the north and south, constructed with pecked ashlar walls (Kent 1988, 28). The east elevation has a large arched doorway beneath a pair of trefoil arched blank windows, flanked by cross-loops (Fig. 4.39). The bark store underneath the tower would have provided tan for the hothouses but may also have served to prevent the water from freezing. The wings have segmented arched doorways under slit loops. The single ground floor chamber has a pointed sandstone tunnel vault with five chamfered transverse arches, supporting an open water tank. The south wing contains a spiral staircase to the roof.

## A vinery external to the walled garden

Wood's 1827 map shows that a new hothouse was constructed external to the original walled garden, a short distance to the north-west of the Gardener's House. This was labelled on an architect's drawing of 1863 (PB 233) as an '*Old Vinery*'. The backhouse element is extant (Fig. 4.40).

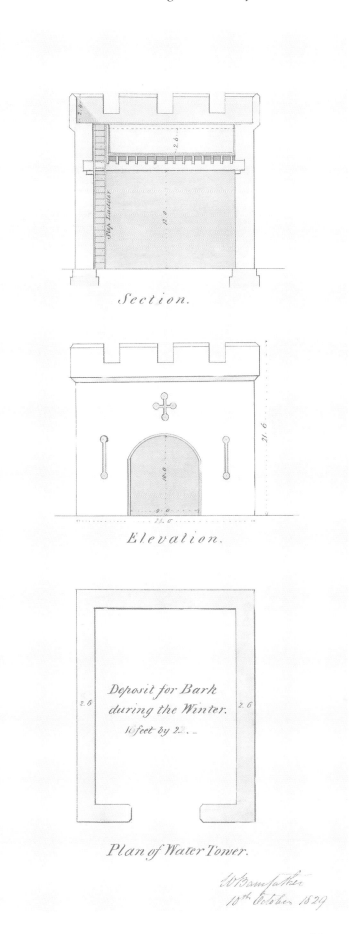

**Fig. 4.38** Detail of proposed water tower from an 1829 plan of the gardens (Barnfather 1829)

**Fig. 4.39** Water tower showing arched doorway in east wall and trefoil-arched windows flanked by cross loops (VR 2015)

**Fig. 4.40** Backhouse of the vinery north-west of the Gardener's House built *c.* 1827, outside and just west of the Alnwick Walled Garden, looking west (VR 2015)

# Chapter 5

## Garden 4, The Garden of the Fourth Duke (1847–1865)

*'In the centre of a broad walk stands the Conservatory, a recent structure, one hundred feet long, divided into three aisles by two rows of iron columns, the centre forming a walk, with flowers on either side... From the Conservatory, the numerous Vineries, and Forcing Houses, the smoke is carried by an underground flue to a distant chimney, where it is so thoroughly consumed, that a little white vapour only is visible at its summit.'*

(Hartshorne 1865)

Algernon, the fourth duke (1847–1865), brought radical changes to the gardens; the original walled garden was transformed and much of the previous layout swept away. By 1859 the duke had purchased land to the south of the existing walled garden and plans were drawn up for a new, extended and largely decorative garden, the creation of which would have been a substantial undertaking. This garden was still in the process of being created at the time of the fourth duke's death in 1865; the 1867 Ordnance Survey map shows the completed new garden (Fig. 8.20). The southern wall of the original walled garden, with the exception of a short segment in the south-east corner, and the eastern wall of the second duke's kitchen garden were demolished. 'The Goose Knows' field on the hillside between the original gardens and the town was incorporated into the enlarged garden; boundaries of this garden remain the same today. An additional hexagonal walled garden (the upper garden) was created to the south of the newly landscaped hillside abutting the rear gardens of properties fronting onto Bondgate Without and accessed internally from the north via a triple-arched gateway. A new, separate, walled kitchen garden was built to the west with an entrance close to the gardener's house; this was presumably intended to replace the second duke's kitchen garden which had been amalgamated into the newly expanded garden.

The garden eventually created was Italianate in design, reflecting the duke's taste and contemporary fashions, the objective being to create a garden to match the recently-restored castle, which included Italianate State Rooms. The Ordnance Survey map of 1867 (Fig. 5.2; see Fig. 8.20) shows Garden 4 as originally laid out; many elements survived as earthwork features and stone structures at the time of the fieldwork as well as being revealed as below-ground archaeology (Fig. 5.1). The garden was laid out along a north–south central axis and two distinct areas, the middle and lower garden, were created, separated by a central ornamental rectangular pond with an apse. Massive L-shaped retaining walls were constructed to support the raised ground levels in the middle garden and the terraces to either side of the pond. Parterre gardens in the lower garden replaced the plots which had previously characterised this area. Ground levels and paths were raised, although the spatial arrangement of the paths which had previously divided the garden into eastern, central and western plots within the central area changed little.

Elements of this design, as excavated in the lower and middle gardens, comprised parterres defined by cobble borders flanking a broad central path, with smaller north–south paths to either side. A central east–west path recorded at the northern limit of excavation formed part of an extensive path which crossed the garden, running between entrances through the garden boundary wall.

Parterres in the middle garden were situated on steeply-sloping ground and were enclosed to the east and west by monumental curving earthwork banks (see Fig. 8.16). The curved southern end of the southernmost parterre and earthwork echoed the shape of the Percy crescent (as shown beneath the legend at the top left of Thompson's map of 1760; see Fig. 1.10). The large raised mounds and associated terracing to create the lower and middle garden entailed substantial excavation and ground level changes and this is reflected in the archaeological record; a significant depth of what appeared to be imported sand was encountered below garden deposits on the sloping hillside. Some of the original layout of the new formal garden parterres survived in the upper garden as main paths defining the parterres.

The fourth duke also rebuilt Hothouse 1 on the northern wall, the basement of which was converted into the furnace room of an impressive new conservatory (Hothouse 6). The above-ground elements of this building comprised a glasshouse built against a new wall which projected to the north beyond the line of the original walled garden, covering the footprint of the glasshouses and backhouses of the original hothouse which stood in this location (see Fig. 8.20).

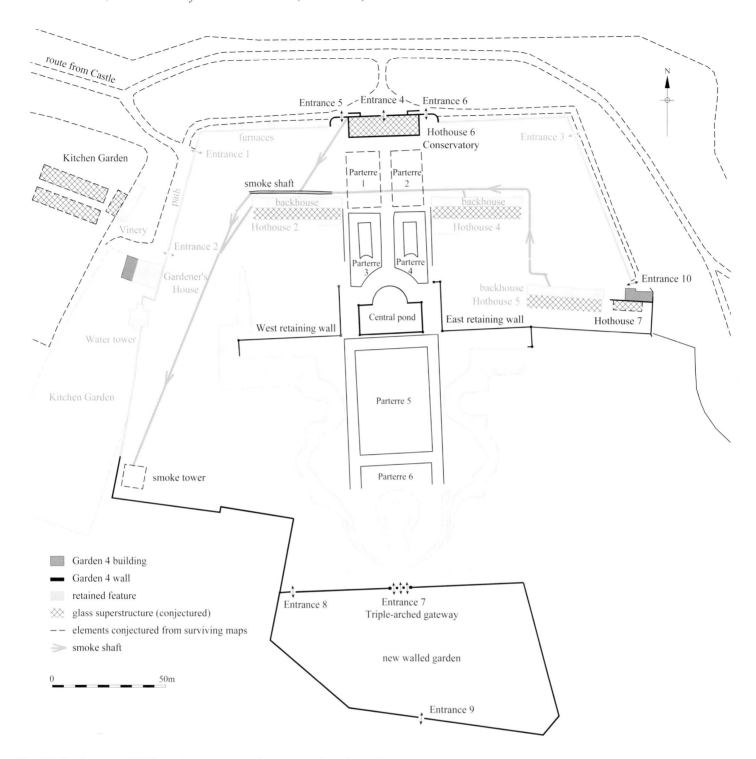

**Fig. 5.1** Garden 4, c. 1860, based on surviving elements, archaeological excavation, conjecture and contemporary map evidence and showing retained elements of earlier gardens (scale 1:1250)

Curved walls were constructed to either side of the new conservatory between which ran the newly constructed east–west stretch of boundary wall, set back to the north from the original perimeter, which formed the rear wall of the new conservatory. Two narrow entrances (5 and 6) were set within the newly-built stretch of wall at either side of the conservatory, replacing the two entrances that had been created here in Garden 3, as illustrated on the Ordnance Survey map of 1856 (see Fig. 8.10, Fig. 5.13). A wide entrance allowed access into the centre of the

conservatory from the north. The centre of this new building, the mound and the triple-arched gate of the hexagonal garden to the south were constructed along a north–south central axis through the garden. The original backhouse of Hothouse 1 was incorporated into a cellar for the northern conservatory, indicating a major change in external ground levels resulting in the structure changing from a semi-basemented backhouse to a fully below-ground cellar; such landscaping was presumably necessary due to the rising ground levels inside the garden, and

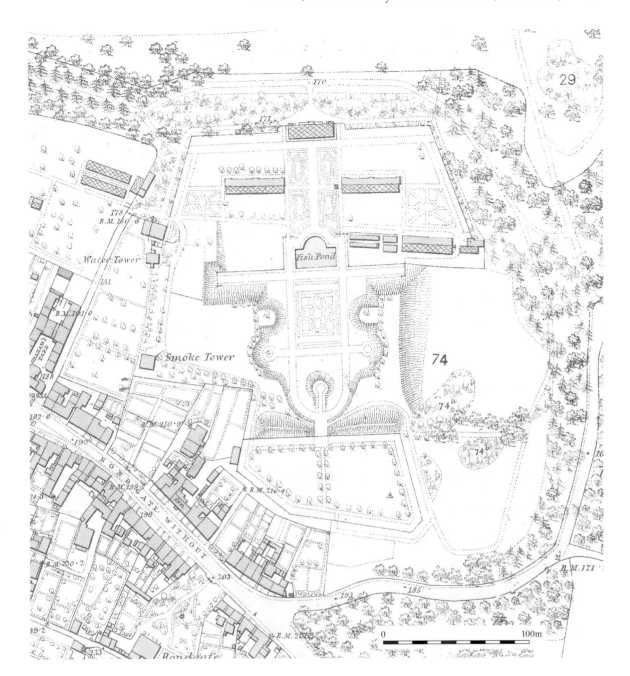

**Fig. 5.2** Extract from the Ordnance Survey map of 1867 showing the fourth duke's garden (see Fig. 8.20 for an illustration of the garden in relation to Alnwick and the Castle) (scale 1:2500)

is also reflected in the need to raise the height of the northern boundary wall. Flights of steps were constructed to provide access at either end of the cellar along with coal bunkers and a new heating system was installed.

Hothouse 2, Hothouse 4 and Hothouse 5 remained in the west, east and south-east, and apparently changed little in use; some modifications to the buildings reflect different methods of providing heat. A new small glasshouse, Hothouse 7, was also built to the east of the pinery, Hothouse 5, abutting the original garden wall at its south-east corner. This is shown on the 1860 map with a glass frontage and is labelled on a design for the new garden as '*New Vinery*'.

Elements of an east–west aligned shaft recorded to the north of Hothouse 2 and Hothouse 4 formed part of an extensive system of smoke shafts installed during this period. The 1896 plan of

the water supply to the garden shows smoke shafts leading from all of the hothouses, including those in the south-east corner, and conservatory and it is assumed that these were constructed at the same time as the smoke tower, to draw smoke away from furnaces or boilers in the hothouses. Map evidence shows that the tower was built between 1856 and 1860; it first appears on the Ordnance Survey First edition in the south-west corner of the extended garden (see Fig. 5.2).

The terrace walls and the pond survived at the time of the fieldwork and were subject to standing building recording; the east–west aligned elements of the terrace walls have been incorporated into the new Alnwick Garden. An earthwork survey was also carried out on the curving mounds in the middle garden, which have also been incorporated into the design of the present garden.

**Fig. 5.3** The Venetian wrought iron gate in the centre of the northern garden wall, as seen at the time of fieldwork; the iron supports for trellis wires can be seen to either side of the entrance (Entrance 4)

# 5.1 Excavated Remains of Garden 4 Pond *c.* 1850

Prior to the purchase of the Goose Knows field to the south of the original garden, the central part of the original walled garden was altered. Bell's *c.* 1849 map and the 1856 Ordnance Survey map, which was surveyed in 1851, show that following the demolition of the third duke's central conservatory (Hothouse 3), a small pond or fountain, which may be the remains of a feature originally housed within the conservatory, occupied the central plot of land, equidistant between the eastern and western hothouses (see Fig. 8.9). Features recorded in plan and section [938] represent the robbing of a curvilinear wall defining a circular structure with an internal diameter of *c.* 3m; this is assumed to be the pond (see Fig. 4.1; Fig. 4.3). Demolition rubble infilling the feature suggests that it was of sandstone construction.

# 5.2 Excavated Remains of Garden 4, Lower Garden

Elements of the formally laid-out lower parterre garden which formed part of the enlarged garden of the fourth duke lay within Area A and were excavated and recorded (Fig. 5.5). The western and eastern hothouses remained standing and continued in use throughout the use of Garden 4, fitting into the symmetrical formal layout of the new garden, and north–south paths between the two remained in much the same position in this garden scheme, despite extensive ground levelling. There is evidence of widespread preparation for this new garden layout, involving demolition and removal of earlier features and sequential levelling events. The layout appears more formal and rigorously designed than previous phases of garden development recorded during the excavations, though this may partly due to differential survival of the remains. This garden had suffered little subsequent damage and most of its components were to some extent visible prior to excavation.

### Levelling and ground preparation

Towards the centre of the excavated part of the lower garden (in Area A), a substantial 0.50m deep feature extended over 10m by 7.50m; this contained a mixed, compact fill overlain by a relatively clean deposit of orange brown sand. The purpose of this feature was evidently wholesale removal of earlier garden features and preparation for a new garden layout; additionally the deposition of sand to such a depth would help to keep the area weed-free and free-draining. Its fills produced 32 sherds of mixed eighteenth- and nineteenth-century pottery along with fragments of moulded stone and two iron strips. Further evidence of demolition of structures and subsequent levelling could be seen at the northern side of the excavation area where a deposit of rubble, glass and clay up to 0.40m thick continued beyond the limits of excavation to the north; this presumably represents demolition debris from the northern hothouse prior to the construction of the conservatory.

Levelling, ground raising and garden soil horizons surviving and recorded in section in front of Hothouse 2 suggests that garden beds extended to the front of the glasshouse, as reflected in contemporary garden layout designs (see Fig. 5.12). In front of Hothouse 4, a 0.62m-thick deposit [206] comprising clayey silt notable for the frequent presence of bone and horn throughout, was dumped upon deposit overlying the surface [312] in front of the eastern glasshouse element (see Fig. 4.5). This deposit had been truncated to the north by a substantial feature [264] which ran parallel and up to the edge of the glasshouse and thus this material may have originally extended to the front of the glasshouse. It may represent a deliberate consolidation layer deposited in front of the vinery to prevent collapse of the border but would have had additional benefits. Campbell (2005, 182) reports that at Pylewell, Hampshire '*as elsewhere, any horse, cow, sheep, cat or dog that died at the farm was buried in this bed.*' The composition of the faunal remains assemblage from deposit [206] suggests that the peculiar combination of cattle horn cores, dismembered horse bones and sheep feet bones represents specialised debris from a knacker's yard or tannery and not domestic food refuse from the castle household (see section 10.2). This material was therefore being imported from outside specifically for levelling. Dating evidence retrieved from the deposit included 35 sherds of late eighteenth- to early nineteenth-century pottery. The build-up of levels to the south of Hothouse 4 would have rendered the glasshouse element of the hothouse semi-sunken. An indication of the original construction level for the glasshouse and the subsequent build-up of soil, through accumulation and landscaping, is provided by the level of the culvert and original pathways relative to the final surviving pathway of the garden (Fig. 5.4). No excavation was undertaken to the north of Hothouse 2 or Hothouse 4, but it can only be assumed that these had originally been accessed via external steps.

Early vineries (*c.* 1770s) were constructed with holes in the front wall so that well-rooted plants could be planted outside, and their stems poked through the wall and into the glasshouse (Campbell 2005, 181). The borders in front of such vineries were relatively narrow at around 1.50m wide, as the vines would be replaced every two years. By the early nineteenth century, vineries were being constructed with arched foundations under the front wall so that the roots of the vines could spread much farther, with the result that the border outside a vinery frequently sinks revealing the tops of the arches (Campbell 2005, 182). Vines would presumably have been trained through the columns which formed the original front of the glasshouse; modifications must have been made to continue to allow vines to be trained through the front of the glasshouse once the brick infilling associated with the construction of the curvilinear glasshouse was inserted between the columns. The vines may have been trained through specially-designed openings in the corner of the windows at the front of the house (see section 9.5).

## Parterre gardens

Three north–south paths and an east–west path recorded in the lower garden defined parts of four parterres (Parterres 1–4) (Fig. 5.5). The 1860 Ordnance Survey map (see Fig. 5.2) shows two rectangular parterres in the north (Parterres 1 and 2) and two in the south with curved southern ends mirroring the apse of the pond (Parterres 3 and 4). This was a sunken area; a detailed survey of this part of the garden dated 1897 in the castle archives depicts steps leading down into the parterre area from the western glasshouse and from the east end of the path adjacent to the eastern hothouse (Acc 444/1–3; see Fig. 5.6). The latter steps are shown on the modified plans drawn up for this area (see Fig. 8.15).

**Fig. 5.4** Excavation to the south of Hothouse 4 showing the raised ground level in front of the hothouse

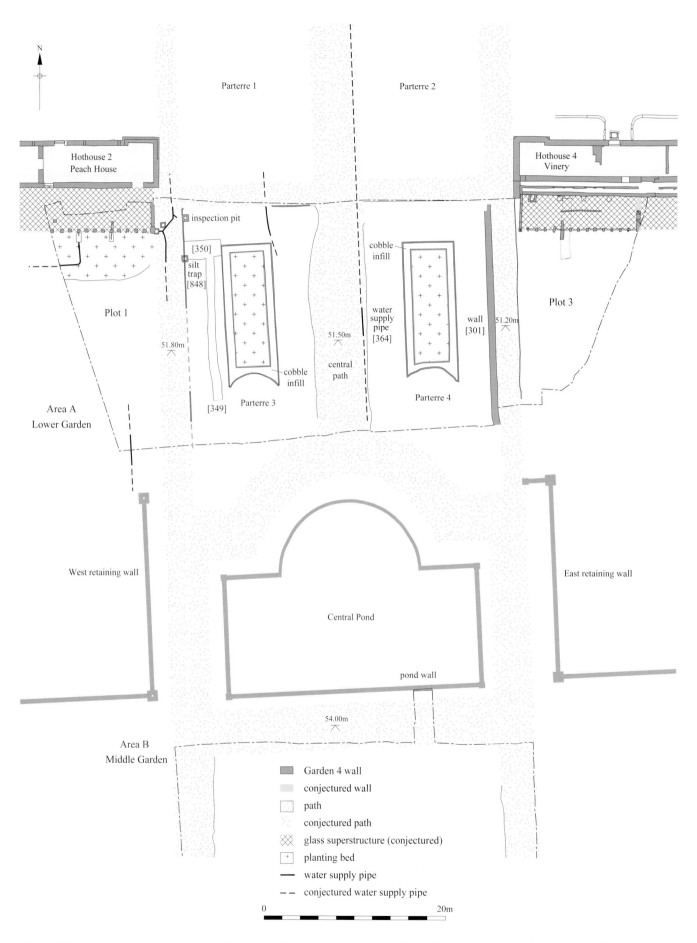

**Fig. 5.5** Garden 4, excavated remains of the Lower Garden as seen in Area A and the northern part of Area B (Middle Garden) (scale 1:400)

West Wall / Peach House / Vinery / East Wall

**Fig. 5.6** East–west cross section (based on architects drawing of *c.* 1860, PB 236) showing the fall in levels between the peach house (Hothouse 2) and vinery (Hothouse 4); note this is later than Barnfather's map, which illustrates the garden in 1829, and reflects levels following the construction of Hothouse 4 and demolition of Hothouse 3

The location of the outer north–south paths were retained from the previous garden layout, despite the ground raising which had occurred, particularly to the eastern side of the excavated area. Modifications included the installation of new salt-glazed drainage pipes, resurfacing and widening. Various drainage elements were exposed beneath the excavated portion of the path, some of which can be dated to this phase of garden. A ceramic drain ran north-eastwards from a silt trap [848], constructed with bricks which dated from the mid to late nineteenth century, and then ran northwards under the centre of the path. This was a salt-glazed drainpipe stamped 'Wm HARRIMAN & Co LD BLAYDON-ON-TYNE'. In 1845, Harriman went into partnership with Mr W Dodds of Lemington to set up a new firebrick works at Blaydon Haugh. In 1858, the works gave preference to manufacture of salt-glazed ware, the firm of Harriman and Company was wound up and a new company formed in 1881 (Davison 1986, 139–144). This dates the installation of the salt-glazed drainage pipe to between 1858 and 1881 and is therefore contemporary with Garden 4.

The north–south paths defined an area with a total width of 40m east–west, exposed for over 28m north–south; the northern edge of the east–west path was not exposed within the limits of excavation. The central north–south path which divided Parterres 3 and 4 was wider than those at the eastern and western sides, being 6m wide and built within a substantial construction cut which at its most extensive was up to 7.90m wide and 0.90m deep, surviving to a level of 51.50m OD. The path mainly survived as a 0.40m thick deposit of brick and sandstone rubble make-up with patches of crushed sandstone path surface surviving intermittently. The western path, smaller at 3m wide, was lined to the east by brick edging, and survived to 51.80m OD. The eastern path was built within a 2.70m-wide and 0.30m-deep construction cut, which contained a series of path construction deposits, culminating in a compact silty sand deposit at a level of 51.20m OD. The path was delimited to the east by brick edging and, following re-surfacing with sand and gravel, an addition to the eastern brick edging was installed, capped with an ornamental cast cement kerbstone. The west side of the path was bounded by a substantial 0.70m-wide wall, built with well-faced sandstone blocks and a rubble core. Parterres 3 and 4 were 14m wide internally and exposed for a length of 25.50m.

This construction had considerably raised the level of this part of the gardens; the level of the western path had been raised approximately 0.20m since first built, but that in the east had been raised by approximately 1.00m as a result of this landscaping event (see Fig. 5.4, Fig. 5.6). It was notable that the east–west height differential had been much reduced and a more level garden created, yet a change in level from west to east across the garden persisted following landscaping. A cross-section of the garden from *c.* 1860 shows the difference in height between the two central hothouses with a flight of steps leading down from the east end of Hothouse 2 and another down to the west end of Hothouse 4 (see Fig. 5.6). At the northern limit of excavation an east–west path formed the northern boundary of the parterre blocks and provided access between the two hothouses. The full width of this path was not revealed within the limits of excavation, but the garden design indicates it was of the same width as the narrower north–south paths on the east and west sides of the garden.

Two rectangular planting beds with curved southern ends were constructed in the centre of Parterres 3 and 4; these measured 15m north–south by 5.50m east–west and were set 14m apart. They were defined by parallel brick walls 1m apart comprising one course of unfrogged red brick with a cobble infill between the walls with inner garden beds *c.* 12m by 3.50m, the fill of which produced 18 sherds of pottery ranging in date from medieval to the nineteenth century, implying material derived from elsewhere as well as reworked garden soils. The walls defining the parterres were composed of machine-made bricks of mid to late nineteenth-century date.

At the north-western end of the western block, a pebble and sandstone surface [350] ran east–west to adjoin the parterre. To the south a narrow north–south cobble path [349], ran between the edge of the planting bed and the main external path. These may have been paths associated with the parterre, presumably providing access, perhaps for gardening, with more substantial north–south paths which defined the plots of land for viewing the gardens. This evidence illustrates the details of use that are not visible on the original garden designs or contemporary maps and may reflect minor temporal changes in use and layout.

## 5.3 Excavated Remains of Garden 4, Middle Garden

### Landscaping

The construction of the southern part of the Italianate garden across the sloping ground of the newly incorporated hillside to the south of the original walled garden necessitated substantial ground raising, landscaping and terracing as well as the construction of retaining walls. Extensive deposits of relatively clean, interleaved sands, silts and clays were recorded wherever excavations were sufficiently deep. A complex sequence of dumps was recorded and it was concluded that these deposits represent an extensive program of landscaping, utilising largely natural deposits imported from elsewhere. The apparent complexity of the sequence is presumably a product of the method of deposition, perhaps by individual barrow loads. The upper surface of the levelling deposits sloped from a maximum of 59.16m OD in the north down to 52.65m OD at the southern limit of excavation, a drop of *c.* 6.50m over *c.* 60m. During excavation attempts were made across this area to reach 'natural' deposits, but the only potentially natural layers were encountered at the far north of the excavation area at a level of 51.55m OD, overlain by plough soil, or buried sub-soil. At this location, overlying levelling layers were only *c.* 0.40m deep; elsewhere depths varied from around 0.70m to 1.20m, but the lower interfaces of those deposits were not reached.

These layers represent a major phase of preparation prior to the laying out of a new garden and may perhaps have fulfilled several functions. Overlying an area previously used as an open field, the deposits would have primarily been used as landscaping, but also being composed almost exclusively of clean sands and silts, would have provided a free-draining and weed-free foundation on which to lay out a new garden. Contemporary with the surrounding landscaped 'banks', a partly sunken garden effect was produced, although levels appear to have been raised across the area as part of an attempt to terrace the ground, and provide vistas across the parterre gardens.

### Initial path layout, repairs and consolidation

Overlying, and cutting into, the ground-raising and landscaping dumps were construction cuts and make up deposits associated with preparation for a network of *c.* 5m-wide paths on north–south and east–west axes. The paths would have surrounded the rectangular parterre garden located to the immediate south of the pond, as shown on an 1865 plan of the castle and gardens (see Fig. 5.12). The entirety of Parterre 5, which had internal measurements of 31m east–west by 44m north–south, was exposed.

The east–west path at the southern end of the excavation area also delimited the northern side Parterre 6 to the south, which was exposed for a length of just 7m north–south. The 1865 plan shows a U-shaped parterre at this location, with the curved end to the south surrounding the earthwork crescent which echoed the Percy crescent (as shown beneath the legend at the top right of Thompson's map of 1760; see Fig. 1.10; see Fig. 5.12).

The resulting path and garden layout remained little changed into the twentieth century. Modifications and additional features added to the corners of the planting bed in the later nineteenth century destroyed any evidence of the original planting scheme here (see Fig. 6.2) and thus the layout of these gardens is presented below (Chapter 6). Some features pertaining to the earliest phase of garden paths were identified, however.

Following the laying out of garden beds and dumping of garden soils, the path layout underwent a phase of consolidation and surfacing. A ceramic drainpipe was evidently inserted along the north–south path, prior to subsequent path surfacing. Various materials were used for this; heavily compacted sand and pea grit, cemented brick rubble and sand and gravel, and coarse sand and gravel surface. Localised repairs had been carried out, although the overall layout of north–south and east–west aligned paths was clear. The slope down to the north remained apparent, seen, for example, in a drop of *c.* 5m over a distance of 39m in the western north–south aligned path, from 60.05m OD in the south to 55.38m OD towards the north.

### Garden beds and decorative borders of the original Garden 4 scheme

Traces of a garden bed and decorative garden borders survived within the north-eastern corner of Parterre 6. A shallow north-east to south-west aligned linear feature and two small curvilinear, or sub-circular, features, may also have formed part of a scheme of decorative borders. In the north-west corner of Parterre 6, several small sub-circular and linear features were presumably part of the original Garden 4 layout and design.

Within the internal area of Parterre 5 traces of garden soils and beds indicate a large flower bed, roughly 30m across and with a downward slope from north to south, apparently devoid of any internal features; the divisions for the five central circles and surrounding borders and as shown on the 1865 plan were presumably formed by planting (see Fig. 5.12).

The garden bed deposits produced an assemblage of pottery of mixed eighteenth- to nineteenth-century date, also incorporating some medieval ceramics. This perhaps implies the introduction of material from elsewhere to build up and improve soil levels. Inevitably, given the creation of a new garden on a relatively clean sandy base, material for garden beds would have been imported and would also, presumably, include compost produced by the household and gardens, which may have incorporated fragments of broken crockery. Some garden soils may have been imported from elsewhere, possibly even from clearance in the Lower Garden to prepare for the newly laid-out parterre gardens in that area.

Map evidence demonstrates that the original internal layout of Parterres 5 and 6 only survived for a few decades as a new design is shown on the Ordnance Survey map of 1897, established by the sixth duke. The redesign seems to have been contemporary with a substantial drainage system in this area, the installation of which evidently required digging up a large area of Parterres 5 and 6.

## 5.4 Standing Structures of Garden 4

### Hothouse 6: the northern conservatory and conversion of Hothouse 1 backhouses

#### Above-ground elements of the northern conservatory

Amongst the substantial changes that the fourth duke brought to the garden was the construction of a new conservatory (Hothouse 6) at the northern boundary wall, on a sight line from the triple-arched gateway leading into the new walled southern hexagonal garden (the upper garden). By the time of the fieldwork the above-ground elements of the northern conservatory had been largely demolished to create a decorative terrace. The lowest portions of the surviving walls formed a balustrade around an ornamental garden, referred to colloquially as the 'old pavilion'. Some features noted during the 1998 evaluation of the garden structures (Kent 1988) were no longer present when the structure was recorded in 2000.

The footprint of this newly-constructed glass element of the conservatory would have extended over the area previously occupied by Hothouse 1 glasshouse and backhouse. The spine wall of Hothouse 1, which had formed part of the original eighteenth-century boundary wall, therefore had to be demolished to below ground level to accommodate the new conservatory, the garden wall was pushed northwards at this point, ground levels were raised and new entrances created.

The surviving remains of the northern conservatory comprised a raised stone platform 34m east–west by 10.70m wide with 'balustrading' along the east, west and south sides set 0.30m in from the edges of the platform. To the north the platform was bounded by a stretch of newly-constructed garden wall which stepped back from the original line of the walled garden (Fig. 5.7). Steps led up to the stone platform from the surrounding

garden; these would have led up to a central entrance into the conservatory and entrances in the east and west ends. The 'balustrades' comprised roughly square uprights topped with chamfered capping stones built of hammer-dressed sandstone which were 1.10m high above the surrounding platform and were set 0.90m apart. There were alternating wide (0.50m) and narrow (0.35m) uprights along the southern side. An architect's drawing of the conservatory shows that the larger stone uprights (marked 'a') were intended to support the cast iron pillars which would have formed the framework of the glasshouse above (see Fig. 5.14). The smaller uprights (marked 'B'), in conjunction with these, would have carried the iron frames of ventilators around the base of the wall. In total there were five large supports for the cast iron pillars to the west and south of a central entrance, with a half-size pillar either side of the doorway. These supported eleven arched bays at the front of the conservatory; a photograph taken in 1898 of the northern conservatory shows each bay with six vertical iron uprights for the glazing, with the exception of the central bay which contained the doorway (see Fig. 6.5). Internally, two rows of ten column bases (five to either side of the central doorway) provided bases for cast iron columns to support the roof; no remains of these survived. The recorded remains of the conservatory balustrade illustrate the stone capping which topped these columns.

The intervening spaces below the chamfered capping and between the stone uprights were 0.90m wide x 0.50m high, with ten either side of the central entrance and two gaps either side of the eastern and western entrances. Kent (1998) noted the remains of an iron top-hung ventilator in the eastern side (Fig. 5.11). This series of ventilators would have facilitated the control of temperature inside the conservatory, similar to those at the top of the spine walls of Hothouse 2 and Hothouse 4. The capping stones were set with numerous iron fittings and sockets into which the iron framework would have been inserted (Fig. 5.7).

Three sets of steps led up to corresponding *c.* 2.60m-wide entrances into the conservatory, one centrally, the others into the eastern and western elevations. They were each formed of four risers, initially two small steps, a wider step at platform level, and a fourth small step into the garden area, the lowest step at 52.12m OD rising to 52.53m OD. Beyond the top steps, the level dropped again to around 52.40m OD. Rectangular iron sockets at each side of the upper steps marked the position of the door frames with a smaller circular central socket indicating that these would have been double doors, each *c.* 1.30m wide. The 1898 photograph shows a side entrance with the arched iron framework of the superstructure above divided by a central vertical column and double doors, one closed (Fig. 5.16). A photograph taken in 1898 of the front of the conservatory shows

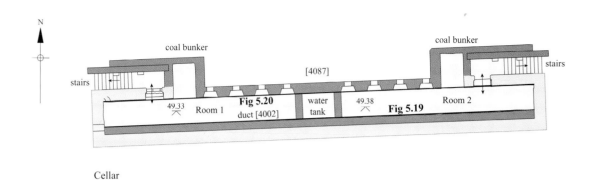

Cellar

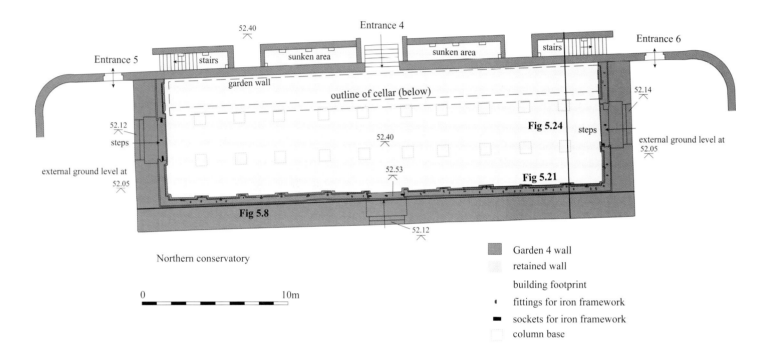

Northern conservatory

0    10m

Garden 4 wall
retained wall
building footprint
fittings for iron framework
sockets for iron framework
column base

**Fig. 5.7** Hothouse 6, Garden 4, plan of surviving elements of the northern conservatory (bottom), showing the converted former backhouse (top), now a cellar providing heat to the conservatory (scale 1: 250)

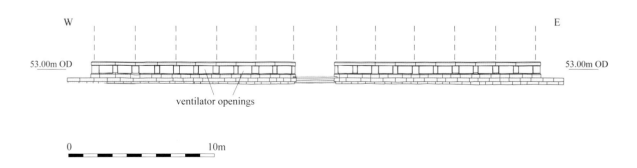

0    10m

**Fig. 5.8** Hothouse 6, Garden 4, elevation of surviving remains of the south side of the northern conservatory; only the stonework of this structure, which had incorporated ventilators, survived and was used as the decorative surround for a paved garden (scale 1:250)

**Fig. 5.9** Hothouse 6, the internal wall of the conservatory, which forms a rebuilt Garden 4 northern boundary wall, looking north-west, with Entrance 4 in centre, Entrance 6 through the eastern curved wall and Entrance 5 through the western curved wall in background

**Fig. 5.10** Hothouse 6, alternate wide and narrow stone uprights, which would have enclosed ventilators and supported the iron and glass superstructure of the glasshouse, looking north (scale 1m)

**Fig. 5.11** Hothouse 6, remains of iron framework for ventilator opening in east wall of northern conservatory, looking west (RK 1998)

the same arrangement at the southern entrance with the arched framework divided centrally (see Fig. 6.5). The internal faces of the stone supports at each entrance bore a vertical socket where the framework would have been inserted (Fig. 5.7). Kent (1998) also noted brass door-keeps in the stonework at the time of his survey, adjacent to the entrances. A fourth entrance in the rear (north) wall of the conservatory led out of the garden (see below), giving a symmetrical appearance to the whole. The latter entrance also appears to have had a glazed door, as indicated on the 1898 photograph (see Fig. 6.5); this permitted light to enter the conservatory from the north and also allowed the garden to be viewed from outside, through the glasshouse.

The northern side of the conservatory was formed by a newly-constructed east–west stretch of garden boundary wall set to the north of the original line with a central arched entrance leading through the conservatory and into the gardens (Entrance 4). The new segment of northern wall was 55m long, 4m high and 0.56m wide and was constructed with regular coursed

sandstone rubble, hammer dressed. The northern external face had ten low rectangular openings in groups of five to each side of the entrance, subsequently blocked, which were presumably associated with the ventilation system of the conservatory and would have functioned in the same way as those around the 'balustrade'. The internal (southern) face of the wall was cement rendered with espalier frames attached.

An 1865 plan of the gardens shows external steps to the north of the boundary wall leading up to the new entrance (Fig. 5.12). This was an arched opening 2.30m wide, which at the time of the fieldwork had a decorative iron gate set within it. A brass plaque on the east reveal of this gate recorded that this was one of four sixteenth-century wrought-iron gates purchased by the fourth duke in Venice in 1871 (Kent 1988, 9). Another hung within one of the openings of the triple-arched gateway opposite this gateway in the new hexagonal garden to the south. This gateway is the main entrance into the present Alnwick Garden and still retains the Venetian gate.

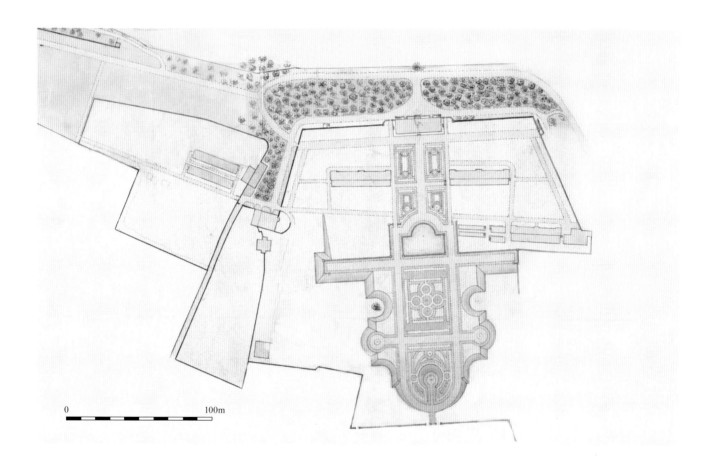

**Fig. 5.12** Extract from 1865 plan of the gardens showing detail of new northern boundary wall and entrances (COW A146) (scale 1:2500)

**Fig. 5.13** Eastern element of the curving wall at the northern boundary, looking north, showing Entrance 6 (scale 1m)

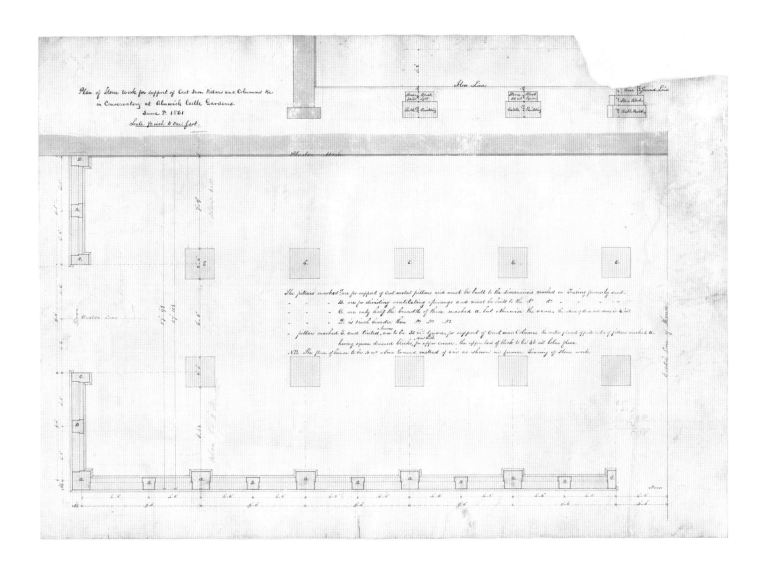

**Fig. 5.14** Architect's drawing showing the western half of the northern conservatory, Hothouse 6 (PB 218)

0                    2m

**Fig. 5.15** Architect's drawing showing a transverse section of part of the iron framework for the northern conservatory, Hothouse 6 (PB 237)

**Fig. 5.16** Photograph taken inside the northern conservatory, Hothouse 6, *c.* 1870 (Shrimpton n.d.)

Beyond the conservatory to the east and west, curving sandstone walls were constructed with two narrow entrances (Entrances 5 and 6), replacing the two entrances shown on the Ordnance Survey map of 1856 (see Fig. 8.10), which had presumably been created here in Garden 3 (Fig. 5.13). At the time of the fieldwork these were hung with wooden doors. These walls met the original eighteenth-century northern wall of the garden to east and west, providing a grand setting for the newly built conservatory.

The new conservatory was constructed by William Shakespear, *'metallic hothouse manufacturer'* of Birmingham, in 1862 (Kent 1998, 5). The castle archives contain a receipt dated 31/12/1863 for £300 relating to payment of costs of building a conservatory in the Alnwick Walled Gardens. This is for iron work provided

by John Meiklejon, Westfield Ironworks, Dalkeith, Scotland (DP/D4/1/262). The structure was evidently fully functional by 1867 when the first Paylist of Workmen for the gardens lists the Conservatory as a weekly task in the garden (Acc 446/1).

The conservatory was described in 1874 as a '*large and elegant conservatory of recent erection 100 feet by 30 feet*' (*c.* 30.50m by *c.* 9.10m) with 'a *lofty roof supported by a double row of pillars, which are entwined by creepers*'. This description matches the 1861 architect's drawing which depicts a plan of the stonework for the support of cast iron pillars in conservatory; this drawing shows the western half of the structure from its central line (Fig. 5.14). Along the front, south, wall of the building large stone supports set 9 feet (*c.* 2.75m) apart for the cast iron pillars are interspersed

with smaller supports for '*dividing ventilating openings*'. Half
of the entrance into the building on the south wall is shown
and in total this entrance would have been *c.* 2.75m wide. The
architect's drawing shows the same arrangement of stone pillars
on the western side of the structure as the south wall, either
side of a 9-foot-wide entrance, but the main stone supports are
smaller. Inside the conservatory two rows of five stone supports
for the internal cast iron pillars are set 9 feet apart with the
rows 6 feet 6 inches (*c.* 2m) apart. Assuming the building was
symmetrical, there would have been two rows of ten columns
inside. Another drawing shows half of the transverse section
of the iron framework of the building which included a central
curved section supporting the glazed hipped roof (Fig. 5.15).
These creeper-entwined pillars can be seen on the photograph
taken inside the conservatory in *c.* 1870 which shows that
the centre of the roof was supported on an arched framework
with square framework to the side (Fig. 5.16). A central path
ran along the length of the structure, with planting behind a
balustrade to one side and large pots and plants to the other.
An arched door can be seen at the end of the building. The
1898 photograph shows arched iron framework at the front of
the glasshouse, with decorative finials above, supporting the
glass roof which was also topped with a decorative fretwork
ridge (see Fig. 6.5). A doorway in the central arch leads into the
conservatory and this photograph shows that the conservatory
was higher than the boundary wall. The conservatory also
appears also appears on a photograph published in *The Gardeners'
Chronicle* in 1902 (see Fig. 10.34).

## Northern conservatory cellar: conversion of Hothouse 1 backhouse

Considerable alterations were carried out to the Hothouse 1
backhouse, which was converted into a cellar containing the
heating system for the northern conservatory constructed above
it. It is assumed that a new furnace (or furnaces) were installed
when the conservatory was built in 1862 and the Hothouse
1 backhouse modified into a cellar. Two coal bunkers newly
constructed at either end of the cellar would have stored the fuel
to supply the furnaces.

Associated modifications included the introduction of light
wells and steps down into the structure to accommodate a major
change in external ground levels, resulting in a change from semi-
basemented backhouse to a fully below-ground cellar (see Fig.
5.24). Such major landscaping may have been necessary due to the
rising ground levels inside the garden and is also reflected in the
need to raise the height of the northern boundary wall. Ground
level external to the gardens at the western end of the structure

**Fig. 5.17** Hothouse 6, steps leading into the western side of the cellar (RK 1998)

**Fig. 5.18** Coal bunker at the eastern end of Hothouse 6 (scale 1m)

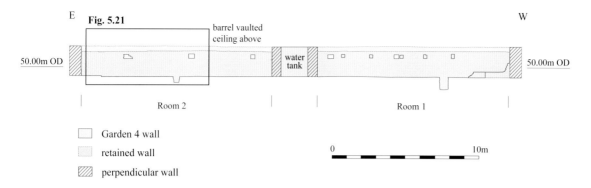

**Fig. 5.19** Hothouse 6, Garden 4, elevation of southern wall of cellar (scale 1:250)

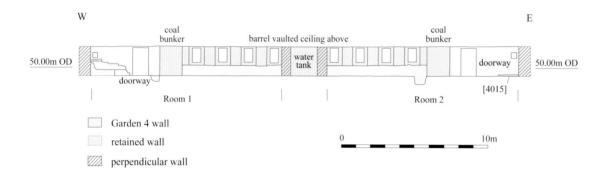

**Fig. 5.20** Hothouse 6, Garden 4, elevation of northern wall of cellar (scale 1:250)

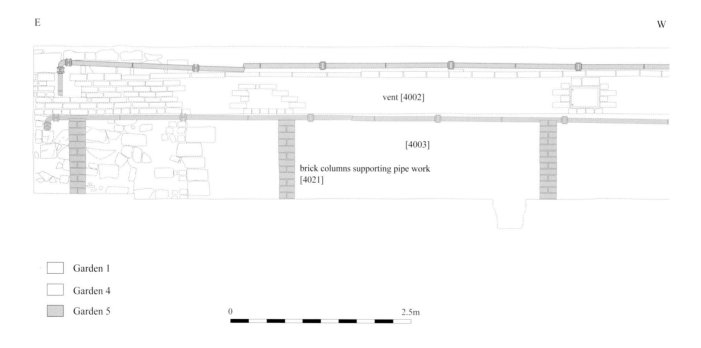

**Fig. 5.21** Hothouse 6, phased detail of elevation of southern wall, illustrating the original structure of Garden 1 Hothouse 1 (just visible behind later brick and stone work), Garden 4 stone wall to support brick duct and Garden 5 modifications (scale 1:50)

was at 52.40m OD and floor level in the cellar was 49.33m OD. At the eastern end of the structure ground level was at 51.80m OD and floor level at 49.38m OD; the cellar was therefore over 3m deep and accessed from east and west by fifteen external stone steps via the two original doorways which were set approximately 3m from either end of the structure (Fig. 5.17). Two coal bunkers were constructed extending northwards from the cellar; these measured 1.50m by 2.20m and were set 4.80m from either end of the cellar (Fig. 5.18). The ceiling of the western bunker was built with substantial, square sandstone blocks. Towards the centre of the ceiling, a circular opening (sealed at the time of survey) 45m in diameter, cut through the blocks forming the ceiling presumably formed the aperture of a coal chute. The ceiling of the eastern bunker was cement rendered.

Between the two coal bunkers, the upper part of the north wall of Hothouse 1 was largely rebuilt [4007] with eight recessed windows, in two groups of four, each group served by a light well to the north of the building (see Fig. 5.7). The sandstone surrounds to the windows were well-dressed (Fig. 5.20; Fig. 5.22); the windows had been subsequently infilled with breezeblocks. In the central part of the basement a large water tank with sandstone wall surrounds, which presumably served the boilers which heated this structure is interpreted as being associated with this reorganisation of the heating system.

Inside the backhouse adjacent to the southern wall, an east–west aligned duct [4002] was supported by a 1.10m high stone wall [4003] constructed adjacent and parallel to the original spine wall [4001] of Hothouse 1. The hollow duct [4002] was constructed with yellow bricks; one course of header bricks with five courses of stretcher above, capped with sandstone slabs (Fig. 5.21; Fig. 5.25). The duct appeared to continue behind the central water tank, enclosed by sandstone walls, to the south. In the western part of the cellar two square openings in duct [4002] with iron surrounds, which presumably originally held two iron doors (subsequently removed and the openings infilled), would have controlled airflow and ventilation. Three similar openings were visible in duct [4002] to the east. At the western end of the cellar, extending out of the southern corner of wall, the duct appeared to continue, utilising an earlier red-brick lined duct. A stone arched opening observed during the watching brief in the area south of the cellar, beneath the former conservatory, was positioned centrally on the east–west axis; it seems probable that this led from the duct and may also have utilised an element of an earlier structure.

The long duct [4002] was most probably constructed to vent the furnaces which heated the conservatory, when first constructed. Presumably this heating system took the form of furnaces associated with water boilers. It is unlikely that this duct was

**Fig. 5.22** Hothouse 6, blocked-in window in northern wall of cellar, looking north-east (scale 0.50m)

**Fig. 5.23** Vaulted brick ceiling in Hothouse 6 cellar with its rendered northern side, looking east (scale 1m)

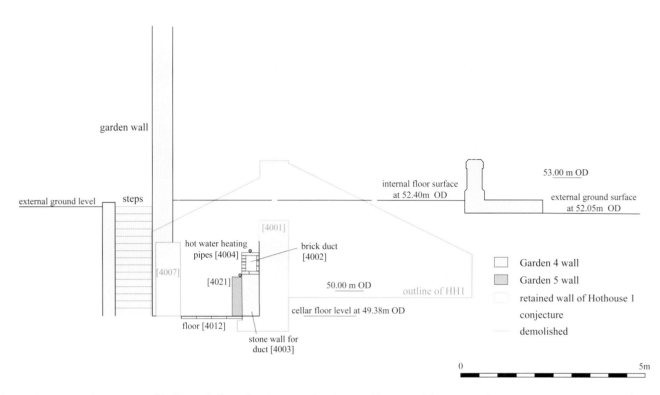

N                                                                                                          S

garden wall

53.00 m OD

internal floor surface
at 52.40m OD

external ground surface
at 52.05m OD

external ground level    steps

[4001]

hot water heating
pipes [4004]

brick duct
[4002]

[4007]

[4021]

50.00 m OD

outline of HH1

□ Garden 4 wall
■ Garden 5 wall
□ retained wall of Hothouse 1
conjecture
— demolished

cellar floor level at 49.38m OD

floor [4012]

stone wall for
duct [4003]

0                                                    5m

**Fig. 5.24** Hothouse 6, schematic profile through the cellar showing the duct and later modifications to heating system represented by pipework; the newly constructed conservatory is shown in relation to the former vinery, which was demolished to make way for the new structure (scale 1:100)

**Fig. 5.25** Hothouse 6, opening in smoke vent [4002] in eastern side of cellar with iron surround, looking south, showing later pipework

intended to supply heating in the form of hot air, since it ran the length of the cellar, internally and below ground, it was only a single brick in thickness, and thus would have contributed to the dispersal of hot air. It seems most probable that this was associated with the installation of a centralised system of venting which saw all the smoke from the hothouses vented away from the buildings to a distant smoke shaft. Evidence for the smoke shaft to the south-west of this building was identified during the watching brief (see Smoke shafts below).

Two north–south aligned sandstone walls were constructed across the cellar, dividing it into two rooms; Room 1 to the west and Room 2 to the east. The walls were constructed of roughly hewn, randomly coursed blocks and enclosed an area 1.80m east–west surrounding a water tank, still containing water at the time of the survey (Fig. 5.7). At either end of the building brickwork had been constructed, which is assumed to have supported cast iron boilers associated with this newly installed heating system. The walls supporting the smoke shaft appeared to be of similar build to these two north–south aligned walls which enclosed the central water tank and it is thus concluded that they are likely to be contemporary. By contrast, hard mortar adhering to the supporting wall is likely to be associated with the construction of piers to support later pipework (see Garden 5 below). The external arrangement of steps leading into the two rooms, with a central baulk between to allow access to the conservatory from beyond the garden, mirrors this internal arrangement.

Thus, it is concluded that the modifications to the cellar associated with the construction of Hothouse 6 (the northern conservatory) were, from the outset, associated with the provision of heat via boilers and hot water pipes. However, there is evidence to suggest that the boilers (and associated pipework) might have been modified or replaced on at least one occasion as they punctured the vent along the southern wall of the cellar (see Garden 5 below); this may be contemporary with the introduction of steam heating in the 1890s. Some of the pipework recorded may have been associated with the original heating system, but, given the significant evidence for modification and damage to the structure of the vent along the spine wall, it seems likely that most of this was associated with later alterations.

In the south-west corner of the cellar, above an opening in duct [4033], an iron door appeared to have been controlled via a pulley on the ceiling. The brick-vaulted ceiling [4006] ran the entire length of the cellar. It had been rendered on its northern side, a division running down the central spine of the ceiling seemingly reflecting a now removed longitudinal division within the cellar, or perhaps rendering to prevent

water damage, after construction (Fig. 5.23). The evidence for extensive rebuilding of the northern wall and the modification of the original backhouse into a cellar indicates that the ceiling was contemporary with this rebuild. This vaulted roof was almost certainly constructed to support the conservatory above; the roof of the original backhouse would not have needed to be of such robust construction and is more likely to have been constructed with timber rafters supporting a tiled roof.

## Hothouse 2: a peach house

There were no apparent modifications to Hothouse 2 at this period. Now furnished with boilers and a new glass and iron frontage, the building was at the forefront of technological developments in the garden, and other structures would be updated to reflect this. Whilst some minor modifications were no doubt carried out during this 18–year period there is nothing which can be definitively tied to this phase, other than the insertion of a smoke shaft.

## Modifications to heating system in Hothouse 4 backhouse

Modifications to Room 2, the cellar, appear to be associated with a change to the heating system in Hothouse 4. In the south-east corner of the room a *c.* 2.50m-long and 0.80m-wide platform [2021] was constructed directly in front of the arched support in the spine wall for the hearth and flue of the original heating system. The structure comprised an east–west brick wall with cement infilling to the south at a slightly lower level than the floor surface of the adjoining room. To the west of the centre of the building, east of the door between glasshouse and brickhouse, an infilled brick arch [2038] had been modified with the insertion of a rectangular structure containing a water tank. The water tanks were presumably inserted when the heating system was modified from hot air flues to boilers and hot water pipes.

At the eastern end of the hothouse, internal to the glasshouse, two brick piers were positioned in the alcove of the brick arch which supported the flue F3 in the spine wall (see Fig. 3.19; Fig. 3.20). These were supporting walls for a cast iron water tank, placed within the thickness of the wall and extending to the south. The central arch supporting flue F2 was also remodelled with two rectangular 1m-high sandstone-lined recesses constructed against it. The western one was 1.30m wide, the eastern one 0.50m wide with the space between the original brick arch and new sandstone structure infilled with brick (see Fig. 3.19; Fig. 3.20). Set within the western niche was a cast-iron water tank set on brick supports. The 1896 plan of the water supply to the gardens shows a water pipe supplying both of these tanks and it is presumed that these tanks fed hot water boilers located in the eastern and central cellars (see Fig. 6.17). No water supply was found at the western end of the building where the arch for Flue F1 was simply infilled. This rendered the cellar in the backhouse redundant as no heat source was required; the room was infilled and a flagstone surface laid at the same level as the rest of Room 1. As described below, the

access into the glasshouse from this room was blocked with only the access from the north remaining; a plan of 1900 shows that by this date the room was being used as a tool shed (see Fig 9.13).

A steep flight of stone steps leading down into the eastern end cellar adjacent to the spine wall represents a modification to the original plan of the structure as a doorway had formerly entered the glasshouse at this location. The entrance was infilled,

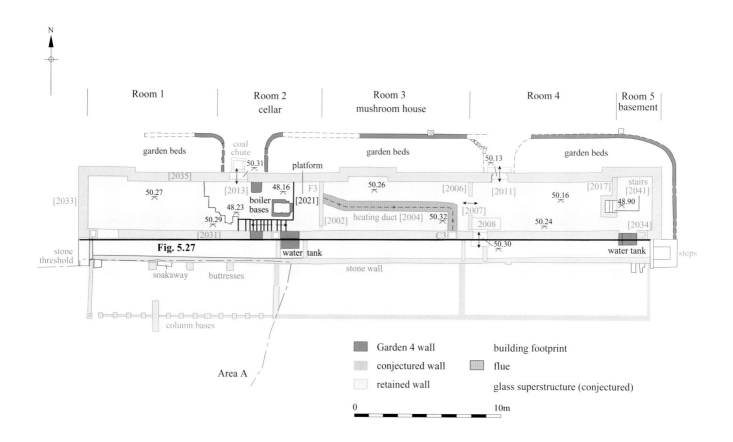

**Fig. 5.26** Hothouse 4, Garden 4, plan showing modifications to the heating system in Room 2 of the backhouse (scale 1:250)

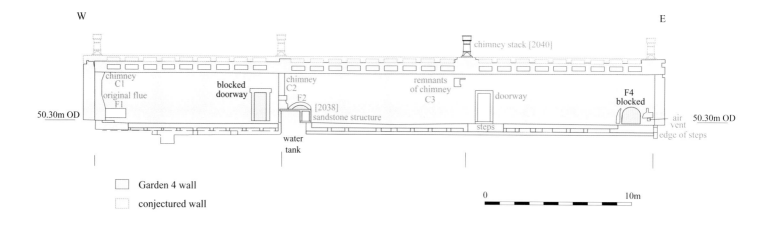

**Fig. 5.27** Hothouse 4, Garden 4, south-facing elevation of spine wall, showing blocking of flues associated with modifications to the heating system (scale 1:250)

**Fig. 5.28** Hothouse 4, Room 2, cellar, with later stone steps, looking west (scale 1m)

**Fig. 5.29** Hothouse 4, Room 2, cellar, detail of internal structures with stone flagged floor and cement platform in the background, looking east (scale 1m)

presumably when the cellar steps were built. This flight of steps dropped a depth of 1.78m over seven steps down into the lowest part of the cellar (beneath the vaulted roof), then stepped up two steps (0.55m) into a higher part of the cellar, platform [2021], which was also a later modification (Fig. 5.28). The steps became narrower as they descended due to the increasing width of the foundations of the spine wall of the building and there was evidence that metal railings had been attached to the steps in the north and to the spine wall. The steps can be seen in this position on the 1896 water supply plan of the gardens which also shows that the door into the glasshouse at the western end of Hothouse 4 was no longer in use (see Fig. 9.12).

Immediately west of the dividing wall [2002] between the cellar and Room 3 was a 1.80m wide and 0.75m high stone and cement platform [2021] (see Fig. 4.27; Fig. 5.29). A line of sandstone slabs ran along the outer (western) edge with cement infilling behind, suggesting deliberate construction in this form rather than the cement being a later repair. Set on the eastern element of the flagged floor of the cellar were the remnants of three structures: [2025], which was built against the northern wall of the building and had originally been capped with sandstone blocks which were badly disturbed during demolition (Fig. 5.29); and [2027] to the south-east which was infilled with ash, charcoal and coal. Iron panning in the vicinity of both of these structures suggests

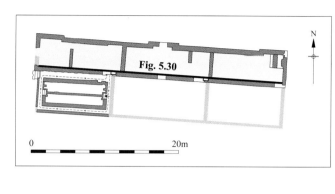

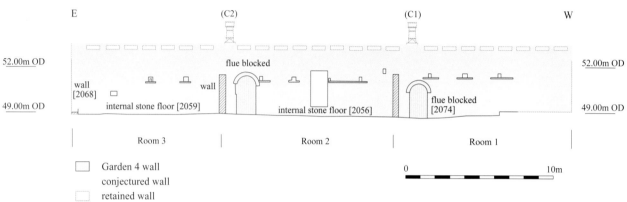

**Fig. 5.30** Hothouse 5, Garden 4, north-facing internal elevation of backhouse spine wall showing blocking of flues (scale 1:250)

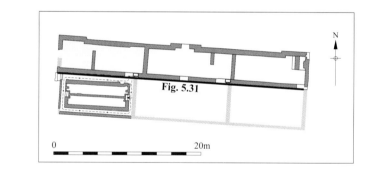

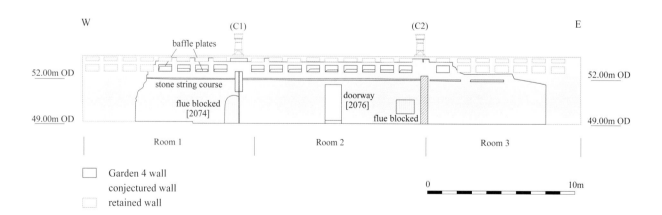

**Fig. 5.31** Hothouse 5, Garden 4, south-facing internal elevation of glasshouse spine wall showing blocking of flues (scale 1:250)

**Fig. 5.32** Hothouse 5, Room 1, showing the infilled brick arched hearth in the back wall [2074] looking south; a later (Garden 5) platform and the opening for a water pipe are associated with the introduction of a hot water heating system (scale 1m)

**Fig. 5.33** Hothouse 5, the infilled wall flue [2074] in the spine wall can be seen to the right of the image, looking north (scale 1m)

the presence of a boiler above. A solitary sandstone block set immediately adjacent and to the east of structure [2025] had a worn upper surface as if from repeated use.

The water tank presumably fed boilers which may have been situated on top of the platforms. To the immediate east of platform [2021] a sub-circular hole through the spine wall with an iron surround, which presumably carried hot water pipes into the glasshouse. It is assumed that the hot water pipes would have run along the original heating ducts in the glasshouse. Water pipes were also observed beneath the floor of Room 1 and through the walls dividing Rooms 1 and 2 and Rooms 2 and 3. On the 1896 plan a pipe runs the length of the backhouse on the

north side of the spine wall with branches feeding tanks in the former furnace rooms (see Fig. 6.17). The plan appears to show a large tank on the eastern side of the wall between Rooms 3 and 4, suggesting that a boiler may also have been fitted in this room. A cement slab was located in the south-eastern corner of the Room 5, in front of the infilled opening through the spine wall. A water tank was also located in the eastern end of the building, through the spine wall in the area of the former flue (F4) suggesting that a boiler may also have been fitted in the eastern end of the building. However this is not conclusive, as water would have been necessary for the irrigation of plants within the glasshouse as well as to supply boilers.

Decorative cast kerbing curved out away from each entrance and continued parallel to the northern wall of the building, at a distance of 2.30m, to form three garden beds, encircling the northern and eastern walls of the building.  At the approach to the western doorway, cobbled paving surrounded the opening for a coal chute into Room 2 (which appears to be part of the original construction see Chapter 4 above). The exact phasing of these external features was not established (there was no excavation undertaken in this area). However, these features presumably post-date the ground raising episodes here. Similar paving probably approached the eastern doorway, but did not survive.

## Hothouse 5

Hothouse 5 was ultimately modified to take a boiler, which replaced the original hot air flues; the boiler was placed within the eastern part of Room 1, which survived as a basement. The exact dating of the conversion of this building to hot water heating remains unknown, but this is likely to have happened by the 1840s at the latest. The modifications, as observed archaeologically, comprised the infilling and blocking of the flues through the central spine wall (see Fig. 5.30 and Fig. 5.31).

The opening from Room 1, was blocked with brickwork, rendered on the southern face of the spine wall and forming an alcove. To the immediate east of the blocked up opening a rectangular aperture with an iron frame and circular section pipe above, visible in the north face, may possibly have been a heating duct associated with the original heating system, or possibly a damper to control the flow of air through the system, but

more plausibly this may be associated with a later boiler system (Fig. 5.32). Evidence of damage to the floor of Room 1 of the backhouse adjacent to the spine wall may be associated with these modifications.

As with the arch in Room 1, brick blocking had also rendered the furnace in Room 2 obsolete. From the south, this blocking appeared as an alcove/rectangular recess 1.30m wide x 1m high and surrounded by a grooved iron frame 80mm wide which presumably had originally formed a hatch with a door, which could be opened and shut, perhaps controlling heat within the glasshouse. Immediately east of the infilled hearth, seen in the northern face of the wall, was a small bricked-up rectangular opening though the spine wall with associated pipework, comparable to those one in Room 1, and presumably representing elements of a hot-water heating system (Fig. 5.34).

## Hothouse 7: the new vinery and modifications to the boundary wall

A new hothouse (Hothouse 7) was constructed in the south-east corner of the garden to the immediate east of Hothouse 5; this is labelled on the plan of the gardens that was amended in 1864 as '*New Vinery*' (see Fig. 8.14). As with the other hothouses, only the backhouse element survived but unlike the other backhouses was extant at the time of writing (Fig. 5.35), although the glasshouse attached to the south had been dismantled. The backhouse measured *c.* 15m east–west and was 4m high and a maximum of *c.* 4m wide; the structure was L-shaped and the eastern end was narrower than the western. The northern wall of the backhouse at this end of the structure formed a new boundary wall for the

**Fig. 5.34** Hothouse 5, Room 2 showing the door through the back wall into glasshouse, and the bricked-in arched opening of a former flue and hearth to east, looking south (scale 1m)

garden in the expanded south-eastern corner of the garden. It is considered likely that the wide sandstone-arched entrance inserted through the southern end of the original eighteenth-century eastern boundary wall of the garden (Entrance 10) is contemporary with Hothouse 7 (Fig. 5.35).

The backhouse to Hothouse 7 was a regular coursed building with a parapet concealing a lean-to Welsh slated roof (Kent 1998, 15), mirroring the roofing arrangement of Hothouse 2, Hothouse 4 and Hothouse 5. The structure had a sandstone flagged floor and was entered via an external door into the backhouse in the west end of the building (Fig. 5.35). Map evidence suggests that the western end of the backhouse was a small separate room (see Fig. 9.12) but the dividing wall which survives appears to be later in date as it cuts off the eastern end of a well-built and substantial stone arch in the spine wall. The upper part of this feature is visible with brick infill below and this marks the location of a wall flue; as with Hothouse 2 and Hothouse 4 a hearth would presumably have been situated lower down the wall. The 1896 plan shows that at the western end of the backhouse was a basemented room, entered by stairs near the external entrance, to accommodate the heating apparatus (see Fig. 9.12). As with the other hothouses the heat source was placed below the level of the glasshouse for maximum efficiency. If this arch relates to a furnace for hot air heating in this building, this would be of note as this is relatively late for this form of heating; the building was constructed in the early 1860s by which time boilers and hot water pipes were the most common form of heating system. It is more likely that the feature identified is a relieving arch for a boiler set within the thickness of the wall.

The spine wall of Hothouse 7 extended west beyond the end of the backhouse and the 1867 OS map shows that glasshouse measured *c.* 15m by *c.* 5m but was not totally flush with the backhouse; the western end of the glasshouse extended beyond, and the eastern end stopped short, of the backhouse (Fig. 5.2).

At some stage, the function of Hothouse 7 changed as a 1928 plan of the water supply to the gardens labels the glasshouse as 'Peach House' and has an added note 'pulled down in 1935' (referring to the glasshouse element; Kent 1998). In recent years the backhouse was converted to a toilet block; the door inserted into the north wall presumably dates from this period.

## Boundary walls

The east, north-east and north-west walls of the original eighteenth-century garden were raised in height; the nineteenth-century fashion for higher walls in kitchen gardens may have been a factor, but an increase in height was also necessary due to the levelling of the external ground on the north side of the garden which was carried out after 1860 (Kent 1988, 8). The northern stretches of wall were raised from 2.80m to 4m. A buttress on the north-west stretch appears to be in the same location as a second furnace for the heated wall, which appears on early nineteenth-century maps but had been completely demolished by the time of the fieldwork. External landscaping to the east resulted in the north end of the east wall acting as a retaining wall, with the outside face of the wall some 5.10m in height in this area and the inside face of the wall 4m high; by the late nineteenth century it was necessary to construct an external buttress in the central part of the wall.

**Fig. 5.35** Hothouse 7, the new vinery, with contemporary Entrance 10 through the original east wall of garden, looking south-east: compare Fig. 4.35, in which this can be seen in relation to Hothouse 5 (VR 2015)

## Smoke shafts

Running parallel *c.* 1.5 m to the north of Hothouse 2 was a 1m-wide duct recorded in plan extending beyond the western end of the hothouse. A rectangular access shaft was located in the centre of the duct, roughly in line with the centre of the hothouse. A watching brief undertaken during groundworks associated with the construction of the new Alnwick Garden revealed a similar brick-lined duct running south-west beyond the cellar and location of northern conservatory, constructed largely of red brick with a stone slab roof (Fig. 5.36). The nature of its floor could not be determined during the watching brief (access to the structure being unsafe). However, it was observed that it had inner walls, one brick thick (110mm) and 13 bricks high (approximately 1m overall height), and that there was then a small vertical gap, running the full height of the wall, with an outer brick wall two bricks (220mm) wide.

Map evidence shows that a smoke tower was built between 1856 and 1867 in the south-west corner of the garden (compare Fig. 8.10 and Fig. 8.20) and it is assumed that the extensive system of smoke shafts shown on the 1896 plan of the water supply were constructed at the same time as the tower (see Fig. 9.12). The plan shows shafts from Hothouse 5 (as well as melon beds etc to the

**Fig. 5.36** Smoke shaft to the south-west of Hothouse 6, as revealed during the watching brief (VR 2004)

west which were not encountered during the excavations) joining a north–south shaft running along the eastern side of the garden. The smoke shaft then turned at right angles to run along the north side of Hothouse 2 and Hothouse 4 and then turned again to run south towards the smoke tower. Short stretches of shaft linked the individual hothouses to the smoke shaft, elements of which were identified during the fieldwork. A length of smoke shaft exiting the south-west corner of Hothouse 6 was observed during the watching brief. A rectangular opening in the spine wall in the corner of the western room in Hothouse 2, which was later infilled with brick [187], may be associated with this smoke shaft.

## The central pond and terrace retaining walls

The major scheme of terracing and landscaping of the gardens instigated in the 1860s by the fourth duke involved the construction of a large pond on the central north–south axis of the garden, views of which would have been provided downslope from the central mound at the southern end of the middle garden. Terrace walls ran parallel to the eastern and western sides of the pond and in the south, turned and ran east–west away from the pond in either direction, as terrace retaining walls. Access to the lower parts of the garden would have entailed a detour around the pond using either of the broad tree-lined sloping walkways built to the east and west.

Similar-sized and dressed stones and construction techniques were employed for all elements of the pond and terrace walls. The pond was rectangular in plan and measured 28m east–west by 13m north–south with a 15m-diameter apse extending 6.20m north from the rectangular element. The pond was terraced into the slope of the hill, with the effect that the southern wall rose up behind the pond and the eastern and western walls sloped down on either side, with adjacent sloping banks. The top of the west wall sloped down to the north from 54m OD to 52.55m OD (Fig. 5.37). In 1988 the pond was empty revealing its full depth of 0.65m and a shelf situated towards its base; damage in some areas showed that its cement render lining incorporated broken china and ashes (Kent 1998, 22). A lead overflow pipe was situated on the southern side of the pond (*ibid.*).

The western, southern and eastern internal walls of the pond were recorded using rectified photography and subsequently digitised (PCA 2004). All had been constructed using the same techniques. Internally the 0.40m-wide western wall as seen was 12.10m long, visible to a height of 2.30m in the south, sloping down to 0.90m in the north. The lower courses of the wall were formed of well-faced sandstone blocks with facetted edges blocks, regularly laid in horizontal courses, one course high in the north to five courses high in the south. Above this were set two courses of sandstone blocks, following the angle of the slope, capped with thin moulded sandstone slabs. The eastern internal wall of the pond mirrored the western in construction, though was exposed to a greater depth and the lower 0.50m of the wall was cement rendered. It was seen to a depth of at least 2.70m in the south, sloping down to 1.10m high at its northern end, where a small buttress, 0.60m square in plan, formed the end of the wall.

The external face of the western wall was up to 0.80m high externally and the finished face was formed of two courses of well-faced sandstone ashlar blocks; in places, these could be seen to overlie roughly-coursed, smaller sandstone blocks, presumably exposed due to erosion. At the northern and southern extents of the wall, for 0.60m at either end, the courses were level, however, between these the wall sloped at an angle of *c.* 7° to the horizontal.

The wall was capped with moulded sandstone slabs *c.* 100mm thick, but originally had a polished granite edging.

**Fig. 5.37** The central pond, as seen from the south-west; the standing remains of Hothouse 4 are visible to the rear of the photograph (RK 1998)

**Fig. 5.38** The internal face of the east wall of the pond, showing planting holes

**Fig. 5.39** Design for the red granite ornamental fountain in the central pond
(PB 227)

A contemporary account of the garden describes the pond as having polished red Aberdeenshire granite margins and fountain (Hartshorne 1865). In 1988 this granite was stored in the gun sheds (Kent 1998, 22). A drawing in the castle archives shows a design for a red granite fountain with water spouting from lion's heads (Fig. 5.39). The fountain is not marked on any of the garden designs, nor on the 1867 Ordnance Survey map which labels the pond as a Fish Pond (see Fig. 8.20) and it had been removed by the time a photograph of the garden was published in the May 3 1902 edition of *The Gardeners' Chronicle* (Fig. 10.34).

Excavation in the middle garden exposed the foundations of the south wall of the pond. The wall was considerably thicker at foundation level, stepping in progressively with height, to enable terracing into the slope. The south wall was built within a substantial 1.38m-deep construction cut at least 1.20m wide. The wall was 3.23m high with a base of randomly coursed stones interspersed with levelling string layers. At a level of *c.* 53.40m OD, presumably at the contemporary ground surface, the wall changed substantially in character. Above this point, regular, well-dressed, faced ashlar blocks were employed for two courses, capped with a decorative course of chamfered sandstone slabs edged with a decorative scroll-work band. The wall here would

have stood to a height of 1.50m above the contemporary ground surface.

Numerous planting holes were set into the east, west and south walls of the pond in a random pattern. These were irregular in shape, but approximately triangular and had been formed by removing adjacent corners of blocks at their base. They generally measured 0.20m to 0.30m across. The irregularity of these holes, combined with the correlation in height of holes on adjacent blocks, suggests that they were a later modification to the wall, provided to allow plants to cascade down the inner faces of the walls above the water level, lightening the effect of the walls.

The east–west element of the eastern terrace wall was recorded by rectified photography and subsequently partially digitised to show details of construction technique (PCA 2004, elevation 65, fig 41). The wall was built with well-faced, regularly coursed sandstone blocks capped with sandstone slabs which were dressed with decorative scrollwork. It was 37m long and 4.20m high at its eastern end where a small buttress, 0.60m wide, formed the end of the wall. The wall returned to the south for a distance of *c.* 8m with a very short return to the west to form the eastern end of a walkway. At its western end, the eastern terrace wall stepped up above a north–south wall element which ran parallel to the east pond retaining wall. The *c.* 4m-wide space between these parallel walls was planted with trees.

Terrace walls ran parallel to the eastern and western sides of the pond at a distance of 7.80m on either side, providing wide sloping walks from south to north. In the south, these turned and ran east–west away from the pond in either direction, as long terrace retaining walls which had a maximum height of 4.20m.

As well as their function as retaining walls, the terrace walls formed the northern sides of two 8m-wide tree-lined walkways on the higher terrace above the pond, 37m long to the east and 45m long in the west. Contemporary accounts describe the walkways as planted with lime trees, also known as linden trees, a large deciduous tree with green heart-shaped leaves (*The Gardeners' Chronicle* 1891, 593). All elements of the pond, retaining walls and terrace walls were evidently planned to present a unified whole using the same stonework, and plans of the garden show a buttress at every corner of these terrace and pond retaining walls, only a few of which survived at the time of the fieldwork (see Fig. 9.13). The terrace walls have been retained within the new Alnwick Garden, to either side of the Grand Cascade which forms the centre piece of the new garden.

## Earthwork mounds

Along with the monumental stone walls, substantial earthworks formed a major design element of the middle garden; an earthwork survey was undertaken of those remains which survived in the early twentieth century. At the far southern end of the middle garden were large east–west aligned earthworks running adjacent to the northern wall of the hexagonal garden, to either side of the triple-gated entrance. These were up to 16m wide and sloped down to north and south from the summits and from each wide end at the corners of the hexagonal garden to narrow ends adjacent to the gate. The western mound was 40m in length and the height at the top sloped down from 69.94m OD in the west to 68.73m OD in the east. At the western end, the base of the slope was at 65.99m OD in the south and 64.93m OD in the north, the mound thus survived to a height of over 5m. The eastern mound extended for nearly 55m in length and was up to 4.60m high.

At the centre of the southern end of the middle garden, in line with the triple-arched gate, was a crescent-shaped earthwork, its shape echoing the Percy crescent. This extended for 25m north–south and was 20m wide with the top of the earthwork at a height of 63.41m OD and the base in the south at 60.37m OD. Sinuous, curving mounds on either side of the middle garden extended down the steeply-sloping hillside, sloping to east and west, thus enclosing a sunken area in the centre of the garden. These commenced as narrow earthworks to either side of a pathway

into the upper garden at a height of 64.17m OD which curved around each side of the crescent earthwork; degradation had evidently taken place with the narrow mounds becoming split in some places. The earthworks enclosed the central decorative area occupied by Parterres 5 and 6, increasing in width as they ran southwards down the hillside. In this area the earthworks mounds survived as fairly amorphous curves which, towards the centre of the middle garden, were *c.* 2m high. The earthwork turned at right angles to run parallel with the terrace retaining walls. The western earthwork was over 6m high, surviving at a highest level of 59.41m OD sloping down northwards to 53.40m OD, it continued around the end of the west terrace wall and extended northwards into the lower garden to run parallel with the pond. The eastern mound terminated at the end of the east terrace wall.

A stylised depiction of the earthworks can be seen on a plan of the gardens dating to 1865, soon after their construction (see Fig. 8.16) and they are also shown as detailed earthworks on the 1867 Ordnance Survey map (see Fig. 8.20). It is evident from the map evidence that the mounds had degraded considerably over time and eventually came to be covered in large trees. When first built the earthworks were sharply defined and included semi-circular mounds surrounding circular paths at either end of the east–west path which divided Parterres 5 and 6 beyond which, to the south, were U-shaped mounds which created viewing platforms. A north–south path internal to the crescent-shaped mound also terminated in a circular viewing area.

## Upper garden

A new irregular hexagonal garden was constructed in the southern part of the extended garden backing onto the streets of the town. This was surrounded on all sides by a 4.20m-high brick wall, the northern section of which divided the hexagonal upper garden from the rest of the garden (Fig. 5.1). The wall, which still survives, is generally 0.60 wide built in Flemish bond with bricks measuring 70mm x 230mm x 115mm topped with sandstone slabs (Kent 1998, 6). The south-west segment of boundary wall is 0.68m wide. Its external face was built with regular coursed sandstone rubble and the internal face brick-built in Flemish bond. The northern boundary wall extends for 107m, is 4.20m high internally and 4.30m high externally. The inside face is again brick-built in Flemish bond with espalier frames and the outside face random sandstone rubble brought to courses, topped with sandstone slabs. A triple arched gateway in the north wall (Entrance 7) approached by a flight of steps provides a 'triumphal arch' motif at the top of the garden which terminates the view from the northern conservatory and provides a dramatic entrance to the upper garden and from the upper into the middle garden

**Fig. 5.40** Sixteenth-century Venetian gate in central entrance of triple-arched gateway (Entrance 7) looking south into the middle garden from the upper garden (VR 2015)

(Kent 1988, 7). An architect's drawing for the gateway held in the archives shows that three entrances were designed to be 7ft 6 inches wide (*c.* 2.30m) (Fig. 8.17). At the time of the fieldwork an ornamental iron gate hung in the central entrances, part of two pairs of sixteenth-century Venetian gates bought by the fourth duke (Fig. 5.40); three of these gates now hang in the entrance to the upper garden with a fourth in the main entrance into the garden. A narrow entrance was also provided through the northern wall at its western end (Entrance 8) and along the southern wall (Entrance 9).

## The new walled kitchen garden

Creation of the fourth duke's garden involved the destruction of the kitchen garden built by the second duke to the south-west of the original walled garden, with this area incorporated into the newly expanded Italianate decorative garden. A new walled kitchen garden was therefore established beyond the boundaries

of the walled garden and the northern parts of several backlots of properties fronting Bondgate were acquired to create this new kitchen garden. The new kitchen garden was accessed via a wide entrance to the west of the Gardener's House, which appears to have been extended further to the west by 1856, as shown on the Ordnance Survey map of that date (see Fig. 8.10). Two north-west to south-east aligned hothouses were built within the new kitchen garden, designs for these buildings date from 1863 (see Fig. 9.6) and these first appear on a map of 1865 (see Fig. 5.12; Fig. 8.16) providing a tight date for construction. The southern building was also extant at the time of writing and although the glass roof panels had been removed, the original wrought-iron roof structure including the venting mechanisms still survived under the modern roof cladding. The drawings also show a detailed plan of the earlier vinery, built during Garden 3 and now straddling the east wall of the new kitchen garden, with the backhouses external to the new garden and the glasshouse inside the garden.

# Chapter 6

## Garden 5, The Garden of the Sixth Duke (1867–1899)

*'I found Mr. Ingram in the midst of improvement. Since his arrival, on the accession of the present Duke of Northumberland, thirteen years since, the improvements have been continuous. At present he is reorganising the heating apparatus of the numerous houses.'*
(*The Gardeners' Chronicle* 1880)

The fifth duke, who held the title for just two years having acceded at the age of 87, was succeeded in 1867 by his son Algernon who brought a new head gardener, Alexander Ingram, to Alnwick. Cartographic evidence indicates that the general layout of the garden established by the fourth duke remained largely unchanged, although the internal layout of Parterres 5 and 6 in the middle garden was redesigned. Extensive new drainage systems installed by the sixth duke were recorded within this area and construction of these evidently destroyed much of the original formal beds of Parterres 5 and 6. Excavated elements of this new layout correspond closely to the 1897 Ordnance Survey map (see Fig. 8.21).

The later nineteenth century was a period of significant technological innovation and substantial changes were made to the heating systems of the hothouses, including a radical overhaul of the heating system for both castle and gardens in 1890 when steam heating was introduced. Substantial modifications occurred to the backhouse of Hothouse 2 with the central portion converted for domestic habitation, presumably providing accommodation for a gardener.

A range of buildings were constructed against the outer northern wall of the garden at its eastern end. These gun sheds first appear on the 1897 map and thus were almost certainly commissioned by the sixth duke, as was a nursery area, which lay to the south-east of the original walled garden. This can be seen on the 1897 Ordnance Survey map as a rectangular garden, walled on the east and south sides and abutting the southern wall of the lower garden on its northern side (see Fig. 8.21).

### 6.1 Excavated Remains of Garden 5, Middle Garden

Elements of an identical system of drains and decorative paths were recorded in five of the six corners of Parterres 5 and 6, the exception being the south-east corner of Parterre 5 where only a tree extraction pit was recorded. Ceramic drain pipes led out from the centre of the large central bed in Parterre 5, flowing into curvilinear drains in the corners, which were overlain by brick-edged pebbled paths. The same arrangement was recorded on the two northern corners of Parterre 6. These ceramic pipes then fed into a system of drains that ran on beneath the two parallel north–south paths. There are indications that the drains were joined by an east–west element in the north, beneath the northernmost path. Inspection pits were provided at each corner and also equidistant from the corners along both north–south paths. Iron pipes led into the drains from above at these points, perhaps added as later drainage measures. The whole system drained down towards the north, probably into the pond, though this was not proven.

The archaeological remains recorded in the north-west corner of Parterre 5 can be used as an indicator of the system as a whole. An east–west ceramic drain pipe was recorded in plan and section in a sondage excavated through the path bounding the northern side of Parterre 5 ( Fig. 6.2), and it is assumed that this ran along the length of the path, joining with pipes flowing northwards at the corners of the path. The construction cut for the drain pipe cut through the original path surface, which was reinstated over the backfilled trench.

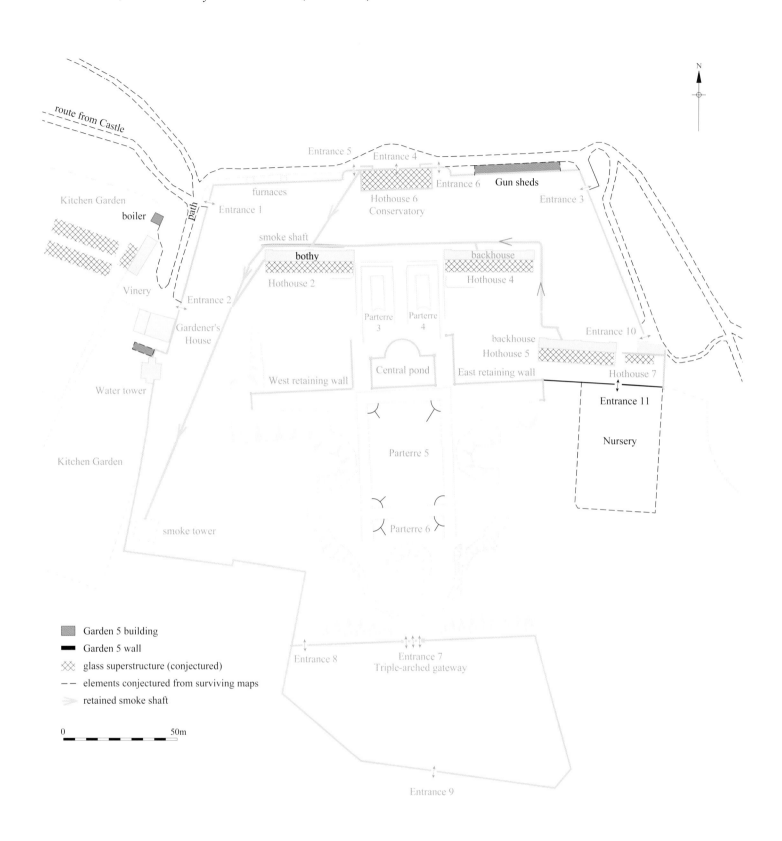

**Fig. 6.1** Garden 5, 1867-1899, based on surviving elements, archaeological excavation, conjecture and contemporary map evidence showing retained elements of the earlier gardens (scale 1: 1250)

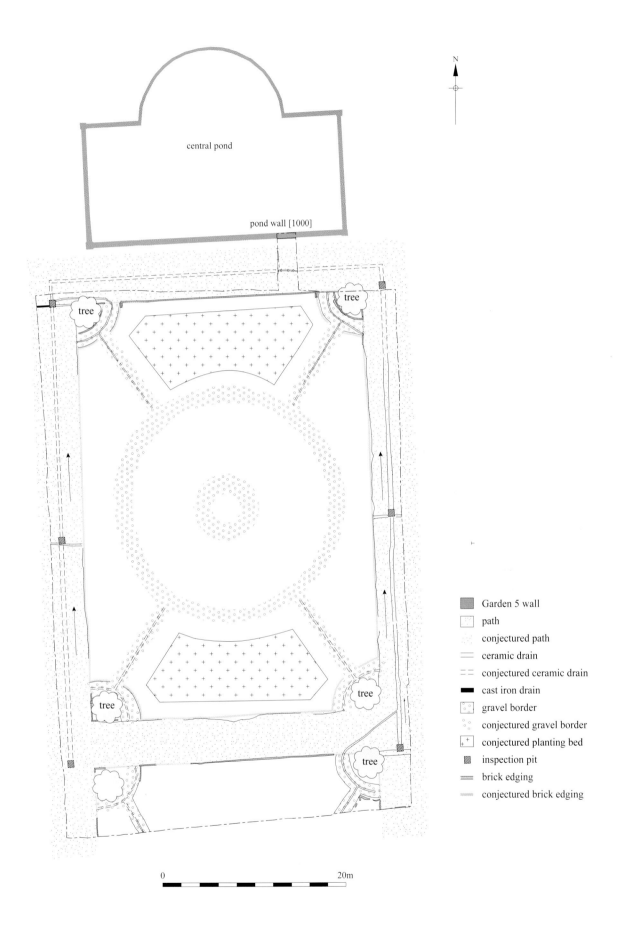

central pond

pond wall [1000]

tree

tree

tree

tree

tree

| | Garden 5 wall |
| | path |
| | conjectured path |
| | ceramic drain |
| | conjectured ceramic drain |
| | cast iron drain |
| | gravel border |
| | conjectured gravel border |
| | conjectured planting bed |
| | inspection pit |
| | brick edging |
| | conjectured brick edging |

0                                    20m

**Fig. 6.2** Garden 5, remains of the late nineteenth-century garden laid out by the sixth duke as revealed in excavation in Area B (scale 1: 400)

A brick-lined inspection pit/silt trap beneath the path at the north-west corner of Parterre 5 was roughly square, measuring 0.66m x 0.72m internally, and was capped with a reused paving slab. A ceramic salt-glazed drainpipe led into the pipe from the south and continued out to the north. A cast-iron drainpipe ran east–west, resting on a brick plinth with a down pipe leading into the structure; it is possible that this was a later addition to the drainage system. The path surface was repaired and reinstated over these drainage features with a sand and pea grit surface bedded on compact sandy gravel. Brick-lined inspection pits were also recorded in the south-east corner of the Parterre 5 and 12m to the north under the eastern north–south path (Fig. 6.2). The ceramic drain pipe under the path was also recorded in a section excavated across the path to the north. This arrangement of drains and inspection pits was mirrored along the western north–south path. The east–west ceramic drain was recorded in the section excavated across the path at the northern limit of excavation (Fig. 6.2) and located towards the centre of the path presumably joined the north–south drains running along the eastern and western sides of the parterre.

In the north-west corner of Parterre 5, a ceramic drainpipe within a *c.* 0.70m wide construction cut ran from the north-eastern corner of the inspection pit under the east–west path for a distance of *c.* 6m and then turned to run as the south-east quadrant of a circle in the north-west corner of the parterre. A north-west to south-east aligned spur from the central point of the quadrant appeared to run from the centre of the parterre. The drainpipe was overlain with patchy gravel and sealed with a surface deposit of fine sub-rounded pebbles. This represents the surviving surface of paths which can be seen on the 1897 Ordnance Survey maps leading from the large central circular path to each corner and then bifurcating around a tree in each corner (see Fig. 8.21). An identical drain construction and part layout was recorded in the northern corners of Parterre 6 (Fig. 6.3). A deposit of purple clinker which survived intermittently in both of the northern corners of this parterre would have formed a decorative surface for the paths around the cypress trees in the corners.

The southern side of the east–west path at the northern end of Parterre 5 was edged in a single course of red unfrogged machine-made brick, and brick edging was also recorded on the internal

**Fig. 6.3** Ceramic drains in the north-east corner of Parterre 5, looking south-west (scale 1m)

**Fig. 6.4** Paths in the north-east corner of Parterre 5, showing brick edging and concrete kerb, the tree extraction pit is in the foreground, looking south-west (scale 1m)

edges of the north–south paths, in some cases only as traces of mortar. Brick edging also survived intermittently along the southern side of the east–west path defining the two parterres at the southern end of the middle garden. There was also evidence to suggest that both sides of the curvilinear paths in the corners of the parterres had been edged as well as the paths leading into the centre, in places topped with a kerb made of decorative moulded ceramic blocks (Fig. 6.4). Bricks used in the construction of drains, wall elements and brick edging included machine made, slop-moulded and handmade types, perhaps suggesting reuse of materials, incorporating whatever bricks were readily available. The inspection pits were constructed consistently with the same machine-made bricks of mid to late nineteenth-century date, suggesting either that better-quality material was required for these features or that these were a later introduction when the iron pipe was installed.

The resulting appearance was of a series of decorative parterres, closely pruned and tightly managed, defined by gravel paths and divisions. The overall appearance of the parterre gardens thus created is illustrated in photographs of the early twentieth century, which illustrate the sheer scale of these gardens (see, for example, Fig. 8.22).

## 6.2 Standing Structures of Garden 5

### Hothouse 6: the northern conservatory

#### Conversion of northern conservatory to a palm house

Internal modifications would have been carried out within the conservatory related to the use of the structure as a palm house during the latter years of the sixth duke's life. A 'Palm House' is first listed as a weekly task in the Paylist of Workmen from 1899 (Acc 446/5; see section 10.2 below). This is considered likely to refer to the northern conservatory, as a photograph taken in 1898 shows large palm trees inside this structure (Fig. 6.5), in contrast to the *c.* 1870 photograph taken inside the conservatory which shows a very different planting scheme (see Fig. 5.16).

An account of the gardens in *The Gardeners' Chronicle* of May 3 1902 states that:

> 'The glasshouses and conservatory have been extensively altered in recent years, much of the staging of the conservatory having been removed and shallow beds substituted for it, and a wide central path formed, together with an artistically-arranged rockery at the back of the house, masking a lot of hot-water pipes, and affording situations for climbing plants.'

**Fig. 6.5** Photograph taken in 1898 of a group of scholars from the Duke's School, Alnwick, described as a souvenir of the Collinson re-union, banquet, and presentation, June 15th 1898 (Library 29739). Note the palm trees visible in the conservatory, Hothouse 6

Modifications to the heating system within Hothouse 6 were attested in the form of amendments to the furnace at the western end of the cellar (Fig. 6.8) in Room 1. The evidence of successive rebuilds here as well as modification of earlier masonry, is perhaps the best reflection of the numerous modifications to the heating system alluded to in *The Gardeners' Chronicle* (1880).

A brick surface [4015] at the eastern end of Room 2, which was laid on the original stone floor [4014] across the width of the cellar, may have formed a base to a furnace (see Fig. 2.7). The bricks were stamped 'Broomhill' and the hard cement mortar suggests that they once supported a boiler similar to that at the western end of Room 1. Broomhill Collieries brickworks, which was located to the south-east of Alnwick near to the coastal town of Amble, produced firebricks from 1866 to 1900 (Pevsner *et al.*. 2002, 95). A similar brick structure at the western end of Room 2 [4016] was perhaps

the support for another boiler, its association with pipe work [4004] suggests that it was associated with the heating system. Damage to the duct near the water tank is indicative of replacement of the furnace and associated heating pipes at the western end of Room 2, above the central hearth location (Fig. 6.9).

Brick columns built against the northern wall in Room 2 and brick additions to the flue in Room 1 appeared to have been inserted to support iron pipework. Two cast-iron water pipes ran through both rooms in the cellar along the southern wall. These all comprised 65mm diameter segmented pipes 1.65m in length connected with collars. In Room 2 the upper pipe was situated on top of the earlier duct at a height of *c.* 1.75m above floor level along the majority of its length; at the eastern end the pipe was raised higher on bricks, sloping from east to west. The lower pipe was supported on four brick columns [4021]

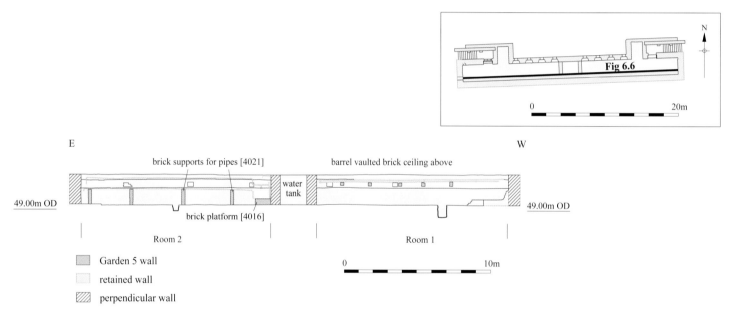

**Fig. 6.6** Hothouse 6, Garden 5, elevation of the southern wall of the cellar showing modifications (scale 1:250)

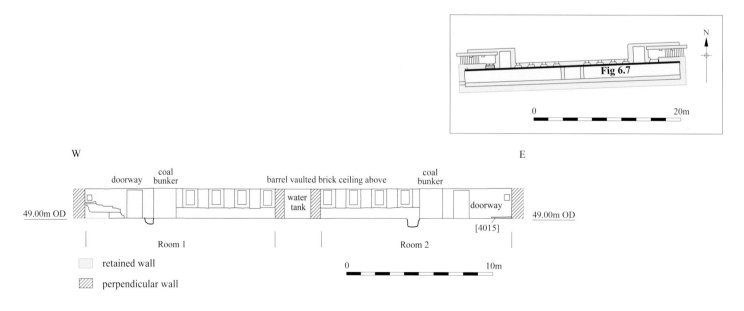

**Fig. 6.7** Hothouse 6, Garden 5, elevation of the northern wall of the cellar (scale 1:250)

constructed against stone wall [4030] (see Fig. 5.21). This pipe was located at a height of 1.05m above floor level at the east end of the room, sloping gently down to a height of 0.95m at the west end. Both pipes turned at 90° at the eastern end of the room, and presumably fed into and out of a boiler located here. At the western end, near to the central tank, the arrangement of pipes was complex; a downpipe from the upper pipe headed towards the centre of a brick platform [4016] in the corner of the room. At the base of this downpipe was a square plate with rivets at each corner which presumably attached to a feature such as a boiler or water tank which would have been set on the brick platform. The lower pipe turned down towards the brick platform at a 90° angle then turned again where it presumably connected to the base of the fitting on the platform. The upper pipe continued through the wall of the central water tank. Another downpipe attached to that wall turned eastwards at its base and also presumably flowed into or out of the bottom of the fitting on platform [4016]. A system of smaller diameter water pipes was also located in this area.

The pipe work and brick platforms in Room 2 were less substantial and complex than in Room 1. Here the two pipes were set close together and were carried on brick supports tied into

the brickwork of the earlier heating duct [4002]. The lower pipe sloped down from 1.40m above level in the east to 1.20m in the west. At the eastern end of the room the pipes entered the duct and presumably the water tank behind.

It is assumed that most of the pipework identified was associated with this set of modifications although it is possible that some was retained from previous heating systems. Once these structural modifications had been made the vent for the smoke tower (assuming that was the original purpose of this part of the structure) would have become redundant.

These modifications to the heating system within the cellar to heat the northern conservatory above, might be reasonably equated with the sixth duke's reorganisation of the heating apparatus in the garden. An 1880 account of the garden relates that the head gardener was reorganising the heating apparatus of the numerous houses (*The Gardeners' Chronicle* 1880) and this is supported by the date of the Broomhill bricks (1866–1900) used in construction of the boiler platforms. The hot water heating, a precursor to modern central heating, used water from the central tank with pipe work feeding into and out of the water tank and to the three possible boilers. Although the boilers, which were connected to the pipe work, had been removed, their presence could be inferred from the

**Fig. 6.8** Hothouse 6, the original western backhouse room, showing the furnace platform [4032] of the original build, a later boiler support [4008] and brick duct (scales 1m and 0.50m)

**Fig. 6.9** Hothouse 6, pipework associated with the central hearth at the western end Room 2, showing damage to the vent along northern wall (scale 0.50m)

surviving pipes and brick supports. The most substantial furnace was located at the western end of the structure. A brick platform would have supported a boiler with a rake-out channel beneath. Hot water exited the cellar and presumably circulated around the superstructure, heating the conservatory, via large iron pipes. Two other possible furnaces were located in Room 2. It was not clear how these functioned together, although conceivably boilers may have been fired alternately, allowing the one not in use to cool down and be cleaned out. The 1896 plan of the garden water supply shows that a pipe led from the main water pipe, which was fed by the water tower, into the north-west corner of the conservatory and along the north-west side of the structure; two right-angled branches presumably fed into the central tank and the main boiler in the west end of the cellar (see Fig. 9.12).

## Hothouse 2: conversion of the backhouse into a bothy

Substantial modifications occurred to the backhouse of Hothouse 2 with the central portion, which had previously been occupied by a mushroom house, converted for domestic habitation (a 'bothy'), presumably providing accommodation for a gardener. The remodelling involved the infilling of doorways through the north–south dividing walls creating three bays with a total of seven rooms. The western bay measured 11m internally, the central bay, which was the bothy, measured 14.50m and the eastern bay measured 12m. Earlier furnaces and associated heating system features had been demolished and infilled within the central portion of the structure. Iron pipework passing through the walls of the building indicates that this form of heating may have continued to be used to heat the glasshouse and the survival of

a basemented area at the western end of the building (Room 1) indicates that this was the location of the boiler at this time. Also associated with this phase of modification was the blocking of the door from the backhouse into the glasshouse at the eastern end of the building, with only the western entrance remaining in use. The two doors into the backhouses from the north remained in use, and another was inserted through the north wall to provide access into the bothy.

The 1896 plan of the water supply into the gardens shows a water pipe leading into the bothy annotated '*put on 1876*' and '*Bothy*' indicating the approximate date of the conversion of the Hothouse 2 backhouse (Fig. 6.11; see Fig. 9.12). Additional pipework was added in 1893 and 1896, indicating the frequency of modifications to the water supply. The 'Paylist of Workmen' first lists a woman as being employed in the bothy in December 1884 (Acc 446/3), the last mention is in June 1899 (Acc 446/5) although the bothy may have continued to be used beyond this date.

### The western bay (Room 1)

The 11m-long western bay Room 1 comprised a basement area and ground level room which apparently remained little altered, other than the blocking-in of the internal doorway at the eastern end of Room 1. Access to the glasshouse, via steps [103], was maintained as was external access through the north wall on the opposite side of the room. The western bay thus comprised a cellar and ground level room, presumably rooms associated with the glasshouse to the front, perhaps serving as stores and/or potting sheds as well as providing housing for a boiler, prior to the introduction of steam heating (see section 9.1, below).

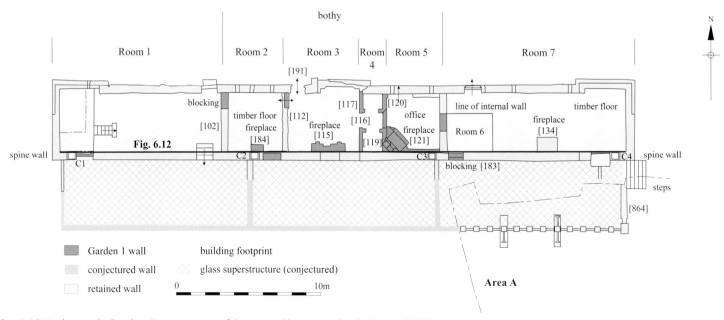

**Fig. 6.10** Hothouse 2, Garden 5, conversion of the central bay into a bothy (scale 1:250)

## Central bay, the bothy (Rooms 2–5)

The 14.50m-long central bay comprised three rooms (Room 2–5 from west to east) with two small storerooms either side of a corridor between Rooms 3 and 5 (Fig. 6.10). This bay was accessed externally via a new doorway [191] in the north wall in the north-west corner of Room 3.

Room 2 measured *c.* 3.70m internally and was provided with a small fireplace; this, along with the plaster rendered walls and wooden floors, indicates that this room was used as a bedroom. The doorway along the west wall [102] was blocked-off and a new doorway in the north-east corner inserted in wall [112] to allow

access to the adjoining Room 3. This room occupied the former basement (Room 2, Garden 3 and 4) which had contained the furnaces for the mushroom house and glasshouse. The room had been infilled with layers of demolition debris culminating in a mortar spread which formed the foundations for parallel north–south walls which formed the supporting joists for a suspended timber plank floor constructed at contemporary ground level (51.92m OD). Adjacent to the south wall, and to chimney C2, was a hearthstone for a small brick-built fireplace [184]. Little of this survived; essentially it was just an aperture lined with brick on either side. The front of the chimney breast was flush with the inner face of the walls and the sandstone blocking of flue

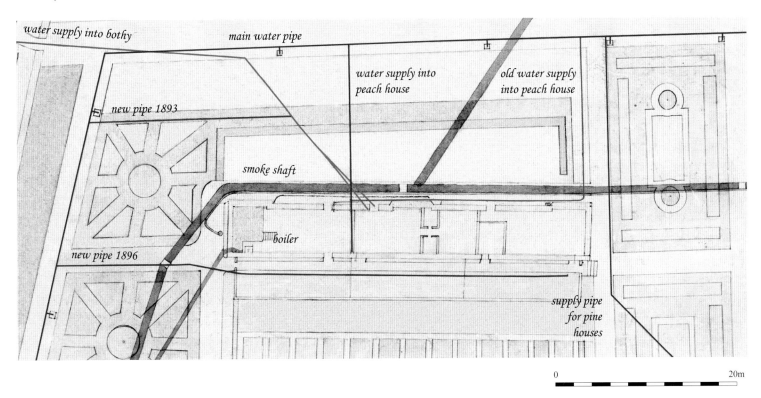

**Fig. 6.11** Extract from an 1896 plan of the water supply to the gardens, showing Hothouse 2 (TAG 2/1/1) (scale 1:400)

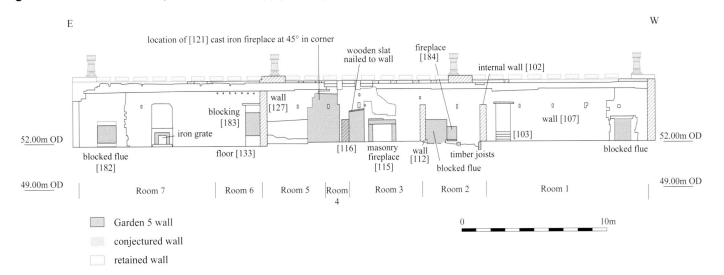

**Fig. 6.12** Hothouse 2, Garden 5, north-facing elevation of spine wall, the internal wall of the bothy and associated stores and potting sheds (scale 1:250)

**Fig. 6.13** Hothouse 2, rectified photograph of spine wall, looking north (scales 2m)

[1102] was visible at the back of the fireplace; the earlier chimney associated with the heating system for the glasshouse was reused as the outlet for the fire.

Room 3 measured *c.* 4.80m internally and was the largest room in the bothy; the provision of an oven and an ornate fireplace suggests that this was the kitchen and living quarters. This occupied the former mushroom house (Room 3, Gardens 3 and 4) and retained the flagstone flooring. A door was inserted through the backhouse north wall in the western side of the room to create the only external entrance into the bothy. The 1896 plan of the water supply in the garden shows that the water pipe for the bothy led into the building through this door (see Fig. 9.12). A brick-built chimney breast with stone surround and mantel [115] was keyed into the southern wall of the room (Fig. 6.14). Two sockets above the mantel, with iron staining inside, presumably held some form of overmantel or façade to the chimney breast. Within the fireplace a damaged iron grate rested on a hearthstone of shale and was bricked in to either side. Above this, set to the east and resting on the brick infilling was an iron box, with internal shelf supports and hinges for a door, forming an oven. The sandstone fire surround and mantel were reasonably ornate, with chamfered edges. To either side of the fireplace the southern wall was plaster rendered and plaster skirting was visible all around the walls of Room 3.

A new brick wall was built to form the eastern end of Room 3 [116] and [117] with a roughly central doorway providing access into two small storerooms, or perhaps larders (Room 4). The storerooms were located either side of a corridor between Rooms 3 and 5 and were bounded to the east by brick walls [119] and [120]. The southern storeroom measured 1.30m square and the northern one 1.30m east–west by 1m north–south. Short east–west returns to the four north–south walls framed entrances and sockets cut into the floor at these returns mark the position of doors. The floor in the vicinity of the entrances to the storerooms was noticeably

worn. Plaster skirting was also visible along the bases of the walls, resting on the flagstone floor.

Room 5 measured *c.* 3.70m internally and also contained a fireplace. The provision of a window in the eastern wall of the room, albeit at a high level, indicates that this may have functioned as an office.

The lower half of the former doorway in eastern sandstone wall [127] was infilled with roughly hewn sandstone blocks, and the upper half with brick, suggesting that perhaps it was originally only half blocked and that a hatch or window was left between the bothy and Room 6. However, it is also possible that the differential blocking of the doorway reflects materials to hand. Above and to the south of this doorway was a high window with a timber frame which suggests it was originally glazed. In the north-west corner of the room, a brick wall [120] was constructed over the earlier sandstone floor and two stretches of low brickwork constructed alongside the northern and southern walls of the room formed supports for a timber floor, subsequently removed, which would also have utilised the partially collapsed heating duct from the earlier Room 3 for support. In the angle of the south-western corner of the room was a brick-built fireplace [121]. This comprised a brick surround and chimney breast, with brick arch over fire surround and single slab sandstone hearth, set above the level of the floor support brickwork (Fig. 6.15, Fig. 6.16). The joist floor would have rested at the same level as the hearthstone, though had been removed by the time of the investigations. Set within the brick surround was a relatively ornate, arched, cast iron fire surround, measuring 760mm by 970mm, with a border of crossed weave on its outer arch and central decorative floral motif on the inner arch. Brickwork visible in the wall above the fireplace extended westwards at an angle, which suggested the chimney for this fire led into and vented via the chimneybreast of fireplace [115] in the central living quarters (see Fig. 6.13, Fig. 6.15).

**Fig. 6.14** Hothouse 2, Garden 5, fireplace [115] in the kitchen/living quarters of the bothy, Room 3, looking south (scale 1m)

**Fig. 6.15** Hothouse 2, Garden 5, office, kitchen/living quarters and southern storeroom, Rooms 3, 4, 5, in the bothy, looking south (scale 1m)

**Fig. 6.16** Hothouse 2, Garden 5, fireplace [121] in the bothy office, Room 5, looking west; the full extent of the bothy accommodation can be seen (scale 1m)

### Eastern bay (Rooms 6 and 7)

The 12m-long eastern bay comprised Rooms 6 and 7 and was entered externally via the original doorway in the north wall, now in Room 6. Room 6 measured 3.10m; there was no surviving wall between Rooms 6 and 7, but traces of plaster on the stone floor indicated the position of a north–south dividing wall and sockets set in the floor in the north-east corner indicated the position of a former doorway. An east–west return observed in plaster on the floor divided Room 6 into two areas, a larger southern area with a small entrance corridor to the north. The spine wall in Room 6 had joist holes for ceiling supports at a higher level than elsewhere. Access to the glasshouse via the doorway in the spine wall had been infilled with brick [183], but the upper 0.30m had been left open and a wooden frame surrounded the aperture, suggesting

a glazed window to allow light to enter the room from the glasshouse. A window was also inserted into the northern wall of Room 7 and light would also have entered via the high window in the west wall through to Room 5 in the bothy. This emphasises the necessity of provision of light into these rooms, where previously none had been required.

Room 7 measured *c.* 9.50m by 3.80m. Brick infilling of the earlier fireplace [134] on the south wall of the room to make a smaller aperture and the insertion of a cast iron grate/surround may imply conversion to coal burning from wood burning. Abutting fireplace [134] and set adjacent to the southern wall and against the northern wall of Room 7, were low east–west brick walls. These would have formed supporting walls for a timber floor, now absent. There was evidence for joists in a plaster spread on top of one of these walls. The original semi-basemented eastern furnace room of the hothouse had been infilled prior to the insertion of four east–west aligned supporting dwarf walls. As with other rooms in this modified hothouse, these formed supports for the joists of a subsequently removed timber floor. Levelling dumps, between the supporting joists, included demolition debris, clinker, coal and brick rubble, including fire bricks deriving from the destruction of a furnace or similar construction, which presumably would have been located within the former eastern furnace room. The function of this part of the building was not apparent; it may have been used as garden offices, stores or similar.

The backhouses thus would have comprised three separate bays, each with a different function. Only the western bay, which housed the boiler, provided access to the glasshouse, and this would have been the functional part of the backhouse. Although smoke appears to have still been drawn away from the building via the smoke shaft at this point (this feature is shown clearly on a 1900 water supply map; see Fig. 9.13), the desire to keep the garden completely smoke free was apparently only limited to the smoke from furnaces, as attested by the provision of domestic fireplaces with separate chimneys.

### Spine wall

The wall was plaster rendered on its south face, internal to the glasshouse. The westernmost third of this elevation had thirteen iron uprights with wires running horizontally through, presumably for the training of fruit. It is not possible to say with any certainty which period of use this relates to. The walls are likely to have been re-rendered and or whitewashed as needed throughout the course of the building's history and supporting trellis work would be modified and repaired as needed and according to the crops grown in the building. Plaster rendering was also visible in some areas on the north face of the wall.

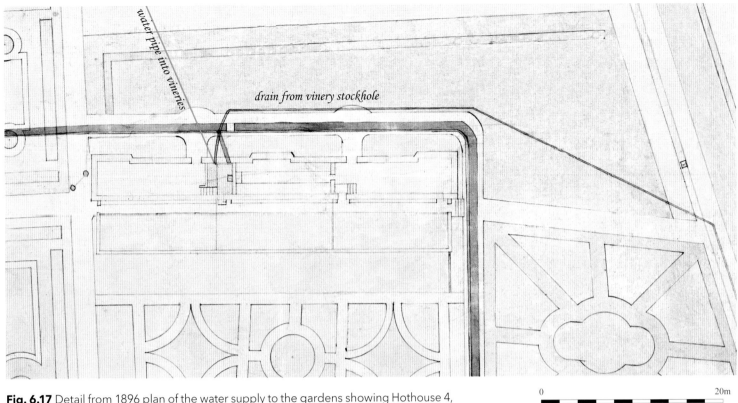

water pipe into vineries

drain from vinery stockhole

0                                                                20m

**Fig. 6.17** Detail from 1896 plan of the water supply to the gardens showing Hothouse 4, with original annotations enhanced for clarity (TAG 2/1/2) (scale 1:400)

## Hothouse 4: modifications to heating systems

The precise dates at which various modifications to Hothouse 4 were carried out are unknown, but some of these may be placed with the sixth duke. Cartographic evidence demonstrates that some of the changes in Hothouse 4 were in place by 1896. Whether the conversion to hot water heating had been completed by the fourth duke, or whether this fell to the sixth duke is not certain. What is clear is that by the 1870s these conversions are likely to have been complete and subsequent reorganisations would constitute a remodelling of the workings of the various heating arrangements; such reorganisation of heating systems appear to have been a recurring event (*The Gardeners' Chronicle* 1880, 523–524). Internal modifications to the glasshouse element of the hothouse were recorded in the form of a spread of brick rubble, perhaps representing the demolition of the internal dividing wall [266] (see Fig. 4.5), overlain by a further dump of rubble and then a clay surface.

Unlike Hothouse 2, which had its back sheds converted with domestic occupation in the form of the bothy, Hothouse 4 backhouses appear to have remained functional. The central boilers served the vinery to the south and the mushroom house to the east, which apparently continued to function as such. The position of the smoke shaft, installed to draw the smoke from the numerous chimneys which had previously served the backhouse

boilers, can be clearly seen on the water supply plan of 1896 (Fig. 6.17). A cast iron pipe exposed close to the surface of the central north–south path between Parterres 3 and 4 was installed between the production of the 1896 and 1900 water supply plans (see Fig. 9.12 and Fig. 9.13). This led from the main east–west water supply pipe which was installed during Garden 3 and replaced in 1896.

## The heated garden wall

The eighteenth-century north-west heated boundary wall was originally heated with hot air which ran through flues in the wall, generated in the external furnace. These flues were utilised for the insertion of hot water pipes, presumably during this reorganisation of the garden heating system by the sixth duke, and then for the steam heating introduced in 1890. Rectangular openings with iron doors in the external face of the wall, the original flue inspection holes and access for cleaning the flues, accommodated valves for controlling the supply of water.

## The gun sheds

The gun sheds first appear on the 1897 Ordnance Survey map as a long narrow range of buildings attached to the external side of the original north-east garden wall, this wall forming the south wall

**Fig. 6.18** Eastern end of the gun sheds, looking south-west (RK 1998)

**Fig. 6.19** Structural remains of the steam plant in the north-east corner of new kitchen garden, built *c.* 1890, looking west (VR 2015)

of the sheds. The precise date of their construction is not known from cartographic evidence, but the garden accounts book record that in May 1880 Arthur Forster was employed 'attending masons' for six days a week at 2'8d for six full weeks; he resumes attending masons for four weeks from August to September (Acc 446/2). It is possible that this may be related to construction work for the gun sheds.

A brief description of the sheds was compiled by Kent (1988, 18). The mono-pitched Welsh slated roof is supported on stone corbels inserted into the north face of the garden wall and braced timber posts on stone plinths. At each end are stone-built rooms with segmental arched doors and raised parapets. The room at the east end had a reused 6–panelled door and frame

and a large cast iron and brick stove with cast iron flue. Kent (1988, 18) suggests that the sheds may have been built to exhibit some of the Percy Tenantry Volunteers' field pieces. The gun sheds have been converted into a public toilet block as part of the facilities of the Alnwick Garden.

## Steam heating

Documentary and cartographic evidence demonstrate that steam heating for the glasshouses was introduced by the sixth duke. The archives contain correspondence relating to steam boilers supplied to Alnwick Castle (DP/DS/I/62). Proposals for the steam heating date from January 1890 and imply that the boiler which heated the castle was placed at some distance from the castle, close to the garden. Accounts from December of the same year record a cost of 11,540/15/4 for insertion of electric lighting, steam apparatus and repairs to a waterway, demonstrating the speed with which it was introduced (see 9.2 below).

A 1900 plan of the water supply system shows a steam main and condensed water pipes running through Entrance 1, past the northern conservatory, skirting around Hothouse 4 and Hothouse 5 and into the backhouse of Hothouse 7, the small vinery (i.e. the Muscat House) in the south-east corner of the garden (see Fig. 9.13).

An article in *The Gardeners' Chronicle* May 3 1902 describes how all of the hothouses were by this time heated by steam with a boiler which had been constructed near to the Gardener's House with a large smoke-shaft nearby. The 1897 Ordnance Survey map depicts a large square structure straddling the east wall of the walled kitchen garden to the west of the original walled garden, close to its north-east corner (Fig. 8.21). The lower portion of this substantially built stone square structure is extant and an opening on its east side facing the west wall of the original walled garden suggests that this is the remains of the steam boiler building constructed in 1890 (Fig. 6.19).

# Chapter 7

## Garden 6, The Garden in the Twentieth Century and the Post-War decline

*'Few residences are of higher historical interest and more stately in an old-world fashion than Alnwick Castle, the seat of the ducal house of Percy,'*
(*The Gardeners' Chronicle* 1902)

No archaeological remains or elements of standing buildings can be tied down to the period of Henry the seventh duke (1899–1918) or Alan Ian the eighth duke (1918–1930) and with the exception of the demolition of the glasshouse element of the northern conservatory, no documentary or cartographic evidence has been discovered to suggest that any significant changes occurred during this time.

The decline of the gardens may have commenced during the First World War, although the Paylist of Workmen in the castle archives August 1907–December 1916 (Acc 446/7) and December 1916– December 1925 (Acc 446/8) lists seven convalescing soldiers working in the garden for a week in June 1916 and more soldiers are listed March to June 1917 (see section 10.2 below). However, a plan of the gardens produced in 1932 provides some interesting details which indicate that on the eve of the Second World War the garden was fully functioning and used both for pleasure and production (Fig. 7.4).

The 1932 plan shows the gardens surrounded by woodland, with pathways running through. The continuing use of elements of the garden for pleasure is demonstrated by a tennis court, within the eastern half of the Upper Garden, as well as the parterre gardens, lily pond, flower beds and borders to the south. The castle archives contain architect's drawings for the construction of the court and shelter. Large parts of the garden, including areas surrounding the decorative parterres, are given over to lawns. Presumably these would be carefully maintained, mowed and rolled, in contrast to other areas of grass, labelled on 1932 plan as 'cut with scythe'. The use of a scythe to cut the grass on the banks surrounding the parterres of the central garden is unsurprising as these areas would be difficult to tend with a traditional mechanical lawnmower. In other areas, for example to the north of Hothouses 2 and 4 and around the tennis courts, the use of a scythe is more surprising; these areas may have been planted with bulbs or wildflowers which demanded a different cutting regime.

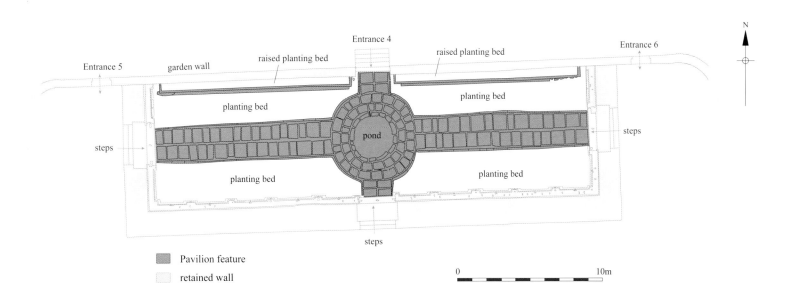

**Fig. 7.1** The pavilion, the formal garden created after demolition of the northern conservatory in the 1920s or early 1930s (scale 1:250)

**Fig. 7.2** Paths within the pavilion, looking west (RK 1998)

**Fig. 7.3** The central pond inside the pavilion, looking south (RK 1998)

Clearly much of the land was given over to fruit and vegetable production; plots of kitchen garden are indicated within the walled garden as well as more extensively in the kitchen garden to the west. With the exception of the northern conservatory (Hothouse 6), which had by this point been demolished and converted to a decorative raised garden, all of the glasshouse elements of the hothouses, as well as the forcing frames, appear to have remained in use at this time. Like many gardens, Alnwick was turned over to intense vegetable growing during the Second World War, as part of the 'Dig for Victory' campaign. From January 1949, just five people are listed in the Paylist of Workmen as being employed in the garden and by 1955 workers are occasionally listed by hours of work carried out (Acc 446/10).

## 7.1 Twentieth-Century Structural and Archaeological Remains

### The 'Old Pavilion'

The glasshouse element of the northern conservatory was demolished sometime between 1923, when it can be seen on an Ordnance Survey Map (Fig. 8.23) and 1932 when the plan of the gardens shows that it was no longer extant (Fig. 7.4). Following the demolition of the glasshouse, elements of the stonework on which the frame was built were incorporated

into a formal garden, known at the time of excavation as the pavilion. The pavilion comprised sandstone-paved paths 2.50m wide which ran along the length and width of the former building, on its north–south and east–west axes (Fig. 7.1; Fig. 7.2). The paths met at a central small circular pond, 2.70m in diameter and 0.75m deep (Fig. 7.3). The pond was surrounded by paving, forming a circular path 1.70m wide. In the four corners of the area formed by this paving were long rectangular planting beds, *c.* 2.50m by 14m maximum. Adjacent to the northern wall a raised, brick-lined planter, 0.50m wide, survived to a height of 0.60m.

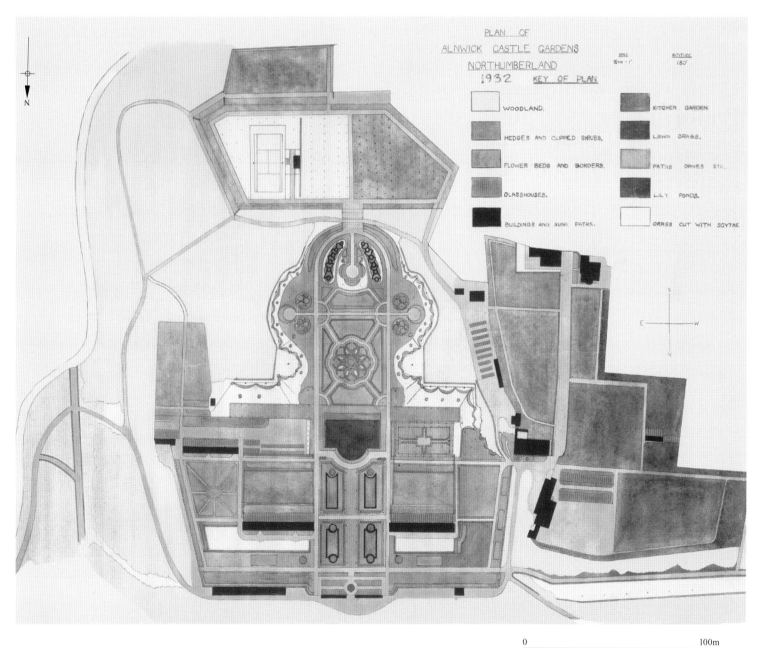

Fig. 7.4 Plan of Alnwick Castle Gardens Northumberland, 1932 (TAG Z/1/15) (scale 1:2000)

(NB North is to the bottom of the image)

## Lower garden

Numerous small linear cut features, interpreted as spade marks deriving from cultivation of the overlying topsoil, truncated the upper surface of the parterre garden in Area A, revealed immediately beneath machined-off topsoil. The garden was turned over to intense vegetable growing during the Second World War and this archaeological evidence for digging over of the parterres in Area A may well date from this period of use of the garden. Subsequent use of the walled garden included a tree nursery, an echo of the earliest years of the garden, a stone yard, a car park and a rubbish dump.

   The glasshouse element of Hothouse 7 was demolished in 1935. The remaining glasshouses were dismantled in the 1950s. To the north of the foundations of the southern side of the Hothouse 4 glasshouse, a substantial 3.80m wide cut was identified in plan extending 12m east–west, continuing to the west beyond the edge of excavation. Where excavated in a 1m-wide sondage this was 0.80m deep; its function is uncertain (see Fig. 4.5).

## Middle garden

Across the central part of the middle garden, in the area previously occupied by Parterres 5 and 6, various small rectangular pits were characterised by loose fills of recent date. Sealing the area was moderately compact mid-brown silty sand topsoil, up to 0.48m thick. In the south-eastern corner of what was Parterre 5, a large irregular feature measuring over 4m across and 0.40m deep, contained a distinctive deposit comprising silty sand and charcoal, frequent burnt tree roots and fragments of plastic bag. The feature was emptied by machine prior to excavation and appeared to represent a burnt-out tree. Information made available to the excavator identified the tree as a cypress. Similar features were identified to the north of the east–west aligned path, in the south-west and in the north-west corner of the excavation area, representing the location of cypress trees at each junction of the paths around the decorative borders.

   Cutting into the garden soil described above was a series of features, variously recorded in plan and section comprising parallel, linear, east-west aligned features, *c.* 20m to 22m in length, varying in width between 0.54m and 0.69m and extending up to 0.31m deep. These features have been interpreted as garden bedding trenches; some intercutting was observed, possibly representing the reinstatement of similar features over numerous years.

# Chapter 8

## Chronological Development of the Alnwick Walled Garden

*'A good Kitchen-garden is almost as necessary to a country seat, as a kitchen to the house; for without one, there is no way of being supplied with a great part of necessary food; the markets in the country being but poorly furnished with esculent herbs… therefore whoever decides to reside in the country, should be careful to make choice of a proper spot of ground for this purpose'*
(Miller 1768)

The preceding chapters detail the built heritage and archaeological evidence to produce a considered chronology of developments within the walled garden, in relation to the evidence gained through this fieldwork. Whilst referencing published and unpublished (archival) material where relevant, detailed background cartographic and documentary information has deliberately been left to a minimum, particularly where it was felt this would interfere with presentation of an overall narrative.

The following chapter therefore, seeks to provide an overall chronology drawing the findings of the fieldwork into a broader account, particularly relating to the background and interests of the various Dukes of Northumberland and their impact not only on the Alnwick Walled Garden, but also on the surrounding landscape and estates. This also allows for a consideration of the reliability and relevance of reference material, both cartographic and documentary. It presents in full the maps and plans upon which details, particularly of conjectural elements, within Chapters 2 to 7 are based. The text follows the chronological framework established above, with reference to the six phases of garden identified during the fieldwork.

## 8.1 The Construction of a Walled Kitchen Garden (1766–1786)

In 1740, before his marriage to Elizabeth Seymour, daughter of the Earl of Northumberland, Sir Hugh Smithson had set about improving the parklands of his estate at Stanwick, North Yorkshire. Elizabeth had inherited Syon House in Middlesex, which had been in the Percy family since the end of the sixteenth century, and this became a residence of Smithson and Lady Elizabeth. By the mid-eighteenth century, Syon already had a 200–year-old reputation as a garden of distinction, being the principal source for William Turner's *Herbal*, the first English botanical study (Shrimpton 1997, 2). Smithson enhanced the Syon gardens and his *'fine taste and liberality are owing the many and*

*great improvements which had made the gardens at Syon so universally admired'* (Shrimpton 1997, 2).

After becoming the Earl of Northumberland in 1750, Sir Hugh embarked on a major program of reorganisation of Alnwick Castle and grounds employing the celebrated Robert Adam as architect for the renovation of the castle, which was restored, inside and out, in a Gothic style, and Lancelot 'Capability' Brown to transform the gardens and parkland around the castle, bringing them up to the forefront of contemporary design. By this time Sir Hugh's reputation as a gardener was already established through his work at Stanwick and Syon and Philip Miller dedicated his *'Gardener's Dictionary'* (1752 edition) to the Earl *'whose knowledge and skill in every part of this subject render you the most competent judge of its merit'*. The botanist John Hill also dedicated *Exotic Botany* to Sir Hugh and many of the plants described in this volume were raised in the stoves and hothouses at Syon (Shrimpton 1997, 2). The restoration of the castle and parklands by the first duke boosted the local economy and he also modernised local agriculture as well as industries such as coal mining and glass making on the Tyne (Shrimpton 2006, 20).

Smithson's head gardener Thomas Call was sent from Stanwick to Alnwick in 1751. When Smithson inherited the Percy Estates at Alnwick, he set about transforming their landscapes and parklands. In 1751 Call produced a plan for the parklands involving walling and planting at Brizlee Hill and the development of the pleasure grounds at Hulne Park, to the north-west of the castle (see Fig. 10.30). In 1756 Thomas was joined by his relation James Call at Alnwick, by which time he is recorded as holding the post of gardener.

The duke employed Lancelot 'Capability' Brown, the most famous gardener and landscape designer of his age, at both Syon and Alnwick. It had long been thought that the duke consulted Brown on plans for the estates on or around 1760 (Stroud 1975, 102). However, evidence has recently been uncovered from the duke's account books for payments made to Brown for work at Syon from as early as 1754 (Christopher Hunwick, pers. comm.).

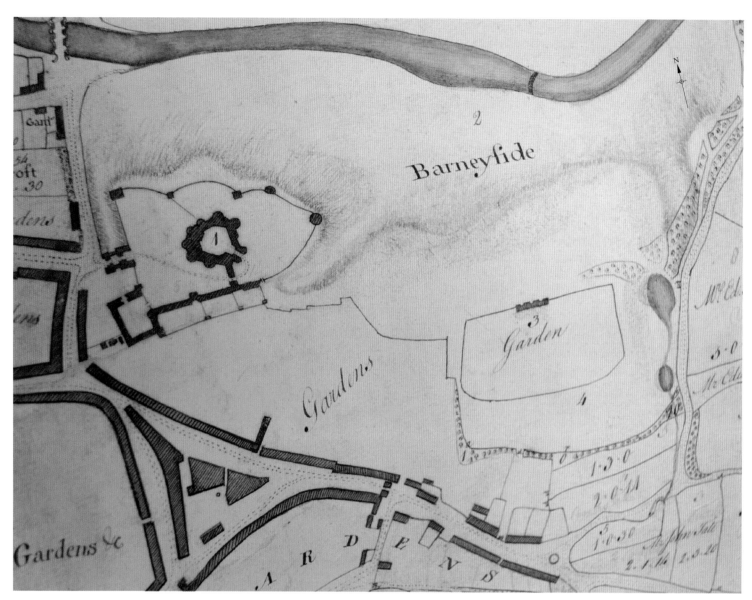

**Fig. 8.1** Extract from a plan of Alnwick, 1772 showing the walled garden constructed by the first duke (Wilkin 1772) (not to scale; NB direction of north is approximate)

The Syon Household Vouchers held in the Alnwick castle archives show that much work was carried out in the gardens and park of Syon between 1754 to 1757, with 1756 a particularly active year for Brown. The estate account books suggest that Brown was at Alnwick in 1759, 1769–1770, 1776 and 1781 (Owen 2014). There is also a record of Brown dining in the castle in September 1770 at the time of his visits to Kirkharle and Rothley (*ibid.*).

Lancelot Brown was born in Kirkharle in Northumberland, *c.* 50km south-west of Alnwick (see Fig. 1.1) and was related to the duke's bailiff of Newburn manor, who was himself related to the duke's commissioner (property manager) at Alnwick; his involvement in the duke's parklands scheme at Alnwick is hardly surprising given such associations (Shrimpton 2006, 42). Three of Brown's foremen, Cornelius Griffin, Thomas Robson and Thomas Biesley, are known to have worked at Alnwick from the late 1760s,

often with large teams of gardeners and labourers. The constable of Alnwick Castle's accounts for 1769 and subsequent years record monthly payments to Cornelius Griffin and his gang of workmen as well as payments to Thomas Call and his workmen indicating that there were two separate planting teams at Alnwick. The work was presumably coordinated by Brown. In 1773 Biesley was leading a team of 78 men at Alnwick while Thomas Call, was working in Hulne Park with 60 men (Owen 2014). This large workforce indicates the scale of the work taking place to transform the landscape around Alnwick Castle (see section 10.3 below).

The Alnwick Walled Garden was sited *c.* 300m to the south-east of the castle on the terrace of land which overlooks the River Aln. The garden does not appear on Thompson's 1760 plan of Alnwick and the earliest known plan depicting the garden is that of Thomas Wilkin (1772) which shows a sub-rectangular enclosure labelled 'Garden' (Fig. 8.1) with a hothouse against the northern wall. No documentary evidence has been discovered to prove a connection with Capability Brown and this walled garden, but the garden was evidently built during the period when Brown is known to have been working at Syon and Alnwick and given Brown's involvement from the mid-1750s with the design of the parklands across the North Demesne on the opposite side of the Aln, it seems possible that he had a hand in the design of the walled garden and locating it in this specific area within the landscape.

The Alnwick Walled Garden was sited to be concealed from the castle, and this was also an ideal position in horticultural terms. Miller's *Gardeners Dictionary*, first written in 1831, provides a wealth of advice on the siting and location of the kitchen garden. A 1768 revision of the work (from which quotations in the volume have been obtained) contains the following dedication, which illustrates the close working relationship between Miller and the duke:

*'Your Grace's kind Acceptance of this Work, has emboldened me to lay this at Your Grace's Feet as a public Acknowledgment of the many useful Observations and Instructions. which Your Grace has at several Times communicated to me for its Improvement. If I have been so happy as to employ them in such manner, as to merit Your Grace's Approbation, I shall have less Reason to doubt that of the Public; since the most skilful Persons in this useful Branch of Science, pay the highest Regard to Your Grace's Judgment.*

*'The many Improvements which Your Grace is annually making so happily upon Your various Estates, sufficiently demonstrate Your Grace's superior Judgment; but more particularly in a Country almost destitute of Timber : Where, if Your Grace continues planting, so ardently as for several Years past, the whole Face of the Country will be much altered for the better, and Your Grace's Estate thereby greatly improved.*

*'That Your Grace may long live to continue these Improvements and to be an Example to others, is the sincere Wish of Your Grace's Most obedient humble Servant, Philip Miller.*
*'Chelsea, March 12, 1768' (*Miller 1768, dedication*).*

The northward sloping topography of the hillside on which the garden was built was, according to Miller in his *Gardeners Dictionary*, advantageous; he advises against levelling land if one part of the garden is higher than another as '*by this situation you will have an advantage which could not be obtained on a perfect level, which is, the having one part dry ground for early crops, and the low part for late crops, whereby the kitchen might be better supplied throughout the season with the various sorts of herbs, roots, &c And in very dry seasons, when in the upper part of the garden the crop will greatly suffer with drought, then the lower part will succeed...*' (Miller 1768, Kitchen Garden).

The Alnwick Walled Garden measured a maximum of 210m east–west by *c.* 70m north–south covering an area of *c.* 1.5 hectares (*c.* 3.7 acres), conforming to the size of 3–4 acres recommended

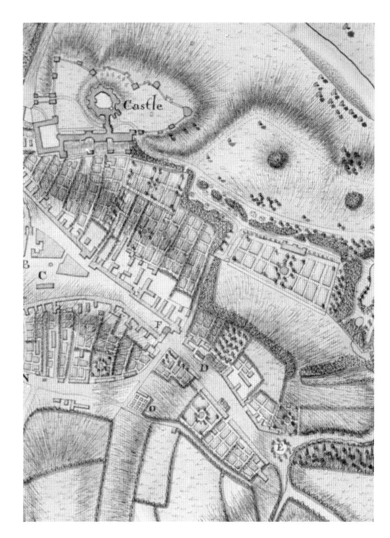

**Fig. 8.2** Extract from C.J. Sauthier's map Alnwick Town and Castle, 1788, showing the garden laid out by the first duke (SY B/II/2b (3) (not to scale)

for a large estate by Miller (1752). The garden was surrounded by a perimeter wall large sections of which are extant (see section 9.2 below), although the south wall was demolished in the 1860s when the garden was extended. Sauthier's 1788 plan (Fig. 8.2) indicates a walk along the southern boundary possibly raised on a terrace to overlook the garden (Green 1998). The Alnwick Walled Garden was trapezoidal in plan, its shape partly determined by land boundaries, but also with the eastern and western walls constructed slightly south facing to benefit the cultivation of wall-trained fruits.

Sauthier's 1788 plan shows the walled garden divided into a series of regular rectangular plots or beds with a central pond; archaeological evidence indicates that this is a reasonably accurate representation of the layout of the first duke's garden. Elements of a central pond were recorded during the archaeological investigations along with a series of paths dividing the garden into rectangular beds which were evidently long-lived features surviving during subsequent periods of the garden. This is a typical plan for formal kitchen gardens of this period; it allowed the garden to be split into manageable sections to cultivate a variety of plants. The wide walks allowed the garden to be enjoyed by the owner and his visitors, as well as providing access to the beds for the gardeners and their barrows (Campbell 2005, 80). During this period borders would have been edged by herbaceous plants, espaliers and box edgings (*ibid.*)

Wilkin (1773) shows a hothouse against the northern wall with four backhouses extending beyond the line of the wall, although this plan may be rather schematic (Fig. 8.1). The building, labelled on later plans of the garden as a vinery, is perhaps more accurately shown on Sauthier's 1788 plan with three backhouses (Fig. 8.2). Elements of the eastern and western backhouses which would have housed the furnaces to heat the glass element to the south were recorded during the building survey along with the spine wall of the structure which formed the south-facing wall of the glasshouse. The hothouse, built for cultivation and display, reflects the first duke's interest in exotic plants (Green 1988). Hothouses specifically for the cultivation of dessert grapes, known as 'graperies' or 'vineries', began to be constructed across the country from the 1770s. The vines were planted outside the glasshouse and trained through gaps in the low front walls (Campbell 2005, 177). In the winter when there was no leaf cover from the vines, vineries would be used for forcing plants and crops such as French beans, strawberries, spring bulbs and early summer flowers. In 1781 the horticulturalist John Abercrombie describes forcing peaches, nectarines, apricots, cherries, early figs, dwarf currants, gooseberries and raspberries in a vinery (*ibid.*).

A contemporary account of the garden by Peter Wadell, one of the duke's gardeners (Acc 163) provides information about the plants being grown within the walled garden; of particular interest is the fact that the garden was used to cultivate trees for the plantations around the castle, as referenced in Miller's dedication '*in a Country almost destitute of Timber : Where, if Your Grace continues planting, so ardently as for several Years past, the whole Face of the Country will be much altered for the better*'. Common vegetables were apparently not grown within the walled garden, instead the Alnwick gardeners were encouraged to grow vegetables in their own gardens.

'*…for here, none of the common esculent plants are cultivated, the Noble Owner wishing to encourage the Growth of such Vegetables in the Grounds of the Gardiners in the Town, not only as yielding a profit to them but being thus the means of promoting the Culture of more excellent kinds than would otherwise have attempted, of which the Town of Alnwick and its Neighbourhood very sensibly feel the Advantage*' (Acc 163).

The great achievement of the first duke in creating the Alnwick Walled Garden is highlighted by accounts written in July 1786 of a visit to the castle and gardens by John Bush (born Busch), gardener to the Czarina Catherine at her palace of Tsorskoze Selo (Shrimpton 1997, 8). The duke's properties and their landscapes featured prominently on the Green Frog Dinner Service of the Russian Empress, made by Wedgwood in 1773 for Catherine the Great. Bush served the Czarina alongside James Meader who had been the duke's head gardener at Syon prior to his move to Russia and it seems likely that Bush came to Alnwick on Meader's recommendation to view the garden and landscape created by the first duke  (Shrimpton 1997, 9). The castle constable John Thirlwall reported to the second duke that Bush considered '*Your Grace's gardener had everything in order here – and observed that he had not seen so fine a show of wall fruit as he found here at any places in his travels when he left London*' (Shrimpton 1997, 9). Following Bush's visit to Alnwick, one of the members of the Call family, gardeners to the duke, joined the group of British gardeners serving the imperial family in Russia. The international reputation of the garden at Alnwick was thus established within just a few decades of its creation.

## 8.2 A Garden for the Production of Fruit (1786–1817)

'*Perhaps at no period since the days of Evelyn and Miller has horticulture assumed so respectable an attitude among rural and economical pursuits as at the present time. The horticultural societies of London and Edinburgh, composed of men of rank and influence, scientific amateurs, and practical gardeners, give a degree of eclat and salutary consequence to the study; and from this circumstance, as well as the known skill and activity of many of their members, the public may expect to reap considerable advantage*' (Loudon 1817, 1).

Like his predecessor, Hugh the second Duke of Northumberland (1786–1817) also made considerable changes to the wider setting of the castle and its gardens, following a distinguished career in the army from the age of 16, having served in the Seven Years War (1756–1763), the American War of Independence (1775–1783) and the Napoleonic Wars. In 1800 the duke purchased a large part of the Alnwick Abbey estate along the north bank of the Aln between Hulne Park and North Demesne, including the abbey itself, along with around 200 acres of land to the east of the existing castle land (Shrimpton 2006, 54). An extensive programme of improvements to the parklands was implemented, which included employing local masons to rebuild the wall around the perimeter of Hulne Park (Shrimpton 2006, 56). Gates, lodges and cottages were also built and drives through the pleasure grounds extended.

The second duke played a direct role in the management of the gardens and continually provided the gardeners with seeds to propagate, including melons from noble acquaintances in Portugal (Shrimpton 1997, 11). He ordered an increase in the number of cherry trees to be grown on the east wall and suggested that his favourite apple, the Ribstone Pippin, should be introduced to

Alnwick from his Stanwick estate (Shrimpton 1997, 11). Hugh's involvement in the garden was practical as well as theoretical; he designed an easy-tipping wheelbarrow for use at Alnwick. The economical running of the garden was of major importance to the duke and he required that all produce should be accounted for, that the soft fruits should be bottled, that the garden should be self-sufficient in vegetables such as carrots for the household, and that the ripening of fruit should be timed to be at its best when the family was in residence at Alnwick (Shrimpton 1997, 11).

Considerable investment took place within the walled garden and in keeping with contemporary trends a major impetus for this was the desire to cultivate exotic fruit. Pineapples exemplify this obsession (see Chapter 10, below). The main function of the garden at this time was to produce fruit principally for consumption by the family when at Alnwick, but also for Northumberland House, the duke's residence in London (Shrimpton 1997, 10). To achieve optimum results the duke invested in several new garden structures to cultivate produce, bringing the latest innovations in garden technology to Alnwick, though not always with successful results.

To cultivate the melon seeds the duke had acquired from Portugal, frames were constructed adjacent to the south wall of the garden; these can be seen on Bell's 1826 map and are labelled as such on Barnfather's 1829 plan (Fig. 8.3; Fig. 8.6). The second duke invested in new hothouses designed by John Hay of Edinburgh, including a fruiting pine stove for pineapples, a mushroom house and two vineries (Shrimpton 2006, 58). Hay was a renowned horticulturist and garden designer and was an expert in the cultivation of the pineapple. Shrimpton records that a peach house of four compartments and a garden seed room were also constructed (Shrimpton 2006, 58), although it is difficult to reconcile this description with either the excavated or cartographic evidence, both of which sources appear to suggest that the peach house had three compartments. The pine stove and two new hothouses were built from September 1808 and 1811 by local masons Nesbitt and Shepherd at a cost of more than £1700 (Shrimpton 1997, 10). The furnaces for these buildings would have required large quantities of coal. A cheap supply was obtained from the duke's colliery at Shilbottle, with coal transported by wagonway from the pithead to staithes (landing stages) at the south end of Alnwick town, which were within close carting distance of the castle; hundreds of tons of Shilbottle coal were consumed each year by the castle and gardens (Shrimpton 1997, 10).

No contemporary maps of this garden have been identified, but a map produced by Thomas Bell in 1826 a few years after the duke's death still largely reflects the arrangement of the second duke's garden and shows that the layout of paths and borders within the walled garden which enclosed the groups of rectangular beds was apparently not significantly modified (Fig. 8.3). The

archaeological excavation confirmed this cartographic evidence with paths evidently maintained in the same position. Bell's 1826 map depicts three structures along an east–west axis within the central part of the walled garden; elements of only the western structure survived. This western building is shown as a long east–west aligned glasshouse with two small backhouses at each end and a central one attached to the north side of the glasshouse. Parts of the three backhouses and of the spine wall were the only surviving elements of this structure which is labelled as a 'Peach House' on the 1829 plan of the garden (see Fig. 4.3; Fig. 8.6).

Loudon (1825, 1080) reported that the kitchen garden at Alnwick was '*lately much improved by a range of hot-houses erected from the designs of J. Hay, Edinburgh.*' Hay was an architect and pineapple expert who invented an improved form of steam heating in 1807 (Kohlmaier *et al.* 1991, 53). A contemporary account refers to the construction of a short-lived pine stove at Alnwick:

*'In 1807, a pine-stove was designed and executed for the Duke of Northumberland, at Alnwick Castle, by Mr. Hay, in which a chamber*

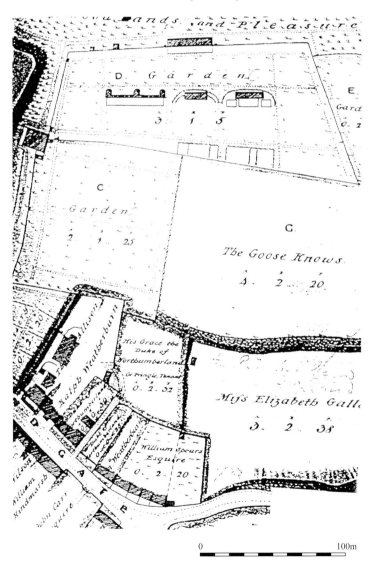

**Fig. 8.3** Extract from an 1826 map of Alnwick, showing Garden 2 as laid out by the second duke (Bell 1826) (scale 1:2500)

*below the bark-bed was filled by stones heated by steam; but as the pipes and supply of steam were too small for the mass of stones, the use of this mode of heating was in this instance not long continued.' (Loudon 1832, 330).*

This may refer to the eastern building in a line of three labelled 'Pines' on Barnfather's map (Fig. 8.6), although, had this been built in 1807, it would have been in use for 25 years by the time this account was written, and thus unlikely to have been described as 'not long continued'. This is therefore considered more likely to be the early, heated forcing frame or pine pit which survived in the centre of Area A (see section 9.2 below) although there was no surviving evidence for the use of steam pipes with this structure. It may be that the western 'flue' extending south from the furnace associated with this structure had carried steam pipes and was replaced by the eastern, brick-lined flue, in a modification to the structure. Whatever the sequence of events, this structure appears to have been short-lived.

The 1826 map and Barnfather's 1829 map (Fig. 8.6) shows the eastern building in the line of three, labelled 'Pines', as three separate glasshouses, a larger central one and smaller ones at each end, with single backhouse which does not span the full length of the glasshouse. No trace of this structure was identified within the excavated area.

A central building is shown on the 1826 map as a rectangular structure, smaller than the flanking buildings. Curved elements of uncertain function are shown on the map encompassing the central and eastern buildings to the north. This may have been one of the buildings designed by Hay but again no traces of this short-lived structure were identified within the excavated area.

The 1826 map also shows that the three Hothouse 1 backhouses at the north wall of the garden had been converted into one long rectangular backhouse, labelled as a '*Vinery*' on the 1829 plan. Evidence for the conversion was recorded within the cellar surviving at the time of the investigations.

The garden wall which formed the north-east boundary wall of the garden continued to function as a heated wall and further investment was made by the introduction of another furnace (Fig. 8.3), suggesting that the original furnace did not provide sufficient heat for the wall. This smaller structure was later converted into a buttress which is extant.

The Alnwick Walled Gardens were extended by the second duke; a new walled garden was added to the south-west, shown on Bell's map as a rectangular garden enclosed on all sides by walls, the northern wall being the western end of the south wall of the original garden (Fig. 8.3). It is labelled as a '*Kitchen Garden*' on Barnfather's 1829 plan and was presumably originally designed as such (Fig. 8.6). A large external building was built at the north-west corner of the new kitchen garden for the new head gardener, George Robson, who was previously in charge at Seaton Delaval in

Northumberland (Green 1988). The house is extant and has been renovated for use as offices for the new Alnwick garden. The new kitchen garden measured a maximum of *c.* 90m by 65m. Bell's map shows paths adjacent to the long axes on the east and west sides of the garden and three paths crossing its width creating two large rectangular beds and two narrow beds at each end of the kitchen garden. Another new walled garden was also built to the east of the original garden defined to the west by the east wall of the original garden with new walls on all other sides with a curving north-east corner (Fig. 8.3). This has a path running through its length parallel and adjacent to the western boundary. This is also labelled as a '*Kitchen Garden*' on Barnfather's 1829 plan.

Construction of these new gardens would have been a major investment and a document dated 1811 in the castle archives may refer to the building of some of the walls for these new gardens:

*'Estimate and proposal for building a wall on the west and south sides of the new kitchen garden. The wall will be three hundred and 55 yards long* [*c.* 324.60m] *and 3 yards* [*c.* 2.74m] *high, clear of the foundations, to be built of common walling on one side and blocked course on the other. The thickness to be two feet* [*c.* 0.61m] *at the bottom and one foot eight inches* [*c.* 0.51m] *at the top. The wall to be ridge coped, hewn.*

*'Total estimate: 425/17/–*

*Mr Stevenson, his Grace's architect, having commissioned to me the particulars of the above estimate, I hereby agree to perform the work for £425:17:0.'* (DP/D2/I/20).

The second duke's investment in the walled gardens and hothouses, his introduction of the latest innovations in garden technology to Alnwick and his role in the day-to-day management of the garden was obviously successful. During his time, it became common practice to pack grapes and other fruits and dispatch them by mail coach from Alnwick to Northumberland House (Shrimpton 1997, 11). By 1815 the fruit from Alnwick was prized so highly by the family that the young Earl Percy considered it to be finer than that produced at Syon, prompting the duke to ask his commissioner to inform the gardener that the fruit he sent to London did the gardener great credit. Thus, by the time of the second duke's death in 1817, the Alnwick Walled Garden was no longer eclipsed by Syon in terms of its produce.

## 8.3 A Garden for Entertainment, Flowers and Fruit (1817–1847)

*'I have this day sent off for Ireland, three boxes containing eleven Pines, and twenty eight bunches of Grapes, also about six dozen green Apricots for preserving in brandy, the Apricots were sent by order of his Excellency.'* Thomas Smith, Head Gardener, 15th August 1829 (DP/D3/I/197).

The second duke was succeeded by his son Hugh in 1817 who held the duchy until 1847. Like his grandfather, the third Duke of Northumberland was considered by his contemporaries to be a distinguished gardener and patron of gardeners; Loudon dedicated his *Arboretum et Fruticetum Brittannicum* to Hugh and cited the encouragement the duke had 'always given to his gardening pursuits' (Loudon 1838). Loudon highlighted the contribution the duke made in introducing new botanical species to Syon from around the world, which were grown in a magnificent conservatory designed by Charles Fowler. Loudon's admiration of the duke's achievements at Syon perhaps overshadows the developments which the duke brought to the Alnwick Walled Garden (Shrimpton 1997, 12). The duchess Charlotte Florentia also played an active role in the development of the walled garden, the castle estate and the wider community.

The expenditure on the parklands and gardens during the time of the third duchy must have been considerable. The third duke continued the purchase of old Alnwick Abbey land including farms at Heckley within the wider landscape surrounding the castle, however the boundaries of Hulne Park were drastically reduced (Shrimpton 2006, 58). At their greatest extent, West and Hulne Park had covered 4,170 acres (*c.* 1,690 hectares) and were enclosed by a perimeter wall 13 miles (*c.* 21km) long (*ibid.* 59). Following the construction of a bridge which carried a public highway over the Aln by the duke in 1823, the highway, which ran through Hulne Park, was turnpiked in 1826. To preserve the privacy of his parkland, the duke moved the park boundary to run along the turnpike road, reducing the area by 1,500 acres (*c.* 610 hectares ; see Fig. 10.31). The duke's new Clerk of Works began a programme of maintenance of the park walls from 1820, and between then and 1825 this had a monthly budget of between £200 and £270 for labour and materials (*ibid.*). In 1820 'Her Grace's Dairy' was built at Canongate on the western side of the town; cows were grazed on the Castle Close and Dairy Ground using an underpass beneath the Lion Bridge for access. Shortly after the construction of the dairy the duke and duchess also developed two home farms in Hulne

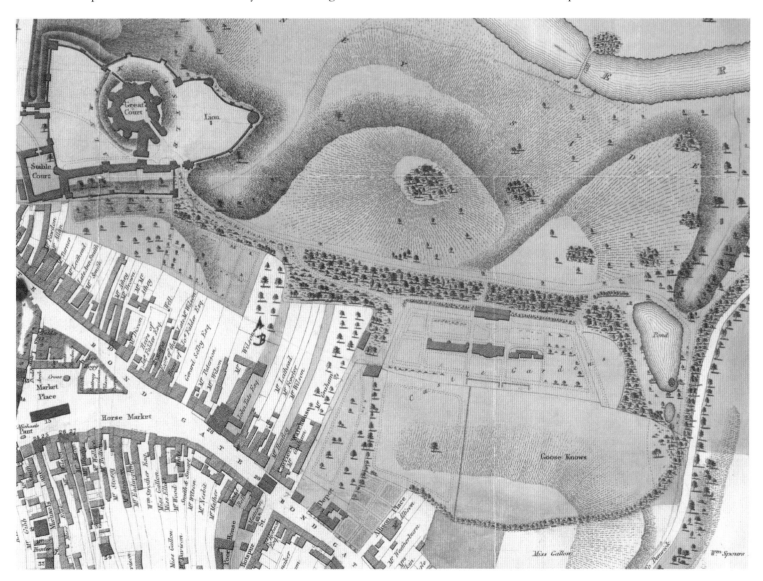

**Fig. 8.4** Extract from an 1827 map of Alnwick (Wood 1827) (scale 1:5000)

0                                        200m

**Fig. 8.5** The new conservatory, parterre and pond with its iron dome awning, reconstruction by Chris Mitchell (c.mitchell02@btinternet.com)

Park which together occupied 500 acres (*c.* 200 hectares) of the park (*ibid.*). Walled compounds which are extant were constructed to the north of the central road through Hulne Park; the walls were set in ditches to create the effect of a ha-ha so that the compounds were visible from the road. The compounds may have been constructed for deer, but it seems that they were to become occupied by Indian water buffalo brought to Alnwick by the duchess from her brother the Earl of Powis who kept a herd at Powis Castle.

As well as the considerable expenditure in the surrounding parkland, the third duke invested heavily in the original walled garden. The role of this changed and as well as focusing on providing fruits from its hothouses and walls, it also became a garden for the entertainment of the family (Shrimpton 1997, 16). A new conservatory, parterre and lily pond formed a central focus point for this new role and areas were given over to the cultivation of flowers (Fig. 8.4). In contrast to the duke's actions to maintain the privacy of the surrounding parklands, the walled garden began to be occasionally opened to visitors (see 10.2 below), a radical departure from its origins as a kitchen garden, albeit of such a large and important household.

The duke also had a great interest in collecting plants and exotic varieties were brought to Alnwick from around the world. In

1818, 32 different types of seeds were imported from 'the Cape' in Southern Africa including eight forest trees, three myrtles, nineteen heaths, ten varieties of proteas (a flowering plant known as sugarbushes) and asparagus (Shrimpton 1997, 14). In 1832 Richard Forrest, the head gardener at Syon, sent a large number of plants and seeds from North America to Alnwick and in the same year a supply of seeds came from Van Diemen's Land (Tasmania) (Shrimpton 1997, 14). In the Syon Conservatory Botany collection 1820–1840 (DP/D3/I/30) there are a series of letters dated from 1837 and 1838 between the duke and Dr Wallick, Superintendent of the East India Company's Botanic Gardens in Calcutta (1817–1846). The letters contain list of plants shipped over for the duke's collections, including many species of orchid, and requests from Dr Wallick for plants from the duke (see section 10.1 below).

The production of fruit continued as a significant function of the garden and as with the previous duke, the gardener had to regulate the hothouses so that fruits would be produced when the third duke's family were in residence in July (Shrimpton 1997, 14). Pineapples, peaches, nectarines, apricots and grapes were produced for the family at Alnwick when in residence but were also sent to the duke's properties in London: Northumberland House and Syon. Fruit surplus to requirement by the family was sent as

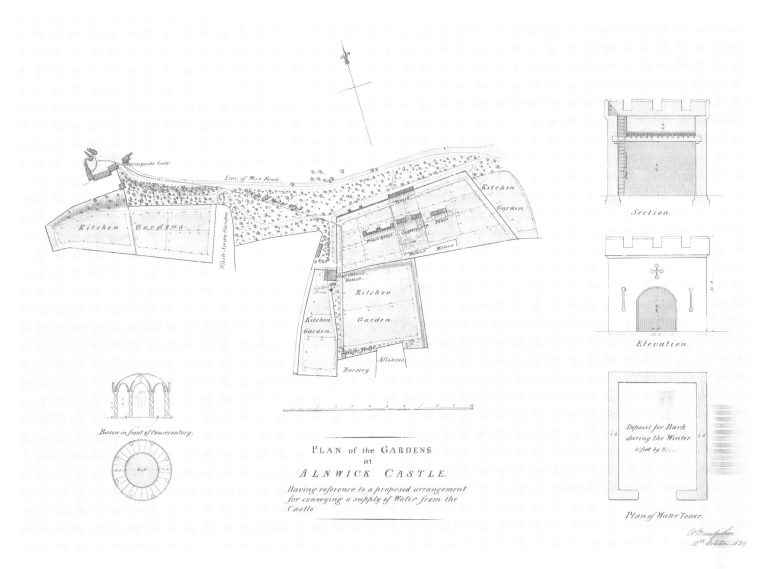

**Fig. 8.6** Plan of the Gardens at Alnwick Castle, produced to illustrate the piped water supply from a water tower (Barnfather 1829)

gifts to the duchess's relatives and to neighbouring gentry and clergy or civic dignitaries, such as the Mayor of Newcastle; there is an account of melons being sent to the mayor by Union coach in 1820 (Shrimpton 1997, 15). The garden also provided cuttings to the neighbouring gentry and apple trees and gooseberry and blackcurrant cuttings were given to the duke's cottage and farm tenants (*ibid.*). Produce was also sent farther afield. In January 1825 the gardener was instructed to select six pineapples to be sent to Paris to grace the duke's table when he attended the French court as ambassador extraordinary at the coronation of Charles X (Shrimpton 1997, 15). A bundle of correspondence in the castle archives from 1829, the year the Duke of Northumberland served as Lord Lieutenant of Ireland, includes letters to commissioners from various correspondents including Thomas Smith, Head Gardener (DP/D3/I/197). Several letters from Smith list pineapples and other fruit sent to Dublin Castle, the seat of English rule in Ireland at the time (see section 10.1 below). The hothouses evidently produced large quantities of fruits as the duke's

confectioners were sent to Alnwick to preserve fruits and make jams (Shrimpton 1997, 14).

To cultivate these large quantities of fruit and display the exotic species brought to Alnwick, the duke invested a great deal of money in constructing new hothouses in the original walled garden as well as modifying earlier buildings and constructing a grand new conservatory. Revolutionary new glasshouse technology was brought to Alnwick and used in the conservatory and hothouses. In 1816 John Claudius Loudon had devised a wrought-iron sash bar that could be curved while maintaining strength and began experimenting with using these bars to build curvilinear glasshouses (Woods and Warren 1988, 112; see Chapter 9, below). Loudon formed an alliance with the manufacturers W. and D. Bailey of Holborn, later D. and E. Bailey, and from 1818 until 1843 the firm had considerable success supplying curvilinear glasshouses across the country (Hix 1996, 36–40).

In the 1820s the central part of the original garden was still divided into three blocks with hothouses in each, but the central

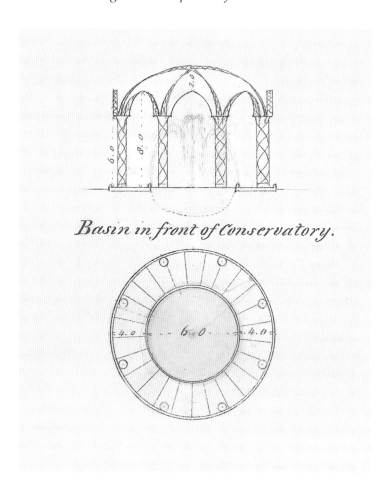

*Basin in front of Conservatory.*

**Fig. 8.7** Detail of pond with iron pergola (Barnfather 1829)

block was completely redesigned (Fig. 8.6). Barnfather's 1829 plan shows an elaborate decorative parterre with a lily pond in front of a new central conservatory which formed the focal point of the new garden for the enjoyment of the family (Fig. 8.5; Fig. 8.6). A detail of this structure on the plan shows a 6ft (*c.* 1.8m) diameter pond under an iron dome awning 14ft (*c.* 4.30m) in diameter and 10ft (c.3m) high supported on eight latticework columns (Fig. 8.7). This structure covered a walkway around the lily pond. Pencil marks on the drawing indicate that the pond may have had a central fountain (Fig. 8.7). Barnfather's useful map, detailed in the extreme and apparently very accurate, was in fact designed to illustrate the route of piped water supply into the gardens from an external water tower.

The construction of the grand central conservatory echoed innovations taking place at Syon. There, a new conservatory, designed by Charles Fowler had been constructed for the Duke of Northumberland (Woods and Warren 1988, 120). One of the finest examples of the period, with a central giant-domed palm house and two curved wings, this housed a range of exotics collected and imported from all over the world. The depiction by Bell (1826; Fig. 8.3) of a conservatory with two long curved wings extending to east and west in this location is somewhat

perplexing. Shrimpton suggests this is a conservatory constructed by the second duke (Shrimpton 1997, 16), although the rationale behind this is not clear. An alternative explanation for this depiction may be that as preparation for the construction of a grand conservatory, smaller than but based on the example at Syon, was underway, Bell depicted what he thought the new structure would look like: a conservatory with projecting curved wings, resembling that at Syon.

The grand central conservatory as constructed at Alnwick is shown on the 1827 and 1829 maps; the latter detailed plan shows it as 100ft (*c.* 30.50m) in length with sixteen ribs along the width of the building (Fig. 8.6). On the south side, the middle eight sections formed a bow front which overlooked the parterre and in the roof of the conservatory was a glazed dome on a square base. A narrow rectangular building shown adjoining the glasshouse element to the north presumably housed the heating apparatus for the structure. Most of the conservatory lay beyond the investigated area; it was demolished by 1851 (Kent 1988, 5) and only traces of the bow front (south) wall were identified in the excavation area, as a robber trench which had removed the structural remains.

After the construction of the central conservatory, the third duke modified the western hothouse and built an almost identical hothouse in the eastern plot; this must have occurred sometime after 1829 as these structures are not shown on Barnfather's plan. The three-celled western backhouse building in the line of three, Hothouse 2, was converted into one long building, although its original form was still echoed in the new plan, with projections to the north in the centre and at each end formed by the original furnace rooms. Evidence for this conversion was identified in the recorded remains of the backhouse and spine wall. A rebuild of the glass frontage also identified within the excavation area is considered a slightly later modification to the backhouse associated with the introduction of a curvilinear hothouse. This hothouse retained its original function as a peach house (Barnfather 1829), as indicated on designs for a new garden drawn for the fourth duke dated 1860 (see Fig. 8.14).

The eastern hothouse (Hothouse 4) was completely rebuilt by the third duke; no traces of an earlier structure were identified in the remains of the backhouse and spine wall and the map sequence shows that the small backhouse structure of the Pine House (Fig. 8.6) was replaced with a much larger one shortly after 1829. This was built to mirror Hothouse 2 with a central projection to the north and one at each end, reflecting the original three furnace rooms of the western structure, and is first shown on Bell's *c.* 1849 map (Fig. 8.9). This structure is labelled as a 'Vinery' on an 1860 plan (see Fig. 8.14).

An architect's drawing in the castle archives dated 1830 shows construction details of the vinery indicating the approximate

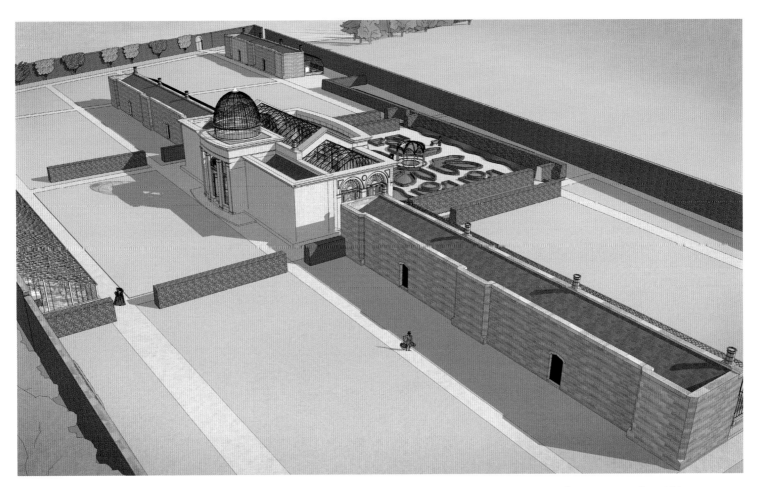

**Fig. 8.8** The third duke's garden at Alnwick, with its central conservatory, seen from the north-west, as it may have appeared in 1830, reconstruction by Chris Mitchell (c.mitchell02@btinternet.com)

date of construction (see Fig. 9.30; Fig. 9.31). A new hothouse (Hothouse 5) constructed in the south-east corner of the garden also reflected the plans of the eastern and western hothouses, although this was slightly smaller, with three projecting bays in the backhouse. The backhouse element of this survived as a standing structure at the time of the investigations and archaeological excavation revealed structural elements of the glass frontage to this hothouse. This is labelled for the first time as a 'Pine House' on an 1864 design for the garden (see Fig. 8.14). The layout of the newly remodelled gardens can be seen on maps of the late 1840s and 1850s (Fig. 8.9; Fig. 8.10).

The backhouses of all three of the third duke's hothouses were substantial buildings of fine stone ashlar construction and would have presented a unified appearance when viewed from the north. Produce was not just grown in the glasshouse elements of these hothouses; mushroom houses with underfloor heating ducts were constructed in the central parts of the eastern and western backhouses. A design for such purpose-built mushroom houses was published in 1816 and by the 1820s they were commonly built in kitchen gardens (Campbell 2005, 230, see section 9.5 below).

As well as the expenditure required for the backhouses and

their heating systems, the glasshouses would have required considerable investment with their construction utilising the latest, costly, technology. A bill dated July 15, 1836 in the castle archives from D. and E. Bailey, Manufacturers and Ironmongers, Holborn, London, for '*A Range of Curvilinear Peach Houses*' refers to the iron framework of a peach house with two partitions dividing the glasshouse into three elements (DP/D3/I/43). It is assumed that this bill refers to a rebuild of the glasshouse element of Hothouse 2. A cross-section of the garden which probably dates from around the same time also shows that the eastern hothouse had a curvilinear glass frontage and was used as a vinery (Fig. 8.13). The invention of Loudon's wrought-iron sash glazing bar in 1816 and his association with the Bailey construction company heralded a new era in curvilinear glasshouses. During the 1830s and 1840s curvilinear structures were increasingly common. A description of a visit to the garden published in 1874 suggests that by this time the eastern and south-eastern buildings (Hothouses 4 and 5) also had curvilinear glasshouse elements (J.T. 1874 *The Garden* 1874, 101).

The wrought iron frame for the glasshouse would have been constructed on stone foundations to a specification prepared by the ironmongers. The new glasshouse was evidently heated by hot water pipes as the bill lists:

> '*three sets of hot water apparatus to heat the above range of peach houses including three improved shape wrought iron boilers with strong double doors, frames furnaces and bearing bars, ? and cover plates, flue doors and dampers, cast iron straight and curved oval and round pipes, Reservoirs, Brackets and slings as well as pipe work and a reservoir*' (PB 236).

The historic map sequence suggests that both the backhouse and the glasshouse of the northern hothouse may have been modified or rebuilt by the third duke at different times. On Bell's 1826 plan (Fig. 8.3) the glasshouse is rectangular but is shown on Wood's 1827 plan (Fig. 8.4) and subsequent plans with the central section projecting. The backhouse has a central projection on the northern side on Bell's map of *c.* 1849 which can be seen on the more detailed Ordnance Survey plan of 1856 which also shows small stretches of the northern boundary wall had been demolished to create two new entrances into the garden to either side of the hothouse (Fig. 8.10).

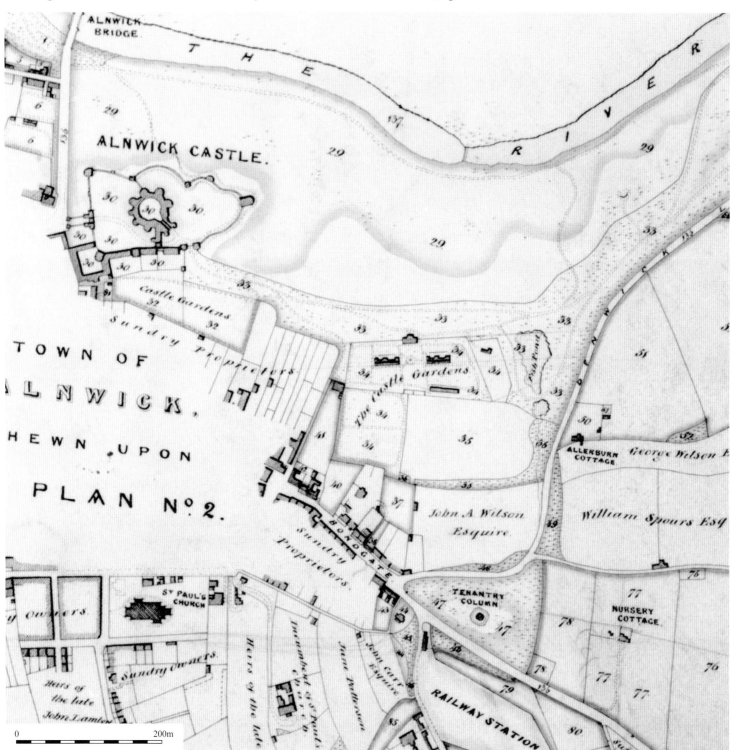

**Fig. 8.9** Extract from a plan of Alnwick, *c.* 1849; note the recently constructed railway station, to the south of the gardens (Bell 1849) (scale 1:5000)

The third duke brought further innovation and radical changes with the introduction of piped water from the castle to the walled garden. Following (extensive) negotiations recorded in the Business Minutes for the Castle for 1826 (BM 14), the resulting 1829 plan of the garden by Barnfather records the final proposals for this new water supply and shows a pipe running from the castle through Entrance 1 adjacent to the western boundary wall to a water tower in the south-west corner of the walled garden and thence supplying the garden (Fig. 8.6; see 9.4 below). The tower, which is extant, was built in this amended location, and is first seen on the 1856 Ordnance Survey map. The design of the tower that was constructed was very similar in design to a drawing on the 1829 Barnfather plan, with a crenelated upper storey, large U-shaped double door entrance and decorative crosses and slits in the stonework. The plan shows that the lower area was used to store bark in the winter; the heat produced by the bark would have prevented the water from freezing. This bark would presumably be

utilized in the pineries (see 9.5 below). The introduction of piped water would have been revolutionary for the gardeners; buckets drawn from the dipping pool in Garden 1 and the well would have been a labour-intensive way to supply water for the garden and hothouses. The need for a reliable water supply became even more essential with the introduction of hot water heating to some of the hothouses in the 1830s.

With the original walled garden no longer in use primarily as a kitchen garden, two more kitchen gardens were created by the third duke to add to the south-west and west kitchen gardens constructed by the second duke. The boundaries of the garden were extended by the piecemeal purchase of town gardens. Eleven separate plots were acquired and as soon as each purchase was made local masons were employed to extend the perimeter wall of the garden across the new parcel; the cost of this was 5s. per yard if the stone came from the Reigham quarry and 6s.5d.per yard for walls built with stone from the Denwick quarry (Shrimpton 1997, 14). By the 1820s just six complete burgage backlots of the Bondage properties survived. A walled kitchen garden was added to the western side of the south-west kitchen garden between 1827 (Fig. 8.4) and 1829 (Fig. 8.6). The Gardener's House stood at the northern end of this long and narrow garden and beyond the walls to the north a long rectangular structure can be seen for the first time on Wood's 1827 map. Although this has the appearance of the backhouse of a hothouse, it is not shown on Barnfather's plan with a glasshouse and the land to the west does not seem to have been owned by the duke at this time. This building is labelled on an architect's drawing of 1863 (PB 233) as an *'Old Vinery'* so it is possible that this structure may be another hothouse built by the third duke. On plans from 1865 onwards a glasshouse element is shown attached to the west of this structure within another kitchen garden created in grounds which were former backlots of town properties (see Fig. 8.16). Barnfather's plan also shows that yet another walled kitchen garden was built close to the south side of the castle, at some distance from the original garden. This was extensive in size, nearly as large as the original walled garden, and the western half was divided into quarters by paths, as was traditional for the layout of a kitchen garden.

The changes made by the duke and duchess led to widespread interest in the garden. The demand for access by visitors and travellers became so great that by the spring of 1828 a set of regulations had to be introduced to control the showing of the garden's greenhouses, conservatory and hothouses (Shrimpton 1997, 17). Access was however limited, not just in terms of the time allowed, but also to the class of visitor; the garden was certainly not accessible to all levels of society. The gardener was instructed by the duke to set aside one day a week for visits by 'ladies and gentlemen of the town and neighbourhood' so that he

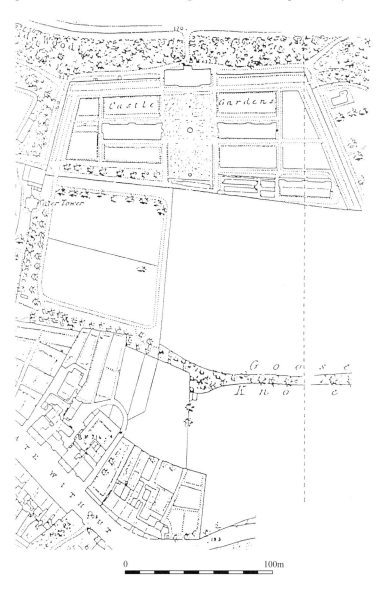

**Fig. 8.10** Ordnance Survey 2 inches to 1 mile map of Alnwick, 1856 (scale 1:2500)

was not continually interrupted by visitors. Strangers to the town were also welcomed to view the garden if the gardener considered them to have 'the appearance of gentlefolk' (Shrimpton 1997, 17–18). In 1843, a few years before the death of the third duke, admissions to the garden were curtailed to just one hour on a weekday between 9am and 10am and only with the written permission of the commissioner (*ibid.*).

## 8.4 An Italianate Garden (1847–1865)

*'Here, again, we are reminded of the possessions of Italian princes in past centuries, notwithstanding the cold skies and keen winds of the 'North Countrie.'…. In the heart of the garden, in the centre of the parterres, is a large fountain, or* carrie d'eau, *with a polished semicircular red granite lip, or rim. And beyond all this are many kitchen*

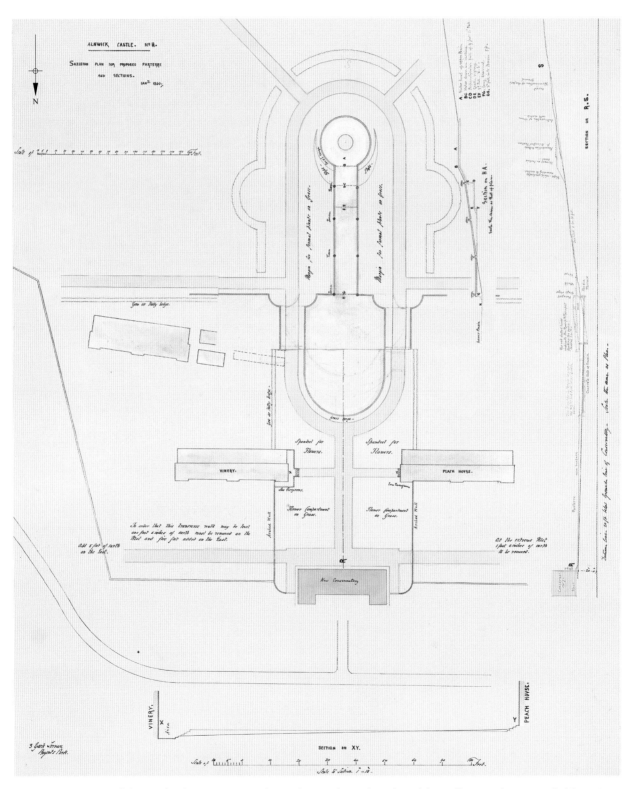

**Fig. 8.11** A proposed design for the parterre garden and central pond at Alnwick by William Andrews Nesfield (PB 230) (NB North is to the bottom of the image)

*gardens, glass-houses where Pine-apples are grown in great numbers, vineries, ferneries, an Orchid-house, and most of the items that go to make up Lord Bacon's idea of man's greatest happiness. The ornamental pleasure-grounds encircle the gardens and extend westwards, where they enclose the river, and finally merge in the parks mentioned, round which runs a stone wall about twelve miles long'. (The Gardeners' Chronicle 1898, 593).*

The changes made to the castle and gardens by Algernon the fourth Duke of Northumberland (1847–1865) were on a vast scale and the original walled garden, the principal layout of which had survived despite the changes made by the second and third dukes, was transformed beyond recognition. These changes, which involved landscaping on an unprecedented scale, were to remain, largely unaltered, for over half a century; many of the features

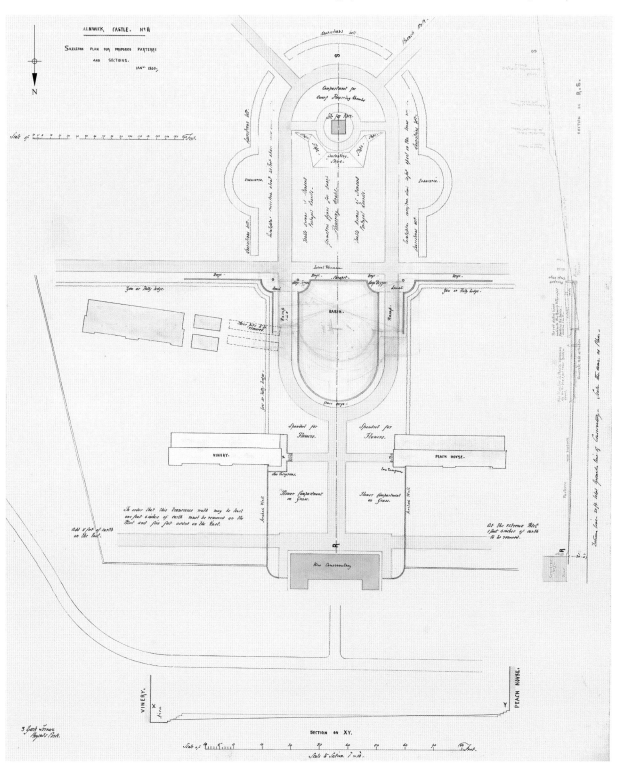

**Fig. 8.12** Modifications to the proposed design for the parterre garden at Alnwick, showing a central cascade descending to the pond as illustrated on a flyleaf to the original design, by William Andrews Nesfield, dated January 1860 (PB 230) (NB North is to the bottom of the image)

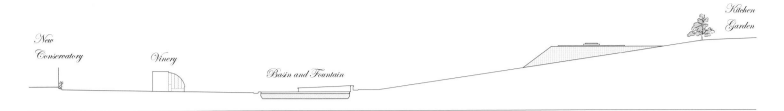

**Fig. 8.13** Garden Cross Section, *c.* 1860, illustrating the slope of the newly designed garden (PB 236)

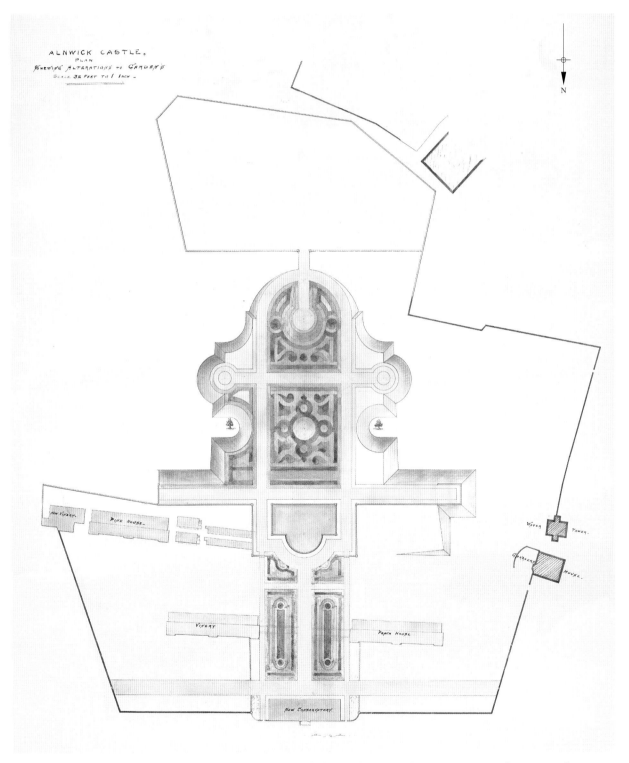

**Fig. 8.14** A proposed design for Garden 4 showing extended walled areas and alterations to northern part of parterre garden marked in pencil April 1864 (PB 220) (NB North is to the bottom of the image)

**Fig. 8.15** Detail of proposed Italianate parterre in the central part of Garden 4 showing modifications to the design of the parterres in northern area (PB 217) (NB North is to the bottom of the image)

that were introduced by the fourth duke survived to the time of the fieldwork.

Following service as a naval officer in the Napoleonic Wars, Algernon had travelled extensively and engaged in archaeological exploration. He had a fascination with the culture of Italy and was a frequent visitor to Rome. On his accession to the dukedom, Algernon embarked on an ambitious programme of restoration of Alnwick Castle, replacing the eighteenth-century gothic with an

Italianate style. The Roman architect Luigi Canina met the duke in Rome in 1853 and discussed a scheme for the restoration of the castle's interior which was based on the style of sixteenth-century Roman palaces (Shrimpton n.d., 25). To carry out this work, the duke created a school of wood carving at Alnwick and employed a Florentine carver to teach the skills required (*ibid.*). Canina visited Alnwick in 1856 with his assistant Giovanni Montiroli to survey and discuss progress with the duke and British architects who

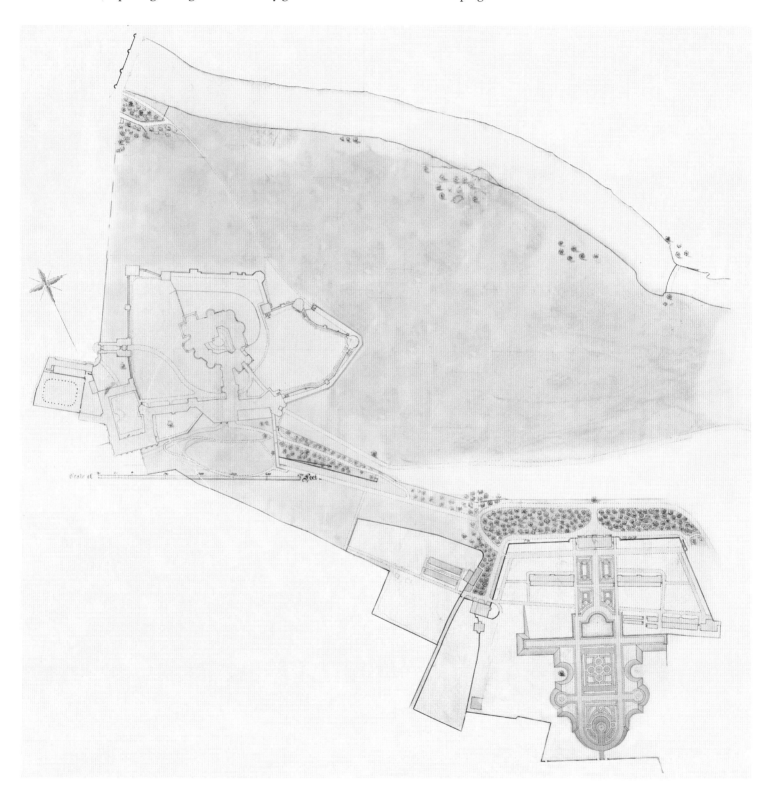

**Fig. 8.16** The fourth duke's Italianate garden in relation to the Castle, 1865 (COW A146)

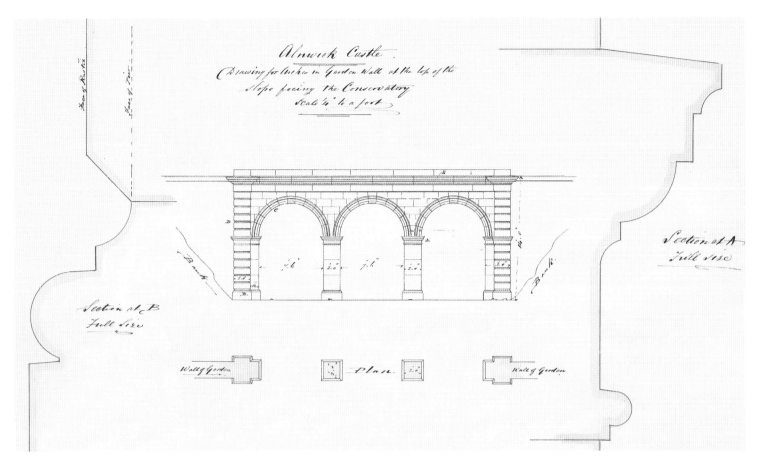

**Fig. 8.17** Architect's drawing of the triple-arched gateway in the northern wall of the middle garden, providing access into the upper garden (PB 235)

approved the scheme, amongst them Anthony Salvin, one of the leading architects of the Victorian castle style (Shrimpton 1997, 15; Shrimpton n.d., 25). After Canina's death, Montiroli supervised the work in Rome, where craftsmen produced marble fireplaces and balustrades, and Alnwick.

The fourth duke had a close acquaintance with Benjamin Disraeli and admired the social stance of his politics and of this early Victorian era (Shrimpton 1997, 19). This was to be reflected in his management of the gardens and parkland where his policies brought about social change in the access allowed. One of Algernon's first requirements of the Alnwick Walled Garden was to supply gooseberry, currant and raspberry bushes to holders of allotment gardens which he had created on some of his town lands (Shrimpton 1997, 19). Within months of his accession Algernon had written to the commissioner asking for the grounds of Hulne Park to be opened to the inhabitants of Alnwick (Shrimpton 1997, 19). He suggested that notices should be placed in the town announcing that the park would be open on Sundays from 1pm until sunset, thus ending the family's exclusive use of the park. Access to the gardens was similarly revolutionised; whilst during his brother's dukedom only selected members of the public could visit the garden during very prescribed times, in keeping with the social and political attitudes of this period, the fourth duke broke

down social barriers by allowing all classes to visit the gardens (Shrimpton 1997, 20). The gardens were opened to the public on Thursdays and the park was opened on Sundays and Thursdays so that both could be visited on the same day. The opening of the east coast railway line from Newcastle to Edinburgh and the branch line to Alnwick made a day visit feasible to visitors from farther afield. The newly-constructed railway station, which lay close to the southern entrance to the gardens, can be seen on Bell's map of 1849 (see Fig. 8.9). The duke's gardens and parks became a popular destination for many Tyneside societies, especially gardening clubs, church fellowships and for work outings from Newcastle manufactories (Shrimpton 1997, 20).

Before embarking on the Alnwick restoration, Algernon had transformed the house and gardens at Stanwick. The eminent garden designer William Andrews Nesfield (1794–1881) was commissioned to produce plans for a sunken parterre at Stanwick (Shrimpton 1997, 21). When Algernon succeeded to the title of fourth Duke of Northumberland five years after this commission, he already had the experience of the transformation of the Stanwick garden on a scale that overshadowed the restoration of the house. The central part of the original walled garden at Alnwick was redesigned during the early part of Algernon's dukedom with the demolition of the third duke's conservatory and

**Fig. 8.18** The fourth duke's expanded garden at Alnwick, as it may have appeared from the north-west, *c.* 1870; compare to the view of the earlier garden shown as Fig. 8.8, reconstruction by Chris Mitchell (c.mitchell02@btinternet.com)

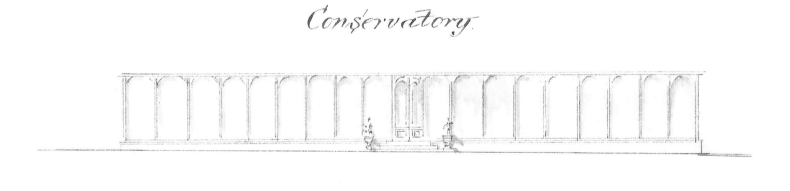

**Fig. 8.19** Detail from one of a series of architect's cross sections across the garden produced *c.* 1860, showing the northern conservatory (Hothouse 6); this representation demonstrates the schematic nature of these drawings, showing nine arches either side of the central entranceway, rather than the five that were ultimately constructed (PB 236)

lily-pond and the redesign of the entire central part of the garden along the width of the walled garden as a formal garden. These inherited garden features can be seen on Bell's *c.* 1849 map and the Ordnance Survey map of 1856, surveyed in 1851; these show a central pond, traces of which were recorded in the excavation area, surrounded by formal gardens to north and south and with a small pond adjacent to the southern boundary wall of the garden on the same axis as the central pond (Fig. 8.10).

The fourth duke's plans to further transform the Alnwick walled garden were equally as ambitious as those he had employed to create gardens at Stanwick, and key to this was the acquisition of yet more land adjacent to the gardens. Properties were purchased along the backlots of Bondgate Within in 1849 and the White Swan Garden was acquired in 1855 along with additional properties between 1856 and 1861; the total cost of these acquisitions came to £7,815 (Shrimpton 1997, 21). The purchase of these plots of land allowed the creation of another kitchen garden to the west of the original walled garden. This is no longer shown as extant on the 1867 Ordnance Survey map (Fig. 8.20). It was however the purchase of the grass paddock known as the Goose Knows field in May 1859 which allowed the duke to implement plans for the transformation of the original walled garden (Shrimpton 1997, 22). This parcel of land lay to the south of the walled garden, as shown on the Ordnance Survey map surveyed in 1851 and published in 1856 (see Fig. 8.10) and its acquisition allowed the creation of a garden nearly twice the size of the original walled garden.

William A. Nesfield was invited to Alnwick in the summer of 1848 to view the gardens and pleasure grounds (Shrimpton 1997, 23). Anthony Salvin, one of the architects involved in the restoration of the castle, was W. A. Nesfield's brother-in-law, and Nesfield's son William Eden Nesfield worked in Salvin's office in Argyll Street, London. Correspondence from W. E. Nesfield in the 1850s demonstrates a maintained contact by the family with Alnwick (Shrimpton 1997, 23). The acquisition of the Goose Knows land allowed W. A. Nesfield to draw up a plan for newly extended garden boundaries. This is dated January 1860 and was produced at Nesfield's drawing office at 3 York Terrace, Regents Park (Fig. 8.11). The drawing is number 11, which indicates that it was one of a series of Alnwick garden plans (Shrimpton 1997, 23).

Nesfield's plan comprises a design for a garden along the north–south axis of the original garden from the northern boundary wall and extending southwards across the land newly incorporated into the garden. A new conservatory is shown at the northern boundary wall; some of the levelling seen archaeologically is attested in this plan, which proposes a wide east–west walk in front of the conservatory. An accompanying note says: *'In order that this transverse walk may be level one foot 6*

*inches of earth must be removed on the West and five feet added on the East.'* A central north–south walk led from the new conservatory, forming the main axis of sight for the garden past the peach house and vinery to a large apsidal-ended basin. The walk was flanked by flower beds and a pair of curved symmetrical walls (arched walls) linked the conservatory to the peach house and vinery and hedges of yew or hollow border walks which run around the basin. An east–west walk at the end of the basin marked the end of the level area of the garden and beyond this two different layouts were proposed for the slope. In one design the sloping area was occupied by an apsidal shaped walkway with a central 'apex' or viewpoint at the southern end. A flyleaf over this design shows the alternative layout of a 'Cascade Canal' leading from a circular basin of water at the southern end of the garden into the large basin in the north (Fig. 8.12). It is recorded that the duke took Nesfield's plans with him when he sailed to Lisbon to convalesce in 1860 (Shrimpton 2006, 64).

A detailed examination of subsequent designs for the garden held in the Alnwick castle archives and comparison with the final garden layout revealed that Nesfield's proposals were not fully carried out, though they were broadly reflected in the new garden layout (Evans, in Kent 1998). Ultimately, a more Italianate garden was constructed, reflecting the duke's taste and contemporary fashions, the objective being to create a garden to match the recently restored castle which included the Italianate State Rooms. A detailed drawing for this Italianate garden design within the central area of the newly expanded garden is held in the castle archives (Fig. 8.14). Shirley Evans, a leading Nesfield expert, considers that this 1864 design was drawn by Arthur Markam Nesfield, Nesfield's son (August 2006, 112). The plan has been amended, with modifications to the layout of the northern parterres drawn in pencil and dated April 1864. This change in design is shown on a detail of the parterre garden along the central north–south axis of the garden (Fig. 8.15) and the 1867 Ordnance Survey map (Fig. 8.20) demonstrates that this modified plan was implemented, and also correlates with the excavated evidence for the position of an east–west path revealed in the excavation area. Parterres were constructed in a sunken area between the eastern and western hothouses.

To create the new enlarged garden the southern wall of the original walled garden was demolished and the kitchen garden of the second duke to the south-east was incorporated into the new garden. A new conservatory was built on the north wall, replacing the vinery (Hothouse 1) which had stood at this location since the creation of the walled garden in the 1770s. However, elements of the original spine wall and backhouses of this earliest hothouse did survive, incorporated within the cellar which housed the heating apparatus of the new conservatory. The

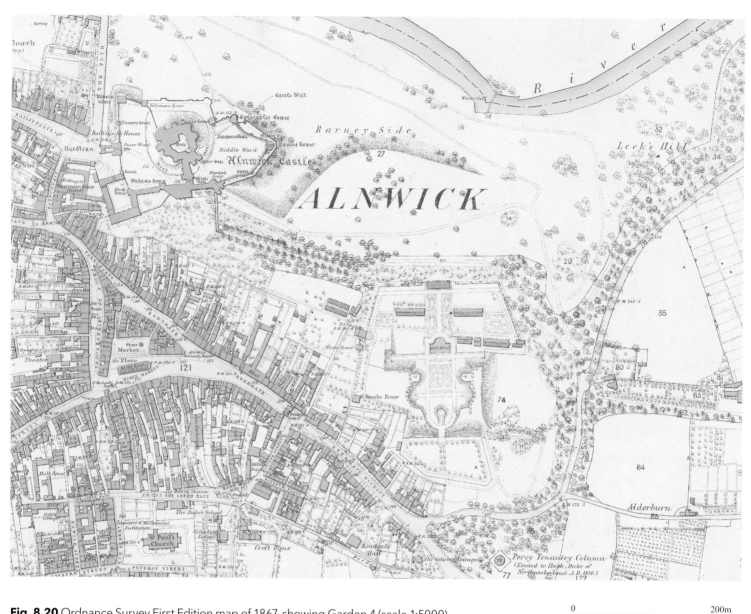

**Fig. 8.20** Ordnance Survey First Edition map of 1867, showing Garden 4 (scale 1:5000)

0                                    200m

third duke's three hothouses were retained in the new garden with the area between Hothouse 2 and Hothouse 4, the peach house and vinery, occupied by four parterres. The ends of the southern parterres curved around a large rectangular fish pond with an apsidal end and contemporary accounts of the garden demonstrate that this would have been a spectacular focal point, in contrast to the dilapidated structure which survived at the time of recording. The pond had polished red Aberdeenshire granite margins and central fountain (Hartshorne 1865; see Fig. 5.39). The area of the lower garden to the north of the sloping hillside was retained by substantial L-shaped retaining walls of ashlar blocks which extended to either side of the pond. Beyond the retaining walls a large rectangular parterre garden occupied the centre of the sloping middle garden surrounded by walkways (Fig. 8.20). To the south of the parterre the walkways enclosed an apsidal area around an earthwork in the shape of the Percy

crescent, an echo of the original 1860 W. A. Nesfield design. This area and the parterre on the steeply sloping ground was retained to the east and west by monumental curving earthwork banks. Beyond two large east–west mounds at the southern end of the middle garden an irregular hexagonal garden was constructed, backing onto the streets of the town, with the entrance way between these two gardens provided by a spectacular triple-arched gateway (see Fig. 8.17).

The fourth duke's new conservatory on the northern wall of the garden was located at the northern end of a central north–south axis which ran throughout the new garden; the centre of the building, the mound and the triple-arched gate of the hexagonal garden were built along this axis through the garden. Construction of the conservatory involved a radical change to the appearance of the perimeter of the garden in this area. The glass element of this new conservatory projected to the north beyond the line of the original walled garden, covering the footprint of the backhouses of the old vinery which had stood in this location. Curved walls were constructed to either side of the new conservatory between the original garden perimeter wall and adjoining a newly-constructed east–west stretch of boundary wall set back to the north from the original perimeter wall. These stone ashlar walls were in great contrast to the original garden boundary walls which were brick-faced internally. A wide entrance led through the wall in the centre of the conservatory and two narrow entrances were set within the newly built stretch of wall at either side of the conservatory, replacing the two earlier entrances in a similar position in the original wall. This allowed the furnace rooms (backhouses) of the former hothouse to be incorporated within the basement of the new building. This is an interesting detail, indicating that it was preferable to rebuild the garden wall, than to provide new accommodation for furnaces or boilers. It is also possible, if the interpretation of Hothouse 1 as incorporating a heated wall is correct, that it was necessary to rebuild this structure, either as a result of collapse or of heat damage.

Architect's drawings and photographs show that the conservatory was an impressive structure, built on a stone plinth and creating a focal point at the northern end of the long axis through the garden. Remnants of the conservatory survived at the time of the fieldwork as a stone platform surrounded by 'balustrading' which represents the stone supports for the iron frame of the glasshouse above. This impressive conservatory with its eleven arches was designed by William Shakespear, a 'metallic hothouse manufacturer' of Birmingham in 1862 (Shrimpton 1997, 25). The archives hold a receipt from John Meiklejon of Westfield Ironworks Dalkeith, Scotland for £300/–/– for the cost of the iron work for the *conservatory in Alnwick Castle Gardens* (DP/D4/1/262).

Westfield Iron Works provided all the smiths' work for the conservatory and other garden houses; local firms were used for all the garden glazing which was undertaken by Wilkin and Dickman of Alnwick and all painting work which was done by Adam Robertson (Shrimpton 1997, 25). The new garden lawns came from seed supplied by Edward Thew, the local seedsman and miller (Shrimpton 1997, 25).

Structures built in the south-eastern corner of the fourth duke's garden demonstrate that the newly-extended walled garden still had an important role to play in the production of fruit and other produce. A new hothouse (Hothouse 7) was built in the south-eastern corner of the original garden, to the east of Hothouse 5, though this was on a much smaller scale to the three large hothouses built by the third duke. This is labelled as a '*New Vinery*' on the 1864 design for the garden and the glasshouse

element is shown to the south on the 1867 Ordnance Survey map. The L-shaped backhouse of this vinery formed part of the perimeter wall of the garden and was extant at the time of writing. The 1860s plans for the design of the garden show two long rectangular and two smaller rectangular structures to the west of Hothouse 5, labelled on a 1900 plan as forcing frames and the smaller structures as Pine House (see Fig. 9.13).

The fourth duke brought further technological changes to the garden with the installation of a network of smoke shafts running from the furnace rooms of the hothouses and conservatory to a tower that was constructed in the south-west corner of the newly-extended garden. This is first shown on the 1865 design for the garden and is labelled as a '*Smoke Tower*' on the 1867 Ordnance Survey plan (Fig. 8.20). The extensive network of smoke shafts from the hothouses, conservatory, pine houses and forcing frames is shown on an 1896 plan of the water supply of the gardens (see Fig. 9.12) and a few elements of the smoke shafts were encountered during the archaeological investigation.

Following the purchase of town backlots by the fourth duke, a new walled kitchen garden was built to replace the second duke's kitchen garden which was amalgamated into the expanded garden of the fourth duke. This was located to the west of the original walled garden with an entrance close to the house of the head gardener. Two north-west to south-east aligned hothouses were built within the new kitchen garden; these are shown as glasshouses on the 1867 Ordnance Survey map (Fig. 8.20). Drawings from 1863 held in the castle archives show plans, cross-sections and elevations of these buildings by John Meiklejon (see Fig. 9.6). Both buildings are semi-subterranean with central steps at each end providing access through a wooden door. The brick walls along each elevation have twelve vented openings and the hipped glass roofs are supported on iron frames. The northern propagating pit is one long building whilst the southern is equally divided into two sections. The archive drawings also show a detailed plan of the earlier vinery, built by the third duke, and now straddling the east wall of the new kitchen garden, with the backhouses external to the new garden, and a plan and cross-section of the furnace house. The plan of the heating apparatus pipes shows pipework leading from the central backhouse of the old vinery to the new propagating pits.

The northern propagating pit was demolished sometime after the 1948 Ordnance Survey map. The archives hold a drawing showing an extension to be built at right angles the western end of the southern building, this is extant and used as a greenhouse. The southern propagating building is also extant and although the glass roof panels have been removed, the original wrought-iron roof structure including the venting mechanisms still survive under the modern roof cladding.

# 8.5 Late Victorian and Edwardian Innovation

*'The upper portion of the flower garden is much higher than that near the conservatory, and rises from the pond in the centre. The latter was recently planted with modern varieties of Water Lilies. On one side of the pond a square area is surrounded with a pergola…of Lime-Trees… The square of turfed area enclosed is used for bowls and croquet. The opposite side of the pond is sunk below the level of the garden and is used as a melonry and co. The flower garden from this point rises considerably and occupies a wide area and the beds on the upper differ from those on the lower level, which are mostly geometric, and filled with spring flowering plants. The beds on the upper ground are formed into many devices, edged with Box and planted with dwarf shrubs having variegated foliage, Hollies being employed much in them…'* (*The Gardeners' Chronicle* 1902).

The gardens entered their golden age in the Late Victorian and Edwardian era; the trees, shrubs and flowers had matured and the reputation of Alnwick as one of the great gardens of Britain had been established (Shrimpton 1997, 26). An account of a visit to the garden in 1880 describes the 'encircling banks' as 'flanked with festoons and chains of low-growing and hardy shrubs' (*The Gardeners' Chronicle* 1880). The substantial earthworks created by the fourth duke had evidently matured into the landscape of the new garden by this time. Throughout this period the garden retained its dual function as a decorative pleasure garden and as a productive garden, with large quantities of fruit being grown in the hothouses and against the walls of the garden. Following in the tradition of his predecessors, the sixth duke brought the latest innovations in garden technology to Alnwick.

The gardeners evidently continued to successfully produce large quantities of quality fruit at Alnwick. Contemporary articles and the 'Paylist of Workmen' from this period which detail the weekly tasks undertaken in the Alnwick Walled Garden demonstrate that many varieties of vegetables and fruit were grown in the kitchen garden to the west of the walled garden (see section 10.2 below; Acc 446/1–10).

An account of a visit to the garden in 1880 published in *The Gardeners' Chronicle* describes the five Grape Houses (wide houses with vines front and back); five Pine Houses as well as pits for suckers; melons which sometimes weigh 6 ½ lbs (*c.* 3kg) and on average 3lb to 5lb (*c.* 1.4–2.3kg). The technology for pineapple cultivation had evidently been perfected by this time as the pineapples are described as perfect and the number grown very great. The Peach houses:

*'yield an average crop of 150 dozen. Among the fruits upon the walls outdoors, 350 miles north of London and 5 miles only from the North Sea, I was surprised to find such Pears as Marie Louise, Chaumontel and Beurré Rance. These sorts ripen here in good years, assisted as they*

*must by management and a warm, dry soil.'* (*The Gardeners' Chronicle* 1880).

During the time of the sixth duke (1867–1899) and his head gardener Thomas Ingram, the garden underwent a period of significant technological innovation with changes made to the heating systems of the hothouses. An article in *The Gardeners' Chronicle* in 1880 refers to this work in an account of a visit to the Gardens at Alnwick (see Chapter 6). This presumably refers to reorganisation of hot water systems which had replaced the hot air flues; contemporary accounts suggest that heating systems were subject to constant change and 'improvement' with increasingly powerful and efficient boilers being introduced. Evidence for the hot water system was recorded in the hothouses and conservatory in the form of pipes, evidence for boiler fixings boilers and the blocking of the arched openings for the fires in the backhouses. However, a radical overhaul of the heating system for both castle and gardens occurred just ten years later when steam heating was introduced by the sixth duke (DP/DS/I/62; see 9.2 below). The boiler, which heated the castle and gardens, was placed at some distance from the castle, within the corner of the new walled kitchen garden just to the west of the north-west corner of the original walled garden. This structure is shown on the 1897 Ordnance Survey map (Fig. 8.21) and the base is extant (see Fig. 6.1; Fig 6.19). A 1900 plan of the water supply system shows steam main and condensed water pipes running through Entrance 1 from the boiler, past the northern conservatory, skirting around the peach house and vinery and into the backhouse of Hothouse 5, the small vinery (i.e. the Muscat House) in the south-east corner of the garden (see Fig. 9.13). By the turn of the century all of the hothouses were heated by steam (*The Gardeners' Chronicle* 1902), putting an end to the original function of the backhouses as providing heat to the glasshouses in front which had persisted since the creation of the gardens in the 1770s and in turn freeing up the backhouses for other purposes.

The sixth duke also added a nursery area to the south-east of the original walled garden and east of the fourth duke's earthworks in the sloping part of the new garden. This can be seen on the 1897 Ordnance Survey map as a rectangular garden, apparently walled on the east and south sides with the northern side formed by the stretch of southern wall which was possibly rebuilt by the fourth duke.

The improvements to the gardens are reflected in the investment in labour for the garden provided by the sixth duke. A 1867–1873 volume of paylists of workmen employed in the garden (Acc 446/1) shows that the number of men employed increased from 14 at the end of 1867 to 25 in 1868, with an unspecified number of women, and by 1895 up to 30 staff were employed by the sixth duke (Acc446/4; see section 10.2 below).

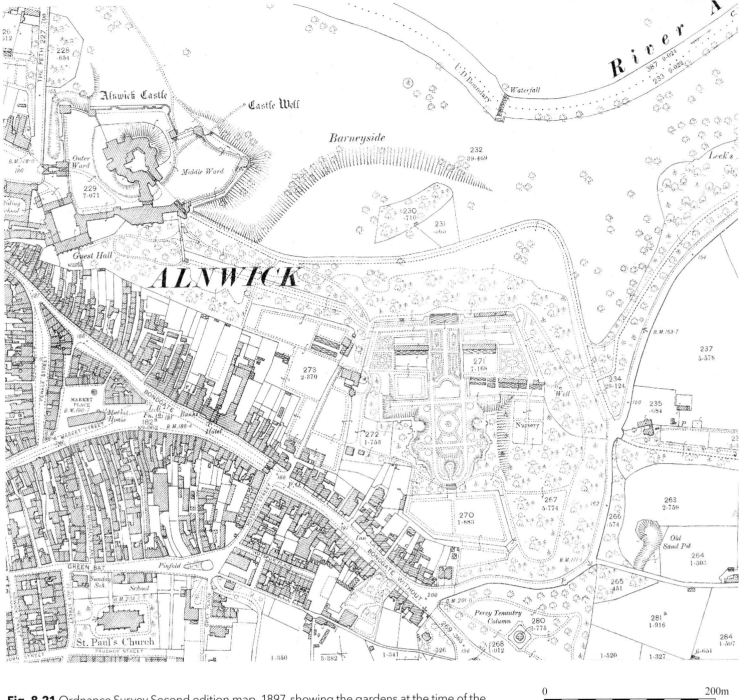

**Fig. 8.21** Ordnance Survey Second edition map, 1897, showing the gardens at the time of the sixth duke (25 inch to 1 mile) (scale 1:5000)

The sloping parterre garden between the two curving earthworks evidently suffered from drainage problems and necessitated the installation of an extensive new drainage system by the sixth duke; the new layout, which corresponds to the excavated remains in this area, can be seen on the 1897 Ordnance Survey map (Fig. 8.21).

Photographs taken at the beginning of the twentieth century add much to the detail shown on the 1897 map (Fig. 8.22; see Fig. 10.34). In the parterre to the south of the pond a central tree was surrounded by a path, encompassed by a large circular path occupying much of this parterre. Paths led from the circular path

towards each corner of the parterre, splaying out in two directions at each corner around a low conical tree. According to information provided by a member of Alnwick Castle staff at the time of the excavation, these were cypress trees which were removed a short time before the excavations began. Within each area bounded by the paths, decorative planting was defined by low shrubbery. Large irregular-shaped features in the six corners of the parterres exposed within the excavation area represent tree extraction pits, created when the cypress trees were removed. An account written in 1891 provides further details about the planting scheme in the parterres:

**Fig. 8.22** The Italianate garden as photographed *c.* 1900 showing the northern conservatory (Hothouse 6) built by the fourth duke; the internal layout of the southern parterres had by this time been redesigned as part of the sixth duke's modifications (Country Life, n.d.)

*'There are terraces sloping up one above another, parterres bright with flowers arranged with geometric precision, parterres green with convolutions of Box and Ivy without flowers, leafy screens of Linden trees, squared edges of Yew and Privet almost as compact as masonry, banks with festoons of foliage on them, wide walks bordered on either side with wide flower-beds all the more brilliant for the contrast with their smooth grass bordering and on three sides of the goodly acres thus treated, stands a high red-brick wall covered with fruit trees…'* (*The Gardeners' Chronicle* 1891, 593).

The garden was described on the eve of the First World War in the *Estate Magazine*. The gardens were approached from the castle through a high hedge of yew and *'tunnel-like openings in a series of hedges set at equal distance from each other and dividing distinct sections give an impression as of gazing through an immense telescope focused upon a perfect blaze of colour'* (Shrimpton 1997, 26). Topiary in the garden included a hound in full cry, a fleeing fox and a straight-tailed Percy Lion. The garden was described as being an August garden, so there were beds of all varieties of dahlias, as this was when the family was in residence at Alnwick for the shooting situation, continuing the long tradition of gardening to suit the habits of the duke's family.

## 8.6 Post-War Decline and Food Production

Wage inflation after the First World War more than doubled the daily pay rates and the huge increase in labour costs forced the eighth duke to drastically reduce the numbers employed in the Alnwick Walled Garden, by more than half, and from the summer of 1920 no more than nine gardeners worked under the head gardener (Shrimpton 1997, 27). The effect of this was that many of the tasks required to maintain such large and varied gardens had to be abandoned or carried out less frequently (Shrimpton 1997, 27). The function of the Alnwick Walled Garden was yet again transformed with the Second World War which saw them turned over to the production of food for the war effort. By 1941 sales of produce reached £308 to offset garden costs of £1284 (Shrimpton 1997, 27). The sale of foods grew throughout the war and into the post-war years until food shortages ended. In 1953 the decision was taken that the glasshouses should no longer be maintained and that they should be dismantled. Thereafter parts of the original walled garden were given over to a nursery for the Woods Department.

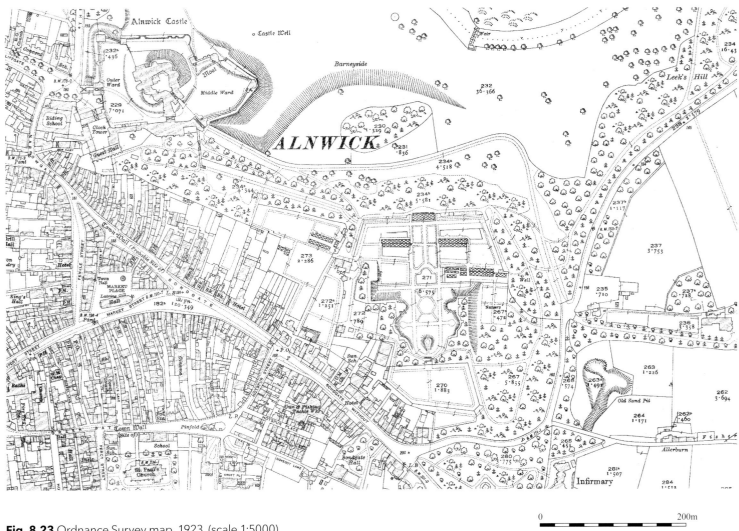

**Fig. 8.23** Ordnance Survey map, 1923 (scale 1:5000)

0                                              200m

# Chapter 9

## Technological Developments within the Alnwick Walled Garden

*'So much difference of opinion prevails amongst gardeners respecting the proper forms of Forcing Houses, that two are rarely constructed quite alike, though intended for the same purposes; and every gardener is prepared to contend that the form he prefers is the best, and to appeal to the test of successful experiment, in support of his opinion'.*
(Knight 1822)

The excavations, building recording and archive work undertaken at Alnwick Castle Gardens provide much evidence relating to the evolution of the kitchen garden, one of the major outcomes of which has been to further our understanding of the development and roles of the various hothouses within the garden. Evidence has been found to suggest that various modes of heating, glazing and ventilation were supplied to these structures. To better understand how that evidence relates to changing technologies, a brief history of the development of such expertise in glasshouses, particularly of the eighteenth and nineteenth centuries, is presented here, before addressing how these were applied to the different demands of specific plants within the Alnwick Walled Garden. Knight's statement (above) provides an important caveat to studies of hothouse construction; early hothouses were rarely constructed alike and thus any information drawn from published sources can only be employed to infer the use of similar techniques. Despite this caveat, as the nineteenth century progressed the advent of glasshouse manufacturers and their catalogues brought about much more standardisation.

### 9.1 Garden Technology

*'Such heat as is required in addition to that of the sun is most generally produced by the ignition of carbonaceous materials, which heat the air of the house, either directly when hot embers of wood are left in a furnace or stove, placed within the house…; mediately, as when smoke and heated air, from, or passing through ignited fuel, is made to circulate in flues; or indirectly, when ignited fuel is applied to boil water, and the hot vapor, or the water itself, is impelled through tubes of metal or other conductors'.*
(Loudon 1825, 312).

The use of heat and protection for plants has a long history. The application of artificial heat combined with 'transparent stone' (*lapis secularis*, or finely sliced sheets of mica) for forcing the early development of plants and extending growing seasons has been known since Roman times (Hix 1996, 10–11), but it was not until the sixteenth century that the practice of providing heated or protective environments for plant cultivation really took hold in Britain. Various mechanisms were used to provide protection to plants, including cloches, hotbeds, heated walls (and temporary structures constructed against them), as well as buildings designed specifically for the nurture of tender plants during inclement weather. The earliest heated growing structures to be extensively developed in this country were orangeries; these allowed the cultivation of citrus fruits by providing shelter throughout the coldest months of the year. From these early seventeenth-century origins (Woods and Warren 1990, 15) developments in hothouse technology were closely linked to the expansion of international trade and the resultant importation of exotic plants, linked with the successful development of portable greenhouses for the transportation of exotics by sea. A desire to cultivate exotic tropical fruit, in particular the pineapple, fuelled developments in hothouse technology. These, in turn, led to hothouses being increasingly used to improve the cultivation and extend the growing season of heat-loving fruits such as the grape and peach, which traditionally struggled in the British climate, particularly in more northerly areas. By the beginning of the nineteenth century the desire for glasshouses had developed into a 'mania' (Hix 1996, 30).

The story of the kitchen garden at Alnwick begins in the mid-eighteenth century and thus it is not necessary to dwell here on earlier developments, except in so much as they relate to the technological advances which influenced the structures encountered. Excellent modern guides to this technological development exist (e.g. Hix 1996; Grant 2013) as well as contemporary accounts in the form of various encyclopaedias and treatises (e.g. Miller 1768; Speechley 1796; Loudon 1825). The pages of contemporary periodicals (e.g. *Transactions of the Horticultural Society of London*; *The Gardener's Magazine*; *Memoirs of the Caledonian Horticultural Society*) are similarly full of discussions of and proposals for improved methods of heating, glazing and ventilating hothouses; the information presented here provides a brief introduction only.

The successful cultivation of exotics and the forcing or extending of the growing season of native or temperate varieties of fruit and vegetable is generally dependent on several factors, including the provision and regulation of a supply of heat, light, shade, humidity and ventilation to create an 'ideal' artificial climate. Technologically, the biggest developments were in glazing and heating and complex developments were made, although ventilation could be provided by simple sliding or opening sashes and shade could be provided using paper or cloth blinds.

Cloches, hotbeds, portable glazed shelters for trees and glass, oiled-paper, or cloth-covered frameworks which could be moved and either placed directly on the soil or propped against sections of heated wall all helped the gardener to extend the growing seasons of plants and protect delicate specimens (Loudon 1825, 291–301). There would also be an attendant need for the storage of such structures when not in use. The forcing pit may have had a permanent base, constructed in brick or stone, with moveable lights (glazed wooden frames) above and could have been used for extending the growing season of asparagus, strawberries and cucumbers as well as for growing pineapples (Loudon 1825, 301). The construction of permanent glasshouses therefore, can be seen to have developed out of the use of temporary structures such as cloches, hotbeds and frames, alongside the use of buildings such as orangeries which enabled citrus and other exotic fruits to be overwintered in a British climate.

The use of glass, essential for conservatories, greenhouses and hothouses, was limited, at least until the mid-nineteenth century, by prohibitive costs of manufacture as well as window tax. Glass was taxed by weight between 1746 and 1845, making the glazing of glasshouses an expensive undertaking. Manufacturers of horticultural glass were encouraged to make the panes as thin as possible, with the result that individual panes were small, as the glass would be too fragile to make these larger. The repeal of the glass tax, combined with the mechanisation of the manufacture of cylinder glass in the mid-nineteenth century, allowed for larger, flat sheets of glass to be produced, transforming the glazing systems in use in hothouses. The earliest orangeries were provided with large windows facing the sun but were ill-lit compared with later hothouses and generally were provided with solid tile or stone roofs. Small glass panes supported in wooden frames were eventually superseded by lighter structures with iron frameworks and elaborate roof pitches, designed to maximise the light entering hothouses (see 9.3 below).

Alongside advances in glazing and building construction came inventions and adaptations designed to provide optimum artificial heat to glasshouses. These followed a pattern of technological development, although it is clear, both from contemporary accounts and from the excavated evidence at Alnwick and elsewhere, that one or more of these innovations may have been in use within a garden at any one time and that there was an apparent need or desire to constantly modify and improve the design of hothouse heating systems.

The earliest forms of heating using fire were provided by the 'smudge pot', an open fire, fuelled with peat, or a charcoal brazier. Such fires were labour intensive and could be dangerous, potentially providing noxious, smoky fumes and occasionally causing hothouses to be accidentally set alight. By the end of the seventeenth century iron stoves had become popular in Germany and Holland. These freestanding boxes, fuelled by peat or charcoal, with iron flues which vented through the roof of the house, provided uneven heat distribution, but could keep plants above freezing through the winter. An indirect heating system developed by John Evelyn in 1691 drew the heat from a fire under a vaulted floor beneath the hothouse and vented via a chimney in the manner of hypocaust systems. Fire was not always used to provide heat to plants; hotbeds might rely on the heat generated by dung or tanners' bark (powdered oak bark which had been used in the tanning process). Such materials fermented giving off heat and could also be used in tandem with other heating methods.

By the eighteenth century, however, the most common form of heating was by hot air, generated by fires and channelled through flues, either contained within walls or constructed around the interior of the hothouse, before being vented via a chimney. This method of heating had the benefit of better and more even heat distribution, although gardeners still had to stoke furnaces through the night. It was labour-intensive and inefficient; temperature control was difficult, and the fires consumed vast quantities of fuel (Hix 1996, 48). There was always a danger of soot accumulating in the flues, leading to structures catching alight (Connolly *et al.* 2012). Nevertheless, flued walls and developments of the flued system of heating appear to have been extensively used at Alnwick where most of the hothouses investigated were initially heated by flues.

The use of steam heating was developed in the early eighteenth century; in 1807 John Hay experimented with passing steam across stones to store heat which would maintain the temperature of glasshouses overnight (Hix 1996, 49). The earliest steam heating devices employed open containers in which water was boiled, causing condensation to gather on both glass and plants, but by 1817 improvements had been made in the way steam was employed, being transported through vaults and pipes to heat gravel and bubbled through water beds. Writing in 1805 Loudon had little time for steam heating, but by 1817 had come to view the technology more favourably (Loudon 1805; Loudon 1817, 59). Steam heating had the benefits of being useable across many buildings; only one furnace, and thus chimney stack, were needed and heat could be transferred great distances. However, steam had its disadvantages; fires had to be constantly stoked, water took a long time to reach the required temperature and there was a threat of explosion. Steam eventually gave way to hot water heating, in which water was carried through buildings in iron pipes in a system little different from that of central heating in use across many homes today. Adoption of this method of heating gained momentum after 1845, following the development of technologies which enabled iron pipes to be cast vertically (Connolly *et al.* 2012). Existing structures with antiquated heating systems could be, and were, adapted to accept hot water pipes, which provided a steady, controllable and even heat.

## 9.2 Heating Systems in use in the Alnwick Walled Garden

*'A garden is not now considered complete without a greenhouse, or conservatory with flued walls and with frames and lights…'* (Nicol 1810).

### The walled garden

Large sections of the original boundary wall of the Alnwick walled garden are extant. The external faces of the garden wall were built in stone, with the internal faces brick-built. When the walled garden was first constructed, in the 1770s, bricks were an expensive commodity and in areas where stone was readily available, such as Northumberland, the external faces of garden walls were sometimes built in stone to reduce expense (Campbell 2005, 52). Brick was much more suitable for fruit walls in a kitchen garden; stone was chilly and damp, it was difficult to nail in supports for plants and garden pests such as snails and earwigs could shelter in the crevices between jointed stones (Campbell 2005, 53). Brick also has the advantage of absorbing heat during the day and releasing it at night, increasing the variety of plants that could be grown. Dark red, highly fired bricks were considered the best type as they absorbed the most heat and were the most weather-durable (Campbell 2005, 53). Walled kitchen gardens on large estates had become commonplace during the seventeenth and eighteenth centuries, the walls serving the purpose of protecting plants from predators and from inclement weather as well as providing a support on which to train fruit trees and other plants (Gray 1998, 114–115). From the mid-eighteenth century the form of garden walls seems to have been the subject of much interest and experimentation, with serpentine or zig-zag forms noted, designed to more readily catch the sun's rays as well as to save money in construction (the form of these walls allowing them to be only one course of bricks thick). There were even attempts to build walls on

a slope to the vertical, and recommendations in favour of darkly painted walls, but these did not prove universally popular (Miller 1754, WALLS; Loudon 1825, 306–308).

*'Walls are absolutely necessary in gardens, for the ripening of all such fruits as are too delicate to be perfected in this country without such assistance. These are built with different materials; in some countries they are built of stone, in others with brick, according as the materials can be procured best and cheapest.'* (Miller 1754, WALLS).

The original Alnwick walled kitchen garden was trapezoidal in plan, its shape partly determined by land boundaries, but also benefitting from the eastern and western walls being constructed slightly south-facing to assist with the cultivation of wall-trained fruits. Until the end of the seventeenth century, kitchen gardens tended to be square in plan or rectangular as dictated by the space available; the direction of the sun was not considered when laying out a garden (Campbell 2005, 29). By the beginning of the eighteenth century, garden design began to take account of the fact that the warmth of the sun could be harnessed by building gardens with a long axis running east–west with the south-facing walls the longest; fruit and kitchen gardens of the period were therefore often trapezoid or rhomboid in plan (Campbell 2005, 29). Alnwick differs in this respect; although the north and south walls formed the long axes of a trapezoidal garden, the south facing wall was shorter than that which faced north.

### Heated garden walls

The walled garden at Alnwick when first built *c.* 1760–1772 included a section of heated wall in the north-west. An original external furnace is extant; the location of the second, later furnace subsequently converted to a buttress can still be seen (see section 2.3 above). The introduction in the early eighteenth century of heated walls which contained serpentine internal flues running up the height of the wall allowed grapes and other tender fruits to be grown outdoors in even the coldest parts of Britain (Campbell 1988, 109). These were particularly common in walled gardens in northern England from the mid-eighteenth to the nineteenth century, such as at Belsay Hall in Northumberland (Hall 1989; Green 2000).

Miller (1754; WALLS) considered that the construction and maintenance of a flued wall need not be a great expense, arguing that there was no need to heat such walls before about the middle of January and that the fires need only remain lit until the end of May, beyond which time there would be no need of artificial heat providing the glass (of any associated shelter or glasshouse) was shut at night or in bad weather. Loudon (1825) suggested that heat may also be necessary in September, to assist with the ripening of fruit and wood. It is clear from Miller's description that heated walls were designed to be used in conjunction with moveable forms of glazing. He further recommends a heated wall of approximately 100 feet in length was sufficient for forcing fruit. Assuming a heated wall of around three times this length is constructed, moveable glazing can be used to force fruit successively, allowing a two-year rest period for trees between forcing:

'*by dividing it into three parts, there will be two years for the trees to recover their vigour between the times of their being forced, whereby a greater quantity of bearing wood may be obtained, and the fruit will be fairer, and in larger quantities, than when they are forced every year, or every other year; and as the glasses may be contrived so as to move from one to the other, the expense of building the Wall so much longer, will not be very great, because the frames and glasses will be the same as for one year's fruit.*' (Miller 1754, walls)

Miller's recommended distance between furnaces is 40 feet; furnaces should be housed in sheds, preferably of brick and tile construction. The necessity of having furnaces underground (to allow the upwards movement of air through the wall) is stressed here:

'*As it is absolutely necessary to have the ovens below the foundation of the first flues, there must be steps down into the sheds; to come to the mouth of the ovens to supply the fuel*' (Miller 1754, WALLS).

Both Miller (1754) and Loudon (1825; 304) recommend that a flued wall should be constructed entirely of brick, unless stone is particularly abundant and cheap, Loudon lays down guidelines for constructing such a structure:

'*The flued wall, or hot-wall, (figs. 236, & 237 [see Fig. 9.1]) is generally built entirely of brick, though where stone is abundant and more economical, the back or north side may be of that material. A flued wall may be termed a hollow wall, in which the vacuity is thrown into compartments (a, a, a, a), to facilitate the circulation of smoke and heat, from the base or surface of the ground to within one or two feet of*

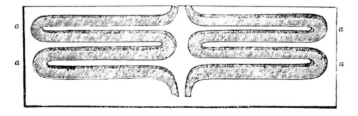
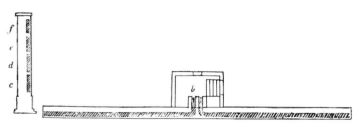

**Fig. 9.1**  Elevation (cut away), cross section and plan of a hot wall and furnace (from Loudon 1825)

*the coping. They are generally arranged with hooks inserted under the coping, to admit of fastening some description of protecting covers… and sometimes for temporary glass frames. A length of 40 feet, and from 10 to 15 feet high, may be heated by one fire, the furnace of which (b), being placed 1 or 2 feet below the surface of the ground, the first course or flue (c) will commence 1 foot above it, and be 2 feet 6, or 3 feet high, and the 2d, 3d, and 4th courses (d, e, f), narrower as they ascend. The thickness of that side of the flue, next the south or preferable side, should for the first course be 4 inches, or brick and bed; and for the other courses it were desirable to have bricks cast in a smaller mould … This will give an opportunity of bevelling the wall, and the bricks being all of the same thickness, though of different widths, the external appearance will be every where the same.*' (Loudon 1825, 304).

Such walls, with their moveable glazing bars, would provide sufficient warmth and shelter to enable the successful growing of cherries, plums, peaches, apricots and nectarines, with a capacity for forcing approximately 1/3rd of the crop to produce early fruit. Strawberries, as well as peas and beans, may have been planted towards the front of the border, benefitting from the heat and protection offered.

It should be noted that if the extant furnace at Alnwick was expected to provide heat to the stretch of wall from the north-west corner of the garden up to Hothouse 1, this would have covered an area of south-facing wall approximately 50m (164ft) long. This scenario seems unlikely and is distinctly at odds with the recommendations of both Miller and Loudon (above); Miller (1754 WALLS) advises a distance of 40ft between flues. In practice these have been observed to be constructed as far as 60ft, or as closely spaced as 30ft apart (Hall 1989, 99). This is somewhat problematic; the presence of cleaning holes along this entire stretch of wall, combined with the wall's width for the entirety of this stretch, suggests that it was heated along the whole of this length. It may be that more furnaces were originally present than have survived, although there was no evidence for such either within the standing buildings record or in historic mapping. That this single furnace was insufficient to heat the entire wall is however demonstrated by the later provision of a second furnace. Whatever the case, it is not hard to imagine how such a wall, provided with temporary glazing to encourage the forcing of early fruit, could be easily developed into a more permanent glasshouse for the cultivation of exotic, or more demanding, fruit.

## The earliest hothouse

Given the evidence which still survives for a heated wall at Alnwick, it might be reasonable to assume that the earliest heated structure, Hothouse 1, was constructed against a flued wall heated by means of the three associated furnaces. This could not be demonstrated by excavation, however some details of the heating system were identified. The earliest system comprised a simple furnace fuelled by coal in each of the three backhouses. With intervals of 15m (around 50ft) between the furnaces, the distribution of heat through flues to the wall would be appropriate for this form of heating. Given that there were three furnaces along a 100ft stretch of wall, each furnace would supply heat to a little over 30m of walling (Fig. 2.8).

It is assumed that the hot air produced by the furnaces would have been directed through ducts in the corner of the rooms (examples were identified at either end of the building, although these may have been later modifications) and thence into the rear wall. The furnaces may have supplied additional heat via flues around the internal perimeter of the structure, but in the absence of excavated evidence this could not be established.

Speechly (1796, 93) recommends that the fireplace should not be too close to the level of the flue or the fire would come back when the wind was in a certain direction. To prevent this, he suggested that the fire grate should be two feet (0.60m) below the level of the bottom of the flue and the top of the fireplace six inches (0.15m) below the bottom of the flue. It would be logical to expect the Hothouse 1 backhouses to have been built as subterranean rooms so that the fireplaces could be constructed at a suitable height for optimum performance of the hot air system used to heat the glasshouse. This assumption has been followed in reconstructing a schematic cross section through Hothouse 1 (see Fig. 2.8).

## Hot air flues

The late eighteenth and early nineteenth centuries were a period of experimentation and the consequent development of new heating techniques. The stimulation for this was the desire to create different environments specifically targeted to the cultivation of imported exotics. Glasshouses built against hot walls developed into buildings with flues constructed against the back wall; later developments along the same theme included freestanding flues, which would allow air to be directed around the glasshouse (Grant 2013, 17–21). In the mid-1820s Loudon was still very much in favour of the use of fire and smoke flues to heat glasshouses:

'The most general mode of heating hot-houses is by fires and smoke-flues, and on a small scale, this will probably long remain so. Heat is the same material, however produced; and a given quantity of fuel will produce no more heat when burning under a boiler than when burning in a common furnace. Hence, with good air-tight flues, formed of well burnt bricks and tiles accurately cemented with lime-putty, and arranged so as the smoke and hot air may circulate freely, every thing in culture, as far as respects heat, may be perfectly accomplished…. As

to the size of hot-house fireplaces, the door of the furnace may be from ten inches to one foot square; the fuelchamber from two to four feet long, from eighteen inches to two feet wide, and of the same dimensions as to height. Every thing depends on the kind of fuel to be used. For Newcastle coal, a chamber of two feet long, eighteen inches broad, and eighteen inches high, will answer as well as one of double the size,' (Loudon 1825, 323–24).

Within the Alnwick hothouses, only one of the original furnaces survived to be excavated, this being the furnace for the mushroom house, Furnace 3 in Hothouse 4 (see section 9.5 below). This had a hearth or fuel chamber with a metal door above and an ash pit beneath and compares favourably with Loudon's (1805, Plate 1; Fig. 9.2) illustration of a furnace. A publication of 1825 describes the common construction of a furnace thus:

'The hot-house fire-place, or furnace, consists of several parts : a chamber, or oven, to contain the fuel, surrounded by brick-work, in which fire-brick (a sort containing a large proportion of sand, and thus calculated by their hardness not to crumble by heat, &c.) is used; a hearth or iron grating, on which the fuel is laid; a pit or chamber in which the ashes drop from this grating, and iron doors to the fuel-chamber and ash-pit'. (Loudon 1825, 323–24).

Loudon recommended that to heat an expanse of glasshouse a larger number of small furnaces are preferable to fewer large ones, because of the heat loss suffered by hot air travelling over a distance. Flues were varied in form:

'The modes of constructing flues are various. The original practice was to build them on the naked earth… or in the solid walls of the backs and fronts of the pits, like the flues of dwelling-houses. The first improvement seems to have been that of detaching them from the soil by building them on flag-stones, or tiles supported by bricks; and the next was, probably, that of detaching them from every description of wall, and building their sides as thin as possible. A subsequent amelioration consisted in not plastering them within, but in making their joints perfect by lime-putty, by which means the bricks were left to exert their full influence in giving out the heat of the smoke to the house.' (Loudon 1825, 323–24).

Loudon concludes that the best sort is 'the common form' with thin bricks, and base and top of tiles, no less than 9 inches wide and 14 to 18 inches high. Dampers allow control over the heat generated and dispersed:

'The direction of flues, in general, is round the house, commencing always within a short distance of the parapet, and after making the course of three sides, that is, of the end at which the fire enters, of the front, and of the opposite end, it returns (in narrow houses) near to or in the back wall, or (in wide houses) up the middle, forming a path; and in others, immediately over or along side of the first course. In all narrow houses this last is the best mode.' (Loudon 1825, 326).

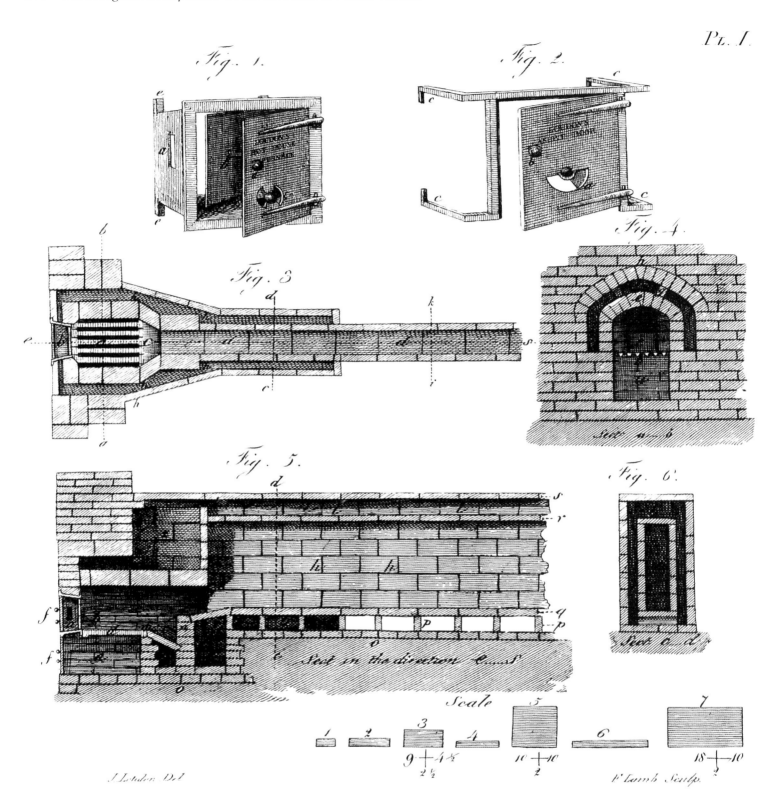

**Fig. 9.2** Illustration of a furnace and flues to supply hot air to hothouses (from Loudon 1805)

FIG. I.
*Loudon's improved Hothouse Furnace.*
a   The opening in each side, which communicates with the air vacuity.
b   The inner furnace door---9 inches square.
c   Valve in the outer furnace door for admitting cool air to be heated upon the inner furnace door, and in the vacuity around the fuel-chamber, & c.
d   Handle, which opens, shuts, and fastens both doors at once.
e e   "Nobbs," which are for the purpose of fixing the furnace more securely in mason work*

FIG. II.
*Ash-pit door to Loudon's Hothouse Furnace.*
a   The valve.
b   The handle.
c   Part of the frame on which the door is hinged, turned inwards and hooked at the extremities in order that it may be fixed more securely in the mason work.

FIG. III.
*Ground plan of the Fuel-chamber, Air-vacuity, and part of the Flue.*
a   The fuel-chamber.
b   Furnace door.
c   Recess for preserving live feul [sic].
d d   Bottom of smoke-flue.
h h   Vacuity around the fuel-chamber, and part of the flue communicating also with the furnace door.

FIG. IV.
*Vertical section of the fuel-chamber, supposing it finished, and cut through in the direction a .... b, fig. 3.*
a   The ash-pit.
b   Bars of the furnace grate.
c   Upright rise of the flue above the recess, for preserving the live coals, see *m ... n*, fig. 5.
d   Throat of the smoke-flue.
e   Arch over the fuel-chamber.
f   Air vacuity.
g   A brick seen projecting down in order to support the upper arch.
h   Mass of bricks around the whole, being part of the wall of the hothouse, as may be seen by the dotted line *a b*, in fig. 3.

FIG. V.
*Longitudinal section of the furnace, and part of the smoke-flue, supposing them finished and cut down, in the direction of e ... f, fig. 3.*
a   Space betwixt the outer and inner furnace doors, in which the hole that cornmunicates with the air vacuity is seen.
b   Fuel-chamber.
c   Recess for live-fuel.
d   Grate.
e   Ash-pit.
f f   Handles of furnace and ash-pit door.
i and g   Vacuity for heated air under the "recess" and part of the smoke-flue.
h·h   Smoke-flue, five bricks breadth in depth.
z   Air-vacuity above the fuel-chamber.
k   Contraction of this vacuity, immediately before the air-flue commences.

l l   The air-flue.
o o   Sole of the furnace and flue.
p p   Supports of the flue.
q   Bottom of the smoke-flue
r   Covers of ditto, which serve also for the bottom of the air-flue.
s   Covers of the air-flue.

FIG. VI.
*Section of the smoke-flue and air-chamber surrounding it, supposing them finished and cut through in the direction shewn by the dotted line c .... d, in figures 3. and 5.*
a   The smoke-flue
b   The air vacuity and flue.

The scale shews the form and the dimensions of the bricks supposed to be used in building the furnace, flues, &c.
1   Is the end of a common brick.
2   The edge of ditto.
3   The face or breadth of ditto.
4   The end of a common flooring or pavement tyle.
5   The surface of ditto.
6   The side and the front of a large tyle cover, supposed made on purpose for covering that part of the air-flue, which from being continued on each side of the smoke-flue, is broader than the other parts. Where the air-flue is continued above the smoke-flue only, common tyles, as No. 5. will answer.
In Scotland pavement will generally be had as conveniently as tyle of this size.
In England the tyle covers, will be most economical.

---

* There is a beautiful variety through all nature, which a person of a contemplative mind is ever admiring. This variety in the animal as well as in the vegetable kingdom, is mightily supported by contrasts or oppositions. The meadow walk at Edinburgh, is shadowed by a row of stately beeches, and though those trees when planted at regular distances are all very much of a shape, yet each of these, are so different from one another, that a person might spend in a most agreeable manner, a very long time in observing their several forms and varied hues of green. In walking along the promenade and examining each tree, how much is the beauty of the whole heightened, when near one end of the row, there suddenly appears an old shattered trunk with its branches greatly scathed and and curtailed------I have already said that during the time the alterations were making upon Dicksons and Shade's hothouse, I had been much amused with variety of opinions, by hearing the workmen relate what some planners and others, purposed as improvements. When the alterations were proven to be of importance, and had in some measure attracted public attention, the author was again amused by reports of what some would call a worse kind. But what a fund of entertainment did he partake of, when after these varied efforts to skath or blast, a "landscape gardener" who happened to be getting some common furnaces made, pleased with the one recommended and sold at the foundry, quietly copied (as the Edinburgh Foundry people told me,) one part of it after another, until at last he produced a furnace almost an exact copy of that in the plate. This person affords like the decaying trunk a strong contrast to the rest of his profession–and like it must strikingly affect the attentive observer, or moral painter.

## Hothouse 2

The original construction of Hothouse 2 appeared similar to that of Hothouse 1, with three furnace rooms (linked by narrow corridors), supplying heat to the glasshouse. Constructed as a peach house, it is quite plausible that when initially constructed (in the late eighteenth century) this building used hot wall technology: the spine wall of the building had been largely rebuilt when the backhouse was modified and extended.

Map evidence, primarily that of Barnfather (1829), suggests that the remodelling of Hothouse 2 and construction of Hothouse 4 occurred in the early 1830s. This conclusion is supported by a document in the Alnwick castle archives, dated March 5 1830, which illustrates the ventilation system of the vinery (Hothouse 4), and presumably constitutes an architect's design (TAG Z/1/4; see Fig. 9.9, Fig. 9.29, Fig. 9.30, Fig. 9.31). The remains of a system of hot air flues, seen directly to the south of the spine wall in Hothouse 2, and paralleled in Hothouse 4, suggests that both buildings would have been heated by means of hot air flues in the early 1830s. Hothouse 5 was apparently similarly heated, with flues extending around the central raised bed (see section 9.5 below).

The glasshouse elements of Hothouses 2 and 4 had been systematically demolished and little remained to give any indication of their original floor level. Hothouse 5 survived better, although this had also been modified to take hot water heating. The actual structural remains of the flue walls adjacent to the hothouses fell between the areas designated for excavation and for standing building recording and were only recorded in plan as exposed and not fully excavated. Thus, the flue system and associated flooring must be interpreted from the surviving evidence, contemporary accounts and existing excavated parallels; consequently, any interpretive cross sections are schematic. The variety in potential shape, size and form of flue is demonstrated by Loudon (1825, 325). The details of the workings of the Alnwick houses are described in detail below (see section 9.5).

There was an apparent chronology to the development of heating apparatus for hothouses in which hot walls were superseded by heated flues adjacent to the walls, then separate heated flues, steam heating and finally hot water heating; however, in practice many technologies were apparently in use at once. Moreover, there was much debate within contemporary literature as to which method was considered best; in 1825 Loudon did not think that hot water heating would succeed (Loudon 1825, 328).

## Flue-heated forcing frames

An early heated structure, with separate furnace (Structure 1), occupied a central location within the garden. This does not appear on any known maps, unless Bell's map of 1826 depicts this structure very crudely and badly-positioned as the central building in a line of three hothouses, a scenario which seems unlikely considering his apparently accurate depictions of buildings to the east, west and north. Shrimpton considers this central structure is more likely to be a conservatory constructed by the second duke (Shrimpton 1997, 16); if so, this would suggest a relatively rapid sequence of rebuilding in the same general part of site. An alternative explanation is that Bell's representation is schematic (see section 8.3 above). Whatever the case, Structure 1 dates to the period between 1788 and 1826; an unmapped period for the garden of almost 40 years providing a chronology which fits with the excavated sequence.

By examining the form of the structure and its apparent date it is possible to suggest parallels for this building and speculate on its use. Many elements of the building had been systematically and thoroughly demolished rendering its exact function hard to elucidate, but it clearly comprised a brick-built structure with two main elements, the northern of which had been subdivided into two cells separated by a central path. The survival of two separate channels, one a brick-lined flue, the other heavily demolished, rising from a small external furnace to serve the building, confirm that the building was heated. The dimensions of the robbed-out features certainly allow for the inclusion of flues adjacent to or within walls. An unexcavated surviving element of brickwork at the south-eastern corner of the building, within cell 3, conforms in dimensions and construction technique to the flue leading out of the furnace to the south. This comprises a brick base with

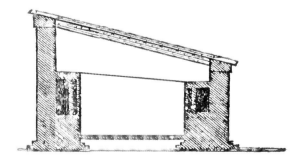

**Fig. 9.3** A 'flued pit' used for the early forcing of plants, or the cultivation of low-growing heat-loving fruit such as melons or pineapples (from Loudon 1825)

brick-built sides having an internal width of 0.22m (or 8.66in, roughly corresponding to the maximum flue dimension of 9in recommended by Loudon 1825). This suggests that the flues which entered the building originally ran adjacent to and inside the walls of the structure, beneath the planting beds.

This heated structure may have served as a forcing frame or propagating pit, providing optimum conditions for encouraging the growth of young or out of season plants. It appears comparable to a 'flued pit', a type of structures described by Loudon (1825, 228) under the heading 'adapted frames'. The Alnwick example is however, clearly more substantial than these small forcing pits. Many variations on the design of such pits are documented (e.g. Loudon 1825, 300–03), which may have developed according to location, the skills of the gardener and the materials to hand. They would have been used for the early forcing of plants, or for cultivation of melons or pineapples, relying on heat provided by fermenting organic matter (manure or tanners' bark) supplemented by artificial heat:

*'a flue, which either makes the circuit of the pit, or runs along and returns by its back wall….whenever the heat of the bark or other fermentable matter subsides, or whenever the air in the pit is too moist, and in danger of generating damps, a fire can be lighted which will remove both evils.'* (Loudon 1825, 228).

## Steam heating

Technologically, as with other forms of hothouse heating, steam heating was a trend which had its proponents and detractors. It was generally quickly superseded by hot water systems; the pages of contemporary periodicals of the early nineteenth century are full of recommendations and discussions on the uses of steam in heating systems. Brown advocated the use of steam in 1817, asserting that it was beneficial to the cultivation of pines, extending the growing season, providing 'sweet' heat (in contrast to that provided by hot air flues), needing less fuel to maintain and allowing heat to be distributed in two different ways. Steam from the boiler would be passed along pipes fitted with safety valves, these valves (or 'steam-cocks') could be opened allowing steam into the growing house, as required; an hour at most would be the maximum requirement (Brown 1817, 322). The application of steam to plants would obviously be of benefit to those tropical species which prefer a moist, humid environment (such as the pineapple). It may not have been so beneficial to the grape or peach. Steam was also transferred along flues, similar to those employed in hot air systems. Archaeologically, therefore, in the absence of any heating apparatus, the evidence of flues might appear similar, whether designed to carry hot air or steam.

Loudon, writing in the same year, also discusses the use of

steam. Clearly extensively employed in the heating systems of factories and larger residences, Loudon (1817, 55–56) suggests that steam may be preferable to the use of hot air flues in hothouses for several reasons, which may be summarised as: greater control of the temperature; a more even temperature throughout a structure; a sweeter, cleaner and pleasanter environment; a more economical mode of producing heat. Yet, steam was clearly not very widely used at this date, and Loudon observes:

*'If the advantages of heating by steam in hothouses are, or promise to be, so considerable, it may be asked why, having been tried for nearly twenty years, it has not become more general. To this I answer, that in respect to the trials mentioned above, they were exceedingly imperfect; and that the steam was applied more as dew or moisture, than as a vehicle for communicating heat'… 'it is not likely that steam will soon, if ever, become so general as to supersede in horticultural buildings the use of smoke flues…'* (Loudon 1817, 55, 59).

Interestingly, with respect to Alnwick, he continues:

*'I shall only add, as a general idea, that in large establishments where the mansion, the family stables, the farm, and the garden, are all at some distance from each other (1) it will be worth while to have separate apparatus for each of these departments'*

The note which accompanies this text *'(1) As at Woborn Abbey, Alnwick Castle, Harewood House, &c.'*, is somewhat equivocal. Loudon may be suggesting that steam was being used extensively in the gardens at Alnwick at this time, although it seems more likely that he is presenting examples of places where separate steam plants would be desirable.

The first definitive reference to the use of steam at Alnwick suggests that it was an early and short-lived introduction predating Loudon's remarks by 10 years and related to the construction of a pine stove by John Hay of Edinburgh in 1807. Hay, who had become interested in the application of steam in hothouses in the late eighteenth century, was commissioned to redesign the hothouses at Alnwick. In 1829 he recalled his early, experimental and unsuccessful use of steam at Alnwick, suggesting improvements. The resulting 'improved plan' was based on his early experimentation at Alnwick and details the application of steam in a chamber filled with round stones. This invention was to result in Mr Hay being awarded the London Medal by the Caledonian Horticultural Society in 1828 (Memoirs of the Caledonian Society, fourth volume, 600; see Fig. 9.4):

*'In the year 1807, I had the honour to be consulted by his Grace the late Duke of Northumberland, with a view to rebuilding the hot-houses at Alnwick Castle, which then chiefly consisted of grape and pine houses, and was desired by his Grace to furnish him with plans for executing the work on the most approved principles. His Grace directed me to provide for the heating of one of the pinestoves by steam, as he had seen an attempt of this kind made in Scotland a number of years before; the*

*particular place was not mentioned. The duke's desire to have one of his pine-stoves constructed, with a view to attain this object, led me to consider the subject attentively. It occurred to me that a close chamber below the pit filled with stones and heated by steam introduced among them, from a boiler placed at a short distance, would answer the purpose; and in this manner one of the stoves was accordingly designed and executed. But the pit was of large dimensions; and the steam-pipe, which had also to supply other two houses, being only two inches bore, was found insufficient to give out the portion of steam necessary fully to effect the heating of the mass· of stones under the pine-pit. The apparatus in this case, not being quite perfect, the use of it was not long continued.'* (Hay 1829).

Hay's text may here be referencing the 'pine-house' range illustrated on Barnfather's map (1829), however, several factors militate against this and it is considered far more likely that this refers to the somewhat enigmatic Structure 1. This furnace and associated pits were apparently short-lived, as was Hay's stove, constructed in 1807 but 'not long continued', whereas the pine-house illustrated by Barnfather was still apparently in use in 1829. Hay's furnace was separate from the boiler, which was placed at a 'close distance' and the pits were filled with stones; both factors correspond well with the archaeological remains of Structure 1,

whereas Barnfather's pine-houses appear to be connected to the backhouse beyond. The relative proportions of the boiler house and associated heated pit might also support this interpretation as would the fact that the furnace was set at a short distance. Any associated fire-surrounds or boilers had been robbed out (presumably for recycling of iron). If this interpretation is accepted, then the second 'flue' leading out of the furnace in the west may have housed the steam pipes which supplied the building. Plausibly the eastern flue may have superseded this.

Steam heating appears thus to have been an early introduction to the Alnwick Walled Garden. The extent to which the method was applied after the first decade of the nineteenth century is unknown. It has been argued here that the Garden 3 hothouses were heated initially via hot-air flues, although, given the lack of surviving evidence for furnaces or boilers, steam may have been employed; the brick flues would have appeared similar in either case. Existing hothouses which had previously been heated via hot air flues could be adapted to take steam, resulting in a more fuel-efficient system:

*'I saw several hot-houses in London heated with metal pipes; iron or copper. But metal, I found, transmitted the heat too rapidly. I therefore have employed stone-flues, with only small subsidiary metal pipes.'* (Rhodes 1829, 512).

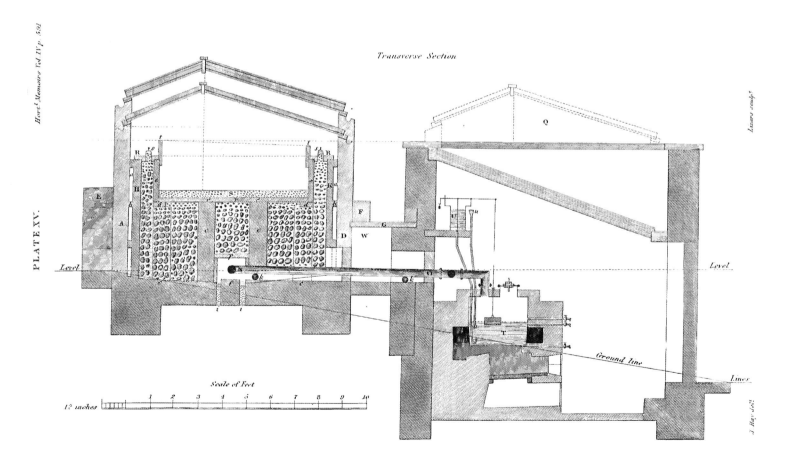

**Fig. 9.4** 'Mr. Hay's Steam-Pit': a cross section showing the improvements effected following the construction of a steam heated pit at Alnwick (from Hay 1829)

## Hot water pipes and boilers

Boilers and hot water pipes appear to have been introduced into all the hothouses at Alnwick in a somewhat piecemeal fashion; although ultimately this form of heating was to become ubiquitous. Archaeologically it can be difficult to precisely date when these systems were introduced to the hothouses. The heating systems were subject to frequent modifications, one system replacing another, often in the same location. The principal of hot water heating was relatively simple, although it developed over time with boilers becoming increasingly sophisticated. Essentially, the system relied on a boiler producing hot water, which circulated through pipes running around the glasshouse, in a manner similar to modern central-heating systems. A design for a boiler, dated 1831, published in the Gardener's Magazine shows the system at its most basic, relying on a simple copper boiler and copper pipes:

*'My boiler, which cost 1 l. 3s. 9d., is constructed of strong copper, is oval, measures 18 in. by J 2 in., and is in the form and size of such a dish-cover as is put over a roast goose. Mr. Smith's boiler is 28 in. by 18 in.; it rests upon its two ends over the fire, and the flames, mounting over the two sides, enter the flue or chimney at the top. The sketch (fig. 18. [reproduced as Fig. 9.5]) will illustrate the kind of boiler which I mean.'* (Mearns 1831, 142).

Mearns goes on to describe how this system may be used in conjunction with hot flue systems; it is thus quite plausible that one or more system may have been in operation at any one time within a single building at Alnwick.

Boiler technology quickly developed from this modest starting point, with the adoption of wrought and cast-iron boilers and pipes; modifications and improvements proliferated. There is little archaeological evidence to suggest the types of boiler in use in the various hothouses at Alnwick. The evidence that does survive mainly takes the form of the pipework and water tanks that would have been part of this system, all the boilers having been apparently systematically removed (perhaps reused to help the war effort in the 1940s).

The earliest evidence for the insertion of a boiler at Alnwick comes from a bill dated 1836 (the 'Bailey bill' 1836; DP/D3/I/43). This account records three new boilers which were inserted into the peach houses (Hothouse 2) at the same time as a new curvilinear frontage was installed. The bill describes the apparatus thus:

*'Three sets of Hot Water Apparatus to heat the above range of Peach Houses including three improved shape wrought-iron Boilers with strong double doors and frames, furnaces and bearing Bars dead and cover plates, flue doors and dampers, cast iron straight and curved oval and round pipes, Reservoirs, brackets and slings…'* (DP/D3/I/43).

It is interesting to note here that while archaeological evidence suggests that ultimately most of the furnace houses were infilled (and thus that the glasshouse ranges were ultimately heated by single boilers) originally, the conversion of Hothouse 2 to hot water heating employed three boilers, presumably located in the three deeper backhouse elements of the structure. The mushroom house in Hothouse 2 appears to have continued to be heated via its original hot air flue, as there is no evidence for the removal or modification of the original furnace.

Hothouse 2 may have been the first of the heated houses to be fitted with hot water boilers, although this could not be conclusively demonstrated. At what point other hothouses may have received boilers and been heated by hot water pipes is unknown, although available evidence suggests they are likely to

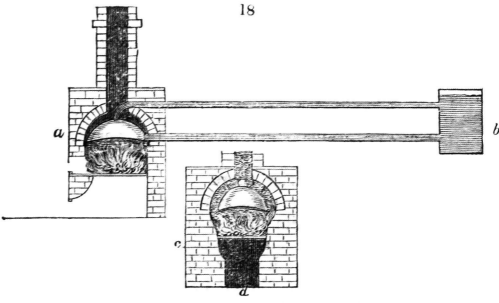

18

**Fig. 9.5** An 'improved boiler for hothouses'; this illustration of 1831 illustrates the principal of hot water heating at its most basic (Mearns, 1831, 142, Gardener's Magazine)

*a,* **Side-view of the boiler.**    *b,* **The feeder.**    *c,* **Front view of the boiler.**    *d,* **The ash pit.**

have been modified more or less contemporaneously and these changes were part of the third garden, presumably around the mid-1830s or later. The chronology of change appears to have been particularly rapid at this period. Barnfather's plan of 1829 illustrates the Peach House and Pinery which preceded the substantial rebuilding of Hothouse 2 and construction of Hothouse 4. The architects' drawings, dated 1830, including details of the ventilation systems for the new buildings (TAG Z/1/4, see Fig. 9.9), provide a date after which Hothouse 4 (and by implication Hothouse 2) were built (or remodelled). Yet these buildings initially included features which appear to be hot flues. The Bailey Bill of 1836 (DP/D3/I/43) records three new boilers being inserted into the Peach House at the same time as a curvilinear frontage was installed. The implication here is that Hothouses 2 and 4 may have been provided with a heating system which lasted no more that 6 years at most. Given the duke's interests in a time of rapid innovation this is perhaps not as surprising as it may at first appear.

Recently excavated evidence from Auckland Castle, some 58 miles (93km) south of Alnwick provides evidence for the change from furnace and flue heating to circulating hot water in the form of stubs of flow and return cast iron heating pipes, which remain undated, within the upper, or northernmost, of the two pinery-vineries. The pipework stubs appeared to be related to a boiler placed in the former western furnace stokehole in the back-shed range and utilising the original exhaust flue. It is considered that the original furnace heating system may have been replaced around 1840 or later, taking advantage of the increasing availability of reliable boilers and cast-iron components. Very little remained of this installation though a damper on the exhaust flue bore a manufacturers casting [Falkirk Iron Company] which suggests the era of catalogue components and perhaps points to a later nineteenth-century date than originally speculated.

Both pinery-vineries were subsequently supplied with heat by a "district main" served by a vertical water tube boiler set up at the base of the slope to the east of the lower pinery-vinery. Elements of the linking flow and return pipe work between the two ranges were recovered and the boiler survived intact, though sadly without an indication of the manufacturer. The seating for a second vertical water tube boiler was also excavated – this system serving the big lean-to range on the north wall via a long brick-built pipe conduit. The structure containing both boilers appears on an undated tracing, apparently based on the Ordnance Survey 1:1250 scale partial revision of 1912–13 (Durham University Library Special Collections: DDR/BP/EST/4/12). The final boiler-heated system, fired by oil in the later twentieth century, was set up above the older boilers and served a combination of reused cast iron pipework in the lower pinery-vinery and smaller diameter steel pipework in the upper pinery-vinery and back shed range.

## Maintaining the heating systems

The provision of heating was a subject which continued to occupy the gardeners at Alnwick throughout the century. The head gardener was notably reorganising heating systems in 1880 (see Chapter 6). Meanwhile, the conversion of the original walled garden to its much more decorative Italianate design in the 1860s presumably necessitated the expansion of the working kitchen gardens including into the western extension which, with the provision of new propagating pits, bore the brunt of the production side of the gardens. The new propagating pits constructed in the 1860s (extant at the time of writing) were heated by a furnace housed beneath the old vinery, subsequently apparently converted for the propagation of pines. Hot water pipes supplied heat to the propagating houses. A cross section demonstrates how hot water was conveyed beneath staging set within the propagating houses (PB 224; Fig. 9.6).

Maintenance and modifications to the existing systems of heating continued into the early decades of the twentieth century. A bill dated November 3 1916 from Henry Walker and Son Ltd of Gallowgate Iron Works, Newcastle on Tyne, provides a quote for installing a new Calorifier in the Castle Gardens (COW-A747).

## A resurgence of steam

There is ample evidence for the much later use of steam in the Alnwick Walled Garden. Correspondence found within the castle archives relates to the insertion of steam boilers to supply the castle and gardens (DP/D5/I/62) and comprises two bundles of papers. The proposals are dated January 1890, with an invoice for the resulting work dated December 1890 and further proposals throughout 1891. The documents include a plan and correspondence which suggests that the boiler was situated at least 500ft (152m) from the castle (to avoid danger of explosions). A series of documents from a Mr G. Reavell relate to the extension of the steam heating system to power the servants' baths and a laundry room and provide heating for the library. The possible insertion of a Bennies Patent Shovel Stoker (self-cleaning camel boiler) is also discussed, presumably to cope with the additional demand. Accounts of December 4, 1890 record a cost of £11,540 15s 4d for insertion of electric lighting, steam apparatus and repairs to a waterway. The document ends with a note demonstrating that the heating had been put in place by late 1890:

*'The Steam Heating has been extended to the following places, viz: Garden Walls, Muscat House, Breakfast Room, Side Entrance, Chapel and Barbican'* (DP/DS/I/62).

This document demonstrates extensive use of steam in both the castle and the gardens. The boiler housing appears to have been

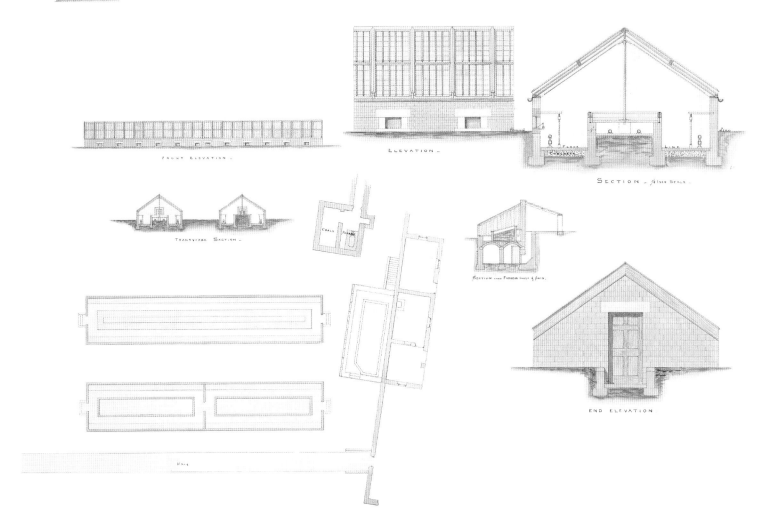

**Fig. 9.6** Plans, cross-sections and elevations of propagation pits and houses in the new kitchen garden of Garden 4, dated 1863 (PB 224)

located to the west of the Alnwick Walled Garden, at the corner of the 'new kitchen garden' (see Fig. 6.19). This building first appears on mapping in 1897 (Fig. 8.21). According to the 1900 water supply plan (TAG Z/1/3, see Fig. 9.13), steam heating only seems to have served the Muscat House (Hothouse 7) within the original walled garden. A report in *The Gardeners' Chronicle* for 1902 however suggests that the kitchen garden was supplied exclusively be steam:

*'There are some excellent span-roofed planthouses in the kitchen garden… The houses have mostly iron and copper ribs. The young gardeners have no stoking to do here, all the houses being heated by steam, which demands the attention of an engineer at all times. The boilers are placed near the Gardener's House, and unfortunately a large smoke-shaft likewise'* (*The Gardeners' Chronicle* 1902, 286–287)

The plan illustrates a smoke shaft, inserted in the 1860s to enable smoke to be drawn away from the garden, which may imply the provision of boilers serving a 'district heating' scheme, using circulating hot water to heat the various hothouses. This would have obviated the need to stoke all the individual furnaces and small boilers around the garden, providing a considerable saving in labour and was a common trend at the time, particularly in larger establishments such as Alnwick (Harry Beamish, pers. comm.).

Evidence of iron pipework within the hot wall at the north-west corner of the garden suggests that at some point this also received either hot water or steam pipes, although the water supply plan does not show steam being supplied, despite assertions within correspondence that a heated wall was supplied by steam. Either the water plan does not illustrate the full supply of steam, or the reference to garden walls (DP/DS/I/62) relates to the new kitchen garden west of the Gardener's House only.

## 9.3 Glazing and Ventilation Systems in use at Alnwick

*'Economy in glass is therefore no economy, and produces effects really as disagreeable to the eye as injurious to vegetation.'* (Loudon 1827, 83)

Initially hothouse glazing would have been held in place by timber sashes; the earliest stoves would have had solid roofs and a progression from solid to glazed roofs in 'stove houses' through the eighteenth century is illustrated in the developments shown between the 1731 first edition and the 1752 revision of Miller's Gardener's Dictionary (Grant 2013, 18).

It is probable that the earliest hothouses at Alnwick would have had glazed panels held in place with timber. The height of the roofs and angle of the lights, particularly in the earlier manifestations of these structures, remains unknown. It is important to note that as none of the glazing survived, any reconstructions presented within this volume are based on the simplest arrangement of low front wall and sloping roof, with roof pitch based on the illustrations contained in Loudon (1825); these would ultimately be replaced by curvilinear frontages, with wrought iron glazing bars.

At the beginning of the nineteenth century cast iron began to be increasingly used in garden buildings, following the recommendations of Humphrey Repton. An increasing awareness and understanding of the effect of sunlight on cultivated plants led to developments in the design of glasshouse glazing systems (Grant 2013, 25). Contemporary accounts demonstrate that much consideration went into the most beneficial angle (or angles) for the setting of glazing panes (Hix 1996, 30–31). It was George Mackenzie (1815) who was to instigate a revolution in the design of hothouse roofs, proposing that these should be hemispherical to maximise the available light entering the glasshouse, whatever the time of year. Knight modified this design, using a segment of a hemisphere (Loudon 1825, 314); a design apparently ultimately adopted at Alnwick. Loudon's invention of the wrought iron sash bar (1816) made the application of these theoretical technological advances more practicable. Despite the revolution promised by Loudon's invention in glasshouse design, this development did not meet with universal approval and there were still those who continued to espouse the use of wood. Nevertheless, the new technology was widely adopted.  Long curved lengths of frame were developed, which allowed the use of a wide variety of 'curvilinear' forms (see Hix 1996, 36–41; the term 'curvilinear' is applied extensively in contemporary literature and refers to a building in which the glazed elements are curved, in whatever plane). Curvilinear glasshouses provided more and better light than conventional sloped roofs; the solid pieces of wrought iron used contained no crevices in which corrosion might develop. They

were solid, yet flexible in any direction and retained strength when bent, in contrast to timber. Wrought iron was more durable than softwood, strong enough to span a large structure. The glazing bars were thinner than those of timber thus casting less shadow. These innovations spawned a plethora of different hothouse and conservatory roof forms, including semi-globes and ridge-and-furrow roofs, although at Alnwick, with the possible exception of the central conservatory (Hothouse 3) which appears to have had a complex glazing arrangement, the hothouses appear to have adopted a relatively simple, albeit elegant, design.

The earliest structure at Alnwick to be provided with a glazing arrangement supported on a wrought iron framework may well have been the central conservatory, Hothouse 3. In 1827 Richards and Jones (who were recommended in the manufacture of glazing bars by Loudon and were working for the Duke of Northumberland at Syon) were 'engaged in erecting a most extensive range of the same kind at Alnwick Castle' (Loudon 1827, 108).

Loudon was also to forge a commercial relationship with manufacturers W and D Bailey, who had patented Loudon's innovative wrought iron glazing bar in 1819. The Baileys are known to have worked on the glazing and heating system for Hothouse 2 and the use of curvilinear roofs at Alnwick can be demonstrated by a Bill of 1836, from D and E Bailey (the successors of W and D Bailey), which gives a date to the construction of iron and glass roofing as well as the introduction of hot water heating systems:

*'A range of Curvilinear Peach Houses with roofs formed of patent moulded wrought iron Sash Bars with cast iron coping plates and Gutters supported by cast iron standards…'* (DP/D3/I/43).

The date at which the glazing of the other hothouses in the garden may have been modified in line with these developments was not established. A cross-section of the garden, produced in 1859, illustrates the vinery with a curvilinear frontage (Fig. 9.7) demonstrating that this form of glazing was in use by this date on the vinery (Hothouse 4). It is important to note that this drawing appears to have been produced in order to illustrate changes in levels across the garden. It is not necessarily precise in its depiction of individual structures, indeed the illustration of the northern conservatory (Hothouse 6) is clearly not accurate, having an incorrect number of arches. Nevertheless, it suggests that Hothouse 4 was provided with curved glazing in a wrought iron framework by this date. The archaeological record suggests a rebuild to the front wall of the glasshouse, from which it may be inferred that the building would have been reglazed. Short lengths of curved glazing bar survived in 1998 (Kent 1998) although these did not survive at the time of the archaeological survey. All the hothouses in the Alnwick Walled Garden (with the exception of the later northern conservatory) are likely to have been provided with curvilinear glazing by the 1870s:

'*Either from necessity, caused I presume by local circumstances, or from the idea that fruit and flowers ought to grow together, all the forcing-houses are within the flower garden. They are fine noble houses made of iron, curvilinear in shape, which makes them externally light and pleasing to the eye, and everything has been done to make them harmonise with their surroundings, so that the visitor, who threads his way through them upon an autumn day, will pronounce them not the least pleasing feature of the flower garden. Grapes, Peaches, and Pines, are all grown here to perfection, which will be noticed in a future number.*' ('J. T.' 1874, 100–101).

With little surviving on which to base reconstruction of the glasshouse frontages, parallels may be sought elsewhere. A recently renovated hothouse at Felton Park, Northumberland, may provide a visual parallel for at least some details of the glazing schemes used, in the absence of surviving remains of the glasshouse frontages at Alnwick. The date of the construction of the glasshouse at Felton Park is unknown, but combined evidence strongly supports a date between 1830 and 1840 (Beamish 2016), which correlates well with the dating provided for the modifications to Hothouse 2. On the basis of this evidence and that of the Bailey Bill of 1836 (DP/D3/I/43), it is presumed that curvilinear frontages were provided for Hothouse 4 and Hothouse 5 at a similar time or soon after.

The small glazing panes used at this time were dictated partly by window tax, cost increasing exponentially with size, as well as by the current technologies of manufacturing crown or cylinder glass (Woods and Warren 1988, 89). Greenhouse glass in the 1830s would have been prone to breakage, meaning that smaller panes were more manageable and easier to replace. Moreover, small glazing panels would better fit within the curving iron frameworks of curvilinear glasshouses. It frequently had a slight greenish tinge, which actually assisted in reducing the scorching of plants by the sun on the hottest days of the year. Hence the glazing which accompanied the use of curving iron frames comprised small, slightly overlapping, scalloped or 'fish scale' panes. As with any aspect of hothouse construction at this time, innovation was the key and a range of thought prevailed on how to glaze and whether to seal with putty, or not. Panes generally had parallel straight sides on the long (vertical) axis, sometimes with curved ends, creating a beautiful effect as well as encouraging condensation to migrate to the middle of the pane and away from the ribs. As evidenced at Felton Park, this glazing technique enabled structures to admit maximum light despite the small panes of glass available (see Fig. 9.10). Moreover, a series of small, overlapping panes would be essential to accommodate the curves of the wrought iron framework of the glasshouse; structural components and

glazing thus complemented one another. A paper of 1818 in the Transactions of the Horticultural Society exemplifies these concerns, recommending the use of glass with a curved lower and upper edge over a simple parallelogram:

'*In a pane eight inches in width, a curvature of five- eighths of an inch deep in the centre will be sufficient. The glazing is to be executed in the usual manner, except that the panes should lap over each other as little as possible; a lap of one-eighth of an inch is ample, less will do; and however small the lap, no rain will ever penetrate… Those who prefer a close house, may bed the panes with putty between them*' (Gowen 1820, 246–247).

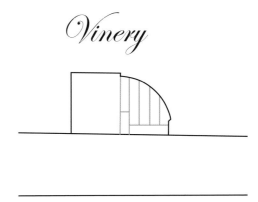

**Fig. 9.7** Detail of the gable end and southern elevation of Hothouse 4, from an architect's drawing *c.* 1860, showing the curvilinear glasshouse front (PB 236)

**Fig. 9.8** Gable end of the Felton Park glasshouse, looking east (VR 2016)

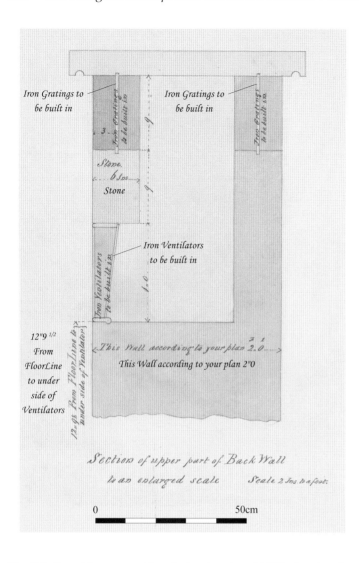

Ventilation, to control temperature and regulate air movement through the glasshouses, would have been as important as heat and light. This may have been provided initially via opening or removeable window sashes and roof lights but, following the rebuilding of Hothouse 2 and the construction of Hothouse 4 and Hothouse 5, a sophisticated system of ventilation was in use which enabled the temperature in the hothouses to be moderated using a series of shutters and associated vents at the top of the walls. Ventilation was supplied by iron shutters at the top of each wall arranged in three groups of nine, corresponding to the three divisions within each glasshouse range. These would have been operated via pulleys. Ventilation would have been needed both along the front wall and at the top of the back wall in order to allow movement of air within the house (Harry Beamish, pers. comm.). This can be seen in the opening sashes along the front wall of the glasshouse at Felton Park (see Fig. 9.10) and at Gibside. At Alnwick, the provision of opening shutters at the base of the walls can be seen in the northern conservatory (Hothouse 6; Fig. 5.10, Fig. 5.11). Whether the frontages of the other hothouses relied on opening sashes, or were provided with shuttered ventilation within the walls, is unknown. Evidence for the earliest phase of Hothouse 4 suggests a series of brick columns; these may have accommodated opening shutters later replaced with glazed openings within the curvilinear glasshouse frontage, as at Felton Park, alternatively this might have been an element of the foundations of the building, designed to accommodate the roots of the vines planted here.

An 1830 architect's drawing for a vinery (given the date and the details on the drawing, presumably Hothouse 4) provides detailed cross-sections of the system at the top of the walls in operation.

**Fig. 9.9** Detail from an architect's drawing dated 1830, showing the proposed ventilation system of the vinery (TAG Z/1/4) (scale 1:12)

**Fig. 9.10** Felton Park Glasshouse looking northeast; the upper parts of the ventilators can be seen above the glazed portion of the structure and opening sashes are visible at the base of the glasshouse; the intact grilles resemble those used at Alnwick (VR 2016)

**Fig. 9.11** Detail of open ventilators at the top of the back wall inside the glasshouse and pulley to operate the shutter inside the curvilinear glasshouse at Felton Park, Morpeth (VR 2016)

The drawing appears to be accurate in representing what was found within the standing buildings survey. An iron ventilator at the top of the internal part of the wall could be opened and shut using pulleys, according to need (Fig. 9.9). The glazing for the glasshouse would have been attached to the stone or wood work above this. Ironwork grilles above glazing level, protected by a coping stone top to the wall, allowed the hot air to escape (see Fig. 4.15, Fig. 4.23, Fig. 4.33). This type of ventilation system appears to have been relatively common within hothouses in the area. The curvilinear glasshouse at Felton Park employs a similar system (Fig. 9.10, Fig. 9.11), as does the peach house in the walled garden at Wallington Hall, Northumberland.

The northern conservatory, Hothouse 6, employed a different system of glazing. Supported on an iron framework, the conservatory had high, vertical, glazed panels with a sloping roof; presumably with opening lights at the top of the roof. Ventilation from the bottom of the glasshouse was provided through shutters set into the base of the walls on all four sides of the building.

## 9.4 Water Supply

*'A copious supply of water is essential to a good kitchen-garden, and, from whatever source it is furnished, should be distributed either in reservoirs or open cisterns, or in pipes, properly protected, over the garden, and in hot-houses'* (Loudon 1825, 463).

A readily available supply of water would have been as crucial to the garden and the successful growing of produce as any of the buildings contained within it, yet the earliest phase of the Alnwick Kitchen Gardens provide little evidence for the nature of any water supplies. The earliest kitchen garden, Garden 1, had a pond at its centre. There was no evidence for the drainage system which may have supplied the pond, nor of any water pipes leading from it. The pond may have functioned as a dipping pool allowing gardeners to extract water by hand, lowering watering cans into the pool. This may have been a necessity at this early date, but rainwater would be preferable to any water conveyed from tanks via iron pipes, and watering by hand essential for delicate young plants and seedlings.

A well, identified during the excavation and assumed to be associated with Garden 2, may have provided for the needs of the garden in the late eighteenth and early nineteenth centuries. Another well lay just outside the central northern entrance to the garden, labelled on the water supply map of 1896 as 'old well' (Fig. 9.12). Culverts, draining water from the downpipes of hothouses, would presumably have led to collecting tanks, or fed into ponds. The construction of Hay's steam heated pine pit in 1807 suggests that the garden must have had some rudimentary piped water supply by this date, although no evidence for such was found.

A report by William Barnfather, the duke's Clerk of Works, in the Business Minutes for 1826 describes the existing water supply and makes recommendations for the provision of water and sewerage and the construction of a cistern:

*'Since the failure of the Spring in the Deer Park, it has been found necessary to use a portion of the Water from the Open Reservoir, in order to Keep up the daily supply for the Castle and Gardens. And as this Water cannot be said to be altogether free from Animalculae, it may be well to suggest that a Close Tank should be constructed capable of containing 20, 30 or 40,000 Gallons, into which the Water might be collected, and the Surplus to pass through the Tank into the present Reservoir, which might be deemed a reserve in case of Fire, or a large quantity being suddenly wanted. This would be a great improvement on the existing arrangement, and the Works would then be perfectly efficient, having a head of water equal to 280,000 Ale Gallons.* (BM 14, 229).

Barnfather's resulting 1829 plan illustrates the proposed plan for a piped water supply to the gardens, providing for the hothouse ranges and a central pond (see Fig. 4.3; Fig. 8.6). A metal pipe runs through the Barneyside Gate of the castle, along the path between castle and garden, through the original north-west entrance and

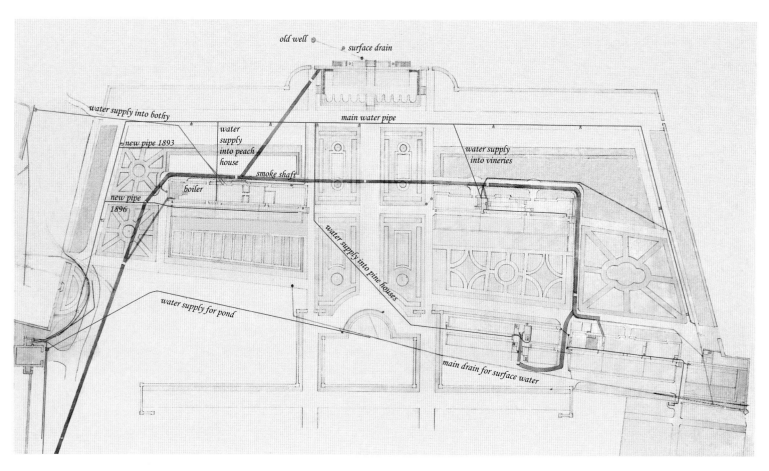

**Fig. 9.12** The Castle Gardens Water Supply 1896, with original annotations enhanced for clarity (TAG Z/1/2)

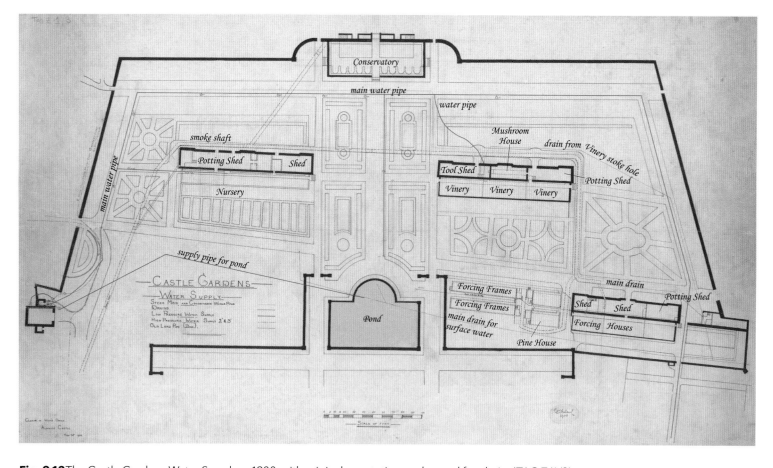

**Fig. 9.13** The Castle Gardens Water Supply *c.* 1900, with original annotations enhanced for clarity (TAG Z/1/3)

along the path running adjacent to the west wall through the original walled garden and to the south-west corner of the later kitchen garden where a water tower is shown. Another pipe runs from the water tower, along the western path of the kitchen garden and original walled garden, adjacent to the supply pipe coming in, along the northern path of the walled garden, with a branch leading off to feed the lily pond, and along the eastern part of the garden into the south-east corner. Ultimately this plan was not strictly adhered to and the water tower was located in a more central position, just south of the Gardener's House, straddling the west wall of the new kitchen garden (see Fig. 4.1). The plan has been amended in red ink to show the new location. Hydrants may have enabled this supply to be tapped into, but when initially laid out the supply lines were simple.

Once boilers had been introduced into the hothouses there would have been a need for each building to be provided with its own water supply, to feed the tanks which were identified archaeologically, and which in turn would have supplied the boilers. The water supply first outlined by Barnfather was to be modified and added to over time. A plan of the water supply in 1896 (TAG Z/1/2; Fig. 9.12) illustrates a palimpsest of water-supply pipes. Each hothouse had its own supply. The dating of individual pipes illustrated here suggests that there was almost certainly a need to replace these over time. The system appears to have been simplified by *c*. 1900 (TAG Z/1/3; Fig. 9.13).

**Fig. 9.14** This tap, a modern replacement of an original feature in the vinery at Felton Park, allows rain-water collected from the gutters of the curvilinear glasshouse to be used inside the building (VR 2016)

Despite this investment, some of the water for watering of plants may still have been collected via drainage culverts and from the gutters of buildings, leading into the drainage system, or plausibly feeding water butts. A complex of drainage culverts was excavated which were apparently associated with the 1830s' construction of Hothouses 3 and 4. Water would always be a valuable resource and it is likely that the head gardener, assisted by those who designed and constructed the buildings within the garden, would have gone to considerable lengths to ensure that when plentiful, rain water was collected and reserved for later use (Fig. 9.14).

In addition to the evidence for culverts, proposals for hothouse construction include drainage holes cut through the foundation walls at the front corners of the glasshouse (see Fig. 9.31).

## 9.5 Technology Applied: Specific Requirements for Particular Plants

*'Consequently gardeners, through trial and error, and the application of innovative techniques, developed glasshouses in exquisite forms; the heating equipment that they advanced to protect the hard won exotics was far more sophisticated than that of any appliance in domestic use at the time'* (Hix 1996, 6).

The discussion above provides a general introduction to the ways in which technologies developed and may have been applied at Alnwick. The following examines evidence for individual hothouses, particularly those recorded during the standing building survey, in relation to the produce grown within them. Specifically, this looks at the ways in which buildings were arranged, glazed and heated to provide the necessary conditions for growing pineapples, grapes, peaches or nectarines and mushrooms; comparing the excavated structures with contemporary descriptions, comparable surviving structures and excavated evidence. With each of these examples, and in spite of the clear labelling of structures on surviving documents, it is important to bear in mind that more than one type of plant may have been cultivated within a single glasshouse. Additional crops may well have been fruited in the walled garden glasshouses, such as early strawberries, which may have been cultivated on high shelves along the back wall. A high stone shelf within the pinery (Hothouse 5) may have been provided for this purpose. Whilst hothouses may occasionally have been used for protecting, or bringing on, tender young plants to plant out in the kitchen garden, in a large establishment such as Alnwick there would most probably have been a separate frame yard where most of the propagation would have been carried out (Harry Beamish, pers. comm.). Melon frames are illustrated on Barnfather's map of 1829 (see Fig. 8.6), towards the south-east of the garden, and were apparently carried on into the design of Garden 4 as they continue to be illustrated in subsequent maps (e.g. Fig. 8.20).

## Pineapple houses and Pinery-Vineries

Since the development of hothouses, whatever the produce grown in them, was driven by the cultivation of the pineapple (see Chapter 10 below) it is logical to begin with a consideration of the technological developments of pineries in light of the evidence from Alnwick.

The method of cultivating pineapples using the heat thrown off during the fermentation of waste oak bark from the tanning process was developed in the Netherlands in the late seventeenth century (Grant 2013, 21). Tanners' bark was found to produce a stronger, moister and longer-lasting heat than manure, qualities which were essential to the successful cultivation of the pineapple. Pineapples would be planted in deep pots plunged into the warm fermenting bark.

The pinery or pine house was a natural progression of this system supplementing the heat thrown off by fermenting tanners' bark with artificial heat, via hot flues, steam pipes and flues and, ultimately, hot water systems. Pineapples take at least two years to mature, requiring different conditions at different stages of growth. For this reason, pineapples tended to be grown in a three-stage successional scheme; after the suckers or crowns had rooted in the first year they were transplanted into a 'succession bed' to be grown on in the second year, before being moved to a final 'fruiting bed' in the third. Under ideal circumstances the pineapple would be started in a low pit and moved to a larger and warmer 'stove'. Practically speaking the whole process would often be housed in one structure and pineries would therefore contain two or three separate sections, divided by partitions and individually heated so that the environments in each could be separately controlled.

The pinery would typically be provided with a low and relatively flat roof to bring the plants close to the sun. Nicol's pinery consists of three pits (Loudon 1825, 502) one for crowns and suckers, one for succession and one for fruiting plants. The fruiting pit was placed in the centre, bark beds and flues provided the necessary heat which was conducted to the front of the house first before proceeding to the back. The fruiting pit itself may have been provided with two furnaces, one flue to run above the other. Flues may have been small, 5–6in. wide and 9–10in. deep.

Developing rapidly out of this emerging technology, the heat generated in the pinery was utilised to extend the growing season of the vines. In the pine and grape stove, also known as the 'pinery-vinery', the stems of vines, grown outside the front of the glasshouse, were trained into the structure and under the rafters of the roof. The scheme had the benefit of providing light and heat for the vines, whilst they, in turn, shaded the pineapples beneath. Elegant as this design was in principle, it was not ultimately a great success, since the two crops have different requirements; the pineapple, being a tropical plant, thrives in a humid environment, whilst the vine prefers a much drier climate. The pinery-vinery form of glasshouse was thus a relatively short-lived trend.

a  pit
b  back path
c/d  flues

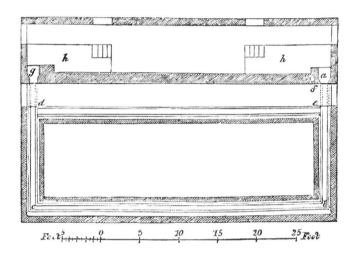

**Fig. 9.15** Plan and elevation of a pinery-vinery at Kew (from Loudon 1825)

**Fig. 9.16** The upper pinery-vinery at Auckland Castle, looking west (VR 2017)

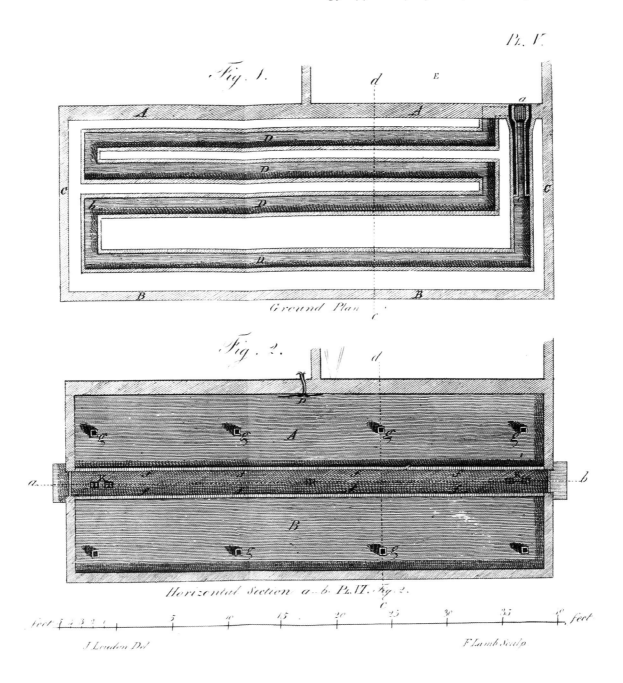

FIG. I

*The ground or foundation plan of the walls and flues.*

A  Back wall.

B  Front wall.

C  End walls.

D  Flues.

E  Back shed.

a  Furnace.

c  Termination of the side vacuity.

b  Termination of the top vacuity or air-flue.

FIG. II

Surface plan supposing the house cut over by the line a .... b, in plate VI. fig. 2.

A and B  Two pine pits.

a ... b  Passage through the centre of the house.

D   A vine introduced from behind intended to cover the back wall (ie spine wall). Vines may also be introduced at the two front corners to run up the sashes.

g g  Air or steam tubes.

K K  Registers or valves for admitting heated air either from the air-flue, or from the large vacuity under the pit, or for pouring in water to cover the surface of the whole pit, or to cover the surface of the air-flue, and thus to produce either steam or moist heat in abundance.

f  The situation of holes made in the parapets for pouring in water to the ruble [sic] stone vacuity under the bed of earth, see B.fig. 2. plate VI.

**Fig. 9.17** Plan of a pinery with a transcript of the original accompanying text (from Loudon 1805)

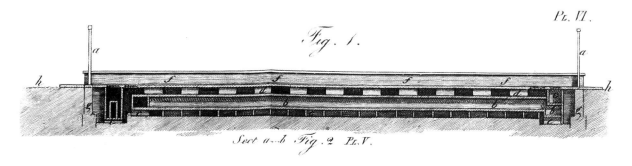

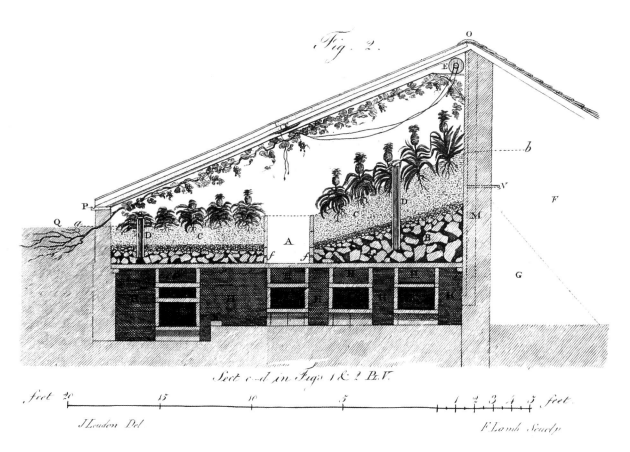

FIG. I

*Longitudinal section of Figure 1 and 2 in Plate V. according to the line a .... b, fig. 2.*

a   Doors at the ends.
b   Smoke flue.
c   Supports of ditto.
d   Support of passage-pavement .
e   The communication of the air-flue with the registers, K K, in fig. 2. plate V.
f   Holes in the wall of the pit for pouring in water, etc.
g   End walls.
h h Ground level.

FIG. II

*Transverse section of fig. 2. plate V. upon a larger scale.*

A   Passage through the house.
B   Ruble [sic] stone vacuity.
C   Earth in which the plants are inserted, either in pots or otherwise.
D   Air and steam tubes.
E   Curtain of the inner roofing.
F   Rack-pully for ditto. Here also may be fixed the hooks for fastening the cords used to pull up or let down the glass sashes.
F   Back shed.
G   A space which may be made an excellent Mushroom-bed.

H  Vacuities around the flues.
I   Air-flue.
K   Smoke-flue.
L  A row of bricks to preserve water over the whole surface of this chamber, when it is poured in for the purpose of creating moist heat, etc.
M Dotted lines shewing the direction of the shaft or chimney.
N  Dotted line shewing the manner in which the damper is placed.
O  The author's mode of coping and roofing hothouses and backsheds.
P   Spout for collecting water from the roof.
Q  Ground level.

**Fig. 9.18** Elevation of a pinery with a transcript of the original accompanying text (from Loudon 1805)

**Fig. 9.19** The planting bed at the western end of Hothouse 5, showing the thickness of the southern wall surrounding the planting bed, the cobble infilling and brick interval supports, looking north (scale 1m)

**Fig. 9.20** The planting bed at the western end of Hothouse 5, showing the thickness of the walls surrounding the planting beds and the central access steps, looking east (scale 1m)

The earliest pine-pit known to have been constructed at Alnwick was Mr Hay's steam pit (see section 9.2 above), which is likely to be represented by the excavated remains of Structure 1. In this short-lived construction a small, separate furnace heated three growing beds, infilled with stones. Flues clearly provided heat to the beds and, if the interpretation as a steam pit is correct, would have been supplemented by steam. A second pine house is also attested and shown on Barnfather's plan of 1829 (see Fig. 4.1, Fig. 8.6). No archaeological evidence for this was found, but the map evidence would suggest a much larger central element (the fruiting pit) with separate, smaller elements to east and west.

Following the 1830s remodelling of the garden (Garden 3) and construction of the new range of hothouses, a pinery was built towards the south-east of the garden and is labelled as such on proposals for the redesigned garden on plans of the 1860s. This building, recorded here as Hothouse 5, displays features which clearly mark it out as a house for the cultivation of pineapples, notably, central raised bark pits with lower surrounding walkways. The lower elements of this structure were not investigated and thus many of the details concerning the exact mode of heating and placing of the flues remain somewhat speculative.

The building range comprised three backhouses, which, it is presumed, would equate to three separate glasshouse elements, the central one presumably being the fruiting house. This is the only part of the glasshouse to have been accessed from the backhouses; a door provided access to the rear of the glasshouse, from the west (see Fig. 4.30). Each glasshouse element would originally have been provided with a separate furnace, which was located in the eastern part of the respective rooms of the backhouse. Associated flues would run around each of the glasshouse rooms, heating the growing beds. Only the western bed was excavated; the details of other glasshouse compartments may therefore have differed from this.

**Fig. 9.21** Detail of the planting bed at the western end of Hothouse 5, showing the thickness of the northern wall surrounding the planting bed, looking east (scale 0.20m)

Based on comparable examples (from excavations and contemporary accounts) there are various ways in which hot air or steam may have travelled around the glasshouse. Loudon (1825) depicts flues beneath the floors of the pathways surrounding the hotbeds, in his plan and elevation of a pine pit at Kew (Fig. 9.15).

This arrangement approximates to that observed during recent excavations at Auckland Castle, where flues surrounded a central bark pit in a building (the more northerly or 'upper' building of two investigated) probably built in the later eighteenth century for use as a pinery-vinery. A newspaper correspondent of the 1840s describes its use as a succession house for pineapples (suggesting that the lower range was at that time the fruiting house). It was a single-celled structure, of simpler design than the three-roomed glasshouse of the pinery at Alnwick and comparable with Loudon's depiction of the pinery-vinery at Kew (Fig. 9.15). Stone flagged pathways enabled access around the central pit with the return flues adjacent to the northern wall running beneath the pathway at a higher level. The range was later remodelled with a circuit of cast iron pipework running around the interior on support piers (see section 9.2 above). By the early twentieth century the two ranges at Auckland Castle were used as early and late vineries.

A further plan and elevation, again for a pinery-vinery, depicts a more complex arrangement of flues extending beneath the hotbeds of a pine pit. Although not provided with a surrounding walkway, this arrangement might be more comparable to that encountered at Alnwick. The provision of heat around or beneath the beds would be preferable to heat beneath the pathways.

Based on the excavated evidence and comparisons with other examples, an interpretative scheme for the workings of the pinery, when first constructed, has been attempted (Fig. 9.22). The furnace at the eastern end of Room 1 almost certainly supplied heat as hot air via flues around the hotbeds to the south. The eastern end of this glasshouse was not fully excavated but here, presumably, the flues would enter the glasshouse element of the building. The southern wall of the central planting bed, as recorded, was 0.43m wide and brick built, topped with a sandstone plinth, internally, with an outer brick element, and cobble infilling (Fig. 9.19). A similar arrangement, 0.50m wide, can be seen in the northern wall. There were no flues excavated within this element of the building, but on the basis of the surviving evidence and the examples cited above, it is proposed that flues would have been housed within the thickness of these surrounding walls. The central furnace was apparently set at ground level, rather than in a basement, suggesting a different layout for the central part of the glasshouse.

Warm, moist air was an important element of pineapple cultivation and the application of steam, to mimic humid, tropical conditions, was certainly desirable:

'*in the growing season, when moisture is wanted, a fine dewing with the steam is much superior to watering them over the leaf, as, by the latter method, the water is left standing in the hearts of the plants, particularly if they be large; but when steam is used it is quickly absorbed by the leaves, and the plants, so treated, wear the appearance of health and vigour*' (Brown 1817, 321).

The presence of three separate furnace rooms in Hothouse 5, one for each element of the house, suggests that, at least initially, hot air may have been the original method of heating the glasshouse, and would have been passed from the furnace

around the outside of, but integral with the structure of, the planting bed, carried through brick-built flues. The construction and thickness of the walls allows for this (see Fig. 9.19–Fig. 9.21). This would enable heat to be passed more directly into the hotbeds, where needed. The flues may have returned down the centre of the structure in a serpentine fashion (as depicted in Fig. 9.17 and Fig. 9.18), possibly beneath the central element of the hotbed, or may alternatively have described a single circuit as reconstructed here. Assuming the proposed reconstruction is correct, moisture may have been supplied to the atmosphere

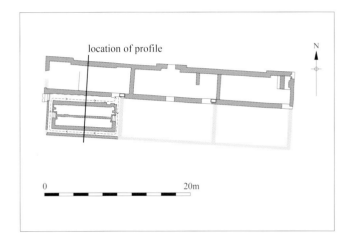

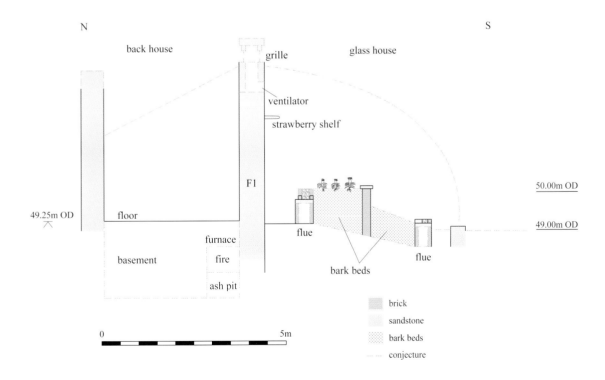

**Fig. 9.22** Schematic profile through Hothouse 5, showing the heating system which is presumed to have operated when initially constructed, illustrating a cross section through the ventilating system (compare Fig. 9.33)

surrounding the plants by pouring water directly onto the cobbles surrounding the bed, or via pipes as depicted by Loudon (Fig. 9.18). The finish of the southern wall of the bed, with its internal sandstone plinth, and the survival of a single sandstone plinth element on the central wall, suggests that this represents the original finished height of these two elements of this structure. The provision of steps up to this central division and a single surviving sandstone slab (presumably similar slabs formed a walkway extending the length of the glasshouse) suggests that the pines may have been tended from the centre of the bed as well as its outside edges. The finished height of the northern element of the central bed was not established and the northern wall appeared truncated. It is assumed that both would have been filled with stones at the base and tanners' bark above, as in contemporary depictions. The southern element would have sloped up towards the north, maximising the available light, while the northern element would presumably have been horizontal.

A schematic profile through the hothouse has been produced based on these surviving elements (Fig. 9.22). A curvilinear roof has been shown on the reconstruction, although this may originally have been plain pitched (The Garden 1874; see section 9.1 above). Generally, the form of the pine pit appears to correlate well with published examples, however, the roof appears to be particularly high for a pinery; generally, pine houses were provided with low roofs. The height of the roof illustrated here is based on the surviving evidence for ventilators at the top of the wall, which must have been below the height of the roof. A sandstone string course, jutting out from the wall (see Fig. 9.19) may have been an integral part of the roofing or glazing system, supporting secondary glazing or shade for the plants, or perhaps a shelf for the cultivation of early strawberries, or similar.

The overly-high glasshouse reconstructed here may have been a design fault which arose from a desire to create a unified appearance to the glasshouses in the garden when constructed. In a section entitled 'Places of interest going North' *The Gardeners' Chronicle* notes of the Alnwick Walled Garden:

'*The Pine stoves are not quite all that a gardener could wish, most of them being too lofty; and then the iron construction and small panes of glass tend to make artificial heat in excessive amount a necessity in cold weather.*' (*The Gardeners' Chronicle* 1891, 282).

The heating system of the hothouse was eventually modified, as indicated by the infilling of the original flues and the provision of iron pipes through the walls of the house. Little evidence for this survived, other than the blocking of the flues through the walls of the hothouse.

## The vinery

Prior to the development of glasshouse technology, vines, as well as peaches and nectarines, may have been cultivated outdoors in Britain. This would not have been particularly successful in the northern climate and the advent of the vinery thus helped to extend both the growing season of the fruit and its geographical range. In a vinery the vine would usually be planted with its roots outside; the fruit would generally have been trained close to the inside of the glass. There are examples of vines being grown inside the house, or with the roots extending beneath the front wall, both internally and externally (Fig. 9.23), although such a method might ultimately have led to subsidence and weakness of the front wall. Vineries therefore, prior to the introduction of curvilinear glazing schemes, tended to have low fronts and sloping roofs. Many different and ingenious methods were applied to facilitate the introduction of the vine from outside the glasshouse, which might be effected through the walls, or via glazing panels.

The construction techniques applied to the front wall of Hothouse 4 suggest that initially the glazing may have been carried on low dwarf walls, formed of a series of columns with spaces between, which would have facilitated the training of stems through the wall from vines planted outside the house. There is evidence to suggest that a broad gravel terrace extended in front of this glasshouse. The area within which vines may have been planted had been truncated by later activity and therefore the planting associated with this initial wall and glazing scheme can only be inferred, however it may be deduced that planting was introduced at regular intervals through this surface into soils beneath.

Subsequent modifications to this low front wall involved infilling the spaces between the columns. It may be that the vines were introduced higher up the wall (although no evidence for this survived); alternatively, they may have entered the glasshouse via specially designed 'cut outs' in the corners of glazing panels. This type of arrangement can be seen in the corners of the lowest glazing bars at Felton Park (Fig. 9.24) and the method of use is described by Loudon thus:

'*…where vines are to be introduced from without, particular care must be had to provide for the withdrawing of the vines, even when their wood is of a considerable age and thickness. For this reason, where horizontal shutters are used, the lower styles or pieces against which they shut, should always be moveable; and, in general… cutting off a corner of the sloping or front sash, is the best; by this means, when the sash is opened, a vine of almost any size may be taken out with ease. A piece of thin board or cork cut every year to fit the increasing diameter of the shoot is screwed to the wall-plate or lower style, as the case may be, and the vacuity, which must necessarily be left around the stem, is closed up with moss.*' (Loudon 1825, 323–4).

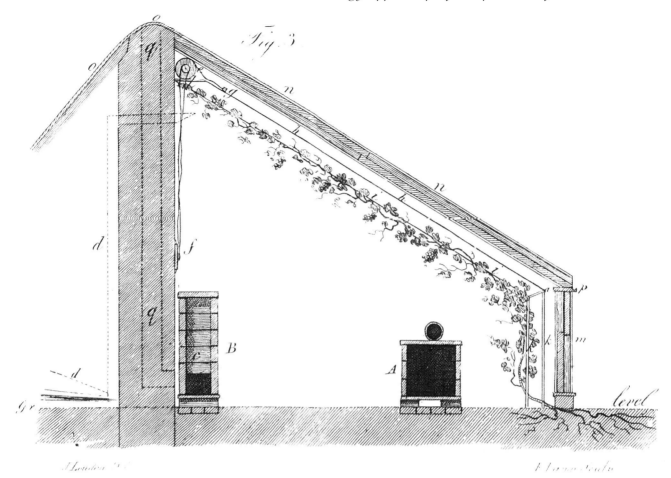

FIG. III

*Section of a vinery supposed to be built according to the proposed plan.--- A vinery of this kind is at present constructing at --- Smith's Esq: Leith Walk, under the author's direction.*

A   The front flue, made broad and shallow, suited to this situation.

B   The back flue deep and narrow agreeable to its situation.

c   Partition seen in this flue.

d   Dotted lines shewing where the air bellows is placed.

e   End of the curtain.

f   Rack pully.

g   End of the rod of wood which is attached to the curtain.

h   Wire upon which it slides down.

i   Trellis on which the vines are trained.

k k Upright rods of wood or iron, each being one inch broad, and 1/4 of an inch thick, to support the wire trellis, and the wire upon which the curtain slides; these rods are fixed to a stone or board at bottom, and joined together at the top. They are also fixed to the rafters at the top, but this only betwixt each curtain, for otherways these fixtures would interrupt the rolling down of the curtain. In this way they only interrupt the hooking on the overlay which can be prevented by making a slit in it, opposite to the fixture.

l   A small piece of iron under each rafter which serves to fix the trellis and wires to the back wall.

m  Upright rafter, placed upon the front parapet.

n   The sloping rafters.

o   Mode of coping by lead and slate, by which are joined the roofs of the hothouse and backshed, approven of by the author, as more ornamental and durable.

p   Water spout continued along the front of the house.

q   Dotted lines in the back wall, shewing how the chimney is carried up .

**Fig. 9.23** Elevation of a vinery showing vines trained under the front wall of the glasshouse and growing partly inside and partly outside the vinery with a transcript of the original accompanying text (from Loudon 1805)

**Fig. 9.24** The glazing arrangements along the front wall of the vinery at Felton Park, looking out; cut-away corners can be seen at the bottom right of each glazed panel (VR 2017)

As with any other hothouse, nineteenth-century opinions regarding heating, glazing, ventilation and other matters of cultivation within the vinery were diverse and occasioned much heated debate (see, for example, Williams 1814; Loudon 1817; Wilkinson 1822; Williams 1822; Knight 1822; Mackenzie 1822; Knight 1841). It is clear, however, that vines prefer a drier heat than pineapples and suffer from too much moisture in the atmosphere. Hence, early attempts to grow pineapples and grapes together were ultimately unsuccessful and dedicated houses for the cultivation of vines were developed.

The Alnwick Walled Garden was provided with three vineries; the earliest being Hothouse 1, of which only the much-modified backhouse element was observed within the excavations. Hothouse 4 appears to have functioned as a vinery from the early 1830s. A third vinery, or muscat house, Hothouse 7, was not subject to archaeological investigation and the following text focusses on the evidence for Hothouse 4.

The surviving evidence from Hothouse 2 and Hothouse 4 has been used to reconstruct the original heating system used in both structures. By the 1830s each building housed four furnaces (F1 to F4 in Hothouse 4), one at each end and two off-centre, set 1/3rd of the way along the building in a semi-basement (see Fig. 4.20). Four chimneys vented these four furnaces, set regularly along the length of the building, two at each end and the others at regular 1/3rd intervals. The vents were topped with what were described as 'octagonal gothic chimneys', four to each hothouse (Kent 1998, 25). Only one survived at the time of recording and this was inaccessible and heavily overgrown with ivy, although it was visible in 1998 and recorded by Kent (see Fig. 4.24).

The western central furnace F3 supplied hot air from a furnace in wall via an underground flue to a mushroom house situated in the structure's backhouse and vented at chimney C3 (see mushroom houses, below). The other three furnaces would have supplied hot air to the glasshouse element of the building via a system of wall flues into its corresponding chimney. These were recorded at ground level (following demolition of the superstructure). The westernmost example was the best preserved – as a brick structure, rectangular in plan, housed within the width of the spine wall. With an overall wall thickness of *c.* 0.6m, this would have been easily achieved. The brick chimney had internal dimension of 0.4m north–south by 0.3m east–west. It is worth noting that the two end chimneys sloped outwards towards the end gable walls – this is visible within the wall thickness for chimney C4. The brickwork of chimney C2 was the most clearly visible in elevation and can be seen on the southern face of the central spine wall, beneath the chimney stack (see Fig. 4.23).

Furnaces F1, F2 and F4 thus supplied heat via flues (subsequently blocked) in the thickness of the wall to three separate sections of low-level flue walls against the spine wall of the building. These appear to form three separate units, each corresponding to a furnace. Reconstruction of the flue walls is hampered by the lack of excavation of these elements, which fell beyond limits of excavation but were planned at 1:50 and partly recorded using rectified photography. The evidence suggests a southern 'main' wall,

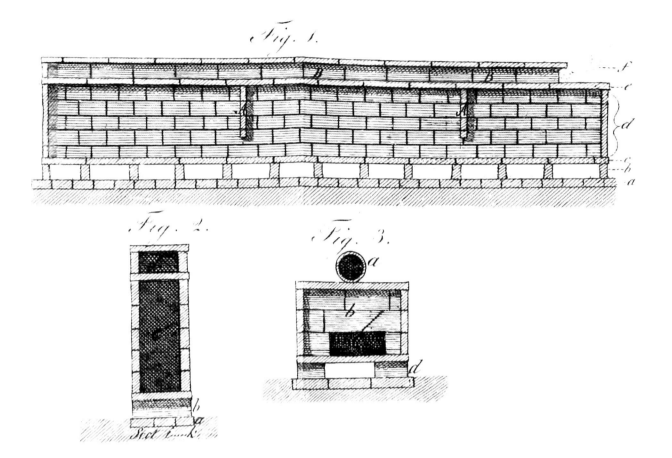

FIG. I

*Longitudinal Section of the smoke and air flue as erected in Dicksons' and Shade's hothouse shewing principally,*

A A The" briggs" or partitions in the smoke-flue.

B B The air flue.

a   Sole of the flue, being bricks laid flat.

b   Supports of the flues (being bricks set on edge.)

c   Sole of the flue being ordinary tyle covers.

d   End of the smoke-flue being bricks on edge.

e   Cover of the smoke-flue.

f   Intended to shew heated air coming out of the air-flue. Here, however it would be better to fix one of the registers described in plate VI, as they would answer better for regulating the quantity of heated air admitted into the house.


FIG. II

*Section of the smoke-flue, and airflue, supposing them cut across at the dotted line i ... k in fig.3. plate I*

a   The sole.

b   The supports.

c   The smoke-flue.

d   The air-flue.


FIG. III

A section intended to shew the manner in which the briggs, or partitions, are formed in wide flues; and also how the heated air may be conducted in an  earthen pipe in certain circumstances.

a   Section of the earthen pipe.

b   Brigg or partition.

c   Hole under it for the smoke to pass through.

d   Supports of the flue.


The covers and sole of this flue are supposed to be made of large brick or stone pavement.


**Fig. 9.25** Illustrations of flues (longitudinal and cross sections) with a transcript of the original accompanying text; note the brick uprights at intervals, which correspond to observations at Alnwick (from Loudon 1805)

**Fig. 9.26** The back wall and return flue of the northernmost hot-house at Auckland Castle Gardens, looking west. The air gap along the south side of the flue can be seen with traces of render sealing the flue to prevent leakage of poisonous gases (VR 2017)

**Fig. 9.27** View of the flue from the eastern furnace running below the floor between the bark pit (left) and the southern wall of the northernmost hothouse at Auckland Castle, looking east. Remnants of the shafts for warmed air leading upward to the floor grilles can be seen (VR 2017)

**Fig. 9.28** View of the vine border along the front of the northernmost hothouse at Auckland Castle Gardens showing the grooves in the front wall allowing the vine stems to enter the range, looking east; the trench in the middle of the border confirmed the entry point for a later cast iron heating circuit linking the upper and lower ranges (VR 2017)

**Fig. 9.29** Hothouse 4, showing flues adjacent to the spine wall, looking east; the drainage at the corner of the building, shown in Fig. 9.31, can be seen at the bottom right of this image and a possible box for distribution of heat at the bottom left (scale 1m)

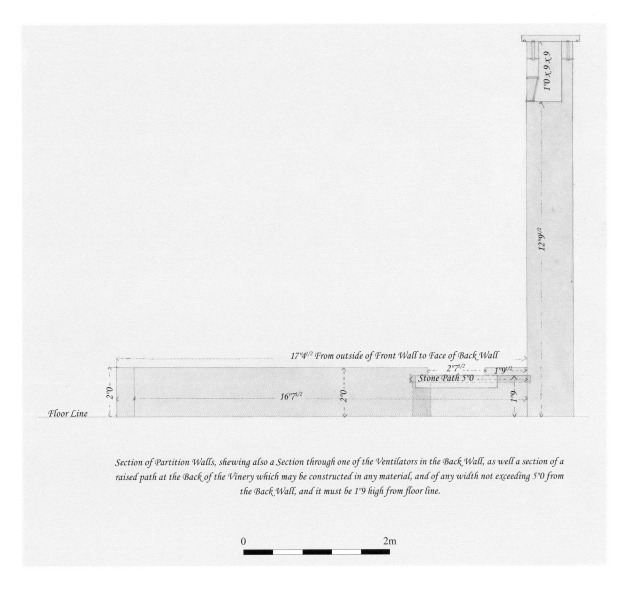

*Section of Partition Walls, shewing also a Section through one of the Ventilators in the Back Wall, as well a section of a raised path at the Back of the Vinery which may be constructed in any material, and of any width not exceeding 5″0 from the Back Wall, and it must be 1″9 high from floor line.*

0                                    2m

**Fig. 9.30** Detail from an architect's drawing dated 1830, showing the proposed details of a partition wall of the vinery (TAG Z/1/4) (scale 1:50)

*c.* 1m from the central spine wall, with an internal brick division, supporting sandstone capping. It is probable that the whole was capped and sealed with sandstone flags but that these elements were removed at a later date, perhaps to accommodate the grilles necessary to provide support above hot water pipes. Contemporary drawings (see above) suggest that it was most likely that these flues would have incorporated two (or more) horizontal chambers, although methods were experimental and varied.

Reviewing the various plans, elevations and cross sections of the furnaces and flues the principle for their construction seems simple enough. However, in practice, interpreting the excavated detail is complex. The remains at Alnwick are fragmentary, but may be usefully compared with contemporary surviving structures. Two pinery-vinery ranges within the southern walled garden at Auckland Castle, visited by the authors in 2017, bear comparison

with some aspects of the Alnwick structures. The arrangement of glasshouses here comprised two heated houses terraced into a steeply-sloping site and descending one below the other. The buildings comprise an early (1750s) pinery range, which had been subsequently converted to a pinery-vinery and augmented by another (probably late eighteenth century) range, the upper pinery-vinery having a backhouse with furnace stoke holes at each end, but the lower structure being heated from a basement furnace (this latter structure being less comparable in terms of construction and date to those at Alnwick). The stepped layout of these structures is considered to be unique, but reflects the topography of the site (Beamish 2014).

The upper pinery-vinery at Auckland Castle, presumed to have been built in the last decade of the eighteenth century, was provided with two circuits of heated flues running around

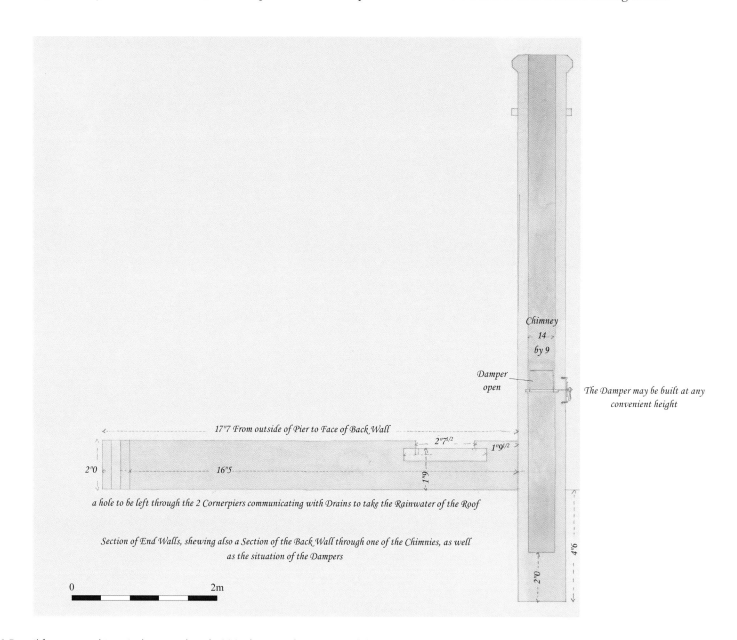

**Fig. 9.31** Detail from an architect's drawing dated 1830, showing the proposed details of the end wall and chimney of the vinery (TAG Z/1/4) (scale 1:50)

the outside of the bark pit within a single celled glasshouse and returning along the back wall (Fig. 9.26) to vent at a distant chimney. The complex of brickwork shown here may be paralleled at Alnwick. The 'double walled' construction of the heating duct is best illustrated adjacent to the southern wall of the building (Fig. 9.27). The flue gases passed through the smaller brick-built chamber and heated air in the surrounding spaces which then passed via vertical 'boxes' set at intervals along the flue run to circular openings in the flooring flagstones above, which could be regulated by brass hit and miss ventilators set into the floor (Fig. 9.27; Harry Beamish, pers. comm.). These boxes may be compared with a similar feature, interpreted during excavation as a soak-away, in Hothouse 4 (Fig. 9.29). At Auckland Castle the level of the flues rose with distance from the furnace enabling the passage of hot air by convection; this allowed the flue gases from

each furnace to complete a circuit of the house to exit via a flue in the western gable and along the north wall of the garden to a chimney against the wall of Castle Lodge. The provision of a planting border to the south and grooves in the front (stone) wall, allowed the stems of the vines grown externally to be trained into the glasshouse and up to roof level. The flues surrounding the central bark pit, filled with tanners' bark, provided the additional heat required for successful growth of the pineapples plunged in pots in the pit (see below; Fig. 9.28).

This building may differ in detail from those excavated at Alnwick, for example there is no surviving evidence to suggest that Hothouses 2 and 4 were provided with heated flues to the front of the house, but the comparison of heating systems facilitates an understanding of the heavily truncated remains.

A detailed cross-section through various elements of the vinery,

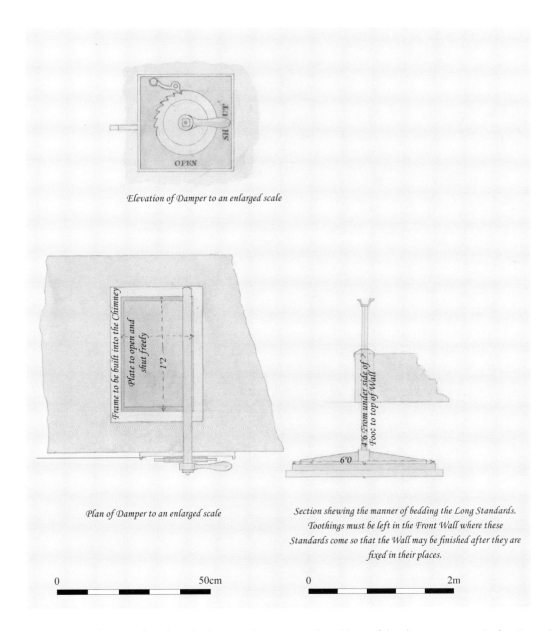

*Elevation of Damper to an enlarged scale*

*Plan of Damper to an enlarged scale*

*Section shewing the manner of bedding the Long Standards.*
*Toothings must be left in the Front Wall where these*
*Standards come so that the Wall may be finished after they are*
*fixed in their places.*

0                    50cm

0                    2m

**Fig. 9.32** Detail from an architect's drawing dated 1830, showing the proposed workings of the damper system in the vinery (TAG Z/1/4) (scale 1:12/1:50)

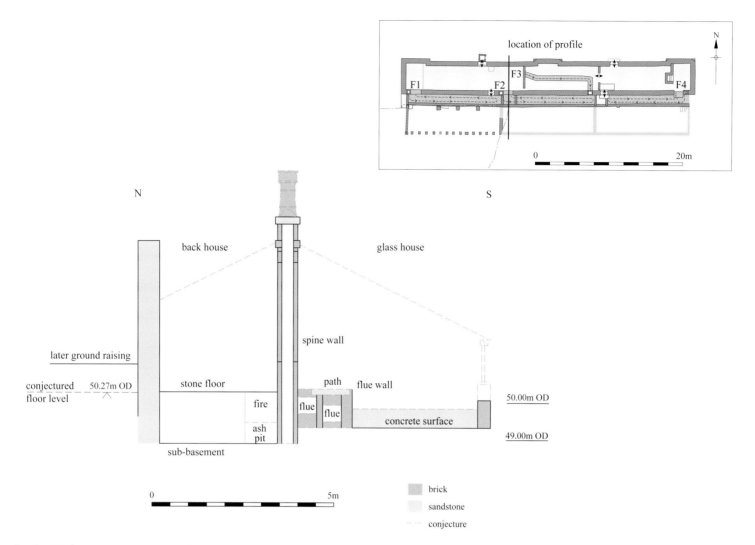

**Fig. 9.33** Schematic cross-section showing the heating system which is presumed to have operated in Hothouse 4, Garden 3, illustrating the chimney in cross section (compare Fig. 9.22 which illustrates the cross section through one of the ventilators; chimneys and ventilators would have appeared the same in both structures)

produced in 1830 to illustrate the ventilation system (Fig. 9.32) is presumably only one of many drawings which would have been produced prior to construction of the vinery and other hothouse ranges; unfortunately, this is the only example which survives in the archives at Alnwick Castle. A section through the partition walls illustrates a raised path; this presumably was set at a level which would correspond with the top of the flues which ran along the back wall of the vinery, 1ft 9in (0.53m) above the floor line. The flues would have been placed between each of these internal dividing walls. Above this level it is assumed that the internal divisions within the glasshouse would have been carried up in glass and iron, as at Felton Park. A section through the end wall shows one of the chimneys. It illustrates that this wall extended 4ft 6in below the internal floor level in the building, a measurement which corresponds well with observations of the furnace houses on site. Using these sections, together with the recorded evidence, it has been possible to suggest the original floor height within the building

(which was not seen archaeologically) and the original height of the flues. A damper within the wall could be used to control air flow through the flue system from within the backhouses.

A schematic cross-section (Fig. 9.33) illustrates how two flues may have been positioned against the spine wall, the front, southern flue, being the one along which hot air initially left the furnace, would have given out the greatest heat. The rear flue, being the return, would have been cooler. Hot air would rise as it passed along the front flue, travel along the back flue and exit via a chimney. Here the chimney is illustrated in cross section. Ventilation would have been provided via the shutters provided at the top of the wall (as illustrated for the pinery, see Fig. 9.22, and in the architects drawing Fig. 9.29 ). A cement bedding layer, identified during excavation, presumably formed a construction horizon for this or a for the floor of the glasshouse; if the architect's drawing (Fig. 9.30; Fig. 9.32) is correct, the internal floor would have been higher. The hothouse is illustrated with a plain pitched roof. Ultimately this would have been replaced with one of curvilinear form. The stone floor of the ground-level elements of the backhouse would have been at the same level as the finished height of the top of the flues. Ground level to the rear of the backhouse would presumably originally have been level with the internal stone floor but was subsequently raised.

Subsequent modifications to this building include the provision of curvilinear glazing, associated rebuilding and infilling of parts of the front wall and the provision of hot water heating, indicated by the blocking of flues, insertion of water tanks and removal of the original furnaces. Ultimately the boilers which supplied this hothouse would all be housed within the central part of the building. No furnaces associated with these hot water heating systems survived.

## The peach house

Peaches and nectarines grow in temperate but warm zones and, in Britain, would originally have been grown against south-facing (or sometimes east-facing) walls, which could be provided with additional glass protection. They will fruit outdoors in southern Britain, given adequate protection and soil conditions but, as with the vine, benefit from the growing conditions of a heated glasshouse, particularly in a northern climate:

'*Scarcely any fruit can be raised in greater abundance, or with fewer chances of failure, than the Peach in a forcinghouse; where the insects…are easily destroyed, and where the tree is subject to scarcely any other disease than the mildew…But though a crop of Peaches, or Nectarines, is very easily obtained under glass, experience seems to*

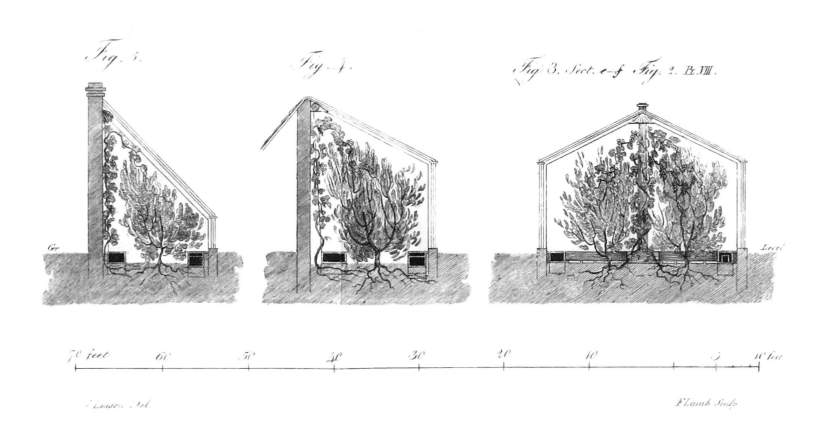

FIG. III.
*Section of both the Plan and Elevation of the improved peach-house, supposing it finished and the trees and vines full grown.*
In this section it will be observed that the inner roofing is made according to the mode shewn in plate III. which will have the best effect in a double roofed house.

FIG. IV. AND V.
*Are Sections of the approved mode of planting the peaches, and also of introducing vines in peach-houses.*

**Fig. 9.34** Elevations of peach houses; the peach house at Alnwick may have resembled that shown as Fig. 4, with flues at the front and back of the house and a backhouse to the rear with a transcript of the original accompanying text (from Loudon 1805)

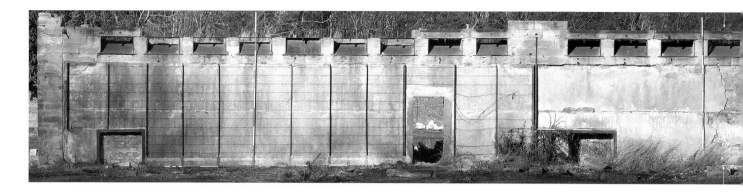

**Fig. 9.35** Hothouse 2, rectified photograph of spine wall, looking north (scales 2m)

*have proved that neither of these fruits acquire perfection, either in richness or flavour, unless they be exposed to the full influence of the sun, during their last swelling, without the intervention of the glass. It has consequently been the practice, in some gardens, to take off the lights wholly before the fruit begins to ripen; and in warm seasons, and favourable situations, this mode of management succeeds perfectly well. But in the colder parts of England, this cannot be done'* (Knight 1841, 186).

The peach house in the Alnwick Walled Garden appears to have occupied the same location throughout the garden's working history; modified from a glasshouse with three projecting furnaces to the rear, it ultimately resembled Hothouse 4 in its appearance and operation, with hot air flues running along the spine wall. As with Hothouse 4, there is no evidence to suggest that these ever extended along the front of the house; however, the original glasshouse element of the building had been removed and it is suggested that this occurred when the curvilinear glazing and hot-water pipes were originally installed (*c.*1836). It is possible therefore that the flue-heated house may have had flues running close to the front of the house, as illustrated by Loudon (Fig. 9.34), however, the flues at the rear of the house appeared to resemble those in Hothouse 4, and were therefore of double construction; it is assumed that they functioned in a similar manner.

Peaches may have been trained close to the front wall of the peach house, as well as on trellises against the back wall of the glasshouse. Wires on which trees may have been trained were still evident in the western third of the glasshouse at the time of excavation (Fig. 9.35).

## The mushroom house

Dark, heated buildings, equipped with wooden staging on which the appropriate compost could be laid, would have been used for raising mushrooms, blanching winter salads, preserving cauliflowers and broccoli and for forcing asparagus and sea kale. Mushroom houses were identified in the backhouses of Hothouse 2 and Hothouse 4. Supplied by a central furnace, beneath the end wall of the mushroom house, the hot air would travel beneath the floor along a central axis, before turning to vent via a chimney in the spine wall. The preparation of the requisite compost was a complex affair, but the principle behind the mushroom house was simple enough (Oldaker 1822).

Isaak Oldaker (1822) provides a plan, elevation and perspective view of a mushroom house (Fig. 9.36). The principle on which his mushroom house is constructed is similar to that noted at Alnwick, differing mainly in that Oldaker's mushroom house was an independent structure, with a flue that ran the length of the house before returning to vent at a chimney above the furnace, although he notes that such houses would more commonly be built as part of the backhouses of a range of buildings. Oldaker's shed is also provided with windows unlike the Alnwick examples. These would need to be shaded for the cultivation of the mushroom, which thrives in a dark environment (Oldaker 1822, 343), and demands very exacting soil conditions:

*'Collect a quantity of fresh horse dung that has neither been exposed to wet nor fermentation, clearing it of the long straw, so as to leave one fourth, in quantity, of the shortest litter, when incorporated with the horse droppings; then add a fourth part of tolerable dry turf mould, or other maiden earth, and mix it well with the dung beforementioned : the advantage derived from the mould or maiden earth, is the union of the whole into one compact solid substance, so congenial to the growth of mushrooms.'* (Oldaker 1822, 339).

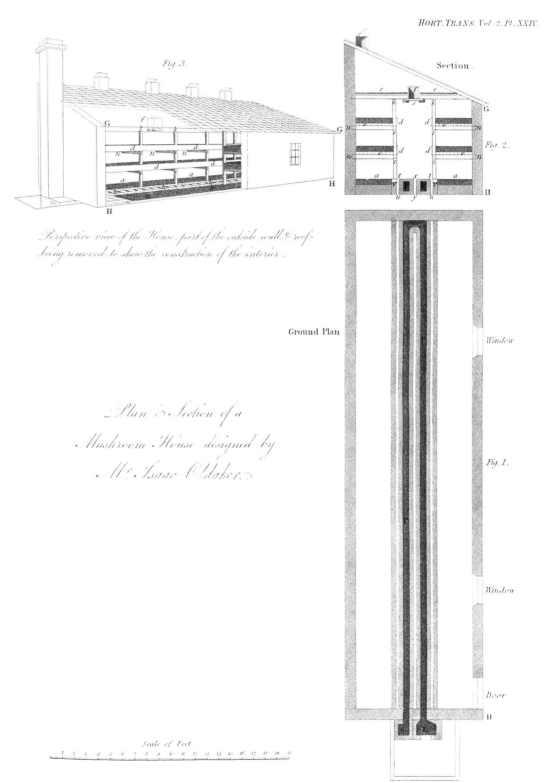

**Fig. 9.36** Plan, section and perspective view of a mushroom house (by Isaac Oldaker, 1822)

**Fig. 9.37** The renovated mushroom house at Audley End, Essex (VR 2003)

## The conservatory

In the nineteenth century conservatories were frequently attached to large houses, forming an outdoor room in which cultivated plants, either permanent or temporary, could be displayed. On the whole, conservatories may have been cooler structures than hothouses, with a temperate atmosphere, designed for the cultivation of plants and flowers for display rather than exotics for consumption. Moreover, the conservatory could be enjoyed by people of the house as additional living space, if attached. The conservatory, as exemplified in Hothouse 6 was generally a more lofty structure than the forcing houses designed for the cultivation of the vine or particularly the pineapple (compare Fig. 5.24 and Fig. 9.22). In the case of the northern conservatory at Alnwick, although detached from the main house (or castle) this space may have been enjoyed by members of the household or visitors as a place in which to appreciate the plants on display as well as vistas of the garden (see section 10.3 below). Little is known of the arrangement or planting within the central conservatory (Hothouse 3). However, limited information is available, which helps to elucidate the planting schemes that might have adorned this structure. A photograph of *c.* 1870 shows that the pillars which held up the roof supported creepers, planted in permanent beds towards the rear (north) of the structure (see Fig. 5.16). The sandstone wall of the conservatory is just visible to the rear of the planting scheme. Similar plants are apparently cultivated in pots along the southern edge of the central path of the conservatory. The planting scheme at the front (southern) part of the house is not visible. The internal arrangements of the conservatory were altered, apparently around the turn of the century. A contemporary description provides an indication of planting schemes and internal arrangements:

> *The glasshouses and the conservatory have been extensively altered in recent years, much of the staging in the conservatory having been removed and shallow beds substituted for it, and a wide central path formed, together with an artistically-arranged rockery at the back of the house, masking a lot of hot-water pipes, and affording situations for climbing plants. The roof is supported by iron columns, to which some very fine climbers, such as Luculia gratissima, a very large plant, which flowers grandly; fine Fuchsias, Cassia eorymbosa, Habrothamnus Newelli, and Jasmins are trained. The portable plants are now arranged in groups or beds, and, of course, more attention is paid to the late summer, autumn, and winter-flowering plants than to others. In this house are some fine Tree-Ferns and Palms.* (The Gardeners' Chronicle 1902, 287).

# Chapter 10

## Plants, Produce and People; the Alnwick Walled Garden in a wider landscape setting

*'The Pines are perfect. The number grown is very great and they are all in the best possible condition. A house of suckers taken off at the January shift, to fruit next year, were getting air day and night, and looked most vigorous and promising. Many Pines are near ripe or approaching ripeness. There is a splendid show of that most useful Pine, the Queen.'*

(*The Gardeners' Chronicle* 1880)

The transition of the Alnwick Walled Garden from kitchen garden to pleasure grounds and back to productive plot has been charted above (Chapter 8). The application of various technologies to encourage longer and more productive growing seasons and to allow the cultivation of exotics has also been presented (Chapter 9). This chapter seeks to consider the evidence for the plants that were cultivated within the garden and the ways in which that garden was experienced by those who toiled or relaxed within it, through archaeological evidence and records and letters held in the Alnwick archives. It is important to stress that these, particularly the records held in the archives, are incomplete; and thus illuminate only snapshots of particular points in the garden's history. They are augmented by descriptions of the Alnwick Walled Garden taken from contemporary published accounts.

### 10.1 The New Exotics

*'Scaly like an Artichoke at the first view, but more like to a cone of the Pine tree, which we call a pineapple for the forme... being so sweete in smell... tasting... as if Wine, Rosewater and Sugar were mixed together.* (*Theatrum Botanicum* 1640, John Parkinson, Royal Botanist to Charles I, describing the pineapple).

A desire to cultivate exotic and unusual flowers, plants and vegetables has a long history, but eighteenth- and nineteenth-century trade connections and travel, particularly to the New World and the East, led to what might be termed an explosion in the pursuit of exotic plants and a desire to propagate and cultivate them. This part of the story, insofar as it relates to Alnwick, probably begins with the pineapple.

### Cultivation of the pineapple

The origins of pineapple growing in Britain are obscure. The first documented occurrence of the fruit being brought to this country dates to 1657; Miller asserts that it may have been introduced as far back as 1690 and a ripened fruit was noted at George London's Nursery in Kensington (Woods and Warren 1988, 60). The rarity of the fruit at this early date is attested by the fact that this particular specimen was destined to be presented to Queen Mary in October 1793. By the early eighteenth century pineapple cultivation began to take off; by the end of the century, foreign species had become so popular it was possible to buy greenhouse plants, and even pineapples, on the streets of London and Paris (Hix 1996, 24).

Widespread publicity for the cultivation of the pineapple in Britain was gained by the gardener Henry Telende in 1721, working for Sir Matthew Decker, using a sunken hotbed or 'pit' filled with waste tanners' bark and covered with a glass frame. Decker was so proud of this achievement that he commissioned a portrait of the fruit from Theodore Netscher (Grant 2013, 22). The earliest evidence for pineapple cultivation at Alnwick does not appear until almost a century later, with the experimental steam pit designed by Mr Hay (see section 9.2 above). An apparently more successful and longer-lived pine pit was established on the site of a later vinery (Hothouse 4) and ultimately a new pine house was built in the south-east of the garden.

The cultivation of pineapples at Alnwick by 1829 was apparently very successful, as is demonstrated by a bundle of correspondence in the castle archives which include letters to commissioners from various correspondents including Thomas Smith, Head Gardener (DP/D3/I/197). The date of these documents suggests that the pineapples under discussion were cultivated in the predecessor to Hothouse 4. Several letters from Smith detail pineapples and other fruit sent to Dublin Castle, the seat of English rule in Ireland at the time; clearly the garden was producing a reasonable surplus.

31st May 1829 '*I sent the Pineapple yesterday to Dublin Castle by the Union Coach.*'

1829 (date illegible) '*The Pines have ripened a little quicker than I anticipated, today I intend sending off six Pines and fourteen bunches of Grapes, also the Apricots….*'

13th August 1829 '*I intend sending two boxes of fruit, by the Union today, for Ireland, containing twelve pines and twenty eight bundles of grapes…*'

15th August 1829 '*I have this day sent off for Ireland, three boxes containing eleven Pines, and twenty eight bunches of Grapes, also about six dozen green Apricots for preserving in brandy, the Apricots were sent by order of his Excellency.*'

There is also correspondence relating to the purchase of pineapple plants. The pineapples which were being cultivated were clearly of a small type. Thomas Smith requests leave to purchase large-fruited pineapples from Sir David Smith, the third duke's Commissioner for the ducal estates. The letter illustrates the three-year successional planting which was required to take a pineapple plant from sucker to maturity.

8th Oct 1829 '*As we have none of those large fruited Pineapple plants here, with the exception of two or three very small plants, which I have had given to me, and they being such very small ones, it will take two years before they come into fruit.*'

'*By your permission Sir David, I should like to have two plants to fruit this next year, also two succession plants for the year following, which will then put me into a complete succession of them, as the fruit swells to a large size, they will be a great acquisition for the Public Days- the four Pine plants will cost about three pounds or three guineas at most.*'

'*I have an excellent stock of the other sorts, which are looking remarkably well. Every garden that has Pines, has a few of these large ones, except this.*'

## Fruit cultivation

Pineapples were, however, only a small part of the story. The kitchen garden, in its heyday, would be expected to feed the duke's household when they were at home in Alnwick, and to help supply the household when they were elsewhere, as the letters above demonstrate. Even following the construction of a new kitchen garden and the radical remodelling of the Alnwick

Walled Garden by the fourth duke, the beds surrounding the walled garden, at least on the eastern, northern and western sides, would be planted with fruit trees. Whilst vines, peaches and warmth-loving fruit such as figs could be cultivated in the hothouse ranges, natives might be at home in the open ground, and more tender or delicate species would be planted against the heated north wall, where they would be afforded both protection and warmth in the colder months. The nurture provided could help to extend growing seasons, whilst the cultivation of different varieties would result in extended cropping times; important considerations at times when fresh fruit might be required for the table on a daily basis. *The Gardeners' Chronicle* for May 9, 1891 records: '*on three sides of the goodly acres thus treated, stands a high red-brick wall covered with fruit trees*' (593).

Apart from the evidence provided by particular structures, built to encourage the growth of specific species, there was little archaeological evidence for the varieties grown. Palaeo-environmental sampling was unforthcoming in this respect. Some indication of the varieties planted is, however, provided by the recovery of lead tags, used to identify species. Prior to the excavations a metal detector survey had been carried out across the original walled garden during which eighteen lead tags were discovered. With one exception, a cypress, all of these lead tags are for fruit trees. Some examples have dates, which may relate to when the particular variety was first planted, and these tags provide evidence for the wide range of fruit trees grown in the original walled garden in the latter part of the nineteenth and into the early twentieth century. Information relating to the varieties grown is given below and, unless otherwise stated, has been taken from the website of the National Fruit Collection (National Fruit Collection 2015). Clearly, this sample does not reflect all the fruit trees planted in the garden. The history of these trees, their development and registration, their display and the awards they won, is further testament to nineteenth-century interests in developing new varieties and improving on them. As well as providing fruits at different times throughout the cropping season, the cultivation of different varieties would aid with pollination.

A lead tag, rectangular in shape with cut corners, was also recovered unstratified during the excavations (Fig. 10.1). Stamped on the front is 'PINE APPLE NECTARINE 1872'. To the left, it has a small hole through which a metal cord was strung; the cord has been cut. Nectarines were grown on walls or in glasshouses, and this tag, found during initial site clearance, would presumably have labelled a nectarine in Hothouse 2. The other tags relate to fruits planted within the open garden adjacent to the heated north wall in the north-west corner. Unfortunately, there is no information relating to their precise location and distribution.

**Fig. 10.1** Rectangular lead tag stamped 'Pine Apple Nectarine 1872'

**Fig. 10.2** Rectangular lead tag for cypress tree Lawsoniana

**Fig. 10.3** Rectangular lead tag for Bismark apple tree

**Fig. 10.4** Rectangular lead tags for Bramley Apples

**Pineapple Nectarine** (Fig. 10.1). Pineapple is a late-season, yellow-fleshed traditional English nectarine which ripens in August to September. It has a strong tropical flavour, which is somewhat reminiscent of a pineapple, hence the name. It is very sweet, but with a characteristic peach or nectarine tang. The plant produces large, greenish yellow fruits with a crimson red flush and can be grown outdoors in the south; at Alnwick it would have been cultivated under glass.

**Chamaecyparis lawsoniana (Lawson's Cypress)** (Fig. 10.2). The Lawson's Cypress was first discovered (by Euro-Americans) near Port Orford in Oregon and introduced into cultivation in 1854, by collectors working for the Lawson & Son nursery in Edinburgh, Scotland, after whom it was named as Lawson's Cypress by the describing botanist Andrew Murray. The USDA officially calls it by the name Port Orford cedar, as do most people in its native area, but some botanists prefer to use the name Lawson Cypress. This is the only tag recovered which does not refer to a variety of fruit.

**Bismark 96** (Fig. 10.3**).** This apple was named after Prince Bismark the German Chancellor. Its origin is variously reported as Bismarck, Tasmania; Carisbrooke, Australia; and Canterbury, New Zealand. This variety received a First Class Certificate from the Royal Horticultural Society in 1887. The fruits have firm, fine-textured, juicy flesh with an acid flavour and cook well.

**Bramley Seedling** (Fig. 10.4). There were two examples of Bramley Seedling tags recorded, one bearing the date 1888 the other 96 (presumably for 1896). The Bramley Apple is recorded as being raised by Mary Ann Brailsford, Southwell, Nottinghamshire, England between 1809 and 1813 and introduced in 1865 by nurseryman H. Merryweather. It was first exhibited in 1876 and received a First Class Certificate from the Royal Horticultural Society in 1893. The Bramley remains the most popular cooking apple grown in the UK.

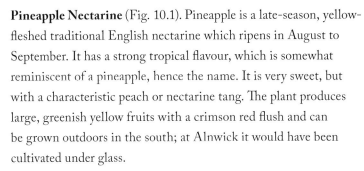

**Fig. 10.5**  Pear-shaped lead tag for Conference Pear

**Fig. 10.6**  Pear-shaped lead tag for Doyenne du Comice Pear

**Fig. 10.7**  Rectangular lead tag for Glenton Green Gooseberry

**Fig. 10.8**  Rectangular lead tag for Gascoyne's apple

**Conference** (Fig. 10.5). The Conference Pear is one of Europe's best known and most widely grown pear varieties. Raised by Rivers Nursery, Sawbridgeworth it was exhibited at the National British Pear Conference, after which it was named. It was awarded a First Class Certificate from The Royal Horticultural Society in 1885. The fruits of the conference pear have pale yellow flesh with a slight pink tinge.

**Doyenne du Comice** (Fig. 10.6). Raised by the Horticultural Society of Maine et Loire, Angers, France, the Doyenne du Comice Pear first set fruit in 1849 and was introduced to England in 1858 by Sir Thomas Dyke Acland. The fruits of the Comice have pale yellow, extremely melting, juicy flesh with a delicate and delicious flavour.

**Ecklinville.** The Ecklinville is a variety of cooking apple, said to have been raised by gardener Logan at Ecklinville, Portaferry, Belfast, Ireland. Its precise origins are not know, but it is documented as early as 1800. The fruits have rather soft, fine-textured, juicy flesh, with a very acid flavour and cook well.

**Glenton Green** (Fig. 10.7). A tag labelled Glenton Green New C3, almost certainly refers to a type of gooseberry, described as having small, oblong, hairy green fruit on pendulous branches. It was considered by Don as being amongst the best fruit of gooseberries (Don 1844, 180). A second tag is labelled Glenton Green G24; this may also refer to the same type of gooseberry, the variation in spelling being just that. Alternatively, it could relate to a local fruit of some other type; the village of Glanton lies some 8 miles west of Alnwick.

**Gascoyne's Seedling** (Fig. 10.8). First raised by Mr Gascoyne at Bapchild Court, Sittingbourne, Kent, Gascoyne's Apple was introduced in 1871 by nurseryman G. Bunyard & Co., Maidstone, Kent. This dessert apple received a First Class Certificate from the Royal Horticultural Society in 1887. It is commonly called Gascoyne's Scarlet, on account of the deep red colour of the fruits which have firm, fine-textured, slightly juicy, sweet flesh with very little flavour. It crops prolifically and is harvested in October.

**Joséphine de Malines** (Fig. 10.9). Developed in Belgium around 1830, Joséphine de Malines was discovered and raised by Major Esperen of Malines, Belgium and named for his wife. The pear is an exceptionally late cropper, which keeps well, and these characteristics may have been influential in the choice of this variety for the Alnwick Walled Garden.  The variety produces small- to medium-sized fruit with russet greenish yellow skin and juicy, sweet white flesh with a smooth, buttery texture.

**Louise Bonne of Jersey** (Fig. 10.10). This early variety of pear was raised by Longueval, in Avranches, Normandy, France around 1780. The name arose probably because it was introduced to England via the Channel Island of Jersey. Cropping between October and November, the tree bears medium sized, conical fruit with smooth pale green skin turning slightly yellow with ripening. It has white, smooth, melting flesh, combining sweetness and acidity.

**Fig. 10.9** Rectangular lead tag for Joséphine de Malines dessert pear

**Fig. 10.10** Pear-shaped lead tag for Louise Bonne of Jersey Pear

**Fig. 10.11** The newly introduced Roosevelt Pear as illustrated in *The Gardeners' Chronicle* 1905 by Charles Baltet

**Northern Dumpling.** The Northern Dumpling is a hardy variety of cooking apple which succeeds even in the coldest parts of Britain. It produces acidic large round, sometimes slightly conical, fruit of a greenish yellow and red colour (Castle 2013). Tag not illustrated.

**Roosevelt Pear.** Named after President Theodore Roosevelt (1901–1909). *The Gardeners' Chronicle* 1905, says: 'M. Charles Baltet, the famous pomologist of Troyes, sends us an account and illustration of this fruit. *"This Pear,"* he says, *"is destined to bring about a revolution in our fruit gardens and orchards. The tree is robust and fertile when grafted on the free-stock or on the Quince. The fruit is very large, sometimes measuring 10 inches round, globular or ovoid; skin smooth, of a pleasing whitish-yellow colour shading into lemon, with carmine or vermilion spots on the sunny side. The flesh is snow-white, delicate, sweet and melting, of an agreeable flavour. It may be said to be ripe during the whole of October, as it really begins at the end of September and continues in use to the beginning of November"* (*The Gardeners' Chronicle* 1905, 243; Fig. 10.11). Tag not illustrated.

Tags for Morello Cherries, Rhubarb (Paragon variety) and Victoria Plum reflect the range of other types of fruit which would have been typical of a garden of the period. The rhubarb is dated 1883 and the plum 1894. A few plant varieties could not be identified, among them Celina; this name is currently given to a very recently registered variety of pear, its meaning in the context of the Alnwick Walled Garden is unknown.

The tags themselves fall into two types, a simple rectangular shape, cut out of lead, between 7cm and 9cm across and generally with the corners clipped, with one or two holes through which wire could be threaded to attach the tag to the plant. Some of these appear to bear dates (presumably the date of planting); and the text appears to have been hand-punched into the tags, presumably by one of the gardeners. A second, pear-shaped, type of tag is much more finely made. The text is regular and raised and the tags appear to have been cast rather than cut and punched. The examples recovered record only the name of pears; this is unlikely to be coincidence. There may also be a chronological development to the style of tag used as the Roosevelt pear must post-date 1901. The dating of these tags confirms that fruit continued to be grown in the Alnwick Walled Garden after its transformation from kitchen garden to flower garden.

An article which appeared in *The Gardeners' Chronicle* on October 23, 1880 describes a visit to Alnwick Gardens, some thirteen years after the accession of the sixth duke, when Alexander Ingram was head gardener, further confirming the range of produce grown in what had by then become the flower garden. The reporter (known simply as 'H.E.') describes some of the produce grown within the 20 acres of walled flower garden and 7 acres of walled kitchen garden. In the flower garden he enthuses over the pines (see beginning of chapter) and mentions apricots as well as the '*Pears, Apples, Peaches, Nectarines, Apricots, Plums, &c. which cover a great extent of wall-surface here…*He adds '*There are five Grape-houses and five Pine-houses, besides pits for suckers… 'The Melons sometimes weigh 6 1/2 lb., and the average weight is from 3 lb. to 5 lb. each. The Peach-houses yield an average crop of 150 dozen. Among the fruits upon the walls outdoors, 350 miles north of London and 5 miles only from the North Sea, I was surprised to find such Pears as Marie Louise, Chaumontel and Beurré Rance. These sorts ripen here in good years, assisted as they must by management and a warm, dry soil.*' (*The Gardeners' Chronicle* 1880, 524).

The number of 'Grape-houses' and 'Pine-houses' presumably refers to compartments in the glasshouses of the hothouses. There were three divisions within Hothouse 4 (vinery) and two rooms are shown within Hothouse 7 on the water supply plan of 1896 (see Fig. 9.12); both these buildings were vineries. The pine house, Hothouse 5, contained 3 compartments and an adjacent frame to the west of this is labelled 'pine house' on the water supply plan of 1990 (Fig. 9.13); presumably the structure to the north of this may also have been use for pineapple cultivation.

Some eleven years later pines were still being cultivated at Alnwick. An article entitled 'Places of interest going North' in *The Gardeners' Chronicle* records some of the fruit varieties grown and reports that vines, first planted presumably when the vinery (Hothouse 4) was initially constructed, were still bearing fruit and being tended. The peach house continued to be maintained:

'*Peach trees are well grown, and have been by Mr. Harris put into perfectly healthy condition as regards soil and drainage of the borders, &c. In one of the first peach-houses entered were found two trees, each seventy years old; these were the old Galande and Royal Hative, and another tree of the same great age yields fine crops every year of pale-coloured fruits – its name was not learned…We entered three of the iron-ribbed vineries, of an old-fashioned style of workmanship, in which there were splendid crops of Black Hamburgh, Alicante, Mrs. Pince, Muscat, &c. It was remarked that Mrs. Pince, a notoriously shy setter, was hung all over with perfect bunches –a result which has followed artificial fertilisation…. Pines have always been well managed at Alnwick, and fine fruits, ripe, and approaching ripeness, were noticed; these were mostly Queens.*

'*The handsome conservatory was gay with plants in bloom… Plums and Pears and Morello Cherries were heavily laden, as were most of the Apricot and Peach trees. A Noblesse Peach, planted so long ago as 1828, was full of nice fruits.*

'*Dwarf Apples on the paradise stock are planted at the sides of the vegetable quarters, and the varieties which almost invariably crop well are Ecklinville, Lane's Prince Albert, Bismarck, Red Calville, a famous dark crimson, and very prolific early fruit; The Queen, Manx Codling, Grenadier, and Lord Suffield.*' (*The Gardeners' Chronicle* 1891, 282).

**Fig. 10.12** The Alnwick seedling grape as depicted in 'Pictorial Practical Fruit Growing' by Walter P. Wright

## The Alnwick Seedling

In much the same way as many of the varieties of apple and pear mentioned above gained their names from either the person or place where they were first raised, Alnwick gave its name to a particular variety of grape, 'The Alnwick Seedling' (Fig. 10.12):

'*A handsome grape, with a very black berry, good habit, but not always setting freely. It was sent out in 1876 by Mr. Bell, of Clive House; raised at Alnwick Castle; always colours jet black; second-rate in quality. A grand exhibition grape*' (Kirk 1909).

There was some initial confusion and debate about the naming of this grape variety, which had initially been named the 'Clive House Grape' and was renamed the 'Alnwick Seedling Grape' as it had been raised from a seedling first planted by a Mr Todd, when foreman at Alnwick (*The Gardeners' Chronicle* 1877, 377).

## Other kitchen garden products

The 1880 article also describes other produce grown for the table at the castle at which '*about one hundred persons dine daily*' (*The Gardeners' Chronicle* 1880, 524). In September and October this would include carrots and green peas, Cocoa-nut cabbages and onions as well as 'coleworts', non-hearting 'greens', such as kale. In conversation with Mr Ingram the reporter for the Chronicle reports:

'"*What capital beds of Carrots!" I remarked. "Yes" said my instructor, and he pulled up the first that came to hand, and showed its shape and quality. Such a Carrot! crisp and tender, and a yard long, more or less*' (*The Gardeners' Chronicle* 1880, 524).

## 10.2 People and the Garden; Staff, Visitors, the Town, the dukes and their Travels

*'I have seen Patten this morning, he has no doubt of the hoes being thrown up to the trees, but can not ascertain which of the women it was that did it, however, I hope this will be a caution for them in future, to keep their hoes in their proper places, that is instead of knocking the pears down, to knock the weeds up.'* (A letter in the castle archives from Thomas Smith of the Castle Gardens to Sir David Smith dated 28th August 1829).

### Head gardeners and other garden staff

The management and upkeep of the walled garden at Alnwick would clearly have been a major undertaking; in times of change, rebuilding or at planting or harvest time there may have been need for greater help and support than at other periods. The surrounding parklands would obviously also create a demand for labour. Information about head gardeners and other garden staff employed at Alnwick has been gathered from a wide variety of sources, including paybooks in the castle archives which list the names of every member of staff employed in the garden each week from 1867 until 1958.

The successful management of the garden would be dependent on the employment of a suitable head gardener. Sir Hugh Smithson, who became the Earl of Northumberland in 1750 following his marriage to Elizabeth Seymour in 1740, and later the first Duke of Northumberland (1766–1786), brought his head gardener Thomas Call from his estate at Stanwick, North Yorkshire to manage the gardens at Alnwick in 1751. Smithson and Call had improved the parklands of Stanwick and by the time he started work on the Alnwick estate, Sir Hugh already had an established reputation as a gardener, as shown by Philip Miller's dedication of his '*Gardener's Dictionary*' (1752 edition) to the earl and John Hill's dedication of his second volume of '*Exotic Botany*' to the duke in 1772. In 1751 Call produced a plan for the parklands and the development of the pleasure grounds at Hulne Park, to the north-west of the castle, and in 1756 was joined by his relation James Call; James is recorded as holding the post of gardener at Alnwick by this date (Shrimpton 2006, 41). In 1758 the Calls each had salaries of £29 per annum (Shrimpton 1997, 3). In 1764 the countess recorded in her notebook that 42 garden men were employed at Alnwick Castle (Shrimpton 2006, 41). Documents in the castle archives record the employment of Cornelius Griffin, one of Lancelot Brown's foremen, from 1769; Brown had placed Griffin in charge of the project to transform the parklands scheme at Alnwick. Three

of Brown's foremen, Griffin, Robson, and Biesley, worked at Alnwick with teams of men between 1771 and 1781. The constable of Alnwick Castle's accounts for 1769 and subsequent years record monthly payments to Cornelius Griffin and his gang of workmen, as well as payments to Thomas Call and his workmen, indicating that from the later 1770s there were two separate planting teams at Alnwick (Shrimpton 2006, 42). In 1773, Call had a team of 60 men and Biesley had a team of 78; a considerable workforce was therefore employed in the latter part of the eighteenth century, both in the newly-constructed walled garden and the surrounding parklands of Alnwick.

A document dating from 1806 in the castle archives lists the ages and years of service of men working on the garden and in this year 21 men and boys were employed in the garden of the second duke (DP/D2/I/163). This reduction in the workforce, though still leaving a large number of workers, presumably follows the initial construction of the garden and development of the surrounding landscape which required large numbers of people. A James Call aged 22 listed in the 1806 document was presumably related to the duke's head gardener. Thomas Call, son of James, was head gardener to the second duke from 1798 to 1808 (Shrimpton 1997, 4). He was replaced by George Robson, ending over 60 years' management of the dukes' of Northumberland gardens at Stanwick and Alnwick by the Calls. The Call family continued as gardeners of the Springfield Nurseries at Alnwick well into the nineteenth century (Shrimpton 1997, 9).

The Gardener's House was built adjacent to the south-west entrance into the walled garden between 1808 and 1811 (Kent 1998, 16) for head gardener, George Robson, who came to Alnwick from Seaton Delaval, also in Northumberland (Green 1998). By 1829 he had been replaced as head gardener by Thomas Smith; letters from Smith are amongst a bundle of correspondence in the castle archives (DP/D3/I/197). That he still held this position in 1843 is known from a notice of the death of Sarah wife of Mr. Thomas Smith, head gardener to His Grace the Duke of Northumberland at Barneyside, Alnwick in 1843 (Carlisle Journal 1843, 3).

A letter from Thomas Smith to Sir David Smith, the third duke's Commissioner for the ducal estates, dated 17th May 1829, reflects the role of the head gardener in negotiating for staff, and illustrates Thomas' shrewd nature:

*'Sir David*

*After duly weighing in my own mind the proposition you made to me the other day of employing two extra men, until I get the dandelions partly up I have come to the following conclusions, that two men at 2/ per day, will be 4/- I can have six strong boys at 8d per day, will be 4/. The boys by being placed amongst the men that is now employed in the pleasure grounds who will keep them right, will do as much of this sort of work as the men will do therefore I will gain four, for the same money. Should Sir David approve of employing the boys, I shall immediately adopted [sic] it, otherwise, I will adhere to the first proposition,*

*I am, Sir David etc…'* (DP/D3/1/197).

Thomas Smith was succeeded as head gardener by Mr. W. Pillans; a Memoriam for John Smith II who began work as a gardener at Alnwick in 1844 aged 18 and worked there for twelve years records that at this time Pillans was the head gardener at Alnwick (Journal of the Kew Guild 1897, 32–33). An 1845 article by William Pillans (*The Gardeners' Chronicle*

*and Agricultural Gazette* 1845, 579) describes bee hives that he had designed to prevent bees from leaving the hive in the winter and perishing from cold, with an accompanying drawing. The 1871 census records William Pillans as a retired gardener from Scotland aged 60 living as a lodger in Howick Street, Alnwick. At the suggestion of the Duke of Northumberland, John Smith II was transferred in 1855 from Alnwick to Syon and in 1857 was appointed head gardener at Werrington Park, Cornwall, also owned by the Duke of Northumberland, then head gardener at Syon. In 1864 he was appointed as Curator of the Royal Gardens, Kew at the age of 38, a position he held until his retirement due to ill health in 1886.

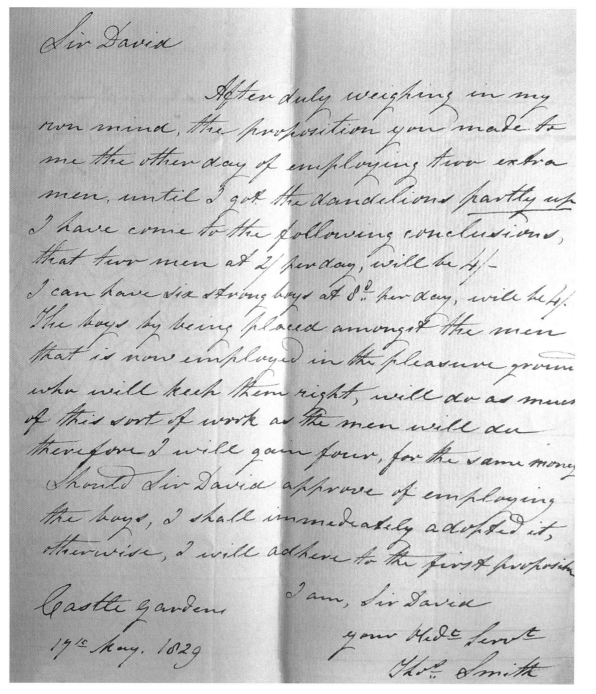

**Fig. 10.13** A letter from head gardener Thomas Smith to Sir David Smith, the duke's commissioner, requesting boys to weed dandelions (DP/D3/1/197)

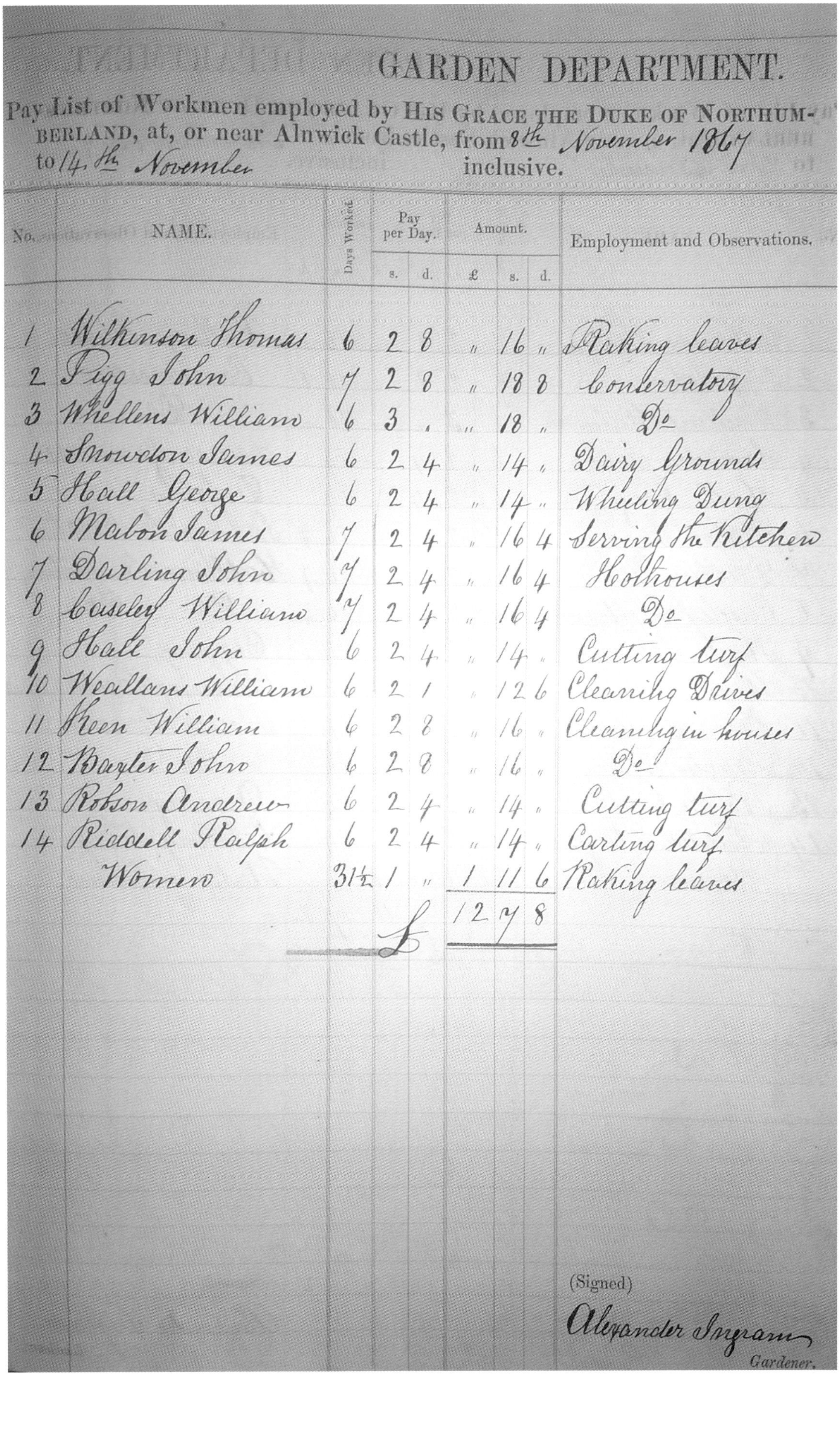

GARDEN DEPARTMENT.

Pay List of Workmen employed by HIS GRACE THE DUKE OF NORTHUMBERLAND, at, or near Alnwick Castle, from 8th November 1867 to 14th November inclusive.

| No. | NAME. | Days Worked. | Pay per Day. s. | Pay per Day. d. | Amount. £ | Amount. s. | Amount. d. | Employment and Observations. |
|---|---|---|---|---|---|---|---|---|
| 1 | Wilkinson Thomas | 6 | 2 | 8 | " | 16 | " | Raking leaves |
| 2 | Pigg John | 7 | 2 | 8 | " | 18 | 8 | Conservatory |
| 3 | Whellens William | 6 | 3 | . | " | 18 | " | Do |
| 4 | Snowdon James | 6 | 2 | 4 | " | 14 | " | Dairy Grounds |
| 5 | Hall George | 6 | 2 | 4 | " | 14 | " | Wheeling Dung |
| 6 | Mabon James | 7 | 2 | 4 | " | 16 | 4 | Serving the Kitchen |
| 7 | Darling John | 7 | 2 | 4 | " | 16 | 4 | Hothouses |
| 8 | Caseley William | 7 | 2 | 4 | " | 16 | 4 | Do |
| 9 | Hall John | 6 | 2 | 4 | " | 14 | " | Cutting turf |
| 10 | Weallans William | 6 | 2 | 1 | " | 12 | 6 | Cleaning Drives |
| 11 | Keen William | 6 | 2 | 8 | " | 16 | " | Cleaning in houses |
| 12 | Baxter John | 6 | 2 | 8 | " | 16 | " | Do |
| 13 | Robson Andrew | 6 | 2 | 4 | " | 14 | " | Cutting turf |
| 14 | Riddell Ralph | 6 | 2 | 4 | " | 14 | " | Carting turf |
| | Women | 31½ | 1 | " | 1 | 11 | 6 | Raking leaves |
| | | | | £ | 12 | 7 | 8 | |

(Signed)

Alexander Ingram

Gardener.

**Fig. 10.14** A page from the paylist of workmen employed by his Grace the Duke of Northumberland at, or near, Alnwick Castle from 8th to 14th November 1867, signed by Alexander Ingram (Acc 446/1/10)

Alexander Ingram (1821–1881) who was born in Aberdeen and was a gardener to J. J. Blandy at Reading in 1854, was appointed head gardener at Alnwick in 1867 (Desmond 1994, 373). The reputation of the gardens attracted important visitors from abroad and in the 1800s the head gardener of Czar Alexander I of Russia visited and subsequently 'head-hunted' Alnwick's head gardener, who left for Russia.

The castle archives contain ten account books relating to staff employed in the garden *'Paylist of Workmen employed by his grace the Duke of Northumberland at, or near, Alnwick Castle'* (Acc 446/1–10). In these are listed the names of every member of staff employed in the garden each week from 1867 until 1958, the number of days worked, wages paid and, in the earlier volumes, the tasks carried out. The early books are signed by the head gardener Alexander Ingram. The late nineteenth-century volumes generally contain four years of accounts, with the years 1874 to 1877 missing, and during the course of the twentieth century staffing levels decrease and each volume spans more years.

In the earliest volume of the records, dated October 1867 to January 1873 (Acc 446/1), the number of men employed in the garden increased from 14 or 15 employees with an unspecified number of 'women' in the three months to end of December 1867 to 25 plus 'women' in March 1868, remaining at between 23–25 employees until the end of this volume in 1873. The highest number was in the week 22nd–28th March 1872, when 26 named employees, a boy and 'women' were employed in the garden. By 1884 up to 30 staff are listed in the weekly accounts (Acc 446/4). This doubling of the workforce was associated with the accession of the sixth duke in 1867 and the arrival of his new head gardener, Alexander Ingram. Contemporary accounts describe the continuous improvements made to the garden by Ingram from his arrival and the technical improvements to the heating system of the hothouses from 1880 (*The Gardeners' Chronicle* 1880). In October 1881 the weekly Paylist was signed by Charles Ingram for Alexander for three weeks, then for another two weeks, and from November 18th 1881 until December 23rd the book is signed by Alex McKiddie (Acc 446/2). This suggests that Alexander may have been ill or incapacitated; by the end of 1881 George Harris had taken up the position of head gardener (Acc 446/5). Harris spent seventeen years in this position and his memoriam following his death in Westerhope, Newcastle upon Tyne in 1940 records details of his career as well as of the history of the Alnwick Walled Garden (Journal of the Kew Guild 1940, 822). After starting his career in Bideford, Devon in 1870, Harris was employed at Kew Gardens in 1872 and was put in charge of the Great Palm House just two years later, before moving to

Syon House where he was 'Foreman' for over three years. His seventeen-year service at Alnwick came to an end in 1899 and his memoriam states that this was due to the great reductions cause by death duties, the sixth duke having died on 2 January 1899. A reduction in staffing levels is recorded in the Paylists after the death of the sixth duke; from 30 named staff to 19 by July 1899 (Acc 446/5). After his employment by the duke ended, Harris became a successful market and flower gardener; his memoriam states that in some years over five tons of tomatoes were grown in the best week of the season and 100,000 Chrysanthemums were planted in a year.

The early twentieth century saw staffing levels increase again to 28 named employees in 1903; the glasshouses evidently required dedicated staff with the Palm House (northern conservatory, Hothouse 6) and Stove Orchids listed as a weekly task (Acc 446/6). With the First World War came a dramatic reduction in staff as men would have left their employment to join the army, or would have been conscripted; by March 1917 just 13 employees are listed (Acc 446/8). From June 9th 1916 for a period of 19 weeks between four and thirteen convalescing soldiers were employed in the garden. Initially they were paid 1s 4d for a week's work (contemporary wages at the time in the garden varied from 3s 8d to 4s 6d); subsequently they were paid by the number of hours worked, generally between 14–25 hours per week, at 6d per hour.

In August 1920 four boys from the Duke's School worked for six days in the garden and in 1921 'duke's School Boys' worked for a few days over the summer holidays (Acc 446/8). The duke's School was founded in 1810 by the second duke and provided elementary education for 200 poor boys; a new school building, extant, was built between 1901 and 1904.

The Paylist of Workmen for the years 1926–1943 shows a great reduction in the number of staff employed; during the 1920s to early 1940s just nine staff remained in employment (Acc 446/9). Heavy death duties had been imposed following the death of the seventh duke in 1918 and the eighth duke in 1930; this evidently had a financial impact on the resources available to staff the garden. Cartographic evidence shows that the northern conservatory was dismantled between 1923 and 1932 and the south-eastern hothouse in 1935 and it is likely that the remaining two hothouses also fell into disuse during this period as the financial resources to run these high-maintenance structures diminished. In March 1939 George, the ninth duke, began making plans to leave Alnwick Castle as a result of the impact of the financial burden of paying death duties twice within twelve years (*The Newcastle Journal*, 4th March 1939). George was killed just one year later in the Second World War.

The last volume of the Paylist spans 1943 to 1958; fifteen years of record in comparison to the six in the earlier volumes, reflecting the reduced resources used in the garden during this period. By 1950 just four people were entered in the book and by 1955 staff time in the garden is recorded in hours worked (Acc 446/10).

## Working conditions in the garden

Of the 21 employees detailed in the 1806 list, the oldest is the 75–year old John Froam who by 1806 had worked for 23 years in the garden (DP/D2/I/163). Four employees were in their 60s, including Matthew Davison, aged 62, the longest serving employee, who had worked in the garden for 42 years. The youngest on this list is George Kisks aged ten who had been employed since the age of seven; two fifteen-year-olds had been employed for four and five years each, illustrating the early age at which young boys might commence working. The very young and people well into their old age were evidently employed by the first and second duke in the Alnwick Walled Garden during the early nineteenth century.

The duke's estates apparently demanded loyalty beyond the working day. A letter of 1829 in a bundle of correspondence to Smith, who was the third duke's Commissioner (property manager) for the ducal estates, indicates that garden workers, presumably as with all of the duke's employees, were expected to obey orders outside of work and vote as instructed (DP/D3/I/197):

*'Pigg and some other unnamed gardeners were trenching at Denwick, Pigg has been accused of voicing his support for another candidate and not Sir David in an upcoming election. Thomas Smith says that he did not hear Pigg saying this, and Sir David should bring Pigg to his office and question him himself about this.'*

The Paylists of Workmen show that in the latter part of the nineteenth-century, employees of the sixth duke worked six to seven days a week, including Christmas day (Acc 446/1–2). John Pigg (paid 2/8 a week) is registered from the first day of the first Paylist, 18th October 1867, as working in the conservatory with William Caseley (paid 2s 4d) in the vineries and peach house. Both men worked seven days week with John Pigg consistently working a seven-day week until 9th July 1872 (there is not a single recorded day off for Pigg for nearly five years), before going down to a six-day week, still in the conservatory.

The weekly jobs undertaken within the garden are listed in the nineteenth-century volumes of the Paylists demonstrating that some employees spent weeks carrying out the same task, some of which would have involved heavy manual labour. Matthew Common trenched in the garden from February 1868 for six weeks, working a six-day week (Acc 466/1). The Garden staff could be treated relatively well by the dukes of Northumberland. John Weallans was first recorded as an employee of the sixth duke in March 1894 when he was paid 17s a week for a six-day week (Acc 446/4). In 1895 John worked in the kitchen garden earning 19s a week and carrying out a wide variety of tasks (Acc 446/5). From December 1901, he was listed as being ill yet continued to be paid 14s a week for a full ten months, until October 1902 (Acc 446/6); he was listed as being away until December 1902, but thereafter until February 1906 again paid 14s a week. He was not recorded in the paylists as being ill, but the amount he is paid and the fact that no jobs are listed indicate that he is unable to work. After his return to work, John was employed for another two years earning 19s for a six-day week, his last week in the garden being December 11 1908. Before the introduction of employees' right to sick pay, John was paid over 80% of his full wages for nearly four years between 1901 and 1906, during a period when he was unable to work. Employees' insurance was first recorded in the Paylists in July 1912 (Acc 446/7).

Autumn and winter were the busiest seasons in the Alnwick Walled Garden in the early twentieth century. *The Gardeners' Chronicle* for May 3, 1902 notes:

*'The ducal owner having other large gardens, and not residing at Alnwick in the period from early spring to early autumn, the gardener has not much early forcing of any kind to carry out, the supplies coming from the other gardens; still, the post of gardener at Alnwick cannot be considered a sinecure, as he has plenty to do in, making preparations on a large scale for an average number of over 100 persons daily in the late autumn and winter.'* (*The Gardeners' Chronicle* 1902, 286).

By 1913 the gardens employed 24 workers with the head gardener receiving a salary of £104 per annum as well as £26 worth of allowances including a house, coals, vegetables and light (Shrimpton 1997, 27). Around half of this labour force lived in a bothy which had been purpose-built at the Bondgate entrance to gardens, to provide accommodation for the garden workers. These men received a monthly salary of £46.16s with an allowance to the value of £6.10s, including vegetables, whilst townsmen who were not accommodated received an annual wage of between £52 and £54.12s with no allowances (Shrimpton 1997, 27).

Living conditions, as reported in 1902, appear to have been quite good:

*'A bothy which permits of each young gardener having a separate bedroom, a common bath-room, sitting and dining-room, and rooms for the foreman, has been erected, and forms a sightly and suitable entrance to the kitchen-garden.'*

Wage inflation after the First World War more than doubled the daily pay rates; from 3s 4d in 1913 to 6s 2d in 1918 and 7s 8d in 1920 (Shrimpton 1997, 27). The huge increase in labour costs may have been one reason that the eighth duke drastically reduced the numbers employed in the Alnwick Walled Garden by more than half and from the summer of 1920 no more than nine gardeners worked under the head gardener.

The 1926 volume of the paylists reveals exceptions to payment of insurance by employers; Thomas Croudace at 70 years of age is exempt as is H. Webster, a boy under 16, and it is also notable that no employer health or unemployment insurance is paid for Mrs Eddy (Acc 446/9).

## The role of women in the garden

Women were clearly part of the garden workforce in the 1820s as the letter relating to the women throwing up their hoes to knock down pears from trees at the beginning of this section clearly demonstrates. Their status is made clear in the earliest volumes of the Paylists; although women are listed as working in the garden, in common with the boys they are not named individually. The numbers of women employed are not recorded so it is not possible to calculate their weekly wage, though undoubtedly they would have been paid less than the men. It seems that they were employed throughout the year to carry out seasonal tasks considered suitable for women. Between November 11, 1867 and December 25 1868, a sample week from each month shows that women carried out the following tasks: washing flowerpots, raking leaves, weeding walks, raking grass, weeding, making hay and cleaning (Acc 446/1). On 10th January 1868 'women' were recorded as 'making blinds', presumably for the glass elements of the hothouses (Acc 446/1).

The names of female employees began to be recorded from the 1880s. Mary Hennessy was employed in the bothy, presumably relating to the domestic quarters which were situated in the backhouse of Hothouse 2 rather than the later, purpose built structure, from December 1884 to November 1895. She was paid 1s 8d per day for a six or seven-day week. From February 3rd 1888 Elizabeth Gardener also worked a six or seven-day week and was paid 1s 4d for cleaning walks, cleaning pots, cleaning flower beds, mending shading (presumably for the glasshouses), cleaning up grass, raking leaves and hay. Cleaning walks is her most frequent task in the 1884–1890 volume (Acc 446/3).

The distinction between wages paid to men and those paid to women is clear in these volumes. From 8th April 1926 a Mrs Eddy was employed in the garden on a rate of 3s 6d per day; the daily wages of the male employees in the same week ranged from

7s 10d to 4s 2d, with the exception of one individual who was paid 3s per day, reflecting a disparity in female to male wages which would have been seen across all employment.

The number of employees working in the garden diminished considerably with the advent of the First World War and by the advent of the Second World War the proportion of named woman working in the garden to men was at its highest. This employment pattern reflected the general trend across the country with women taking on traditionally male jobs to fill the void left by men joining the forces. In November 1939 a Miss Iron and Miss Pollard were employed at a rate of 2s 4d per day and by April 1940 six men and four unmarried women were employed at 4s 4d per day. In May 1941 four women were employed at 6s 4d; this seems to be seasonal work, with one or two women employed in latter part of year. The rise in pay does not reflect an improvement in wages for women, but a steep rise in inflation caused by the war. During the Second World War the garden was used to cultivate vegetables for the war effort, and women would presumably have been employed in the garden to help with food production, with the pleasure and flower gardens and the hothouses for display no longer being maintained.

## Tasks in the garden

The Paylists of Workmen provide information about the wide variety of tasks which would have been required to maintain both the original walled garden, with its three hothouses, growing frames and conservatory, and the walled kitchen garden to the west. Some of these tasks were seasonal, others would have been carried out throughout the year, and some of the listed tasks provide information about the varieties of fruit, vegetables and flowers grown in the gardens.

The highest paid employees tended to carry out the same tasks most weeks in the Paylists and were evidently placed in charge of the running of the hothouses, variously listed as conservatory, hothouses, planthouses, vineries, peach houses and pine stoves. The 'Palm House' is first listed as a weekly task from 1899; contemporary photographs show that the northern conservatory was at this time used to grow large palms (see Fig. 6.5).

The less well-paid employees carried out many different tasks over the year; some examples are given below. Matthew Common, whose employment in the garden began on 26th December 1867 on a rate of 2s 4d per day for a six-day week, performed the following tasks over the course of 1868: trenching in flower garden, trenching slopes, trenching, planting shrubs, rolling grass, cleaning walks, digging, planting in flower garden, bedding out, weeding, pegging in flower garden, cleaning in flower garden, cleaning in grounds, laying pinks, rolling walks, mowing, shifting pines, propagating, transplanting, making walks, shifting manure, mixing manure and wheeling dung (Acc 446/1). The weekly tasks allocated to John Weallans, employed in the kitchen garden from November 15th 1895 provide an insight into the wide variety of jobs needed to maintain these productive fruit and vegetable gardens throughout the changing seasons: pruning apples, root pruning, trimming bushes, nailing wall trees (x 5 weeks), digging, cleaning fruit trees, nailing (x 4 weeks), digging, nailing (x 2 weeks), planting potatoes ( x 2 weeks), tying raspberries (x 2 weeks), digging, hoeing walks, clipping hedge, hoeing walks, staking peas, planting broccoli (x 2 weeks), mulching potatoes, planting celery, staking beans, mowing, hoeing weeds (x 2 weeks), planting savoy, planting coleworts (x 2 weeks), planting lettuce (x 2 weeks), cleaning up, pruning wall trees, cleaning up, planting cabbages, cleaning up, loading loam, tying raspberry canes, planting onions, planting flower garden, moulding celery (x 2 weeks), raking soil, planting trees, pruning fruit bushes (x 2 weeks), pruning shrubs and pruning bushes (Acc 446/5).

As well as the regular garden tasks, seasonal jobs are noted in the Paylists. The entry for 22nd to 28th October 1880 records extra money paid for smoking wasps' nests at night with one person paid for 80 nests, another for 50 nests (Acc 446/2). All the fruit cultivation would clearly attract wasps and it is perhaps no coincidence that this was the week that a journalist from *The Gardeners' Chronicle* was to visit the gardens. On June 16, 1882 an extra payment is recorded for washing blankets for the bothy.  Ice would be an important commodity for the castle and on November 19th 1880 John Darling was paid 2/8 per day for six days for filling the icehouse. A note at the bottom of the page records that the park pond produced ice 2¼in thick. This was obviously a cold winter; on January 28, 1881 it is recorded that 25 loads of ice off the river 8 inches thick were stacked. The icehouse was located under the walkway from the castle to the gardens, in an area where the former ditch of the catle had been filled in:

'*To open an easy and commodious Communication between the Castle and the Pleasure Grounds, a Part of this Fosse has been filled up and over it a Road 12 feet wide made; And even this part has been with great Judgment appropriated to a very useful purpose, for under this Road is a large Ice House.*' (Acc 163).

Monthly accounts for the garden provide an insight into the expenditure on goods and the range of different purchases made. In 1829, the monthly expenditure varied from £6 2s 9d in November to £28 15s 5½d in May (*c.* £2000 today - www.nationalarchives.gov.uk/currency-converter), with expenses including 'Ale for reaping corn', presumably supplied to slake the thirst of those bringing in the harvest, to grass and oats for horses, and bread and barley for servants. Ale was also needed for hothouses, presumably for those working in them. Hardware was necessary in the form of bricks for the garden walls, slates, frames, flue covers and glazing. Sundries ranged from candles and besoms to wheelbarrows. Joiners, bricklayers, chimney sweeps, blacksmiths and slaters were all employed to carry out repair work and construction in the gardens.

## The garden and the town

At its peak the Castle Gardens would have provided much employment in the town, but from the early nineteenth century onwards also provided a place of rest and respite; by 1828 regulations were introduced which controlled when visitors were allowed to see the gardens, hothouses and conservatory and the gardener was instructed by the duke to set aside one day a week for visits by ladies and gentlemen of the town and neighbourhood so that he was not continually interrupted by visitors. Strangers visiting town would also be welcomed to view the garden if the gardener considered them to have 'the appearance of gentlefolk' (Shrimpton 1997, 17).

In 1843, a few years before the death of the third duke, admissions to the garden were curtailed to just one hour on a weekday between 9am and 10am and then only with the written permission of the commissioner (Shrimpton 1997, 17).

As a keen promoter of the allotment garden movement, one of Algernon, the fourth duke's, first deeds was to arrange that gooseberry, currant and raspberry bushes should be provided to holders of allotment gardens he had created on his town lands. The gardens were further opened to the public at this time (see section 10.3 below).

In times of plenty the townspeople might receive some produce; in the 1820s the head gardener helped serve the local populace with the 'duke's bounty' during the July fair, he dealt out potatoes to chosen needy families of the town and supplied Alnwick's soup kitchen with leek and potatoes (Shrimpton 1997, 13). Such acts of generosity were not limited to consumable produce and gifts of flowers were extended to the sick of Newcastle by 1880:

'*I ought to mention that the sick poor of Newcastle probably derive as much keen delight from the flower-gardens of Alnwick as almost any other persons. A basket of flowers, from the borders and greenhouses, is sent every week to the nurses' home, and thence the gift is distributed to many a sick bed, where a flower, like the Passion-flower in " Picciola," may prove a physician, and something more.*' (*The Gardeners' Chronicle* 1880, 524).

## Tanners' waste and fertilizer; evidence for animal husbandry and craft industries

### Kevin Rielly

Animal bones were found throughout the excavations, although with a notable concentration within that part of the garden associated with Hothouse 4 (the vinery). This collection forms the basis of the following comments and a more detailed discussion presented in Appendix 2, both of which are based upon a full report, held with the archive (Rielly 2016; see Gidney 2004, 136). This animal bone collection has enabled a consideration of breeds farmed within the vicinity and the use of post-mortem products, for consumption and within local craft industries as well as the opportunistic use of animal bone waste as a convenient source of fertilizer. Tabulated data which supports this text is reproduced in Appendix 2.

## Description of the faunal remains

In total, 161 bones were recorded primarily from Period 4 layers in front of Hothouse 4, in particular layer [206] (see Appendix 2; Table 1), an extensive dumped soil as well as the underlying deposit, from a brick soakaway within Hothouse 4 and from the fill [264] of an extensive robber trench [265] which truncated [206]. The latter is most likely to represent redeposited material.

Most of the bones were identified as cattle, equid (horse) and sheep/goat (see Appendix 2; Table 1); equid numbers may well have been higher than indicated, as many of the 'cattle-sized' ribs identified could have derived from horses. Post-mortem use of this collection is demonstrated by butchery marks, which include carcass sectioning chops as well as defleshing marks. The horse bone element of this collection shows a general range of skeletal parts (Fig. 10.15), generally comprising disarticulated elements, with the notable exception of the central part of a right

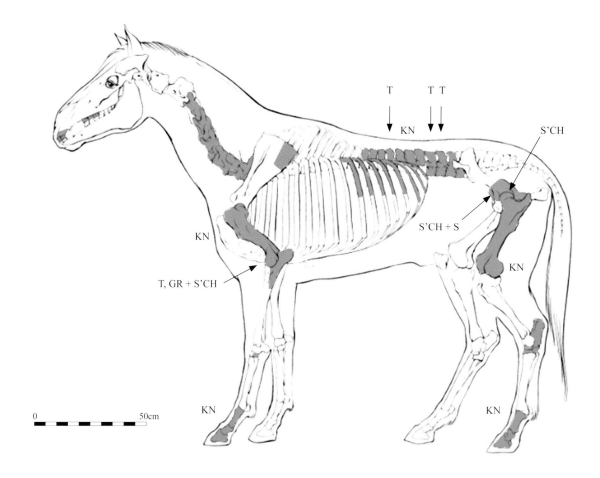

**Fig. 10.15** The distribution of skeletal parts (shaded grey) and butchery cuts within the equid assemblage. Butchery abbreviations include T for transverse cuts (separating vertebrae and removing a distal humerus), S splitting (through a pelvis acetabulum), GR grazing cuts, S'CH superficial chops and KN knife cuts.

hock joint. This level of disarticulation is undoubtedly related to some post-mortem usage, as indicated by a high proportion of butchery marks, including skinning cuts and various jointing cuts. Potential age or work-related pathologies include probable osteoarthritis (exotoses and surface pitting); marked osteophytic lipping; and severe degradation and extension of the posterior aspects (anguli) of a third phalange either side of the articular surface (Fig. 10.16, Fig. 10.17).

The cattle skull pieces represent a minimum number of 26 individuals, generally comprising horncores with some part of the adjacent skull, but including two polled specimens (Fig. 10.18).

The skull fragments are likely to mainly derive from relatively young oxen, possibly culled before their fourth year, and certainly prior to their sixth (after Armitage 1982). This is indicative of animals principally bred for their meat, although, as not all of the horncores could be sexed, the collection may possibly include some cows bred for milk production. The horncore size and nuchal shapes suggest an assortment of 'types', including polled as well as horned cattle varieties. The concentration of particular cattle skeletal parts (see Appendix 2) strongly suggests they were derived from a craft source, probably hornworkers' or tanners' waste (see Conclusions).

A craft source, again probably tanners, could also account the sheep/goat metapodials, following an accepted view that skins (cattle, sheep and goat) were usually provided to the tanner with the horns and the feet still attached (after Serjeantson

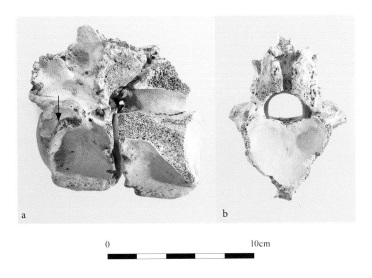

0          10cm

**Fig. 10.16** Equid vertebrae (18th thoracic and 1st lumbar) from [206] showing severe pitting and osteophytic lipping indicative of osteoarthritis – a) left lateral view (also showing butchery – arrowed) and b) showing posterior view of the 18th thoracic vertebra

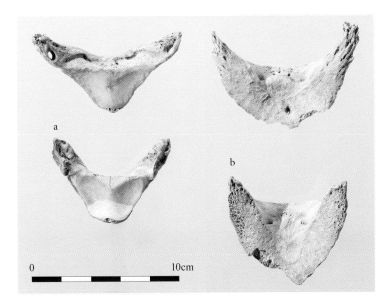

0          10cm

**Fig. 10.17** Equid 3rd phalange with elongated and heavily pitted posterior extensions (above) compared to a 'normal' example (bottom) showing the posterior (a) and ventral (b) aspects

0          10cm

**Fig. 10.18** A polled cattle skull from [206] viewed from posterior (top) and dorsal (bottom)

1989). The excess components would then be sent on to other craft establishments (hornworkers, glue makers, boneworkers, fertilizer producers etc; see Rielly 2011 and Stevens 2011). Both items, head and feet, may have been disposed of en masse following a secondary use; in the case of the skull parts after the removal of the horn sheaves.

The remaining part of the bone assemblage consists of a small number of heavily butchered domesticate vertebrae (cattle) and limb bones, a single goose tibia and a few unidentified fish bones. The butchery was clearly intended to produce joints and this part of the collection can essentially be described as food waste.

## Conclusions

The derivation of various components of the [206] and associated assemblages raises a number of interesting points. Horncore/ skull fragments as well as the sheep metapodials can arguably be categorised as tanning waste, following the premise that skins would generally be delivered with these parts still attached (see Appendix 2). Conveniently, the historical evidence documents tanning establishments within the nearby town. While present in the late medieval period, this industry undoubtedly grew in importance following the Reformation, with no less than 22 tanyards within this urban centre by the mid-sixteenth century. Tanning continued throughout the post-medieval era with at least five tanneries, situated at the southern periphery of the town, dating to the first quarter of the nineteenth century (information taken from Tate 1866 and 1866–9 in Derham *et al.*, 2009). Judging by the presence of cattle skull pieces as well as sheep metapodials, and obviously assuming they came from one or more of these local tanyards, it follows that the town was involved in the production of heavy as well as light leathers i.e. using cattle skins and then those from all other species, but mainly sheep and goat, respectively.

There is clear historical evidence for the former industry. Quoting a court record dating to 1726 (Tate 1866, 344 in Derham 2009, 30), a certain Robert Hyndmarsh was called before court for 'a nuisance caused by teaming and emptying bark and other rubbish in the well course or runner at the foot of Hunters Orchard which annoys the stone well.' Oak bark was one of the major ingredients used in the tanning of cattle hides, while sheep and goat skins were generally prepared/cured using a variety of other substances as for example alum (see Thomson 1981 and Rielly 2011, 173). These two industries were traditionally separate concerns (*ibid.*, 160) and from this evidence it can be further assumed that the Alnwick Castle craft waste was procured from at least two tanyards. Unfortunately, there seems to be little archaeological evidence for this local industry, and this limited

to the recovery of faunal remains from just two sites, both in the grounds of Alnwick Castle. Apart from this present collection, a concentration of cattle metapodials was recovered within a stone lined pit just beyond the castle walls and dated to the eighteenth or early nineteenth centuries (Swan 2006 and Gidney 2013, 248).

There are two main potential sources for the equid collection found at this site, either from the local knacker's yard or from one or more of the urban tanyards. Evidence for the latter source can be found amongst the copious quantities of equid bones found at various post-medieval tanning sites in Bermondsey, London and also in Northampton (Rielly 2011, 169 and Shaw 2011, 125). These collections, in comparison to Alnwick, and indeed with other concentrations of equid remains, here divorced from an industrial setting, as at 14th century Kingston-upon-Thames (Serjeantson *et al.* 1992) and the sixteenth to seventeenth century London site at Elverton Street, Westminster (Cowie and Pipe 1998), all feature a general distribution of skeletal parts, mostly disarticulated and several with butchery marks. In addition, they tend to be from animals of varied stature, no doubt representing a cross section of the local horse population, all either of advanced years or infirm, indicated by often gross pathologies, or both old and infirm. The evidence clearly shows post-mortem usage, the cut marks and disarticulation suggestive of skinning and some exploitation of their meat. Now such meat may have been intended for human consumption and while difficult to prove otherwise, there is undoubted evidence from the post-medieval era regarding the use of horsemeat as pet food. A description of horse trading in Tudor and Stuart England refers to low priced animals as 'dog horses', these to be sold to country estates, essentially as food for hunting dogs (Edwards 1988 in Wilson and Edwards 1993, 52). Dismembered and butchered horse bones have indeed been found at a number of these estates, including Witney Palace in Oxfordshire dating to the eighteenth century (*ibid.*). It can be proposed that a similar purchase may explain the occurrence of the equid remains at Alnwick Castle. While there is an undoubted link to upper class rural society (*ibid.*), it can perhaps be assumed that the aforementioned urban collections, perhaps including Alnwick (assuming a tanyard or knackers yard derivation), were providing meat to some other source. Maybe they were still 'dog horses' supplying food for a variety of pets, working or otherwise. This was certainly in evidence in London by the latter part of the nineteenth century, the yearly cull of some 126,000 horses supplying meat for a burgeoning pet food industry (Bailey 2005, 42).

A proportion of the cattle bones (the food waste) and the two pig bones were clearly from large animals. These, and in particular the pig, may well represent improved 'types', here following the breeding experiments of certain gentlemen farmers in the latter part of the eighteenth into the nineteenth centuries.

In this part of England there were the Colling Brothers, based in County Durham instrumental in the production of a Shorthorn breed of cattle and also the Culley brothers, who established a herd of Dishley Leicester sheep crossing this improved type with a local variety, the Old Teeswater (after Hall and Clutton-Brock 1995, 153 and Rixson 2000, 217). It can be conjectured that these Shorthorns are included amongst those identified at Alnwick as shorthorns (following Armitage 1982) or amongst the larger bones; while the varieties of sheep represented could include this new Leicester variant or perhaps one or more of the older 'types' such as the Teeswater (Hall and Clutton-Brock 1995, 135 and 153). There were undoubtedly a number of such old 'types' amongst the cattle being driven past this area on their way to the London meat markets, the described horn types maybe allowing for the presence of Ayrshire cattle amongst the smaller varieties and maybe Highland cattle amongst the larger (*ibid.*, 23 and 30). In addition, there may have been examples of either unimproved or improved longhorns, the latter famously produced by Robert Bakewell, the Dishley Longhorn, this becoming very popular in England and especially in the midland counties by the early nineteenth century (*ibid.*, 63). The polled animals could be either Aberdeen Angus or Galloway, the lack of horns being a positive asset considering the trials and tribulations associated with driving cattle over long distances (*ibid.*, 19). The pig bones may well represent a cross between one of the older types with Chinese and/or Neopolitan varieties, this dating from the last few decades of the eighteenth century (see Rixson 2000, 220–2).

The previous discussion raises another major point of interest concerning this collection, and that is the relationship between the Castle and a notable concentration of bones which are almost entirely composed of non-food waste. The equid bones are included in the latter category as even though they may represent the remains of dog horses, it is perhaps unlikely that the bones as well as the meat would be transferred from the knacker's yard/tan yard to the Castle. In addition, the completeness of the bones and the lack of dog gnawing counter any arguments concerning the use of these bones for chewing purposes. The dumping of such waste can hardly be seen as a convenience being somewhat removed, most probably, from their points of origin even supposing the highly unlikely scenario that fly tipping would have been allowed within the Castle grounds. The only possible explanation is that there must have been some benefit to the garden or rather to the soil with the juxtaposition of this collection to the vinery in Hothouse 4 offering a major clue. Of interest in this respect is a contemporary account, dated to the nineteenth century,

referring to the growing of vines in hothouses at Pylewell in Hampshire (Campbell 2005,182). Here it is mentioned that any animals which had died at the farm would be buried in the ground next to the vineries, a precursor no doubt of the 'blood and bone' fertilizer used by later gardeners. This would appear to involve entire carcasses rather than the partial remains found at Alnwick, perhaps suggesting that the choice of parts/carcasses would depend on availability. At Alnwick, it was obviously easier to make use of waste from the tanneries and knackers yards available in the nearby town. Tanneries would no doubt also have been called upon to provide the used tanners' bark required for pineapple cultivation.

## Connections with China and Calcutta

A hardbound notebook dated 1796 contained within the castle archives may provide some of the earliest evidence for plant collecting connected with the dukes of Northumberland, apparently illustrating the second dukes' far-flung connections and interests in acquiring exotics (DP/D2/I/182). A letter, accompanying the collection and contained within the book, gives some idea of the background; plants here are being procured from China for the Botanic Gardens in Calcutta. The notebook contains illustrations of some of the species gathered, labelled in Chinese. Some of these are readily recognisable, others less so. There is no evidence to suggest whether any of the plants illustrated in the notebook made their way to Alnwick, although later evidence suggests a strong link back to Britain from China; the passage from Canton to Calcutta being only the first leg of the journey. The letter is directed to Richard Hall esq, President etc of the Select Committee [of the East India Company], and details the ships and captains by which the plants would be sent:

'Gentlemen,

 *In compliance with a letter from the president of the 19th of September requesting I would use my endeavour to procure such Chinese plants etc as are wanted for the honourable company's botanic garden at Calcutta I have the honour to inform you that I have sent by the Nancy Grab, Captain Carnegy, and Upton Castle, Captain Thomas, the following packages, being the only articles of the list now procurable. I have given the necessary directions for those remaining to be in readiness for the ships of next season.'*

The consignment shipped included two boxes of sugar cane (and a miniature model of a sugar mill), hemp seed, cotton seed and 'linkock' or the lin kio nut, the water chestnut, also known as the 'calthrop nut' on account of its shape.

The letter continues *'Drawings of the Aquatics are likewise sent on… [to] the gentleman who has the Superintendence of the Botanic Gardens in Bengal'*, with apologies for lack of identification according to Linneaus' system. The letter goes on to describe many aquatic plants dispatched and is signed by A. Duncan (surgeon) at Canton, 30th October 1796.

Sadly, few of the illustrations of aquatic species described in the letter survive within the book. Under the heading 'Lin-Faa' Duncan writes:

*'This beautiful aquatic is difficult to be procured at this season, I have consequently only sent on the drawing of the double red Water Lily. It is divided into different genus as the red, white, double red and double white. It is used as an ornamentation in tanks or pots, & produces a seed, which when boiled is in great estimation as a cooling vegetable in sickly habits.'*

The illustrations generally relate to terrestrial plants some of which are clearly identifiable, others less so. An illustration of what appears to be a persimmon, or Sharon fruit, is accompanied by the following description: *'a flat soft reddish fruit with a smooth skin, containing a slight acid pulp with a kernel in the middle. The fruit is of the size of a middling orange, and looks as if flattened by weight from a globular form'*.

Some illustrations are of flowers, such as a probable Convolvulus, or morning glory (see images in the inside covers). Other illustrations clearly represent fruits, resembling almonds, peaches and apricots. A green and red coloured, elongated fruit with a leaf and kernel resembling those of a peach or nectarine is labelled in English 'China Peach', whilst an image of a lychee bears the Chinese symbols for this fruit.

The surviving archives at Alnwick Castle clearly only contain a fraction of the correspondence which must have existed regarding the movement of exotic fruits and plants around the globe. Chronologically, the next set of surviving correspondence relates to the movement of plants between the Americas, Britain and the Indian subcontinent. In the 1830s there was extensive correspondence between the third duke, a keen collector of exotics, and Dr Wallick (DP/D3/I/30). Dr Wallick was Superintendent of the East India Company's Botanical Garden at Calcutta (Dutt 1916, 277) and was actively engaged in shipping species from there to the Duke of Northumberland. These documents clearly illustrate the complex movement of plants around the world.

A letter dated 25th February 1837 from Dr Wallick, at the Botanic Gardens, Calcutta includes a list of the contents of two closed cases of plants which are to be sent to his grace the Duke of Northumberland (Case 1 contains 20 plants, Case 2 contains 19 plants). The letter from Dr Wallick to 'my lord duke' contains an apology for not having sooner acknowledged a favour sent by the duke; the unfortunate doctor had been severely ill, his wife and children sent back to England on account of their illness. Dr Wallick

had dispatched 'closed cases' of orchids (*orchidae*) to the duke.

The exchange of plants went both ways, however, the duke having sent seeds to Dr Wallick, sadly only a few of which had germinated, these included: Coreopsis, Lupinus, Stocks and Nigellas. Dr Wallick requested different varieties of orchid in exchange for the plants he sent: *'I shall feel grateful for an orchidae with which you Grace may indulge me, natives of Australia or of south America. I entreat you to order the two cases to be returned to me filled with Orchidea and other rare plants…'* (DP/D3/I/30)

The duke clearly honoured this request. A document dated 25th September 1837, records the transfer of some 59 plants to Dr Wallick in Calcutta by the ship 'Phillip Manion', under Captain McCarthy; many of the species listed originated in the Americas (a full list of the species transferred is held with the project archive). Around half the plants dispatched were species of orchid, these are accompanied by many lilies, in particular varieties of Alstromeria, as well as Fuschia (*onagracae*) and Thunbergia (*acanthceae*). Perhaps one of the most ambitious transfers concerns rice sent from Nepal to the third duke; unfortunately, there are no records to suggest how successful (or otherwise) the cultivation of rice may have been once it arrived in Britain:

*'East India House,*
*16th October 1838*
*My dear Lord Duke,*

*I have the honour by command of the Court of Directors of the East India Company to forward for your Grace's acceptance a sample of Mountain Rice in the Husk grown at Joomlah in Nepal and transmitted to the Superintendent of the Company's Botanical Gardens at Calcutta, Dr A Wallick. (DP/D3/I/30)*

*It will be gratifying to the Court to learn of the result of any experiment which your Grace may be pleased to institute with the accompanying sample.'*

A second exchange contained within the same bundle of correspondence contains three letters from a Thomas Nightingale. Nightingale appears to be travelling to Penang and Manilla plant-collecting, funded, or at least financially assisted, by the duke.

*'May 16th 1838, Trincomali*
*My Lord Duke,*

*Permit me to express my most grateful thanks for the permission to draw for hundred pounds to complete my expedition to the South Seas contained in your Grace's letter of 30th January…'I regret to find of your Grace's letter the rhododendrons did not reach England alive, but hope that other plants which I have made arrangements to procure will be more fortunate...'* (DP/D3/I/30).

**Fig. 10.19** Illustration of the double red Water Lily from a notebook of 1796 portraying Chinese imports to Calcutta (VR 2015; DP/D2/1/182)

**Fig. 10.20** Illustration of what appears to be a persimmon fruit from a notebook of 1796 portraying Chinese imports to Calcutta (VR 2015; DP/D2/1/182)

**Fig. 10.21** Illustration of a 'China Peach' fruit from a notebook of 1796 portraying Chinese imports to Calcutta (VR 2015; DP/D2/1/182)

**Fig. 10.22** Illustration of a lychee from a notebook of 1796 portraying Chinese imports to Calcutta (VR 2015; DP/D2/1/182)

**Fig. 10.23** Illustration of an orchid, in Chinese called 'Lan-Fa' from a notebook of 1796 portraying Chinese imports to Calcutta (VR 2015; DP/D2/1/182/15)

## 10.3 Views and Vistas; the Alnwick Walled Garden in its Landscape Setting

*'The gardens at Alnwick Castle, the best in the county of Northumberland for fruit growing under glass, and a certain style of bedding-out pursued there, that is well adapted for the cool climate, should not be omitted from the list of places worthy of being visited by gardeners going North… as befits a modern garden and its glass erections, it is removed some distance from the hoary old stronghold of Alnwick Castle, whose flagstaff on the keep is about all that one can see of it from the area round the glasshouses. One cannot say too much for the fine style of keeping the beauty of the turf and walks, and the general air of tidiness and cleanliness prevailing, not only in this part of the garden, but everywhere else…'* (The Gardeners' Chronicle 1891, 282).

When the kitchen garden at Alnwick was first established in around 1770, it was quite deliberately set 300m or so away from the castle. Where earlier, seventeenth-century, kitchen gardens had commonly been situated close to the house for ease of access, the developing aesthetic of the naturalistic landscape resulted in kitchen gardens being placed at some distance from the house. Consideration for the visibility (or otherwise) of the walled garden was paramount, with the garden being hidden from any views of the landscape. Similarly, the castle remained hidden from view within the garden. Whilst the dimensions and internal arrangements of the garden changed, this aspect did not, and the Alnwick Garden remains to this day an enclosed space, very much separate from the surrounding landscape.

**Fig. 10.24** A view of Alnwick Castle from the Aln, painted by Canaletto in 1747 this shows the landscape before it was modified

## Lancelot 'Capability' Brown at Alnwick

It is generally accepted that Lancelot 'Capability' Brown was influential in redesigning the landscape and gardens surrounding the castle in the 1760s and 1770s although sadly no plans of the garden by Brown survive. Brown, born at Kirkharle, some 30 miles south-west of Alnwick, is likely to have been influential in the design of the grounds of Kirkharle Hall and Rothley Lake (at Wallington). Willis argues in favour of Brown's hand in the redesigning of Alnwick Gardens, citing Brown's links to the architects Daniel Garrett, James Paine and Robert Adam and the gardener Cornelius Griffin, who worked for Brown (Willis 1981, 176). Cornelius was one of three foremen, the others being Thomas Robson and Thomas Biesley, all of whom are known to have worked for Brown at Alnwick from the late 1760s, often with large teams of gardeners and labourers.

Two pieces of documentary evidence attest to Brown's connections with Alnwick; a payment of £300 made to one Mr Brown on 10 July 1769, and a note dated 7 September 1772 relating to the payment of 18s for a 'Postchaise to Hampton Court to Mr Brown about a Man to conduct the Works at Alnwick on the Death of Mr Griffin'. The implication here is that Brown, working in London at the time, was called on to advise on both the original design (the £300 payment) and to suggest a way forward on the death of the foreman of the works that were taking place. Brown, at this time, is known to have been working at Syon House, also for the Duke of Northumberland; it seems logical to surmise that he planned and advised on the works at Alnwick, even if he did not personally oversee their realisation (Willis 1981, 176–177).

A recent review of Capability Brown's landscapes concluded that there was a 100% likelihood that the parkland at Alnwick was designed by Brown, citing correspondence as the principal form of evidence (Phibbs 2016). The certainty of this attribution rests on a new understanding that Brown acted as a type of 'employment agency' for gardeners and foremen whose work he was responsible for overseeing. In the case of Alnwick this relates to Cornelius Griffin, foreman from 1769 to 1772 and his successor Thomas Biesley, who was paid directly by the Alnwick estate.

**Fig. 10.25** A view of Alnwick Castle from the Aln, showing the Lion Bridge; J.M.W. Turner, Britain, 1775 - 1851, Alnwick Castle , *c*.1829, London

**Fig. 10.26** A view of Alnwick Castle across the Aln as it appears today. Comparison with Canaletto's depiction (Fig. 10.24) illustrates the changes made by Brown; the ground in front of the Castle has been smoothed and rounded, the river widened, deepened and tamed (Darryn Wade)

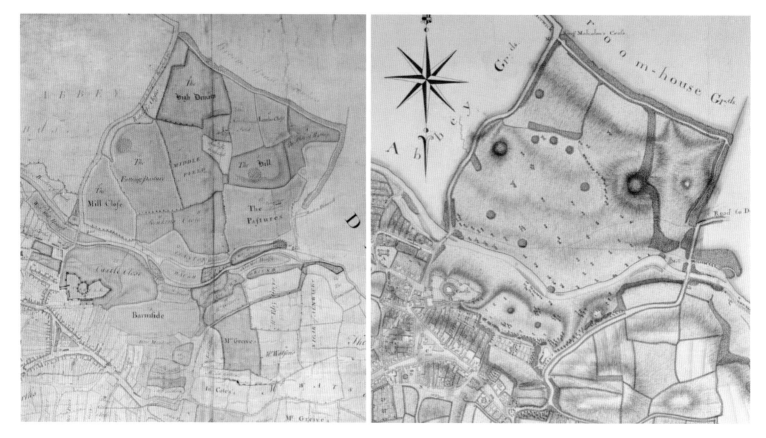

**Fig. 10.27** Details from 1760 (Thompson) and 1778 (Sauthier) maps showing the extent of the transformation of the landscape attributed to Capability Brown, including unification of pastureland and clearing of the river

**Fig. 10.28** View eastwards from Alnwick Castle along the line of the driveway, towards the walled garden, which remains obscured by trees (VR 2015)

The transformation of the landscape at Alnwick by Brown was described thus by Tate:

*'Naked and bleak was the country round Alnwick in the early part of the eighteenth century. ...Many of the forests and woods had been destroyed in the days of border warfare; but this duke began to adorn the lands around his castle…the tops of the hills were planted with lumps of trees; other clumps mostly of a circular form were scattered over the slopes, and on other parts were long belts of plantations, while in the valleys larger forests were created; the old parks too were extended and enclosed by high walls. Greatly beautified and enriched was the scenery by these improvements'.* (Tate 1866, 358).

The area known as the North Demesne, a large expanse of land north of the river Aln which had been divided into over a dozen plots of land (see Thompson's 1760 plan, Fig. 10.27) was to form part of the newly designed landscape. The field divisions were removed and trees planted in clumps across the now unified pasture land, in lines or individually to break up the view, creating a characteristic Brown landscape (Shrimpton 2006, 47) which can be seen depicted on Sauthier's 1778 map (Fig. 10.27). One of the most important parts of Brown's scheme at Alnwick was his transformation of the River Aln. The duke had wanted to create a huge lake at Alnwick, however this plan was dropped and Brown worked with the canal builder James Brindley to

make the river into the main feature of the landscape. Brindley advised on the creation of a series of cascades, which slowed the flow of water making the river calmer and giving it more of the appearance of a lake (Owen 2016a). This created wide surfaces of water to complement the newly-landscaped North Demesne and reflect the newly restored castle. The great flood of 1771 swept away the cascades which were rebuilt by a local millwright. The causeway bridge which was also swept away was replaced by the 'Lion Bridge', a single-arched bridge designed by James Adam, the younger brother of Robert (see Fig. 10.25). The slopes below the castle walls were smoothed and turfed, the river banks cleared and levelled, and the river bed cleared of boulders, making the river fit for sailing.

Brown's scheme for Alnwick also included a carriageway to cross the valley from the east of the castle stretching along the length of Barneyside and skirting the north side of a newly created large pond to the east of the walled garden (Owen 2016a). This gravel walk, which can be seen on Sauthier's 1788 plan (Fig. 8.2; Fig. 10.27), was overhung by trees and gave views down river towards the Gothic-style mill and Denwick Bridge, which had replaced the old ford. A walkway branched off from the route to lead to the entrances into the walled garden through the north wall. Construction of this carriageway was a major undertaking;

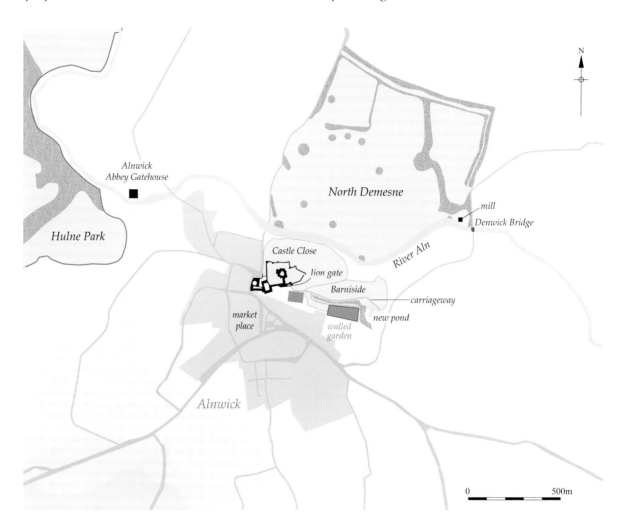

**Fig. 10.29** The environs of Alnwick Castle *c.* 1770, illustrating the principal landscape features mentioned in the text (based on Sauthier 1778) (scale 1:20,000)

a gate, the 'Lion Gateway' was put through the castle walls and a causeway built over the castle ditch. This involved culverting a stream (visible on Thompson's 1760 map; Fig. 10.27) which flowed through Alnwick along the side of the castle and under the causeway (Shrimpton 2006, 42). Construction of the garden also had a major impact on the town. To create enough space for the garden, grounds at the back of the town were purchased by the duke and one of the roads in the town, which ran between Barneyside and Dew Meadows, was lost (see Fig. 10.27).

This landscape was described in 1785, thus:

*'At some Distance from the Gate, a winding Path turns on the right, through a Plantation of Trees towards the Garden, but pursuing the Road above mentioned leaving a fine Clump of Beech & other Trees on the Left, and descending a gentle Hill there is a piece of Water, with several foreign Water fowl on it. A little beyond this pond the Road divides to the right and left, the part on the right towards a Gate opening to a Road leading to the Town of Alnwick and that to the left, to a Gate opening to the same Road leading northwards to the Village of Denwick.*

*'The Pleasure Grounds are bounded on this side by a Stone Wall, between which and the Road or Path is a thick Plantation of various Trees mixed with flowring shrubs; And as the land is every where*

*elegantly diversified by Hills and Dales, small Clumps and single Trees scattered on the Tops and in the Vallies have a most beautiful Effect; but advancing still further to the left, and walking up a gentle Hill, on which is placed a small Rustic Seat, a Scene presents itself which at once delights and charms the Spectator, for from hence is seen in the Bottom the River Alne meandring through the Vales, and falling over a beautiful Cascade at the Foot of the Hill. At some little Distance up the River is an elegant Bridge of Three Arches with a fine Statue of a lion on its Center; and beyond, Hills with Woods on them terminated by Brisley Tower. From this spot is also the most compleat prospect of the Castle standing in Majestic Pride, and finely contrasted by an extensive Pasture on the other or North Side of the River, on which Flocks of Sheep and Herds of Cattle are grazing, and which, rising with a gentle Ascent, is every where bordered by Plantations of Wood...'* (Acc 163, 54–56).

Brizlee Tower (also Brislee or Brisley) was built by the first duke in honour of his wife and provided a focal point on Brizlee Hill (Fig. 10.30). The tower bears an inscription in Latin, which illustrates the duke's impact on the surrounding landscape, which translates as: '*Look about you. I have measured all these things; they are my orders: it is my planning; many of these trees have been planted by my own hand*'.

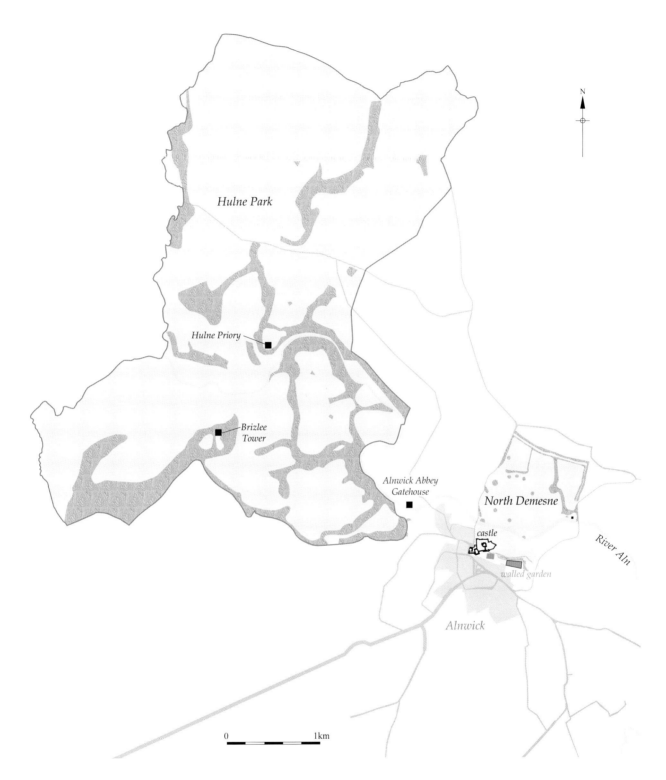

**Fig. 10.30** The wider environs of Alnwick Castle *c.* 1770, showing the castle and garden in relation to North Demesne and Hulne Park (based on Sauthier 1770; Shrimpton 2006, 78) (scale 1:40,000)

An essential element of many of Brown's landscapes, a walled garden, was included in the design of many of his landscaped parks around great houses, and often sited at some distance from the house. The plans drawn up for Kirkharle, which date from *c.* 1770, include a rectangular walled garden located some distance from the house (Owen 2016b). This included a hothouse on the north wall and a small circular pond along the central axis in front of the building with the garden divided into four segments by paths, a very similar layout to the original walled garden at Alnwick. Brown was following contemporary trends in gardening, in both the location and design of the Kirkharle walled garden. The extent of Brown's influence in the internal layout of the original Alnwick kitchen garden remains unknown, but the principles regarding its setting were well established and would have been closely adhered to; the kitchen garden was a prominent feature of the transformation of the landscape.

Throughout the seventeenth century kitchen gardens had been located as close to the house they supplied as possible but, as the fashion changed from formal to natural landscapes throughout the eighteenth century, with the development of the English Landscape Style, the kitchen garden would be placed out of sight of the main house or concealed behind shrubs or belts of trees (Campbell 2005, 23–24). Internally, the symmetrical, regular layout of a kitchen garden was not in keeping with the naturalistic landscapes of Brown and contemporary fashion, whilst the high stone or brick walls surrounding a kitchen garden, along with the smoking chimneys of hothouses, did not fit easily into a picturesque setting. The garden would have been screened from view by planting; belts of trees disguised the high walls. Ultimately the kitchen garden would have been hidden from views from both the castle and the River Aln, but it is worth remembering that when first planted trees would not totally obscure, but only soften the lines of the walled garden. They may also have provided shelter from northern and north-easterly winds.

Once inside the garden, views of this surrounding landscape would be hidden by the high enclosing walls. The original garden was 3.7 acres in extent and trapezoidal in shape; this form was designed to maximise the sunlight hitting the walls, particularly on the north, west and east sides. The main entrance to the kitchen garden, i.e. the entrance used by family or visitors to the garden, would commonly be along one of the short sides providing the longest views of the garden, where a walkway would lead towards a central pool, fountain or similar. Gardeners, wheeling in barrow loads of manure, removing weeds and bringing in vegetables and trees to plant would typically use a separate entrance (Campbell 2005, 45). The location of the original gates, within the western wall, is typical for gardens of the period; a description of the garden in the 1780s suggests that the family used that in the north-west and gardeners would use a gate in the south. Approaching the gardens from the pond to the north-east, visitors may have entered the garden via gates on either side of the vinery (Hothouse 1):

*'on turning to the right and again passing the Pond, another small path leads among a Plantation of Trees to the Garden, or rather Nursery – from whence the extensive Plantations in the Neighbourhood are principally supplied with young Trees…Having passed through these Gardens, a path to the left leads through a gate to a pleasant field, beyond which is another Nursery of young plants, and a Gate opening near the South Extremity of the Town - this is the way by which all Refuse Matter is carried from the Garden, and the Manure brought in without in any degree incommoding the more conspicuous parts of the Grounds, which are kept in the greatest State of Neatness'* (Acc 163, 56–57).

Alternatively, visitors from the castle may well have entered the garden via the entrance in the north-west. This being the case the visitor, entering the garden, would be faced with a long walk leading to, and alongside Hothouse 1. The position of the original hothouse, central to the northern wall, with furnaces external to the garden itself was common for the period. More unusually, however, the description of 1785 suggests that much of the kitchen gardens at this date were originally given over to growing trees with which to supply the ample grounds surrounding the castle:

*'The Nursery Grounds are divided into five parts surrounded by high walls well furnished with peach, Nectarine, Plum and other Wall Fruit Trees: within these walls are also Pineries, Grape Houses, Melon Frames, &c – And in the Borders are great numbers of Currant, Gooseberries &c – but the Beds are occupied by Firs of various kinds, Oaks, Ash, Beech, and a great variety of other young Forest Tree…'* (Acc 163, 57).

## Expansion of the parklands and early hothouse construction

The second duke, Hugh, also invested heavily in the landscape surrounding the castle, extending the property by around 200 acres, and rebuilding the crumbling walls around Hulne Park (Shrimpton 2006, 56); the castle and gardens thus formed part of a much wider landscape. This land acquisition included the purchase of part of Alnwick Abbey estate, north of the Aln between Hulne Park and North Demesne. Here the duke's 'improvements' were destructive as well as constructive and he was responsible for the demolition of the Abbey buildings and for razing them to the ground, saving only the gatehouse (see Chapter 8.3). Investment in the construction of metalled drives through the pleasure grounds enabled these extensive parklands to be enjoyed by carriage. The walled garden remained a separate world, within which Hugh's enthusiasm for plant collecting and gardening resulted in the construction and modification of numerous hothouses while the expansion of the kitchen gardens to the south and east provided additional growing space. The garden at this time would still have been entered from the west; although an entrance in the north-east corner now supplemented the access. The basic layout of the kitchen garden, with its rectangular plots dividing the garden into a series of regular beds, interspersed with walks and with a pond on the central north–south axis, remained little changed. A proliferation of glasshouses of different, and experimental, designs, along with forcing pits for melons and the like, emphasise that this was very much a practical and productive kitchen garden and one in which the interests of cultivation may have taken precedence over an overall aesthetic.

## Flowers and fruit: a new central conservatory and rebuilt hothouses

By 1829, the kitchen gardens had been extended to the south-west, south and east (see Fig. 8.6). A plot of land closer to the castle and covering approximately the same area as the original kitchen gardens is also marked as Kitchen Gardens; it may have been that this provision of additional growing space allowed the role of the original walled kitchen garden to change. Writing in 1839 McIntosh makes it clear that by this period opinion on the location of kitchen gardens was divided. Some felt it should be situated close to the house, for convenience, others at some distance, so as to remain out of sight (McIntosh 1839, 1–4).

'*however convenient it may be to have the kitchen garden so near to the house, that convenience can seldom counterbalance the difficulty of screening the garden, so as completely to hide it from the windows, without the creation of plantations, which will either shade the garden itself, or produce a heavy appearance, as an artist would term it, that ill accords with that free and graceful arrangement which should be so carefully studied in the disposal of trees throughout every domain, but more particularly in the immediate vicinity of the mansion.*' (McIntosh 1839, 2–3).

Wherever the garden was located in relation to the house, it was important at this period that it should remain hidden from view. This aspect of the garden was to remain constant; throughout its history the garden remained hidden and enclosed by high walls. Maintenance of the surrounding landscape was clearly as important as the walled garden:

'*The estate was splendidly cared for from both the forester's and gardener's point of view, during the last century, as duke Hugh and*

**Fig. 10.31** The wider environs of Alnwick Castle c. 1830 showing the castle and expanded garden in relation to North Demesne and Hulne Park; note the reduced size of the latter compared with Fig. 10.30 (based on Barnfather 1829, Shrimpton 2006, 79) (scale 1:40,000)

*duke Algernon were great planters. The splendid woods in the park testify to this. These woods afford charming effects, the trees being of large size and richly diversified, and when these woods are viewed from the Castle walls stretching away for many miles, with the Brislee Tower in the distance on one side…, and the castles of Warkworth, Bamborough, and Dunstanborough near the coast in the far distance, and the long stretch of sea and rock-girt coast, the river Aln meandering in various directions, and at one point lapping the hill on which the castle stands,'* (*The Gardeners' Chronicle* 1902, 273).

The third duke had invested heavily in the parkland surrounding the castle, but these grounds remained very much private pleasure grounds for the enjoyment of the Ducal household. This privacy came at a cost however. The boundaries of Hulne Park were much reduced by the third duke, in an attempt to maintain the secluded nature of his lands, with the addition of a turnpike on the highway which formerly crossed the park and the construction of a new enclosing wall alongside the turnpike road (Fig. 10.31). The cult of the exotic did not only encompass plants, but could be extended to the animals occupying the landscape as exemplified by the

walled gardens within Hulne Park, constructed perhaps originally for deer, which were occupied by Indian water buffalo brought to Alnwick by the duchess from Powis Castle (see section 8.3 above). The walled garden, however, changed significantly and was, for the first time, opened to the public. The focus of the garden was much more related to display, and attention was turned to the cultivation of flowers, and of exotic fruit for the table.

The duchess Charlotte Florentia, had an enthusiasm for flower gardens and would have played an active part in the design of the garden. The duke's commissioner relayed information from the duchess to the clerk of works' masons on the finish to be given to the borders of the flower beds which were to be edged by stone slabs half an inch thick and standing two inches above the walls (Shrimpton 1997, 17). Instructions were given to the gardener to have the flower gardens ready for her visit in July 1827. The garden was stocked by the duchess with Chinese asters, double *hanea elegans*, scandises, red cock's comb, primulas and green *colchium*; seeds were sent from France by Lady Pembroke (Shrimpton 1997, 17). Some of the flower stock was brought on in cold frames. In

**Fig. 10.32** The third Duke of Northumberland's conservatory at Alnwick as it may have appeared in the 1830s, seen from the south-east. Constructed by the same builders as the conservatory at Syon and just a few years later; this reconstruction is based on the latter example, but lacks the extensive projecting curved wings seen at Syon. Excavation revealed the curving frontage of this building only, at foundation level; evidence for the pergola, decorative parterre garden and glazed cupola are based on evidence from Barnfather, reconstruction by Chris Mitchell (c.mitchell02@btinternet.com)

**Fig. 10.33** The approach to the garden from the south-west as it may have appeared by the late 1830s, following the construction of the curvilinear frontage to Hothouse 2, reconstruction by Chris Mitchell (c.mitchell02@btinternet.com)

1828 slag was sent from the glass and iron works on the duke's land at Newburn on the banks of the Tyne west of Newcastle to the staithes at Alnwick to help establish the correct soil composition for the duchess' rockery (Shrimpton 1997, 17).

A major investment, and change in the garden's layout, came with the renovation and building of a grand conservatory and new hothouses. The conservatory, constructed around 1825, formed the centrepiece to the garden. Little of the building was revealed archaeologically, but Barnfather's plan (1829) suggests a complex design with a central glass cupola or dome to the rear, flanked by houses which presumably housed the furnaces to heat the structure and with an extensive glasshouse 100ft in length in front. A central bow provided views over a parterre garden laid out to the south with a central basin and surrounding pergola.

The construction of the grand central conservatory (Hothouse 3) is paralleled by similar developments at Syon, where the duke had commissioned a new conservatory designed by Charles Fowler (Woods and Warren 1988, 120). This had a central giant-domed palm house with two curved wings and housed a range of exotics, collected and imported from all over the world. John Claudius Loudon described a visit to Syon in 1827 where the

metallic hothouse manufacturers Richards and Jones of Cheapside, Birmingham had built a hothouse which:

*'exceeds 400 feet in length, and is intended for pines and early forcing. This magnificent range is constructed entirely of metal, even to the wall-plates, the doors, and the framing of the sashes'* (Loudon 1827, 107).

The conservatory at Syon has been recently renovated, it actually measures 382 feet in length and, whilst the dome, glazing bars and sashes are all, as Loudon reports, of metal, the facades of the structure employ Bath stone, echoing the designs of earlier orangeries (Woods and Warren 1988, 120).

The new conservatory at Alnwick (Hothouse 3) was built in the centre of the walled garden in 1827; Loudon reported that Richards and Jones (builders of the magnificent glasshouse at Syon) were *'now engaged in erecting a most extensive range of the same kind at Alnwick Castle'* and payments for the wages of 'Birmingham men' are mentioned in the Alnwick accounts for January 1827 (Shrimpton 1997, 16). There are other references to large sums of money as 'greenhouse' weekly wages (£77, £52, £168 and £40) from late 1826 to summer 1827 which most probably also refer to the construction of the conservatory (Shrimpton 1997, 16). This grand central conservatory is shown on the 1827 and

**Fig. 10.34** The view of the garden from the raised central mound as it may have appeared in 1860. Planting schemes, which would have changed with the season, have been deliberately kept simple in these reconstruction illustrations, reconstruction by Chris Mitchell (c.mitchell02@btinternet.com)

1829 maps; the latter detailed plan shows it as 100 feet (*c.* 30.50m) in length (the sixteen ribs along the width of the building may be indicative only; Fig. 8.6). On the south side, the middle section formed a bow front which overlooked the parterre and in the roof of the conservatory was a glazed dome on a square base. Narrow rectangular buildings shown to the east and west of the cupola and adjoining the glasshouse elements to the north presumably housed the heating apparatus for the structure. Given Loudon's comments and the fact that the same builders were employed, it seems reasonable to suggest that the new conservatory at Alnwick resembled that at Syon; it certainly seems to have been topped with a similar high dome. The principal difference between this and the building at Syon is the lack of projecting, curved 'wings' as seen on the Syon example. The overall impression would have been imposing, but nevertheless very light and would have formed a centrepiece to the newly designed garden, set off by a decorative parterre (Fig. 10.32).

This apparently magnificent glasshouse seems to have been a relatively short-lived feature of the garden; constructed by 1827, it is not shown on Bell's map of 1849, indicating that it survived for only 20 years or so. Why this might be the case remains unknown.

Perhaps the design of the structure was ultimately too ambitious and the building collapsed (a relatively common fate of many glasshouses of the period); however, given the longevity of the Syon example, constructed by the same builders, this interpretation might be questioned. It may be that there was no place for such a structure within the fourth duke's plans for a redesigned and much expanded garden, yet designs for Algernon's garden were not drawn up until around 1860.

By the nineteenth century it had become common for the main entrance into kitchen gardens to be sited in the southern wall (Campbell 2005, 45), particularly where the gardens contained glasshouse ranges. The southern wall of the garden did not survive later expansion of the garden and there are no indications of a centrally located entrance within it, although an entrance was present in the south-west corner, leading from the expanded kitchen garden to the south (see Fig. 8.6), adjacent to the Gardener's House. From this entrance the visitor would proceed eastwards along a path which skirted the southern edge of the original garden, to arrive in the centre of the parterre garden. Clearly the vista of the conservatory would have been best appreciated from this direction (Fig. 10.33).

**Fig. 10.35** The garden in its landscape setting, as it appeared in 2000, before the commencement of the fieldwork

**Fig. 10.36** View westwards along the Aln, towards the castle, the walled gardens are obscured by trees to the left of the image (Darryn Wade)

**Fig. 10.37** The Italianate garden, as it may have appeared from a vantage point east of the central conservatory. The construction of the back of Hothouse 2 is visible to the centre right of the image, with the gardener's house and water tower beyond. The steeply sloping nature of the southern part of the garden can be appreciated, reconstruction by Chris Mitchell (c.mitchell02@btinternet.com)

The parterre garden had a decorative pond at its centre. This feature is depicted by Barnfather as being 14ft in diameter, with a central pond 6ft across surrounded by a stone walkway, the whole being covered by an octagonal pergola 10ft in overall height (see Fig. 8.7). A later addition drawn onto the plan suggests that it may have had a central fountain. There had clearly been some debate about this fountain and the provision of water to supply it as an 1826 document shows:

*'With respect to a Fountain as suggested by Mr Rawlinson, it is only necessary to remark, that in Situations like the Castle Dairy Grounds, or the Gardens, they have a very pleasing effect, but the Water proposed to be used for this purpose is highly objectionable, being so strongly impregnated with iron, as highly to discolour every article in contact with it. It is understood to be the Drift Water from some of the old Coal Workings on the Moor.'* (BM 14, 230).

Barnfather's map demonstrates that a piped supply to the central pond was provided with presumably clean water from the newly-constructed water tower; whether the accompanying fountain was ever constructed remains unknown.

Sometime in the early 1830s the duke modified the surviving western peach house (Hothouse 2) and constructed a second structure (a vinery; Hothouse 4) to the east of the conservatory, mirroring the construction of the peach house almost perfectly. A pinery was set to one side of the garden in the south-east away from the main vistas. Smaller in length, it nevertheless mirrored the construction of the other hothouses; the same arrangement of three groups of nine vents was positioned at the top of the walls of all three houses, but those on Hothouse 5 were correspondingly reduced in size. The overall impression would have been one of unity and harmony, which may contrast with the more haphazard and *ad hoc* approach seen in the second garden.

Despite these dramatic changes, and the shift in emphasis from production to display, the basic layout of the garden remained constant, divided by broad walks into rectangular plots. There is archaeological evidence to suggest that Plot 3 south of Hothouse 4 may have been sub-divided by a north–south aligned hedge. The garden was by no means symmetrical, in fact it had an irregular, trapezoidal shape in plan, but the regular arrangement of planting beds, features and buildings within it would add to a feeling of symmetry.

**Fig. 10.38** The Italianate garden as it appeared in the early twentieth century, looking north and showing the decorative parterres, central pond and the northern conservatory in the background, taken from the east-west path defining the two southern parterres (*The Gardeners' Chronicle* 1902, 286)

## Italian influences in an expanded garden

The fourth duke Algernon, Hugh's brother, transformed the size, appearance and use of the walled garden almost beyond recognition. The key to this transformation was the purchase of land to the west of the Alnwick Walled Garden, between 1849 and 1861 (see section 8.4 above). Crucially this allowed a new dedicated kitchen garden to be constructed, replacing the small western kitchen garden extension and freeing up the existing walled garden for redevelopment. The purchase of Goose Knows field in 1859 almost doubled the area of land which could be occupied by the new garden, the boundaries of which continued to be walled to the north, west and south, whilst the south-eastern boundary, with a steep slope to the east, was planted with trees and shrubs.

New gardens, inspired by the duke's love of Italy and created following restoration of the castle itself in an Italianate style, were influenced by plans produced by W. A. Nesfield, although the original design was not strictly adhered to (see section 8.4 above). The defining elements of this new garden comprised a conservatory (Hothouse 6), constructed centrally on the northern wall, over the basement and demolished glasshouse of the former vinery (Hothouse 1), a large central fishpond with fountain and extensive parterre gardens. The new garden was arranged on a north–south axis, with an entrance in the middle of a new southern wall, via a triple-arched gateway leading from a hexagonal garden which could be entered directly from Bondgate, thus bringing the garden into immediate contact with the town. An important element of this transformation was that both the gardens and the surrounding parkland were to be opened to the public; unlike the third duke, Algernon allowed access to any member of the public who cared to visit (providing they came on a Thursday), whilst the surrounding parkland was open on Thursdays and Sundays. This seemingly philanthropic move would have given the townspeople somewhere to stroll on a Sunday afternoon, but at what cost? The duke had purchased land within the town to the rear of Bondgate, including the garden of the White Swan public house. In reference to the transformation of the landscape by Brown, Tate was to comment:

*'Alas ! that in carrying them out the ancient privileges of the people were encroached on, and a policy begun which destroyed the independence and importance of the corporation, and put a bar to the development of the natural resources of the town'* (Tate 1866, 358).

Following its transformation, the garden would have remained hidden from view from the castle, and from the Aln to the south, as contemporary depictions of planting suggest (see Fig. 8.16); whilst the surrounding southern wall would have hidden it from view from within the town.

The opening up of the Alnwick Walled Garden to visitors may, in part, explain the profusion of contemporary descriptions of these grounds and the surrounding parkland, which had become a focus for day trips from Tyneside and Newcastle. The east coast railway from Newcastle to Edinburgh, meanwhile, included a branch line to Alnwick, allowing visitors from further afield. These contemporary descriptions, as well as plans drawn up for the garden's redesign, help to illustrate its appearance and have aided the creation of reconstructions.

The excavations revealed one of the most extensive undertakings of the whole project: a massive landscaping event which dramatically changed the appearance and vistas of the gardens. The original slope of the garden was not ideal; running from the south down to the north this would have been the least beneficial aspect a kitchen garden could possibly have. Although the slope on the original walled garden was only slight, the incorporation of the Goose Knows field to the south brought in an area of higher ground, whilst the land also sloped away to the east (see Wood's 1827 map, Fig. 8.4). The transformation involved levelling the lower, northern parts of the garden and the dumping of vast quantities of sand to create a raised mound to the south, from which views of the gardens could be appreciated (Fig. 10.34).

The construction of a new conservatory was accompanied by a significant rise in levels at the north end of the garden. Levelling of the slight slope from east to west, proposed by Nesfield (see cross section at base of Fig. 8.11), was recognised in the archaeological record. This exceptional feat of landscaping was reported in 1874, thus:

*'We soon see, from the very nature of the locality, that it has taken all the practical skill and ingenuity of the landscape gardener to make the flower garden what it is. Hedged in on the western and north-western sides by the old town of Alnwick, from which the ground slopes irregularly to the east—where it is enclosed by a Peach-wall, well covered with fine young trees just beginning to bear excellent crops—the broad border along the base of this wall is very striking and effective, when filled, as it has been this season, with choice bedding plants. A large and lofty conservatory divides it into nearly equal parts, the promenade along the border leads into the conservatory.'* (The Garden 1874, 100).

It is unlikely that much of the landscape beyond the garden to the north was visible from within the garden, even if not hidden by trees, the high garden walls and tall conservatory would have created an enclosed space (Fig. 10.34). The wider landscape setting of the castle and parkland, however, retained many of the aspects of the open landscape created by Brown. A description published in *The Garden*, January 31 1874, epitomises this preservation of the past (artificially created) landscape, which still persists today:

*'we experience a feeling of thankfulness that so grand a memorial of the past has been spared to us, and that no attempt has been made to introduce modern innovations, in the shape of flower-beds, upon the green sward that surrounds the Castle; and it is with feelings of pleasure that we look down from the battlements upon a landscape every way in keeping with the noble building. Right below, the river Alne (with numerous water-fowls floating upon its surface) winds its way eastward to the sea through a vale rich in the varied beauties of nature.'*

The inclusion of a dedicated smoke tower, with shafts leading away from each of the hothouses and the conservatory, would also have had a transformative effect on the appearance of the garden: there would no longer have been unsightly smoke emanating from the chimneys of these structures. It is perhaps interesting to note that the subsequent conversion of the backhouses of Hothouse 2 into dwelling rooms and offices in the later nineteenth century, with the insertion of 'domestic' fireplaces and a cooking range, would once more have resulted in smoke escaping from the chimneys of the peach house.

Shrimpton (1997, 24) suggests visitors entered the garden near Bondgate Tower. The new garden could have been accessed via a gate in its southernmost wall, through the hexagonal walled garden and thence via the triple-arched wrought iron gates. However, there is much to suggest that this garden, hidden from view from the castle, was also designed to be approached from a northerly direction. The new conservatory had been cleverly constructed in a manner which utilised the existing space available in the backsheds of the former vinery to accommodate a heating system within an underground space. This construction had entailed extending the central garden wall backwards to accommodate the new structure. Whether this was necessitated by some weakness in the former (possibly flued) wall which resulted in a need to rebuild, or was simply a device employed to enable the existing structure to be accommodated is not known. All of the proposals for the garden's redesign incorporate this element, which both enclosed the new structure and provided three new entrances; one each to the east and west of the new building and a third entering the conservatory centrally from the north. The latter entranceway would provide a vista of the gardens looking south, and entrance into the conservatory via this route would enable the view of the gardens to be enjoyed however inclement the weather (see cover image). This may have been a privilege largely reserved for the duke's household and guests.

A series of plans drawn up for the redesigned garden all depict south to the top of the drawing, suggesting that this was the direction from which the new garden and parterres could be best appreciated (see Fig. 8.11, Fig. 8.14, Fig. 8.15). From this vantage point the vinery and peach house would frame the central pond and high retaining walls to west and east would echo this symmetry. Within kitchen gardens usually the main entrance would be sited in the southern wall, at least from the early nineteenth century onwards; this would allow the glasshouse ranges to be shown to their best effect (Campbell 2006, 45). However, this was no kitchen garden, moreover, the backsheds of the glasshouses were elegant sandstone structures, presenting a unified appearance.

*'Looking from the conservatory, the visitor obtains perhaps the best general view of the flower garden. From its arrangement and situation the flower-beds have to be large to give them effect, and, as the eye runs up the centre walk, which becomes rather steep at the higher end, it is arrested by the pleasing effect produced by a chain of beds tilled with evergreens, and arranged in the form of drapery along the face of the steep green terrace that overhangs the garden.'* (The Garden 1874, 100).

The inclusion of a glazed double door into the conservatory from the north, as visible on a photograph of 1898 (see Fig. 6.5) would have rendered the garden visible from outside through the conservatory. This approach from the conservatory is also that described by Hartshorne, in 1865:

*'Leaving the Conservatory, a broad gravel walk, flanked on both sides by flower borders in sunk panels, leads to a large basin of water, with a polished red Aberdeenshire granite margin and fountain. Here the walk divides, and passing round both sides of the basin, ascends to a terrace four hundred feet long. Crossing this the walks ascend a slope, laid out in flower beds, and surrounded by high grass banks, surmounted by rows of lime trees, unite again at the top and enter a walled garden by three large stone arches. The view from the Conservatory over the beds of flowers, the water, and rising ground, covered with masses of gay colours, and terminating at the three arches, is very striking. Beyond the Gardens, walks extend to woods clothing the banks of the river and from various points command extensive views of the Castle and the Park, backed by the wild scenery of Ayden Forest.'* (Hartshorne 1865).

The inclusion of the Goose Knows field and associated substantial levelling deposits had brought landscaping within the walled garden, which would also be seen to advantage from the south, particularly from the newly-created raised mound. From this viewpoint the splendid new conservatory, framed by flanking

curvilinear glasshouses, would be seen to its best effect, as would the gardens laid out beneath:

*'Looking down from the higher end of this centre walk, the whole of the flower garden is seen to good effect;....'* (The Garden 1874, 100) and *'the higher ground, extending to the pinetum in one direction, there are beds boldly placed, and containing many interesting devices, floral and evergreen. There is a great deal of originality about this part of the grounds, especially in the encircling banks which form their background, planted as they are with festoons and chains of low-growing and hardy shrubs'* (The Gardeners' Chronicle 1880, 523–524).

Today, even from the Alnwick Garden's highest vantage point, the trees planted to screen the walls of the garden from views of the surrounding landscape obscure views northwards from within the garden. However, when initially constructed the view from the northern raised mound would also permit a vista of the distant hills, beyond the walled garden, bringing the walled flower gardens into the wider landscape. This may have been part of the rationale behind creating this artificially elevated platform. The hills would form a backdrop to the formal parterres and elegant conservatory, whilst the curvilinear glasshouses of the vinery and peach house would neatly frame the view.

*'At the lower end of this division, or opening, stands a fine conservatory, 100 feet long, with two other glasshouses about as long on either side of it, at a little distance, wing-fashion. At the upper end, at the full height of the sloping terraces, is an Italian-looking gateway of three arches filled with ornamental ironwork of the lightest workmanship, which gives access to other portions of the gardens and grounds. To the west of the fountain is a quadrangular* allee verte *of Linden trees trained to form a green colonnaded cloistral walk round a central Paradise, to use an old word for the grassy square enclosed by it; to the east is the Rose garden—some thirty beds of choice Roses cut out of greensward, which is an addition to an older starlike device of Roses near it, originally thought of, probably, by Capability Brown.'* (The Gardeners' Chronicle 1891, 593).

The maintenance of this landscape setting and the distinction between castle parklands and productive or flower gardens persisted into the twentieth century:

*'Fortunately, there are no flower-beds in the vicinity of the Castle, and this is in keeping with the rugged character of the old fortress; but ample breadths of turf give a charm in a position where flowers would be obviously out of place.'* (The Gardeners' Chronicle 1902, 274).

The distinction between the castle and its landscape setting and the walled garden remained up until the time of the fieldwork (Fig. 10.35) and persists to this day, with the newly-created Alnwick Gardens enclosed within the walls first constructed in the 1760s and last modified by the fourth Duke of Northumberland.

# Appendix 1: The Hothouses

The following provides a brief description and history of each of the hothouses within the garden. Since their histories have been quite long and, at times, complex, and have been provided above as part of a phased narrative, the following provides a brief synopsis of each individual structure, using the various terms by which they have been historically known and referencing relevant map evidence.

## Hothouse 1, the northern vinery

Hothouse 1 (Garden 1) was built on the northern boundary wall shortly after the garden was first constructed, presumably at some point between the preparation of Thompson's map of 1760 and Wilkin's map of 1772 (see Fig. 1.10; Fig. 8.1). The latter shows it with four backhouses, but no evidence for this could be found within the building, and it is considered that the original structure is probably more accurately shown on Sauthier's 1788 map, which shows a building with three backhouses straddling the boundary wall (see Fig. 8.2), this map seems relatively accurate regarding the layout of individual beds within the garden as well as the overall shape in plan of the garden and associated planting schemes and might thus be generally considered a more accurate representation than that of Wilkin (compare Fig. 8.1 and Fig. 8.2). The excavations identified remains of the eastern and western backhouses, although all trace of the central one had been obscured by later modifications. By 1826 the structure had been modified with the original three backhouse rooms amalgamated into one long rectangular structure (Garden 3; see Fig. 8.9; Bell 1826). Evidence for this was recorded in the surviving structure. On Barnfather's 1829 plan of the garden (see Fig. 8.6) the structure is labelled for first time as a 'Vinery'. There is no contemporary mapping which might reflect the layout of this building during the time of the second duke, although evidence suggests that the changes to the layout indicated in 1820's mapping may have occurred during this period. Records in the castle archives show that the second duke invested in new hothouses designed by John Hay of Edinburgh, including a fruiting pine stove for pineapples, a mushroom house and two vineries (Shrimpton 2006, 58). The pine stove and two new hothouses were built from September 1808 and 1811 by local masons Nesbitt and Shepherd (Shrimpton 1997, 10). This may provide a date for the conversion of the original structure into one long backhouse and possibly an associated rebuild of the glasshouse which by this time would be approaching 40 years old and would presumably have been in need of repair or replacement. There was no evidence recovered for the glasshouse associated with this building as it had been completely demolished and obscured

by the construction of the Garden 4 conservatory, Hothouse 6. The form of heating used remains unknown, but it is likely to have employed hot air flues, or perhaps more plausibly, to have incorporated a heated wall.

The backhouse and the glasshouse of the northern hothouse may have been modified or rebuilt by the third duke at different times. On Bell's 1826 plan (Fig. 8.3) the glasshouse is rectangular but is shown on Wood's 1827 plan (Fig. 8.4) and Barnfather's 1829 plan (see Fig. 8.6) with the central section projecting, suggesting a tripartite glasshouse, with a wider central element. The backhouse also appears to have been modified; a central projection on the northern side is shown on Bell's plan of 1849 (see Fig. 8.9) and the Ordnance Survey plan of 1856 (Fig. 8.10). No evidence of this was seen within the standing remains, unsurprisingly since this would presumably not have been visible due to later modifications and the insertion of a large water tank; the nature of this projecting element is unknown, and it may simply represent steps providing access to the structure.

With the fourth duke all above-ground elements of this structure were demolished. However, the backhouses were to remain, with modifications, and were utilized as a subterranean furnace house, with coal bunkers and a water tank inserted, for a new conservatory above (see Hothouse 6, below).

## Structure 1, a pine pit or forcing frame

The remains of the foundations of a forcing frame and associated furnace identified during excavation do not appear on any known plans of the garden. In Garden 1 this part of the walled garden was occupied by a central pond and by the mid-1820s (Bell 1826; Fig 8.3), the heated building had evidently been demolished. This structure is most plausibly interpreted as a documented, steam heated, fruiting pine stove contemporary with Garden 2, designed by John Hay of Edinburgh and constructed in 1807 (Shrimpton 1997, 10; see section 8.2 above). Ultimately this experimental structure proved unsuccessful and was of short-lived duration.

## Hothouse 2, the western hothouse or peach house

In its earliest phase of construction (Garden 2), Hothouse 2 comprised three small semi-basemented backhouses to the north of a spine wall, elements of which survived to be recorded. Possibly one of the structures designed by Hay and built by masons Nesbitt and Shepherd between 1808 and 1811 (Shrimpton 1997, 10), this first appears on Bell's 1826 map (Fig. 8.3), and is labelled as 'Peach House' on Barnfather's plan (1829; Fig. 8.6). It would originally have had a timber glasshouse. Modifications to turn the three small backhouses or furnace rooms into one long backhouse occurred after 1829 (Garden 3) and evidence for this conversion was recorded in the form of well-faced stone ashlar walls connecting the initial elements with clasping buttresses around the original furnace buildings. The structure first appears as one backhouse on the 1856 Ordnance Survey map (Fig. 8.10). The spine wall and elements of the original heating system to the south within the glasshouse survived. The central part of the backhouse functioned as a mushroom house; three original furnaces supplying three elements of the glasshouses to the front, with a fourth (for the mushroom house) would have vented via four separate chimneys along the length of the building. A rebuild of the glass frontage revealed within the excavation area to the south-east of Hothouse 2 is considered likely to postdate the modification of the three furnace rooms into one continuous backhouse and may have been closely followed by the introduction of hot water heating systems. A curvilinear glasshouse was added in 1836 as documented by a bill from D. and E. Bailey, Manufacturers and Ironmongers, Holborn, London, for 'A Range of Curvilinear Peach Houses' referring to the curved and glazed iron framework which would have contained two partitions dividing the glasshouse into three elements (DP/D3/I/43). A smoke shaft added by 1856 (Garden 4) would have directed the smoke away from any furnaces within the building to a large chimney at the southern limit of the garden, keeping the garden free of noxious fumes. Ultimately (Garden 5) the mushroom house was made redundant and the central part of the backhouse converted into a bothy with living areas (bedroom and kitchen) and office accommodation for a gardener. Interestingly the introduction of domestic fireplaces within this building would have meant that chimney once more poured out smoke. The 1896 plan of the water supply into the gardens shows a water pipe leading into the bothy annotated 'put on 1876' indicating the approximate date of the conversion of the Hothouse 2 backhouse (see Fig. 9.12). A 'Paylist of Workmen' first lists a woman as being employed in the bothy in December 1884 (Acc 446/3). By 1900 (Fig. 9.13) the backhouses were used as 'potting shed' and 'shed'. On a 1928 plan of water supply (see Kent 1998) the glasshouse is shown as one continuous structure with no divisions and labelled as a 'Peach House'; the glasshouse was still standing in 1932 as shown on a contemporary plan of the garden (TAG Z/1/15).

## A pine house

A building labelled 'pine house' is shown to the east of Hothouse 2 on maps of the 1820s (Bell 1826, Wood 1827 and Barnfather 1829; Fig. 8.3, Fig. 8.4, Fig. 8.6). This had a long central backhouse with three, separate, glasshouse elements to the front extending to east and west beyond the length of the backhouse. This building appears to have been demolished and completely replaced by

Hothouse 4 and no definite traces of the original structure survived. This may well have been one of the structures built by John Hay of Edinburgh from September 1808 and 1811 by local masons Nesbitt and Shepherd (Shrimpton 1997, 10), but if so, given its longevity, it is unlikely to have been Hay's short-lived and highly experimental 'pine stove' (see Structure 1 above).

## Hothouse 3, the central conservatory

In 1827 Loudon reported that Richards and Jones were 'now engaged in erecting a most extensive range of the same kind at Alnwick Castle', in relation to the construction of a conservatory along similar lines to that at Syon, associated with the Third Duke's garden. Payments for the wages of 'Birmingham men' are mentioned in the Alnwick accounts for January 1827 (Shrimpton 1997, 16) and there are other references to large sums of money as 'greenhouse' weekly wages in the months of late 1826 to summer 1827 which most probably also refer to the construction of the conservatory (Shrimpton 1997, 16). This grand central conservatory is shown on maps of 1827 and 1829 but was short-lived and had been demolished by 1849 (probably by the Fourth Duke; see Fig. 8.4; Fig. 8.6; Fig. 8.9). The robber trenches which removed this building's curved southern wall were excavated as was a pond, originally sited within the building. Possible elements of heating system were seen in section. The appearance of this structure has been recreated by reference to map evidence and by comparison with the contemporary structure at Syon (which still survives).

## Hothouse 4, the eastern hothouse or vinery

Built after 1829, Hothouse 4 first appears Bell's 1849 map (Fig. 8.9). Excavation as well as the surviving map evidence demonstrate that this was built to mirror the modified Hothouse 2, apparently in the early 1830s (Garden 3). The backhouse survived as a standing structure, with the spine wall, while elements of the original heating system to the south within glasshouse and parts of the external glasshouse walls were identified in excavation. First labelled as a 'Vinery' on a plan of the gardens dated 1860, the central part of the backhouse was built as a mushroom house as in Hothouse 2, although unlike the Hothouse 2 this use persisted apparently throughout the life of the building. Elements of column bases for the original glasshouse frontage were excavated, modified by the insertion of walls between, which would have strengthened the structure. A cross-section of the garden shows the western gable end of Hothouse 2 as a curvilinear glasshouse attached to the backhouse (see Fig. 9.7). This modification may be associated with the rebuild of the front wall of the glasshouse perhaps around the same time as Hothouse 2, *c.* 1836, suggesting that the original glasshouse, presumably built using timber, would have been short lived. The hot-flue heating system was replaced and converted to piped hot water powered by boilers. By 1900 the western end of backhouse was used as 'tool shed' and the eastern as a 'potting shed', the mushroom house was still labelled as such and the glasshouse was still used as a vinery (Fig. 9.13). The glasshouse was extant in 1932 as indicated by contemporary mapping (Fig. 7.4).

## Hothouse 5, the south-east hothouse or pine house

The entire length of the backhouse and western third of the glasshouse of Hothouse 5 survived in very good condition. Externally it would have resembled Hothouses 2 and 4 in its construction. This hothouse is labelled on a plan of the garden from the 1860s as a 'Pinery' and its initial construction belongs with Garden 3 (see Fig. 8.14). The raised central bed visible in the glasshouse element clearly marks this building out as a house for the propagation of pineapples. In common with the other hothouses in the garden this pinery benefitted from the addition of the smoke shaft by 1856, which would have vented smoke from its furnaces. Hot water heating had been added by c 1880, if not earlier. One single furnace would have supplied the necessary heat to the glasshouse by 1896, when the building is illustrated with a basement in the eastern side of western backhouse room only (Fig. 9.12). Over time, and presumably with an increased availability of imported pineapples, its function changed. On the 1900 water supply plan it is labelled as a 'Forcing House' with two 'sheds' and 'potting shed' in the backhouses (see Fig. 9.13) and on a plan of the gardens from 1928 as for 'Pears, Figs and Plums' (Kent 1998). The glasshouse remained standing until at least 1932 (see Fig. 7.4).

## Hothouse 6, the northern conservatory

The footprint of the glass element of a new conservatory (Hothouse 6) was constructed over the area previously occupied by the Hothouse 1 glasshouse and backhouse, and beyond the line of garden boundary wall to north. The boundary wall was modified and pushed back to the north, incorporating curved elements either side of the conservatory. First seen on an 1865 plan of castle and garden and also illustrated on the 1867 Ordnance Survey First Edition map (see Fig. 8.16; Fig. 8.20), this conservatory was built as part of the fourth Duke's extensive remodelling of the gardens. The original Hothouse 1 backhouse was converted into a cellar containing heating elements for the conservatory, with coal cellars, light wells and steps leading down from outside the garden, providing access (all of which were extant at the time of recording). The 1896 water supply plan shows pipes supplying the hothouses with water (see Fig. 9.12); and this hothouse would almost certainly have been supplied with hot water boilers on its conversion. The glasshouse element of the northern conservatory

was demolished sometime between 1923 (see Fig. 8.23) and 1932 (Ordnance Survey, see Fig. 7.4). The lower, stone, structural elements of the building were converted into a paved 'pavilion' garden with a central pond.

## Hothouse 7, New Vinery

Hothouse 7 (Garden 4) is the only building within the garden of which structural elements remain (the backhouse and spine wall are extant). This was not recorded as part of the fieldwork. It was constructed in the south-east corner of the garden to the immediate east of Hothouse 5. It does not appear on the 1856 plan or Nesfield's 1860 designs; but is labelled as 'New Vinery' on the plan of the gardens that was amended in 1864 (see Fig. 8.10; Fig. 8.11, Fig. 8.12; Fig. 8.14). The date of this building suggests that it was always heated by hot water. The smoke shaft is not shown extending to this building, but by 1900 it is illustrated as being heated by steam. The glasshouse remained standing until after 1932 (Fig. 7.4). It is labelled as a 'Peach house' on a 1928 plan of the gardens water supply and annotated as being pulled down 1935 (Kent 1998).

# Appendix 2: Animal Bone

The following provides a summary report of the animal bones recovered from the excavations, which are interpreted as material primarily deriving from tanyards within the town and dumped to raise ground levels and improve the soil in front of Hothouse 4. The conclusions are presented above (see section 10.2).

In total, 161 bones were recorded from the selected deposits. The major part of this assemblage was taken from layer [206] (see Table 1), an extensive soil deposit situated just to the south of Hothouse 4, with the remaining parts taken from the underlying deposit, the fill [264] of an extensive robber trench [265] which truncated [206] to the south of the glasshouse wall, and finally from a brick soakaway within Hothouse 4. Feature [265] would appear to be associated with the robbing of this hothouse, with [264] forming an upper deposit within this feature. While this collection may therefore somewhat postdate those from the other three deposits, it nevertheless demonstrated similar attributes suggesting perhaps a similar source or redeposited material.

Most of the bones were identified as cattle, equid (horse) and sheep/goat (see Appendix 2; Table 1), the former largely composed of skull pieces and sheep/goat by a concentration of metapodials (see Appendix 2; Table 2). The proportion of equid bones is likely to have been larger, as a majority of the cattle-size ribs may well belong to equid rather than cattle. As well as ribs, the equid collection features a rather general range of skeletal parts (see Fig. 10.15), for the most part incorporating disarticulated elements, with the notable exception of the central part of a right hock joint, consisting of the central, third, first/second and fourth tarsals. This level of disarticulation is undoubtedly related to some post-mortem usage, as shown by the large proportion of equid bones with butchery marks (11 out of the 36 bones from [206]). These include skinning cuts (knife cut to 1st phalange) various jointing cuts (chops through the distal humerus and pelvis acetabulum plus cut marks noticed on or adjacent to the distal humerus and acetabulum, as well as the proximal and distal femur), carcass sectioning chops (noticed on thoracic and lumbar vertebra) and finally two bones with defleshing cuts (thoracic vertebra and humerus). There are at least four equids represented within the [206] deposit, as shown by four left femurs, all fused, and therefore representing individuals in excess of 3 to 3.5 years in age. However, this may rise to five individuals taking into account a maxilla fragment with a deciduous toothrow featuring a well-worn fourth deciduous molar and therefore representing a horse aged approximately 2 to 3 years. With the exception of this maxilla fragment, the equid remains can all be classed as deriving from fully adult individuals. Indeed, there is evidence of some longevity as shown by the height of a maxillary second adult premolar (using

Levine 1982) and the wear patterns of a set of upper incisors (after Goody 2008, 100–103), giving ages of 10 to 11 years and about 9 years respectively. Potential age-associated and/ or work-related pathologies were observed on a few of these bones, including probable osteoarthritis (exotoses and surface pitting) at the dorsal/ posterior and dorsal/anterior articulations of two adjoining thoracic/lumbar vertebrae; marked osteophytic lipping at the distal articulation of a calcaneus; and severe degradation and extension of the posterior aspects (anguli) of a third phalange either side of the articular surface (see Fig. 10.16, Fig. 10.17). Finally, some corresponding exotoses and pitting was observed at the distal surface of the central and the proximal surface of the third tarsal within the partial articulation. This could represent an early stage of spavin (a disease of the hock joint of horses) or perhaps, due to obvious damage to the articular surfaces, may relate to an arthritic infection (after Baker and Brothwell 1980, 119).

There is considerable variation amongst the size of the equids, although perhaps with more larger than smaller animals. The range of sizes is shown by the lengths of the two calcaneii, one at 109.8mm and the other measuring 137.3mm. Comparing these lengths with the large collection of equid bones found within an early post-medieval site in London (Cowie and Pipe 1998 with data taken from MoLA archives) as well as from archaeological skeletal finds within the PCA archives, it is possible to suggest that these correspond to shoulder heights averaging about 1295 and 1645mm or about 12.7 and 16.2 hands respectively (height calculations based on von den Driesch and Boessneck 1974). In addition, there are two similarly sized humerii, although not a pair, one of which provided a length measurement of 348mm, from which can be calculated a shoulder height of 1695mm or 16.7 hands. From this evidence it appears that this collection features small to medium-sized ponies as well as large horses, the latter certainly suitable for riding purposes or perhaps for heavy pulling (following size categories described in Clark 1995, 22–3).

The cattle skull pieces represent a minimum number of 26 individuals, essentially comprising horncores with some part of the adjacent skull, with the exception of two polled specimens. There were no obvious paired horncores amongst these fragments, the total of 24 skull pieces amounting to 13 on the left and 11 on the right. The great majority of these bore butchery marks demonstrating that an oblique chop from the anterior/dorsal direction was used to remove the horns, the cut exiting or snapping through the bone just dorsal to the occipital condyles. It could perhaps be suggested due to the lack of pairing that each horn was separately removed. However, the angle of the cut as well as the recovery of much of the nuchal ridge with several horncores, suggests they were generally removed as a pair. There was one fragment where the dorsal/anterior cut was angled to exit between

**Table 1** Species representation

| Context: | 206 | 264 | 308 | 309 | Total |
|---|---|---|---|---|---|
| **Species** | | | | | |
| Cattle | 34 | 8 | 2 | | 44 |
| Equid | 46 | 1 | 2 | 1 | 50 |
| Cattle-size | 30 | | 1 | | 31 |
| Sheep/Goat | 25 | | 1 | 1 | 27 |
| Pig | 3 | | | | 3 |
| Sheep-size | 3 | | | | 3 |
| Goose | 1 | | | | 1 |
| Fish | 2 | | | | 2 |
| **Grand Total** | 144 | 9 | 6 | 2 | 161 |

**Table 2** Selected species and skeletal part representation

| | | Context | | | | |
|---|---|---|---|---|---|---|
| **Species** | **Bone** | 206 | 264 | 308 | 309 | **Total** |
| Cattle | Skull | 25 | 7 | | | 32 |
| | Scapula | 3 | | | | 3 |
| | Vertebrae | 3 | | | | 3 |
| | Femur | 4 | | 1 | | 5 |
| | Tibia | 2 | 1 | 1 | | 4 |
| | | | | | | |
| Equid | Skull | 4 | | | | 4 |
| | Mandible | 1 | | | | 1 |
| | Maxilla | 2 | | | 1 | 3 |
| | Scapula | 1 | | 1 | | 2 |
| | Humerus | 3 | | | | 3 |
| | Ulna | 1 | | | | 1 |
| | Carpal | 1 | | | | 1 |
| | Vertebra | 15 | | | | 15 |
| | Pelvis | 2 | | | | 2 |
| | Femur | 5 | 1 | | | 6 |
| | Tarsal | 4 | | | | 4 |
| | Calcaneus | 2 | | | | 2 |
| | Phalanges | 5 | | | | 5 |
| Cattle-size | rib | 27 | | 1 | | 28 |
| | | | | | | |
| Sheep/ Goat | radius | 3 | | | | 3 |
| | ulna | 2 | | | | 2 |
| | tibia | 4 | | | | 4 |
| | metcarpus | 3 | | | | 3 |
| | metatarsus | 13 | | 1 | 1 | 15 |

the horncores which would have removed just a single horn. Yet in most cases it can be assumed that separation of the individual horns took place as a secondary part of this process, although no splitting cuts were observed in the nuchal area of these skull pieces. Both of the polled specimens were neatly sawn through starting just posterior to the orbits and exiting or snapping through some way down the posterior surface (see Fig. 10.18). Following Armitage (1982) it can be seen that there is some age variation amongst the horncores with a preponderance of those in his subadult category, aged between 2 to 3 years (see Appendix 2, Table 3), although a proportion of these were probably on the cusp of the young adult age group at 3 to 7 years. An additional indication of age was provided by the degree of closure of the skull sutures. Notably none of these specimens demonstrated an open suture at the mid posterior part of the nuchal area (frontal/parietal) which fuses at 1 year while there were also no examples of a fully closed frontal/parietal suture within the temporal fossa (the lateral part of the skull below the horncore), this fusing at 5 to 7 years (suture closures after Grigson 1982). It was noticed that the majority of the subadult examples exhibited an unfused parietal/occipital suture, just above (dorsal to) the occipital condyles (as for example shown by the polled specimen in Figure 4). Unfortunately, there does not appear to be a closure time for this suture in the available literature. Armitage (1982) also refers to the 'type' and sexual characteristics of post-medieval horncores with the proviso that distinctions can only be made once growth has abated i.e from his young adult stage. Nevertheless, an attempt was made to categorise the subadult horncores, particularly, as several were on the cusp, probably subadult/young adult (see Appendix 2, Table 3 and see a full list of length measurements from the complete specimens in Table 4). Notably each of the three types is represented with a majority of those in the medium-horned category. There were just two longhorns, each reaching this size when subadult. Both of these horncores, though young, clearly compare to the castrate characteristics, with a broad oval base, a marked twist in the shaft with the point up or slightly back with reference to the dorsal plane. Each of the other complete cores appears to follow an approximately similar shape although less pronounced amongst the smaller horncores; the assemblage includes cores with lengths of 170mm, 238mm, 148mm and 414mm, so within the shorthorn, mediumhorn, shorthorn and longhorn categories (Fig. A2.1). These few examples also show a probable defining characteristic in that the smaller cores tend to show a more pronounced frontal (nuchal) eminence (viewed from the posterior), either rounded or pointed (as shown in this figure), the medium horn examples tend towards a more shallow eminence, while the larger examples are shallower still or close to flat, some with a pronounced concavity below the middle area of the nuchal

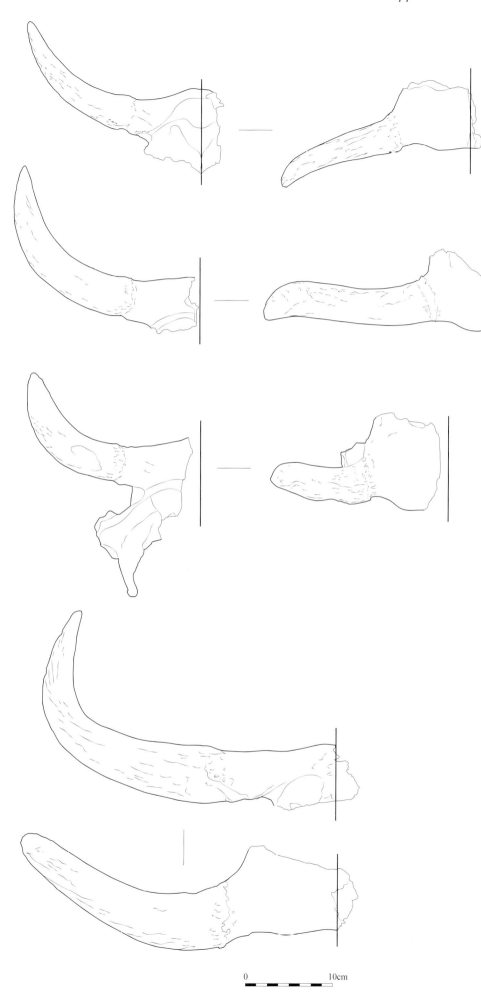

**Fig. A2.1** Four cattle skulls from [206] demonstrating the range of sizes and shapes of the horncores and associated nuchal area (posterior and dorsal views), categorised (from top to bottom and referring first to posterior and then the dorsal profile) as well rounded/narrow shallow concave, shallow rounded/ narrow shallow concave, pointed/narrow shallow concave and shallow rounded/ wide deep concave. The vertical line is at the nuchal centre orientated dorso-ventrally

0            10cm

**Table 3** The distribution of cattle horncore types and ages from [206] and [264] (in brackets), where SA is subadult (2-3yrs), YA is young adult (3-7yrs) and A is adult (7-10yrs); while SH is shorhorn (length less than 220mm), M is mediumhorn (220-360mm) and L is longhorn (over 360mm) using real and estimated values, the latter using data given in West (1995, 28); where age and type data is taken from Armitage 1982.

| Age: | SA | YA | A | Total |
|---|---|---|---|---|
| Type | | | | |
| SH | | 2(1) | 2 | 5 |
| M | 12 | 1 | 1 | 14 |
| M/L | 2(1) | | | 3 |
| L | 2 | | | 2 |
| Total | 16(1) | 3(1) | 3 | 24 |

**Table 4** The size of cattle horncores from [206] and [264] (in brackets) sorted by age group (after Armitage 1982 and see Table 3) where length refers to the length of the outer curvature (see von den Driesch 1976).

| Age Group | Age (years) | Length (in millimetres) |
|---|---|---|
| SA | 2–3 | 170, 210, 265, 312, 414, 420 |
| YA | 3–7 | 137, (156) |
| A | 7–10 | 145, 148, 238 |

**Table 5** Sheep/goat shoulder heights illustrating the data from the combined metapodial evidence (All) and also from the two metatarsal 'types' labelled S/S short and slender and L/B long and broad. The two incomplete L/S (long and slender) examples provided estimated lengths of 670 and 690mm.

| Type | Ht (in mm) | Average | N |
|---|---|---|---|
| SS | 545.7–550.2 | 547.9 | 2 |
| L/B | 595.6–625.6 | 613.1 | 3 |
| All | 545.7–635.7 | 601.4 | 8 |

ridge (though not shown in the longhorn specimen in Fig. 10.18). There is some variation in the nuchal shape viewed from the dorsal aspect although not to the same degree as that observed from the posterior aspect, the descriptions given referring to the shape of the indentation either side of the frontal eminence.

It can be suggested that these skull fragments are likely to derive from relatively young oxen, certainly culled prior to their sixth year (the suture data) and maybe before their fourth year (after Armitage 1982). This age range would be indicative of animals principally bred for their meat, with the possibility of some usage for work purposes perhaps including, as not all of the horncores could be sexed, some cows bred for milk production. The horncore size and nuchal shapes would suggest the local meat markets were provided by an assortment of 'types', here including polled as well as horned cattle varieties. In addition, it can be observed that the concentration of these particular cattle skeletal parts would strongly suggest they were derived from a craft source, probably hornworkers' or tanners' waste (see Conclusions).

A craft source, again most probably tanners, could also account for the availability of the other major constituent of this bone assemblage, the sheep/goat metapodials. This follows the generally recognised view that skins (cattle, sheep and goat) were usually provided to the tanner with the horns and the feet still attached (after Serjeantson 1989). These excess components could then be sent on to other craft establishments (hornworkers, glue makers, boneworkers, fertilizer producers etc) which would often be in close attendance with the tanners (see Rielly 2011 and Stevens 2011). Both items, head and feet, may have been disposed of en masse following one of these secondary usages; in the case of the skull parts after the removal of the horn sheaves.

Twelve out of the sixteen sheep/goat metapodials are complete and it can perhaps be assumed that the remainder were probably whole when deposited into these layers. There is a general mix of ages in this collection, comprising seven fused and six unfused distal ends, thus with about 50% from animals younger than 2 years old (after Schmid 1972, 75). There is no evidence to show how they were removed from their respective carcasses although one metatarsus displayed grazing marks to the anterior shaft perhaps signifying soft tissue removal. Finally, a comparison can be made with the cattle horncore evidence concerning the representation of a variety of 'types'. Notably the eleven complete metatarsals from [206], though undoubtedly a small sample, appear to conform to three size groups: short and slender (3 S/S), somewhat larger and broader (6 L/B) and tall and slender (2 L/S). The single complete specimen from [309] fits into the second group (see Appendix 2, Table 5). The two metatarsals categorised as L/S had unfused distal ends, however comparing the proximal to distal diaphyses lengths of these bones with the complete metatarsals indicates heights between about 670 and 690mm. Any comparison of size must entertain the possibility of sexual dimorphism, and it could be suggested that S/S are female, L/B are intact males and L/S are castrates, the latter assumption based on evidence that wether limb bones tend to increase in length in comparison to rams (Albarella *et al.* 2009, 63). However, the presence of a range of types/breeds could also be indicated. Notably, the larger 'type' would appear to conform in size and shape to one of the longwool varieties, these amongst some of the largest British sheep in the post-medieval era, which in the north-east of England would have been the Teeswater (Hall and Clutton-Brock 1995, 135; and see Armitage 1984 in his discussion of Lincolnshire and Leicestershire longwools in eighteenth century London).

The remaining part of the bone assemblage from these selected deposits can essentially be described as food waste. It consists of a small number of heavily butchered domesticate vertebrae (cattle) and limb bones, with a single goose tibia and a few unidentified fish bones. The butchery was clearly intended to produce joints: the sheep/goat including one radius and two tibias chopped through the midshaft; a pig radius and ulna from the same large individual sawn through the shaft; and cattle with two sawn scapulae, a tibia chopped through at the midshaft and a femur with its distal end removed using a cleaver. Jointing was also achieved using less cumbersome butchery utensils, as shown by knife marks close to the distal end of another tibia. The vertebrae, all lumbar, include three split by sawing, with two of these also showing sectioning chops. The sheep/goat follow the metapodial evidence regarding a mix of adults and subadults (generally second year animals); the pig is subadult; while the cattle bones are probably all from older individuals with the exception of a femur belonging to a first-year animal and a scapula which is clearly foetal or neonate. Most of the cattle bones and the pig bones are clearly from large individuals, probably representing a preponderance of males, although the presence of 'improved' types cannot be discounted.

# Bibliography

## Primary Sources

### The Archives of the Duke of Northumberland at Alnwick Castle

AC O/I/1b, 1624. A platt of the town and castle of Alnwick and the grounds adjoining, by Robert Norton.

AC O/I/7, 1760. A plan of the town and castle of Alnwick and of the demesnes with divers other lands near the town, by I Thompson.

Acc 163, 1785. Alnwick Castle described and Illustrated with Drawings by P[eter] W[adell].

Acc 446/1, 1867–73. Paylist of Workmen employed by his grace the Duke of Northumberland at, or near, Alnwick Castle.

COW A146, 1865. The Fourth Duke's Italianate garden in relation to the Castle.

COW A747, 1916. Letter from Henry Walker & Son Ltd. regarding supply of a calorifier for the Castle Gardens.

DP/D2/I/20, 1811. Estimate and proposal for building a wall on the west and south sides of the new kitchen garden.

DP/DS/I/62, 1890–91 Correspondence relating to insertion of steam boilers to supply the castle and gardens.

DP/D2/I/163, 1806. Details of men employed in the garden, their ages etc.

DP/D2/I/182, 1796. Book listing Chinese plants and various descriptions - hardbound notebook.

DP/D3/I/30, 1820–1840. Syon Conservatory Botany collection 1820–1840.

DP/D3/I/43, 1836. Bill on headed paper from D and E Bailey Manufacturers and Ironmongers, 272 Holborn, opposite Red Lion Street.

DP/D3/I/197, 1829. Letters to commissioners from various correspondents including Thomas Smith, Head gardener, Mark Smith, stationer and Sir John Swinburne and information on association for protection of agricultural property against incendiarism.

DP/D4/1/262, 31/12/1863. Receipt of payment of costs of building conservatory in Alnwick Castle Gardens.

DP/D5/I/62, 1890–91 Correspondence relating to insertion of steam boilers to supply the castle and gardens.

Library 29739. The Duke's School, Alnwick. An Account of the Reunion, Banquet, and Presentation to Mr Thomas Collinson (After nearly 50 years' service as headmaster,).... Souvenir of the Collinson re-union, banquet, and presentation, June 15th, 1898.

PB 217, n.d. Castle Gardens, pond and ornamental gardens.

PB 218, 8/6/1861. Stone work for iron pillars, conservatory, castle gardens.

PB 220, WM 1861 (altered Apr. 1864). Plan showing alterations to gardens.

PB 224, 30/4/1863. Propagation pits.

PB 227, WM 1863. A fountain.

PB 230, 1/1860. Plan for proposed Parterre, Alnwick Castle garden with fly leaf to show introduction of Upper Basin and Cascade Canal.

PB 233, 14/5/1863. Castle Gardens propagating houses heating apparatus.

PB 235, 9/10/1862. Alnwick Castle Gardens, arches in garden wall.

PB 236, WM 1859. Cross Section.

PB 237, no date. Garden building.

TAG Z/1/2, 1896. The Castle Gardens Water Supply 1896, with original annotations enhanced for clarity.

TAG Z/1/3, *c.* 1900. The Castle Gardens Water Supply *c.* 1900.

TAG Z/1/4. 1830. Detail from an architect's drawing dated 1830, showing the proposed details of a partition wall of the vinery.

TAG Z/1/15 1932. Plan of Alnwick Castle Gardens Northumberland, 1932.

### Durham University Library Special Collections

DDR/BP/EST/4/12. Undated tracing of boiler housing structure at Auckland Castle Gardens apparently based on Ordnance Survey 1:1250 partial revision of 1912–13.

### Syon

SY.B.II.2b(3), 1788. A plan of the town and castle of Alnwick with the demesne and other lands belonging to the Duke of Northumberland by C.J. Sauthier.

## Published sources

Albarella, U., Beech, M., Curl, J., Locker, A., Morena Garcia, M. and Mulville, J. 2009. *Norwich Castle: Excavations and Historical Survey, 1987–98, Part III: A Zooarchaeological Study.* Dereham: East Anglian Archaeology Occasional Paper 22.

Alnwick Castle Gardens, 1928. Plan Showing the Water Supply Existing July 1928.

Armitage, P.L. 1982. A system for ageing and sexing the horn cores of cattle from British post-medieval sites (17th to early 18th century) with special reference to unimproved British Longhorn cattle. In B. Wilson, C. Grigson and S. Payne (eds) *Ageing and sexing animal bones from archaeological sites. Oxford: B.A.R. British Series* 109, 37–54.

Armitage, P.L. 1984. The Faunal Remains. In A. Thompson, F. Grew and J. Schofield. Excavations at Aldgate, 1974. *Post-Medieval Archaeology* 18, 131–44.

August, I. 2006. *The Making of the Alnwick Garden.* London: Pavilion.

Bailey, C. 2005. Harnessing horse power. *Ancestors* 35, 34–42.

Baker, J. and Brothwell, D. 1980. *Animal Diseases in Archaeology.* London: Academic Press.

Banks, J. 1811. On the Forcing Houses of the Romans, with a List of Fruits Cultivated by Them, now in our Gardens. In C. Taylor (ed) *The Literary Panorama Volume 10.* London: Cox and Baylis, 871–6.

Barnfather, W. 1829. Plan of the Gardens at Alnwick Castle, having reference to a proposed arrangement for conveying a supply of Water from the Castle.

Beamish, H. 2014. Establishing a context for the pinery-vineries and other early buildings in the walled garden at Auckland Castle. Unpublished Report.

Beamish, H. 2016. The Nineteenth-Century, Curvilinear Lean-to Glasshouse Range at Felton Park, Felton, Northumberland. Unpublished Report.

Bell, T. 1826. Survey of lands in the Townships of Alnwick. Denwick and Cannongate, in the Parish of Alnwick, in the County of Northumberland belonging to his Grace the Duke of Northumberland.

Bell, T. 1849. Map of Alnwick township.

British Geological Survey 1975. *Alnwick: England and Wales Sheet 006 Solid Geology 1:50,000.* Nottingham, Keyworth.

Brown, J. 1817. *On the Application of Steam, and its salutary Effects in Forcing, but particularly as applied to the Pine Apple:* *Transactions of the Horticultural Society of London.* London: M. Bulmer & Co.

Campbell, S. 1988. Glasshouses and Frames, 1600–1900. In C. A. Wilson (ed) *The Country House Kitchen Garden 1600–1950.* Stroud: Sutton Publishing, 100–13.

Campbell, S. 2005. *A History of Kitchen Gardening.* London: Frances Lincoln.

Campbell, S. 2006. *Walled Kitchen Gardens.* Oxford: Shire Publications.

Carlisle Journal, 1843. Register of Births Marriages and Deaths, 04 February.

Castle, L. 2013. *The Apple, With Chapters on Propagation, Grafting and General Pruning.* London: Smith Press.

Clark, J. 1995. *The Medieval Horse and its Equipment c.* 1150–c. 1450. London: Museum of London.

Connolly, D., Dinning, S., Rocks-MacQueen, D. and Struckmeier, M. 2012. Central Glasshouse Investigation, Amisfield Walled Garden, Haddington, East Lothian. Peter Potter Lost Landscapes and Amisfield Preservation Trust Unpublished Report.

Cowie, R. and Pipe, A. 1998. A Late Medieval and Tudor Horse Burial Ground: Excavations at Elverton Street, Westminster. *The Archaeological Journal* 155, 226–51.

Davison, P.J. 1986. *Brickworks of the North East.* Gateshead: Portcullis Press and Gateshead Libraries and Arts Services.

Derham, K., Williams, A., Finlayson, R. and Hardy, C. 2009. *Alnwick Northumberland Extensive Urban Survey.* Morpeth: Northumberland County Council and English Heritage.

Desmond, R. 1994. *Dictionary of British And Irish Botanists and Horticulturalists.* London: Taylor and Francis.

Dix, B. 1999. Alnwick Castle, Northumberland. Gardens Project. Archaeological Recording Action Brief. English Heritage Unpublished Report.

Don, G. 1844. *A general history of the dichlamydeous plants, comprising complete descriptions of the different orders: together with the characters of the genera and species, and an enumeration of the cultivated varieties : their places of growth, time of flowering, mode of culture, and uses in medicine and domestic economy: the scientific names accentuated, their etymologies explained, and the classes and orders illustrated by engravings, and preceded by introductions to the linnaean and natural systems, and a glossary of the terms used: the whole arranged according to the natural system: vol. iii: calyciflorae.* London: John Van Voorst.

Driesch, A., von den and Boessneck, J.A. 1974. Kritische Anmerkungen zur Widerristhöhenberechnung aus Längenmaßen vor- und frühgeschichtlicher Tierknochen. *Saugetierkundliche Mitteilungen* 22, 325–48.

Dutt, R. 1916. *The economic history of India under early British rule, from the rise of the British power in 1757 to the accession of Queen Victoria in 1837.* London: Kegan Paul.

Edwards, P.R. 1988. *The horse trade of Tudor and Stuart England.* Cambridge: Cambridge University Press.

Evans, S. 1998. Report on the Conservatory Garden at Alnwick Castle, Appendix 1. In R. Kent, The Conservatory Garden, Alnwick Castle, Historic Buildings Evaluation. Unpublished Report. Appendix 1.

Fairhurst and Partners 1998a. Report on the condition of Boundary Wall, Cellar, Gunsheds and Retaining Walls, all located on and around the 'Old Garden' at Alnwick Castle. Fairhurst and Partners Unpublished Report.

Fairhurst and Partners 1998b. Report on the condition of the remains of two existing Vinery Buildings located in the 'Old Gardens' at Alnwick Castle. Fairhurst and Partners Unpublished Report.

Fairhurst and Partners 1998c. Report on the condition of a) the Water Tower and b) the Toilet Block, located in the 'Old Gardens' at Alnwick Castle. Fairhurst and Partners Unpublished Report.

Gidney, L.J. 2004. Faunal Remains. In Assessment of excavations at Alnwick Castle Gardens, Alnwick Castle, Northumberland (ACG00). Archaeological Services University of Durham Unpublished Report, 133–6.

Gidney, L.J. 2013. Offspring of the Aurochs: A comparison of a reference collection of Dexter cattle skeletons with archaeological and historical data. Doctoral Thesis, Durham University. Online at http://etheses.dur.ac.uk/10561 [accessed 05/04/2018].

Goody, P.C. 2008. *Horse anatomy. A pictorial approach to equine structure.* London: J.A. Allen.

Gowen, J.R. 1820. Observations upon the Glazing of Hot-houses, and Conservatories (paper read to the Society 1818). *Transactions of the Horticultural Society of London, Volume III.* 244–9.

Grant, F. 2013. *Glasshouses.* Oxford: Shire Publications.

Gray, T. 1998. Walled Gardens and the Cultivation of Orchard Fruit in the south-west of England. In C. A. Wilson (ed) *The Country House Kitchen Garden 1600–1950.* Stroud: Sutton Publishing, 114–28.

Green, F. 1998. Report on the Conservatory Garden at Alnwick Castle, Appendix 2. In R. Kent, The Conservatory Garden, Alnwick Castle, Historic Buildings Evaluation. Unpublished Report. Appendix 2.

Green, F. 2000. The Heated Garden Walls at Belsay Hall. *Archaeologia Aeliana 5th Series* 28, 223–30.

Grigson, C. 1982. Sex and age determination of some bones and teeth of domestic cattle: a review of the literature. In B. Wilson, C. Grigson and S. Payne (eds) *Ageing and sexing animal bones from archaeological sites.* Oxford: B.A.R. British Series 109, 37–54.

Hall, E. 1989. Hot Walls: An Investigation of Their Construction in Some Northern Kitchen Gardens. *Garden History* 17 (1), 95–107.

Hall, J.G. and Clutton-Brock, J. 1995. *Two Hundred Years of British Farm Livestock.* London: The Natural History Museum.

Hartshorne, C.H. 1865. *A Guide to Alnwick Castle.* London: Longmans, Green, Reader and Dyer.

Hay, J. 1829. Account of a mode of introducing a steady and uniform Bottom-Heat in Pine-apple or Melon Pits, or in Stoves for Exotic Plants, by means of Steam introduced into a close chamber filled with waterworn stones. *Memoirs of the Caledonian Horticultural Society* 4, 582–99.

Hix, J. 1996. *The Glasshouse.* London: Phaidon Press.

J.T. 1874. The Gardens of England: Alnwick Castle. *The Garden. An Illustrated Weekly Journal of Gardening in all its Branches* 5 (January 31st 1874), 100–1.

Journal of the Kew Guild 1897, 1:5.

Journal of the Kew Guild 1940, 5:46.

Kent, R. 1998. The Conservatory Garden, Alnwick Castle, Historic Buildings Evaluation. Architecture and Historic Buildings Conservation Unpublished Report.

Kirk, A. 1909. *Grape Culture Up-To-Date.* London: Simpkin, Marshall, Hamilton, Kent & Co. Ltd.

Knight, T.A. 1822. On the Ventilation of Forcing-houses. *Transactions of the Horticultural Society of London* 2, 224–227.

Knight, T.A. 1822. A Description of a Forcing House for Grapes; with Observations on the best method of constructing Houses for other fruits. *Transactions of the Horticultural Society of London* 1. 99–102.

Knight, T.A. 1841. *A selection from Mr. Knight's Physiological and Horticultural Papers published in the Transactions of the Royal and Horticultural Societies, by the Late Thomas Andrew Knight Esq., President of the Horticultural Society of London etc. etc.* London: Longman, Orme, Brown, Green and Longmans.

Kohlmaier, G. and von Sartory, B. [translated by J.C. Harvey] 1991. *Houses of Glass: A Nineteenth-Century Building Type.* Cambridge: MIT Press.

Levine, M. 1982. The use of crown height measurements and eruption-wear sequences to age horse teeth. In B. Wilson, C. Grigson and S. Payne (eds) *Ageing and sexing animal bones from archaeological sites.* Oxford: BAR Brit Ser 109, 223–50.

Loudon, J.C. 1817. *Remarks on the Construction of Hothouses, pointing out the most Advantageous Forms, Materials, and Contrivances to be used in their Construction; also a Review of the Various Methods of Building them in Foreign Countries as well as in England.* London: Richard and Arthur Taylor.

Loudon, J.C. 1825. *An Encyclopaedia of Gardening.* London: Longman, Hurst, Rees, Orme, Brown, and Green.

Loudon, J.C. 1827. *The Gardeners Magazine Volume 2.* London: Longman, Rees, Orme, Brown, and Green.

Loudon, J.C. 1838. *Arboretum et fruticetum britannicum; or, the trees and shrubs of Britain, native and foreign, hardy and half-hardy, pictorially and botanically delineated, and scientifically and popularly described; with their propagation, culture, management, and uses in the arts, in useful and ornamental plantations, and in landscape-gardening; preceded by a historical and geographical outline of the trees and shrubs of temperate climates throughout the world.* London: Henry G Bohn.

Loudon, J.C. 1805. *A short treatise on several improvements, recently made in hot-houses: by which from four-fifths to nine-tenths of the fuel commonly used will be saved, time, labour, and risk, greatly lessened, and several other advantages produced: and which are applicable to hot-houses already erected, or to the construction of new hot-houses: illustrated by nine large copperplates.* John Turnbull, Edinburgh.

Loudon, J.C. 1832. *The Gardeners Magazine Volume 8.* London: Longman, Rees, Orme, Brown, Green and Longman.

Mackenzie, G.S. 1822. On the Form which the Glass of a Forcing-House ought to have, in order to receive the greatest possible quantity of Rays from the Sun. In a Letter to the Right Hon. Sir Joseph Banks, G. C. B. P. R. S. etc. *Transactions of the Horticultural Society of London* 2, 171–177.

McIntosh, C. 1839. *The New and Improved Practical Gardener.* London: Thomas Kelly.

McMaster, A.R. 1998. Alnwick Castle Walled Garden: Report on an Archaeological Evaluation. Tyne and Wear Museums Archaeology Unpublished Report.

Mearns, J. 1831. On an Improved Boiler for heating Hot-Houses by Hot Water, and on some other Modifications of Hot-Water Apparatus. *The Gardener's Magazine and Register of Rural & Domestic Improvement*, 141–3.

Miller, P. 1752, 1754, 1768. *The Gardeners Dictionary, Volume 2.* London: privately printed.

National Fruit Collection, 2015. National Fruit Collection. http://www.nationalfruitcollection.org.uk/search [accessed 31 August 2018].

Nicol, W. 1810. *The Gardener's Kalendar. or Monthly Directory of Operations in every branch of Horticulture.* Constable, London.

Oldaker, I. 1822. Account of the Method of growing Mushrooms in Houses. *Transactions of the Horticultural Society of London 2*, 336–46.

Ordnance Survey, 1856. 1st edition, 24 inch to 1 mile.

Ordnance Survey, 1867. 1st edition, 25 inch to 1 mile.

Ordnance Survey, 1897. 2nd edition, 25 inch to 1 mile.

Ordnance Survey, 1923. 25 inch to 1 mile.

Owen, N. 2014. Alnwick Castle. http://www.capabilitybrown.org/garden/alnwick-castle [accessed 31 August 2018].

Owen, N. 2016a. Alnwick Castle. http://www.capabilitybrown.org/garden/alnwick-castle [accessed 31 August 2018].

Owen, N. 2016b. Kirkharle. http://www.capabilitybrown.org/garden/alnwick-castle [accessed 31 August 2018].

Pevsner, N and Richmond, I. Revised by Grundy, J., McCombie, G., Ryder, P. and Welfare, H. 2002. *The Buildings of England: Northumberland.* New Haven and London Yale: University Press.

Phibbs, J. 2016. *A list of landscapes that have been attributed to 'Capability' Brown.* Online at http://johnphibbs.uk/wp-content/uploads/2016/05/160506Attributions.pdf [accessed 04/12/2017].

RCHME 1991. *Recording Historic Buildings – A Descriptive Specification.* London: English Heritage.

Rhodes, J. 1829. On heating Hot-Houses by Steam. *Memoirs of the Caledonian Horticultural Society* 4, 511–9.

Ridgeway, V. 2004. The Alnwick Castle Gardens Archaeological Project. Post-Excavation Assessment Report. Volume 1: The Text and Plates. Volume 2: The Figures. Pre-Construct Archaeology Unpublished Report.

Ridgeway, V. 2005. Archaeological Investigations at the Northern Conservatory, The Alnwick Garden, Alnwick, Northumberland. Post-Excavation Assessment Report. Pre-Construct Archaeology Unpublished Report.

Rielly, K. 2011. The leather-production industry in Bermondsey - the archaeological evidence. In R. Thomson and Q. Mould (eds) *Leather Tanneries - the Archaeological Evidence.* Exeter: Archetype Publications Ltd in association with the Archaeological Leather Group, 157–86.

Rielly, K. 2016. Report on the animal bone recovered from excavations at Alnwick Castle Gardens, Alnwick Castle, Northumberland *(ACG0*0). Pre-Construct Archaeology, Unpublished Report,

Rixson, D. 2000. *The History of Meat Trading.* Nottingham: Nottingham University Press.

Schmid, E. 1972. *Atlas of Animal Bones for Prehistorians, Archaeologists and Quaternary Geologists.* London: Elsevier.

Serjeantson, D. 1989. Animal Remains and the Tanning Trade. In D. Serjeantson and T. Waldron (eds) *Diet and Craft in Towns.* Oxford: B.A.R. British Series. 199, 129–46.

Serjeantson, D., Waldron, T. and Bracegirdle, M. 1992. Medieval Horses from Kingston-upon-Thames. *London Archaeologist* 7 (1), 9–13.

Shaw, M. 2011. Late Medieval to Early Post-Medieval Tanning: The evidence from Northampton and its wider implications. In R. Thomson and Q. Mould (eds) *Leather Tanneries - the Archaeological Evidence.* Exeter: Archetype Publications Ltd in association with the Archaeological Leather Group, 117–29.

Shrimpton, C. 1997. History of Alnwick Castle Gardens. Unpublished document?

Shrimpton, C. 2006. *A History of Alnwick Parks and Pleasure Grounds.* Derby: Heritage House Group Ltd.

Shrimpton, C. n.d. *Alnwick Castle. Where History Lives.* Peterborough: Jarrold Publishing.

Speechly, W. 1796. *A Treatise on the Culture of the Pineapple and the Management of the Hot-House Together with a Description of Every Species of Insect that Infest Hot-Houses with Effectual Methods of Destroying them (second edition, with additions).* Nottinghamshire: Peacock.

Stevens, P. 2011. Can we identify a tannery from waste products? In R. Thomson and Q. Mould (eds) *Leather Tanneries - the Archaeological Evidence.* Exeter: Archetype Publications Ltd in association with the Archaeological Leather Group, 187–91.

Stroud, D. 1975. *Capability Brown.* London: Faber and Faber.

Swan, N. 2006. Alnwick Castle, Alnwick, Northumberland: Archaeological Monitoring. Archaeological Services Durham University Unpublished Report.

Tate, G. 1866. *History of the Borough, Castle and Barony of Alnwick, Volume 1.* Charleston: Nabu Press.

Tate, G. 1868–9. *History of the Borough, Castle and Barony of Alnwick, Volume 2.* Charleston: Nabu Press.

Taylor-Wilson, R.H. 2000. The Gardens Project, Alnwick Castle, Northumberland. Project Design for Archaeological Works. Pre-Construct Archaeology Unpublished Report.

The Gardeners' Chronicle and Agricultural Gazette, 1845.

The Gardeners' Chronicle, 1877, 1880, 1891, 1898, 1902, 1905.

The Newcastle Journal, 4 March 1939.

Thomson, R. 1981. Leather manufacture in the post-medieval period with special reference to Northamptonshire. *Post-Medieval Archaeology* 15, 161–75.

Wilkin, T. 1772. Plan of the Demesnes with divers other lands near the Town of Alnwick in the County of Northumberland.

Wilkinson, T. 1822. Observations on the Form of Hothouses. *Transactions of the Horticultural Society of London* 2, 161–4.

Williams, J. 1822. On the Cultivation of the Vine in Forcing Houses, with Observations on Forcing Peaches. *Transactions of the Horticultural Society of London* 2, 108–13.

Willis, P. 1981. Capability Brown in Northumberland. *Garden History* 9 (2), 157–83.

Wilson, R. and Edwards, P. 1993. Butchery of horse and dog at Witney Palace, Oxfordshire and the knackering and feeding of meat to hounds during the post-medieval period. *Post-Medieval Archaeology* 27, 43–56.

Wood, J. 1827. Plan of the Town and Borough of Alnwick from actual survey.

Woods, M. and Warren, A.S. 1988. *Arete Swartz Glasshouses: A History of Greenhouses, Orangeries and Conservatories.* London: Aurum Press.

Young, R.E. 1998. Alnwick Castle Walled Garden, Northumberland: An Archaeological Evaluation. Tyne and Wear Museums Archaeology Unpublished Report.

# Index

Illustrations are indicated by page numbers in *italics*.

# ASSIOUT –
# THE SAGA OF AN EGYPTIAN FAMILY

# ASSIOUT –
# THE SAGA OF
# AN EGYPTIAN FAMILY

## HANNA F. WISSA

The Book Guild
Sussex, England

This book is sold subject to the condition that it shall not, by way of
trade or otherwise, be lent, re-sold, hired out, photocopied or held
in any retrieval system or otherwise circulated without the
publisher's prior consent in any form of binding or cover other than
that in which this is published and without a similar condition
including this condition being imposed on the subsequent purchaser.

The Book Guild Ltd.
25 High Street,
Lewes, Sussex

First published 1994
© H.F. Wissa 1994
Set in Baskerville

Typesetting by Acorn Bookwork, Salisbury

Printed in Great Britain by
Bookcraft (Bath) Ltd

A catalogue record for this book is
available from the British Library

ISBN 0 86332 908 X

# CONTENTS

# The Reason Why, an Apology and Acknowledgement

It has been said that everyone has a book in him. But the word book frightens me. It reminds of school books, which I hate. So when I decided to write about my mother, I did my best not to write a book. I did not feel I was up to it; but I'd write a story instead. I liked stories, I liked listening to stories and telling stories. As a child I loved fairy stories, frightening stories, and romantic stories; and when I grew older I liked dirty stories. I liked hearing about people I knew, and those I did not know. I liked myth and legend and folk stories, which I either heard or read. But always in story form, nothing stodgy or overwhelming. As a child I loved Bible stories told to me by my mother in the piano room, in the evenings, and by Sister Gerschen, a Dutch missionary who used to spend the summer months with us, on the balcony in the mornings. I liked weird stories, parts of Greek legends told to me by our Greek maid Sophia on Wednesday evenings when our English nanny had her day off. I loved Arabic folk stories, about Goha*, or from *The Thousand and One Nights*, told to me by the gardener Osta Ibrahim, whom we were not supposed to mix with, including all their sexy undertones.

I loved telling stories to my children and watching the reaction on their faces. My two daughters had very different reactions. I knew I could influence one of them, catch her imagination. I could see her living through the story, and I'd soar away with her into the clouds. I could never be sure of my other daughter, who'd suddenly come out with a very logical question or remark, that would bring me quickly back to earth. My two daughters married foreigners and live abroad. Their children's reactions and outlook on life are very different from ours. They are more practical, worldly, and tuned to our modern times, they know more of life and its problems than we ever did; and yet they still have a romantic streak in them, and like to hear stories about their family, and they encouraged me to write it for them. They had only known their great grandmother Esther as an infirm old lady, whom they used to see for a few minutes at a time, when they came to Alexandria for the summer. They could not imagine the person

*Goha – An Egyptian folkloric character.

viii

she really was, or had been. There were eighty three years difference in age between her and her eldest great grandson. Other young members of our scattered family and relations, whose parents had married foreigners and lived abroad, knew little of their family, or Egypt or days gone by. They hardly knew what relationship they were one to another. They knew they were distant cousins somehow.

It was under these circumstances, and because I had a good memory, and listened all my life to stories of our family and Egypt, that made me decide at first to write the story of my mother, which developed into a story of the family, their origins and the times they lived in. I apologise to all those to whom I am telling this story, for the way I tell it, jumping from one subject to another, making statements which may seem irrelevant, but which I find in my peculiar way to be either amusing or interesting. I have not tried and would not be able to write a comprehensive study of the times I write about. I can only give my impressions of what I have read, or heard, or felt about Egypt in the nineteenth and twentieth centuries. The books I have read on the subject are very limited, and this in itself should preclude it being intended as a scholarly work. It never was meant to be. I apologise to all those scholars whose ideas I have used, and I hope I have not misquoted or misread them. I have throughout tried to refer to any quotation or information used, and I apologise for references that may have been omitted inadvertently. A full list of all the books I have read on the subject is mentioned in the bibliography.

I take this opportunity of acknowledging and thanking all those who have helped me in writing this story, by lending me books and photos, giving me advice or information, or listening to me for the past two years.

I would like to thank the publishers, The Book Guild Ltd, Lewes, East Sussex.

I would like to thank Mr Mohammed Salmawy, author and playwright, and Managing Editor of the *Ahram Weekly* who read carefully through the manuscript and took the trouble of making some very valuable comments.

I would especially like to thank Miss Martha Roy, that learned and dedicated scholar, an American missionary who has loved and lived in Egypt most of her life, for elucidating a subject that I had always wondered about, of how the American missionaries were able to convert a considerable section of the Copts, members of the Coptic Orthodox Church to Protestantism. It did not seem logical that the Coptic Monotheist, who had withstood persecution and ostracism by the Byzantine Orthodox and the Roman Catholic Churches was so easily wooed away from his beliefs and customs within a few years by a bunch of American missionaries.

I would like to thank my cousin, Mrs Sylvia Nicolaier (née Khayatt) for documents and pictures of her family, and great grandfather Wassif el Khayatt.

I would like to thank Mrs Phoebe Choucri for all the information she supplied me with, of the work of the YWCA in Egypt and its National General Council which my mother chaired for several years, as well as being President of the Alexandria YWCA for many years.

I would like to thank Mrs Nadra Sarofim who translated some of my mother's articles from Arabic which can be found in the appendices.

I would like to thank Dr Soheir Bakhoum the well known numismatist at the Centre National de Récherches Scientifiques Paris for her help in finding reference to the coin struck for Lycopolis (Assiout), and providing me with a photocopy of it.

I would like to thank Dr Mohamed F. Awad, architect and historian on Alexandria, for the valuable information he gave me on Alexandria and its sites.

I would like to thank Mrs Gertie Wissa for all her help and for the photos she gave me.

I would like to thank Miss Mariann Wissa Hvelplund for all the trouble she took in designing and producing the book jacket.

I would like to thank my aunt Aida Fanous whom I telephoned whenever I wanted to elucidate certain stories and dates about her sister Esther and the family.

I would like to thank my wife Philae, for putting up with me for the last years, with all my tantrums, my books and papers strewn all over the living room and dining room table, and for all the advice she gave me, trying to correct my bad punctuation.

I would like to thank Mr and Mrs Fields of Fields Secretarial Services, Dover who word processed, typed and photocopied much of the manuscript, trying to teach me at the same time how to use a word processor.

I would also like to thank Mrs Soheir Kallini, Miss Amani Salib of Cairo, and Mrs Lucy El Semine of Alexandria for helping me out with the typing of parts of the manuscript when I was stuck.

I would like to thank my secretary Mr Adel Badawi for all the photocopying, finding my papers and reference books, sticking in photos, and a lot of the drudgery and running around.

And last but not least I would like to thank my thirteen year old grandson, David John Massad of New Jersey, USA, who is a wizard with a computer and wordprocessor, for having retyped and spellchecked most of the manuscript during his summer holidays.

# PROLOGUE

This is the story of an Egyptian lady, her family and times; her pioneering grandfather and his brother, and the town in which they were born.

The background is a short outline of Egypt, its people, their beliefs and prejudices; its geography and history throughout its different periods, Pharaonic, Christian and Islamic; until the emergence of the Egyptian Renaissance under Mohamed Aly at the start of the 19th Century, when our story begins.

The Egyptian lady was my mother, Esther Fahmy Wissa, née Esther Akhnoukh Fanous (1895–1990), who through much of her life was at the forefront of the emerging feminist movement, and political aspirations of the country.

The pioneers were my grandfather Hanna Boctor Wissa, and his brother Wissa Boctor Wissa, my great grandfather*, whose life story on how they made a fortune, and created a dynasty is more like a tale from *The Thousand and One Nights* than reality.

The town is Assiout where some of the leading Christian families were converted to Protestantism by the American Riverboat Missionaries, 'Nile Evangelism', who sold the Bible translated into Arabic, and explained the gospel in the villages on the way up the Nile in Upper Egypt, eventually settling in Assiout in the 1860s, making it their main stronghold.

In order to understand what made a personality like Esther Fahmy Wissa tick, one should take into consideration the different forces, beliefs and prejudices that she was subject to, from her immediate surroundings, over and above the historical facts of her people and their roots.

She was the daughter of one of the leading Coptic families of Assiout, capital of Upper Egypt, and the fourth largest city after Alexandria and Tanta in Lower Egypt. Assiout was also the bastion of the Copts, the indigenous Christian natives of the country called Egypt, who alone can trace an unadulterated descent from the race to whom the civilization and culture of the ancient world was so largely due. Thanks to their religion they were able to keep their blood pure from admixture with the Arabs, Kurds, Caucasians and Turks.

*See family tree.

Originally, the word *Copt* was a corruption of the word Egyptian and indicated *nationality* and not *creed* – as *Aigyptos* was the Greek form of one of the names of Memphis[1] Ha-ka-ptah which was afterwards applied to the inhabitants of the whole country. So *Gubti* or *Agbat* were the Arabic corruptions of the root which remains in the ancient Egyptian language (Coptic) as Egypt and Egyptian. The Europeans further altered the Arab words to Copt or Coptic.

When the Arabs invaded Egypt in 641 AD the word *Gubti* came to mean the natives of Egypt who retained their Christian faith, and had not been converted to Islam. It became the name of a *creed* and not a *nation*. By contrast Islam considered itself a nation and not a religion, no matter from what part of the world their members came. Over the years the Copts, or the natives of Egypt who retained their Christian faith, became a minority in the land of their ancestors. At its lowest ebb, it is reckoned that there were no more than a hundred and fifty thousand[2] pure bred Christian Egyptians in the country.

Esther's family had, however, been converted to Protestantism by the American missionaries who had come to Assiout in the 1860s, thus causing a minority within a minority. All the different sects of the Protestant missionaries, together with the Catholic teachings of the Jesuits and Fréres, further weakened the native Coptic Church, causing a rift within the Coptic Christians themselves, due to the fact that members of one family were at loggerheads with each other, that is, if they had nothing better to do.

Esther was brought up at the American Mission School in Assiout, imbibing many of their ideas, whether they were religious, political or social. Her English governess gave her a love of poetry. Her natural intelligence and searching mind led her to delve deeply into the vast library of her father and her brother, Louis, a scholar and political being, a graduate of Oxford. Her reading of many books on many subjects gave her ideas and knowledge extraneous to her immediate surroundings.

Assiout, being one of the stops of the Cook's tours up the Nile, enabled her to meet many foreign personalities of different nations, who were entertained by different members of the family, giving her the possibility of developing a cosmopolitan outlook on life and at the same time recognising the anomalies in Egypt's position.

Egypt was paying Britain to rule her in the Khedive's name, but as a vassal of Turkey. This rule or occupation was supposed to be temporary, to help Egypt regulate her finances, and pay off her foreign debt. However, at the same time Britain's real interest was to perpetuate or at least prolong

---

[1] Memphis, an ancient Egyptian town 10 miles south of modern Cairo
[2] *The Coptic Community in the 19th Century* by Boutros Sourial, page 210

the occupation, in order to defend her Empire, her lines of communication to India.

Together with the abuses of the foreigners who had obtained privileges under the capitulary system of the Turkish Empire; the difference in wealth and style of life of the inhabitants; the ignorance and sophistication that was found in the different strata of the community; all helped to make up the paradox that was Egypt, and the character that was Esther Fahmy Wissa.

# PART ONE

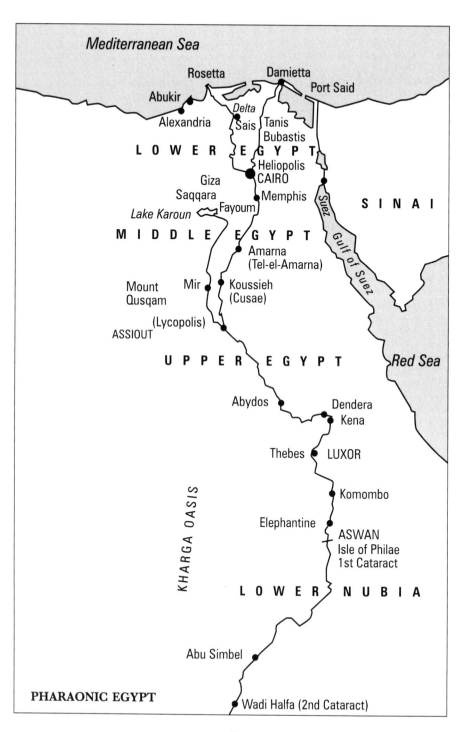

Mediterranean Sea

Rosetta    Damietta
Abukir                Port Said
Alexandria    *Delta*
Sais    Tanis
Bubastis

L  O  W  E  R    E  G  Y  P  T

Heliopolis
Giza    CAIRO
Saqqara    Memphis
*Lake Karoun*    Fayoum

M  I  D  D  L  E    E  G  Y  P  T

Amarna
(Tel-el-Amarna)

Mount    Mir    Koussieh
Qusqam    (Cusae)

(Lycopolis)
ASSIOUT

U  P  P  E  R    E  G  Y  P  T

S  I  N  A  I

*Suez*

*Gulf of Suez*

*Red Sea*

Abydos    Dendera
Kena

Thebes    LUXOR

Komombo

Elephantine    ASWAN
Isle of Philae
1st Cataract

KHARGA OASIS

L  O  W  E  R    N  U  B  I  A

Abu Simbel

**PHARAONIC EGYPT**

Wadi Halfa (2nd Cataract)

# HOW IT ALL HAPPENED

*Pharaonic Egypt*

Ten thousand years ago while the rest of the world was deep in slumber, there lived in the north east corner of Africa, where it links with Asia, a highly developed people, 'an oasis of civilisation' cut off from the rest of the world by the desert and the sea. These were the inhabitants of Egypt, who lived on the raised areas of land in the valley of the River Nile, out of reach of the annual floods. They cultivated the arable lowland on both banks of the river, once the waters of the flood had receded leaving its rich and fertile silt on the land's surface. The Egyptians by this time had developed from a hunting to a farming community.

From Egypt's southernmost border at the first cataract at Aswan, the Nile, over the ages, had carved out of the valley a course northwards to the Mediterranean Sea. For 800 miles the arable land on both sides of the river was restricted to a strip, never exceeding eight miles in width, being sandwiched between the Western and Eastern deserts. This strip of country is known as Upper Egypt ending at what was known as Memphis, a few miles south of modern Cairo. For the last 200 miles of its meandering journey towards the sea, the Nile branched out into seven main and five auxiliary rivulets, forming what is known as the Nile Delta of Lower Egypt. It was created over the ages by the rich mud deposited on the sandy ground and marshes of the sea, having been brought down by the annual torrents emanating in the highlands of Ethiopia, over four thousand miles away. At some time in far off ages, the waters of the Mediterranean washed against the limestone ridge of the Mokattam Hills south-east of Cairo.

Herodotus said 'Egypt was the "gift of the Nile" and without the Nile there is no Egypt'. The Greeks rightfully observed that 'the Nile flood, was to the farmer of Egypt, what the rain of Zeus was to the European peasants'. Too high a flood, or too low a flood were equally disastrous for the Egyptian farmer. Too high a flood could mean catastrophe, as it could wash away their mud dwellings, destroying their meagre possessions; too low a flood could mean famine, as there would not be enough water to inundate the land.

According to Manetho, a scribe, and chronicler of the Egyptian Dynasties who lived at the time of Ptolemy II (282–246 BC), the people of the

Nile Valley were already co-operating with each other in prehistoric times over 3000 years before what is known as the beginning of the Archaic period 3200 BC. They cooperated out of necessity, guarding the Nile banks in case of breaches, making small retaining walls of mud to trap some of the waters of the flood, in order to grow more and better crops.

These prehistoric people worked in stone and ivory, then copper, stitched their clothes, domesticated their animals, 'cooked their food, glazed their beads, slept on beds, played such games as ninepins and enjoyed the artistry of shaping and decorating their earthenware pots.'[3] They lived as independent families or tribes, loosely attached to the cultivatable parts of the valley. Each group had its individual god, whose emblem was set up on top of a pole and took animal forms to suit the hunting communities of the early days.

Just as the chieftains became princelings, then minor kings, so did the villages become principalities, then minor states, called *nomes* by the Greeks, then two Kingdoms, Lower and Upper Egypt. The individual gods were also transformed into hybrid gods and through it all the castes of priests were increasing their influence over the people and their rulers alike. They guarded their secrets of magic and mumbo jumbo jealously, for their own aggrandisement, wealth and power. The people in time came to realise that the petty squabbles of their rulers were usually for selfish reasons, and were not conducive to their well-being, which depended on order as represented by the god Ptah who created the world by means of his heart (thought) and his tongue (utterance), pure reason wherein all creation takes place. 'In the beginning there was the word and the word was God' who controlled the Sun, the Moon, the Stars, the Flood, the Nile; all of which were deified, believing that these forces controlled everyone, including their rulers. The idea that the ancient Egyptians deified their pharaohs is not far from the conception that the pharaohs represented these natural forces on earth, especially if it could be seen that the pharaoh was a good administrator and was able to rule his people justly and in security.

The more intangible were these ideas of supernatural powers, of life, and life after death, the more the priests' influence increased.

The ancient Egyptian's religion was based on observation. He saw in the natural forces around him a duality of opposites, life and death – the Nile with its black mud represented Life, the desert with its red sand represented Death – Night and Day, the Moon and the Sun, Good and Evil, Osiris and Seth. Such forces became the basis of his religion; he knew he could not control them, he knew that there was some power that kept them in equilibrium. His need to establish equipoise can be seen in the symmetry of his art and architecture, in his creation of the political duality of the Two

---

[3] *Modern Egypt* by Tom Little

4

Lands, Lower and Upper Egypt, and in his conception of *Maat*, the incarnation of Truth and Justice, that kept everything in balance. The forces of Evil could upset *Maat*, but it could be re-established by Pharaoh, by his authoritative utterance, and his understanding. (*Maat* was represented in the painted scenes as a gracious little lady, seated and wearing an ostrich feather on her head this symbol was used for writing her name.) Since Pharaoh was the representative of God on earth, *Maat* was stability. The cosmos is essentially static; change is only a recurring rhythm, not a progression. The struggle between the opposites is evenly matched. The land may be parched in summer, but it will be followed by the inundation. The victory of the sun god is proclaimed with every dawn, though his death will occur at dusk of every day.

The view of the Egyptian was that, though it was the nature of man to transgress, yet it was in the nature of the gods to forgive, 'for their wrath is finished in a minute'. The Egyptian felt no guilt, which has given the rest of the world a motive force either for good or evil. The Egyptian felt he was not compelled to put himself right with God, but he had to attune himself to the system of *Maat* which had been created by God. *Maat* was said to rule when the kingdom was unified and peaceful. A strong ruler was her chief upholder. Without *Maat* creation could not be sustained but would fall into chaos.

All the gods that the Egyptians worshipped were only symbols of different manifestations of the one God who had created the world and who ruled everything.

There is no doubt that the unification of the ancient Egyptians into one nation was one of the earliest recorded unities on this earth. It came about when Egyptians realised that their welfare depended upon greater cooperation amongst themselves, leading to fewer man-made catastrophes and more ability to withstand the vagaries of nature. This led to the idea that maybe someone could control everything by the union of Upper and Lower Egypt as one nation kingdom.

It only needed a strong leader with a sense of purpose to carry it out. That person was Menes, the first recorded dynastic king of the Archaic period – the First and Second Dynasties 3188–2815 BC – who drove down from Upper Egypt, making his capital at Memphis, eventually conquering the different princelings of the Delta and unifying the whole country into one nation wearing the double crown, the Red Crown of the Delta, together with the White Crown of Upper Egypt. From Memphis he divided the country into thirty-six provinces, creating a government administration to supervise the control of the Nile by regulating the man-made canals; he also passed laws of equality of labour and gave the people justice and security.

From 3188 BC to 2394 BC, a period just under 900 years from the Ist to the end of the VIth dynasty known as the Archaic and the Old Kingdom, Egypt was unified under one crown, that of Lower and Upper Egypt. During this period she developed a centralised administration whose bureaucracy went hand in hand with pharaonic grandeur. This enabled her to mobilise and organise great sections of the people in the construction of dykes, thus mastering the annual flood, creating new man-made canals, as well as maintaining the old ones with the subsequent result of larger and better crops.

Egypt developed its architectural technique to the point that by the year 2600 BC, the Step Pyramid of Zoser was built at Saqqara; and by the year 2400 BC both Khufu's and Khafré's pyramids were built at Giza and the Sphinx was carved out of solid rock. Several generations of able builders had created a true architectural style in the manner of building and decoration that became fixed in general lines by the middle of the Old Kingdom. The first six dynasties were considered the first and most creative period of Egyptian history.

However, with life becoming easier the rulers became lax, the power of the princelings and priests increased and Egypt was ruled from the VIIth to the Xth dynasty by several princelings for 140 years. During this period, which is known as the First Intermediate period, Egypt stagnated though she was still protected from the outside world by the surrounding deserts and the sea.

The XIth and XIIth dynasties known as the Middle Kingdom of 2132 to 1777 BC saw Egypt united again. The XIth dynasty included three kings named Mentuhotep.

Mentuhotep I, whose reign was for fifty years, was able to reunite the country under his own rule. Thebes, which was until then a provincial town, became the capital of the whole country. His successors Mentuhotep II and III did not know how to consolidate his work, which had to be undertaken again after an interval by the kings of the XIIth dynasty. They brought an end to a long period of trouble and civil war and brought the country to the apogee of its power and prosperity, with the help of its protector Amun, an obscure god whom the dynasty raised to the rank of the great gods.

The reigns of the kings named Amenemhèt and Senwosret (XIIth dynasty) were brilliant; in every town temples and fine architecture sprang up; literature and art were held in honour. During this period the story of Sinuhe was written, which was particularly popular in Egypt even eight hundred years after it was written. Pupils in the scribal schools on the left bank at Thebes still copied passages from it as an exercise. Kipling said that the story of Sinuhe deserved to be counted among the masterpieces of world literature. Senwosret III (1878–1841 BC) finally abolished the authority of the great provincial nobles who had governed the nomes independently of the crown. He consolidated the conquest of Lower Nubia which was annexed to Egypt up to the Second Cataract. Semna, south of the Second Cataract became the frontier of the kingdom and from there, as far as Elephantine, a system of fortresses protected communications.

A hymn to Senwosret III declares: 'He who massacres without striking a blow, he who shoots an arrow without touching the bow.'

By the time Amenemhet IV's reign was drawing to a close, this great era known as the Middle Kingdom was being eroded from within. Nomads had been infiltrating the Delta, settling there. This regularly happened whenever the country was not strong enough to guard its frontiers.

From the end of the eighteenth century BC to the beginning of the six-teenth century BC, a period of 140 years, between the Middle and the New Kingdom, which was known as the Second Intermediary Period, Egypt was overrun by these local nomads who declared their independence and fought against their lawful sovereigns together with a people of an 'ignoble race' who crossed the Sinai with horse and chariot. This was the period of the Hyksos[4] or Shepherd Kings, during which Egypt became completely deca-dent, and in the course of which nearly all the monuments built by the great kings of old were destroyed.

There were two Hyksos dynasties, the XVth and XVIth. At the begin-ning, they were able to rule the fringes of the eastern part of the Delta. Gradually they extended their control over the whole of the Delta, finally dominating the whole country.

It seems that Lower and Middle Egypt became reconciled to them. The national reaction came at last from the Theban princes of the XVIth dynasty, who drove out the Asiatics, fighting at the same time successfully in the south against the Hyksos' allies, the Nubians. The invader was finally driven out by Ahmas (Ahmose), the founder of the XVIIIth dynasty, whose descendants raised Egypt to the culminating point of her greatness.

Once Egypt's frontiers had been breached, from the time of the Hyksos to the final fall of Egypt, no king could maintain his dependence on the Nile without first subduing the forces that were arrayed against him. This was impossible in the long run. Egypt could not equal the resources of manpower of Asia. However, the descendants of Ahmose, the Thutmoses and the Amenhoteps, pushed their frontiers outwards in order to defend themselves. They conquered Palestine and the Lebanon (where timber which is so rare in the valley of the Nile was to be found) and northern Syria as far as Aleppo, and reached the Euphrates, where they came into conflict with the Chaldean Empire and were stopped.

The sanctuaries which had been destroyed were rebuilt and enriched with the spoils of the conquered nations; the temples of Karnak and Luxor

[4]*Hykos* meant in Egyptian 'Princes of foreign countries' quoted from an article by G Posener in '*A dictionary of Egyptian Civilization*' page 133.

attained gigantic proportions, and artists rivalled the skill of their predecessors of the finest periods, decorating these monuments or the tombs of high officials.

The heresy of Amenhotep IV (1372–1354 BC, known as Akhnaton, the son of Amenhotep III and the husband of Nefertiti,) introduced a new religion which was in reality a re-statement of an earlier belief in one sole god, Aton. When the ancient Egyptian wanted to express in words the great vital force of the sun, he said *Re*. But he said *Aton* when he meant the sun as a positive experience. Amenophis IV repudiated the overlordship of Amun Re the king of the gods, lord of the empire, father of the royal house, and the foremost capitalist of the country due to the wealth its priesthood had accumulated over the ages. He refused to tolerate an insolent priesthood, as did his forebears.

He changed his name from Amenhotep, meaning 'Amun is satisfied' to Akhnaton, meaning the 'one in whom the sun disk is satisfied.' He decided to make Amarna (Tel-el-Amarna) the centre of his personal religion instead of Thebes (Luxor), bastion of the priests of Amun. The age-old temples around which the spiritual life of the whole people revolved were neglected. He erased all mention of Amun or other gods. 'The beautiful child of Aton'[5] and his wife Nefertiti only thought of raising the fruits of the earth and increasing their offerings in honour of the visible sun, giver of 'all prosperity'. Everywhere altars were built in great open courts suffused with light. The king sang of his wonderstruck devotion in a 'great Hymn' which is generally known through its many translations to have inspired indirectly one of the Psalms. Akhnaton as a mystic was remarkable, but as a king he was a disaster. Like someone lost in a dream he allowed his empire to crumble away and the government of the country to fall into pieces. The light of Aton was supposed to benefit all the races of mankind, but Akhnaton's faithful vassals in Asia appealed in vain for help; bedouins overran the country, his representatives betrayed him and the Hittites conquered Syria. A new faith was supposed to grip the hearts of the people. Admittedly in Amarna there were believers, but all over the country it was difficult for the peasant to disown the god of the town, and for the whole people to break with their traditional pattern, which embraced their life, body and soul.

All the old customs were restored under his successor Tutankhamun and were never disturbed again. The generals Ai and Horemheb, rulers after Tutankhamun, wiped out every trace of Akhnaton, the latter dated the dates of his reign from the death of Amenhotep III for he would not recognise as legitimate any of the supporters of the heresy, even those who had repented.

Then the general Rameses began the XIXth Dynasty. He was one of the

---

[5] *A Dictionary of Egyptian Civilization* by Jean Yoyothe

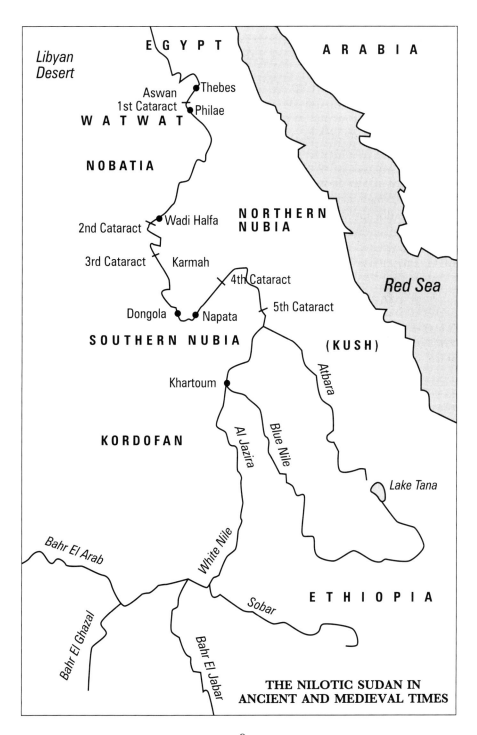

EGYPT

Libyan
Desert

ARABIA

WATWAT

Aswan
1st Cataract
●Thebes
●Philae

NOBATIA

NORTHERN
NUBIA

2nd Cataract
●Wadi Halfa

3rd Cataract
Karmah

4th Cataract

Red Sea

5th Cataract

Dongola●
●Napata

SOUTHERN NUBIA

(KUSH)

Khartoum●

Atbara

KORDOFAN

Al Jazira

Blue Nile

Lake Tana

Bahr El Arab

White Nile

Bahr El Ghazal

Bahr El Jabar

Sobar

ETHIOPIA

THE NILOTIC SUDAN IN
ANCIENT AND MEDIEVAL TIMES

9

generals who liquidated the regime of Akhnaton, he was very elderly when he became king, and he left the real control of affairs to his son Seti, who became Seti I (1312–1300 BC) who consolidated Egyptian power in Palestine and signed a peace treaty with the Hittites.

Numerous monuments are attributed to Seti I's reign in which relief sculpture attained one of its peaks, as seen at Abydos and the tomb of Seti in the Valley of the Kings.

His son Rameses II (1301–1235 BC) did everything on a grand scale during his long reign of sixty-seven years. He was a lover of pomp, erected monuments to his own glory everywhere, but quality was sacrificed to quantity; the sculpture does not show all the old care, and as the artists were not sufficiently numerous to execute the royal orders, they contented themselves in many cases with effacing the names of previous kings on existing statues and substituting that of Rameses II. The great rock temples of Abu Simbel in Lower Nubia were constructed in his reign.

After the reign of Rameses II Egypt was exhausted; she had already lost Syria and was about to lose Palestine.

In the reign of Merneptah, son of Rameses II, and until the reign of Rameses III, of the XXth Dynasty, she had to struggle in the west against the Libyans, who were invading the Delta, whilst the tribes of Asia Minor were attempting to land on the Mediterranean coast, and she could with difficulty stem the tide of invasion.

Deprived of its conquests in Asia and in the Sudan, the country became impoverished; but the priests of Amun, enriched by the booty which the conquerors had bestowed on their temples, still remained wealthy and under the XXIst Dynasty forced the kings to divide their power with them. The kings of the XXIst to the XXIIIrd Dynasties resided at Tanis (San el-Hagar) or at Bubastis (Zagazig) in Lower Egypt, whilst the First Prophets of Amun at Thebes governed Upper Egypt and sometimes appropriated all the royal titles. The sovereigns of Lower Egypt found themselves unable to maintain control over the military governors of the provinces who, supported by bands of Libyan mercenaries, made themselves more or less independent.

At this point it is interesting to note the relationship of pharaonic Egypt and Nubia – the area between Aswan at the First Cataract and Dongola at the Fourth Cataract – this area was divided into two parts:

a. Lower Nubia from Aswan at the First Cataract to Wadi Halfa at the Second Cataract was known as Wat Wat; it had its capital in Aswan. It was considered by the pharaohs as Egypt's natural expansion area, and its defendable borders; they therefore built temples and fortresses along both sides of the Nile. They also recruited their mercenaries for their armies from this area;

b. Upper Nubia from Wadi Halfa at the Second Cataract to Dongola at the Fourth Cataract was known as Kush, and had its capital at Napata in the vicinity of the Fourth Cataract. Kush however was more remote, and Egypt's grip and influence over it depended on the strength of the pharaoh at the time, and the economic desire for expansion.

At its apogee during the New Kingdom, the ancient Egyptians ruled both Wat Wat and Kush (known as the biblical Ethiopia). They appointed a viceroy responsible to Pharaoh alone called 'The King's son of Kush'. He was assisted by two deputies, one for Wat Wat, and the other for Kush.

Under Thutmose III, Egypt initiated a truly imperial Egyptian rule in Napata; much of the land became estates of institutions of Egypt; sons of Nubian chiefs were educated at the Egyptian court a few returned to Nubia to serve as administrators.

The products of Nubia added greatly to the wealth of Egypt, particularly in gold, ivory, ebony, cattle, gums and semi-precious stones.

In fact according to Cyril Aldred in his book *The Egyptians* 'The egyptian-isation of Lower Nubia and Kush was so effective, that at the end of the New Kingdom, the Viceroy intervened decisively in the affairs of Egypt in the name of law and order'.

Thus it came to pass that under the XXIIIrd Dynasty one of the petty kings of the Delta known as the Tefnakhte was attempting to get control over all Egypt and was proceeding south past Memphis. He was met by Pianche, King of Kush, who had taken possession of Nubia and Upper Egypt, and who descended the Nile valley in the name of order and ortho-doxy, and who eventually received the so-called submission of the Delta princes. Upon Pianche's return to Kush, Tefnakhte reasserted his authority over the princes of the Delta. He was eventually succeeded by his son Boc-choris, sole king of the XXIVth Dynasty. Meanwhile Pianche's brother Shabaka who formed the rival XXVth dynasty, defeated Bocchoris and brought all Egypt under his control (719–703 BC). He had Bocchoris burned alive, and removed all other claimants to the throne of Egypt.

The Kings of Kush held Egypt only a few decades, for rivals arose in the persons of the Kings of Assyria who had just seized Palestine and were invading the Delta.

Profiting by the general confusion, the princes of Sais, who lived in the north-west of the country, near Kafr el Zayat, with the aid of the Greeks to whom they had given permission to settle in certain parts of Lower Egypt, drove out the Kushites and Assyrians, and brought the country up to the First Cataract, under the rule of the XXVIth Dynasty.

By 656 BC the Kushites had withdrawn from the Egyptian scene, but their culture survived for another 1000 years in the Sudanese Napatan and Meroitic Kingdom.

11

The epoch of Psamtik, Necho II, Apries, Amose II, was not without splendour. Trade with Greece provided Egypt with new resources. A canal was dug between the Nile and the Red Sea and many buildings arose, particularly in the Delta. An artistic renaissance set in, but with a partiality for over-refined forms, which look feeble in comparison with the best of Old Kingdom work.

But by this time Egypt had lost her strength and, relying only on mercenaries to protect her independence, she fell a prey to Cambyses and the Persians in 525 BC.

Recovering her vitality somewhat she regained her liberty from the XXVIIth to the XXXth Dynasties (404–340 BC), and Nectanebus I and II carried out repairs to the temples and sanctuaries.

The Persians again occupied Egypt, but only for a short time, for in 332 BC Alexander the Great came as conqueror and founded Alexandria.

After his death, Egypt remained in the hands of one of his generals, Ptolemy, whose descendants, all bearing the same name, ruled her for 300 years, ending with Egypt's last Pharaoh Cleopatra, who bore a son to Caesar, but Caesarion was not a true pharaoh and died before ascending the throne.

The Ptolemys were Greeks by education but they nevertheless adopted Egyptian customs and declared themselves direct heirs of the ancient pharaohs. Magnificent temples were constructed (at Philae, Kom Ombo, Edfu, Dendera etc.) but the country, overburdened by taxation and torn by constant family wars, was flourishing in appearance only. Upper Egypt rebelled several times and Thebes was devastated.

On several occasions Rome intervened in order to restore peace. Finally in the year 30 BC Octavian (Augustus) took possession of Alexandria, and Egypt became part of the estate of the Emperor governed by a prefect in the Emperor's name. The latter was given all the titles and attributes of the ancient kings and in the temples completed or built during this period (at Dendera, Esna etc.), no difference can be discerned between the scenes pictured in relief, where the Emperor plays a part in religious rituals, and those engraved 1500 years earlier.

During the Roman period Egypt was no more than a granary for Rome, ruled by a dictatorial absentee landlord with no thought given to the welfare of the native Egyptian.


*A little bit about Assiout 'The Everlasting'.*

Assiout province (now a governorate) stretches for 160 km along the Nile lying between the governorates of Minieh and Sohag.

Its settled area is limited to the river valley, its widest point across the Nile is 20 km, bordering on the western desert.

Assiout. From *La Description de l'Egypte.*

*The Overflowing of the Nile.* Belzoni's sketch of the disaster near Thebes

13

Its history dates back to the prehistoric Badarian period, renowned for its thin baked pottery, distinguished by a band of black at the top.

Assiout lies midway between Cairo and Aswan, its capital is Assiout city.

In ancient Egypt it was known as Siout. It was the centre of worship of the wolf-headed god Wapewet, also known as Upuaut, who was depicted as a standing wolf, or a wolf-headed man, sometimes wearing armour and carrying weapons. Joseph was supposed to have used the caves in the Assiout mountains as stores for grain during the seven years of famine mentioned in the Old Testament.

During the Middle Kingdom it was the capital of the seventeenth nome (province) of Upper Egypt, and later during Hellenistic times it was known as Lycopolis, or Wolf City. Wolf mummies were found in small excavated cells in the rock behind the town itself. During the Roman Empire, the coin of the Lycopolite nome bore a wolf on its reverse, together with the word Lyco.

The sheep was sacred in Upper Egypt, particularly in the vicinity of Thebes and Elephantine.

However, the Lycopolites, contrary to the customs in other cities in Egypt, sacrificed and ate this animal because according to Plutarch 'the wolf did so, whom they revered as god'.[6]

Eighty kilometres downstream on the east bank of the Nile, lies Tel-el-Amarna (the hill of Amarna), which got its name from a Bedouin tribe, Beni Amran, two centuries ago when they settled on the outskirts of the ancient site of Akhet Aton – 'the horizon of Aton' built on a great dry circle of barren land, away from nowhere, by Akhnaton about 1370 BC as the city of his personal god Aton. It lasted only as long as Akhnaton reigned and was completely destroyed by his successors.

As it lies on the border between Assiout and Minieh, it has been attached administratively at different times to one or the other. It remains a barren spot until this day, frequented by tourists, visiting its archaeological remains.

When central rule broke down in Egypt during the first Intermediate period (c. 2180–2080 BC) Assiout became the battle ground for rival princes.

Princes living at Herakopolis near Fayoum, were able to extend their influences over most of the Delta and Middle Egypt up to Abydos.

While never being able to challenge the power of Thebes, the rulers of Assiout tried always to be on the right side, but their sympathies were usually with the northern princes, trying to curtail the ambitions of their southern neighbours, who were just on their doorstep.

---

[6] *The Customs and Manners of the Ancient Egyptians*, by Sir Gardner Wilkinson, Part III, page 304, published by John Murray, 1878.

A ruler of Assiout at this time was buried with two companies of model warriors, to render services in some troubled after-life.

Another monarch from the same region boasts of how the land was in terror before his soldiers, and how all were afraid when they beheld smoke in the south.[7] But it seems that Assiout accepted the change of new masters without revolt.

After the Middle Kingdom the ancient history of Assiout becomes obscure. But it is known that the philosopher Plotinus was born in Lycopolis (Assiout) in 205 AD, and died in Campania in 270 AD. Plotinus was the centre of an influential circle of intellectuals in the third century in Rome. He is regarded by modern scholars as the father of the Neo-Platonic school of philosophy.

Assiout was also the birthplace of the Christian mystic, John of Lycopolis, who spent his life secluded in the mountain. But it is principally during Islam, that Assiout became famous. It is mentioned by the historian and geographer Abu-el-Feda a descendant of Ayoub the father of Salah El Din who became a local Sultan of Hama (Syria) under Memluke rule.

Its prominence grew with the increase of commerce, as it was the terminus of the caravan routes that crossed the Eastern and Western deserts. The Darb-el-Arbaeen, the Beaten Forty-Day Route from Assiout to Darfour in the Sudan, was famous for the caravans that traversed it, taking cereals, textiles, silver, *appliqué*-worked shawls made in Assiout, and other goods to the Sudan, and returning with ivory, ebony, ostrich feathers, vegetable dyes and slaves.

Assiout has always had a large Christian community, known for their business acumen.

A story told about why there are no Jews in Assiout recounts that in far gone days a Jew thought he'd travel to Assiout, and start business. But before entering the town, he wanted to test the type of people who lived there. So he stopped a young boy and asked, 'Can you bring me lunch for myself and my donkey, and dinner for myself and my donkey, and provide me with entertainment?' He then gave him five millimes. The boy took the five millimes and returned a little later with a water melon which he had bought for four millimes. He said 'Cut this water melon in two, eat one half for lunch and give the skin to your donkey, the other half you can have for your dinner and give the skin to your donkey; and you can entertain yourself by cracking and eating the pips.' The Jew got on his donkey and went back sighing to himself, 'There is no bread for me in this town.'

The inhabitants of Damanhur in Lower Egypt recount the same story about their town.

[7] *The Egyptians* by Cyril Aldred. Page 103

The Assioutites have a keen sense of humour, relating stories about themselves as well as their neighbours.

An amusing story is told about a well-known money-lender, in the early twentieth century, who got fed up with one of his debtor friends, who made a point of coming to pay his monthly instalment at lunch time, in order to be asked to stay for lunch.

One month the money-lender espied his friend together with a few companions, making his way to the house as usual at lunch time. So he closed his shutters and pretended he was not at home.

His friend, who knew that he was never away at lunch time, stood under the window calling out: Mr so and so, Mr so and so, why don't you answer me, don't you know that even God answered Moses when he called to Him on the mount?' A voice answered from inside the house, 'But Moses did not bring with him the tribe of Israel.'

### An Extraordinary Magician

It would be impossible to talk about Assiout without mentioning Sheikh Selim, who was around in the twenties.

Egypt since the times of the pharaohs has been reputed for its magic, the miracles that its priests were able to perform in their monasteries. The Egyptians are a superstitious people whether they be Moslem or Christian, and many of them believe in talismans, love potions, spells and spirits.

It is reputed that there lived in Assiout a holy man or at least a magician. Father and other members of the family knew him personally.

According to the stories I heard, Sheikh Selim was able to produce things out of the air. He could not steal anything, but he could produce something for you which you had left behind in another town. It had to be your property. He could also shop for you in another town, but you had to know the price and pay. He would put out his arm and produce it from thin air; at the same time the price given him would be put in the till of the shop denoted to him.

He was supposed to be able to accomplish his magic with the help of good spirits. Egyptians believed in benevolent as well as wicked spirits.

A reputed story related about him was about the time he was travelling by train from Minieh to Assiout. The ticket collector came into the compartment and asked for his ticket. Sheikh Selim answered: 'I haven't got a ticket'.

'Well then I'll have to fine you,' said the collector.

Sheikh Selim tried to explain that he was Sheikh Selim and he always travelled free. 'Well you're not travelling free on this train today,' said the collector.

'Well what do you want?' asked Sheikh Selim.

'I want a ticket,' answered the collector.

'You want a ticket,' said Sheikh Selim. 'Well here is a ticket.' He put out his arm, and tickets flew in through the window. Every time he'd stretch out his arm more tickets would fly in. The poor collector nearly fainted with fright.

'Stop, stop,' he cried. 'I want no more tickets.'

Another time father had left his sapphire ring behind in the safe in Alexandria. As Sheikh Selim was visiting someone at Granny's house, father asked him if he could produce the ring for him. He just put out his arm and in a few minutes produced it for him. According to father it actually happened, it was his ring, and it was not found in the safe in Alexandria on his return since he had it. It was difficult to trick or influence father, as he was a very sceptical and down-to-earth sort of person. He believed that Sheikh Selim actually and physically brought the ring from his safe in Alexandria. There are many more stories about Sheikh Selim which are just as fantastic and difficult to believe.

## Language

The Egyptian Language which is classed among the Hamitic or North African languages, has both in structure and vocabulary much in common with the Semitic family. From its state under the first dynasties, it gradually underwent modifications in pronunciation and syntax. In the New Kingdom, there were two quite distinct written idioms, one traditional, learned and classical, and the other an expression of the spoken language.

## Writing

From the First Dynasty the Egyptians used two scripts: one decorative, the signs being little figures carefully drawn – hieroglyphic, the other cursive – hieratic, used for writing on papyrus.

The hieratics are merely abridged hieroglyphs. From the Ethiopian period, and above all during the Ptolemaic period, a third script – the demotic – was used. This was a simplification of the hieratic and served to transcribe the popular language.

In 1799 an engineer officer in Napoleon's army named François Xavier Bouchard was working at Fort Julien near Rosetta (a fort about forty-three miles east of Alexandria) noticed a curious stela re-used in the masonry of an old wall. He informed General Minou of his discovery who had the stela removed to Alexandria. This stela bears a copy of a decree issued by Ptolemy V (196 BC) written in hieroglyphs, demotic and Greek. It became the key to the reading of hieroglyphs twenty-three years later by Champollion.

It was removed to England in 1801 by the British. The stone is known as

17

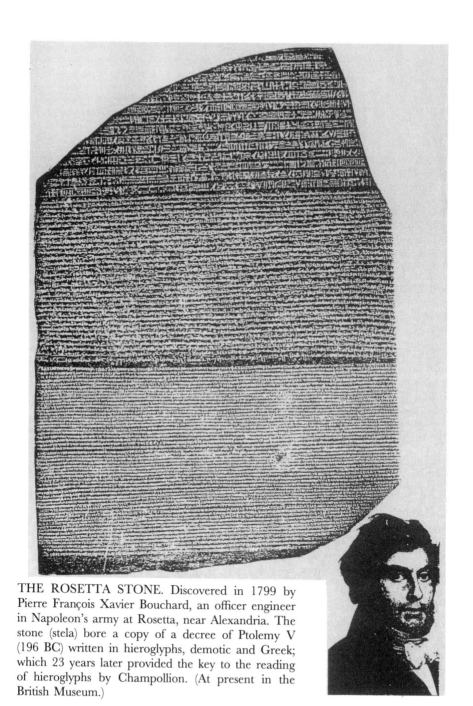

THE ROSETTA STONE. Discovered in 1799 by Pierre François Xavier Bouchard, an officer engineer in Napoleon's army at Rosetta, near Alexandria. The stone (stela) bore a copy of a decree of Ptolemy V (196 BC) written in hieroglyphs, demotic and Greek; which 23 years later provided the key to the reading of hieroglyphs by Champollion. (At present in the British Museum.)

Jean François Champollion by Leon Cogniet.

18

The step Pyramid of Zoser (Saqqara) about 2600 BC

By 2400 BC the pyramids of Giza were built by Khufu, Khafrē and Menkaurē, and the Sphinx was carved out of solid rock.

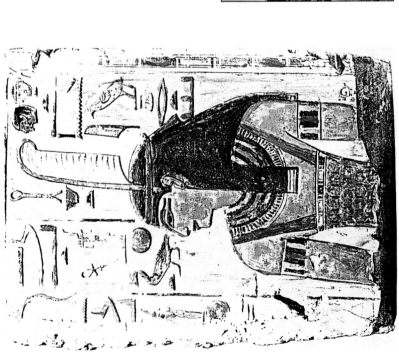

Maat, goddess of truth and justice and personification of divine order wearing her symbol, an ostrich feather, on her head.

A company of Nubian archers. Wooden model. Assiout. First Intermediate Period. Cairo Museum.

A company of spearmen. Wooden model. Assiout. First Intermediate Period. Cairo Museum.

Al-Mu'allaqah Church (Hanging Church) dating from the late 4th and early 5th century, the basilica was named 'Al-Mu'allaqah' because it was built on top of the south gate of the Fortress of Babylon

The Virgin's Tree. This is the tree where the Virgin rested with the Child Jesus when they came to Egypt

The Deir-el-Muharraq on the Mount Qusquam, site of where the Holy Family were supposed to have sojourned for 6 months

Church of the Virgin at Deir-el-Muharraq

Minarets of El Azhar Mosque

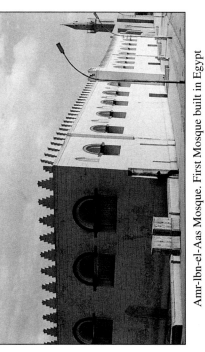

Amr-lbn-el-Aas Mosque. First Mosque built in Egypt

Mohammed Aly Mosque. The Citadel

the Rosetta Stone and is one of the most treasured monuments of the British Museum.

When the Egyptians became Christian they abandoned the ancient scripts, finding them too complicated, and adopted the Greek alphabet, with the addition of seven special signs to represent the sounds unknown in Greek. By the end of the fourth century AD, people had forgotten how to read hieroglyphs.

Similarly, Coptic, a mixture of ancient popular Egyptian with Greek and foreign words, ceased in its turn to be employed as the common tongue on the invasion of the Arabs in the seventh century AD, and made way for Arabic, but has continued in the Coptic Church as a liturgical language.

# THE BIRTH OF A NEW ERA

*The Legend of the Holy Family in Assiout, Egypt*

One of the most ancient and reputed Christian monasteries in Egypt can be found in the governorate of Assiout, near the modern town of Kossieh. It is known as Saint Mary's Monastery of Al-Muharraq built on the mount Qusqam. The name *Qusqam* given to the mount means in Pharaonic and Coptic, 'Everlasting'.

The Virgin Mary, her husband Joseph, the child Jesus and their maid Salomé were reputed to have lived for six months on this mount before returning to Israel. The Copts believe that Isaiah's prophecy, stating:

> And in that day, shall there be an altar in the midst of the land of Egypt. Isaiah 19.19

refers to this monastery.

Elaborating on Joseph's dream, mentioned in the Gospel of Saint Matthew, in which the angel of the Lord told Joseph:

> 'Arise and take the young child and his mother, and flee into Egypt, and be thou there, until I bring thee words, for Herod will seek the young child and destroy him.'
> When he arose he took the young child and his mother by night and departed into Egypt. And was there until the death of Herod.' Matthew 2.13–15.

A legend has been built up which relates that after the Holy Family fled from Bethlehem to Egypt, they passed through several towns and villages, where they rested for a time. Many of these have shrines or churches commemorating these events; but on the final stage of their long and weary journey the Holy Family found their peace and rest on the Mount Qusqam which was at the time barren and uninhabited, except for an abandoned small house, with a room on top built of mud bricks, with a thatched roof of palm branches, which the Holy Family occupied, the Virgin Mary and her child Jesus making use of the top room.

Joseph repaired as best he could this house, which lay on a slope on the east side of a range of hills. To the north of the house they discovered a well, which had been dry for many years, but which suddenly became filled with good fresh water. Joseph was able to provide the bare necessities of life for his family, in this remote place, by the will of God.

Some way up the hill as related in the legend, there was an empty cave, where frequently the Virgin Mary used to rest with her young child Jesus. Nowadays the nearest cave to the house is five kilometres away, which is reputed to have been used by Matthew before he became Patriarch in

1378–1408 AD during his retreats into seclusion when he was living at the monastery of El-Muharraq.

The legend also relates how a man named Youssa, from the tribe of Judah, who may have been a relative of Joseph's, who, after searching all over Egypt trying to find the Holy Family arrived at Qusqam, in a very sore and exhausted state. He came to warn them that Herod had sent ten men to Egypt to look for the child and kill him. This bit of news greatly perturbed the Virgin Mary and Joseph, but an angel came to Joseph in a dream and assured him that they would come to no harm. It was not long after Youssa delivered his message that he died at Qusqam. Joseph buried Youssa not far from the porch of the house.

A spot claimed by the monks as being the grave of Youssa lies to the south west of the old church, which was originally the house in which the Holy Family lived.

The Virgin Mary and her family lived on Mount Qusqam until Herod died, when:

> 'An Angel of the Lord appeareth in a dream unto Joseph in Egypt saying "arise, and take the young child and his mother, and go into the Land of Israel; for they are dead that sought the young child's life."
>
> And he arose, and took the young child and his mother into the land of Israel.'
> Matthew 2.19–21.

According to writings found in the Coptic Church the Holy Family lived on Mount Qusqam, from the seventh day of the Coptic month of Baramoda, which coincides with Monday 2nd April until the sixth day of the Coptic month of Baba, which fell on Wednesday 3rd October – a total of 185 days – in the year in which Herod the Great died.

There is no controversy in the fact that the Holy Family returned to Israel in the year that Herod the Great died; but there would be, if one tried to tally chronologically the Christian era to historical fact. For historically, Herod died in the year 4 BC, which would mean that he died four years before the birth of Christ.

The reason for this discrepancy was that the Christian era was calculated five centuries after the birth of Christ by Dionysius Exigius, about the year 525 AD to settle a long dispute over the correct method to calculate Easter. He argued that the Christian world should have a date with which to start its era, since Christianity was becoming dominant in the Roman Empire.

The Jews calculated their era from Adam, the Alexandrian era was calculated from the time of the building of Alexandria; whereas the Roman era which was being used at the time, started from the year of the foundation of the city (Rome) or *Anno Urbis Conditae, AUC*. Dionysius used the term BC to denote the time before the birth of Christ, and *Anno Domini* (in the year of the Lord) denoting the year of the birth of Christ. So the year 1 AD was supposed to be the year Christ was born, or 754 AUC.

Somehow Dionysius reckoned the birth of Christ to have occurred in the year 753 AUC. But the Gospel of St. Matthew states that Christ was born some time before the end of Herod's reign. Herod is reckoned to have died in 750 AUC. Dionysius's dating was questioned by the English Saint Bede in the eighth century, and rejected outright by the German monk Regino of Pruüm, at the end of the ninth century[8].

Other evidence tends to prove that Christ was probably born a few years before Herod the Great's death in 750 AUC, due to the fact that Caesar Augustus decreed that there should be a general census, in 745 AUC, by which he wanted to tax the whole world. According to the Gospel of Saint Luke:

'And it came to pass in those days, that there went out a decree from Caesar Augustus that the world should be taxed.

And this taxing was first made when Cyrenius was Governor of Syria.

And Joseph also went up from Galilee, out of the City of Nazareth into Judea, into the City of David which is called Bethlehem, because he was of the house and lineage of David, to be taxed with Mary his espoused wife, being great with child'.
Luke 2.1–5.

However it is not known how long the census took, nor if it was followed by minor censuses. Also it is not known how long the Holy Family remained in Egypt, but this evidence denoted that Christ was born some time between 9 BC and 4 BC, the date of Herod's death.

In spite of these discrepancies the Christian Church never thought it worth while to try to reconcile the date of the Christian era chronologically with historical facts by back-dating the commencement of the Christian era.

They agreed that all historical facts which had occurred before 1 AD should be dated BC, and all historical facts that occurred after that date should be dated AD. In other words the Church got out of its chronological dilemma by just ignoring it. So Dionysius's erroneous dating continues in use to the present day.

The Monastery of Al-Muharraq was built in the fourth century AD on Mount Qusqam, which was still uninhabited except for the poor small church that had been transformed out of the abandoned house in which the Holy Family had lived. Due to its remoteness from anywhere, a few devout Christians had built their mud houses around the church, to be able to carry out their Christian rites without fear of persecution. Similarly a few

---

[8]The *Encyclopedia Britannica*: Macropedia: The Christian Era

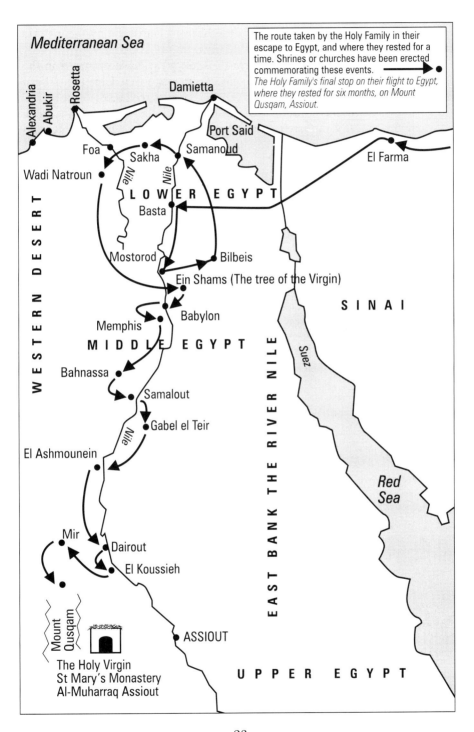

Mediterranean Sea

The route taken by the Holy Family in their escape to Egypt, and where they rested for a time. Shrines or churches have been erected commemorating these events. ➤●

*The Holy Family's final stop on their flight to Egypt, where they rested for six months, on Mount Qusqam, Assiout.*

Alexandria
Abukir
Rosetta
Damietta
Port Said
Foa
Sakha
Samanoud
El Farma
Wadi Natroun
Nile
Nile

**L O W E R  E G Y P T**

Basta

Mostorod
Bilbeis

Ein Shams (The tree of the Virgin)

**S I N A I**

Memphis
Babylon

**M I D D L E  E G Y P T**

Bahnassa

Samalout

Gabel el Teir

Nile

El Ashmounein

**E A S T  B A N K  T H E  R I V E R  N I L E**

Suez

**Red Sea**

Mir
Dairout
El Koussieh

Mount Qusqam

ASSIOUT

The Holy Virgin
St Mary's Monastery
Al-Muharraq Assiout

**U P P E R  E G Y P T**

**W E S T E R N  D E S E R T**

small mud houses had been built by the church to shelter the poor and needy, or those who search for a life of solitude and contemplation.

This church was named the Church of the Virgin, and is supposed to be the first Christian church built in Upper Egypt. It became the nucleus around which the great monastery of Al-Muharraq was built. The history of this monastery, its expansion, and the miracles that are reputed to have occurred between its walls, could fill many volumes. But it is sufficient to say, that it has become a place of learning, meditation, and pilgrimage up to this day.

## Christianity Came to Egypt

The religion of Egypt changed little in the 4000 years prior to Christianity. It absorbed a little from the invading occupiers but basically it remained the same.

Christianity came to Egypt with the first visit of St Peter accompanied by St Mark, the founder of the Church of Egypt. This visit was to Babylon in Egypt[9]. As St Peter's first epistle is dated from that city, 'The Church of Babylon' of which he speaks (Peter 5.v.13) was clearly intended for the Egyptian disciples of his friend St Mark. It was likely that a good deal of the gospel of St Mark was written during his stay at Babylon with St Peter, the Apostle's intention being to use it in the evangelisation of Egypt. All the early writers speak of St Mark as living in Egypt until his death as a martyr in the year 62 AD.

The Egyptians took readily to Christianity. By the fourth century AD there were about six million Egyptians who were Christians. This figure made up the bulk of the population. These people retained their faith in spite of them being martyred under the Roman emperor Diocletian. This savage martyrdom lasted from 284 AD until Constantine succeeded to the throne in 324 AD. He became a Christian and thus brought an end to martyrdom and relief to the harassed Egyptians.

During this period St Anthony of Egypt (c. 251 AD) disciple of Paul of Thebes, began to practise an ascetic life. At the age of twenty he withdrew in absolute solitude to a mountain near the Nile in Middle Egypt, where he lived for twenty years. With the end of martyrdom in Egypt, St Anthony moved to another mountain in the Eastern desert between the Nile and the Red Sea, where a monastery named after him, Deir Mari Antonious, still stands.

---

[9]Babylon was originally a fortress built by the Romans in c. 100 AD and became one of a series of military settlements which developed in time into the city of Cairo. It has nothing to do with Babylon of the Old Testament, or the Hanging Gardens of Babylon in Southern Mesopotamia (Northern Iraq).

The spiritual struggles and temptations he envisioned induced his followers, the early monks, to fast and perform his ascetic practices, considering themselves the vanguard of God's army. Because of the rules attributed to him St Anthony emerged as the sane and sensible father of Christian monasticism. These rules are still observed by some Coptic and Armenian monks. So inspiring was St Anthony's endurance, that the subject of his temptations have often been used in literature and art, notably in the paintings of Hieronymus Bosch, Mathias Grünewald and Max Ernst. St Anthony's popularity as a saint reached its height in the Middle Ages. The Order of Hospitalers of St Anthony was founded at La Motte (c. 1100).

In 389 AD an edict of Theodosius proclaimed Christianity as the religion of the state and all of its provinces, which included Egypt, and ordered the ancient temples to be closed. This was the definite end of the pagan period.

At the time of St Mark's visit Egypt was a province of the Roman Empire, and continued to be so until the death of the Emperor Theodosius (AD 395), when the empire was divided between his two sons, Arcadius and Honorius. Egypt went to the eastern division of the empire, henceforth known as the Byzantine Empire. Up till the reign of Theodosius, the Patriarch or Pope of Alexandria was the recognised doyen of the Universal Christian Church.

When the Egyptians embraced Christianity, the people cast off most of the ancient beliefs. They adopted the Greek alphabet and Byzantine art, and threw themselves passionately into religious quarrels that led to so much schism in the East.

Rome had always shown some jealousy of the precedence of Alexandria for many reasons, one reason being the encyclical letter which yearly fixed the date of Easter. There had been no formal settlement of precedence for the first two centuries. The five Sees of the first rank had been Alexandria, Rome, Antioch, Jerusalem, Caesarea, and of these Alexandria was generally reckoned the first, while by a canon of Nicea, Jerusalem was ranked second.

When Constantine became a Christian, his new imperial city at once took rank with the earlier Patriarchates. At the Council of Nicea (AD 325) the first blow was given to the prestige of Alexandria by the adoption of the Western date for the celebration of Easter.

At the Council of Constantinople AD 381, Theodosius the Byzantine Emperor agreed with Rome to give Rome the primacy, Constantinople the second place and degraded Alexandria to the third place, in order of precedence. Timothy, the Pope of Alexandria at that time, indignantly left the Council and withdrew his bishops to Egypt.

These squabbles caused no lasting disagreement; the different branches of the Church remained as they were for another century. But the Church of Alexandria usually resisted the innovations and pretensions of Rome, and from the Western point of view the Egyptian Church was the first to break away from the Christian unity.

The ancient Egyptians loved splitting hairs in their arguments, and the fathers of the Egyptian Church had inherited the habit, as was manifest in their writings. St Anthony himself protested against this Egyptian weakness. He said the devils which possess man come with tumult and wrangling. However, the straw that broke the camel's back which split the Coptic Church from all other Christian churches, happened at the Council of Chalcedon, AD 451, and was no doubt a political, rather than a religious difference.

An accusation of heresy was in that age the only weapon thought serious enough to crush the Egyptian Pope. Even this failed. Dioscorus the Patriarch of Alexandria was not crushed; he refused to submit either to the Greeks or to the Roman Pope and broke off all connections with Europe. The controversy is known as the heresy of one nature (monophysitism), a dispute, so far as words go, having a more trivial basis than any before – for it practically turns on the words 'in' or 'of'. Nestorius had previously asserted that the two natures of Christ, the human and the divine, were so separate and distinct as to prevent one nature from qualifying the acts of the other nature. This was condemned in the Council, and the unity of two natures asserted.

The Egyptians like their opponents acknowledged, and acknowledge, that Christ was God and Man. Only they said that both natures were united 'in' Him, instead of being co-existent 'in' Him. Therefore it is irreverent to speak 'of' two natures, as that implies imperfect union, whereas 'in' Him there was no imperfection the two natures were absolutely one God-Man. The whole squabble began with the persecution of an old abbot named Eutyches, whom the Greeks and the Romans insisted on excommunicating for talking in this way. It was because of him and this interpretation which Dioscorus the Egyptian Patriarch espoused, refusing subsequently to submit to the decision of the famous Council of Chalcedon.

It would seem that Rome used this whole business of semantics as a weapon to finally crush the claims of Alexandria, rather than to purge the Christian doctrine of error. This decision was made the excuse by Marcian (consort of Empress Pulcheria) not only to dethrone the Patriarch, but also to confiscate the property of the Church.

The Copts remained loyal to their true Patriarch and ignored the authority of the Patriarch appointed by the Emperor, who was consecrated by four bishops who had deserted Dioscorus. This small minority formed what was known as the Melkite Church, representing Byzantium, as opposed to the Coptic Church, representing the Egyptian point of view, which was now subjected to waves of persecution by the Byzantines.

Heraclius attempted in the seventh century to reconcile the two factions, but the Coptic Church would have nothing of it; the doctrine which had been made the excuse for their persecution now became to them the emblem of their most cherished aspirations. Their Patriarch had become more to them than a religious head, he was to them as the king of the land of their birth.

The Emperor Heraclius then sent a man called Cyrus to assume the government of Egypt both as Patriarch of the Melkite Church and as viceroy for himself in civil matters. However, no Egyptian would acknowledge the authority of an alien Patriarch, nor fight for their Byzantine masters against the invading Moslems under Amr Ibn el Aas. Cyrus unable to hold the country against Amr made terms for the escape of the Byzantines, leaving Egypt open to the invading Arabs.

# ISLAM COMES TO EGYPT

According to S.H. Leeder in his book *Modern Sons of the Pharaohs*, Egypt under Byzantine rule had become depopulated, due to the fact that monasticism had taken a grip over the country. 'In Sohag alone there were at one time ten thousand monks and twenty thousand nuns. The holy man, Aba Thor, in his desert monastery ruled over a thousand monks, but he was quite eclipsed by one of the great cities in Thebais, where it was computed that there were no less than ten thousand monks and twenty thousand virgins; and this was far from having reached its zenith.'

It was in an Egypt weakened by depopulation and persecution that the Arabs found it easy to occupy, and encouraged 'a great stream of emigration from Arabia into Egypt, which was kept up for many years to save the rich and fertile land, watered by the Nile from depletion.'

No doubt, in the early days of the conquests there were a great many conversions to Islam, and it is this mixture with the Arabs that has, when one considers the matter on broad lines, made of all the people of Egypt one nation, as near together in ethnic appearance as in manners and customs.

Esther's father, Dr Akhnoukh Fanous, a man of culture and a great orator, declared to a great gathering of his fellow Christians at Assiout, that the Copts and the Moslems 'have indeed been divided, yet really they are one, and united, and the only difference is one of faith. From this point of view they cannot be looked upon as distinct elements. Whatever they may be called, the Moslems and the Copts are the veritable descendants of the people of Egypt of seven thousand years ago'.

## The Arabs and the Kurds

AD 706 is a date that every Egyptian should have engraved in his mind. For in that year the ruler Abdallah Ibn El Malik issued his decree enforcing the use of Arabic instead of Coptic *for all official documents*. For 4000 years of recorded history the Egyptians spoke the same language. What the Persians, the Greeks, the Romans were unable to do, this Arab ruler accomplished with the stroke of a pen.

In AD 642 Egypt was invaded by the Arabs. The Egyptians helped them as they wanted to get out of the Byzantine yoke which was continually persecuting them because of their loyalty to the Patriarch of Alexandria, representative of the Monophysites' interpretation of the nature of Christ. The Egyptians at the beginning did not mind the Arabs; the Moslem religion seemed little more than another Christian sect, more acceptable than the dogmatism of Rome and Byzantium. The pure monotheism of the Arabs, who were not bothered by priests and their squabbles about ideas that the ordinary man did not understand, attracted the ordinary Egyptian. It resembled Pharaonism in its optimism, and the acceptance of the world as it is, the world harmony, equilibrium, *Maat*.

The Arabs were good soldiers and had the extra virtue of being spartan in their way of living. Their food was the simplest, their couch the roughest, and they despised the refinements of the ruling Egyptian. Amr Ibn El Ass justified his conquest of Egypt in his statement: 'Its land is gold, its people are sheep, and it belongs to whoever is strong enough to take it'. However, he was aghast at the wealth and splendour of Alexandria, and wrote to the Caliph Omar in extravagant terms of his conquest. But though he makes much of the baths and the shops, he writes nothing of the books or works of art which adorned the city. In fact, once Arabic became the language of the country, and once the Arabs started to intermarry with the Egyptians converted to Islam, they were absorbed by Egypt and the Nile. The ordinary Egyptian peasant and workman led a very simple life. The Arabs were not able to change Egypt. The Egyptian peasant remained the same; instead of Coptic speaking, he became Arabic speaking. They had come to Egypt and found it a country well adorned in arts and crafts, in methods of government and trade; they knew nothing of the earlier civilizations such as Greece and Rome, having been sheltered from worldly affairs by the barrenness of their desert. They were armed with nothing but their faith in one God, the Koran, the sword and their Arabic language: 'The great period of Arab learning was created by Arabs, and other peoples converted to Islam and put in the Arabic language. Most of the converts themselves submitted to Islamic traditions, and in Egypt itself little else of learning was finally left. The Greek language had disappeared and with it Hellenic idealism, Rome was forgotten and Byzantium rejected[10], what remained of the Coptic language withered in the sanctuaries of the Coptic Church; yet the residues of pharaonic wisdom and culture were so ingrained in the inhabitants that they were never eradicated completely but infiltrated into the cultures that came into contact with them.

'But as they ate the fruit of knowledge' the Arabs were corrupted.

'Deal gently with the Copts of Egypt' was the injunction of the prophet, and at first the conquerors did their best to obey. They were a military caste who were forbidden to buy land outside the Arabian peninsula. They lived in their own camps apart from the people they conquered. At the same time the converts to Islam, though benefiting by remission of taxes, the Gizzia were not allowed into the caste. Similarly the natives who retained their religion, whether Jew or Christian, were given a certain degree of autonomy under their own leaders as People of the Book, but

---

[10]*Modern Egypt* by Tom Little

were denied the final degree of citizenship, the right and honour to fight alongside the Arabs in the army; they paid a special tax instead.

But in time the need of the military caste, and their imperial army made the Arabs forget their good intentions, with the result that the wealth of the inhabitants was plundered, and their opponents were either killed or sold into slavery.

The Arab rule of Egypt lasted for 500 years. They governed from different parts of the Islamic Empire; the Ummayads from Syria, the Abbasides from Baghdad, the Fatimites, the Kurds under Salah el Din, and the Memlukes – a military caste, mixture of Turk, Mongol and Circassian descendants of the slave mercenaries of Salah el Din – all ruled from Cairo. The Memlukes ruled indirectly for a further 300 years under the Turks who invaded Egypt in AD 1517. For long periods until the reign of Mohamed Aly in the nineteenth century, Egypt was either a subject province or a dominant state in a restless Islamic Empire.

But never at any time between AD 642, the date of the Arab invasion of Egypt, and the Egyptian Revolution in 1952, did a native Egyptian rule Egypt.

The Egyptians had welcomed the Arabs as helpmates in getting rid of a hateful foreign rule, but at the same time had yoked themselves to rulers from every quarter of the Islamic world, who came to Egypt either to convert, build, philosophise or make peace; with the result that the Egyptians whether Moslem or Christian, until their independence, lost all the attributes of a nation. In spite of this, the Egyptian never lost his consciousness of his 'separateness' from all others and of self-identification. He could at least distinguish between the oppressor and the oppressed.

The ordinary native whether Copt or Moslem had for centuries felt that they were victims of their rulers; whether they be Pasha, Khedive, Memlukes or Turks, or those that could be associated with them; the Coptic tax collector, the government official carrying out his duty or exploiting them, the local money lender whether he be Greek or Jew. They were equally opposed to the French and the British, whether they be advisers or occupiers, and all foreigners who had privileges denied to them.

'If they sided with one against the other at any time, it was only to get rid of the first as soon as possible.' From the ninth to the nineteenth century the history of Egypt under different individual rulers was at times positive but mostly negative. For the natives of the country, the relief from oppression was always short-lived; and the time of neglect and persecution always long.

'Ahmad Ibn Toulun, as Viceroy of the Abbasides who seized Egypt for himself, was a man with some nobility of character who patronised learning and is reputed to have behaved justly to the people, however, his policies were ruinously extravagant to the detriment of the country, which led

The Mosque of Al Azhar University

Ahmad Ibn Toulun Mosque

31

indirectly to the rule of a mad Ethiopian eunuch'[11].

For several years Egypt had had a low Nile, canals had been neglected, famine and disease were rampant in the country. On the throne was a child of eleven who presented an easy prey to the Fatimite Arabs who came from the West. They simply marched through the country, and took possession of Fostat in 968–69 AD.

The Egyptians put up no resistance, the Christians as usual looked with relief and hope on any change of masters. The Turks and Arabs who had writhed under the agony of the mad Ethiopian, welcomed the Greek general named Jawhar, who had been educated in the faith of Islam as representative of the Caliph Moez. In 971 AD the Nile rose once more to its full height and this was regarded by the Egyptians as a sign of God's favour towards the new dynasty.

There now existed on the East bank of the Nile three cities – distinct yet almost touching one another. To the south lay Babylon occupied mostly by Christians, and considered by the Western world as the capital of Egypt. Next came the Arab city of Fostat, built by Amr for his followers. North and east of that lay the city founded by Ibn Toulun, which lay further from the river and nearer to the Mokattam Hills than the other two, known generally as Masr-el-Askar.

The term 'Masr' alone, properly signified the country of Egypt, but was often loosely applied to designate the two Moslem cities together.

When bidding farewell to his general Jawhar, the Caliph Moez turned to the Sheikhs who were to accompany the expedition and said 'By God if Jawhar were to march alone he could conquer Egypt. You shall enter Fostat in your ordinary clothes, you shall have no need to give battle to the inhabitants thereof, you shall inhabit the forsaken palace of the children of Toulun, but you shall found another city surnamed El Kahira (Victorious) to which the whole world shall own submission'[12].

Jawhar, having carried out the first part of this programme, lost no time in undertaking the second. The foundations of the new town – the nucleus of the present Cairo – were laid in 970 AD. A new mosque was to be built, superior in magnificence and sanctity to the great mosques of the older cities – Amr and Ibn Toulun. The Gamaa El Azhar, still the most important university in the Islamic world, was founded in the same year 973 AD as the Caliph Moez came to take possession of El Kahira. He brought with him great treasures, the spoils of various countries which he had conquered.

But the Caliph Moez had not the religious scruples of his predecessor Ibn Toulun; and of the forest of clustering pillars in this far-famed

---

[11]*Modern Egypt* by Tom Little, page 23
[12]*The Story of the Church of Egypt* by E.L. Butcher. Vol. II page 9

mosque there is scarcely one that has not been taken from some Christian church.

The capital of Egypt now became fourfold, but for strategic purposes it was twofold. To the North were the two Masrs or Cairo. To the South, with a desert space between them which had once been covered with houses and gardens, lay Fostat and Babylon, the former half Moslem, half Christian; the latter inhabited almost entirely by Christians. In 1168 at the end of the Fatimide and Arab rule, 'Babylon was set on fire in so many places that the whole town seemed to burst at once into flames.'[13] The country had for years been passing through a period of decline. The taxation by the extravagant Caliphs, and the extortions of their troops, so crushed the people that thousands in despair abandoned all efforts to farm the land. 'For Moslem, Christian and Jew alike, the Era of Arab Rule ended, as it had begun, in hunger and poverty'.[14]

During this period the Christians and Jews under Caliphs such as El Hakim subjected the 'People of the Book' to all sorts of indignities and persecutions. According to the Moslem historian Makrizi among the persecutions, 'the Christians were obliged to wear distinct dress, and a sash around the loins, he further obliged them to wear a wooden cross weighing five rolts (about 5 lb) and forbade them to ride on horses, but made them ride on mules and asses, with saddles and bridles on which no gold or silver trimmings were allowed, made of black leather. They were also ordered that their turbans should be black and that the Jews should wear round their necks outside their dress a round piece of wood weighing five rolts (about 5 lb)'[15].

Under the Kurdish rule of Salah el Din in 1169 some efficiency was restored to the management of the Nile and the country, but most of his reign was spent in war. In 1174 he substituted his own name for that of the Abbaside Caliph in Baghdad in the public prayers. By that act he declared himself independent sovereign of Syria, Egypt and part of Asia Minor. One of his first tasks was to secure Egypt against attack and set in motion the ambitious plan for the re-fortification of Cairo. He ordered the construction of a massive fortress – the Citadel – on the Mokattam spur, overlooking the deserted plain between Fustat and El Kahira, to serve as a military stronghold and royal residence. Its central location dominated the two earlier cities, which were linked to the new fortress by a series of walls. Work started in 1176 and ended in 1186. One of his most cherished dreams was to eliminate the Crusaders from the Middle East.

---

[13] *The Story of the Church of Egypt* by E.L. Butcher. Vol. ll page 97
[14] *Modern Egypt* by Tom Little. Page 24
[15] *The Story of the Church of Egypt* by E.L. Butcher. Vol. ll page 26

An Ayoubic lamp 12th century at the time of Salah el Din and the Crusades, denoting the solidarity between the Christians and Moslems in the country. The lamp denotes light.

The emblem of the Crescent with the Cross denoting the solidarity between the two parts of the nation, the Moslems and the Copts, was not used for the first time in the 1919 Revolution, but was used in Ayoubic art during the 12th century under Salah el Din. The above was probably part of an oil lamp. Salah el Din was a staunch Moslem yet he respected Christianity, and although he fought the Crusaders and wanted to drive them out of the Middle East he was an honest opponent.

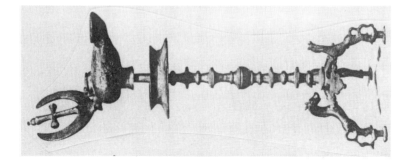

34

Salah el Din however was more than just another ruler. He was a man with a vision that elevated him above the petty ambitions of his day. He made it a matter of principle to base his life on the tenets of Islam. In an age when perfidy was the norm, Salah el Din never once broke a truce with either his Moslem or Christian enemies. Ultimately it was the strength of Salah el Din's personality rather than the size of his army, that finally forged Egypt and Syria into a unified Empire. He died in 1193 leaving sixteen sons, who divided his great Empire unequally between themselves resulting in the usual quarrels and civil wars.

## Memluke Egypt

The next dynasty was that of the Memlukes, descendants of the slave mercenaries of Salah el Din.

Sultan Beybars was a great soldier who can be considered the first real sultan of the Memlukes though in reality if you did not count Shagaret el Dor, he was fifth of those who had usurped supreme power in 1260.

He was a tall, fair European with blue eyes, who soon showed he had some idea of the responsibilities of a ruler. He regulated the taxes with some regard to justice, and received with great honour the Caliph of Baghdad, who had lost everything but his life in the invasion of Baghdad by the Tartars. When in 1262 a terrible famine broke out in Egypt, Beybars opened his granaries and fed thousands of people daily, while he sent hastily abroad for further supplies. He organised the pilgrimage to Mecca which had been suspended for twelve years.

After the famine was over he celebrated the circumcision of his son with great pomp, and as a thanksgiving to God he paid the expenses of 645 other children's circumcisions, who were carried in a solemn procession in the robes which he had given them. The presence of the Caliph gave additional solemnity and splendour to this public spectacle. During his reign public works were carried out such as digging canals, improving harbours and creating a fast mail system by relays of horses, between Cairo and Damascus. Salah el Din could only mitigate the effect on the people of his costly wars, for which they had to pay, whereas Beybars heralded an era of regal fantasy that was ruinous to the country. Nothing could make headway against the ultimate waste of wealth by the Memluke rulers.

'The Memluke Caliph Al Nasir dug a canal on which 100,000 men worked connecting Alexandria to the Nile, built an aqueduct from the river to the Citadel in Cairo; founded thirty mosques and a number of monasteries; public drinking fountains, baths and a number of schools; encouraged trade with Europe; but his exorbitant taxes caused widespread misery and hastened the downfall of his own caste, the Bahari Memlukes. His reign was followed by civil wars and famine, and plague ravaged a people unfit to resist it.[16]

Thereafter the unhappiness of the Egyptians was seldom relieved. Memluke sultan followed sultan, the situation becoming such that by the middle of the fifteenth century Memluke Emirs 'repeatedly set fire to various parts of the cities – probably those quarters inhabited chiefly by Jews and Christians – in order to create opportunities for plunder.'[17]

In 1461 a Greek slave who had risen to eminence in one of the Memlukes' reign, was elected Sultan. Unlike the Turkish and Circassian slaves who had attained the throne, Kochkadem endeared himself to the Egyptians by his kindly government and courteous manners. The six years of his rule were reckoned as golden days. European pilgrims were not afraid of visiting the holy places of Egypt, particularly Heliopolis and the balsam gardens of Matarieh. These had been regarded as sacred, since the time that the Holy Family had rested there on their way to Babylon and where there was an unfailing spring of pure water which was regarded as the miraculous gift of Jesus. It is said that Kait Bey, a later Sultan, had enclosed the sacred fountain and tree in his own Palace at Heliopolis, but only pilgrims were permitted to enter and visit the sacred spots.

Kait Bey, one of the best known of the last Memluke Sultans, spent most of his thirty years' reign in fighting the growing Ottoman power, which was to soon overthrow the Memluke rule in Egypt. His beautiful tomb is one of the interesting sights.

One of Kait Bey's greatest generals was an Emir called Ezbeki, who gave his name to a mosque, built in commemoration of his Syrian victories, and to the open space *Midan* surrounding it. The mosque is gone, but the once waste space is still known as the *Ezbekieh* in modern Cairo. During Kait Bey's rule, the Christians were not persecuted, and were mostly employed as architects of the mosques and colleges of Cairo.

After several rulers were deposed or murdered within a space of five years, the outraged Egyptians for once insisted on taking the matters into their own hands. They deputed the principal Moslem Sheikhs to elect a Sultan. The popular feeling in Egypt and Syria was so strong that the Memluke Emirs did not venture to oppose it, but associated themselves with the Sheikhs and accepted their choice.

The Sheikhs on their part did not venture to propose anyone but a Memluke Emir for the post. They chose an old liberated slave who had belonged to Kait Bey, whose name was Konsu El Ghouri, who was without ambition, and who had not sided in any of the intrigues of their other Emirs. Since he had obtained his freedom he had lived a quiet life and had

[16]*Modern Egypt* by Tom Little. Page 25
[17]*The Story of the Church of Egypt* by E.L. Butcher. Vol. ll page 232

The Grand Square of Ezbekiya, Cairo from *La Description De L'Egypte*

shown himself considerate and kind to all who were dependent on him.

The Emirs were astonished at the choice and so was Konsu, who was reluctant to accept, and exacted a promise from all and sundry that if they were dissatisfied with his rule, he should be allowed to retire into private life unharmed. There should be no rebellions or murders.

Konsu El Ghouri took the throne in 1501 and for more than fifteen years enforced order, even among the Emirs, with a strong hand; he carried out important public works and founded schools and mosques. Among his mosques, the one that bears his name is still one of the show places in Cairo. But he burdened Egypt with excessive taxation due to the expenses of defending the country. However, he made the mistake of backing the wrong son of the Ottoman Sultan Bajazyd, with a result that El Ghouri was killed in battle. The last Memluke Sultan, Tuman Bey, who succeeded him, was hanged like a common criminal at Bab Zawileh, and the unhappy kingdom of Egypt passed under a new form of tyranny, no better and in many ways worse than that of the Memlukes.[18]

## Egypt under the Turks

Three days after the murder of the last Memluke Sultan, Selim I the Turkish Sultan entered Cairo in triumph. This was during the month of April 1517. Egypt was once more reduced to the position of an outlying province belonging to an Empire across the sea. Selim forced the reigning Caliph who lived in Cairo and who still exercised a real, though undefined jurisdiction over their Moslem world, to abdicate in his favour. He then caused it to be publicly proclaimed that henceforth the Ottoman Sultan was also the legitimate Caliph, sole lord, both spiritual and temporal, of the Moslem world. From the Memlukes, whose lives had been spared on their submission to the Turkish conqueror, Selim chose twelve who were set over the twelve military

---

[18]Memlukes or slave soldiers were the Sultan's private bodyguards (the word *Memluke* is Arabic for 'owned'). Military slaves were a common feature of medieval Islamic armies. Young boys, usually Turks, were bought as Memlukes and raised in the Sultan's household, acting as cup-bearers, sword-carriers, and poison-tasters. When they reached maturity, they were freed, but remained trusted advisers and protectors of the Sultan. The officers held the title of Amir (commander) and led the Sultan's armies into battle. In time, after the reign of Salah el Din they were able to rule in their own right. Twenty-four of the greatest Amirs controlled all of Egypt's resources and governmental posts. The most powerful among them was elected Sultan. Although the position possessed certain military advantages, the Sultan was rarely strong enough to rule without the support of the Amirs who had brought him to power. The dream of all Memluke rulers was to eliminate the Amirs of previous Sultans and replace them with men from their own commands. Struggles for supremacy among the Amirs was endemic throughout the Memluke period, and only those exceptionally able, ruthless or lucky survived.

districts into which Egypt was divided with the title of Bey. His successor Soliman II increased the number of Beys to twenty-four, and issued an edict confiscating the whole land of Egypt to himself as the sole landowner. He then farmed out the districts to any man who would bid the highest for the privilege of collecting the taxes, reserving to himself the right to revoke the concession whenever he got less money out of them than expected. This system of farming out districts to the highest bidder was a type of leasehold and was known as *Iltizam* meaning 'commitment' or 'concession'. The concessioner known as the *Multazim* was bound to collect the rent which included the tax, and pay it to the Pasha, or ruler representing the Sultan of Turkey. All government bodies and the law were supposed to help the Multazim collect the rent or tax from the peasant, the sub-tenant who actually farmed the land. In collecting the rent the whip, imprisonment, cutting off ears and hands, confiscation of crops, were rules of the day.

In return for the *Multazim's* bond, he was allowed to reserve for himself a fixed percentage of the land rent or tax free known as the *Wassieh*. He could sub-let it if he wanted to, but he usually had it farmed for his own account. The rest of the land of his concession was sub-let by him to the local peasants, in plots of three to five acres – enough for a family to work on, as well as work on the land of the *Wassieh* for free or a very small wage, in return for having the privilege of renting these small plots. The peasant was usually allowed to grow the crops he chose, and sell the produce without the interference of the concessioner, as long as he paid the rent or tax on time.

The Multazim was allowed to sell the Wassieh or part of it as long as the buyer took with it the same percentage of land that was rentable or taxable with all its obligations. The Multazim could also leave the land to his heirs under the same condition of obligations. This system lasted during the Turkish rule until it was changed by Mohammed Aly and replaced by the system under the name of *Ihtikar*, meaning monopoly. Moslems and Christians in Egypt were thus involved in a common tyranny and the country sank year by year into deeper degradation.

A Pasha was appointed to represent the Turkish Sultan in Egypt, but he was also liable to be recalled at any moment, and the one idea of almost every government official was to make as much money as possible during their brief and uncertain tenure of office. From the conquest of Egypt by Selim to the invasion of Egypt by Napoleon in 1798, a period of 281 years, the Pasha, the Governor of Egypt, was changed 119 times, not taking into account those caused by the temporary revolts of the Beys, and the consultative council (*Divan*) that had been set up originally to help and give advice to the representative of the *Porte*.[19]

[19]The word *Porte* was the name given to the Turkish Court under the Caliphate of all the Moslems.

The council was made up of the military chiefs, the Chancellor (Finance) the Emir el Hag who was nominated each year to lead the pilgrimage to Mecca, the Grand Kadi (Justice) the four Muftis (the interpreters of the four different sects in Islam), the Sheiks and the Ulema, (the sages and learned men). A smaller Divan was composed of the Beys, the governors of the districts who carried out the daily administration. The governor of Cairo had the extra title of Sheik El Balad (meaning the head of the country) he gradually grew more important until he became the actual ruler of the country.

This system functioned normally for a century but in 1624 the Divan decided it had the right to depose the Pasha the representative of the Porte. There was no reaction from the Porte. The same happened in 1631 and 1644 and the Porte did not seem to express much concern.

In this way authority was slowly removed from the hands of the Pasha to that of the Divan. By 1756 just before the French expedition to Egypt the real power lay in the hands of the Beys and their allies, whom the Sheik El Balad manipulated.[20]

The idea that the Porte had the right to appoint or depose the Pasha – his representative – and the Divan had only the right to ask for the Pasha's removal only strengthened the belief of the allegiance of the Divan to the Porte, who could either acquiesce or refuse the request.

But when the Divan, composed of local aristocracy and the clergy emanating from the inhabitants of Egypt, took it into their own hands to depose the Pasha, it soon followed that they would want to appoint their ruler. It was only the fact the Porte was the Caliph of all the Moslems that postponed the final split. The following is a story showing the state of affairs.

When a Pasha was no longer popular with the Beys, a Memluke would go to the Citadel where the Pasha resided, who no longer dared leave his abode. Jumping off his horse he would present himself to the representative of the Porte. He would prostrate himself in front of him, and before the Pasha had the time to recover from his surprise, the Memluke would pull the carpet on which the Pasha was standing from under his feet at the same time shouting to him 'Enzel Pasha' which meant literally 'Get down Pasha'.

It was in such an atmosphere that for a short while Egypt was able to detach itself completely from Constantinople, during the rule of Aly Bey El Kebir.

Aly Bey El Kebir was a freed slave of one of the principal Emirs. His master had met with the usual death by assassination. Aly Bey had been able to amass great wealth under his late master and he spent it on buying

---

[20] *The Egyptian Question* by Emile Selim Amad

Memlukes or military slaves to strengthen himself in case of attack. By intrigue and bribery and playing one against the other he was able to reign supreme in Egypt for ten years. The Ottoman Sultan tried to have him killed by sending a *Firman* (an Imperial decree) to Egypt in 1768 demanding the head of Aly Bey, who ambushed the Imperial messenger, killed him and took from him the Imperial decree. Aly Bey then called a meeting of the Memluke Beys and convinced them that if the assassination attempt had succeeded the Sultan had meant to have them all massacred. He invited them to throw off the Ottoman yoke and elect a Sultan from among themselves as they had done before Turkish rule.

They elected Aly Bey; the Pasha was packed off to the Ottoman Sultan, and Egypt was declared independent under Aly Bey. He declared himself Sultan, and had money minted in his name. During his reign he massacred and exiled his enemies, but he was betrayed in the end by one of his own generals, Mohamed Abul Dahab.

After the death of Aly Bey, Mohamed Abul Dahab, ordered that all the new coinage that had been struck by Aly Bey be withdrawn from circulation. He wrote to the Sultan assuring him of his allegiance and expressed himself ready to receive a Pasha from the Sublime Porte. Mohamed Abul Dahab died soon after.

Under the Ottoman rule the bulk of the population whether Moslem or Christian were worse off than ever. They suffered from a new form of injustice. Up to that time the ancient arts and handicrafts of Egypt had never quite died out. Most of the beautiful work to be seen in the mosques and churches date from the latter half of the thirteenth century and the whole of the fourteenth century, during which time the European Memlukes reigned.

As Christians, the Egyptians were relentlessly persecuted; but as artists, as architects, as physicians, as illuminators and scribes, as wood carvers, as embroiderers, as silk manufacturers – and in short in any job that was conducive to luxury and beauty of life, they were tolerated. And if they adopted the Moslem religion, they were rewarded and encouraged.

At the time of the Ottoman conquest, many of the artistic classes became Moslem, but Selim does not seem to have distinguished between the Moslem Egyptian or the Christian Copt, in the wholesale order he gave for the forcible deportation of the best of these artists and artisans to Constantinople. The result being that as from the beginning of the sixteenth century, the artistic industries in Egypt deteriorated in standard and have never recovered since.

Generally the Moslems and Christians suffered alike under the Turks in Egypt, but occasionally there was a special persecution of the Copts. At the end of the eighteenth century, Egypt was perhaps in a worse position than she had ever been since the Roman Conquest. Her industries were paralysed, her commerce ruined, her people, especially the fragment of the nation which had still kept its Christian faith, were reduced to a condition of absolute slavery and misery.

## *The French Invasion of Egypt*

In 1798 Napoleon Bonaparte conquered Egypt, posing as a deliverer of Islam. He brought with him 120 scholars, and the excellent *Institut Français* which he created for research and which ultimately did much to spread knowledge of Egypt abroad. This gave Egypt a glimpse of the science and skill of the outside world. In particular his introduction of the Arabic printing press, and his use of the printed propaganda sheet, taught the Egyptians how to communicate, and thus became vital elements in their national movement. But the Egyptians were wary of conquering foreigners and Cairo rose in arms at the call of the Imams.

At the time the Egyptians were not able to take advantage of what they could learn from the French, who within a few months had contrived to set every class, nationality and creed against them.

The English who were than at war with the French followed them into Egypt in February 1801, and drove them out in the same year. But the English were concerned with the French, not the Egyptians, and made no attempt to keep the country for themselves.

No matter how indifferent the Egyptians were to the French knowledge and techniques introduced by Napoleon, they were never the same again. The seeds of restlessness which had been sown were at the bottom of all the later upheavals, and Egypt started to wake up from its sleep.

French soldiers on parade in the
desert. From *La Déscription de l'Egypte*

View of Cairo from the Citadel,
with Turkish soldiers

43

Napoleon in Cairo

Napoleon Bonaparte by J. Guerin

A view of Cairo with a caravan in process of formation. From *La Déscription*

# PART TWO

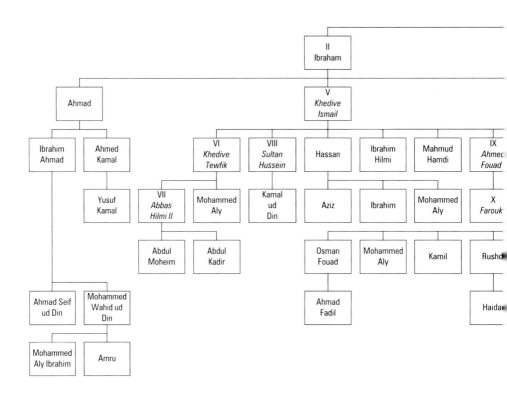

46

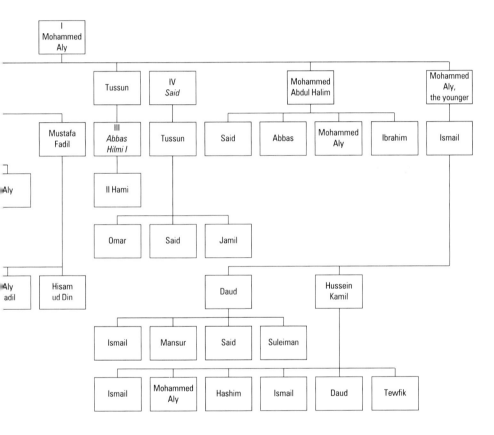

47

# BOOK ONE – THE PIONEERS. MOHAMMED PASHA ALY THE GREAT (1802–1849) TILL KHEDIVE ISMAIL WAS DEPOSED IN 1879

## The Wily Pasha and his Warrior Son

*The Reigns of Mohammed Aly Pasha and Ibrahim Pasha*

Napoleon was not able to wake Egypt out of her long sleep into which she had fallen during the centuries of Turkish rule from 1517 to the date of his invasion in 1798. It only took a few years after his departure for Egypt to emerge out of her torpor.

The continual decline of the population in the Nile valley which had persisted for some centuries seemed to have stopped with the birth of a new century. It seemed as if Egypt had needed the breathing space that had been accorded her after the invasion. Turk and Memluke were fighting each other, giving the people the hope that if they were united they might be strong enough to get rid of the hated foreign rule, as they had got rid of Napoleon.

When Napoleon left Egypt, the Sublime Porte thought it was time he reasserted his authority over the unruly Memlukes, so he named a new Pasha – Khosruf – as his representative, and was backed by the British in his policy. On the withdrawal of the English in 1802, the Memlukes tried to oust the Pasha.

They were beaten, however, by the élite troops of Albanians led by a young Albanian Moslem lieutenant of European and Christian descent, Mohammed Aly. His boss was called Taher Pasha who then informally assumed power. However he was murdered twenty days later leaving Mohammed Aly virtually at the head of the Albanian troops, the only troops with any real military clout in the country.

But Mohammed Aly was not master of Egypt, he was still nominally in the service of the Turkish Pasha, representative of the Turkish Sultan. Moreover, if he ever wanted to be the master of Egypt, he would have to get rid of the Pasha, dispose of the Memlukes, who, in spite of their intriguing and fighting among themselves and the Turks were still a force to be reckoned with. Then he would have to neutralise his Albanian soldiers, and get the Porte to appoint him Pasha of Egypt, with the acquiescence of the

Egyptian people. A tall order, but still a worthwhile goal if he was to realise his ambition.

An interesting digression:

> 'Mohammed Aly was of Albanian origin, born at Kawala in Macedonia. Alexander the Great, the founder of the Ptolemaic dynasty, also came from Macedonia. Mohammed Aly was born in 1769, the same year as Napoleon Bonaparte.'[1]

The genius of Mohammed Aly lay in his ability to judge the situation and use it to his own advantage; to plan his campaign, then to ruthlessly and unscrupulously carry it out. His ambition was to become the sole master of Egypt, to form a dynasty for himself and his heirs after him. He wished to be a good master and do his best for the country he had adopted; yet it was not for the love or the welfare of the country itself, but for his and his descendants' power and glory. He professed Islam as many of the world's greatest tyrants professed Christianity, because it was the wisest thing to do in the circumstances, but he was wholly unaffected by faith in any religion. If a man, or a whole race of men, stood in his way they were simply swept out of it by treachery or open attack, with utter disregard of their faith, nationality or family.

He first attracted the Egyptian man-in-the-street's attention when he supported his protests to the Pasha against some excesses of the Turkish soldiery in 1803. He allied himself with the remaining Memlukes, who were at least less detested by the people than the Turks, helping them with his Albanian troops to get rid of the Pasha of Yambo in Arabia, at the request of the Porte[2]. In 1804 he suddenly changed sides when he heard that one of the leading Memlukes named Elfy Bey – who had just returned from England – was conspiring with other Memlukes against him. He did not wait for the opposition to materialise, but led some of them into a trap and had them butchered. Elfy Bey was just able to escape with his life. The British were annoyed and intimated their fears of this untrustworthy Albanian to the Sublime Porte.

Still wary to assume power openly, Mohammed Aly sent for an Ottoman officer named Khorshed, who was Governor of Alexandria, and caused him to be appointed Pasha of Egypt. Upon Khorshed fell the responsibility and odium of extracting money from the overburdened country to carry on the government and pay the army, whilst Mohammed Aly posed as the friend of the people and blamed Khorshed for his tyrannous exactions.

On May 14th, 1805 after all his plans had been carefully prepared, a

---

[1] Edouard Driault, *Précis de l'Histoire d'Egypte*. Tome III page 205
[2] *La Question d'Egypte* by Emile Selim Amad

# MOHAMMED ALY DYNASTY

H.H. Mohammed Aly Pasha the Great,
Viceroy of Egypt, Founder of the Dynasty.
1808-August 1849

H.H. Ibrahim Pasha, Viceroy of Egypt. Son
of Mohammed Aly the Great, founder of the
Dynasty. 1848-November 1848

H.H. Abbas Hilml I Pasha, Viceroy of
Egypt. 1849-1854

H.H. Said Pasha, Viceroy of Egypt. 1854-
1863

# MOHAMMED ALY DYNASTY

Khedive Ismail, First Khedive of Egypt.
1863-1879

Khedive Tewfic, Son of Khedive Ismail.
1879-1888

Khedive Abbas Hilml II, Son of Khedive
Tewfic. 1888-1914

Sultan Hussein Kamel, Sultan of Egypt.
Brother of Khedive Tewfic and son of
Khedive Ismail. 1914-1917

Hanna Boctor Wissa - (1832-1907)

Wissa Boctor Wissa - (1837-1906)

popular revolt broke out in favour of appointing Mohammed Aly as Pasha of Egypt. It was led by the Rector of the Azhar University, Sheikh el Sharkawy, and Omar Makram, head of the religious nobility. The Sheikhs, followed by a delegation of the notables and chiefs of the city's guilds, implored Mohammed Aly to assume the government and depose the Pasha. Mohammed Aly affected unwillingness, but then complied, sending a messenger to Khorshed, informing him that the people had forced him to accept, and asking him to step down. Unlike most Turkish Pashas in the past Khorshed answered that he was the appointed representative of the Sultan and would not resign at the dictates of his inferiors, he barricaded himself in the Citadel, and complained to the Sultan. Mohammed Aly then laid siege to the Citadel, at the same time appealing to Constantinople to arbitrate. When the answer arrived, Khorshed was ordered to Constantinople and Mohammed Aly was appointed Pasha of Egypt, but only on a temporary basis. Mohammed Aly had not yet reached the ultimate aim of his ambition. He appreciated the need of both caution and courage. Caution to him meant intrigue, treachery and assassination. The Memlukes that had been intriguing with Elfy were still at large, though outside the city, and were in hiding.

Mohammed Aly caused one of his tools to write to the Memlukes' chiefs offering, in return for a big bribe, to admit them into the city, enabling them to reorganise, on a day that Mohammed Aly would be outside the walls with his followers, attending the ceremony of the cutting of the Khalig.[3]

The offer was accepted and a very large body of the principal Memlukes fell into the trap. His faithful Albanian soldiers surrounded and shot down without mercy those Memlukes caught in the narrow lanes. Mohammed Aly now sent for his family to come and settle in Egypt. On the appointment of Mohammed Aly as temporary Pasha of Egypt, the Sultan promised to send him 20,000 men as reinforcements to help keep order, but the British who felt that it was not wise to let Mohammed Aly get any stronger, advised the Porte to send the contingent, with a further 3,000 men under a Captain Pasha, to join the Memlukes. The Porte acquiesced, but when the troops arrived in Alexandria, the Captain Pasha and his troops went over to Mohammed Aly. All attempts by the Porte to dislodge Mohammed Aly were foiled. He then promised the Porte that if he would just leave him in peace, he would fulfil all the agreements that had previously been given to the Sultan by the Memlukes, and at the same time he swore allegiance to him. How could the Sultan resist? He went back on his decision to try and get rid of Mohammed Aly, and on November 2nd 1806, the Porte's

---

[3] *The Story of the Church of Egypt* by E.L. Butcher. Vol. II page 362

Firman was read in Cairo, confirming that Mohammed Aly was appointed governor of Egypt.

The British government clearly misunderstood the situation. Elfy Bey, who was still at large, though in hiding, had greatly impressed them when he had visited London a couple of years previously. A British expedition landed in Egypt in 1807, but the Memlukes had already been dispersed. 'Six years had made a great difference, instead of marching easily on Cairo, the British force was resoundingly defeated by Egypt's chosen leader, and the heads of the British were paraded on pikes in Cairo.'[4]

In February 1811 Mohammed Aly got rid of the rest of the Memlukes by treachery. He ordered an assembly in the Citadel of all the troops, in honour of his son Toussun Pasha's departure on an expedition to Arabia against the Wahabist reformers. A grand military procession was formed to accompany him after his investiture. A reception was held in the Great Hall, situated then in the place of the present Mosque. After coffee was served, the procession was re-formed to proceed down a steep narrow lane. The Memlukes' band was last but one in the procession, between a corps of Albanians and another of the regular troops who had received their instructions. When all the army preceding the Albanians had passed out, the gates were suddenly shut. The Albanians turned on the Memlukes and began cutting them down, while the regular troops fired volley after volley into the devoted band. Except for two or three Frenchmen who had turned Moslem, and Memlukes who had been prevented from taking part in the procession for different reasons, not one escaped. Four hundred and sixty bodies were counted the only Egyptian Memluke who escaped had been shut outside the gate by accident.

There is a story that one other Memluke escaped by leaping with his horse down the sheer wall from the top. Nor were these the only victims. An order was sent through the country that the Memlukes were to be pursued and killed wherever they were found, and within a few days more than 1000 of them had been killed. In Cairo their houses were pillaged, and their women raped, and until this day the name of Memluke has scarcely been heard of in Egypt.[5] It only remained for the Pashalick of Egypt to become hereditary to the line of Mohammed Aly and his Albanian soldiers neutralized, for the ambition of his youth to be realized. As he did not want to rely on his unruly Albanian soldiers to further his ambitions, he decided to create what was known as the *Nezam el Guedide* or New Order which was in reality a reorganisation of his fighting force.

Under the command of Colonel De Sève later known as Soliman Pasha El Fransawi, an officer of Napoleon who had turned Moslem and remained

[4] *Modern Egypt* by Tom Little, page 321
[5] *The Story of the Church in Egypt* by E.L. Butcher. Vol II page 365

THE JUMP OF THE MEMLUKE

53

in Egypt, and other French instructors, a regular army of Egyptian peasants was formed and were trained into an efficient fighting force. 'By 1826 he had an army of 90,000 men with an artillery train equal to the best in Europe'[6].

On Mohammed Aly's first audience given to Colonel De Sève the following conversation is reputed to have taken place[7]:

'Es-tu Militaire?' – demande Mohammed Ali au Colonel Sève.
'Uniquement', aurait répondu le Français.
'Saurais-tu m'organiser ma nouvelle armée à votre maniére?' demande le Vice-Roi.
Fière réponse: 'Sous Napoléon j'ai bien su en battre plusieurs.'
'Alors tu est prêt à exécuter mes projets?'
'Oui, à condition que votre Altesse me donne trois choses; du temps, de l'argent et Son Auguste aide'.

At the same time it was decreed that the Albanians should be given the choice of either joining the Nezam or going back to Albania. In order to give them an incentive to choose the latter, he allowed them to take the spoils that they had acquired in the country.

He was intent on making Egypt a modern state, on the European model, and then to take from the weakening hand of the Ottoman Sultan the hereditary authority for himself and his family in Egypt[8]. The Turkish Sultan Mahmud was having difficulty in subduing the Greeks, who were fighting for their independence, and knowing that he could not do it on his own, called on Egypt, his vassal state under Mohammed Aly, to come and help. Mohammed Aly agreed, but sensing his strength he demanded that his Pashalick should include Syria, Damascus and Crete. The Greeks who had been used to dealing with the undisciplined Turks were powerless against the European trained troops of Egypt, and city after city was taken by the Egyptians. Mohammed Aly's several campaigns, the increase of his army to 250,000 men, the defection of the Turkish navy to Alexandria, and his fighting peasants under the leadership of his son Ibrahim Pasha – a brilliant field commander – made the European countries sit up.

In 1841 the united wills of England, Austria, Russia, Prussia and Turkey made Mohammed Aly give up the gains he had acquired till then[9], and in return gave him and the eldest male of his line the right to govern Egypt

[6]*Modern Egypt* by Tom Little, page 33
[7]*Une Mission Militaire Polonaise en Egypte.* Adam George Benis, Cairo 1938
[8]*Modern Egypt* by Tom Little, page 33
[9]By the treaty of Kutahia Sultan Mahmoud agreed to recognise Mohammed Aly governor of Sinnar and Candie, Pasha of the Pashalicks of Syria: Aleppo, Safada, Siyda, Beyrouth, Tripoli, Jerusalem, and Nablos. His son Ibrahim Pasha was named Wali of Abyssinia, governor of Sandjac, Jeddah and Mecca, and Mouhassil of the province of Adana. It is interesting to note that Lord Palmerston did not recognise that there had been a treaty of Kutahia.

under an International Guarantee. They also established Egypt's future relationship with the Porte. By Mohammed Aly obtaining the hereditary right for himself and his family to govern Egypt as a vassal of Turkey, it could be said that he had attained his ambition.

Anything more ambitious had been aborted by Britain with the support of the European nations, who did not want another Napoleon on their hands. The treaty of 1841 humiliated Egypt, and rubbed it in that Egypt was just a province of Turkey, whose laws were valid over Egypt, but took into consideration local circumstances and customs, justice and equity. It limited Egypt's army to 18,000 men, thus making sure that the Egyptian peasants would never again threaten the peace of Europe. The treaty remained in principle in force, till Egypt became a protectorate of Britain in 1914, except for amendments obtained by Khedive Ismail in the Firman of 1873. However there were other factors during the rule of Mohammed Aly, that completely changed the history of Egypt and its future destiny, and indirectly that of the Middle East.

One of the important results of Mohammed Aly's rule was the regaining of the country's self-esteem, for although it might be said that his policies were for his family's aggrandisement, yet they resulted in dragging Egypt up from centuries of stagnation and oblivion, and putting her on the map again, as a country with great potential which could go far if it was united and well governed, a country that should be reckoned with. In spite of the fact that Mohammed Aly came to Egypt as a foreigner and usurped power unscrupulously, once he became the ruler he considered himself an Egyptian and patriot, making no difference in the treatment of his subjects, no matter what their religion was. One must recognise that Mohammed Aly and all his family after him were not fanatical, although giving lip service at times to the more fanatical elements of the Islamic world. In spite of individual instances of religious persecution and imported ideas and policies, since Mohammed Aly's time there has been a tolerance of all religions, and no open persecution of the Christians as such, has been permitted.

Jean and Simone Lacouture in their book *Egypt in Transition* quote a statement made by Mohammed Aly to the French Consul Drovetti, when the latter proposed to him on Polignac's behalf that he might join the French expedition against Algiers. He said, 'If I did so, I would be dishonoured in my people's eyes, I am not reasoning thus for religious motives, for I am no more Moslem than Christian in my politics, but I am something if at all, thanks to my national reputation and the opinion in which my people hold me.' His remark about being no more Moslem than Christian in his politics goes all the further as it is the expression of a truth, and marks a revolution[10], in the idea that Egypt was not just a member of the

[10]*Egypt in Transition* by Jean & Simone Lacouture, page 52

commonwealth of Islam, but an individual country, a complete entity in itself which had originally elected him, or called for him to be their ruler. He abrogated all the laws that had been promulgated by different rulers against the ethnic minorities in the country, and severely punished any outbreak of fanaticism. At the same time if possible he invariably chose an Armenian, Roman Catholic or other European Christian to occupy posts of authority, in preference to the Copts of the National Church, in order to mitigate any preponderance of influence of the Copts, who could never forget that Egypt was theirs by inheritance.

Similarly when Ibrahim Pasha was reorganising the government of Syria on the same lines as that of Egypt, absolute toleration was enforced for Druses, Maronites and all sects of Christians, and the best men were employed irrespective of nationality or religion. It is said that a delegation of Moslems of Damascus complained to Ibrahim Pasha that the insolence of the Christians was becoming so great that they even appeared in the streets on horseback. Ibrahim coolly advised the malcontents to ride camels, if they wished to be mounted in a superior manner to the Christians[11]. This neutrality between politics and religion was adopted by Saad Zaghloul during the 1919 revolution, with its motto 'The Crescent with the Cross' which has been followed by the Wafdist party ever since.

Mohammed Aly's agricultural policy, it could be argued, was implemented for his own benefit since he had expropriated most of the land when he had exterminated the Memlukes and farmed it under a system known as *Ihtikar* monopoly. One of the main features of this system, was that the peasant was not allowed to sell his produce, which had been allowed under the system of *Iltizam*, which had been established for 300 years when the Turks had invaded Egypt.

This system of *Ihtikar* – according to Dr Riad Sorial in his book *The Coptic Community in the 19th Century*, pages 74–5 – had the following features:

1. The land was distributed to the peasants in three to five-acre lots, which he used to grow in return for a certain tax or rent.
2. The peasant was given seed, manure, cattle and tools for which he had to pay at the time of harvest.
3. The peasant had to grow only the crops prescribed by the authorities, nothing else.
4. Any peasant who did not obey orders given to him by the authorities, or neglected his work, was subject to punishment, which could be flogging (the *korbag*), cutting off ears, prison or even death, which induced a lot of peasants to flee the country.
5. The peasant had no right to sell his harvest on the market, but had to

[11] *The Story of the Church in Egypt* by E.L. Butcher, page 371

Clot Bey

Mohammed Aly

deliver it to government stores, where it would be weighed and the crop priced. He was not allowed to keep any part of it, even for his family's use.

6. His purchases could be from government stores at prices imposed by them.

The peasants were also co-responsible for the debts of other peasants whose land adjoined theirs.

Soliman II of Turkey had confiscated all the land of Egypt in the sixteenth century when Egypt was conquered by Turkey. The land was farmed out to the highest bidder, under the privilege of collecting taxes under the system called *Iltizam*. So in reality, ownership of land in Egypt was leasehold. Whoever had the power to seize and administer the land, be it State, Pasha or Memluke, was the owner; the peasant who grew the land was the leaseholder, no matter what system was imposed.

This can be seen in the 1952 Revolution, when the land was taken away from the supposedly feudal landowner, who in the majority of cases leased most of it to the small peasant, under different systems, replacing it by the bureaucratic Agrarian Reform Board who cultivated the land through probably the same small peasant also under different systems. Those peasants who were given title deeds to the small parcels of land were not allowed to exploit it as they saw fit but were subjected to cooperative farming under the supervision of government officials. It is to be noted that tenure of land in Egypt is confined to the top soil – any oil, minerals or antiquities taken out of the ground belong to the State.

The encouragement that Mohammed Aly gave to growing cotton was due to the development of a new type of cotton with the longest and softest fibre ever seen. It was called *Jumel* after a cotton plant with these characteristics was found by a Frenchman called Jumel in his friend Maho Bey's garden near Cairo. The result was the increase in the cotton crop from 1000 cantars[12] in 1820 to 243,000 crs in 1835. The production of cotton was further enhanced by the American Civil War, and over the years it became Egypt's main cash crop, its main foreign currency earner, and the main factor in the development of the spinning and weaving industries in Egypt. The expansion in growing cotton developed services such as transport, insurance, banking and financing the crop in the interior and for export. New types of cotton were carefully bred. Egypt became, with the help of her cotton exporters, a seller of specialised cottons with certain specifications which commanded a higher premium over other cottons grown in the rest of the world. A great many people were employed directly and

---

[12]1 cantar = 315 pounds of cotton in seed, or half a hundredweight

indirectly by the expansion of the cotton crop, both in the interior by growing and marketing it, and in Alexandria by selling the cotton either to the local spinning mills or by exporting it to foreign spinners. In 1961, when Egypt nationalised the cotton industry, she was growing over ten million cantars of cotton, handled by 54 export firms and 110 ginning factories.

Another important factor that affected Egypt's interior policy was the mobilisation of the *fellah* in the army. It was not a popular move, some even mutilated themselves to get out of being conscripted. A popular wail at the time was

'Ya Baladi, Ya Baladi
El Solta Akhadet Waladi'

which could be translated:

'Oh my country, oh my country
The rulers have taken my son away'

The Copts at the time were exempt from conscription, and instead had to pay a tax. It was in a later reign that both Copts and Moslems were mobilised. However, the officer class was always popular, but was reserved for the privileged members of the community, not for the *hoi polloi*.

During Mohammed Aly's reign a great many public works were carried out. He dug new canals – notably the Mahmudieh to Alexandria – and established hospitals and medical schools under French instructors. He made the roads of Egypt safe and for the first time for many centuries the towns were policed and supervised. The trade and mail routes were once more resumed across Egypt to India and the other countries of the East.

Moreover he set up a printing press on a large scale at Boulak which published translations into Arabic of European books at very low prices, in order to spread knowledge among Egyptians.

The last project in his life was the Barrage, a dam built at the southern end of the Delta at El Kanater, whose original concept was due to the genius of a Frenchman. Its foundations were laid in 1847, but the structure proved faulty and it had to wait till 1882 before the genius of an Englishman found a way to make it work. Mohammed Aly thus started the permanent irrigation network in Lower Egypt which was a great source in creating, in the long run, the wealth of the country. It is debatable whether it would have been better for Egypt if Mohammed Aly had fulfilled the aspirations of patriots like Sheikh El Sharkawy and Omar Makram, who had called him to power hoping he would get rid of the hated foreigner and develop Egypt at its own pace; or to try and make Egypt a modern state. This meant turning more and more to the foreigner to train his army, build and manage his industries, and teach his people the ways of the Western world, resulting in a rich, largely alien ruling class, a growing nation with a subservient population of Egyptian farmers and peasants, labourers, craftsmen, and petty traders.

Since 1835 Egypt had been plagued with a series of outbreaks of cholera. The heroic conduct of a Frenchman Clot Bey, a scientist and physician to the Viceroy, in mitigating the suffering of the afflicted, so excited the admiration of the Pasha, that he named one of the streets in Cairo after him. In his book of observations on Egypt *Aperçu Général de L'Egypte* Clot Bey enumerated the beneficial properties of the Nile waters for those who partook of them.

Under the heading *The Qualities of the Nile Waters* he says:

'During the flood the Nile waters are murky, but they clear slowly by easily disposing of their clayey contents. The waters are of a pleasant taste and never upset the digestion. Being extremely light, one can drink to satiety without coming to any harm. They are excreted easily through perspiration and urine. Chemical analysis has recognised their purity, as well as distilled water – which is difficult to obtain in regions where fuel is short. The Ancient Egyptians not only paid tribute to the kindness of the Nile but they attributed miraculous properties to their waters. If one believes Pliny they had the virtue of making women fertile which probably was the reason Ptolemy Philadelphus made sure that his daughter Bernice had a supply of Nile waters for her exclusive use, when she got married to Anthiochus King of Syria.

The great value that these ancient civilisations placed on the waters of the Nile, have carried through to the present times. For a long time there were always stocks of Nile waters at Constantinople for the sole use of the Sultans and their families.'[13]

Mohammed Aly's problems increased through the years; his luck seemed to have changed since the Treaty of 1841 was imposed upon him by the Powers.

In 1843 a terrible cattle plague visited Egypt, as well as a rather long flood, which did not give the people much time to prepare the ground for agriculture. Cholera appeared to have become endemic, and Egypt was plagued by waves of locusts. By 1848 Mohammed Aly had been reduced to senility and the government had devolved on his son Ibrahim. Father and son died within months of each other, Ibrahim dying in November 1848 and his once great father, almost unnoticed, in August of the next year.

## A Reactionary

*The Reign of Abbas Pasha Helmi I (1849–1854)*

On the death of Mohammed Aly in 1849 his grandson Abbas I succeeded

[13]Much the same as different spring waters are imported nowadays

him. He was the complete opposite to his grandfather and being a fanatical reactionary, could see no good in expansion and tried to reverse the trend of modernising the country started by his grandfather, who had encouraged foreign investment and technique.

He tried to do this by procrastination, by referring everything back to Turkey, who was only too pleased to get back some of her influence which had been lost under Mohammed Aly. However his reign did not last long as he was strangled in Benha in 1854, by two of his Memlukes.

## An Aquiescent Dupe, and a Grand Seigneur

*The Reigns of Said Pasha, and Khedive Ismail (1854–1879)*

This was an Egypt of great change and expansion in which fortunes were made and lost.

On Abbas's death, he was succeeded by his uncle Said, his complete opposite in character and aspirations. He intended to do well for Egypt, but was vain and a great spendthrift on his friends and whims. He had been a great friend of de Lesseps in his youth, when the latter was French Consul, and they both had dreamt of building the Suez Canal. Said opened the doors wide to foreign speculators, businessmen and adventurers. As Egypt was a vassal of Turkey, the privileges that had been accorded to foreigners in the Ottoman Empire to encourage them to invest in the *Wilayas* (provinces) of the empire were law in Egypt as well.

These privileges were known as capitulations and differed slightly between one European country and another, as they had been negotiated individually between the Porte and the European country. According to Henri Lamba in his work *Evolution de la Condition des Etrangers en Egypte,* (Paris 1896), capitulations were concessions given freely by the Porte and could be revocable at his will. They had to be renewed on the accession of each Sultan, based on the idea that war was the only reasonable state of affairs between Moslems and the Christians of the West. It necessitated that each reign should prolong the 'peace' or truce, which is why the capitulations were renewed between France and the Porte sixteen times between the years 1535 and 1740.

However, with the passage of time the character of the capitulations changed, and instead of being retractable concessions freely given, they tended more to resemble treaties between countries which could be imposed on the Porte by the right of the strongest (Auguste Benoit, *Etude sur les Capitulations entre l'Empire Ottoman et la France, et sur la Reforme Judiciaire en Egypte* (Paris 1890), page 14). The conditions of these capitulations at the time of the Khedive Ismail in Egypt were:

1. Foreigners would be able to live in the country, and carry on business.
2. Exemption from the *Gizia* – a tax on non-Moslems.
3. Protection from the local authorities, who could not enter the special quarters in which foreigners lived.
4. Religious immunity.
5. Independence of the local courts, as all civil, criminal and commercial cases between natives and foreigners had to be tried in the foreigners consular court.

Said reigned for nine years from 1854 to 1863, accomplishing much during those short years. He improved the army, considering himself its head, built railways, improved communications between villages, and redistributed land which had been reclaimed by Abbas I for the State. He obtained permission from Turkey to form the Suez Canal Company, but the conditions were weighted against him. However at the same time he lost much of the sovereignty of the country which had been achieved by Mohammed Aly by getting into debt, thus increasing the power of the foreign consuls who put in claims for real or imagined damages, incurred by the business projects of their compatriots.

'Button up your coat dear Consul, button up your coat,' said Said to a Consul General who had just sneezed in his presence, 'you'll only catch cold if you don't. Your government will then ask me for an indemnity.'

Lord Milner best described this looting of Egypt, which had fallen a prey to the Khedive's frenzy of modernisation, as 'It is hard to imagine the complete unscrupulousness with which diplomatic agents used their influence to make a weak Egypt yield to their most extravagant demands. At the time the purpose behind obtaining a concession was not to carry out some project but to invent some complaint which would allow the contract to be broken and then turn to the government for compensation.'[14] A French observer summed all this up with 'the most profitable industry was the exploitation of compensation from the Khedive.'

To Said Pasha is due the credit of having under French guidance, interested himself in the ancient Egyptian civilization, which was scattered around the country. Whereas Mohammed Aly had pulled down ancient temples for the material he could use on building his new factories, Said, on the contrary, repaired old monuments and carried on excavations in all the known sites in Lower and Upper Egypt. He also founded the Egyptian Museum in Cairo. During his reign both the Cairo–Alexandria and the Cairo–Suez railways were completed.

All through Saids' and his successor Ismail's reigns Europeans, principally Greeks, Italians and French, poured into the country. It was they who

[14]Quoted by Jean and Simone Lacouture: *Egypt in Transition*, page 67

usually benefited by exploiting the economic boom caused by the growth and the inclination of the rulers to modernise Egypt. Both under Said and Ismail the Copts were still permitted to enjoy the freedom and tolerance accorded them by Mohammed Aly. They benefitted by the rise in cotton prices that accompanied the American Civil War, taking advantage of their ability to purchase and farm land, due to the redistribution of land by Said, with the result that many of them became large landowner farmers. However, the Copts were dismayed and did not appreciate that, because of their new status in the community, they were now liable to conscription due to the decree passed by Said that: 'Henceforth all Egyptians irrespective of religion were liable to military conscription.' Whereas previously they had been prevented from enlisting in any of the various armies of occupation, not that they really wanted to, instead they had to pay a tax.

Said died on January 18th, 1863, leaving Egypt practically ruined, with a government debt of nearly 376 million gold francs, and a similar amount, being the total of the cost of the Suez Canal shares plus the Anglo-German loan of 60 million gold francs, contracted on March 18th, 1862, over and above amounts due on Treasury Bonds, a sort of floating debt.[15]

Said was succeeded by his nephew Ismail, the son of Ibrahim Pasha, who began working at once for the removal of the humiliating clauses of the Foreign Powers Convention of London, July 15th, 1840, which dictated the relationship between Egypt and Turkey, resulting in the firman of 1841 curtailing Egypt's autonomy. Ismail had the same passionate desire for self-aggrandisement which had characterised his ancestors. One of his paramount ambitions was that of changing his title – which would denote that he was an independent ruler in his own country and was free in his actions. Through continued presents and bribery to those in power in Turkey, Ismail obtained the title of 'Khedive Pasha of Egypt' instead of 'Wali Pasha of Egypt' thus becoming a unique ruler amongst Turkey's vassals. Egypt had been upgraded from a simple *Welayet* or province to a *Khedeviate*, a concocted relationship denoting something else, though still a Turkish vassal.

The title Khedive meant nothing in Arabic or Turkish, but was derived from a Persian word meaning glorious. Ismail was helped in his aim by his sinister Armenian banker, Abraham Pasha Karakekhia, who lived in Constantinople. He was able to obtain the firman of 1866 which settled the order of succession, giving Ismail the hereditary right to rule Egypt and the Sudan according to the law of primogeniture, whereas previously it had been the eldest member of the family who became the ruler.

The danger of the old system was that with princes from different

---

[15]*La Question d'Egypte* – Selim Emile Amad.

mothers, it was possible that the country would be adversely affected, as a ruler who knew that his son was not going to rule, because of there being older cousins or nephews, would tend to accumulate as large a fortune as he could to leave to his son. Another firman of 1867 changed his title from Wali to Khedive. At the same time the military restriction of the size of the Egyptian army was rescinded. The firman of 1873 abrogated the firman of 1841, thus enabling Ismail to achieve the aims that eluded Mohammed Aly. The following are the concessions he obtained:

'Direct hereditary rule from father to son, by order of primogeniture, as in European courts; substituting the name Glorious Khedive for that of Wali – or simple governor of a province. Autonomy in administration both civil and financial in the largest sense; complete legislative autonomy; liberty in contracting public loans, without permission of the Porte; the right to mint coins in Egypt in the name of the Sultan, but with different denominations from those used in Turkey; extension of the Egyptian territory to Suakim and Massawa; liberty to negotiate with the powers, with a view to establishing different conventions to do with customs and postal services; and to establish the relationship of the 'Police of the foreigners', their position, and their relationship with the Egyptian government and population; and to enlarge his army and navy at will.'

With the signing of the firman of 1873, Turkey had no more rights in Egypt except for an annual tribute.

According to Angelo Samarco's *Précis de l'Histoire d'Egypte*, 'One should consider the expenses and presents that Ismail incurred in order to obtain success in his aims from political and not economic criteria and, since he was successful in his endeavours, the 500 million gold francs that he spent were now more than justified.'

The public works that were accomplished during his reign, included railways to Upper Egypt where previously none existed. To aid irrigation he put up barrages, and he dug canals of which the Ibrahimieh in Upper Egypt and the Ismaileh in Lower Egypt were the most important. The revenue of the 22,000 acres of the domain of El Wadi was concentrated in education, earmarked for the *Kouttabs* (village schools) for the populace, where Christians and Moslems were admitted without discrimination. He sent many scholastic missions to Europe, reorganised the Azhar University, extended the planting of sugar cane, with the result that eighteen new sugar refineries were built. He took an interest in the embellishment of Cairo and Alexandria, made new roads, improved lighting and grew trees on both sides of the road. He created public gardens for recreation – in Cairo the Ezbekieh and in Alexandria, Nouzha.

However, the most splendid, the most costly and (to the Egyptians) the least useful achievement of Ismail's reign was the Suez Canal. It was a great French triumph, a great British convenience; but for the Egyptians, it has been a doubtful benefit, purchased at the cost of thousands of lives.

In the first place, Said's concession to his friend Ferdinand de Lesseps was heavily weighted in its terms against Egypt. It granted for ninety years a lease of valuable land and mineral rights, and the right to use forced labour for four fifths of the work.

'One of the first acts of Ismail was to agree with the Porte and the British Government that the onerous terms of the concession should be revoked. While prepared to meet the liabilities of Said in respect of shares in the company, he demanded a complete revision of the concession, including the restoration of land and mineral rights and the abandonment of the system of forced labour.'[16]

The matter was put to the arbitration of Napoleon III who acceded to the Egyptian claims, but assessed the indemnity to be paid to the company at eighty-four million francs, about half the original capital of the company. As Ismail was already committed to take half the shares, it meant that Egypt had paid for the Canal in full.

Ismail secured immunity from any further claims by the company by the payment of £3 million, secured by the interests of the Khedive's share in the Canal until 1895. Ismail wished to raise Egypt to the level of a European state. He felt that justice under the capitulary system was greatly weighted in favour of the foreigner, and set up a Council of State. Then he sent his Prime Minister, Nubar Pasha, who was very capable and intelligent, to negotiate with Turkey, allowing Egypt to establish something new: the Mixed Courts which were to be composed 50% of Egyptians and 50% of Westerners drawn from all the countries. They would judge mainly civil cases. This was great progress over the Consular Court, which would arbitrate in future between Egyptians and foreigners in criminal matters. There were therefore three types of courts in Egypt the National Courts for litigation between Egyptians both civil and criminal, which included the Religious Courts, the Consular Courts for criminal offences involving a foreigner, and the Mixed Courts which litigated between Egyptian and foreigner, or foreigner and foreigner. According to Mr Sabry[17], the well-known historian, 'The capitulary system tended to make Egypt a court of appeal for all the dubious characters thrown out of Europe. The creation of the mixed tribunals put an end to this miscarriage of justice. It cannot be said that Egyptians then began to enjoy equal treatment; but European delinquents were no longer able to rely on a shameful immunity.'[18] Nubar

---

[16] *Modern Egypt'* by Tom Little, page 39

[17] *L'Empire Egyptieanne sous Ismail et l'Ingérence Anglo-Française*: Paul Gauthner, Editeur, Paris, 1933

[18] *Egypt in Transition* by Jean and Simone Lacouture

Pasha was successful in obtaining the acquiescence of the Porte and of the other powers. To celebrate the establishment of the Mixed Courts, Ismail also created a Ministry of Justice.

In spite of the great strides in the modernization of Egypt, the reign of Ismail ended in his formal removal. Ismail had cost the country millions of pounds in money, and thousands of lives and misery of his peasants. He had squeezed the last piastre from the peasant, and borrowed in every country which he could get to lend him money. When it became evident that the great boom in cotton prices had ended, that Egypt was going into a recession and that unless strong measures were taken, neither principal nor interest would be forthcoming, the bondholders and the banks pressured the Great Powers to interfere.

Several attempts were made to curb Ismail's excesses, and although he professed his willingness to comply, yet they all failed. When the Mixed Courts decided in some cases in favour of the German government, which claimed certain sums from Egypt, Ismail ignored the decisions and refused to pay. He was abandoned by his European friends who pressured the Porte to depose him. Ismail was deposed in June 1879, and the dual control of Egypt's finances by Britain and France was imposed for a few months.

Egypt was declared bankrupt and in July 1880 a law was promulgated 'liquidating' some of the assets. The Porte wished to go back on his firman of 1873, but the British and French resisted, and his son Tewfik became Khedive. However, one positive result of Ismail's rule was that Egypt was recognised as a *state* and not a province, though still a vassal of Turkey.

Since the first days of the Arab conquest, the Moslems did not deem fit to allow non-Moslems the right and the honour to fight alongside them, since they were the bearers of the banner of reform. They taxed the conquered instead. During the reign of Ismail, Copts were recruited into the army. Said had passed a similar law which was never put into effect. Ismail told Gabriel Charme, a French writer who was visiting him, during a parade of his troops:

> 'Voyez ce battalion, il y'a des Arabes et des Coptes, de Muslemans et des Chrétiens, qui marchent dans le même rang. Je vous assure qu'aucune d'eux ne s'occupe de culte de son voisin, l'egalité entre eux est complète.'[19]

Ismail's concern in recruiting the Copts into the Army, was to improve Egypt's image in the outside world. He wanted to show that all Egyptians, no matter what their creed, were treated equally under the Law. He also wanted to abolish the idea amongst the Moslems that the Copts were privileged, by not being recruited. It is interesting to note that for two thousand

---

[19]Sylvester Chauleur, *Histoire de Coptes d'Egypte*, page 152

years, from the days of Alexander the Great to those of Mohammed Aly in the nineteenth century, there had been no general conscription of the native Egyptian.

The different conquerors had their own soldiers – usually mercenaries – except under the reign of Ptolemy IV in 217 BC, when a contingent of native Egyptians helped to win the battle of Rafa.[20] There used to be risings of the Egyptians against invaders, but not as a regular army, for example, the resistance of the population against the French invasion in 1799.

In spite of the presents that Ismail had lavished for years on the Sultan's entourage, he was refused asylum by the Porte. However, he was welcomed with open arms by the House of Savoy (Italy) which may account for the traditional friendship between the royal families of Egypt and Italy. Ismail wrote to his suzerain, the Sultan of Turkey, from his palace near Naples the following:

'I have just terminated sixteen years of dedicated service. Under my administration a network of railways has covered the country; the area under cultivation has been increased, the soil enriched by the building of new canals, two large ports have been created: Alexandria and Suez; the sources of slavery in Central Africa have been destroyed, and the flag of the Empire has been raised in countries, where until then it was unknown. The canal of the two seas has been built and given to the world; and lastly after a long resistance, the reform of the judiciary system has been inaugurated, which will prepare a means of establishing a true justice between the civilizations of the Orient and the Foreign Powers.'

---

[20] *Egypt in the Days of the Ptolemies* by Dr. Ibrahim Noshi, quoted by Dr. Riad Sourial in his work *The Coptic Community of Egypt during the 19th Century* page 207

## Egypt and the Sudan

It is opportune at this time to mention Egypt's relationship with Nubia and the Sudan, since the withdrawal of the Kings of Kush from the country. Both the Roman and Byzantine rulers of Egypt never really established themselves for any length of time beyond the limits of the Isle of Philae at Aswan.

Meanwhile the bloodless conquest of Paganism by Christianity southwards had been progressing steadily. Christianity at the time of the Arab invasion of Egypt, was professed not only in the valley of the Nile, but as far as Abyssinia's southern border on the eastern side of the African continent.

There were a number of Christian Kingdoms between Aswan and Abyssinia, who all acknowledged the head of the National Church of Egypt as their Pope.

In 643 AD, Amr Ibn El Aas sent an army into Nubia under the command of one of his Emirs. In the *Book of Conquests* by Ahmed El Koufi, the author writes as follows:

'Amr Ibn El Aas was in Egypt, when he received a letter from Omar, commanding him to march on Nubia, and conquer this country; the country of the barbarians.'

For several years skirmishes and raids were carried out by both sides. However, when Mohammed Ibn Said became Governor of Egypt in 653 AD he was able to defeat the Nubians by using a stone-throwing machine unseen before, which demolished the principal church of the city. The fall of a great church intimidated the Nubians to such an extent, that they eventually concluded a peace treaty with the Arabs.

The conditions of the treaty were as follows:

a. The Arabs agreed not to invade Nubia, who in return was to give aid to the Arabs – if called upon – in the wars of the latter.
b. The Nubians were to allow a mosque to be built in Dongola for those Arabs who might desire to settle there, and to see that no harm was done to it, and no Moslem annoyed or hindered in the exercise of his religion.
c. The Nubians were to hold themselves responsible for cleaning and lighting this mosque.
d. Moslems were to be allowed free entry into the country, but no fugitive slaves from the Arabs in Egypt were to be given shelter. At the same time, immigration into and out of Egypt was discouraged by both sides.

But the worst feature of this treaty was the clause that stipulated – and which laid the foundation of the slave trade – the imposition on the

EGYPT

Nile

NUBIA

ARABIA

Red Sea

KORDOFAN

Atbara

Khartoum

Blue Nile

White Nile

Al Jazira

DARFUR

Lake Tana

Bahr El Arab

Fashoda

Sobar

ETHIOPIA

Bahr El Ghazal

Bahr El Jabar

EQUATORIA

Lake Rudolf

Lake Albert

Lake Victoria

BUGANDA

THE NILOTIC SUDAN FROM
THE 17th TO THE 19th
CENTURY

Extent of Egyptian Influence
at dates indicated

| EGYPTIAN BORDER | |
|---|---|
| After 1885 | ▬ ▬ ▬ ▬ |
| Before 1885 | ·· ·· ·· ·· |
| 1820–1881 | ▬·▬·▬· |
| 1820–1849 | ▬··▬··▬·· |

Nubians, to supply the governor of Aswan, for the use of the Imam, with 360 slaves of both sexes from the interior among whom should be found no old man, or old woman, or child below the age of puberty. In exchange the Arabs were to send presents of wine, wheat and barley and fine robes for the Nubian King. Occasionally the Arab Governor had scruples about sending the wine.

Another question of conscience which subsequently arose among the Arabs was whether, so long as the tribute of slaves was duly paid, it was just to take slaves from Nubia beyond the stipulated number? After some deliberation the *Muftis*[21] finally came to the conclusion that all slaves taken in wars, or all those who had been reduced to a condition of slavery in their own country, were legitimate trade.

With but few interruptions this peaceful commercial arrangement lasted for six centuries. When non-Arab Muslims acquired control of the Delta under the Turkish Tulunid Rulers in the ninth century, they encouraged the nomad Arab tribes to migrate southwards into Nubia. There they did a bit of pillaging, lured by prospects of gold in the Nubian deserts, but the heartland of Nubia remained free of hostilities until the Memlukes established their control over Egypt in the late thirteenth and early fourteenth centuries.

The Memlukes carried out regular military expeditions mainly to get rid of the unruly Arab bedouins and subdue them. They were never able to occupy Nubia, though the constant hostilities greatly devastated the country and left it an easy prey to Arab immigration.

In the fifteenth century, once the Arab nomads felt that the lands beyond Aswan could support their herds and that no authority had the power to turn them back, they began to migrate southwards introducing Arab and Moslem culture to the Christian inhabitants. Through intermarriage and conversion, Islam became the dominant religion in the Sudan.

In 1820 Mohammed Aly, Viceroy of Egypt under the Ottoman Turks conquered the Sudan up to the Ethiopian foothills; he was interested in the gold and slaves that the Sudan could provide, and wished to control the vast hinterland south of Egypt. He appointed a Governor General Ali Khorshed Agha whose policy marked a new era in the Egyptian-Sudanese relationship; he reduced taxation, and cooperated with the Sudanese sheikhs and notables.

Khartoum was developed as the administrative capital of the whole region, and a host of agricultural and technical improvements were undertaken. Trade routes were protected and expanded, and he had a well contented army, who in return for regular pay and tolerable conditions helped in the expansion and the consolidation of the Egyptian administration.

---

[21]The word *Muftis* denotes appointed legal officials who gave opinions on Islamic law

However towards the end of Mohammed Aly's reign, and during the next two decades the country stagnated because of ineffective government at Khartoum and the vacillation of the viceroys in Cairo.

This state of affairs persisted until the more dynamic Ismail took over the guidance of Egyptian and Sudanese affairs. Ismail was ambitious for Egypt; he hoped to get vast areas of Africa and the Sudan under Egyptian control, for which he hired Europeans and Americans to administer both the civil and military sides of his aspirations, trusting them more than Egyptians. To finance these vast undertakings, Ismail turned to the capital-surplus nations of Europe, where investors were willing to risk their savings at high rates of interest in the cause of Egyptian and African development. Such funds could only be attracted as long as Ismail went along with the ideas of the Europeans of abolishing the slave trade; Ismail needed no encouragement. He genuinely opposed the slave trade, and made sincere efforts to suppress it, and cooperate with the European powers towards that end.

In 1869, he sent Sir Samuel Baker in charge of an Egyptian force to curtail the slave trade in the Upper Nile, and to set up garrisons to secure Egyptian hegemony over the Nile basin as far as the equator. Sir Samuel was able to do this; he established an equatorial province as part of the Egyptian Sudan which remained under Egyptian rule until the Mahdist revolt in 1882.

Sir Samuel Baker was succeeded by General Gordon who became Governor of the Sudan in 1874, which included the equatorial province. Outside his jurisdiction to the west lay the vast area of Bahr el Ghazal, bastion of the slave traders, who had large garrisons of slave soldiers. These were ruled by the largest slaver of them all, known as Zobeir Pasha.

When Baker retired in 1873, the Khedive Ismail appointed Zobeir as Governor of Bahr el Ghazal. It had not been possible for the Egyptian forces to abolish slavery in this district, as Baker had accomplished on the Victoria Nile. It was the only way Ismail felt he could at least nominally control this vast area under the Egyptian flag. Difficult conditions were caused by the deposition of Khedive Ismail in 1879, who left the finances of Egypt in a shambles. Then there was the appointment by the creditors of a British and French commission, with the specific duty of sorting out Egypt's finances, and paying off her debts. Taking into account the reluctance of the commission to spend more money on the Sudan plus the preceding circumstances, Gordon felt he was unable to continue running the Sudan. So he resigned and many of the ablest European and Egyptian administrators either resigned or were dismissed by him.

In 1881 the Mahdi, a religious fanatical leader, led a revolt against the Egyptian Turkish occupiers and Christian foreigners in the country. He was aided by the slave traders who felt this was the chance they were waiting for to obtain a free hand in the country. They were able to massacre an

Egyptian force sent against them, with very few casualties to themselves.

In 1882 the British occupied Egypt, after the Europeans were massacred in Alexandria, due to a military revolt of Egyptian officers led by an Egyptian Colonel Ahmed Arabi. They were protesting against the Turco-Circassian privileges and foreign control.

The vacillation of the Khedive Tewfic, the eldest son of the deposed Khedive Ismail; the fear of Britain and France that Arabi was becoming a military dictator and would eventually default on the debts due to Europe and threaten Britain's lifeline to India, the Suez Canal, led to the occupation of Egypt by the British after Arabi and his troops were defeated at the battle of Tel el Kebir. It was at this time that the British advised the Egyptians to evacuate the Sudan. Egypt was reluctant to do so. It made a feeble attempt to retrieve what prestige it had left, and sent a force under General Hicks against the rebels in the Sudan. But when this venture failed, Britain gave orders to evacuate the Sudan, 'She could not collect Europe's debts and at the same time recover a million square miles in Africa.'

Gordon was sent back to the Sudan, to arrange the evacuation of the remaining garrisons. He tried to do this by remitting taxes and releasing prisoners; he even tried to win over the fighting slave traders on the promise of leaving them alone. He pledged not to leave until everyone was brought back to safety. However he was isolated and cut off from his main forces. A relief force was sent by Britain under General Sir Garnet Wolseley which arrived at the gates of Khartoum in October 1882, one day after Gordon had died at the hands of the Dervishes.

In June 1885 British and Egyptian troops were withdrawn to a line across the river at Wadi Halfa. One should note that prior to the Mahdist revolt Egypt bore all the costs in the Sudan. She created a communications system, instituted law courts, built schools, offices for administration, and barracks for her troops. The financial cost included all salaries, the price of arms, provisions, and other expenses. In manpower she provided for officers, soldiers, engineers, administrators and others. It is true that a percentage of the men she employed were foreigners, but they were all paid by Egypt. There were hardly any British civilians living in the Sudan at this time.

According to Prince Omar Tussoun, in his work *Egypt's Sacrifices in the Sudan*,

'The Mahdist revolt cost Egypt 79,900 officers and soldiers, and nearly 200,000 men, women and children of its nationals in the Sudan. England lost 1400 men in all, being one percent of the soldiers, three percent of the officers, and zero percent of the civilians.'[22]

[22]Quoted by Emil Selim Amad in his book *La Question d'Egypte*, page 189

Although Ismail was not able to achieve complete unity with the Sudan, he planted the seed which grew and became an important element in future nationalistic thought – that of the political union of Egypt and the Sudan – which was to become a stumbling block in Anglo-Egyptian relations for years to come.

# BOOK TWO – A UNITED PIONEERING FAMILY: HANNA AND HIS BROTHER WISSA APPEAR ON THE SCENE IN 1845

*Ten Piastres, a Donkey and a Silk-Shop*

Esther's parents and grandparents were born at a time when there were great changes in the country, in religion, economics and ways of life. The story of her maternal grandfather Wissa Boctor Wissa, known as Wissa Wissa, and his brother Hanna Boctor Wissa, known as Hanna Wissa, and how they made their fortune in a lifetime, is more like a tale from *The Thousand and One Nights* than reality.

It all began when a small merchant from Assiout named Boctor Wissa married a second time about the year 1846. His first wife, Sara, had died leaving two sons, the eldest Hanna named after her father was born in 1832, the younger Wissa named after his father was born in 1837. When Hanna was about twelve he came home from his father's shop and found his brother crying. On asking why, he was told that his stepmother had beaten Wissa. Hanna, who was impulsive, resented his father having married again after his mother's death. He went to her, they had a quarrel and he slapped her. When Boctor came home he was so angry at his son's behaviour that he kicked him out of the house. Hanna took Wissa by the hand and they left their father's house. Wissa was crying that he hadn't had his dinner and was hungry, Hanna had a loaf of bread and they each ate half. They went to their mother's sister and asked if they could stay with her; she agreed.

Next morning Hanna, who had ten piastres, which was a lot of money in those days, went and bought some pins, needles, thread, etc. and taking his brother with him, went from house to house selling their wares. They found it paid more, selling out of town in the villages and farms along the banks of the Nile. They tried to supply their customers' needs at their front doors. After several years they had saved enough to buy a donkey, which allowed them to go further afield and get to know their surroundings. After about ten years they had saved forty pounds.

Hanna was then twenty-two and Wissa fifteen; on their rounds they'd heard that a barge had sunk in the Nile near a village where they used to sell their wares. The insurance company, which was based in Alexandria, did not know or did not think it was worth while getting the barge out, and the surveyor was offering it and its contents where it lay in the Nile for forty pounds.

Wissa, who was a gambler by nature, told his brother, 'Let's buy the barge and persuade the villagers to help us get it out. We'll pay them later.' Hanna did not want to risk losing the forty pounds that had taken them ten years and a lot of walking to save. Wissa was adamant and threatened to break up the partnership and take his twenty pounds. Hanna was very fond of his brother and could not bear the idea of separation, and agreed to part with the forty pounds.

They were able, with the help of the *Omda* (mayor) of the village and his men, to raise the barge out of the water. To the brothers' great surprise and good luck the cargo was made of cases of pure silk and other materials that were packed so well that they were hardly damaged at all, which enabled them to open a shop. They were now well on the way to making a fortune.

### Beaten Forty-Day Route

The brothers Hanna and Wissa now traded in their shop. They were hard working and enterprising in their different ways. They were willing to take risks where others feared to tread. They became large traders in cloth and similar merchandise having it brought to Assiout from Cairo. They always had a large variety and plenty of stock on hand, and were thus able to supply other traders mainly from centres south of Assiout. They also carried on brisk business with those who traded with the Sudan, Assiout being the crosspoint where the Egyptian trade route to the Sudan started. This overland route to the Sudan was known as the *Darb-el-Arbaeen* translated as the 'Beaten Forty-Day Route'.

Their big chance came when the Khedive Said came to power, turning aside the economic experiments of both his father Mohammed Aly and his nephew Abbas I. He had been educated in France, he did not believe in state monopolies, he exacted taxes in money instead of kind, and introduced a type of private ownership of land. This was a sort of leasehold, known as the *Saidiya* system, in which the farmer was free to grow whatever crop pleased him, and to sell the produce freely on the market. He could also sell his leasehold, or leave it to his children, or bestow it or relinquish it to another. However, the freehold of the land still belonged to the state, who exacted a land tax and could repossess the land if the taxes were unpaid.

The Copts and foreigners were not prevented from owning land under this system, but there was not much land to be had for any would-be purchaser of leasehold. The large landowners at the time had been created by Mohammed Aly, who gave to his relatives, friends and followers large tracts of uncultivated land in order to reclaim it and grow cotton. Abbas had tried to confiscate all this land for the state, meaning himself, but he only reigned for five years and Said, his successor, discontinued his policy.

Once the peasants were allowed to sell their produce on the free market, the brothers expanded their business to include trading in cereals, cattle, cotton, etc. The two brothers were united in their aims; whereas Wissa would look after the business side making the deals, Hanna would be looking after the administrative side. They also started dabbling in purchasing land and becoming farmers. They knew the districts of the Assiout Mouderieh (province) very well, they knew the land, they knew the peasants on the land, and could be on the spot if anything was going cheap. But they did not launch into buying land on a large scale until the 1890s when the situation looked clearer. More land became available during the reign of Khedive Ismail, and still more when the state domains and the Daira Sanieh[23] were liquidated in 1890 under the Khedives Tewfik and Abbas II.

Over the years the debts the State incurred purchasing the land of the Daira Sanieh and the domains that the princes gave up, were all settled; at first the government sold part of the land thus procured in large auctions. The balance was sold in 1898 to a company who again re-sold it in lots to the population. Thus ownership of land was spread, instead of it being in the hands of the ruling family and their cronies, and the new emerging large landowners.

During the reign of Khedive Ismail in 1870 the Saidiya system of land tenure was changed slightly so that leaseholders became freeholders in order to encourage the ownership of land. As the treasury of the Khedive

---

[23]The Daira Sanieh was a sort of ministry of agriculture whose job was to administer the agricultural land belonging to the Khedive, *Daira* meaning a farming administration. This land was divided into *Teftiches* (inspectorates), each Teftich was responsible for at least 60,000 *feddans* (acres). The Teftiches were all over Lower Egypt and Upper Egypt. They extended over an area of more than half a million acres.

The inspectors who ran the Teftiches had influence over all the government officials they came in contact with. Their authority was without limit.

At the time when the financial position of the Khedive became precarious, and it was becoming difficult to service the debts incurred by the Khedive, Nubar Pasha the then prime minister, was able to convince Khedive Ismail to sell all the lands of his estates (Daira Sanieh) to the State, who would run it in the future, to cover the deficit of the budget either by its income or by selling part of it. Nubar Pasha also induced other members of the Khedive's family to give up their land to the state, in the same manner as the Daira Sanieh, receiving in return monthly emoluments for the owners – the princes and their families – drawn on the state treasury.

grew hungrier, they thought of all sorts of means for increasing its income. A law was passed in 1872 known as 'The Law of the Moukabala'[24].

However, the pressure put on the administration to collect more money during Khedive Ismail's reign made life unbearable for the ordinary peasant, due to the treatment he was subjected to. 'Taxes were increased and great cruelty was perpetrated in collecting them. The *korbag* or whip was an ordinary event. The *corvée*, or forced labour, was general, the peasant had to work free on the Khedive's domains, or even the executive officials' land by force. The collectors of taxes were dictatorial and unfair, as the illiterate peasant did not know exactly what he owed.'[25]

The peasants became so fed up at this period that they did not want to own land, they left it uncultivated and tried to find work elsewhere by running away. A curse which the peasants coined up at that time was *Gak-el-Teen* which meant 'may you get the mud' – as if by having land you contracted a disease.

Lady Duff Gordon who lived for several years at Luxor, and whose letters of observations described what was going on in the country at the time, wrote in 1867 in *Last Letters from Egypt* 'I cannot describe the misery here now, every day some new tax. Every beast, camel, cow, sheep, donkey and horse is made to pay. The Fellaheen can no longer eat bread; they are living on barley meal mixed with water and raw green stuff, vetches, etc. . . . The people in Upper Egypt are running away on a large scale, utterly unable to pay the new taxes and do the work exacted.' The situation became so bad that Khedive Ismail even thought of reverting to the monopolistic system of his grandfather Mohammed Aly. A well-known historian, Dr Mohammed Fahmy Leheta says in his book *The Economic History of Egypt in the Last Centuries* on page 358:

'The free peasant was no happier or luckier than a slave, by nature he

---

[24]Lord Cromer in his book *Modern Egypt* comments on this law, Part I Chapter III, as follows:

'By this law, all landowners could redeem one half of the land tax to which they were liable by payment of six years' tax in one lump sum. They could redeem the fifty percent in instalments over twelve years, or in one sum at the convenience of the state.'

Mr Stephen Cave in his report of the financial situation in Egypt in 1876 says, 'The operation of the "law of the moukabala" is perhaps the most striking instance of the reckless manner in which the means of the future have been sacrificed to meet the pressing needs of the present.'

Lord Cromer commenting on this remark says:

'This is quite true, but the explanation is also quite simple; there was never the least intention to adhere to the engagements taken towards the landowners. When the proper time arrived, it was intended to find means of reimposing taxation in some form, and thus recoup the loss to the Treasury incurred by the partial redemption of the land tax.'

[25]*The Coptic Community in the 19th Century* by Dr Riad Sourial.

was attracted to the land that he grew, and was forced to work on trying his best to get the most out of it, but found that all his effort was no use, as all the produce that was engendered by his labour was taken away by government officials, leaving him barely enough to live on.'

However, things changed dramatically in the following reign of Tewfik. A Commission of five was set up to liquidate the debts of Egypt under the presidency of Sir Rivers Wilson. It consisted of an Englishman, two Frenchmen and a German, the extra Frenchman was to give France the same degree of representation as England. Two controllers were appointed, M. de Blignières, a Frenchman, and Sir Evelyn Baring (Lord Cromer), an Englishman. They were not members of the commission, since it was thought that the interests of the creditors were strongly represented by the commission, and that it was both just and politic and that the controllers should be neutral, and represent the interests of the Egyptian Government and people rather than those of the creditors.

The period was known as that of Dual Control and lasted from November 1879 to December 1880. This period was a great success, the controllers pulled the strings behind the scenes but appeared on the stage as little as possible. During this period the following reforms were put in force:

a. On January 6th, 1880 the Law of the Moukabalah was abolished.
b. On January 17th, 1880 the Poll Tax was abolished. This tax had yielded a revenue of £205,000 per year.
c. Direct duties, such as highway, market and weighing levies were suppressed in the villages, whilst in the towns direct duties were abolished on 105 articles, which were mostly agricultural produce.
d. Twenty-four petty taxes of a vexatious nature were abolished by a stroke of the pen.
e. A law had been passed in 1873, that everyone in Egypt was supposed to consume a certain amount of salt a year. A tax was levied on salt. The population of each village was roughly calculated at the time the law was passed, and the tax divided amongst the villagers. No account was taken of changes which might have occurred since 1873 in the population of each village. This tax was abolished and in substitution for it, salt was constituted a government monopoly.
f. Any land tax that had been paid in kind in some parts of the country, which had given rise to numerous abuses, was suppressed. The payment of taxes since then could only be carried out in money.

One of the most important reforms and most beneficial to the cultivators, was the system initiated on the manner in which the taxes should be collected. In Lord Cromer's book *Modern Egypt Part II*, Chapter X, he describes this reform as follows:

'The dates at which the instalments of land tax were to fall due, were fixed in a manner which was convenient to the cultivators. At the same time the names of the taxpayers belonging to each village were inscribed in one register. An extract from this register was given to each taxpayer showing the total of the sums which were due from him under the several heads of account, and the dates on which he would be called upon to pay.'

He continues:

'It was not so much the amount of the land tax which had heretofore weighed heavily on the country, as in fact the dates of collection which had been regulated without any reference to the convenience of the taxpayers. Further insomuch as none of the taxpayers knew with any degree of certainty how much they had to pay, a wide door was opened for extortion and illegal taxation.'

It was under these ameliorated circumstances and the feeling of security that the Wissa brothers realised the potential in acquiring land, reclaiming and improving it by turning land which had previously been 'basin land' and had been covered by the yearly floods, which could only grow one crop a year, into perennial land on which they could grow three crops a year. This they were able to do by building dykes around their land, using steam engines which they installed in the farms they acquired to draw water from the Ibrahimieh Canal, built by Ismail, or from the Nile wherever their land was situated.

The brothers cooperated as usual in their new enterprise, they took the risk of trusting the new state of affairs, and went into purchasing land on a large scale. They had accumulated wealth in their trading days, which they now used in purchasing land, thus engendering more wealth, whereas other traders were slow to take advantage of the times.

There were neither profits tax nor income tax to worry about, they had to pay their land tax on time, and pay for the labour in building their dykes, and working in the fields. Hanna who was a good organiser was on his horse from sunrise to sunset supervising the work on different farms. Wissa who had a flair for business was looking out for a chance of purchasing more land. According to Dr Riad Sourial in his book *The Coptic Community in the 19th Century*, page 54–56, he says:

'It was in the reigns of the Khedive Tewfik and Abbas Helmi II that the Wissa brothers became large landowners. By 1898 they owned 12,000 acres in Upper Egypt in eighty villages in the Province of Assiout. They also went into the manufacture of sugar, building a sugar refinery in Beni Kora in 1896.' They built a cotton seed oil extraction plant and refinery, and a ginning factory also at Beni Kora later on.

At about that time they bought 14,000 acres in the Fayoum province, owned most of the shares in the Fayoum Light Railway. When Wissa died in 1906, followed by his brother Hanna in 1907, they left their children –

Wissa two boys and three girls and Hanna four boys and five girls – 28,000 acres of agricultural land, a sugar and an oil refinery, and a ginning factory. There were also several buildings and a hotel in Assiout proper, and other buildings in the farms scattered in the villages, both in the Assiout and Fayoum provinces.

It just shows how unity and hard work and love between members of one family may lead to the building of a fortune.

## Tales and Stories of the Wissa Brothers

I do not pretend to know the details of all the transactions that the two brothers accomplished, I can only repeat a few anecdotes that have been passed down over the years about this family of pioneers.

There is a saying in Arabic, *Kirat bakht wala feddan shatara*, which means 'It is better to have a kirat of luck (*bakht*) and not have a feddan of cleverness (*shatara*)'. Kirat and feddan are both measures of land, the kirat is $\frac{1}{24}$th of the feddan which equals approximately one acre. Shatara is a mixture of sharpness and cunning, it is not considered disparaging: in fact *shater* (the adjective) is considered a word of praise, i.e. sharpness or cleverness above the average. All the heroes in children's fables are either called Shater Mohammed or Shater Hassan. The Wissa brothers were supposed to be proverbially lucky, as well as Wissa being extra sharp, or shater, a flair for making money, realising the advantages in a situation and being quick to act upon it.

When the state started selling the land of the Daira Sanieh and the domains which had been relinquished by the princes, the would-be purchasers were canny enough not to go out of their way accumulating land in provinces where they had no influence. Communications were not easy, and the Egyptian, by nature, likes to buy land in his own district. Therefore a landowner tended to concentrate in buying land in his own province, leaving land being sold in the next province to the landowners living there. They did not compete with each other, thus keeping the price down. Consequently you would find that certain families accumulated thousands of acres of land in one province, whereas other families would be concentrated in another province barely forty miles away.

A story handed down about Wissa's luck goes like this: Wissa was travelling by train from Cairo to Assiout. He had a touch of gippy tummy and got down at Minieh, the province before Assiout, either to see a doctor, relieve himself or get some medicine. He waited at the station café. As it happened, there was a big sale of land taking place the next day; Wissa did not know about it and, if he had, had no intention of buying land in Minieh where it could not be administered by his brother.

Some of the would-be purchasers recognised him and thought that he had come down for the sale. So they went and sat at his table, offered him coffee and then asked innocently what brought him to Minieh. If it had been me, I'd have said, 'Look at my bad luck, I've got a tummy ache and had to get down, and here I am having to wait for a few hours for a train.' But canny Mr Wissa answered, 'I'm coming here on business,' not saying what.

Then one of the would-be buyers asked, 'How much will you take to leave it?' Wissa answered, not knowing what he was supposed to leave, 'How much do you offer me to leave it?' The would-be buyers then offered him £1000 – to get on the next train. Wissa then asked for £2000. The would-be buyers then said, 'Let's split the town in two,' meaning to compromise at £1500. Reluctantly, Wissa accepted the deal and left on the next train.

The American Protestants had come to Assiout, and they were able to convert two of the notable families, the Khayatts and the Wissas. How they were able to convert Copts to Protestantism and nurture their mission will be told later, but the result of the American invasion of Assiout was that the converted families imbibed much of their foreign ideas; they were avant garde in their thoughts and actions. Wassif Khayatt became consular agent of America, whilst Wissa Wissa became consular agent of Portugal. It did them no harm in their own eyes, they were protected by the privileges accorded by the Capitulations, but they were disliked by the Copts of the National Church. Another example of the Wissa luck or shatara is the following story:

A certain farm was being advertised by the state and was put up for sale. In the conditions of sale it was mentioned that the farm had a wall built all round it. Wissa knew there was no wall around it at the time, he'd probably walked all over the land when he was selling pins and needles. He bought the farm, and it was mentioned in the deed of sale that he bought a farm with a wall built all round it. There probably was a wall when the Turks took it from the Memlukes, but there was no wall when Wissa came to take delivery. He insisted on getting a reduction in price, and was able to persuade the sellers to acquiesce. However, he had second thoughts, maybe he had been too sharp it was dangerous to thwart a Khedive or the state, you could easily be bumped off. He thought of a way to make amends. The local farmers had a lot of paper debts owed them by the state, which they had crossed off as bad. Wissa bought a lot of these debts for practically nothing, and took them to the palace as a token of his allegiance. They were given to the Khedive who asked to see him. The courtiers answered 'What do you want to see him for, he is a *nouveau riche*; he used to sell cloth in the villages on a donkey.' The Khedive insisted on seeing him, and when he presented himself the Khedive asked, 'Is it true, Mr Wissa, that you used to sell cloth in the villages on a donkey?' Wissa answered, 'Before the donkey your Highness (Affandina) I used to sell it on foot.'

In order to buy land in auctions you had to be sure of your cash flow, no matter how much land you owned. Wissa soon found out that if he intended to continue buying land he would have to find a bank to finance him. The Mosseri bank, a well-known Jewish bank, used to lend money on crops. Wissa did not know Mr Mosseri but had heard of him. He went round to the bank when he knew Mr Mosseri was away and asked to meet him. He was told he would be away for a week. Wissa brought out a bag of gold and asked if he could leave it as he wanted to open an account. The employee said, 'Take a receipt,' but Wissa refused and said he'd come back later. Wissa came back after two weeks and asked to see Mr Mosseri; the employee asked, 'Where have you been Mr Wissa? Mr Mosseri has been asking about you, and he was very angry with me for not insisting on giving you a receipt.' He was then shown into Mr Mosseri's office, who asked him how it was that he left the gold without taking a receipt. Wissa answered, 'How could I take a receipt from Mr Mosseri's bank, which was so honest and well-known?' It was usual for work to be done in Egypt, with a simple *Esta bene*, an Italian sentence meaning 'O.K. I agree.' Papers would be drawn up later. They started talking and Mr Wissa indicated that he was a big landowner who entered into the purchase of large parcels of land which needed hard cash at the time of the sale. Mr Mosseri asked him what sort of collateral could he give. He answered that he had lots of boats of cereals continually coming down the Nile for sale in Cairo. The bank sent down an inspector to see these sailing boats, wheat, lentils, etc. Most of the boatmen were from Upper Egypt and they had probably been coached by Wissa's stooges. Every boat about which the inspector asked, 'Who was the owner,' most of them answered, 'Mr Wissa.' I don't know how truthful they were.

The result was that Wissa became a big client of the Mosseri bank, the overdrafts accorded him were always paid in time, and he had no difficulty in cash flow for many of his purchases.

Another story told in the family about Wissa and his shatara is about an incident that happened between him and one of the Khayatt family. The Wissas and the Khayatts were great friends, who later intermarried, but a bit of *shatara* between friends is sometimes allowed in good grace, with no lasting bad feeling.

It is said among family members that the Wissas are witty and impulsive, whereas the Khayatts are more poised and think a hundred times before taking a decision.

The story that is told was that Wissa, who had come back from Cairo the same day, with the intention of staying a week or two in Assiout, was dining with Hanna as guests of one of the Khayatts. At dinner the host started talking about some land he had heard of that was being put up for sale, and had to be negotiated in Cairo. He was asking everyone their opinion before making up his mind whether he should buy it or not. Wissa felt it was a very good deal, but he could not get up from the table and get on the next train to Cairo to clinch the deal. It was not done. But the temptation was too strong. He bent over and whispered to Hanna, 'I'm going to swear at you, and you answer by giving me a slap.' A little later Hanna said something, Wissa contradicted him, an argument resulted and Hanna, who was known for his impulsiveness and hot temper, slapped Wissa. Wissa swore that he would not spend the night in Assiout, but would leave for Cairo on the next train. He left on the next train and clinched his deal whilst the Khayatts were still talking about it. The Khayatts followed a few days later, in order to get Wissa back to Assiout, to make it up with his brother Hanna. The unity of the brothers and their love for each other was what made a success of the partnership which lasted until separated by the death of Wissa in 1906.

Still another couple of anecdotes showing the relationship between the brothers can be seen in the following:

Wissa and Hanna decided to get married, some time in the 1860s, and decided to have a double wedding. Wissa had asked for the hand of the daughter of an old respected aristocratic family, whose ancestor, El Gohari, has his portrait hung up in the Louvre in Paris. He had also asked on behalf of his brother Hanna for the hand of Firdous, the daughter of a family whose nickname was *Maalaka* which means spoon, as their ancestor was supposed to have been the first person to own a silver spoon in Assiout.

Both grooms had not seen their brides before the ceremony of the engagement, and as they were sitting there Hanna noticed that his would-be bride was plump and white, whereas Wissa's was skinny and dark. Hanna turned to Wissa and said, 'Before it's too late, if you want we'll exchange. You take the nice fat one and I'll take the other.' Wissa answered, 'I'm not marrying a woman, I'm marrying a family!' Hanna was a very good husband, he never looked at another woman all through his married life. Wissa spent most of his time in Cairo on business and mixing with all the *mondaines* for weeks on end, leaving his wife in Assiout with the children.

Another story of the relationship of the brothers happened when their eldest sons were young men. George was the eldest son of Wissa, he was domineering and autocratic. Guindi, who was the eldest son of Hanna, was supposed to be an easy-going chap.

However, the two boys had an argument one day and George told Guindi, 'You shut up, you are only servants in this family, all the land is in my father's name and you have nothing.' That night Guindi asked his father, 'Is it true father, that we are servants of uncle Wissa and that you have nothing, all the land being in uncle Wissa's name?' Hanna did not answer, but left next morning by the first train to Cairo, and went to the

84

club to which Wissa belonged. He found Wissa gambling. When Wissa saw him, he asked, 'What has brought you?' as he knew Hanna did not like coming to Cairo. Hanna answered, 'Is it true Wissa, that I and my family are your servants and that nothing is in my name, and everything is in your name?' Wissa answered, 'Who told you that?' Hanna answered 'George told Guindi.' Wissa realised then that he used to sign all the deeds of the purchase of land, and that he had not thought it necessary to put both names in the deeds. Wissa burst into tears. 'You can never be sure of children. All that is in my name belongs to both of us equally. Don't you remember the loaf of bread and the ten piastres were yours and you gave me half.' Next day they went to the courts and all the deeds of the property bought were put in the names of both of them, by having them endorsed with the words '*Wissa Boctor wa Hanna Akhih*', which in Arabic means 'Wissa Boctor and his brother Hanna.' You can see that endorsement on all the deeds of our property. Wissa also tore his coat into two, giving Hanna half, stating dramatically, 'All that I have, half of it is yours.' When people say 'Oh, weren't the Wissa brothers lucky,' or in other instances, 'Weren't they particularly sharp,' my comment would be that they were blessed with the gift of concord.

The French say *L'homme propose et Dieu dispose*, the Arabs always end their declarations of intent with the words, 'but God is the master of concord,' or in other words 'may our intentions or deeds be crowned by success by the concord of God.'

The Wissa brothers were religious by nature and paid their tithes meticulously according to the tenets of the Bible. They did not consider themselves as grabbers, but hard workers whom God had blessed with success.

# Famille
## ASSIOUT

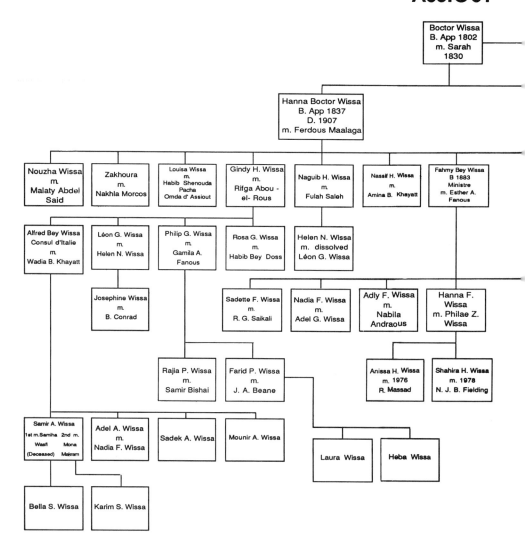

Boctor Wissa
B. App 1802
m. Sarah
1830

Hanna Boctor Wissa
B. App 1837
D. 1907
m. Ferdous Maalaga

Nouzha Wissa
m.
Malaty Abdel
Said

Zakhoura
m.
Nakhla Morcos

Louisa Wissa
m.
Habib Shenouda
Pacha
Omda d' Assiout

Gindy H. Wissa
m.
Rifga Abou -
el- Rous

Naguib H. Wissa
m.
Fulah Saleh

Nassif H. Wissa
m.
Amina B. Khayatt

Fahmy Bey Wissa
B 1883
Ministre
m. Esther A.
Fanous

Alfred Bey Wissa
Consul d'Italie
m.
Wadia B. Khayatt

Léon G. Wissa
m.
Helen N. Wissa

Philip G. Wissa
m.
Gamila A.
Fanous

Rosa G. Wissa
m.
Habib Bey  Doss

Helen N. Wissa
m.  dissolved
Léon G. Wissa

Josephine Wissa
m.
B. Conrad

Sadette F. Wissa
m.
R. G. Saikali

Nadia F. Wissa
m.
Adel G. Wissa

Adly F. Wissa
m.
Nabila
Andraous

Hanna F.
Wissa
m. Philae Z.
Wissa

Rajia P. Wissa
m.
Samir Bishai

Farid P. Wissa
m.
J. A. Beane

Anissa H. Wissa
m. 1976
R. Massad

Shahira H. Wissa
m. 1978
N. J. B. Fielding

Samir A. Wissa
1st m.Samiha   2nd  m.
Wasfi          Mona
(Deceased)   Makram

Adel A. Wissa
m.
Nadia F. Wissa

Sadek A. Wissa

Mounir A. Wissa

Laura  Wissa

Heba Wissa

Bella S. Wissa

Karim S. Wissa

# WISSA
## EGYPTE

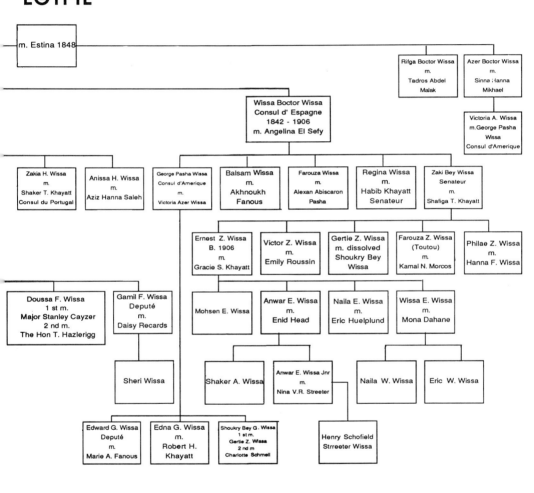

m. Estina 1848

Rifga Boctor Wissa
m.
Tadros Abdel
Malak

Azer Boctor Wissa
m.
Sinna Hanna
Mikhael

Victoria A. Wissa
m.George Pasha
Wissa
Consul d'Amerique

Wissa Boctor Wissa
Consul d' Espagne
1842 - 1906
m. Angelina El Sefy

Zakia H. Wissa
m.
Shaker T. Khayatt
Consul du Portugal

Anissa H. Wissa
m.
Aziz Hanna Saleh

George Pasha Wissa
Consul d'Amerique
m.
Victoria Azer Wissa

Balsam Wissa
m.
Akhnoukh
Fanous

Farouza Wissa
m.
Alexan Abiscaron
Pasha

Regina Wissa
m.
Habib Khayatt
Senateur

Zaki Bey Wissa
Senateur
m.
Shafiga T. Khayatt

Ernest Z. Wissa
B. 1906
m.
Gracie S. Khayatt

Victor Z. Wissa
m.
Emily Roussin

Gertie Z. Wissa
m. dissolved
Shoukry Bey
Wissa

Farouza Z. Wissa
(Toutou)
m.
Kamal N. Morcos

Philae Z. Wissa
m.
Hanna F. Wissa

Doussa F. Wissa
1 st m.
Major Stanley Cayzer
2 nd m.
The Hon T. Hazlerigg

Gamil F. Wissa
Deputé
m.
Daisy Recards

Mohsen E. Wissa

Anwar E. Wissa
m.
Enid Head

Naila E. Wissa
m.
Eric Huelplund

Wissa E. Wissa
m.
Mona Dahane

Sheri Wissa

Shaker A. Wissa

Anwar E. Wissa Jnr
m.
Nina V.R. Streeter

Naila  W. Wissa

Eric  W. Wissa

Edward G. Wissa
Deputé
m.
Marie A. Fanous

Edna G. Wissa
m.
Robert H.
Khayatt

Shoukry Bey G. Wissa
1 st m.
Gertie Z. Wissa
2 nd m
Charlotte Schmell

Henry Schofield
Strreeter Wissa

# Famille
## ASSIOUT

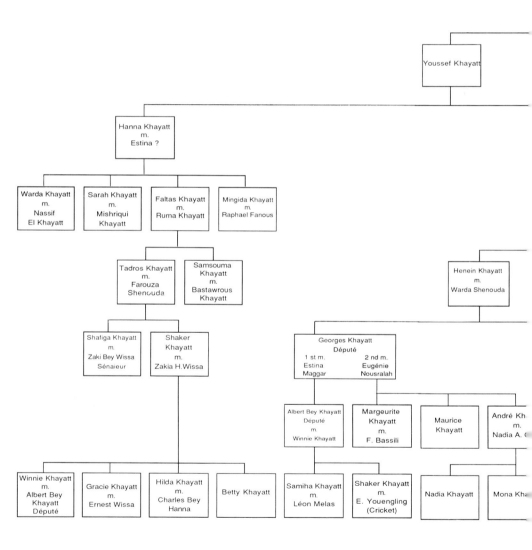

# KHAYATT
## EGYPTE

Gad El Karim
Khayatt
B. aboutt 1754
m.
?

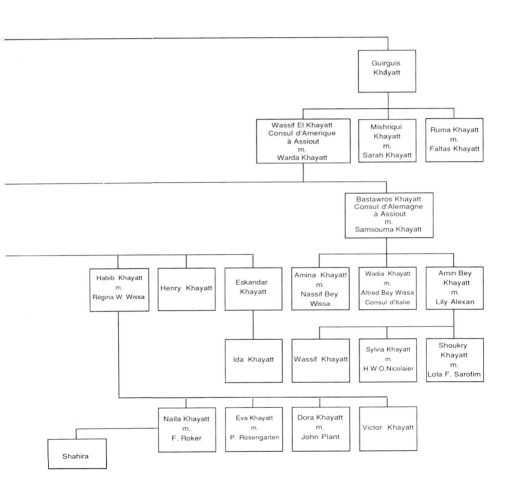

Guirguis
Khàyatt

Wassif El Khayatt
Consul d'Amerique
à Assiout
m.
Warda Khayatt

Mishriqui
Khayatt
m.
Sarah Khayatt

Ruma Khayatt
m.
Faltas Khayatt

Bastawros Khayatt
Consul d'Alemagne
à Assiout
m.
Samsouma Khayatt

Habib Khayatt
m.
Régina W. Wissa

Henry Khayatt

Eskandar
Khayatt

Amina Khayatt
m.
Nassif Bey
Wissa

Wadia Khayatt
m.
Altred Bey Wissa
Consul d'Italie

Amin Bey
Khayatt
m.
Lily Alexan

Ida Khayatt

Wassif Khayatt

Sylvia Khayatt
m.
H.W.O.Nicolaier

Shoukry
Khayatt
m.
Lola F. Sarofim

Naila Khayatt
m.
F. Roker

Eva Khayatt
m.
P. Rosengarten

Dora Khayatt
m.
John Plant

Victor Khayatt

Shahira

# Riverboat Evangelists at Loggerheads with Monotheists

*Conversion to Protestantism, mainly from the Coptic National Church*

Peter VII was Patriarch of the National Coptic Church in the first part of the nineteenth century. He was a man of high character and would have liked to reform the church, in the interest of his flock. Yet he was suspicious of Western influences, especially of the Roman Catholic Church, whose missionaries in the eighteenth century were able to establish a Catholic Church in Egypt, drawing their support mainly from the Melkite Church, but were able at the same time to convert members from the Coptic National Church. However, when the Reverend Tattam came to Egypt in 1836, to see if he would be able to buy a few old manuscripts, he saw the state of the Coptic National Church. He wrote to Archbishop Howley and urged him to get the British to do something to help the Church of Egypt, which had deteriorated to such an extent that the ordinary churchgoer – the man in the street – knew nothing about Christianity.

The priests themselves were ignorant, repeating liturgies in the Coptic language which they read from Arabic writing, which neither they nor the masses understood.

The Coptic religion had turned into a mixture of superstition and the adoration of saints. The help was to take the shape of a college to train young Egyptians desiring to be ordained as priests of their own church. This college was not supposed to convert them.[26]

Before this the Bible Society had published the four gospels in Arabic and Coptic, edited by Mr Tattam. The school was actually opened and kept up for a few years by Mr Lieder, who grew discouraged at the comparatively small success of the work, and in 1848 it was closed. Despite the closure some of the pupils were ordained priests at the time, one of them becoming the Patriarch known as 'Cyril the Reformer'. During his reign Cyril allowed no pictures to be set up in his new cathedral, and collected all those that had furnished the old building and had them burnt. I elaborate on this incident, as well as a similar one which happened twenty years later by a group of Protestant zealots in Assiout, under the title Iconoclasts.

The work that the Church of England, through the Church Missionary Society, had abandoned in the year 1848 was taken up ten years later by the American Presbyterian Mission. They came in the first place not to help the Copts but to convert the Moslems. The Church Missionaries found the work so slow and discouraging that they drew their converts from the Coptic National Church. The Coptic Church had welcomed help from the Church of England, as she believed that her emissaries were not trying to teach her children heresy or lead them to acknowledge the supremacy of

---

[26] *The Story of the Church of Egypt* by E.L. Butcher. Vol. II, page 396

1. William Harvey; 2. John Hogg; 3. Gulian Lansing; 4. S.C. Ewing; 5. A. Watson;
6. C. Murch; 7. J Giffen; 8. E. Lansing, M.D.; 9. J.R. Alexander; 10. J.K. Giffen;
11. T.J. Finney

John Hogg, D.D.
The founder of the American Mission in Assiout

91

Rome, which the Copts had been fighting for fourteen centuries. However, they resented and fought the American missionaries who attracted, through their modern methods and teachings, a great many converts from the Coptic Church, causing what was thought to be disloyalty to their ancient church and a schism among the Egyptian Copts.

The early American Protestant missionaries saw the Coptic Church, and the various orthodox and catholic communities, as having exchanged purity of true worship for the adoration of saints, 'being dominated by hopeless superstition, and the victims of abysmal ignorance.' The clergy lacked competent leadership and spiritual insight through lack of education and moral decay.

One of the aims was to extend the Kingdom of God further into Africa from Egypt, and by Egyptians. 'The evangelical church which came into being through the efforts of missionaries was founded on the conception of the school as the handmaid of the church.'[27] The immediate results were achieved by the printed page. This was accomplished by the sale of Scripture and other Christian literature. Journeys by boat up the River Nile offered occasions for distributing books and tracts.

The missionaries at the beginning thought that the best way to propagate their message was to influence the clergy by convincing them of their erroneous ideas and getting them to reform their churches. But they found that idea almost impossible to accomplish. They found it easier to get their message across by circulating Scripture, and where possible to explain it, thus correcting the people's conception of Christianity. Schools opened in Alexandria and Cairo were not very successful. People were better educated than those in the villages all along the Nile banks, mainly in Upper Egypt, and the Coptic Church had much more influence over their flock in Cairo and Alexandria than they had in the rest of the country.

The success the missionaries had through circulating Scriptures led them to buy in 1860 a houseboat called *Ibis* for use on the Nile and the larger canals.

In the same year Dr McCagne recalled, 'that the five weeks he spent between Cairo and Luxor with the boat as the base of operations were still vivid in his mind.' Four Egyptians accompanied the McCagnes.

He particularly remembered the stop at Assiout, when they went through the streets with a donkey laden with books, calling out 'The Holy Bible for sale. The Holy Bible for sale.'[28] In the same year, in December,

---

[27] *Vindicating a Vision* by Earl E Elder

[28] The new Arabic version of the Bible, published in Beirut, appeared as the result of many years of research and meticulous scholarship of Dr Eli Smith and Dr Cornelius Van Dyke, and their learned Syrian assistants. Using their findings of scholarship at the time, they foresaw many of the changes and corrections that appeared later in the American Revised Version. Today it is found in many Coptic homes. When the Liberation Rally of the 1952 Revolution wanted to give copies of Scriptures, sacred to the soldiers of the Egyptian army, the Christians received copies of the Beirut version.

Mr Lansing headed out with the *Ibis* again on a similar campaign. Luxor became his headquarters until March 1861. He was helped greatly in his work by Lord and Lady Aberdeen who were wintering on their houseboat at Luxor. 'Reports tell of a trip to Esna where, from a tent pitched nearby, they presented the Gospel by spoken word and printed page.' He visited seventy villages between Luxor and Cairo. During that winter, their total sale of literature was $625.

In 1862 the Reverend Hogg and his family first used the *Ibis*. They left Cairo on March 1st and returned on May 8th, they had travelled 1,160 miles and visited 63 villages, and talked with 7000 people, among them 62 priests, 45 monks and two bishops, all members of the Coptic Church. They talked in Arabic about subjects ranging from the unique atonement of Jesus Christ to the sacraments. The pattern of travel was that the only stop was on the Sabbath (Sunday), except when they passed an important town such as Beni Suef, Minia, Assiout, Girga or Luxor. The routine was to call on the notables, government officials, Coptic leaders, and other interested persons. Books were made available for sale, invitations were given to visit the boat, or the house of some willing friend, where a service was held in the evening. After the service, at night, the anchor was raised and the boat was carried by the current to another town or village. The next day the rounds, visits and conversations started in a new situation, with new people. This procedure became the pattern of Nile Evangelism for many years to follow.

Before the close of the nineteenth century there were scores of evangelical groups scattered along the river, and many churches had been organised. They became the centre of missionary Evangelism, and found it the best way of reaching villages which allowed them to be thrown daily into the teeming life of the country. They carried their house with them, which gave them a measure of independence as they did not have to ask the villagers for lodging, it relieved them of sleeping in strange beds or imposing on the famed Egyptian hospitality.

I would like to tell a story of how the American missionaries involved themselves in the lives of those around them. This they achieved by their sympathetic behaviour towards the community, which attracted many converts, who would not have been so easily lured if they had been met by aloofness. The result of this policy enabled the missionaries to cover much of the expenses of building their churches and schools, by involving the more affluent members of the converted to take an active part in their work and thought. The story I am about to recount is that of an Indian Prince, and the girl he met in Egypt, and of his financial help he gave to the missionary cause. I call it an Indian romance and also because of an incident to do with the family as mentioned in the Iconoclasts.

H. H. Dulup Singh.　　　　　H. H. The Maharanah (Bamba).

The House-boat *Ibis*
(in which the American missionaries travelled up and down the Nile
distributing Bibles translated into Arabic)

## An Indian Romance

Early in 1864 the young Indian Prince Dulep Singh came for a short visit to Egypt. He was the heir to the throne of Punjab – which his father, Punjit Singh who was fabulously rich had lost to the British. Dulep Singh had intended to stay only a short while in Egypt, but his secretary became ill, forcing him to extend his visit. Dulep Singh had an annual income of about £2,000,000 which he received from the British Government. In addition he had an enormous wealth in jewels and estates in England. He was educated in Great Britain where he had been converted to Christianity by the Reverend William Jay of the Church of England. He wanted a wife suitable to 'his peculiar tastes and mode of life.' Queen Victoria, with whom he was in high favour, advised him to marry an Indian Princess who had been educated in England. He too preferred someone from the East, yet he was not anxious for a life partner whose tastes were for 'the gaieties and frivolities of a fashionable aristocratic life.'[29]

To while away his time one morning on February 10th, 1864, he called on the American missionaries whose quarters were near his hotel. Having ascertained the various activities of the mission, he gave them a donation of $100 – as prizes for deserving children in its schools. 'His modesty, simplicity, and humility and the genial loving of his Christian character'[30] impressed those who met him. A few days later he donated a further $250 – for the general purposes of the mission, asking them to earmark $100 to the girls' school library.

Dulep Singh usually wore European clothes but now and then he'd appear in Indian dress, with a profuse display of diamonds and other jewels. Following a church service one Sunday, when he came in Indian dress, he wrote a note to Mr John Hogg, intimating that he was leaving shortly and wondering whether there might be in one of the mission schools, 'A truly Christian girl who had joined the church and whom you and Miss Dales could recommend to me for a wife.' This note caused no little excitement, and called for prompt action.

It brought to their minds the name of a girl whose short history was remarkable. Bamba, a fifteen year old girl, had an Abyssinian slave for a mother and a wealthy German merchant residing in Egypt for a father. He, knowing that his daughter would not be happy in an Abyssinian marriage, sent her to the American Mission school for an education. Some time before, the child had a deep religious experience, had publicly expressed her faith in Jesus Christ and had been accepted into the fellowship of the church. The Prince was told that this girl, Bamba, might suit his require-

[29] *Vindicating a Vision* by Earl E. Elder
[30] The Maharajah's intercession with Queen Victoria. See The Iconoclasts

ments. He was informed of her background and parentage as well as her charm, grace and winning manners. The Prince answered that her racial origin did not matter, he thought he had seen her and liked what he saw, but what concerned him was whether she'd share his ideals of Christian life and service.

The next day he appeared at Mr Hogg's house, intimated that he had thought and prayed over this matter and now came to make a formal proposal for Bamba's hand. The next thing was to get the girl's approval. Miss Dales now gave the girl the first intimation of all the planning and proposing that had been going on for the past twenty-four hours. The character of the girl could not have been portrayed better than in the unaffected composure and straightforward sincerity with which she considered the proposal of the Prince. She expressed her happiness with life at school as a student teacher. When urged to consider the proposal as a call to wider service she said, of course, her parents must give their opinion.

Before departing the Maharajah gave the girl a costly bracelet and ring, asking her to wear them for his sake even though she might refuse his proposal. Her father, Mr Muller, decided to let Bamba decide for herself. After much heart-searching and courting by correspondence between the Prince and Bamba, and considerable prayer and counsel, Bamba decided to accept the Prince's offer as a call from God. Her fear had been that since she knew nothing of society life in Cairo, how could she be expected to mingle with royalty in London? She thought her usefulness for Christ was best served in the school where she learned and taught. The Maharajah was delighted with the decision, feeling assured that the marriage would have God's blessing since it was through God's guidance that he was able to find a suitable Christian wife.[31]

In the next few weeks the mission played the role of fairy godmother to the young girl. They tried to teach her as much as they could of Western customs such as to sit at table and to use a knife and fork. Although she seemed to adapt easily to new ways, her health gave way under the strain. After an attack of jaundice she went to recuperate in Alexandria at her father's. She was there when the Prince came back to Egypt. After the six weeks of residence required by law prior to marriage, the ceremony took place in Alexandria, where Bamba maintained her grace and calm throughout the pomp and display of the evening, which culminated in a princely dinner. Two weeks after the wedding the couple paid a visit to Cairo and remained for a fortnight. Bamba assumed no airs of a grand princess, but spent the greater part of each day among her former companions. The last Sabbath of their visit was marked by a celebration of the

---

[31] *Vindicating a Vision* by Earl E. Elder

Lord's Supper together with the small Protestant community. Before the Maharajah departed with Bamba from Egypt he donated $5000 – in her name to the mission, promising to send them $2400 a year to support two missionaries. There was also a promise of establishing a printing press for the mission.

In January 1865 the Maharajah returned with his bride to Egypt for a trip on the Nile. He purchased the *Ibis* from the missionaries, for that was really the happy pair's honeymoon. They took the opportunity of distributing scriptures on their journey.[32]

On leaving Egypt the *Ibis* was left in the care of the missionaries to be used as formerly in Evangelism. Finally in 1874 the Maharajah, after completely refitting the boat, gave the boat to the mission in Assiout towards a fund for the college.

## *The Wissas become Protestant and the Story of the Carpenters*

It was not all plain sailing for the American missionaries. The National Coptic Church was doing its best to stop defection. It was in the 1860s that Hanna Boctor Wissa and his brother Wissa joined the Protestants. Hanna, true to character, was more voluble and outspoken, whereas Wissa was more diplomatic in words, manner and deed.

At the beginning Hanna, although sympathising with the Protestant cause, used to attend the meetings of the American missionaries, without actually joining them, or leaving the National Church.

An act that made some of the would-be converts bolder in their stand than they hitherto had been happened in September 1865. It was due to the Bishop of Assiout's nephew, at the instigation of the clergy, taking down the names of those who were attending the Protestant meetings. Among those attending these meetings were two families of carpenters, Athanasius and his brothers, and Morcus and his brothers, besides Hanna Boctor Wissa. These two families of carpenters were singled out by the priests and a special bull or church decree (*haram*)[33] was issued against them.

Although Hanna Wissa attended these meetings his name was left out of the *haram*, whom the priests dared not mention by name because of his influence.

I will quote from Dr Andrew Watson's book *The American Mission in Egypt 1854–1896*. Dr Watson stated:

'This bull or church decree took place on Friday, October 2, the feast of St Badir, the patron saint of the church of Assiout. Mr Hanna Boctor called on the Bishop, and

[32] *Vindicating a Vision* by Earl E. Elder
[33] *Haram* was a colloquial word coined by the orthodox Church meaning a sort of excommunication. It was derived from the Arabic word *haramme*, meaning to forbid.

Training College at Assiout

A bird's-eye view of the campus of Assiout College

asked him why he had omitted his name, since he was as great a defaulter as the poor carpenters.

"I know that quite well," replied the old man, "but you and your brother and Mr Wassif Khayatt got a special dispensation from the Patriarch last year."

Hanna replied that he did not want a special dispensation from the Patriarch or anyone else. If it was a sin for the carpenters to attend Dr Hogg's meetings, it was a sin for him to do so too, and no dispensation of the Patriarch could alter the moral character of his action in the matter. "I am ready, moreover," he added, "to give up attending the night meetings at the mission house upon two conditions. Firstly, that you read a haram next Sabbath against all who use intoxicating drinks; and secondly, that you have a night meeting in the church for the study of the Scriptures, and grant permission to all of every creed to attend it, even the American missionary, if he chooses to do so."

The Bishop actually gave Mr Hanna permission to read a paper against the drinking of arrack[34], and the latter, satisfied with the concession, and hoping that the other would be granted ere long, came straight to the mission house along with Mr Wassif and another man, and begged of me to draw up as strong a paper as possible against the use of arrack, as a counterblast to the haram of the previous day.

I set to work at once and prepared an article such as Mr Hanna Boctor wanted, exposing the vice of drunkenness, especially in those who held the sacred office of the ministry of the gospel. It was written chiefly in the words of Scripture, and there was added to it at the close the orthodox apostolic haram: "If any man that is called a brother be a fornicator, or covetous, or an idolater, or a railer, or a drunkard, or an extortioner, with such a one, no-one should eat."

Next day at the close of the mass, Mr Hanna Boctor called out aloud to the officiating priest that he had an address which he wished to read to the congregation, and that the Bishop had given his consent.

"We know what you wish to read," the priest replied, in great indignation, "you wish to lower us in the eyes of the people, in order to lead them astray at your will. We know our duty without asking you to come and teach us."

Mr Hanna replied that if he did, perhaps others did not. "The paper I wish to read would do no harm to you or anyone else who wanted to lead a Christian life." Only two days ago people had been publicly reproved for the sin of reading the Bible. There was another sin of which a much greater number of them were guilty, the sin of drunkenness. "The paper which I hold in my hand exposes this sin, and I am resolved that it shall be read."

"It shall not be read," was the curt reply.

"Then you hold it is unlawful to read the Bible, and lawful to drink arrack."

"Yes, it is lawful to drink arrack," replied the priest.

A scene of indescribable confusion followed, some calling out one thing and some another. An attempt was made to read the paper, but not a word of it could be heard; and at length, seeing the uselessness of persisting in the attempt, Mr Hanna Boctor called out to his companions to come off with him to the mission house, "and leave Ephraim to his idols."

The priest then became thoroughly alarmed at the aspect of affairs. With Mr Hanna Boctor and Mr Wassif Khayatt at their head (two of the richest men in Assiout), the Protestant sect would become a power in the city. Something must be done. Several attempts were made to bring about a compromise, but Mr Hanna

[34]*Arrack* are spirits distilled from dates

Boctor stuck to the second condition mentioned above, and that was that a meeting be held in the church for the study of the Bible, to which all be invited to come if they wished.

"I am quite willing," he said one day to a deputation of the leading members of the laity, who called on him to try and bring him round.

"I am quite willing to allow you to decide for yourselves as to the propriety or impropriety of allowing the Protestants to attend our meetings, and I am prepared to abide by your decision. Let us invite Dr Hogg to any place you may fix upon, and ask him to read and explain a chapter of the Bible. If his expositions please you, invite him to our meetings. If it does not please you, I will not press my proposal."

"He will be with us," was their reply.

"No," said he, "the Gospel book will lay hold of you."

This negotiation failed. Hanna continued to attend all our meetings, and he never came alone. In their perplexity, a special messenger was sent to Cairo to inform the Patriarch of Mr Hanna Boctor's defection, and asking him to do whatever his wisdom might direct in the circumstances.

The Patriarch's reply was very different from what the priests had expected. Not a word of reference was made to the White Nile[35] or to the viceroy's wrath. The priests were blamed for having acted foolishly, and charged to try what they could do to win him back. He apostrophized his dear son, Hanna, and told him he never expected this of him, and concluded by beseeching him to beware of causing his weak brethren to offend, and bringing upon himself the woes mentioned in the Gospel.'

Before this letter arrived, Hanna had already joined the Protestant Church.

'But what of the carpenters? The haram of October 2nd had been mainly directed against them, and indeed they were mentioned in it by name. Their case was very different from Mr Hanna Boctor's. He, as the elder of two brothers whose parents were dead, and who had risen from poverty to the highest position in the town, was free to act as he chose.

Morcus and Athanasius had each a number of brothers and sisters older and younger than themselves, and three of their parents were still alive, and all their relatives were brought under the haram, as well as they. To complicate matters still more, there was a proposal of marriage between one of Morcus's brothers and a sister of Athanasius, and the wedding had been fixed to take place on the evening of the 4th of October. The Bishop was aware of this, for he had been asked to perform the ceremony and had intimated his willingness to do so at the time.

The priests saw the opportunity, and obliged the Bishop (who was a mere tool in their hands) to issue a second haram before the marriage would take place, and to state distinctly at the close of it that if any priest should venture to marry them until Morcus and Athanasius had recanted their errors and returned to the bosom of their Mother Church, he would be degraded from his holy office and reported to the Patriarch.

Morcus, who had previously invited us all to the marriage, and had consented, at my request, that it should take place on Saturday afternoon instead of Sabbath evening, did his utmost to persuade his parents and brothers to allow me to conduct the ceremony, and leave the priests to bite their fingers in impotent despair.

[35] An expression of punishment meted out by the State for being exiled to the Sudan.

His brothers were all willing, except the one most deeply interested, that is the bridegroom, but the old folks would not hear of it, and his father went off to the Bishop on Saturday morning, accompanied by Athanasius, the bride's brother, and several of the leading members of the Coptic sect, in order to settle matters, if possible.

Morcus followed them, determined in his mind that they should not bind him over to any course of conduct of which his conscience disapproved.

"You must give your solemn promise," said the Bishop to him, "that you will cease henceforth to frequent the meetings at the American mission house, otherwise the haram shall continue in force against you and all your relatives."

"Here is my answer," Morcus replied, with great spirit, while some of those present tried to prevent him from speaking. "Though your haram may be stretched from heaven to earth, I trample it under my feet. You have no right to prevent me from reading God's Word, nor from hearing it expounded by those who can explain it to me."'

## A compromise was arrived at.

'After a long fruitless discussion, it was decided that Priest Gabriel should be sent for from Tahta, a town about thirty miles south of Assiout, and that Athanasius should receive him into his house and listen to his instructions. The said Gabriel is a one-eyed monk of considerable mental acumen, who is regarded by the Copts of Upper Egypt as a very Solomon. Even Athanasius, up to the date of his visit, regarded him with great respect.

The priest Gabriel came after being sent for by the Bishop and took up his quarters at the house of Athanasius but after two or three weeks found his own faith wavering. Athanasius made several attempts to bring him to the mission house, but, failing in this, some of the brethren called repeatedly on him and spent the evening in long discussions with him, until they fairly drove him out of town.

And what of the marriage? Well, when Athanasius promised to place himself under priest Gabriel's instructions the Bishop felt inclined to yield the point, and gave a kind of half promise to perform the ceremony next Sabbath evening, on his return from marrying two other couples that were to be married on the same night.

On the strength of this promise preparations were proceeded with, and the bride was conducted to the house of the bridegroom. It became apparent, however, in the course of the day that the priests were resolved to prevent the Bishop from performing the ceremony, and when evening came they sent to the governor for a bodyguard to protect the Bishop from being seized by the carpenters and obliged to perform the ceremony by force.

As the hours of the night advanced and no Bishop appeared Morcus repeated his previous proposal that I should be sent for, but still the old people held out. At last, when it was near midnight and all hope had vanished, it was agreed upon by all that ex-priest Boctor, who, before he became a Protestant, had occupied nearly as high a position in the Coptic Church as the Bishop himself, should be asked to marry the forlorn pair. In twenty minutes they were one.

The Bishop, accompanied by the lay head of the Coptic Church at Assiout, called on the governor next morning and accused ex-priest Boctor of insubordination, but the governor pretended not to hear them, and turned the conversation to something else, thus giving them to understand that they must settle their ecclesiastical quarrels among themselves. An effort was made by the priests to induce the married pair to allow them to perform the ceremony over again, but it failed. Only one resource –

the inevitable haram – but this bugbear had lost its power in the family of the carpenters.'

This story shows how the members of the Coptic National Church were intimidated by their clergy. It took people with great courage and purpose to break away after years of tradition.

## A Steadfast Family and their Headstrong Son

As mentioned before, the American missionaries did not always have it all their way. One of the villages they found difficult to penetrate was Abnub, inhabited mostly by Copts. It was situated about twenty miles north-east of Assiout on the eastern bank of the Nile and to reach it you had to cross the river by boat. In the 1860s the Assiout barrage linking the west bank with the east bank of the river had not yet been built. One of the leading Coptic families living in Abnub was that of Raphael Fanous, grandfather of Akhnoukh, Esther's father. Raphael was a staunch member of the Coptic National Church, his grandfather having been a bishop. It is said that when Dr Hogg visited Abnub on one of his evangelisation trips, he was entertained by Raphael, as being the head of one of the main Christian families, but after lunch he left him to his own devices, and went off to have his afternoon nap, without giving any further help to Dr Hogg's mission.

His son Fanous married twice, his second wife named Mingida was second cousin to Wassif El Khayatt. She was a lady with a strong personality, and in spite of the fact that her cousin was a staunch convert to Protestantism, she did not encourage it in the family, even when years later Akhnoukh became a Protestant, and brought up all his children as Protestants.

The rest of the Fanous family remained staunch members of the Coptic National Church.

Akhnoukh was an intelligent, strong-willed and ambitious boy. Born in 1854, he was twelve when he asked his mother to send him to study at the American College in Beirut. He could not understand why his mother was so reluctant to send him, when his second cousin Bastawrous, the son of Wassif El Khayatt, had been sent there by his father.

Mingida did not want to be torn from her youngest son; she felt he was too young to leave the family fold, nor was she enthusiastic about what she heard of the new ideas of those foreign missionaries that her cousin Wassif was so fond of expounding. The only way to get to Beirut was to get onto a Cook's boat and travel down the Nile, and then continue by sea from Alexandria. The railway had not yet come to Upper Egypt. There were no visas or passports to worry about. If you could afford the price of your passage, you just had to get on a boat.

Mingida thought that her son was only being a copycat, and that if the Cook's boats did not call at Abnub for a couple of times, Akhnoukh would forget all about it. So she had it arranged that the Cook's boat should stop at Beni Mohamad, the adjoining village mainly inhabited by Moslems, instead of Abnub; but she did not take into account the obstinate nature of her son, who had arranged with his cousin to lend him the price of the tickets to Beirut, and prepared himself to leave. When he found that the Cook's boat did not stop at Abnub, and had stopped at Beni Mohamad, he got on his donkey and caught the boat at Beni Mohamad. Once Mingida saw that Akhnoukh was determined to study in Beirut, and that he had been encouraged by her cousin Wassif, who persuaded her that it was the best education her son could get, she became reconciled to the idea.

Akhnoukh graduated from the American College in Beirut; he was awarded an honorary doctorate, and became a very good and well-known lawyer, and was considered one of the best orators in the country. In 1882 when Akhnoukh was twenty-seven, he thought it was about time he got married. He had been converted to Protestantism by the American missionaries when at college in Beirut. He was modern in his ideas and outlook, when compared with other people in Assiout. The Fanouses had not yet intermarried with the Wissas. They lived in a village on the east bank of the Nile, whereas the Wissas lived in Assiout proper, the capital of Upper Egypt on the west bank.

Akhnoukh by then was a successful practising lawyer in Assiout, and had heard of Balsam, the eldest daughter of Wissa, who was ten years his junior. She had been sent to Dr Hogg and Miss Martha J. McKowan when they intimated to Wissa that they wanted to start a girls' school in Assiout in the mid-1860s. Balsam was one of the first three girls who joined the new school. Wissa had stipulated to Dr Hogg and Miss McKowan that he wanted his daughter to be brought up as a good Christian, able to read and write, but at the same time he wanted her to be able to look after a large house and family. Wissa was willing to help finance this project which he did. Akhnoukh was a good-looking young man, and a good talker, so it was not difficult for him to persuade Wissa to consider him as a suitable suitor for his daughter. His mother Mingida was a Khayatt – a cousin to Wassif El Khayatt and a good friend of Wissa's – and it only needed her to come officially and ask Wissa for his daughter's hand in marriage to her son for him to accept. The story of the arrival in Assiout of Mingida to ask Wissa for the hand of Balsam shows the mentality of the people at the time. Mingida arrived on the appointed day with her retinue by boat across the Nile from Abnub to Assiout. Wissa was waiting for his guest on the quay, with donkeys and liveried attendants, to take the party to the Wissa mansion, situated barely 200 yards away from the bank of the Nile. But when the boat arrived, and Mingida saw that the donkeys were from the Wissa stables, she would not get off the boat. Didn't her father, who was from the House of Khayatt, have as good a donkey as the Wissas? She insisted on sending for donkeys from her father's house, and waited until they came. She could not bear being transported to her son's future in-laws on any donkey other than those in her father's stables!

The El Khayatt family was reputed for the donkeys they bred. In Judge Jasper Brinton's book *The American Effort in Egypt*, he mentions that donkey riding seemed to have played a singularly large role as a contribution to physical fitness of the American Consul General Thomas Shelton Harrison 1897, for it appears as his daily exercise, across the English Bridge (Kasr El Nil) to El-Ghezireh Club and around the race course.

He mentions that the Consul General's diary was replete with such opening notes of the day's events as 'donkeyed as usual', where the writer in some cases descended to such details as the following:

'On March 25, I rode my donkey for the first time this morning, starting at 7.30 from the Agency. This donkey was sent down to me from Assiout as a present by the Consular Agent there, Bestauros W. Khayatt.

He sent two – a white and black; but I returned one of them, the black, being unwilling to accept them both. The white one is the best I have ever seen; he has a long, fine, and well bred looking neck, a sturdy body, and legs as clean as a whistle.

He is the only donkey that I ever rode that had a good mouth. He has been well bitted and is neck-wise. I had a delightful ride on him around Ghezireh Island ambling and trotting.'

The two families agreed that the wedding should take place in a year's time. The couple were officially engaged, but the custom was that they should not see each other except on special occasions, when both families would be gathered, until they were married. But Wissa was broad-minded he did not mind Akhnoukh coming to the house to court his daughter. Akhnoukh was always in Assiout as he practised there. He also started building his future house, which was not far from Wissa's. Balsam became daily more enamoured of her handsome suitor.

As usual in small towns people gossiped, and Wissa's neighbours the Elias Ballashes criticised this behaviour to all who would listen. This soon came to the ears of Wissa and his would-be son-in-law. They both decided to give the people of Assiout something to talk about. Akhnoukh took Balsam next day on horseback through the town and market. Subsequently, they went riding together most days. It was unheard of at that time, but people soon got used to it. The couple were married in 1883 and it was a splendid affair as most oriental marriages are. They had fourteen children of whom ten survived to adulthood. Esther was the seventh child. Before she was born her father dreamt of an old man who came to him, and told him that his wife Balsam would bear him a daughter, and that he should name her either Fatma or Esther. He wanted a daughter two older daughters had died as babies. So when Balsam was delivered of a baby girl, they named her Esther, as Fatma was a name only used in Egypt by Moslems. Esther interpreted this dream as meaning that she was destined to try to unite the Jewish, Christian and Moslem faiths.

Just when the American missionaries reached the conclusion that Assiout in Upper Egypt was a strategic centre to be occupied in enhancing their mission, is hard to determine. But certainly when Dr Hogg was appointed in Assiout the movement received a big push.

The Evangelists were opposed by practically the whole Coptic nation in the big cities, and their converts were mostly in the villages, especially in Upper Egypt. Even there, members of one family were divided. It was easier to get to the masses through the women who were thirsty for knowledge and felt it was a way towards emancipation, especially if they were able to go to the American Mission schools. Most men went to government schools and they were not greatly influenced, except through their women-folk.

It was more difficult to get to the older women, who had not been influenced by the Americans. They could not really believe in the newfangled ideas and forget their old habits, beliefs and superstitions. The following story demonstrates the above ideas.

Hanna Wissa was an ardent Protestant, had been convicted and pardoned for Iconoclasm and had all his children baptised as Protestants. His wife Firdous, who loved her husband very much and according to custom should never have thought of disobeying him, nevertheless took her youngest son, Fahmy, my father, as a baby and had him re-baptised in the Coptic Orthodox Church. My father always considered himself Orthodox in spite of his wife, Esther, being Protestant. He never interfered in the religious upbringing of his children. When he got married he was married by both churches, as can be seen in the description of the wedding.

The opposition of the Copts in the towns, who were in a position to be near the leaders of the Coptic Church, can be seen from a statement made in a book by Gallini Pasha Fahmy, a notable of Minieh who dedicated it to his Majesty, King Fouad I, recounting his recollections of the reigns of the Khedives Ismail, Tewfik and Abbas II. He says under a heading: *The Copts of Minieh and the American Missions*:

'It was under the reign of Khedive Ismail that the American missionaries first made their appearance. They went round the country trying to convert the Copts of the National Church to Protestantism. They were successful in converting two notable families in Assiout: the Wissas and the Khayatts. These were the first of the Coptic families who abandoned the Coptic Orthodox Church to embrace Protestantism.

The American missionaries next came to Minieh. At the time, the Orthodox Copts had a great respect for my grandfather, Youssef Abdel Chedid Bey. He advised them not to go to the meetings organised by the missionaries.

The missionaries – at whose head was Doctor Hogg – were very annoyed and complained of my grandfather to the Consul General of the United States in Cairo, who transmitted the complaint to the Ministry of Foreign Affairs, who in turn conveyed the grievance to the Ministry of the Interior, who then sent all the papers to the Mudir (governor) of Minieh to investigate the matter. The Mudir called my grandfather and asked him what the whole story was about. Abdel Chedid Bey replied: "The matter is very simple – these missionaries came and asked us to abandon our religion and embrace theirs, which we refused to do. They then complained that we remained faithful to our religion. If the Government wants us to help the foreigners in their task in trying to make us change our religion to theirs, they might as well tell us so openly, in order that we can know what we are up against."

When the Khedive heard of my grandfather's reply he was very pleased, he asked to see him, congratulated him and accorded him a decoration which was greatly appreciated at the time.

The Khedive Ismail was very discontented with American Missionaries' doings. He used to get very annoyed when he heard that an Orthodox Copt had changed his religion to Protestantism.

To combat the actions of the missionaries he suggested that the Anba Demetrius, Patriarch of the Copts, should make a tour of Upper Egypt. He put at his disposal one of his boats, with all its staff, and ordered all governors of the provinces to be at the orders of the Patriarch.

The honours that the Patriarch received, the enthusiasm and respect that was offered him was a great set-back for the American Missionaries' mission, that of converting Orthodox Copts to Protestantism, which was a way in turning the Egyptian from his nationality to that of the American. All the merit for this opposition to the American Missionaries lies at the feet of the Khedive Ismail.'[36]

One can sense from the above memoirs the strength of feeling against the missionaries by the Copts in power. The appointment of John Hogg and Miss McKowan to the Assiout Mission in Upper Egypt, where the Coptic Community was particularly strong was considered an affront to the Coptic Church. Although Mr Hogg attended part of the services in the Coptic Churches, he invariably left before the celebration of the Mass. The clergy did not appreciate the fact that Mr Hogg, at the afternoon meetings which were held in the mission schoolroom, made the basis of his sermons the Scripture lesson, used in the Coptic Church, whereas Mr Hogg considered it as a complement.

In his tour of Upper Egypt the Coptic Patriarch on his arrival at Assiout ordered the flogging of a Coptic priest from a nearby village who had permitted his brother, a Protestant, to conduct Evangelist services in his church. Following his humiliation the priest was degraded from his office and driven out. The Patriarch did not dare to offend Mr Wassif Khayatt, who had openly espoused the Protestant cause, since he was a prominent member of the community and wielded considerable influence. Furthermore, Mr Wassif Khayatt was American consular agent in Assiout. The

[36]*Memoirs* by Gallini Pasha Fahmy

Coptic Patriarch could not do much to hinder the infant Evangelical Church except to threaten and excommunicate any Copts who dared to attend the services.

The Patriarch thought he could ruin the schools – the Wissas' boys' school, the Khayatts' girls' school and the newly founded seminary – by issuing bulls of denunciation against any who would support them. This he proceeded to do.

With the acquiescence of the Khedive and the help of the government officials, the clergy tried to browbeat the parents and get them to withdraw their children from the schools. For a time it succeeded, but it did not last long. Other matters came to the front in Egypt: the opening of the Suez Canal, the rise in the Khedive's reputation when as late as 1876, on the eve of the crash, Egypt was described by the Cairo correspondent of *The Times* as a marvellous instance of progress. The abolition of slavery, in which the missionaries played a part, the financial difficulties the country and the Khedive got into with the result that 'never again did the Egyptian government take such decided action in favour of the Copts against the Protestants', though there is no doubt that it continued to prefer the principles and practices of the former to those of the latter.[37]

### Market Day

One marked effect of the spread of Scriptural Christianity was the successful effort to bring about a change in the time of the weekly market at Assiout from the first day of the week to the seventh.

For some 1800 years Sunday had been the day when people from surrounding villages and countryside came with their camels, cattle, donkeys, sheep and goats for sale. It was the time for buying supplies of vegetables, cereals, cheese, butter, fat and other foodstuffs. Itinerant merchants with cloth of different descriptions and manufactured articles of many kinds all came to the market. People laid in supplies for weeks. In short, for merchants large and small in Assiout it was the great trading day of the week.

For a community that was beginning to take Sunday seriously as a day devoted to worship and good works, it became imperative that the market day should be changed to some other time. A petition, sponsored by such leading men as Mr Wissa and Mr Khayatt, was signed by many Moslems as well as many Copts in favour of the change. When the government agreed to the change, the common people believed this was another evidence of the zeal of the reformers. They are reported to have said 'What will these Protestants do next?' They have actually changed Sunday

---

[37] *Vindicating a Vision* by Earl E. Elder

(market) into Saturday (market). Other market days changed from Sunday to other days in the week in different parts of the country, and the Protestant missionaries said that through their prayers 'The Sabbath market was abolished.'[38]

[38] *Vindicating a Vision* by Earl E. Elder

## The Iconoclasts

Cyril the Reformer, when he succeeded Peter in 1854 as Patriarch to the Coptic National Church, saw the decadence into which the Church had fallen. The Copts of Cyril's time were inclined to pay the same kind of excessive veneration to their sacred pictures as the members of the Greek Church. There was no evidence in times past of any tendency to picture-worship by the Copts. As Cyril was building a new cathedral, he felt that his people might fall into idolatry in the worship of sacred pictures, and therefore decided that none should be put up in his new cathedral. He collected all those which had furnished the old building, and burnt them solemnly in the presence of an immense crowd. He made them an address on the occasion explaining his action, and ended, as he pointed to the burning pile:

'Behold these wooden pictures you used to honour and even worship! They can neither avail you or harm you. God alone should be adored.'[39]

I am mentioning Cyril IV's action because of a similar event in my grandfather's life which caused an uproar in the country at the time. It was in 1870, as recounted in the family. A few years after he had been converted to Protestantism by the American missionaries, he and a few friends, because of excess zeal, went in to the Coptic National Church one night, took out the icons and had them burnt. Next day, crowds went round the town shouting, *Hanna Wissa, Harak El Kanissa* which meant 'Hanna Wissa has burnt the church.'

He was condemned to exile and imprisonment, and was put on a boat to the Sudan, but received a pardon from the Khedive by the time he arrived at Esna due to the intercession at the request of the missionaries of Bamba, the Maharani of Punjab, who had been appointed Lady in Waiting to Queen Victoria as Empress of India. His wife had had in the meantime a baby girl, and he called her Nouzha meaning a 'pleasant promenade'. I will give you the exact wording written in a book called *A Master Builder on the Nile*, a record of the life and aims of John Hogg, D.D. Christian missionary, by his daughter Renah Hogg of the American (United Presbyterian) Mission in Egypt.

She says:

'King Edward VII, then Prince of Wales, was wintering on the Nile and the Royal party spent a few hours at Assiout. They expressed great pleasure at what they had seen of the missionary's work and the tone of the Princess's voice when she remarked

---

[39] *The Story of the Church of Egypt* by E.L. Butcher

that the missionary 'Mr Hogg' was Scottish won his heart at once as betokening a warm affection for Auld Scotia's children.'

She continues:

'But adversity was now at hand and discredit was soon to fall on the cause thus publicly honoured. In the house of Mr Hanna Wissa, the missionary's "new friend", a few kindred spirits sat late one evening reading their favourite Book. "And the Lord said unto Gideon, Throw down the altar of Baal that thy father hath, and cut down the grove that is by it. And it came to pass, because he feared his father's household and the men of the city so that he could not do it by day, that he did by night." Judges 6 v 25.

Near at hand on the walls of an ancient church, hung the "Grove" of their race (the pictures of saints before which the people, the intercessors, bowed in prayer). Was Gideon's call not their call? Why not go at once, while their hearts were hot, and purify their Church's worship from its idolatry? They prayed earnestly for God's blessing, and stole out into the silent street. Tanassa's (Athanassius) house adjoined the church and from its roof, entrance to the building was easy. In his absence his brothers helped the conspirators. The task was triumphantly accomplished, and again joining in prayer, the devoted band returned exultant to their homes.

But Old Testament stories may prove dangerous precedents, and actions that seem parallel lead to divergent issues, as the sequel proved.

The Coptic Church was filled next morning by a wailing and excited people. Dismay, fear, and rage were inextricably mingled. Under threat of excommunication, the whole sect was summoned to appear, and marched in a body to the Governor to demand redress. Investigation soon led to discovery, the names of the culprits being revealed by Tanassa's brother while under the lash. When brought to book the men surprised their accusers by making no denial, telling frankly their story and claiming God's warrant in the Bible. The Copts were exasperated at being exposed, and the Moslems were amazed by a glimpse of a new Christianity and the discovery that the Protestant's Bible forbade idolatry. "Truly," they exclaimed, "this is the Book of God." The eight men were sent to prison to await judgement on their case.

Perhaps only to a resident in Egypt can the full force of the cataclysm be immediately apparent, There the names involved and the interests at stake explain at once the tumultuous excitement it awakened. The Coptic clergy saw in the event the finger of God. The name of Hanna Wissa had become hateful to them, and God had delivered their enemy into their hands.

The Governor granted Mr Hanna Wissa's brother twenty-four hours in which to conciliate his foes, but they were as deaf to appeals as an angry sea, and, like the chief priests of old, "stirred up the people," two thousand of whom invaded the Governor's presence to demand the full satisfaction of the law. As punishment was deserved, no effort was made to secure consular help, and when peace measures failed, Mr Hogg awaited with his friends in unceasing prayer the execution of justice, cheering meanwhile the poor men whose exultation had evaporated, and turning the prison into a schoolhouse where all who entered learnt without effort and without charge lessons that they could not soon forget.

A week later the Moslem feast of Fida dawned, and Assiout was electrified by a telegram from the Khedive granting the culprits free pardon. Moslems joined with Protestants in their rejoicing, about 200 of them being present among the hundreds who gathered in the court of Mr Wissa's house to welcome the prisoner home. A thanksgiving service was held, and the missionary sought to make the most of a grand opportunity and preached a sermon on the importance of breaking idols in their own hearts and to seek henceforth, to win them brothers by works and deeds of love.'

However, the inexplicably speedy release was followed by a further charge of robbery. This may have come about because the Patriarch was moved to action by the threats of the Coptic Bishop of Assiout and others that they would desert to the Catholic Church, or to abandon Assiout because of the offence to the honour of the Church.

Investigations were re-opened by Sherif Pasha whilst the Khedive was away in Europe, and the culprits received sentences of one, two, and three years' imprisonment in the South, and were fined $1750 to replace property, for the theft of which, no evidence was produced.'

The case dragged on for some time awaiting the return of the Viceroy. Finally, on August 10th, after the men had served a month of hard labour at Esna, in addition to the time of incarceration in Assiout, they were released. Miss Rena Hogg concludes the story as follows:

'Great rejoicing awaited them in Assiout. Over a thousand Copts and Moslems visited the chief culprit on the day of his return. Their long trial had not been wholly in vain. Protestants had gained from it a firmer grip on the great realities of their faith. Interest had quickened among the Copts, and throughout the length of Egypt Moslems had learnt that Scriptural Christianity is a purer faith than they had yet imagined.'[40]

[40]No mention of the Maharani of Punjab's (Bamba's) intercession with Queen Victoria on Hanna's behalf can be found in any of the American missionary's books that I have read. Although plausible it might be a good story made up by someone in the family.

Assiout, where General Ulysses S. Grant and party dined at Wassif el Khayatt's home on 19th January 1978 as recounted by John Russell Young: *Around the World with General Grant.* Extract of signatures from American Consulate, Assiout, Visitors Book for 1875–1879

## Men of Influence, and the Visit of Ulysses Grant to Assiout. The Wassif Khayatt Girls' School, the Building of the First Protestant Church in Assiout, and the Start of the Wissa Boys' School

The early 1870s saw a marked development in the spread of Evangelical teaching in Upper Egypt. Although the commanding figure of Dr Hogg and his associates continued to exercise their influence, the centre shifted to Egyptian leadership just as their strategy had been planned. Three congregations were organised in the Assiout district in 1870 at Nikhaila and Mutia the next year. All through the stirring days of early witnessing and resultant persecution, Hogg was sure of the loyal support from Wassif Khayatt, Wissa Wissa and his brother Hanna Wissa.

Wassif Khayatt, a man of considerable wealth, had united with the church in Cairo previous to the sending of missionaries to reside in Assiout. This fact was not widely known at the time, but on the occasion of the Patriarch's visit to Assiout in 1867 he seemingly was the only one in Assiout who openly identified himself with Protestantism. Because of his position as the American Consular Agent in Assiout and his wealth, he was only upbraided by the Patriarch for having adopted the foreigners' religion, but was not subjected to threats and persecution.

Reports of the Board of Foreign Missions from 1865 to 1882 (Wassif Khayatt died in 1881) repeatedly speak of his liberal contributions, his share in establishing the Church in Assiout, his assuming all the expenses of the day school for girls, at the time when the mission established the girls' boarding school, and his unobtrusive humility. One reference, in a statement by Dr David R Johnston dated February 1st, 1875, reveals the great service he gave the mission. 'For the past 10 years he has cashed all our orders, on the general treasury, often at a loss and inconvenience to his business, thus advancing all the money that was used for the mission work in Upper Egypt.'

It may be interesting to the reader to have some idea of Assiout and its inhabitants at the time we are writing about. The following is the description of the dinner party given by Wassif Khayatt for General Ulysses S. Grant, an American Civil War hero, and future president, when he was visiting Assiout in the third quarter of the last century, the time about which this writing is concerned.

The following is taken from the book *Around the World with General Grant* by John Russell Young:

*The Nile*

On the morning of the 19th of January, that being the third day of our journey, we came to the town of Siout, or Assiout, as some call it. We have a vice-consul here,

Wassif Khayatt and his Son Bistawrous Khayatt

School Buildings

and tokens of our coming had been sent, as could be seen by the flags which decorated the bank and the crowds on the shore. Siout is the capital of Upper Egypt, and is a city of 25,000 inhabitants. The city is some distance back from the river, and grew into importance as the depot of much of the caravan trade from Darfour.

Upon arriving, the vice-consul and his son came on board and were presented to the General. Congratulations were exchanged, and we offered our friends coffee and cigars in the true Oriental style. The name of our consul here is Wassif Khayatt. He is a Copt and a landed proprietor. He is a grave elderly person, who speaks only Arabic, but his son had been educated in Beyrouth, at the mission school, and knew English. We all drove to the town. It was over parched fields, through a country that in more favourable years would bloom like a garden. But the Nile is bad this year, and a bad Nile is a calamity second only to a famine in Egypt. We rode into the town and through the bazaars. All the town seemed to know of our coming, for wherever we went crowds swarmed around us, and we had to force our donkeys through masses of Arabs and Egyptians of all ages and conditions, some almost naked – crowds crying for baksheesh or pressing articles of merchandise upon us.

The bazaars are narrow covered ways, covered with matting or loose boards, enough to break the force of the sun. The stores are little cubbyholes of rooms, in front of which the trader sits and calls upon you to buy. As these avenues are not more than six feet wide at best, you can imagine what a time we had in making our progress.

The town had some fine houses and mosques, but in the main it was like all towns in Upper Egypt, a collection of mud hovels. We rode beyond the town to the tombs built in the sand, and climbed the limestone rock on our donkeys. This was our first evidence of the manner of sepulchre in the olden time. These desert rocks of limestone were tunnelled and made into rooms, and here the mummified dead found rest. The chambers appointed for them were large and spacious, according to the means of the deceased. In some that we entered there was a chamber, an antechamber, and sometimes connecting chambers. There were inscriptions on the walls, but they had been defaced in their way. The ceilings of the tombs had been once decorated, but modern Christians have deemed it their duty to deface them by firing pistol shots. When you visit a tomb and note the blue stars and astronomical forms that the ancients painted with so much care, it is tempting to try the echo by firing your pistol. Consequently the roofs are spotted with bullet marks.

Here also came the wanderers for shelter, and you see what the fires have done. What the tombs may have been in the past, when they came fresh from pious, loving hands, you can imagine. But what with ancient Christian iconoclasts, modern Christian wanderers, Bedouins, Arabs searching the grave for ornaments, nothing remains but empty limestone rooms filling with sand and a few hieroglyphic memorials on the walls. We were bidden to an entertainment at the home of Wassif Khayatt, and seven being the hour, we set forth. We were all anxious about our first Arab[41] entertainment, and after some deliberation our naval men concluded to wear their uniforms. The Doctor rode ahead in the carriage with General and Mrs Grant and the consul general. As the Doctor wore his uniform and the others were in plain dress, he was welcomed by the awestricken Moslems as the King of America. Hadden and the rest of us rode behind on our trusty and well-beloved donkeys, Hadden in uniform, followed by wondering crowds. I suppose he was taken for a minor potentate, as in the Oriental eyes all that lace and gold could not be wasted on anything less than prin-

[41]There are no Arab Copts in Egypt. Mr Young should have used the word Copt or Egyptian.

115

cely rank. But we all had more or less attention, although we could feel that the uniforms were the centre of glory, and that we shone with borrowed splendour. As we came to the house of Wassif el Khayatt we found a real transformation scene. Lanterns lined the street, servants stood on the road holding blazing torches, a transparency was over the gate with the words, *WELCOME GENERAL GRANT.* The 'N' was turned upside down, but that made no difference, for the welcome here in far Africa made the heart throb quicker. As we rode up, torches blazed, rockets went up into the air, various coloured lights were burned, and we passed into the courtyard glowing with light and colour, passing into the house over carpets and rugs of heavy texture and gorgeous pattern.

Our host met us at the gates of his house, and welcomed us in the stately Oriental way, kissing the General's hand as he clasped it in his two hands, and then touching his own heart, lips, and brow. Here we met the governor, and, more welcome still, the Rev. I.R. Alexander and his wife. Mr Alexander is one of the professors in the missionary college, and is under the direction of the United Presbyterian Church. The dinner came, and it was regal in its profusion and splendour. I should say there were at least twenty courses, all well served. When it was concluded the son of the host arose, and in remarkably clear and correct English proposed the General's health.

You will allow me, I am sure, to give you a fragment of this speech. "Long have we heard and wondered," said the speaker, "at the strange progress which America has made during this past century, by which she has taken the first position among the most widely civilized nations. She has so quickly improved in sciences, morals, and arts, that the world stands amazed at this extraordinary progress which surpasses the swiftness of light. It is the hard work of her great and wise men that all this advance is imputed, those who have shown to the world what wise, courageous, patriotic men can do. Let all the world look to America and follow her example – that nation which has taken as the basis of her laws and the object of her undertakings to maintain freedom and equality among her own people and secure them for others, avoiding all ambitious schemes which would draw her into bloody and disastrous wars, and trying by all means to maintain peace internally and externally. The only two great wars upon which she has engaged were entered upon for pure and just purposes – the first for releasing herself from the English yoke, and erecting her independence, and the other for stopping slavery and strengthening the union of the States; and well we know that it was mainly under God due to the talent, courage, and wisdom of His Excellency General Grant that the latter of the two enterprises was brought to a successful issue."

The speech closed by a tribute to the general and the Khedive. General Grant said in response that nothing in his whole trip had so impressed him as this unexpected, and generous welcome in the heart of Egypt. He had anticipated great pleasure in his visit to Egypt, and the anticipation had been more than realised. He thanked his host, and especially the young man who had spoken of him with such high praise, for this reception.

The dinner ended with coffee, conversation and cigars. Mrs Grant had a long talk with Mrs Alexander about home – Mrs Alexander being a fair young bride who had come out from America to cast her lot with her husband in the unpromising vineyard of Assiout, and when the evening grew on we rode back to our boat, through the night and over the plain. Torch-bearers accompanied us through the town. Donkey-boys and townspeople followed us to the riverbank. The moon was shining, and as we rode home – you see we already call the boat our home – we talked over the pleasant surprise we had found in Assiout and of its many strange phases of oriental life.'

## The Wassif el Khayatt Girls' School

This was founded and built in the late 1860s by Wassif el Khayatt, in part of one of his gardens. His son, Bistawrous enlarged it in the early 1900s he also entailed enough agricultural land to cover its expenses. His daughter Amina, widow of Nassif Bey Wissa, further enlarged it with the help of her sister Wadia, wife of Alfred Bey Wissa, and the heirs of her deceased brother Amin Bey Khayatt in the late 1940s and early 1950s. In the 1960s, when it was decided to nationalise all private schools, Amina asked the authorities to allow her to retain the school until her death, at her own expense bearing all the costs. She did not want to see any of the staff uprooted whilst she was alive. Her request was accepted and she kept the school for a few years until her death, selling much of her belongings and jewellery in the process. After her death it was officially taken over by the Ministry of Education.

## Building of First Church

Wissa Boctor and his brother Hanna also shared in many ways the establishing of the church in Assiout. Beyond what has already been mentioned, this family assumed responsibility for the boys' school in Assiout, much the same as Wassif Khayatt had done for the girls' school. They initiated a church building project on the west side of the town which began on November 29th, 1869, assuming full responsibility.[42] This project was terminated on March 6th, 1870 and was considered the nucleus of the first Protestant Church in Assiout.

However in September 1896 the church's elders presented a demand to the Ministry of the Interior asking to be allowed to build a larger church than that built in 1870, and on November 8th, 1896 they received the following letter:

> 'To the honourable Mr. Hanna Boctor Wissa, following your request and those of your companions to build a church for the Protestant sect in a piece of land belonging to you and your brother Wissa in your garden planted with palm trees situated North of the town, we have pleasure to inform you that a high ministerial order dated the 15th Gamad el Awal 1314 Hegira the 22nd October 1896 under permit number 15, allows you to build a church in the above piece of land.
>
> Therefore the Modireya is advising you and your companions of the above, under advice number 1742 dated the 29th October 1896.'

The church was built and started working in 1899 and was considered as the first Protestant Church in Assiout.

---

[42] *Vindicating a Vision* by Earl E. Elder

A Khediveal decree issued in 1896 permitted the Wissa brothers to build a church in part of their gardens. The church was built and in use in 1899. It is known as the First Protestant Church in Assiout, in replacement of a small building donated by the Wissa brothers in 1870 and used as a church until this date.

The Wissa Boys' School, Assiout – 1933

118

In 1870 the Wissa brothers founded a school for boys, very much the same as the Wassif el Khayatt's school for girls.

When in 1898 they inaugurated the first Protestant church in a garden owned by them, the Wissa brothers decided to rebuild and enlarge the school. This was terminated in the early 1900s and inaugurated by the Khedive Abbas Helmi II. A marble monument to that effect was placed on the stairway. The school was a masterpiece of advanced structural engineering and beautiful design. The plans were drawn and the school constructed by British engineers. Many people called it 'The Castle' because they thought it looked like one. It was built on four acres of the garden in which the church was built, and enjoyed a motor driveway and full sized soccer field. I do not know the names of the first principals who ran the school, but the late Mr Aziz Abas was chosen to take over the duties and management in the year 1932. He was a graduate of the American College, Assiout and Cairo University. He was God-fearing, a non-smoker and tee-totaller, and respected, appreciated and trusted for his academic as well as his moral character. He was a dedicated principal of the school until his untimely and sad death on January 9th, 1963.

The following details and pictures have been supplied by Mr Momtaz Abas CPA, who lives in Beverly Hills, California. His mother and family emigrated to the USA after the death of his father. He states that the school day started with the raising of the flag and salute. Then the students and staff would go to the chapel and sing hymns to the sounds of a piano, when his father would give a short sermon. Simultaneously the qualified Arabic language teacher would minister to the Moslem students in a separate class and teach them the Koran.

The school was built on two storeys, part of the ground floor was for the junior and elementary classes, the rest for a cafeteria and hobbies such as music, drawing, making nets, carpentry, etc. The upper level was for secondary classes and comprised the school administration's office, a large library, and fully equipped chemistry and biology laboratories. There was a separate building for boarding students. The buildings comprised over 100 rooms for classes, conference rooms, etc.

*Music.* One of the main hobbies was music. There were three separate bands, the largest was for copper instruments with approximately a thirty-piece band. The band enriched the students with its music each Wednesday during recess, and when the sports teams competed against other schools. This band was also hired out by the school for funerals and weddings.

The second band was for string instruments where the violin, mandolin and oude were taught. The third band was Scots inspired and taught the bagpipes and horn.

THE WISSA SCHOOL TEACHING STAFF
Aziz Abas (Principal)
Sheikh teaching Arabic and Koran          Sheikh teaching Arabic and Koran

THE WISSA SCHOOL BRASS BAND
with Teacher and Aziz Abas, Principal

120

*Sports.* The school was in constant competition for first place in soccer, basketball, volleyball, boxing and gymnastics.

*Facilities.* Full time workers were employed as carpenters for the production of students' desks and chairs, printers, plumbers, electricians, armed security guards, cleaning staff and gardeners – a hydraulic machine was used to water the soccer field.

Mr Abas established a new section for those students who wanted tuition in bookkeeping, typing and basic accounting in order to supply the ever-growing banking and commercial needs. Approximately 100 typewriters were in the lab for both English and Arabic touch-typing students. Adding machines and cash registers were also available for student training. Many graduates of the Wissa school were employed all over the country in government and private establishments.

Evening extension education, crash studies for higher school diplomas were started at the time in secondary schools in Cairo. The Wissa School was the only school in Upper Egypt that had such classes.

But with the advent of the 1952 Revolution there was a great change in the system of education and government intervention, which was to the detriment of the school, and led to its final closure and erasement in 1964.

In the first place new government rules stated that the third year secondary classes should be divided into three: Science, Arts and Maths, previously it was Science and Arts – Maths was part of Science. The Wissa School had only the first two specialities, hence those students who wanted to specialise in Maths had to enrol elsewhere. Furthermore schools were forbidden to comprise elementary and high schools in one building, even though a complete structural division was established. In 1960 the Governor of Assiout wanted the upper level of the school for a nurses' technical school, since it could not be used as a secondary school. And although the principal was trying to have the order rescinded, the Governor of Assiout at the time stated he had given the law a holiday, and demanded that the Wissa family should donate the land to the government. As most of the older members of the family were either too old or too worried or not available at the time, my brother-in-law for the Wissa branch, and I for the Hanna branch, signed that we agreed to 'donate' the land. It was no use at the time to protest, the Governor had already laid hands on the school and workmen were removing walls between classes on the ground floor. On January 9th, 1963 at 8 a.m. a section of the building collapsed onto the ground floor. The late Mr Aziz Abas, the principal, and one of his servants were buried and died under the rubble of the demolished walls. The government then decided to raze the buildings.

Other individuals in other provinces sacrificed their time and money in supporting the cause of Protestantism. At Sanabu, thirty-five miles north of Assiout, Mr Mikhail Faltas not only established a school for boys and another for girls, but for a time conducted an orphanage.

One of the weaknesses of the Protestant movement in Egypt was that there were many different Protestant missions trying to do the same thing. They stepped on each other's toes and there were sometimes petty misunderstandings among themselves. It was worse among the converted Copts who were supposed to carry the torch. Petty squabbles, arguments and the splitting of hairs have always been our nation's weakness; they were not helped much by the inflow of missionaries trying to increase their flock.

The missionaries could not understand why the Coptic national priests were so much against Protestantism. One of the main reasons for this attitude as with most people, was dictated by self-interest and the desire for survival.

We can glean an inkling of the above from what was mentioned in a report to the board of the missionary movement when it recounted how in 1866 the Bishop of Assiout was rebuffed in the course of his annual visit to Mutia, where the men who were the nucleus of a Protestant movement refused to give their annual donation of grain to the church under the pretext that they did not wish to support idolatry.

An echo of such a cause for schism came to the writer of the book *Vindicating a Vision* more than eighty years later when a Coptic priest told him that, 'There would be no conflict with the Protestant-Evangelists if the people would continue to give the Coptic priest their annual contribution of grain.' In the long run the movement was beneficial to the country and the Church of Egypt in general. It brought a breath of fresh air and got the Coptic Orthodox Church out of its centuries-old rut, made it more outspoken and fearless, helped to educate and emancipate the Coptic women and developed a competitive spirit among the different churches.

However, the Patriarch and the higher clergy of the Coptic Church still remained adamant in their unrelenting opposition to the Protestants. But it is interesting to note that a Coptic bishop told Mr Theodore Roosevelt when he was visiting Egypt, 'The American Mission has done a great deal of work for Egypt; for it has taught us to read our Bibles.'[43]


*The Family During the 1890s: Wissa's Abduction or Forced Invitation, and his Death in 1906*

It was in 1897 that Hanna, Wissa, and Akhnoukh got together and decided that Fahmy, youngest son of Hanna, Zaki, youngest son of Wissa, and Louis, first-born of Akhnoukh, should complete their studies abroad. They

---

[43] *Vindicating a Vision* by Earl E. Elder

Fahmy Wissa as a young student at Oxford

Oxford 1902

Hertford College, Oxford – 1902

124

The Study, Oxford

Egyptian Students at Oxford, 1902
Back Row, left to right: Fahmy H. Wissa, William Makram Ebeld, unknown.
Seated, left to right: Louis A. Fanous, Arabic teacher at Oxford, Ragheb Hanna

Fahmy Wissa with tutor and family out for a drive (Oxford)

Fahmy Wissa with tutor and family and other students

126

Fahmy Wissa out riding with a young lady at Oxford

Outings

were all about the same age having been born in 1885. They were all sent to the American School at Beyrouth, then to Oxford in 1902. For the first year at Oxford, they lodged at their respective tutors' homes cramming to get into college.

Zaki had to go back after a year, as he had been recalled by his elder brother George, announcing that Wissa had suffered a stroke, and was demanding to see his youngest son before he died. Fahmy was able to enter Hertford College where he spent five years playing sports, and seemingly, from the photographs he took, having a good time.

Louis Akhnoukh Fanous was the eldest of Akhnoukh Fanous's fourteen children, and was spoilt by his parents. He was a brilliant scholar, was sent to the American College in Beyrouth, and then went to Oxford where he obtained a first at New College in Political Economy. When he came back to Egypt, he thought that no job was good enough for him, unless it was that of a cabinet minister. In spite of being brilliant and having a great career, he just missed out, due to his character. Most people found him difficult to get on with, due to his overbearing manner. He talked down to people and believed he was more knowledgeable than anyone else, treating everyone as schoolboys. The Wafdist Committee in Assiout disliked Louis because of his manner (see letter in Appendix 3), and when the Wafd refused to nominate him as a candidate representing the Party in Assiout, he put himself up for election as an independent, and won the seat with a resounding majority. Once elected to the Senate, he was able to retain his seat until 1952 in which year parliament was dissolved. During his tenure he became a Wafdist Senator, but always with independent views. He was an eccentric member, would never stop talking. Once all the members in the House left, and he remained alone with the Speaker, who told him, 'I agree with everything you say Louis, but let's go home.'

Louis answered, 'I am not talking to you, I am talking to the nation, and I insist that my words should be registered in the minutes.'

Another time a vote was passed to remove him forcibly from the chamber, when the Speaker had guillotined the discussion, and he remonstrated vehemently, and had become objectionable to all who advocated reason. Father tried to remonstrate with him on this occasion, but he pushed him aside. Father said nothing more. He just left the chamber; he did not want to be present when his brother-in-law was being chucked out.

In the 1930s he took a case against the Suez Canal Company, which lasted for years and which he lost, because he believed that the company should pay their dividends in gold, and that their price should be quoted in gold. They had stopped payment in gold when the world went off the gold standard. He based his argument on the articles of foundation of the Suez Canal Company. He would rush into an argument or fight where angels feared to tread. He also used to chew each mouthful fifty-two times, believ-

128

ing it was good for the digestion, and wanted everyone to do the same. One day he threw the sardines I was eating out of the window, as he insisted tinned food was bad for our health. As children we thought him a great bore when he turned up. He was always trying to boss us. Although an eccentric he was brilliant in many ways, but he would never take no for an answer. When I call Esther a Fighting Soul, I call her brother Louis, a Pedantic Fighter.

There were other Copts at Oxford at the time. William Makram Ebeid, who was better known later as Makram Ebeid, became a secretary of the Wafd and Minister of Finance. He was exiled to the Seychelles with Saad Zaghloul. He later founded his own party, the Kotla, after falling out with the Wafd. Ragheb Hanna, a landowner, became a senator. I don't know where or when Fahmy became a freemason, but he belonged to a British lodge when he was at Oxford as can be seen from the photographs which I found among his belongings. I mention this because freemasonry played a big part in his life.

Wissa had been ailing for several years; his wife, Angelina, had died in 1895. She adored her youngest son Zaki, but was intimidated by her eldest son George, as were most of the family, because of his domineering nature. The death of Angelina was one of the reasons that decided Wissa on sending Zaki abroad to complete his education.

During this period George had become Wissa's right hand in running the business. Since the properties of the Wissa brothers had been divided, Hanna did not always participate in Wissa's new purchases or projects, as he had done in the past, though he still managed the land for both of them. The Wissa branch of the family have always reproached the Hanna branch for being too conservative and trying to hold Wissa back from some of his bolder ideas. They reproached him for inducing Wissa to change his mind in favour of buying 14,000 acres of agricultural land in the Fayoum, instead of desert land on the outskirts of Cairo – which later became the Garden City – prime building land.

Enough digression and back to our story. In 1903 Wissa was negotiating to buy several blocks of buildings in Cairo, in the new smart quarter called Tewfikieh, in memory of the Khedive Tewfik who had died in 1897. The deal had been clinched, but the final deeds had not been drawn up when Wissa suffered a stroke while he was in Assiout.

Wissa was living in his mansion built on the Nile front, within sixteen acres of gardens. The mansion was built by Italian architects and decorators; Italian painters were employed in painting frescoes on the ceiling of the main reception rooms. Wissa lived on the first floor, with its huge dining room, billiard room, different reception rooms, and four bedrooms with their adjoining bathrooms. The second floor had been divided into two separate apartments. One with its view of the Nile, the fountains, marble statues and the French garden had been given to George, the eldest son. He was married to his cousin Victoria, daughter of Wissa's stepbrother Azer.

Zaki had been given the apartment at the back overlooking the huge orange grove and outhouses. He was not married at the time, but later married Shafika, the daughter of a large landowner, Tadros Khayatt. She was considered a very beautiful woman by everyone.

Wissa's daughters Balsam, Farouza, and Regina all lived with their respective husbands: Dr Akhnoukh Fanous had married Balsam, Alexan Abiskharoun (later known as Alexan Pasha), a nephew of Akhnoukh had married Farouza. Both of them lived in Assiout. Regina, the youngest, married Dr Habib Khayatt and lived in Cairo, but she had come to Assiout to help look after her father when he suffered his stroke. It was under these circumstances that the daughters used to take it in turns to supervise the staff that were looking after their father. They accompanied him on his daily outing by carriage.

Akhnoukh feared that George would influence his father, Wissa, to sign the deeds of the Tewfikieh buildings in George's name, thus cutting out Zaki and his three sisters. He persuaded his wife Balsam and her sisters that it was in the interest of all, and especially for Wissa's health, that he should come and live with Balsam where he would have 24-hour loving care and service. The sisters could come daily and help, which would ensure that nothing was signed by Wissa to their detriment. This they accomplished by carting Wissa off to Balsam's house after one of his outings. The master bedroom had been made up for him. Balsam was his favourite daughter, being his first-born. He did not mind at all staying with the Akhnoukh Fanouses, whose house was full of laughter and life with their numerous children. George could say nothing as Wissa was quite contented.

Wissa died in 1906. The deeds of the Tewfikieh had been registered in his name, before he returned to live in his mansion. His heirs had inherited their respective shares, according to the laws of inheritance. But George administered the running of the buildings until his death in the 1930s. The annual revenue was distributed to the heirs at his own convenience.

I will try and write a little about the two Wissa-Wissa sons George and Zaki.

Whenever I mention George, I make him out as a cantankerous old man, trying to have his way, and rule everyone's life. That is what it would seem to the reader, but one must remember that he was Wissa's right hand for several years before his death looking after much of the business and holding the purse strings, and continued to do so after his death, having to liquidate Wissa's estate. Zaki was much younger, as old as some of his nephews, and George considered him more of a son than a brother and treated him that way. George was a good businessman, a hard nut to crack. He was the only one of Wissa's heirs who increased his inheritance. When in Assiout, he lived in his own quarters of the Wissa house, but he built himself a lovely house in Garden City in Cairo on the Nile, just opposite the Meridian Hotel built a few years ago. There are several stories told about uncle George but I'll only mention one or two.

George Wissa loved his food and before he got married he met an American girl of a good family and was thinking of marrying her. She in return had asked him to the States to meet her parents, who invited him to dinner. He conjured up in his mind all sorts of good food that lay in wait for him. At dinner the maid came in with a huge covered dish. Could it be a young stuffed turkey, or maybe some game in a delectable sauce, thought George. When the cover was taken off the dish, to his surprise they were serving him with *corn on the cob*. He had one look at it and without thinking he exclaimed, 'We give that to the pigs.' That was the end of that romance.

After World War I he bought a big property in Austria when there was huge inflation. The property was confiscated at the time of Hitler.

As mentioned before George loved his tummy. He had a telephone fixed between the dining room and the kitchen in his Cairo house, and whenever he found something he didn't like he'd pick up the phone and curse the cook and bang the phone down again. Many a cook tendered their resignation and Victoria was finding it very difficult keeping any cook. She decided on the quiet to cut the wire. Uncle George as usual at lunch picked up the phone, cursed the cook, and banged the phone down again. For many a month uncle George was able to keep his cooks, to Victoria's relief. One day he picked up the phone and asked the cook to come up to him; he wanted to describe to him personally a dish that he had tasted somewhere, and which he wanted him to prepare. When the cook did not appear all was found out, and poor Victoria had to start looking for cooks again.

One afternoon, trying to reach for something outside the window on the first floor, he fell out on to his *valet de chambre* a Sudanese called Fadl, who looked like someone out of *Uncle Tom's Cabin*, who was passing under the window. George broke his leg, as did Fadl. For the rest of their lives they both hobbled along with a walking stick.

Once he got so annoyed with his niece Esther who was arguing with him, that he said, 'If you were my wife, I would throw you out of the window every day.'

'What do you think I am, a ball to bounce back at you?' answered Esther.

When he lived with his family in Assiout at the Wissa house, as did Zaki with his family, he used to scare the wits out of them. Zaki loved having his sons and nephews around him playing cards. He used to give them all money so they could gamble with him and win it all back. But uncle George would not permit any of his sons gambling, so one of the staff had to keep watch at the door, and whenever George Pasha was around they'd give a prearranged signal and the cards and chips were put away very quickly.

*

Zaki Bey Wissa my father-in-law was a very different person. He had a clear brain, was an entrepreneur who did not mind taking a risk. He loved singing, dancing, gambling, and had a keen sense of humour. Working hard all his life, he was the type of person who wanted to renew, to explore, a pioneer in a sense. But once he put a project into effect, he would leave it to others to run, although he would supervise it at times. He would then start something else. Such a system was not very conducive to making and keeping a fortune. He was very ambitious. He felt the fortune left him by his father was not enough, he wanted to be another Wissa. He rented a huge property, about 1000 acres in Maragha, to grow cotton for his ginning factory and seed for his cotton-seed oil refinery at Beni Korra. It was run at first by an English manager, a Mr Boyse, and later by his sons Victor and Ernest. For many years he was refining edible oil at a loss selling a 14-kilo tin of oil at thirty-four piastres when it was costing him thirty-six piastres.

He also bought a couple of thousand acres of marshy land at Daman-hour, Lower Egypt and spent years and thousands of pounds in reclaiming it.

He was a pioneer in prospecting for oil. He was the first Egyptian who took a huge concession prospecting for oil in the Red Sea. He found some oil and spent a lot of money extracting it. He was able to, but it was not very profitable. He employed geologists from England but their reports were not very encouraging. He refused to go into partnership with one of the big oil companies. He was a loner, and did not believe in partners out-side the family, with the result that after years of just covering expenses, he gave up the concession, which was grabbed by an Egyptian joint stock company owned by Shell called the Anglo-Egyptian Oilfields who were able to extract oil in large quantities just about a mile away from uncle Zaki's wells at Abu Derba.

Uncle Zaki was one of three founders of the Rotary Club in Egypt. They decided to found it over a drink at Shepheard's bar.

Uncle Zaki was a very charming person, who shed money from his pockets wherever he went. He had many friends in all walks of life, and in spite of him being a gambler and illogical in some of his actions, he could face reality, with optimism about the future, and act in a practical way. He was one of the first to receive his Agricultural Reform Bonds after 1952. He just accepted whatever the authorities said, made no difficulties, giving them his farmhouse with its contents in the Fayoum gracefully although he could have kept it. It broke his heart giving up the Fayoum house as he loved entertaining there and showing his guests around the garden. He was a very energetic person, got up in the early morning, did his exercises, had his breakfast and if on one of the farms would ride for hours.

He was very particular in many things. His house was well run, no non-sense from the staff. It was run by his wife Chafiga Tadros Khayatt, who came to his rescue several times in his life, when he was passing through difficult times.

The crisis of the 1930s was very hard on the Zaki Wissas. He arranged with the banks to consolidate all his debts with the Bank Misr, selling both the ginning factory and oil refinery to the bank, with a proviso that both his sons should be appointed managers for life, Ernest to run the oil mill and Victor the ginning factory. He had liquidated his reclamation project in Damanhour,. and stopped prospecting for oil. He gave up renting land at Maragha as he had no need for large quantities of cotton. Cotton acreage had been restricted during World War II, and Ernest did not wish to live in Beni Korra as he had a growing family. So Victor remained manager of the oil mill until he retired in the late 1970's.

It was just bad luck that Uncle Zaki had to give up the oil mill, for once the war started it made pots of money. He was able to pay off all his debts a few years before the Revolution by selling a part of his property on the lake at Fayoum. A new company had been formed which wanted to turn the Fayoum into a tourist resort. They built the Auberge du Lac on part of the land Zaki Bey sold them.

*

The Hanna Wissas' and Wissa Wissas' grandchildren lived in Assiout during the twenties until most of them got married, and then they gravi-tated to Cairo.

At that time there was a social life of the young. Today you would prob-ably call them the jet set. A couple of pages were written in a book by Thomas Rees titled *Egypt and the Holy Land* which gave the following description of Alexan Abiskharoun Pasha's house in Assiout and the enter-tainment he and his friends received on their stop in that town on their way up the Nile:

'While in Cairo, before starting up the Nile, I met a United States Consular Agent, a gentleman of title, George Pasha Wissa, a native Egyptian, who although spending most of his time in Cairo, has a very fine residence in Assiout one of the cities on the Nile and has also large estates in the same locality and in the Fayoum, being one of the largest landowners in Egypt.

After learning that we were going up the river he said that he would write to his family at home to call on us when the boat reached that city. When the boat arrived, his son and daughter called upon us, and after taking us for a delightful ride about the city invited us to their residence for the evening. They further requested us to bring along such friends from the boat as we cared to bring with us, especially all the young people who danced. We accepted their invitation and went to their home in the evening, with a party numbering in all about twenty persons.

It appeared that the gentleman whom we first met had a brother-in-law Alexan Pasha living in the city where he resided, and their two houses were near each other. It was finally decided that the party should be held at the brother-in-law's home. Both residences were beautiful structures and each had a considerable garden or park surrounding it, as is usual with the best homes in this country. The premises of each were surrounded by high iron fences and hedges of flowering shrubbery. The gardens within were beautifully cared for. I will try to describe one of these houses so that my readers may have an idea as to its appearance and arrangement.

The house where we were entertained was a large white structure. It was imposing in appearance, with balconies, porticoes and terraces. Standing back in the grounds, it was almost concealed from the street by the shrubbery and the great flowering vines between it and the thoroughfare. At the entrance to the grounds was a Lodge for the gatekeeper. Between the house and gateway were gravel paths and roadways leading through the gardens to the house.

Arriving at the door, we were ushered into the residence by Arab servants who were dressed in their native costumes of snowy white gowns, confined about the waist with wide red sashes, and wearing slippers and fezes of the same colour. They received us with ceremony. There were plenty of servants, for these two households maintain a retinue of fifty or sixty in all.

On entering the house we found it a magnificent structure. To the right was a fair sized reception room, finished in French style, with furniture to correspond, upholstered in delicate brocades.

Immediately to the rear of this was the large reception room, furnished even more elaborately.

The corridor from the front door led directly to a large circular room in the centre of the building. This room had a hardwood floor which made it suitable for dancing. The second floor and the floors above that were supported by two tiers of white columns one above the other, and the whole was surmounted by a considerable dome.

To one side of this circular room and opposite the reception room was the grand stairway and gallery leading to the floors above. To the left of the corridor and opposite the reception room was a large state dining room, elegantly furnished with heavy furniture, upholstered with leather embossed with gold. The dimensions of the dining room were ample for a very large assembly.

The interior of the house was highly ornamented but not overdone. Some gold leaf was used in the decorations, but all with the very best of taste. The premises, including the grounds and the house, were lighted with electric lights and the fixtures were of late and elegant design. The construction was planned and supervised by an Italian architect and in designing this residence he maintained the high reputation of the master builders of that country.

We found these people royal entertainers and very proficient in culinary art. While the refreshments were what would ordinarily be referred to as light refreshments, such as would be appropriate at an evening party, they were served by and under the direction of the hostess of the occasion and our ladies said that they counted on the table at least twenty-five varieties of the most delectable cakes and sweet-meats, all of which had been prepared by our hostess.

Prohibition is not in vogue in Egypt and refreshments which that custom might have interfered with were served by the young men of the household, and while they were partaken of moderately both by the hosts and some of the guests, there were at least twelve or fifteen varieties of refreshments offered in that line. Dancing was indulged in, and the younger members of the two households, who spend most of their vacations in France, Switzerland or some of the more northern European countries, proved to be proficient in the latest dance steps.

They are also well educated and speak the English language fluently. While being descendants, in a direct line, of the old families of the Pharaohs of Egypt, in their religious belief they are Copts, or in other words followers of the early Christians of Egypt.

Our Egyptian friend also showed us over his dehabyeh, which is a sort of sailing house boat and was, at the time we visited it, tied up on the Nile at Cairo. This boat is equipped with kitchen, dining and sleeping facilities for a party of a dozen or more. While this mode of travel is slow, it is most restful and delightful. For business trips our friend maintains a motor launch for quick trips between his home and Cairo.'

Alexan Abiskharoun is the third character I should write about, he was Akhnoukh Fanous's nephew, and was training as a lawyer in his uncle's office in Assiout which was situated in the garden of Akhnoukh. He was very good looking. I knew him as an elderly gentleman with a big white curled up moustache. He married Wissa's third child, Farouza, who visited her sister Balsam regularly. She espied Alexan one day when she was looking out of the window into the garden. They met and they fell in love and got married. They built their house on the river bank. It was a very grand house, as previously mentioned. The Alexans dropped the name Abiskharoun and kept Alexan as their surname. Alexan Pasha was a very simple and straightforward man, a staunch upholder of the Protestant cause and church. He was head of the synod until he died and influenced many other members of the family to contribute lavishly in building the Protestant Church at Palais in 1920 which they used for many years during the summer months only, when they were in Alexandria. He was the head of the elders of the church. His sons Emile and Alphonse were well-known businessmen, whereas Freddie and William occupied themselves mostly in growing the family land.

Alexan and Farouza were a very close couple. It was said that she used to pinch him if ever he became too outspoken. He had the Fanous trait of not always thinking before speaking. Other than his sons, he left four daughters, Margaret who married Sadek Pasha Wahba, Laura who dedicated her life to charity and good works and looking after her father and mother, Lilly who married Amin Bey Khayatt and Ena who married Wahba Adib Wahba Bey.

135

The Wissa Wissa house in Assiout facing the Nile

136

H.E. George Pasha Wissa (in Pasha's dress)
(Eldest son of Wissa Boctor Wissa)

The Alexan Abiskharoun house in Assiout

A view of its rear taken from the Nile

At a reception given to Sultan Hussein when he was Prince. He can be seen in the centre surrounded by his retinue. Fahmy Bey Wissa is two steps down on the right and his elder brother Nassif Bey Wissa is on the bottom step on the left.

The Sultan Hussein as Prince with a member of his retinue standing in front of him, when he visited Guindi Bey Wissa at his house. He is standing on the step below.

# BOOK THREE – EGYPT ASSOCIATES WITH GREAT BRITAIN FROM 1880, UNTIL DECLARED A PROTECTORATE IN 1914, AND THE START OF THE 1919 REVOLUTION

*A Vacillating Ruler and his Ambitious Successor*

Tewfik was a unique character among the Khedives who ruled Egypt. He was misunderstood during his lifetime, and scant justice has been done to his memory.

Both Europeans and Egyptians found difficulty in believing that such a character existed, quite unlike the usual product of his education and surroundings. His self-restraint was taken for stupidity. His hesitation, in self-preservation, was taken for weakness, and since he tried to cooperate with the different conflicting elements in the country, he was considered insincere. He was a good Moslem and at the same time was free of all intolerance of other religions. He was devoted to his one wife, yet he showed compassion and tried to help the concubines abandoned by his father Ismail.

When he succeeded as ruler of Egypt, he inherited a bankrupt country, whose finances were under the dual control of England and France. A country with a feudalist upper class of Turks and Circassians, an emerging middle class of Egyptians imbibing all sorts of imported revolutionary ideas, in politics, ideas of liberty, freedom, and constitutional government.

In religion, the ideas were far removed from the teachings of their parents: the Christians, with their Protestant and Catholic missionaries, the Moslems, with the teachings of thinkers and revolutionaries, such as Sheikh Jamal el Din el Afghani, a *Shi'ite* chameleon, posing as a *Sunnite*[44]. He advo-

---

[44]Shi'ite is a member of the smaller of two major branches of Islam – Shi'ites and Sunnites. The Shi'ites were the followers of Ali, son-in-law of the Prophet, and believed that the Moslem leadership should belong to his descendants alone. They are much more fanatical and their followers are mainly in Iran, Iraq, Syria, and Pakistan whereas the Sunnites are more flexible and tolerant and hold that the Caliph must be descendant of a member of the Prophets tribe, Koreish. Its followers are the Egyptians and most of the inhabitants of the rest of the Arab world.

Boutros Ghali Pasha

Nubar Pasha

Ryaz Pasha

Gallini Pasha Fahmy

cated a renewal of Islam by its unification under a single ruler, a Caliph, whose nationality was unimportant, but was strong enough to rule all his territories far away from the influence of foreigners. Such talk attracted the ordinary Egyptian, who considered all those in authority whether Turkish or European as foreign usurpers.

The banner was taken up by Sheikh Mohammed Abdu, after Afghani was exiled from Egypt. He was a different type of person, not a politician at heart, nor a revolutionary by temperament. Spiritual and intellectual, his teachings left their imprint on national thought for years to come. He became a journalist, then a judge and was considered an authority on the *Sharia* (Moslem law). In 1900, he was appointed Mufti of Egypt, the highest religious authority in the state, but his moderation in interpreting parts of Islamic law lead him into conflict with conservative members of the community whether political or religious.

It was under such circumstances that Tewfik was confronted by a situation not of his own doing or inclination, but inherited from previous rulers of his family, due to the fact that the top posts in the state were reserved for the Turks, Circassians and Albanians and all those with Turkish origins or strong connections.

Egyptians were excluded. At times Egyptians had been appointed to positions of authority, on a temporary basis, such as those who were appointed by Ismail to collect his new tax, the Moukabala, in the interior. The same sort of discrimination took place in the army. The top posts went to officers of Turkish or Circassian descent. The Egyptian officers were confined to the lower ranks.

It was under those conditions that the Khedive Tewfik was unable to suppress the rise of Egypt's first nationalist movement, which came about when Colonel Ahmed Arabi, a soldier of pure Egyptian descent, nicknamed later on as *El Waheed* (The Unique), and his subordinate Egyptian fellah officers protested against the privileges and treatment of officers of Turkish descent, demanding similar treatment. The Khedive vacillated in his reactions, playing it hot and cold, depending on the advice given him by his ministers and different advisers. He sacrificed his Prime Minister Nubar Pasha, which he did not really mind doing, then his War Minister Osman Rifki, and appointed Arabi as Secretary of War, bestowing him with the title of Pasha.

The population went wild with joy. Instead of an army revolt, a revolution had taken place. They felt that at last a true Egyptian was able to stand up against what they considered to be the oppressive ruling class and the foreigners.

The foreign powers, especially France, felt that Arabi was a potential dictator who might one day lead Egypt to renege on her debts, and maybe hinder France's ambitions in North Africa. Britain was equally concerned,

143

in spite of Britons like Wilfred Blunt seeing events as a mild nationalistic movement trying to ameliorate the fate of the Egyptians.

With Sheikh Mohammed Abdu, Blunt drew up a document named *The Programme of the National Party of Egypt* which recognised that the dual control of Egypt's finances was necessary to pay off Egypt's debts, notwithstanding their object of seeing Egypt some day ruled entirely by Egyptians. England's official position was that if Arabi had to be removed, it should be done with the help of Turkey, who was the natural suzerain of Egypt.

Such a situation had not been envisaged by the powers. The idea of the British encouraging the Turks to intervene suited the Sultan, who wished to occupy Egypt immediately by sending a Turkish army. He feared Arabi might introduce a constitutional government as demanded by the nationalists. He was dead against allowing any constitutional government to rule in any part of the Ottoman Empire.

The Sultan was afraid that it might be the spark which would cause a general revolution in the whole Turkish Empire. Turkey acted immediately by sending envoys to Cairo to reconnoitre and take charge if necessary. The British and French became alarmed at the quick Turkish response; they decided to protest against Turkish intervention without prior consultation. They backed their protests by sending a joint British and French naval force to Alexandria with instructions only to return once the Turkish envoys were withdrawn. This they did one day after the Turks left Egypt, on June 19th, 1881.

French policy at the time was led by an impulsive and energetic Minister, M. Gambetta, who wanted to perpetuate the dual control in Egypt, without an actual Anglo-French occupation, but was willing to consider doing so if no other way was possible. However the British preferred that if any military occupation was to take place, it should be accomplished by the intervention of Turkey. Gambetta was able to persuade the British that the French plan was better for all concerned.

Britain agreed to go along with France but hedged her bets by adding a proviso to the agreement stating that His Majesty's Government must not be considered as committing themselves thereby to any particular mode of action. Britain and France carried out their plan by announcing in a joint note that 'the maintenance of the Khedive on the throne of Egypt, was alone able to guarantee order and prosperity in Egypt,' and that they would back the Khedive if he stood up against any excesses by Arabi or the nationalists. In short, they would support the status quo notwithstanding any gradual improvement to self-government, in response to nationalistic sentiment. This was conveyed to the Khedive by the representatives of Britain and France in Cairo.

Lord Cromer who was not in Egypt at the time commented on the joint note in his book *Modern Egypt*:

144

'The note was taken to mean that the Sultan was to be thrust still further into the background; that the Khedive was to become more plainly the puppet of England and France; and that Egypt would sooner or later, in some shape or other be made to share the disastrous fate of Tunis.

The general effect was therefore mischievous in the highest degree. The Khedive was encouraged to oppose the sentiments of the Chamber. The military, and national and popular party were alarmed; the Sultan was irritated, and the European powers uneasy.'

Events followed fast and are a part of history M. Gambetta resigned office on January 31st, 1882 and was succeeded by M. Freycinet who completely overturned the policy of the French Government as it concerned Egypt. Prior to M. Gambetta, the Egyptian movement was not altogether beyond control. When he left office, England and France were alike mistrusted by the Egyptians, and unable to influence the course of events. It became impossible for anyone to put the hands of the clock back, maintaining the pre-Gambetta status quo.

As the situation got worse it was apparent that France's new policy opposed the occupation of Egypt by a joint British and French force. The French proposed to ditch the Khedive Tewfik and persuade the Sultan to depose him in favour of Halim Pasha.

Britain rejected this proposal, and Lord Granville pointed out 'that after the declarations of support so recently given to the Khedive, in the name of the British and French Governments, it would be an act questionable in point of good faith, if we were now not only to abandon him, but to combine for his removal without any new or more apparent cause than can at present be shown to exist.' The growing atmosphere of panic and confusion came to a head in the summer of 1882 when Tewfik asked for British cooperation in any invasion or occupation of Egypt.

In July 1882 the British went it alone. Alexandria was bombarded, the British landed 20,000 troops, and at the battle of Tel-el-Kebir, Arabi was defeated and sent into exile[45]. This started the British occupation of Egypt which lasted for seventy-two years. Britain promised to withdraw her troops from Egypt as soon as a strong Egyptian government could ensure the Canal's security.

From 1882 to 1914 the Khedive remained the only legal authority in Egypt, which continued to be an autonomous state within the Turkish Empire.

---

[45]Arabi was later allowed to return to Egypt with a pension of £1000 a year, on which he lived pleasantly in Cairo, and could be seen as a placid and forgotten gentleman, driving around Cairo in his carriage at the fashionable hour. *Modern Egypt* by Tom Little, page 45.

## A Disguised Occupation

Britain intended originally to occupy Egypt as a temporary measure, maintaining the status quo, enabling Egypt to pay its creditors and ensuring for Britain the security of its lines to India, through the Suez Canal. In 1883 alone Britain asserted eighty-three times that her occupation of Egypt was only a temporary measure, until matters could be straightened out.

Sir Evelyn Baring, later better known as Lord Cromer, was brought back to Egypt in 1883. He had left Egypt during the dual control, when he was one of the controllers. He returned to Egypt as Consul General of England, a post giving him great potential, since British forces were now occupying the country. He had a freer hand in controlling affairs, than he had under dual control. France had not the same influence; she had forfeited it by refusing to join England in the occupation of the country. She now regretted her naivety in allowing Britain to overthrow Arabi alone.

Cromer had no illusions; he prepared himself for a long stay. The different departments were headed by Egyptian ministers, paid by the Egyptian exchequer, and responsible to the Khedive vassal of Turkey. However, he made sure that all those in authority were vetted by the British advisers, appointed and paid by the Egyptian Government, but whose first loyalty was to Britain.

Similarly in the Egyptian army, the top command and senior officers were British, the Egyptians were all promoted as officers only if they were judged as absolutely loyal to British rule or completely docile. It was under this position of strength that Cromer was able to become the actual ruler of Egypt for twenty-four years. He found 'nothing wrong in occupying a part of the Turkish Empire with British troops and at the same time punctiliously avoiding infringement on the legitimate right of the Sultan.'[46] He was a financier by upbringing and a pragmatist by nature, as well as an honest public servant who made it his first concern to provide for the debt, and balance the budget. This he was able to do by 1887.

He then proceeded to give Egypt fiscal relief, instead of additional expenditure, by abolishing the *corvée* which was in reality a heavy and objectionable tax, at a cost to the treasury of £400,000 a year. Land tax was also reduced by a further £430,000 a year. In fact, he was able to reduce direct taxes by £1,100,000 a year as well as a number of indirect taxes.[47]

In 1897 the surpluses were spent on remunerative projects such as drainage, railways and hospitals. But he neglected those services which he

[46]*Napoleon to Nasser* by Raymond Flower. page 124
[47]*Modern Egypt* by Tom Little, page 48

CROMER, Evelyn Baring
1st Earl 1841–1917
British Administrator

thought were not remunerative to the exchequer, such as education and industrial projects, which he thought risky.

Cromer paid very little attention to the national aspirations of the country. He discouraged demagoguery from no matter what quarter. He remarked, 'What Egypt most required was order and good government. Perhaps after a long interval, liberty would follow.'

Such an attitude was abhorred by the emerging articulate nationalists such as Mustapha Kamel, whose aspirations for Egypt began to be felt in and out of the country. His newspaper *El Lewa* (The Banner) expressed the rising feeling of nationalism in the country, especially among the younger population who knew little of the conditions of the country under the Khedive Ismail.

Wealth had spread during the British occupation, but it had not reached as far as the Egyptian fellah or the new emerging *Effendi* class, who felt that the cream of the country was being lapped by its rulers, the Pashas, the Beys, and foreign merchants. They blamed the British occupation for it.

Mustapha Kamel found an eager ear and mouthpiece in France. A French writer and journalist, Juliette Adam, took up his case and helped him air his views all over Europe. In fact she considered him as her foster son. The movement engendered by Mustapha Kamel sowed the seeds of future political thought by such leaders as Mohammed Farid and Saad Zaghloul.

Egypt under Cromer became a rich and prosperous agricultural country, derived mainly from the Nile and its rich soil, helped by a remodelled irrigation system, and introduced by the British engineers from India. Egypt exported its produce of cotton and onions and other agricultural products mainly to England, who returned the finished goods to be sold in Egypt and other parts of the British Empire.

Cromer did not pay any attention to Egyptian political thought or feeling, and he rarely left the Residency, except maybe to go to the Gezira Sporting Club or to Abdine Palace if he needed to meet the Khedive.

On the death of Tewfik and the accession of his son Abbas Helmi as Khedive, Cromer made a point of humiliating him, to bring him down a peg, when he made him apologise to Kitchener who was at the time commander of the Egyptian army. The reason was a remark made by the Khedive criticising the turn-out of the regiment he was inspecting. Cromer accomplished a lot for Egypt but he was not regretted by the people when he left in 1907. For the last year of his service in Egypt, 'Lord Cromer moved under the protection of British bayonets, through silent and angry streets.'[48] This was due to a tragic accident and a revengeful punishment of an incident at Denshway, a village in Lower Egypt which Egyptians have

[48] *Modern Egypt* by Tom Little, page 51

never been allowed to forget. The Denshway incident is summarised in Raymond Flower's book *From Napoleon to Nasser*, page 127, as follows:

'On a hot June day in 1906, some British officers out shooting were suddenly surrounded by an angry crowd of villagers who objected to the pigeons – of tremendous importance in their meagre diet – being shot. In the uproar, a gun went off, wounding a woman, and the officer had to run for it. One of them, who had been hit on the head, fell dead on the road from shock and sunstroke, and angry soldiers from the dead officer's unit seized a young villager, who had nothing to do with the matter but had come over to help, and clubbed him to death. The foreign communities in Cairo panicked, imagining that a general massacre was imminent, and a special tribunal of three British officials and two Egyptians condemned four of the villagers to death, three of them to fifty lashes each, and a number of others to long terms of hard labour. Cromer confirmed the sentences and Egypt simmered with hatred.'

From 1882 to 1907 Cromer was virtually the ruler of Egypt. In 1885 on the instructions of Britain, Egypt withdrew from the Sudan to its borders at Wadi Halfa, and reconquered the Sudan in 1898 with the help of British troops.

In 1885 Egypt had only withdrawn from the Sudan on the insistence of Cromer, after several attempts by the Egyptian army had failed to regain territory lost to the Mahdi's hordes of Dervishes. The last attempt resulted in the annihilation of an Egyptian force under General Hicks. England's declared policy under the Liberal Government of Gladstone, was that England was in Egypt at the request of the Khedive to guard its borders, and restore order after the rebellion of Arabi. They were there on a temporary basis to protect the minorities and at the same time help Egypt manage her finances, in order to enable her to pay her foreign debts.

The Sudan could only make the task more difficult. Gladstone could see no use in throwing away good money after bad. The Sudan at the time was not vital to England's interests. If anyone should foot the bill for the retention of the Sudan, it should be the Sultan of Turkey, since it was conquered in the name of Turkey by Egypt, her vassal. The Sultan of Turkey did not appreciate this line of thought.

The Egyptian point of view was different. Egypt had always considered the land of the blacks (*Belad El Sud*), the Sudan, as her natural expansion area. It was a land of mystery and riches, from which her lifeline the Nile emerged. For enterprising Egyptians it could mean wealth, a source of trade in ivory, ostrich feathers, ebony, gold and slaves. As long as it was left to nature the Nile flood would arrive each year, and they were not bothered with the activities of local tribes. Egypt had conquered the Sudan in the days of Mohammed Aly as a vassal of Turkey. Ismail had extended Egypt's boundaries eastward creating an equatorial province, and westward her influence penetrated into the vast area of the Bahr El Ghazal. Egypt felt that it was only because of British insistence that she had been forced to withdraw to Wadi Halfa. However, ten years later things looked very different, Egypt's finances had improved under British administration, the foreign debt was under control, and the surpluses in the budget were turning Egypt into a prosperous country.

European powers were starting to scramble for colonies in East Africa. Britain did not want a foreign power threatening the Nile waters, as long as she had an interest and was occupying Egypt. She was able to come to a hands-off policy with Germany and Italy with regard to the Nile valley. It was very different with France, who was smarting under what she considered was Britain's perfidious behaviour. France felt she had been out-manoeuvered with regard to Egypt, and feared that the occupation of

Kitchener of Khartoum 1898

Egypt by Britain was turning into a permanent relationship. France believed that she was entitled to a predominant role in Egyptian affairs, due to her financial investments, her cultural activities, and the building of a French project – the Suez Canal. She was determined to undermine Britain's position, and if possible, drive her out of the Nile valley.

In 1893 an elaborate scheme was concocted by which a French expedition would march across Africa from the west coast to Fashoda on the Upper Nile where a dam could be constructed threatening the Nile waters. The expedition set out in 1896 under the command of Captain Jean Baptiste Marchand.

A Conservative government had replaced Gladstone's Liberals in 1895. They did not mind having a crack at the Dervishes, and if possible retaining a foothold in the Sudan.

In 1897 under the pretext that Britain had to remove a threat to Egypt's southern border, the British in the name of the Sultan of Turkey, sent an Anglo-Egyptian army under the command of General Kitchener, the Sirdar of the Egyptian army, financed by the Egyptian treasury to reconquer the Sudan. It was to ensure that the Sudan remained under British influence and not French. The Anglo-Egyptian force was able to defeat the Mahdi's successor, the Khalifa and his forces, at the battle of Omdorman on September 2nd, 1898, when the flags of Britain and Egypt were hoisted over Khartoum on the same day.

Kitchener then pressed forward with a small force, and met Captain Marchand at Fashoda on September 18th. The French refused to withdraw and for a time it looked as if it might come to an all-out war between England and France. But cooler heads soon had their way, and it was finally agreed in March 1899 that the French expansion eastward in Africa would stop at the Sudan borders.

In the meantime an agreement had been signed between Egypt and England, turning the Sudan into an Egyptian condominium, whereby the Sudan was given a separate political status in which sovereignty was jointly shared by the Khedive and the British Crown. In reality there was no equal partnership between Britain and Egypt. From the first moment the British dominated the condominium. Just as the British occupation of Egypt could be described as a 'financial condominium', so could the annexation of the Sudan to the British Empire be considered a political condominium. Britain's claim for equal partnership was based on the right of conquest.

The condominium agreement signed in 1899 between Egypt and Britain governed the Sudan status until 1953. One of its conditions was that the supreme military and civil commands should be vested in a Khedivial decree on the recommendation of the British government. It did not mention Turkish sovereignty, and in fact abolished all the privileges the foreign powers enjoyed in Egypt. It stipulated that no foreign consuls should reside in the Sudan, without the British Government's consent.

The first Governor-General was Lord Kitchener, but he was succeeded in the same year by his aide Sir Reginald Wingate, who ruled the Sudan from 1899 to 1916. Taxes were kept low purposely to win the sympathy of the people. Any deficits of the Sudan budget were covered by the Egyptian treasury. While British administrators and troops pacified the region and built a new country on the debris of the old, they charged it to Egypt from which the Sudan was administratively separated.

The Egyptians were not happy with this agreement, but they could do very little to change it, except grumble, and later on demonstrate.

# The British Occupation from 1907–1914

## *The Awakening and a Murmur of Discontent*

During this period British policy vacillated. Sir Eldon Gorst, the newly appointed Consul-General, was a completely different character from Lord Cromer. Gorst had worked in Egypt since 1890 in different posts. He had occupied a job at the Foreign Office for a short time before becoming Consul-General in Egypt. Gorst had definite ideas of how he should carry out his mission. He thought he had grasped all the weaknesses in the system, and he was sure he would get the loyal support of his former colleagues. But 'familiarity breeds contempt', and he could never command the personal authority of Cromer. Furthermore, it would seem that he had been instructed by Sir Edward Grey, the Liberal Secretary of State, to try and liberalise the mode of government without losing Britain's grip over matters.

During his last years in office Cromer had intended to encourage the moderate opinion of the country in the art of government. This was in response to liberalism in England, criticism in France, and national agitation in Egypt.

He started by encouraging the new party *Hezb-el-Umma* (Party of the Nation) formed by moderately minded Egyptians, who, whilst acknowledging the benefits of the British connection, yet wanted to attain Egypt's aspirations by caution and constitutional methods. They were equally as patriotic as the members of *Hezb-el-Watan* (Party of the Fatherland) led by Mustapha Kamel who was encouraged and financed by the Khedive, but they were less vociferous. Cromer tried liberalising education by creating a new department of education to which he appointed Saad Zaghloul Pasha.

Saad Zaghloul was a true Egyptian, a fellah, lawyer by profession, who was appointed by Princess Nazli Fadel[49] to take charge of her legal affairs. It was at the instigation of that great lady that he learned French, which helped him greatly in his future career. Saad Zaghloul married Safia, the daughter of the Prime Minister Mustapha Fehmy Pasha, a moderate, and a friend of Cromer.

Saad Zaghloul was considered an honest, straightforward man with moderate ideas, which led him to join the newly-formed party, *Hezb-el-Umma*. Although a nationalist at heart, he believed in the British connection, which he felt had saved Egypt from the misrule of the Khedives, and placed her

---

[49]Princess Nazli Fadel was a great intellectual lady at the end of the nineteenthth century whose salon was frequented by writers and thinkers. She had a great influence on Kassim Amin who started out being very conservative, but was converted to become a champion of women's emancipation.

Saad Zaghloul Pasha

on the road to prosperity. Through all his career, he was at loggerheads with the policy adopted by the Palace. Destiny was to decree that Saad Zaghloul, whom the British thought would strengthen the British connection, due to a series of unfortunate circumstances, twelve years later became the instrument that helped to sever it.

In trying to carry out his policy Gorst felt he could either pander to the Nationalists, or try and win over the Khedive. Many believed that the Khedive had been badly treated by Cromer, and would possibly have been more amenable had he been handled with velvet gloves. Gorst chose the latter policy.

Mustapha Fehmy, the Prime Minister and friend of Cromer, resigned on grounds of ill health, when he felt that the new policy of harmony with the Khedive would be to his disadvantage. He had never been one of the Khedive's favourites. The Khedive accepted Gorst's suggestion to appoint Boutros Pasha Ghali as Prime Minister who had a long experience of politics and administration; he was clever, honest, capable and acceptable to the Khedive.

Gorst in return agreed to the appointment of Mohammed Said Pasha as Minister of the Interior, although he was known as one of the Khedive's stooges. The one drawback of having Boutros Pasha Ghali was that he was a Copt. Relations between Copts and Moslems were usually good during the reign of Khedive Ismail, but after the occupation of Egypt a creeping change took place, due to Britain's well-known policy of divide and rule. Also Turkey hoped that it might again secure control of Egypt, by secretly keeping the spark of pan-Islamism alive through its sympathy with the National Party. This came to a head after the assassination of Boutros Pasha Ghali in 1910, when there was no one leader of the Copts with any real influence, which led to the recriminative Coptic and Moslem conferences of 1911.

In spite of the fact that Gorst tried to improve relations with the Khedive, he felt that liberal opinion in England would appreciate a diluted democracy in Egypt; this would eventually curb any tendency to excesses by the Khedive or the ruling class – as long as such policy did not endanger England's position. Gorst brought this about by increasing the power of the Provincial Councils in 1909, by making them act as genuine Advisory Councils to the Moudir or Governor of the Province on local matters. Previously the principal function of these councils had been to elect from amongst their own numbers the members of the Legislative Council. Similarly the Legislative Council was strengthened when the government announced that in future it was to be in permanent session from November 15th till the end of May, instead of meeting every other month.

It has been suggested that the Khedive, who was getting tired of British interference and policy, wanted to embarrass Gorst, and intimated to the

Coptic leaders, who came mainly from Assiout, that if they held a congress stating their grievances, he would try to get the British and the government to accept them. Recriminations were bandied about left and right. The British stated that when they occupied Egypt the Copts thought that because the British were Christians, they would or should get preferential treatment, whereas the British stated that their policy was 'rule without discrimination.'

The Copts denied the British allegation, stating they only asked for justice and equality with other Egyptians, and for a full participation in the fruits which resulted from the new regime. The Copts maintained that prior to 1882 there had been no accusation of an incapacity of the Copts to fill the higher administrative posts in the government, but when the Copts felt that there was discrimination against them, they tried to get redress. They were then either courteously received and told that the matter would be looked into, or were curtly informed that there was no foundation for their grievances.

At this point it must be admitted that the Copts in the private sector under British rule had waxed rich, and had become prominent and articulate members of society. They held a conference in Assiout in March 1911, and I quote from *The British Agent's Report:*

'The organisers of the congress, are a small clique of wealthy landowners from Upper Egypt, do not claim to represent more than 12,000 of the 700,000 Copts in Egypt, they are purely self-constituted representatives of their co-religionists an influential section of whom, including the Patriarch, head of the Coptic Church in Egypt, disapprove and deprecate their proceedings.'

He continues that the Coptic grievances could be formulated under five headings as follows:

1. Right of the Copts to take advantage of the educational facilities provided by the new Provincial Councils.
2. Recognition of capacity as the sole test for admission to Government appointments.
3. Representation of the Coptic community in the representative institutions of Egypt.
4. Permission for non-Moslems in Government offices and schools to substitute another day for Friday as their day of rest.
5. Conferring of Government grants on all deserving institutions without invidious distinction.

Gorst had tried to forbid the convocation of the congress, but he was overruled by London. The resolutions taken at the Coptic Congress greatly irritated the Moslems to a point that they boycotted the Copts and convened a counter congress known as the 'Moslem Congress'. This was the idea of Prime Minister Mohammed Said Pasha, who wanted to please Gorst by saving his face after the rebuff he had received from London, when it had countermanded his decision to ban the Coptic Congress. Fortunately, the chairman of the Moslem Congress was a clear-sighted and wise politician, Ryaz Pasha. It was due to his wisdom in conducting the congress that a headlong collision was avoided between the Copts and the Moslems.

When Lord Kitchener succeeded Sir Eldon Gorst as Consul-General of Egypt in September 1912 after the latter's untimely death, he convened the leaders of both congresses and ordered their immediate dissolution. He was obeyed and harmony started to reign again among the Copts and the Moslems. The rupture was further healed during the 1919 revolution when the Copts joined with the Moslems under Saad Zaghloul in a struggle for independence where their slogan was, 'The Crescent with the Cross' (in Arabic *El Hilal Wal Salib*.[50])

## Kitchener 1911–1914

*The Overbearing Pro-Consul*

Viscount Horatio Herbert Kitchener arrived in Egypt in September 1911. He had accepted the post of Consul-General of Egypt, in spite of his disappointment at not being nominated as Viceroy of India, a post which he had aspired to, after his long service in that country. On his arrival in Egypt, he behaved like a Pro-Consul of the Roman Empire. This was in contrast to his predecessor, (Cromer's successor) Sir Eldon Gorst, who had tried to accomplish his mission by improving relations with the Khedive and the ruling class.

Before setting off from England, Kitchener was asked by a reporter: 'What do you intend to do in Egypt?'

He answered: 'I'm going to step on a molehill.'[51]

Kitchener like Sir Eldon Gorst imagined he understood Egypt and the Egyptians, because of his previous service in Egypt. (He had served as *Sirdar* of the Egyptian army (Commander-in-Chief) from 1892 and for a year as a Governor-General of the newly created Condominium of the Anglo-Egyptian Sudan in 1898.) In contrast, unlike Sir Eldon Gorst, who had tried to achieve his aim by diplomacy, Kitchener, the soldier, enforced his will like a Gauleiter, tolerating no opposition. He was not interested in placating the influential or the Khedive, whom he ignored most of the time.

---

[50]See Appendix No. 1. Letter to George Khayatt from Saad Zaghloul dated November 24, 1918

[51]*Vingt Années d'Egypte* by Baron Firmin Van der Bosch, page 7. Printed Paris, Librarie Académique Perran 1932

Lord Kitchener 1914, British High Commissioner

He pushed around the Pashas, and sent short notes to the Ministers telling them what to do.

He did not believe in encouraging Egyptian political aspirations, since he was convinced that the party system in its Western form would have a disastrous effect on oriental races. Kitchener did not hesitate to express this view officially. 'Party Spirit,' he wrote, 'is to them (Oriental Nations) like strong drink to uncivilized African natives'.[52] However, he did have a real interest in improving the lot of the falaheen. He yearned to be considered by the peasants as a father-figure and in that he succeeded. He perceived that the small fallah was beggared by debt, and wanted to save him from the clutches of the money-lender.

He went straight to the point and in 1912 he promulgated what is known as the 'Five Feddan Law' wherein the agricultural holdings of a farmer who did not own more than five feddans of land could not be seized for debt. This exemption included the dwelling house on the farm as well as two draught animals, and the agricultural implements necessary for cultivation. Similarly his main concern was the development of rural Egypt. The population had been increasing rapidly and since the drainage system had not been able to keep pace with the development of irrigation, a certain amount of land had gone out of cultivation, as it had become water-logged. Furthermore, the matter was made worse by the peasants' misuse of the extra water available, without regard to the land's actual need.

Kitchener attacked this problem by planning an expensive scheme of drainage and reclamation of new land, and by the erection of a chain of pumping stations.

He was opposed in this scheme by both his financial and technical advisers. And when he took no notice of their protest the financial adviser Sir Paul Harvey resigned. This did not bother Kitchener. The new financial adviser, Lord Edward Cecil, had little technical experience in finance and was willing to carry out the Consul-General's orders. However the scheme was destined to be held up due to the outbreak of the 1914 war.

Egypt had been plagued for some years by agricultural pests, and the cotton crops were ravaged. Kitchener's remedy was to create a Ministry of Agriculture in 1913. Such a ministry was long overdue in a country where agriculture was so important. The development of transport, the promotion of light railways, the opening of village Saving Banks, the establishment of *halakas* (areas for the weighing, storage and sale of cotton in seed) all helped to raise the morale of the rural population, and an atmosphere of confidence and optimism was engendered among the peasants.

[52]Annual Report 1912. Quoted in *Egypt since Cromer* by Lord Lloyd. Volume 1, page 133. Macmillan 1933

The World War put an end to Kitchener's mission in Egypt and his plans. He left a memory of fear and affection. He had been dreaded by the great and loved by the small.

## The Protected Sultanate

When World War I descended on Europe in 1914 Khedive Abbas Helmi was vacationing on the Bosphorus, Kitchener was on leave in England, and the Egyptians were busy with their local problems. For some time it had become evident to Britain that Egypt's strategic position and the Suez Canal had to be held on to, as it was her gateway to her empire in the East, and she had no intention of slackening her grip in the area. The problem was that Egypt was still nominally a vassal of Turkey, and she did not want to rock the boat.

The Turks, for their part, had their own problems. The movement of the 'Young Turks' had weakened the temporal power of Islam, and the authority of the Caliphate; but at the same time they did not mind using Pan-Islamism, if it would help them to hold on to whatever was left of the Ottoman Empire, or to regain, if possible, any of it that had been lost.

Tunisia, Egypt, Morocco and Tripoli were virtually lost, and were occupied by European powers. Russia and Austria-Hungary were competing for influence in the Balkans, which were at one time part of the Ottoman Empire, and although the 'Young Turks' were not thinking about the Balkans, the spark that led to the outbreak of war was struck there.

On June 20th, 1914, the Archduke Franz Ferdinand was assassinated in Sarajevo. The chain of events that followed embroiled the world in war. The 'Central Powers', Germany and Austria-Hungary, joined by Turkey in November 1914, were on one side, and the 'Allies', France, Great Britain, Russia, Italy and Japan, were on the other side. In 1917 the USA joined the allies.

As mentioned before, the Khedive Abbas Helmi was in Constantinople at the outbreak of war, and though he professed his intention to return to Egypt, he did not do so. It has been said that the Turks were reluctant to let him go, and kept him virtually as a hostage, in order to help them regain Egypt from the British in the future. It has also been said that Abbas Helmi, sensing the weakness of the Caliphate, and believing in the eventual defeat of the Allies, was dreaming of becoming Caliph and renewing the grandeur of Mohammed Aly.

Lord Lloyd commenting on the legal status of Egypt at the time, says:

'Constitutionally the ruler of Egypt was the Khedive, and the Council of Ministers were his advisers.

The British had no place in the Constitution, they were legally nothing more than the servants of the Khedive.

There was however one limitation of the power of the Khedive, which was universally recognised in law, and that was that Egypt was a part of the Ottoman dominions, and that the Khedive held office by deed of the Sultan, whose suzerainty he acknowledged.'[53]

It was this legal status and the uproar that would have ensued, that had stopped Britain annexing Egypt to her empire in the past.

Theoretically the Egyptian Constitution provided that, in the absence of the Khedive, the Prime Minister should act as Regent, together with his Council of Ministers and was competent to carry out all policy and government. But in reality the British Consul-General with his British advisers, backed by the occupying army, were the real rulers working behind the scenes.

The Prime Minister at the time was Hussein Roushdi Pasha, an astute politician, a pragmatist, who gauged the situation perfectly. He knew that Egypt had to fall in line behind the British. It was therefore natural that shortly after the declaration of war the Council of Ministers issued a proclamation stating:

'That the presence of the British Army of occupation in Egypt, renders the country liable to attack by the enemies of his Britannic Majesty. And in order to guard against the danger of such a possibility, Egyptian subjects were forbidden to take certain actions. Among which they were not to conclude any agreement, or to subscribe to any loan issued by a country at war with Great Britain. They were to do no business with enemy subjects and finally they were urged to lend all possible aid to Great Britain'.

Britain was quite content at the time with the solution. Turkey had not yet entered the war, although they were sure she would sooner or later, and when she did, they felt it would be on the side of the central powers.

The British authorities in Egypt and the Government in England were undecided on what policy to take in such a contingency. The options considered were either direct annexation to the British Empire, or to declare Egypt a Protectorate with the acquiescence of the Egyptian Government. When Turkey entered the war, Khedive Abbas Helmi made the following appeal to the Egyptian people:

'It has been thirty two years since a foreign nation has occupied our beloved country. And now the decisive hour of our destiny has just struck. Rise up my dear children, both Egyptians and Sudanese, the time is right for our liberation. Let our motto be "Liberate Egypt but respect the foreigners and their property". Our enemies are the British army of occupation and those who collaborate with them. May the Almighty help us to realise our aspirations based on right, justice and liberty'.
Abbas Helmi Pasha, 2nd November, 1914

[53] *Egypt since Cromer*, Lord Lloyd Vol. 1, pages 192, 193

General Maxwell placed Egypt under Martial Law and the Khedive Abbas was virtually deposed. However another two weeks passed before Egypt was *unilaterally*[54] declared a Protectorate of Great Britain. Negotiations had taken place behind the scenes to prevail on Prince Hussein Kamel becoming ruler of Egypt with the title of 'Sultan'.

Prince Hussein Kamel was the son of Khedive Ismail, and the eldest male descendant of Mohammed Aly. He was an honest, amiable man, greatly interested in agriculture and horticulture, with a keen concern for the welfare of the fellaheen. He also had a great love for Egypt. He had not dabbled in politics in the past, as he was afraid of antagonising his nephew Khedive Abbas Helmi, who was very jealous and suspicious of any prince who might be a threat to his position. The Egyptians believed that the British in declaring the Protectorate had promised to lead Egypt to self-government and independence. 'The temporary nature of the Protectorate had been confirmed in a letter sent by King George V to Hussein Kamel in 1915' (*Egypt in Transition* by Jean and Simone Lacouture, page 86).

The following sentence occurred in the body of the note declaring the Protectorate:

> 'His Majesty's government were convinced that the clearer definition of Great Britain's position in the country will accelerate toward self-government'. To which the new Sultan answered when accepting the position offered him, that he expressed his definite wish to associate the people more closely with the government of the country, and asked for a 'more precise definition on Great Britain's position in Egypt, by removing all causes of misunderstanding, will facilitate the collaboration of all the political elements in the country'.[55]

Commenting on both statements Lord Lloyd states:

> 'The immense variety of possible interpretations, while fraught with every kind of future danger, was probably at the time one of the chief reasons why the Egyptians accepted the Protectorate so easily; for them all these vague phrases were in the nature of post-dated cheques, which could not be presented until the war was over.'

Whereas the Egyptians felt that if Britain helped Egypt in getting rid of the Turkish suzerainty, and Egypt received her independence after the war, they had all to gain and nothing to lose in helping England in her war

---

[54]This point is important. According to Lord Lloyd: 'It had previously been understood and accepted that Protectorates overall but quite uncivilized countries had at their basis an agreement jointly subscribed to by the Protector and the Protected. But the British Government either carelessly, or wilfully, disregarded the implications of this usage. And thus the legality of their position in Egypt remained assailable'. *Egypt since Cromer*, Lord Lloyd, Vol. 1, page 207.

[55]*Egypt since Cromer*, Lord Lloyd, Vol. 1, page 208–209

effort. Such help she gave unstintedly. One must remember that Egypt felt it was not her war, she was not threatened, nor had she to defend her country. The British had agreed at the onset that Egypt would not be called on for active war service. But soon a labour corps was raised, at first by voluntary recruitment, and later by conscriptions.

The Egyptians were not affected by Pan-Islamic propaganda:

'The Egyptian army of 30,000 men loyally policed the Sudan; the labour corp contributed 8500 men to the campaign in Mesopotamia, and 10,000 men in France. More Egyptians were recruited for camel transport work in Palestine and Syria. There were eventually 135,000 Egyptians taking part in the Syrian campaign, and official records including General Allenby's despatches bear witness to their reliability. Of the 21,000 Egyptians in the camel transport service in 1917, 220 were killed, 1400 wounded and 4000 died in hospital'.[56]

The Government was compelled by the heavy demands of the British war effort, to requisition the country's corn, cattle, camels and men, which caused a lot of distress among the people.

The British, occupied with their war, paid little heed to this discontent. They considered that the Egyptians had nothing to grouse about. Weren't the conscripts well paid? And wasn't the country receiving good money for any goods supplied? Nevertheless, most Egyptians felt they were being exploited in every way. Whatever money was being spent in the country did not benefit the majority of the people. It was the contractors and the suppliers, not to mention the foreign merchants who creamed off the benefits.

In 1917 Sultan Hussein died. His son, Prince Kamal el Din, did not wish to succeed as Sultan, and renounced all claim to the succession. The next in line was Prince Ahmed Fouad the youngest son of Khedive Ismail. As he had been brought up in Italy, he spoke better Italian than he did Arabic. Although the Prince had played a considerable part in the public life of Egypt, it can't be said that he was overpopular, or influential among the Egyptians. And since he was not considered as an anglophobe by the British, he was selected as the next Sultan.

During the war years political activity in Egypt was at a standstill, due to the declaration of martial law by General Maxwell, and the dissolution of the Legislative Assembly. The people themselves were more concerned with their own private problems than they were with politics.

Saad Zaghloul, until his resignation[57] from the Ministry of Justice in

---

[56]*Modern Egypt*, Tom Little, page 70

[57]Saad Zaghloul resigned as Minister of Justice when some project of legislation of his was rejected by the Khedive and confirmed by Kitchener. He is reputed to have said at a meeting of the Council of Ministers: 'I'm responsible for my department, and my project must pass'.

1912, was always considered by the extreme nationalists as a moderate, and a traitor since he collaborated with the British. He had been appointed Minister of Education by Cromer which post he kept until 1910, when he was appointed Minister of Justice until his resignation. On leaving the Ministry, Saad put himself up for election to the Legislative Assembly. He was elected and within a year he had rehabilitated himself in the eyes of the nationalists, becoming Vice-President of the Assembly in 1913. During his tenure as member, and then Vice-President of the Aassembly, he became known for his outspokenness, his criticism of the Government and the Khedive, his courage, and fiery speeches. However during the war years he tried to calm the anger and frustration of the Nationalists, restraining the hot-heads who always wanted to do something against the British.

But at last the day he had waited for arrived. On November 13th, 1918 two days after the Armistice had been declared Saad Zaghloul Pasha accompanied by Aly Chaaraoui Pasha and Abdel Aziz Fahmy Bey – all former members of the dissolved Legislative Assembly – called on Sir Reginald Wingate the British High Commissioner. They stated that they were a delegation (*Wafd*), the true representatives of the Egyptian people – not the Government of the day – who were asking that the Protectorate should be abolished, and replaced by a treaty of alliance. They also asked to be permitted to travel to England to negotiate the details of such a treaty directly with the British Government.

When their demands were refused, the long struggle for Egyptian independence ensued.

# PART THREE

Esther Fahmy Wissa

# BOOK ONE – A FIGHTING SOUL: ESTHER FAHMY WISSA, HER FAMILY AND TIMES (1895–1990)

*Preamble*

'I think women everywhere will feel a sense of kinship in her interests and ideals' wrote Mrs Eleanor Roosevelt in her column *My Day* of Madame Fahmy Wissa, when that distinguished Egyptian feminist first called on the President's wife at the White House on October 7th (1936). 'I only hope she has a chance to talk in many places throughout the nation. In response to an invitation of the New York Telegram, Madame Wissa has written an article on Egypt's women, their efforts to change social conditions in their country, and their interest in world peace.'

Esther Fahmy Wissa was the product of her immediate surroundings and upbringing, plus what she gleaned from the long and continuing history of Egypt of which she felt she was an incarnate part, and in which she believed she had a great part to play. She linked her destiny to that of Egypt, and a favourite quotation of hers from the Old Testament was:

'In that day shall there be an altar to the Lord, in the midst of the land of Egypt, and a pillar at the border thereof.' (Isaiah 19.19) also 'And it shall be for a sign and for a witness unto the Lord of Hosts in the land of Egypt: for they shall cry unto the Lord because of the oppressors, and He shall send them a saviour, and a great one, and he shall deliver them'. (Isaiah 19.20.)

I don't know if she thought she was the pillar at the border of Egypt, she never said so in so many words, but she believed she had a message which she had to deliver, which may account for the risks she took for the many causes she espoused during her long life.

To her, Egypt was the glorious days of the Pharaohs which were to return according to biblical prophesy:

'In that day shall there be a highway out of Egypt, to Assyria, and the Assyrians shall come into the land of Egypt, and the Egyptian into Assyria, and the Egyptians shall serve with the Assyrians.

In that day shall Israel be the third with Egypt and Assyria, even a blessing in the middle of the land. Whom the Lord of Hosts shall bless, saying, Blessed be Egypt my people and Assyria the work of my hand, and Israel mine inheritance'. (Isaiah 19.23–25.)

Esther interpreted Assyria as being the Western developed nations.

She was interested in Egypt's history insofar as it showed up its inherent strengths and weaknesses. It mattered not that much of Egyptian history resulted from its geography.

To her Egypt was strong during much of her long history, when the country was united, under dedicated honest leaders, her own sons. Whereas she was weak when the country was divided, when their leaders were at loggerheads with each other, when her people were in disarray, a prey to whatever foreign usurper was able to seize power.

She believed that Egyptians, of whom the peasants made up the large majority, were an easy folk due to the country's mild climate. They were good, simple, kind, family-loving, hard-working when in need, obedient to their overlords, and God-loving, but easily aroused by their emotions. But they were also easily calmed, and had a great sense of humour. Their greatest ambition was to be left alone and to be allowed to live in peace. They could be led astray by the wicked, but could be redeemed by the righteous.

Esther Fahmy Wissa, born on February 19th, 1895 as Esther Akhnoukh Fanous, daughter of Doctor Akhnoukh Fanous and Balsam Wissa Boctor Wissa, was the seventh child of fourteen children. A brother and two sisters had died before she was born. She had three older brothers, Louis, Sami and Riad born in 1886, 1890 and 1893 respectively.

Being the first girl that survived, she was spoilt by both her parents. The children were brought up by an English governess when they were older. However, the person who helped her mother run the house and look after the children was a Sudanese liberated slave girl, the daughter of a Sudanese chieftain. She had been captured by Arab slave traders, who had found her playing on the banks of the Nile in her village in the Sudan, and had sold her in the slave market in Assiout in 1850.

She was about nine years old at the time. Her name was Bahr el Nil, known by everyone as Dada Bahr el Nil. Doctor Fanous's grandfather, Raphael, had bought her and she had been given to his grandson Akhnoukh by his mother Mingida to help the newlyweds run their home when he married in 1883.

Dada Bahr el Nil ruled the house with an iron fist. All the servants obeyed her implicitly; even the children respected her and obeyed her. My grandmother, Teta Balsam, never used to countermand any of her decisions. She had been liberated when slaves were freed in Egypt during the reign of Khedive Ismail, but had stayed on as one of the family. She adored Esther, who could do no wrong in her eyes. When she died in 1920 she left her gold bracelets and other jewellery to Esther and her sisters.

Akhnoukh Fanous owned a big house with a basement (within a built-in courtyard) used as a kitchen, servants' quarters and store-rooms. A dumb-

The Akhnoukh Fanous family – 1910
Back Row (left to right) Bahr el Nil (a liberated slave), Joseph, Riad, Louis, Sami, Herbert
2nd Row Ida, Balsam, Akhnoukh Fanous, Esther
3rd Row Gamil, Marie, Gamila

171

The Akhnoukh Fanous family and progeny −1937
Top Row (left to right) Sami Fanous, Gamil Fanous, Joseph Fanous
2nd Row Gamil F. Wissa, Doussa F. Wissa
3rd Row Riad Fanous, Fahmy Wissa, Herbert Fanous
4th Row Hanna F. Wissa, Adli F. Wissa, Ida Fanous, Esther Wissa (Fanous), Louis Fanous
5th Row Adel Fanous, Mae Fanous (Roberts)
6th Row Marie E. Wissa (Fanous), Basma Fanous, Balsam Fanous (Wissa), Gamila P. Wissa (Fanous), Nadia F. Wissa
On the Floor Sadette F. Wissa, Kamal Fanous, Rajia P. Wissa

172

waiter brought up the meals from the kitchen to the pantry to be taken into the adjoining dining-room. The courtyard was surrounded by rooms for the use of any traveller, either Copt or Moslem, who was passing through Assiout and asked for food or shelter.

It had always been the custom, both with Arabs and the Egyptians, that the heads of the gentry of the community, if they were able, kept an open house, offering shelter and food to travellers or strangers passing through the town.

The Akhnoukh Fanous house was such a house. Their gates were never closed. On each side of the gate was a little room for the *Bawab* or gatekeeper. When I used to go to Assiout as a child these two rooms were inhabited by two very old men, with long white beards and moustaches stained yellow round the mouth and nostrils from the nicotine of the hand-rolled cigarettes they used to smoke. One porter was called Mutashaleh or Methuselah, the other Nooh or Noah.

Lunch was always ready for any of the family or their friends who popped in. It was served continually between 2 p.m. and 6 p.m.; dinner from 9 p.m. to midnight. There was no difficulty with the servants, it was part of their life. There was plenty of food for them and their families; they were treated well, and were happy and willing. The cooks and staff could prepare a banquet for fifty within a couple of hours' notice, without grumbling or pouting. They loved parties, probably because of the many different kinds of food that would be prepared, of which they would get their share.

You entered the living area of this one-storeyed house by a large marble staircase leading to a veranda. At each end was a balcony which opened windows from the salon and library on one side, and the visitors' sitting-room and master bedroom on the other. The main entrance was from the veranda into a vestibule, on the left wall of which hung a huge Louis Philippe French mirror, with its accompanying gilt jardiniere. On the right was a door leading into the visitors' sitting-room, with its Arabesque furniture, for those visitors whom you did not want to receive into the house proper. Opposite the main entrance was a small wall, with a curtained archway at each end leading into a huge dark hall. A large Louis Philippe gilt marble-topped table, under a huge French brass and crystal chandelier stood in the centre of this hall, which had a smaller chandelier at each end. Unless the lights were on there was barely enough light from the surrounding rooms to get you around. On each side of the table were S-shaped love-seats, and against the empty walls were sofas with their accompanying armchairs and small tables. On the right was a door leading to the library with its piano, then the salon with its French gilt furniture.

All this furniture was bought from the sales of the Khedive Ismail's furniture when they were liquidating some of the scattered palaces. Next came a door leading to the dining room. At the other far end of the hall were two doors; one led to the main bedroom with its bathroom en-suite, the other to a second bedroom. The dark hall led to an inner hall, by two doors at each end. This hall was very well lit, as a large part of the roof was a light well. In the centre of the hall was an oblong opening in the floor, fenced by a low wall over which were windows, enabling one to see the inner court-yard of the basement. On three sides of this hall were doors leading to the bedrooms, bathrooms and pantry. One end of the opening was nearer the pantry, at the other end was a large living space which was furnished with a comfortable sofa and easy armchairs, where my grandmother used to sit. In winter the centre of this living space was occupied by a large, brass coal brazier to keep us warm; here we would drink hot cinnamon tea, topped with crushed hazelnuts.

Esther was brought up in this large family of brothers and sisters who had to fend for themselves. When they grew up, the brothers had all sorts of schemes and projects which were not always successful. But they were united in that they all were attached to their mother, 'Teta'[1] Balsam, who kept a rein on them. In spite of being hard up at times, she never changed her way of life and kept an open house to all and sundry. A story my mother always liked to tell was that of a relation of hers, Amin Khayatt the only son of Bastawrous Khayatt, one of Assiout's large landowners, who had no appetite and would never eat. His parents were very worried. Someone suggested sending him to the Fanous house to have his meals; maybe the Fanous boys, who were always hungry at meal times, would give him an appetite. The first day he went over, the children were served their food in the nursery. The food disappeared before he could say 'Jack Robinson'. He was too polite to say anything and he went home hungry. The next day he came for lunch and before anyone could serve himself he jumped up saying 'Give me my share, give me my share.' He grew up to be a great gourmet.

When I was young, in the late 1920s and early 1930s, my mother used to take us children from Alexandria to Assiout to spend our three weeks' Christmas holiday. It was a great treat to stay at Teta Balsam's house. I would look out of one of the bedroom windows onto an orchard of man-goes and orange trees. In a walled part of the garden one could see the pigeon tower with its pigeons flying in and out. One could also see chickens picking their food off the ground amidst the gobbling turkeys strutting around.

Out of one of the bathroom windows you could see another part of the yard where women were kneading dough for *shamsi* or sunny bread. This

---

[1] *Teta* is the word used in Egypt to denote 'grandmother'. Maybe it originates from Ancient Egypt.

bread had to be left on wooden plates to rise in the sun before being baked in the oven, which was always lit in the yard.

You could also see a woman squatting in front of a hanging goatskin, full of fresh milk, jogging it backwards and forwards, making lovely balls of fresh butter which we would have on hot shamsi toast with home made grape jam and cream, served by the *suffragi*[2] nicknamed 'Noss', meaning 'Half', as he had been taken on as a small boy. This was when we got back in the afternoon from our donkey rides at Uncle George Pasha Wissa's fruit garden. We would have been taken out in a horse-driven carriage by my father's old liveried coachman, Osta Mohammed, who looked after the different carriages and coaches that were in the coach house of my father's house. This had been closed when Father and Mother decided to make their residence in Alexandria instead of Assiout.

On the way to the garden we would have to cross the Assiout Barrage which had been built in 1906, past the Assiout Sporting Club and Lillian Trasher's well-known orphanage. On the way back, to our delight, Osta Mohammed used to whip the branches of the *nabag* (crab apple) trees that grew on the banks of the Nile, causing their fruit to drop into the carriage.

As a child one of the things I loved about going to Assiout was being taken to father's house by the coachman caretaker Osta Mohammed and shown the automaton kept in the piano room.

It was made up of a porcelain cobalt pedestal divided into sections with gilt brass mounts about five feet high, topped by a music box which looked like a cushion on which sat crosslegged a very good looking negro figure, a hubble bubble next to him, its pipe in one hand and a cup of coffee in the other. Once you wound it up and the music started playing, the figure would turn its head towards the hubble bubble and his arm would raise the pipe to his mouth, he would then bring down the arm and turn his head to the other side and take a sip from the coffee cup. The puppet was dressed in beautiful silk clothes and turban. It must have been stolen some time after the death of Osta Mohammed, because it was not found when we emptied the house in the 1970s.

In 1898 work was started on the Assiout barrage and ended in 1906. It was an 833-meter bridge, 12.50 meters high crossing from the west bank of the Nile in Assiout town to the east bank. It was built by a British company with British engineers. One of its employees, a supervisor of construction, was a young Egyptian engineer Elias Andraous, a Copt, who became in the late forties a crony of King Farouk, and was considered together with Karim Thabet a Lebanese journalist as one of the corruptive elements in the King's entourage. Part of the barrage had a lock that could open to

---

[2] *Suffragi* denotes in Arabic 'he who serves at the table' – assistant butler or footman.

allow boats to pass. It had steel gates in the river with which it was possible to regulate the flow of the Nile.

On the east bank was the Assiout Sporting Club with its tennis courts and its nine-hole golf course, with pressed sand greens instead of grass greens.

The members had fantastic teas on the lawn with homemade American cakes, yearly gymkhanas, football matches, and other entertainments such as tennis tournaments arranged with other clubs from Minieh and elsewhere.

## The Lady on the Donkey

On the east Bank of the Nile, Lillian Trasher built her well-known orphanage.

The story of Lillian Trasher, her orphanage and her life is more like a fairy tale than reality. I will tell you a little about this remarkable lady whom I knew quite well, and her work in Assiout and her achievements from 1911 to her death in 1961 at the age of seventy four. Lillian Trasher was a very beautiful young girl, daughter of a religious farming family in Georgia. She first volunteered for missionary work at a neighbouring orphanage and Bible School in her home country. She was engaged to be married to another missionary, but ten days before her wedding was to have taken place, she got her 'call', she was to become a foreign missionary – in what land she did not know – she had been stirred by a sermon given by a woman missionary who had just returned from India. After hearing this message Lillian felt so burdened within her soul for the people of Africa, that she tried to convince her fiancé to join her on a mission somewhere on that continent. As he would not go with her, she broke off her engagement. Shortly afterwards, with a small sum of money donated by some of her friends, she left her home to travel to Egypt, the land she felt God was leading her to. She arrived in Assiout in October 1910. On February 11th, 1911 Lillian was called to the bedside of a poor widow who was extremely ill. Lillian's heart was moved with compassion when she saw this lady's baby girl of a few months old trying to drink rancid milk from a dirty tin can.

Though Lillian tried to save the mother, she died of complications and the tiny child was left homeless. Finding no one who would care for the baby, Lillian took it home with her. Thus began Lillian's lifelong mission for the destitute Egyptian children in Assiout, which became known as the Lillian Trasher orphanage.

The growth of the orphanage was greatly hampered by lack of funds, but by 1916 Lillian was caring for fifty children. To adequately house her growing family, she bought half an acre of land on the east bank of the Nile. It was there she built the first building.

176

Mama Lillian with some of the children

Christmas present from Mrs Alfred Wissa (née Wadia B. Khayatt) bringing with her Father Christmas with his bag of goodies. Miss Lillian can be seen in the photo next to Santa.

Since Lillian made it a rule never to turn anyone away, the need for food and money never abated. When a new dormitory was needed, the children and Lillian built a kiln, made their own bricks, and raised the building themselves.

Over the years as more people heard of her work, donations of money and materials started coming to her. Additional land was purchased and more buildings were constructed. These buildings included a church, a clinic, a primary school. When she died in 1961 the orphanage had expanded to thirteen large buildings. She was helped by the large Coptic land-owning families of Assiout as much as they could but the demands of the orphanage with the expansion were ever increasing.

Lillian never sent anyone away and was continually expanding; she had difficulty in covering expenses and never knew where the next meal would come from.

Habib Bey Doss a well-known lawyer who married Rosa Guindi Wissa asked Lillian if it was not time for her to put a limit to the number of children she accepted in the orphanage. She told him that it was impossible for her not to take in new children, as people kept dying and leaving orphans.

'Well you'll have to stop some time,' he said.

'Yes,' she said, 'when God stops sending in enough money to support them, I'll stop taking in new ones.'

Money, wheat, meat came in from many different sources. Her sister Jenny who was several years her elder, had come out with her and although it was not her vocation she helped her in her new way of life in this far off town in Upper Egypt, Assiout, which Lillian considered her home until her death.

The orphanage never knew from day to day how it was to meet the cost of its daily needs for its orphans and widows, and it differs not much today. She was known by all in the orphanage as Mama Lillian. She said she had made a deal with the Lord early on in her mission. She told Him:

'I will take care of the babies; You will look after the provisions of food and clothing.' And throughout these many years, this deal has been honoured by God and by those who have followed in Lillian Trasher's footsteps, in the way they operate the orphanage.

Jenny, Lillian's sister, who had come out with her did not feel she had the vocation of a missionary. She loved her sister Lillian, helped her and remained with her for many years. She then travelled back and forth to Egypt, but finally decided to remain permanently with her beloved sister in Egypt. She bought a small villa in Alexandria in 1957 for herself and Lillian, and during the hot summers the two of them would go there for six weeks together with a few children, who had never seen the sea.

In the autumn of 1959, a new car had been sent by a group of missionary-minded young people in the United States. It arrived at an Egyptian port, but was held in bond for a large sum 100% of customs dues. It was impossible for her to raise the necessary amount, so she appealed to the Egyptian Government. When President Gamal Abdel Nasser was informed of her plight, the new car was released without charges. She received a letter later from President Gamal Abdel Nasser which read in part: 'It gives me great pleasure to learn that you got your car free of charge as requested. I would like to tell you that your work for the orphans is very much appreciated by everyone in this country. I wish you continued success in your philanthropic endeavour.'

Her life story is told in a fascinating book called *Lady on the Donkey* by Beth Prim Howell, published by E.P. Doulton and Company, 300 Park Avenue South, New York 10, N.Y.

If any of the readers would like to know more about the orphanage or make contributions please write to:

Lillian Trasher Orphanage
Division of Foreign Missions
1445, Boonville Avenue
Springfield M.065802 1894

or write to the Lillian Trasher Orphanage, Assiout, Upper Egypt.


But let me get back to Esther's childhood. At six she went to the PMI, the American Mission School. She was precocious, idealistic, romantic, superstitious, greatly interested in myth and legend, Ancient Egyptian history and religion. At an early age she started reading the Bible and other books out of her Father's immense library. He was one of the best orators and lawyers in the country; he was also a nationalist, farmer and speculator. Esther got to know the Old and New Testament thoroughly. She could also quote from the Koran, she felt she was destined to be a saviour of Egypt and had a message which she had to deliver.

The missionaries encouraged their pupils to debate and to think and to give their opinions without fear. Esther's father also encouraged her to speak out. She used to tell us how in her teens she used to preach to the fellaheen, telling them stories from the Bible; they were mostly Copts. She was in the habit of taking one of her father's *ghaffirs* (guards) and going into the fields at Walladia, a village on the outskirts of Assiout town proper, just about where the Assiout University is now, and talking to the peasants and answering their questions from the printed Arabic Bible that the American Protestants had introduced.

She was fond of recounting one particular incident that happened to her. One day she was telling her stories in Walladia near a tent that had been erected for some function. As it was hot she stood in the shade of the tent, talking. One of the onlookers went and told the Sheikh of the mosque that there was a Christian girl who was trying to convert them. The Sheikh came back with him and stood listening, and every now and then he would exclaim:

'She's said nothing wrong, she's said nothing wrong.'

Later she got to know the Sheikh very well and many a time they would discuss the Bible and the Koran together.

In my research for this biography I read a very similar story in *Modern Sons of the Pharaohs* by S.H. Leader, who knew Esther and the family well, but he mentions no name. I asked my Aunt Aida, who is a lady of eighty-eight years, if many of the girls from the PMI knew the Koran and the Bible well, and used to go and talk to the fellaheen. She said that she did not think so. She thought it was only her sister Esther who believed she had a message for uniting religions and was in the habit of discussing religion with both Copts and Muslims.

As a very young girl Teta Balsam's uncle, Hanna Boctor Wissa, used to call for Esther in his carriage to take her to school. He was over seventy years old and very cantankerous. He liked talking to her, but she didn't like going with him very much as he was very impatient, and used to call out, '*Ingirii ya bint Ingirii*,' which meant in Upper Egyptian slang, 'Come down girl at once. Come down at once.' He would also leave her at the beginning of the road leading to her school, whereas if she had gone to school in her father's carriage it would have taken her right up to the door. He used to tell her, 'We'll marry you off to Fahmy, we'll marry you off to Fahmy.' Fahmy was his youngest son who was studying at Oxford at the time. In fact they got married ten years later, but that is another story.

The reader might wonder, how is it that Copts marry their first cousins, in spite of the fact that it is banned without special dispensation by the Church in the rest of Christendom. There are many stories giving the reasons. One is that it is common among the Arabs to marry their first cousins, but it is not probable that the Coptic Church would imitate the Arabs in what could be considered Church dogma. It has been suggested that it is an old Egyptian custom, as can be seen by the Pharaohs marrying their sisters.

Another basis mentioned is that Copts loved keeping the money in the family.

But the reason I heard, and which I think most plausible, is that some time during the period when the Memlukes ruled Egypt, I have not been able to find out which ruler it was, a decree was issued fining or punishing any non-Moslem of over sixteen who was not married within a very short time limit. It was not easy to find a wife on command, people did not get about and did not mix except within the close family. So the Coptic

Patriarch at the time, permitted the marriage between cousins, but in order to absolve that sin in the eyes of God, Copts, then and for all future generations, had to fast for an extra fifteen days. This was added to the fast of the Eucharist (Lent) making it fifty-five days instead of forty. During this fast the people were forbidden to eat butter, meat, eggs or fish, they were not to drink milk, coffee or wine and no food had to be taken between sunrise and sunset.

If you ask a Coptic priest the reason for the extra fifteen days of fast, he will reply that it is to prepare ourselves for Lent, or maybe to expiate our sins or to ward off evil days.

## Engagement and Marriage

In July 1912 Zaki Bey Wissa, brother of Balsam, Esther's mother, came to ask if Esther would marry his cousin Fahmy Bey Wissa. The would-be bridegroom was twenty-nine, Esther was seventeen, and although he was her first cousin once removed, they had not mixed much as he was much older. He was an Oxford graduate and had inherited a big fortune, and was well introduced at the palace where the Khedive Abbas Helmy II received him regularly. They were both Freemasons. Fahmy was considered quite a catch. He had always admired Esther.

Zaki, who was the youngest son of Wissa Wissa, was a great friend of Fahmy, they had both gone to the American College at Beyrouth and then went to Oxford together. Being Esther's uncle he used to go to his sister's house often, and was very fond of his niece. He also loved matchmaking. It was usual that the family of the would-be bridegroom would go to the family of the would-be bride and ask for her hand. It was most probable that the bride and bridegroom did not know each other very well, even if they were cousins. Balsam and her husband Akhnoukh, who were quite avant-garde, were delighted but said they would have to ask Esther.

Esther was a romantic and rather liked the idea as Fahmy was a smart young man about town. He had just opened a bank and was very glamorous with his horses and carriages. Esther said she could not decide right away but that she would like to know him better, and gave Zaki a poem to give to Fahmy asking them both to tea next day. The poem she wrote was

'With wavering joy and wondering heart I'll wait
your words of love, which will decide my fate.
If they be true, a red, red rose you'll bring
Which I will cherish more than anything.'

Next day Fahmy came with Zaki for tea. He had forgotten all about the roses, but when he saw her and the expression of disappointment on her

The ceremony

Khedive Abbas Helmi's band

# ESTHER AND FAHMY'S WEDDING

Part of the wedding reception

Bride and Groom, empty plates!

face he looked around and saw a vase of red roses on the table. He went up and took a rose out of the vase and gave it to her.

The period of engagement was about a year, by which time Esther was madly in love with Fahmy, who had had quite a lot of experience with girls in Cairo. On July 24th, 1913 they were married. The Khedive sent his representative to the wedding, together with his private band. A description of the wedding was given in a book written by S. H. Leader called *Modern Sons of the Pharaohs. A Study of the Manners and Customs of the Copts of Egypt*. A picture of the wedding is on the frontispiece. The description reads:

'One of the most gorgeous weddings of recent years, unequalled in Oriental magnificence, it is said, since the spacious days of Ismail, took place at Assiut, between two of my acquaintances, shortly after I had left Egypt after my last visit, in 1914. Miss Esther Fanous, the bride, had read to me some of her charming poems, written in English, and I had often had the pleasure of hearing her speak of her deep joy in the beauties of her beloved country, and of its magnificent, time-old history; and I had also seen her, type of the new Egyptian womanhood, using her gifts to uplift the poor fellaheen by her eloquent pleading in the name of the Cross. I had also met Mr. Wissa, the bridegroom, a graduate of Oxford, and a member of one of the great Coptic families of Upper Egypt.

I give a short account of this wedding, for which I am indebted to a Coptic friend who was present, because it illustrates several things to which reference has been made, and especially shows how the native customs assert themselves on such occasions, in spite of the use that is made of some of the Western modes of life.

Nothing had been spared to make the ceremony the complete success it proved to be. Eastern beauty and Western science blended harmoniously in the gorgeous marquee (suvan) with the myriads of ancient oil lamps and the gorgeous modern electric chandeliers. In this pavilion no fewer than 8000 guests were entertained on one night. Khedivial banners and a magnificent triumphal arch adorned the streets leading to the bridegroom's house. The preparations were said to have cost £20,000.

The entertainment lasted for three days continuously, and the guests, who came from all over the country, included native Pashas, Beys, Omdehs, sheiks, and other notables, besides European Government officials and a host of minor folk.

On the first day eight hundred village notables were entertained to lunch and dinner, a la Turque, by the parents of the bride; and in the evening Abdulhalim Effendi Nahas, the renowned singer, and Sami Effendi Shawas, the violinist, displayed their talents to the delight of a select audience, being accompanied on the mandolin (kanoun) by Mohammed Effendi Omar, most of the pieces being rapturously and repeatedly encored.

On another day the guests from Cairo and Alexandria, and many from Assiut, including native and foreign officials, distinguished residents and their families were entertained to lunch at the Wissa mansion, and in the evening they attended a special reception given by the bride's mother, Mme. Akhnoukh Fanous, whose house was beautifully decorated with flowers and coloured lights. At 8 p.m. the guests began to arrive, being greeted by the band of the Wissa school with Arabic and European airs; and at nine o'clock Fethy Pasha, the Mudir of Assiut, led the way to supper. After this, the toasts and speech-making ended, the male guests proceeded to the Wissa mansion to hear Arabic songs by Mohammed Effendi el Saba, accompanied by Mohammed Effendi Omar's orchestra.

Another day was devoted to the entertainment of the native ladies, who lunched with the bride's family, and took part in the procession to the bridegroom's house, the Wissa's meantime entertaining hundreds of native villagers, Moslem and Christian, to a Turkish luncheon.

On the afternoon of each of the three days, splendid displays of horsemanship were given in front of the bride's house by members of leading local families on richly caparisoned steeds, each performance ending with a procession around the house, the horsemen beating drums and shouting such phrases as, "Amar ya beit Fanous" – "May the house of Fanous flourish for ever!"

An interesting incident took place when the leading horseman, noting Dr. Fanous (who was an invalid) on the balcony, rode his horse up the great flight of steps to salute him, the doctor rising to his feet to grasp the hand of the cavalier, who then rode down again, amid the frenzied shouts and cheers of the vast crowd below.

At 8 p.m. on the evening of the wedding itself, the procession, preceded by the band and torch-bearers, and a contingent of mounted police, and composed of over a hundred carriages, proceeded to the large marquee. Here it was met by Coptic choristers, chanting a hymn of welcome, who accompanied the bride and her party to the dais, where the wedding ceremony was performed by the Coptic bishops and clergy. The officiating clergy included Orthodox and Protestant representatives, the Patriarch having delegated two bishops to represent him, writing at the same time his great regret that age and infirmity prevented his personal attendance. There were also present the Bishops of Assiut, Khartoum and Kena, the latter being accompanied by the full choir of his church.

The five prelates, and the Reverend Mouawad Hanna, united the bridal pair with full Orthodox and Protestant rites, according to the desire of the patriarch, the Coptic Orthodox and Protestant choirs chanting sacred verses and selected psalms. Both bride and bridegroom belong to the Protestant Church, Dr. Akhnoukh Fanous being President of the Church Council, the Megliss el Milli.

After the ceremony, which lasted an hour, Khalil Moutran, the native poet, and others, recited beautiful epithalamia in prose and verse.

At 11 p.m. a sumptuous supper was first served to three hundred guests, and afterwards to several thousands of the poorer people, the feasting going on until 2 a.m. The Moslem and Christian ladies were privately entertained meantime in the house. The festivities were not over until 5 a.m., when they ended in singing and dancing.'

The couple honeymooned in Alexandria. Mother did not conceive in the first year, and she became very worried. The Copts followed the Islamic laws of inheritance, which provided that a deceased *with no direct male issue* could not ensure that all his estate would be inherited by his daughters and/or wife. Depending on the data of each case a certain percentage of the estate devolved on any living sister or brother, or even nephews, sons of deceased brothers, if no living brother existed at the time of death who had priority over a nephew.

It was also very important in the eyes of the young brides that they should provide a male heir as soon as possible to ensure that any future estate should devolve on the deceased's children, after providing for the wife and any living parent. It was the bride's way of self-preservation. Esther was no exception; in spite of her idealism, broadmindedness and generosity, she had a streak of pragmatism. She was very down to earth in business matters.

Mother and Father decided that under the circumstances they should go for a cure in Europe, as well as taking a second honeymoon. They boarded a ship in Alexandria accompanied by Father's *valet de chambre* and Esther's sister Gamila. My aunt Aida, Gamila's elder sister, was supposed to have left with my parents, but she had trouble with her teeth, and the would-be honeymooners were afraid of complications. So they took Gamila instead.

Aida has always said that it was very unfair of my grandmother sending Gamila, since she was the one that wheedled the money for the trip out of her uncle George, who always considered her as his favourite niece, and who was the liquidator of the Wissa estate, and still administered a large part of it. They went to one of the spas in Hungary for a cure and then to Paris and Austria, where they were caught when war was declared. They had a difficult time on their return as all trains had been requisitioned by the German army. England was at war with Germany, and Egypt had been declared a Protectorate.

A *wagon lit* guard had been persuaded by Father to allocate them a compartment and lock them in for the night. He had refused to give the same compartment to an English family from Alexandria, who were livid that Egyptians should have received better treatment than they. When they arrived at the next junction Father stayed with the luggage and Mother rushed off to get similar treatment on the next part of the trip. By persuasion she was able to obtain the required compartment. The same English family were pipped at the post once again. When the English lady saw that Father and Mother had obtained what she considered should have been her compartment she cried out: 'That girl has done it again!' Esther and the English family became friends when Father and Mother built their residence in Alexandria fifteen years later.

In 1915 Mother bore her first son whom she named Wissa, but was known generally as Gamil, which means 'beautiful.' Her next son born in 1917 was named Adly, which means 'just'. In 1919 she had her third child, a girl whom they named Firdous, which means 'Paradise', after her paternal grandmother. Firdous is generally known as Doussa. Mother was very proud of her young family and her life was totally tied up with them. She was not yet interested in politics, but she was still very interested in religion and Biblical prophecy.

Towards the end of 1914 Father's bank got into financial difficulties. Clients were not paying back their overdrafts and a moratorium had been declared in the country. Father had to mortgage his land in order to save himself from bankruptcy. He was even toying with the idea of accepting an offer from George to buy all his land, pay off his debts, and give the family a perpetual annuity, but then thought better about it and refused the offer.

Fahmy and Esther and first three children
(from left) Doussa, Gamil, Adly (who died in 1921)

At one time Father was very worried. A big instalment on his mortgage was due and it had to be settled in the near future. Mother decided to go off on her own bat and offer one of our best farms at Beni-Zeid to Amin Khayatt, a rich relation. He received her courteously but said he had just bought another farm. She went back home and Father found her sobbing. She felt she had made a fool of herself and let Father down by losing face. Father was very angry with her and told her so.

That afternoon she prayed, asking God to find a way out of her predicament. She felt that she should have prayed instead of taking things into her own hands. Suddenly, the suffragi knocked at the door and said that a fellah (farmer) was asking for Father, and as Father was not at home she went out to meet him. He told her that he came from a village called Gallanish, where the land was not very good, and where we had a farm. He asked if we wanted to sell the farm. She replied in the affirmative and as he wanted to know the price demanded, she asked for the exact price of the instalment, which he accepted. A few hours later another farmer called and asked if we wanted to sell a whole lot of bricks that were lying in one of the farms. She had never heard of the bricks. But as he offered a big price, she got in touch with our overseer and clinched the deal. When father came home he found that one of his worries had been resolved. Mother always said that God always answered her prayers when she was in a tight corner.

The reader will by now have had some inkling of Esther's character, and although it mellowed in time, yet the inborn streak was always there. She had been protected all her life, and therefore knew no fear. Her impulsiveness resulted from a self-esteem that did not allow her to accept statements of situations that she considered unfair or disparaging to Egypt, or the Egyptians, whether they were Moslems or Copts. She'd jump into the fray. A typical example of the above will be seen from the letter she wrote to the *Sphinx* in its issue of March 30th, 1918. She was then twenty-three years old. She wrote as follows:

'Dear Sirs,

Reading the article in the "Sphinx" of March 30th 1918 entitled the "Native Woman" I've taken the liberty of answering that special column about the Coptic Woman which has been very unjustly treated by the writer.

The writer says that he deals only with the women of the upper classes, so we take it for granted that he is dealing also with the upper class of the Coptic woman. Henceforth, I shall only speak of this class, and I think I'm justified in what I shall state hereafter:

There is not one Coptic girl of the upper class in my generation, that I know who has not had a fairly good education, most of which is equal to that of any Syrian or Moslem girl educated in Egypt. The Coptic parent sends his daughter to the best school in the land, which can be proved if a report could be taken from the most prominent schools in the country, where the exact number of Coptic girls are given

188

ycarly.

All the families with whom I am connected, and they are numerous, and many others besides, have English nursery-governesses and governesses for their children since their very early childhood, and our babies learn to prattle in at least two languages from their very beginning.

Every Coptic girl of the upper class and many a one of the middle class, studies English, Arabic, French and music, the perfect acquirement of which of course depends solely on her intellectual capacities and skill. And I am pleased to say that with our Moslem sister we still study the Arabic language and it is most fortunate that we know our parents' language as well as we know English or French. Quite a few of our girls have had their education abroad, either in England or France, a matter which is not in my opinion to be recommended as it makes all Egyptian girls dissatisfied with their life in Egypt after their return.

I find very amusing the statement that the suppression of the primary certification annoyed the Copts. I hardly know of any Coptic girl of the upper class who have had their education in government schools, and nowhere else is that primary certificate of education given. The few ladies of my acquaintance who have been educated in government schools have attained the baccalaureate and teacher's certificate, and more than one holds a prominent position as an advanced teacher in government schools.

It is true that most of our girls marry when they reach a certain age, and that perhaps is the reason why we do not find as many Coptic teachers as there are Syrians, although we have a good number; and, since I think that every girl should benefit of the chance of a good husband which is the cherish of all womenkind all over the world, I do not find in this any place for criticism.

The matter of early marriages also accounts for the scarcity of literature written for public perusal by Coptic girls, as domestic duties and social engagements take up most of a married woman's time.

But we are somewhat to blame, for we should prove to the world that the Coptic Woman's mind is as strong and educated as any other, and her upbringing is as sound and advanced, and her manner is as refined, and her morals are unblemished.

It is true that the Copts have not adopted a uniform costume, but most of the younger generation of the upper class dress in the European fashion and most of them are as smart and as well dressed as any European. If the writer had not written an anonymous article, we could have proved to him the fallacy of his statement, for in all his criticisms and praises we find a lot of prejudice, exaggeration and wrong information.

What the writer has said of the home of the Syrian woman of the higher class, may be equally said of the Coptic woman of that same class, and it is not such a rare thing among them to see "the waiter at the dining table dressed in the traditional evening coat, and wearing white gloves".

The Coptic girl is free to go out as much as she wants and we do not see her staying at home as much as the writer speaks of. It is true that we do not care to mix with all kinds of men but we all meet our husbands' friends, at least those of them who are deemed worthy to have free entrance into the Coptic family. And here I would take liberty to advise my fellow sisters and country women not to follow blindly in the footsteps of what is termed civilization, for we could soon approach the stumbling block.

It would be more useful for us to acquire what is good in nations, and still cling to our own sound morals and ideas. Till now the Coptic woman is neither bold nor forward, neither is she a flirt, but she fulfils her duties to the best advantage and is a very good help to her husband and a very good mother to her children.

189

The writer says that:- "The best gauge by which the enlightenment of a native is measured, is the marriage of their daughters with foreign men of a superior civilization".

This is not so, in the case of the Coptic girl, because it is practically impossible for a Coptic parent of good standing to consent to the marriage of his daughter to a foreigner.

Our men find a lot of opposition from their families when they marry foreigners. It would therefore be unthinkable for a young girl who was still under her parents' control to attempt to do so.

I, myself disapprove of foreign alliances, for in every nation there clings some peculiar customs or habits cherished by one nation and despised by the other, that causes a friction in the home and it is more advisable for every nation to keep to its own. If the writer's love of intermarriage which is apparent from his article was carried into execution, it would be a very mixed world indeed and very different from what it has been in every way.'

It is amusing to note that within fifty years of this letter three of Esther's six children were married to foreigners.

## *Where Are the Hats?*

It was in March 1919 that Makram Ebeid, a well-known lawyer, orator and politician, a friend of Father's, who had been at Oxford with him, paid the family a visit. He told them that Zaghloul Pasha and some of his colleagues intended to travel to England to ask the British Government to abolish the protectorate over Egypt and to give her complete independence. They wanted to know the attitude of the leading Copts on the matter. The family expressed great enthusiasm for the idea and promised to collaborate wholeheartedly.

The following is the exact wording of a speech given by Esther at a meeting celebrating the Jubilee of the emancipation of Egyptian women, and their freedom from the veil, which gives a short outline on the subject throwing some light on Mother's life:

'Ladies and Gentlemen,
Today as we celebrate the Jubilee of the emancipation of Egyptian women and their freedom from the veil, I would like to mention the circumstances and events that brought this about. The cause of emancipation of women was taken up by Mr. Kassem Amin and Mrs. Bahisat el Badia, but did not reach any satisfactory result. So when the revolution of 1919 under the leadership of Saad Zaghloul Pasha arose, and women played such an important part in it, a chance was given them to realise their hopes.
I shall relate what happened from my personal experience. One day a friend of ours, Maitre Makram Ebeid, came to see my husband and told us that Zaghloul Pasha and some of his colleagues intended to go to England to ask the British Government to remove the Protectorate over Egypt and to give her complete independence. They wanted to know the attitude of the Copts towards that step. We

H.E. Saad Pasha Zaghloul, founder of the Wafd Party, and main force behind the 1919 Revolution, demanding the abolition of the Protectorate by Britain, and the union with the Sudan.

Madame Safia Zaghloul, wife of Saad Pasha, and daughter of Mustapha Fehmy Pasha, Prime Minister of Egypt under Cromer. Madame Zaghloul was known as the Mother of the Egyptians, and her house was known as the House of the Nation (*Beit-el-Omma*).

expressed our great enthusiasm for that project and promised to collaborate whole-heartedly.

I then went to Assiout with my children, and the next day heard that Zaghloul Pasha and three others were arrested by the British and deported to Malta. I sat down and wrote an appeal to President Wilson in verse asking him to see that our leaders would be allowed to travel and present their cause. The students in Cairo had demonstrated and some of them were shot by the British soldiers. I was so worked up that I wrote this appeal,

'For four we gave that cause and furthermore
We'll give, four hundred, four thousand
Four million and a half to free the four
And thrice that number are resolved to see,
That justice in our land will come to be.
Our old rejuvenated, our young men brave
Our women turned to men, our children grown
Will all unite, to fight a cause so grave.'

I decided to leave for Cairo at once. My mother said, "You have just arrived; how can you leave so soon." I said, "If I don't go now, I shall not be able to leave." That was a true prophecy, for riots broke out and the railways were damaged and all communications between Cairo and Upper Egypt were disrupted for a long time. In the meantime revolution was seething, riots everywhere, strikes, and demonstrations all over the country.

On my arrival in Cairo I went to see Madame Zaghloul Pasha and expressed to her our wholehearted cooperation in the movement, to see that the leaders were liberated and that our country was given her independence. I showed her the appeal I had written to President Wilson, of which she approved. She told me to get this appeal signed by three women, and sent to President Wilson immediately.

A few days afterwards, My aunt, Mrs. Khayatt, received a telephone message telling her that if she loved her country, she was to go to a certain house in the Rue Kasr el Nil. The next morning we went to that address and were met by an imposing lady who looked at us and said, '*What, where are the hats?* Are there only three of you?' Esther Mangabadi was the third lady in a hat. By '*hats*' she meant the Coptic women who had been emancipated forty years earlier. My aunt answered, 'It is true we are only three, but each one of us is worth a thousand.'

There were about a thousand ladies in that house, all veiled. We signed the protests that were prepared and started out in a big manifestation carrying flags and slogans. After a little march we were stopped and surrounded by the British soldiers with pointed guns and bayonets. We started to remonstrate with them and one of the ladies said pointing to her chest, "Shoot me if you will. You will only make of me a second Nurse Cavell."

After keeping us standing about an hour in the hot sun we were allowed to disperse and go home.

That same evening I received a visit from three distinguished ladies, Mme. Riaz Pasha, Mme. Omar Sultan Pasha and Mme. Abousbah Bey. They told us how much they admired our stand before the British soldiers and asked us to join them in the cause of Egypt's freedom. Next day they introduced us to Mme. Hoda Chaarawi, and we decided to form a committee, representing the women of Egypt to work alongside the Wafd. We held a big meeting at the Morkosiah Church, as political meetings were forbidden. There were about three thousand women there and they voted for

A reception given for Madame Saad Pasha Zaghloul in the summer of 1924 at Fahmy Bey Wissa's residence in Alexandria.

Safia Hanem Zaghloul in the centre, Esther at the bottom of the stairs, hanging on to the author at 3½ years of age, next to him Doussa holding some flowers and a little flag, Gamil in a sailor suit holding a flag, other members of the family and friends. It is interesting to note that some of the Moslem ladies, who have lowered their veils still have them hanging on their shoulders.

the committee. Mme. Hoda Chaarawi was elected President, Fikreya Hosni, Ihsan el Kousy and myself as Secretaries.

We started by sending protests, writing articles in the daily papers, and our work was of great value. After the liberation of Zaghloul Pasha from Malta we held a big meeting to celebrate his return and welcome him and his colleagues. As Miss Fikreya Hosni rose to give her speech, being veiled, Zaghloul Pasha got up and removed her veil. Since that time all women went about unveiled.

One day we were invited to a Mosque for another political meeting and we made speeches there. This was the first time that women ever entered the Mosque with men.

When Zaghloul Pasha and three other leaders were deported to the Seychelles, we wrote several protests to Lord Allenby defending our cause and asking for the immediate liberation of our leaders. And when other members of the Wafd were arrested and were sentenced to life imprisonment where they suffered under very hard conditions, we wrote to Lord Allenby stating these facts, asking him to see that they were given more comfortable quarters. He immediately ordered that they be removed to other quarters with better conditions. I must admit that Lord Allenby was very courteous to us at the time and often answered our letters in his own hand-writing. Some of these letters I still have in my possession.

We women then started to form societies for social welfare. One of these societies inaugurated in April 1919 was named *The New Woman Society* which still exists, and now has a school and a charity workshop and a training centre for nurses. They are also now preparing a home for the aged and infirm.

In 1923 the Feminist Union was inaugurated under the leadership of Mme. Hoda Chaarawi and took part in many world Congresses. This society also has a school and a charity workshop and is doing good social work until now. The 'Mobarat Moham-med Aly' was inaugurated in 1908 and has several hospitals both in the big cities and in the Provinces. Several other welfare organizations were formed and there are now more than 150 different women's benevolent societies, besides many others where they work side by side with the men.

The universities then opened their gates wide to the Egyptian girl, and we have many thousand graduates from all the Universities. We now have many women doc-tors, lawyers, teachers, head mistresses, engineers, pharmacists, agriculturalists, civil servants, etc. We have even had one woman Minister in the Cabinet, thanks to the 1952 Revolution under the leadership of President Gamal Abdel Nasser. What a dif-ference between the women of today and the woman of yesterday when a girl of ten years old was removed from school and kept at home, where she saw no men except for her father and brothers, where she never saw her fiancé except on the eve of her marriage! Today things are different, she goes everywhere, meets men, works side by side with them, and goes out everywhere with her fiancé. All this arose from her par-ticipation in the Revolution of 1919, and the first step taken in demonstrating with her veil in the streets of Cairo, and her demand for the recognition of her rights and her freedom.

So now the women of Egypt enjoy full rights, both civil and political as you can see by the number who have been elected as members of Parliament.'

There are a couple of points mentioned in Esther's speech which could be food for thought. I don't think she intended us to ponder over them, she was just relating what had happened. I will try and elaborate on her state-ments, as I think they are important, if one is trying to understand Egyp-tian history in the twentieth century. The first point was that enlightened

A feminist meeting at Esther Fahmy Wissa's residence in Alexandria, addressing the meeting is Madame Hoda Chaaraoui Pasha, President of the Feminist Movement in Egypt – seated Esther is looking up at her and listening.

195

thought in the country was advocating the emancipation of women, and the improvement of their lot, for at least thirty years before men allowed it to happen. It took a charismatic national leader, Saad Pasha Zaghloul, to captivate the minds of the people, inspiring women to participate in the national struggle for independence; who at the same time took advantage of the political upheaval in the country to further their own ends, and express their yearnings. Even then, it took thirty-seven years of long and weary struggle and another upheaval in the country for women to achieve their political rights, which were granted to them by another charismatic national leader, the late President Gamal Abdel Nasser in 1956.

Esther's speech gives the impression that the abolition of the veil, and the emancipation of women in Egypt, came about accidentally, and directly from the 1919 revolution. This may be partly true, in that the uprising of 1919 gave women a chance to express their views in public, thus loosening the fetters of their traditional society.

Many Egyptian intellectuals had pondered and argued in the later years of the nineteenth and early twentieth century, about ameliorating the plight in which the Egyptian woman on the whole, and the Moslem woman in particular found themselves. They advocated the necessity for change by ameliorating some aspects of degradation seen in the norms and ways of the life of Egyptian women. There is no doubt that Islam was further advanced than most of the rest of the world, with regard to the rights of women in administering their own financial matters, before and after marriage. These rights were sacrosanct, whereas many other cultures subjugated women's property rights to their husbands once they were married. Criticism however lay mostly in the segregation of women, their marital status and the upbringing of their children. Coptic women had followed the customs of the majority, and were not seen publicly but mixed within a close circle. Although they were not restricted by religious tenets, they were traditionally conservative in their behaviour. However, under the influence of the American missionaries and Western culture and education they were able to discard the veil in most parts of Egypt towards the end of the nineteenth century. As regards their marital status and the upbringing of their children, there had been no problem, as polygamy and divorce were non-existent.

However tradition was so strong that in some parts of Upper Egypt, Christian women still covered their faces when moving about in up-country towns as late as the 1930s and for a very long time into the 1940s, there was a distinct role for women, and another for men in Egyptian society.

It was left to a judge, a friend of Saad Zaghloul, Kassim Amin, to express these thoughts in print, which he did when he published a book in 1907 entitled *The Liberation of Woman*. This struck public opinion like a thunderbolt and his ideas were attacked as sacrilege by traditionalists, the guardians of fanaticism and ignorance; and although Saad Zaghloul and his like sympathised with these thoughts, believing that a country aspiring to liberty could not afford to have half the population shackled and inarticulate, no practical steps were taken to amend the situation. These writers expounded that Egyptians should liberate themselves before trying to liberate their country; and since man was his mother's creation, a woman who was born a slave, accepting her fate without protest, could not expect to nurture anything but a slave as her son.

In spite of such ideas expressed by Kassim Amin and his followers, and later by women like the poetess Malek Hefni Nassef nicknamed Bahissat El Badia, it was not until 1919 that the seed that had been sown twenty years earlier flowered, and it was as late as 1956 before women were given their political rights by men during the 1952 Revolution. It was in 1969 that the late President Gamal Abdel Nasser convened a conference to commemorate fifty years since the emancipation of the Egyptian woman, and her freedom from the veil. Delegates from world feminist movements were invited. Amongst the speakers were the representatives of Lebanon, Sudan, Kuwait, Iraq and Syria. Speeches were also made by Miss Eva Bloomer, representing the World Feminist Federation, as well as by its former President Mrs Margaret Kurt Ashley, a friend of Madame Hoda Chaaraoui, founder of the Egyptian Feminist Union.

Mme Amina Saied, the well-known writer, gave a discourse on how Egyptian women persevered until they obtained their political rights.

It was at this celebration that the late President Gamal Abdel Nasser honoured four of the many women who participated in the 1919 struggle for independence with the Order of Perfection (Wissam el Kamal). These were Hadiyat Barakat, Ihsan El Koussi, Esther Fahmy Wissa and Gamila Attia. The last three named attended the reception, the fourth lady, Hadiyat Barakat, did not attend as she died the same morning.

It was under these circumstances that Esther was propelled in 1919 into the political storm demanding the independence of Egypt and the Union with the Sudan. Her interest in the emancipation of women and her demand for the vote developed as a result, as did her involvement in social and public affairs.

Until then although idealistic, religious, and a searcher after truth, Esther was not active in politics as such. This was part of a man's domain, for in spite of her being brought into contact with political ideas, having had Akhnoukh Fanous as a father, she did not imagine at the time that it was her call of duty. However, she was always opinionated, willing to champion a cause which she felt was right; and when she was asked to join in the struggle for independence, she rushed in headlong. Her father whom she idolised, had been paralysed in 1912 before her marriage. It was believed that he had overtaxed his health in political matters at the time. He died in 1918, and she saw in Saad Zaghloul, a father figure, an idealist who was

197

willing to sacrifice everything for his principles, and who could do no wrong in her eyes.

The political developments that took place in Egypt after Saad Zaghloul and his companions had called on Sir Reginald Wingate, the British High Commissioner, were swift and unpredicted by either the British establishment in Egypt or the politicians at Whitehall. Both were totally unprepared.

The Egyptian Government during the war years had been occupied with helping the British war effort, running the government smoothly, and keeping the status quo. The Legislative Assembly had been dissolved and the country was ruled by decree, and since political parties had been banned, all aspirations for a revision of the relationship between Egypt and England had been put on ice. But that did not mean that the Egyptians had given up the thought of independence. They had helped England because they believed she would help them get rid of the hateful Turkish rule. The principles of peace proclaimed by President Wilson in his famous Fourteen-Point Plan, including self determination for every race and tribe after the war, encouraged the Egyptians to believe that no doubt these principles would apply to them. After an allied victory they wanted to be free from all interference and live happily ever after. The Arabs had been invited to the World Peace Conference to state their grievances and present their case. The Egyptians felt they were not inferior to the Arabs, and should be given the same chance.

Saad Zaghloul during the war years had not agitated against the British. On the contrary, he had always tried to curb any excesses thought up by young hotheads expressing the general discontent of the occupation. Egyptians had become fed up with being pushed around by foreigners in their own country, meddling in their daily affairs.

At the same time as Saad was restraining extremists he was working among educated Egyptians to procure a strong and united demand for a radical revision of Anglo-Egyptian relations after the war. Saad was not only a nationalist but a humanist as well. He loved animals, and voiced 'his convictions in simple but picturesque phrases', appealing to the ordinary man. He once told a donkey boy who was beating his beast 'Animals cannot talk but they understand', whereas 'Human beings can talk but they do not always understand'. When Saad Zaghloul and his companions presented their demands to Sir Reginald Wingate, they tried to be both courteous and forthright, having stated that they considered England as the highest and most liberal of powers, and as such they asked for her friendship in the name of the principles of freedom which guided post-war policy. They then proceeded to state Egyptian aspirations. Sir Reginald could not believe his ears, 'They constituted a programme for complete autonomy of Egypt, reserving to Great Britain the supervision of the country's debt, and special facilities with regards to the Suez Canal.'

The High Commissioner did not consider Saad Zaghloul and his companions as spokesmen for Egypt, as there was an Egyptian Government and Prime Minister in office at the time, whose demands were less radical. In fact the government had no definite demands but at the same time expressed their desire to reopen the whole question of the interpretation of the Protectorate by negotiation and that, as soon as possible, although this had been tacitly understood when Sultan Hussein accepted the Sultanate, as mentioned before.

Sir Reginald replied to Saad that he was not in a position to announce the intentions of His Majesty's Government. However, within a few days Saad asked to be allowed to proceed to London with his companions, to lay the case directly to His Majesty's Government, and when that was refused, the Prime Minister of Egypt suggested that he and his colleague Adly Pasha Yeghen should leave for London to discuss the Egyptian question with the British Government. Although the later course was recommended by the High Commissioner, Whitehall answered that on no account did they want to open talks with Egyptian ministers as the time was not opportune.

The argument that Saad did not represent the Egyptian people now became invalid, since the British Government did not wish to negotiate with the Prime Minister of Egypt. In fact they did not want to negotiate with anyone. Such an attitude adopted by Britain only helped to consolidate Saad's position in Egyptian eyes. He became their champion, the magnet to which all national thought gravitated.

Local committees were formed both in the villages and towns where people aired their grievances. They blamed the high prices and scarcity of commodities on the British and their war. The quality of British officials in the administration had deteriorated with their increase in numbers, and 'whereas at one time the British were feared and respected rulers, they now had become feared and hated exploiters.'[3] The Egyptians felt that they were being milked dry. Britain did not realise the depth and change in political thought and opinion in Egypt that had taken place in the country since the death of Mustapha Kamel in 1907 and the end of the war in 1918.

Mustapha Kamel had been a dreamer, and aimed at gaining the sympathy of the élite and educated of national and international opinion, whereas Saad Zaghloul, a pragmatist, touched the heart of the Egyptian people themselves. He was encouraged by his wife and helpmate Safia, whom the emerging feminist movement symbolised as their leader. Furthermore, the Egyptian people by 1918 longed for a change, but they could not envisage how this might come about. They needed a leader who would

[3]*Napoleon to Nasser* by Raymond Flower, page 135

light the way, whom they could understand as one of their own, whom they could associate with, who talked the same language and had the same thoughts. It was not as if there were no politicians or leaders in Egypt. There were intelligent, well-educated and capable leaders, but they appealed to the educated and élite of society, not to the man in the street, the fellah, the small effendi. In spite of the fact that these potential leaders were sincere and dedicated to the national cause they were not appreciated by the masses. To the ordinary man they were foreigners, of a different class, the Turco-Circassians, not Egyptians. Saad had a certain charisma for the crowds, just as the spawn of the French Revolution with their cry of *liberté, egalité, fraternité* had appealed to the masses in the Paris streets.

Saad, to them, was a fellah who had succeeded, who had attained the pinnacle. He understood their problems; having lived with them himself, he was one of them. He had been sent as a child to the Kouttab (a village elementary school) where he had learnt to read and write. As he was bright, he entered a mosque where he perfected his understanding of the Koran, a source which gave him a great command of grammatical and literary Arabic. Due to his perseverance and hard work he joined the University of El Azhar, where he was influenced by the teachings of such reformers as Sheikh Mohammed Abdu. At the age of twenty-one he became an editor on the staff of the *Official Journal*, which at the time was not confined to the printing of decrees and laws, but included a section in which the great writers and thinkers of the time expressed their views. In 1892 he was appointed a councillor to the Court of Appeal, and since Egyptian law emanated from the *Code Napoléon* he decided to improve his French, which he had started to learn at the age of forty, to obtain a degree in law from Paris. Having climbed up the ladder of success and married the then Prime Minister, Mustapha Fehmy's daughter, Safia, he was appointed Minister of Education by Lord Cromer in 1907 who stated in his parting speech from Egypt, 'Due to his capacity, sincerity, straight-forwardness and courage, if I am not mistaken, I predict that Saad Pasha will have a brilliant future'. To the followers and admirers of Saad and his policies between the years 1918 to 1927, Lord Cromer's prediction was not far wrong.

Although coming from poor beginnings Saad's capacity, character and success made him acceptable both politically and socially, to the main body of Egyptian society.

Saad Pasha's career between 1907 and 1912 was routine, and although he accomplished much in the departments he was responsible for both as Minister of Education and Justice, he was not particularly in the limelight. But when he resigned as Minister of Justice in 1912 on a question of principle, because he would not kow-tow to pressure from the Khedive or Kitchener, he became a centre of attraction, and rose in the eyes of some of the members of the Nationalist party who had previously regarded him with suspicion because of his modcrate ideas.

Perhaps one of his weaknesses was his lack of magnanimity towards those he considered his enemies or detractors, which became noticeable during his political career later on, a trait observed in many fellaheen.

In 1913 Saad put himself up for election to the legislative assembly, and rose to become its Vice-President. His eloquence, clear thinking and fiery speeches criticising the government and the Khedive, spotlighted him as a potential leader, whereas previously he had been considered as an honest, hardworking, government administrator. He became the Prince Charming of the masses, who expected him to perform miracles for the country. He was the pole to which nationalists of all colours gravitated for a time. But when these miracles were not forthcoming his opponents blamed him for being intransigent and trying to profit from the Egyptian political scene and circumstances, to build his reputation and crown his life in glory. In spite of such accusations, Saad Zaghloul was the catalyst that broke down and amalgamated the conflicting elements that made up the Egyptian nation, forging them into a political party, the Wafd, that dominated the scene until the 1952 Revolution. The second fact mentioned by Esther in her speech that needs elaborating, was that the Coptic Egyptians were invited by Saad Zaghloul and his followers to unite with them in their demand for independence. I have read time and again, whenever there was any sectarian trouble in the country, of the strength of the unity of the Copts and Moslems during the 1919 Revolution under Saad Zaghloul Pasha. But no one seems to have wondered why there was such a unity. Perhaps articles have been written on the subject which I have not read, and no doubt a lot could still be written. I must admit I have not delved deeply into the subject. But what I feel from observing Egyptian politics from afar, from personal experience, and from the little knowledge I have of human behaviour, is that the Copts backed the 1919 Revolution wholeheartedly because they were invited to do so.

They became willing members in the struggle for the future of their beloved country. They became articulate participants, whereas previously they were stammering onlookers. They felt it was not only a toleration by the majority of a minority, but an appeal by the majority to the minority to unite with them under one banner to fight for a common cause, to which the minority responded enthusiastically. Some cynics and detractors were inclined to state that Saad felt he was in a minority when dealing with the majority of the old politicians, who emanated from the old Europeanised Turko-Circassian families, the rulers by birth, who maybe in their heart of hearts looked down on him. Whereas he, a fellah, had climbed to the summit by his own ability, as had the large Coptic landowners who joined and backed him. They not only bolstered his prestige as followers, but helped fill his party's coffers. At the same time these detractors stated that it was the self-interest of the Coptic landowners, not their nationalism, that was behind the Copts' fervour, who wanted to hold on to, and increase any privileges or influence they had in the country, by joining Saad. But the real reasons are less cynical and deeper than that. The large Coptic land-owners and their followers who joined the Wafd were flattered when they felt they were needed and accepted as useful members of the community.[4] They helped the government by raising and ameliorating the state of affairs by combining with the majority and becoming one happy family. '*L'unité fait la force*'; it was a novel and exhilarating feeling for them.

We have all heard of the principle 'Divide and Rule' invented by imperialism, to which British policy during the occupation of Egypt and elsewhere was no stranger. Prior to 1919 the Copts had participated in government as individuals, but not *en gros*. The majority so employed were in minor posts. They were never made to feel that they were part of an entity struggling for the welfare of their country, fighting for the same cause.

The ordinary Egyptian Moslem fellah did not feel also at one with his rulers, let alone the Copts. But during the 1919 Revolution the Copts felt they were counted amongst the country's leaders to such an extent that when the former politicians broke with Saad and the Wafdist party, the Coptic leaders stood steadfast with Saad, and backed the Wafdist party for years to come.

All through Egyptian history the country was never as strong in all aspects as when she was united under one leader. Their greatest architectural achievements, such as the Pyramids, were built when the country was united during the old Kingdom. It mattered not that the population may have suffered at the time, and probably could have been happier and better occupied doing something else, but the fact remains that they were united in their effort in building their Pharaohs' tombs, who represented to them their gods on earth. There is a saying in Arabic: 'My brother and I are one against my cousin, and my cousin and I are one against the foreigner'. This is a natural reaction in a crisis, when hatchets are buried, but which reappear soon enough when the crisis is over. A true enough saying with regard to future political development in Egypt. This idea of strength through unity when facing one's problems can be traced throughout the history of nations. In the present century the former USSR was strong vis à vis the outside world when she was united, in spite of any financial difficulties, or the bleak life of her inhabitants compared to individual comfort and progress in the West. Similarly Yugoslavia seemed united and strong under Tito, able to withstand pressures both from the East and the West. But with disunity one only has to observe what is happening in the former Yugo-

---

[4]See Appendix No. 1. Letter from Saad Zaghloul to George Khayatt

slavia today. Before World War II, Germany was strong when she was united, which was one of the reasons why the allies split her in two after the war.

The same can be said about Israel. They may have their differences within their parties, but they rally in a crisis, and their strength lies in their unity, when facing whom they consider as their enemies.

What is true about nations is also true about individuals and families. The Wissa brothers made their fortune when they were united; but their heirs spent it fast enough, when each member was looking after himself and went his own way, squabbling at times over details in the partition of the estate. But to get back to the events that followed fast and furious. Signatures were collected all over the country for a mandate investing Saad and his companions with the authority to speak on behalf of the Egyptians. Similar mandates were collected all over the country, signed by women members of the leading families, in favour of certain named ladies, to form a committee, to be known as the Central Women's Committee of the Egyptian Delegation to represent them in all nationalistic activities, which aimed at the country's full independence, according to the principles laid down by the Egyptian delegation (Wafd). (A photocopy of one of these signed original mandates is on the following double page spread.) An amusing story was told me by a friend whose mother was one of the signatories on this mandate. She used to send her young brother of ten years old on his donkey to the different ladies to obtain their signatures; he was able to visit them because as a young boy he was allowed admittance to the harem.

There had never been such a scene before and it caught the imagination of the whole country, to such an extent that when it became evident that Saad had the majority of the nation behind him, Whitehall at the recommendation of the High Commissioner Sir Reginald Wingate, reluctantly tendered an invitation to Roushdi Pasha, the Prime Minister, and Adly Yeghen Pasha to come to London and present their case. But by then the country was seething. Roushdi Pasha asked that Saad Zaghloul should accompany them, as it was obvious to him that nothing acceptable to the nation could be accomplished unless it was endorsed by Saad Zaghloul. Sir Reginald Wingate thought that the delegation should include Saad; he even went so far as to travel to London to explain the situation. When the request was refused the Egyptian Government resigned, and Sir Reginald never returned to Egypt.

The resignation of the Prime Minister and the government on March 1st, 1919 was approved by the Sultan Fouad, and as there was no Egyptian willing to form a new Ministry under the circumstances, government had to be carried out ad hoc by permanent officials. Sir Miles Cheetam was acting as High Commissioner at the time. He had obtained permission from Whitehall to deport Saad Zaghloul, and any of his supporters he sought fit,

نقدم حرخه ـــ ... ... براع توفيلاوس  
ـــ زينب محمد حسن ... نسبت السيدم الدكتور السيد ... فاطمة السيد كرية الكنزر السيد  
... والده محمد ثابت بكرادة ...  
... ... ... كريمة السيد ... إبراهيم السيد  
بقيسة هرم سيد حتيم ... والده مراد ثابت بكرادة  
ناظه سيد حتيم ... ... عائشة احمد جمال الدين  
ناظم على ض م ... لطفيت مراد ثابت بكرادة ...  
ـ لبيبة محمد الهلالي ... نينب لطيفه محمد ثابت بكرادة ...

## SPECIMEN OF MANDATES COLLECTED ALL OVER THE COUNTRY

### The Central Wafdist Committee of Egyptian Ladies

We the undersigned declare that we have mandated the following
ladies:- Hoda Chaaraoui, Esther Fahmy Wissa,Sherifa Riad, Regina
Khayatt, Olfat Ratib, Mounira Elwi, Neemat Hegazi, Naima Abusbaa,
Faika Fathi, Ihsan Ahmed Shaker, Farida Sinout Hanna, Sadika
Mahmoud Ezzat,Betsy Takla, Enayat Sultan, Berlanti Wissa
Wassef,Miss Fikria Hosni to establish a central Wafdist
Committee,of Egyptian ladies, to carry our all the national
functions which would lead to complete independance according to
the principles of the Egyptian delegation, (Wafd), and to enable
them to represent us before all institutions, and to accept any
new members whom they consider fit to join them, and would be an
asset to the cause, they are also mandated to carry out all
administrative and financial operations that are beneficial for
the smooth function of their mission.

Signatures

Faika Mohamed Sabet      Soad Sobhi  
Naila Haram Hussein Sabet   (wife of assistant governor  
       etc.              of Assiut) etc.

Note: The word Haram means the wife of...... or the forbidden of.

Specimen of mandates collected all over the country

نحن الموقعات على هذا اقتر أننا وكلنا حضرات السيدات التى هى شهود هذا . واستدفى
ويهما . وشرفى باسب . ووهبنا خياط . والفت ثابت . ومنيره علوى . ونعمت
محانيك . ونعيمه ابو الهيج . وفاليه فتحى . وامل محمد شاكر . وفريده سينوت
منا . ومدىقه محمود عزت . وبتى تفقد . وهنايت سلطانه . وبراتنا وبهما
وامف . والانت قدر مى . لتشكيل لجنه وفد مركزيه للسيدات المصريات
للقيام بكل الاعمال الوطنيه التى تؤدى الى الاستقلال يتم على مبادئ الوفد
المصرى . واللجنه المذكوره اننا نمثلنا امام جميع الجهات وانه نقم لهم راسه
الاعضاء من تشاء ومن ترك فى ضوبه معلم ولها ايضا انه تقوم بجمع
الاعمال الاداريه والماليه التى نقتضيط مصلحة العمل
وقد مد هذا التوكيل وامضى منا

to Malta, but before doing so on March 6th, he demanded Saad Pasha to abstain from future agitation. He reminded him that Egypt was still under martial law, which had not been abolished with the cessation of hostilities.

Saad Zaghloul answered the next day, 'We have a mandate from the people to defend their interests, and only the people can withdraw this mandate'.

The British reply next day was to arrest Saad Pasha Zaghloul, and with him Hamed Pasha el Bassel, a village magnate of bedouin descent with considerable influence in the Fayoum, Ismail Pasha Sidki, an ex-minister, who became in later years a rabid opponent of the Wafd, and Mohammed Mahmoud Pasha, an Oxford graduate from Assiout in Upper Egypt who also became a political opponent of Saad and the Wafd forming his own party, the Liberal Constitutionalists (El Ahrar el Dastouriin).

The result was that within a few days the whole country was alight, communications had been disrupted, and Cairo was completely isolated from the rest of the country. Railway lines had been destroyed, telephone and telegraph lines had been cut. Parts of the country declared their independence, and chaos ruled supreme. Regrettable incidents occurred on both sides. It was at this time the famous demonstration of women took place. Women in their veils bearing flags whose emblem was the Crescent and the Cross, denoting the solidarity between both parts of the nation, the Moslems and the Copts, announced to the whole world that Egypt was united in her demands. This demonstration could be considered the beginning of the feminist struggle, when women became articulate and first appeared on the political scene. It was at this demonstration that Esther in the forefront confronted the British soldiers, the circumstances of which were mentioned in her speech at the celebration of the jubilee of women's emancipation in Egypt in March 1969[5].

Field Marshal Lord Allenby was appointed the next High Commissioner to Egypt. He was born on April 23rd, 1861, and therefore was fifty-eight when he came to Egypt. He had had a brilliant career as a soldier, and arrived with a reputation for clear thinking, courage and probity. He arrived in Egypt on March 25th, 1919. Unfortunately the day before his arrival Lord Curzon made a speech in which he described the circumstances as 'predatory rather than political'. He then praised the behaviour of many Egyptian officials, who had carried on their jobs when the Minis-

---

[5]This incident was mentioned by Madame Hoda Chaaraoui in her memoirs as having happened to her, but according to two well-known historians Abdel Rahman Fahmy and Abdel Rahman El Raffi it was a young demonstrator as mentioned in the notes of Dr Amal Kamel Bayoumi El Soubki's book, *Women's Movement in Egypt between 1912–1952*, page 38.

Mustapha Pasha Kamel
        Adly Pasha Yeghen

Hussein Pasha Rouchdi
    Mohammed Pasha Mahmoud

try resigned. The immediate result was a strike of these officials to show that they were not as amenable as Curzon thought.

It is interesting to note that the strikes were encouraged by women, who picketed the offices, and taunted with treason any official who tried to go to work.

On his arrival Lord Allenby stated that he had been appointed by His Majesty the King as High Commissioner in Egypt, and the intentions were:

> First, to bring the present disturbances to an end. Secondly, to make careful enquiry into all matters which had caused discontent in the country. Thirdly, to redress such grievances as appear justifiable.

Lord Allenby never deviated from this policy. On March 31st barely a week after his arrival, Lord Allenby telegraphed London recommending the release of Zaghloul and his companions. Wingate who was consulted thought it would be a mistake, but the Foreign Office reluctantly acquiesced on April 7th to free the prisoners, and allowed them to travel where they would.

The recommendation of Allenby was criticised both at the time and later. The foreign community in Egypt were not sure what this apparent weakness of the British authorities would lead to, and politicians like Lord Lloyd believed that it was a capitulation to violence when other methods had failed, notwithstanding the pros and cons of the subject.

General Wavell recounts in his biography of Allenby an incident that throws a light on his character. He states: 'One of his staff brought him in a report, in which a subordinate constantly referred to "the difficulties of my position". "What does this mean – 'the difficulties of his position'? I have never been in a difficult position in my life – I have sometimes been in an impossible one, and then I have got out of it as soon as I could".' Wavell goes on to say that this remark revealed Allenby's whole character: 'It showed the strength of the man who was prepared to face any situation, and to admit difficulty in carrying out what he thought right, and yet had the common sense to realise when a task was impossible and the courage and honesty to admit it.'

Allenby realised that in spite of instigation by agitators, it was the pent-up feelings of indignation and frustration that had boiled over, and not without cause.

General Wavell mentions the following incident in a lighter tone, of a dialogue between Lord Allenby and one of his Generals at a conference in April 1919. The relaxation of certain measures of punishment and control were being discussed:

*Allenby*: I hear you are fining the villages in your area somewhat heavily, General X.

208

*General X*: Well Sir, when a village misbehaves itsclf I fine it ten percent of its ghaffir tax.

*Allenby*: That's not what I've heard, I'm told you fine them ten times their ghaffir tax.

*General X*: Yes that's right, ten percent.

*Allenby*: But that's not ten percent, that's a thousand percent.

*General X*: Oh is it Sir? (Pause) Well anyway, it's what I call ten percent, and when I say ten percent, they know what they've got to pay, and they pay it all right, Sir.[6]

It was this humane sense of fairness, that Esther saw in Lord Allenby, and that was what made her appeal to him time and again as you can see in her letters to him, and although she never wavered in her belief in the righteousness of her cause, she appreciated the strength of character and honesty of her opponent.

For about two months there were troubles all over the country, but they were becoming less violent after the arrival of Lord Allenby, and the release of Zaghloul and his companions from Malta.

Lord Allenby had realised what the average Englishman in Egypt and England had not considered seriously, that although Egypt had been a vassal of Turkey, she had enjoyed almost complete autonomy since the days of Mohammed Aly; and except for an annual tribute to Turkey, and a capitulatory system that had been negotiated and granted by Turkey to foreigners residing in her Empire, she had been virtually free. Egypt was now claiming back her right of autonomy which she had partly relinquished by becoming a protectorate of Britain, and breaking with Turkey in 1914, throwing in her lot with the allies. This partial sovereignty was now being exercised by Britain, which she felt was illegal. The average Englishman also had not grasped the fact that executive power was exercised by Egyptian ministers and administrators, on the advice of British advisers, backed by an occupying army. This made the British *de facto* not *de jure* rulers, and without the cooperation of Egyptian ministers, the administration of Egypt would become very much more difficult and costly. Allenby was therefore concerned with having an Egyptian ministry in tow at all times, even if it meant convincing timid or unwilling politicians that it was their national duty to take office.

Lord Allenby, when carrying out a policy he thought right, paid little attention to the criticisms of weakness levelled at him by the local British community and others, who feared the loss of the privileges they enjoyed, if Britain should relinquish her control, or Egypt gain her independence.

[6]*Allenby, Soldier and Statesman* by General Wavell, page 271

Lord Allenby was not helped much by the vacillating policy of Whitehall, whose instructions he was supposed to carry out. He had the force at his command to command instant obedience, but he knew he could not solve the Anglo-Egyptian question by brute force. He knew he had to execute the policy of the Cabinet, but at the same time he used his common sense and his principles to guide him in dealing with the situation on the spot.

According to General Wavell in his book on Lord Allenby, he quotes a passage from one of Lord Allenby's letters to his mother about a disturbance on May 21st, 1921. On page 280 he writes:

'I bide my time, as I want the Egyptians to settle their politics for themselves. I don't want to interfere with my troops unless the life, limb, or interests of the Europeans are in danger.'

On the release of Saad Zaghloul and his companions from Malta, the situation calmed down in Egypt for a few days. Rushdi Pasha agreed to take office again as Prime Minister and to cooperate with the British, but the Wafdists were now demanding that Rushdi Pasha should endorse their policy and a clash between the government and the mobs ensued. Picketing of offices continued, and on April 21st Rushdi Pasha resigned once more. Egypt was without a government again, and Britain gave up all pretence of governing through Egyptians, and the High Commissioner, under martial law, declared that all officials who were not at their posts next day would be considered as having resigned. Schools were threatened with closure if students did not return to their studies immediately. Egypt was ruled for a month under strict martial law, until Allenby was able to persuade Mohammed Said Pasha to form a Cabinet. But Allenby was now convinced that he either had to capitulate to what was termed the extremists, or try to carry on as best as he could with what he thought were the moderates. It is now opportune to mention the Sudan briefly. Since the Condominium of 1898, England had ingeniously accorded Egypt a partial sovereignty in the Sudan, in return for which Egypt covered any of the deficits of the Sudanese budget out of Egyptian resources. Britain concentrated upon the sole task of improving the welfare of the Sudanese people and her own popularity by keeping taxes low. People were becoming richer. By developing a semi-educated class of Sudanese through creating elementary schools, and vocational instruction which was provided by the Upper School of Gordon College, the British ensured Sudanese recruits for junior posts in government service, and thus eliminated the need for Egyptians. For a time although Egypt did not like the situation, she did not protest, she could do nothing about it. At least her lifeline, the Nile, was not threatened by any of the other major powers. But when the British started in 1911 growing cotton successfully in the Sudanese Gezira Plain, she tried to persuade the Egyptians in 1913 to finance irrigation schemes in the Upper Nile. Egypt would get a larger share of the extra water produced which allowed the Sudan to increase her cotton acreage. But Egypt would have no control of such projects, and she felt threatened, and declined. She felt she could not provide large capital sums out of her budget, for a project which might prove a potential threat to herself. The British now felt free to go it alone. However, with the outbreak of war and the increase in the price of materials, the Sudan Government slowed down the development of the Gezira Plain; it seemed too expensive and risky. But now Egypt had woken up to the threat to her lifeline – the Nile. She started clamouring for the abolition of the Condominium and complete unity with the Sudan.

*

## Egypt's Aspirations and Struggle – Saad Zaghloul

Going back to the events of 1919, and the ensuing feminist movement. When Lord Allenby with the acquiescence of Whitehall liberated Saad Zaghloul and his companions from Malta on April 7th, 1919, they went straight to Paris to present their case to members of the Peace Conference, who were not interested. Saad Zaghloul paid courtesy calls to all the delegates of the countries attending, but the only country that bothered to return his call was Italy. However, he did not lose heart, but presented Egypt's case in a written appeal in French to the French parliament which was about to ratify the peace treaty. At the same time he tried to propagate his views through the media, but was not very successful. The main points in his appeal were as follows:

(a) The proposed treaty up for ratification was in contradiction to all previous allied declarations made during the war, which had obtained for the allies much sympathy throughout the world.
(b) Egypt had proposed to Britain at the outbreak of war, that she was prepared to go to war against Germany on the side of Britain in spite of Turkey being neutral at the time, in order to rid herself of her vassalship to Turkey. Britain vacillated for a little while and asked Egypt to take certain measures, which she did. But when Turkey declared war on the side of Germany and the ex-Khedive Abass Helmi called on the Egyptian people to rise up against Britain, England declared Egypt a protectorate, without even consulting the Egyptian people.
(c) In spite of the above, the Egyptians believed in the promises made to them by the British authorities, that this was only a temporary situation necessitated by the war. Consequently Egypt did not try to hinder the British war effort, but on the contrary contributed 1,200,000 workers

employed on all fronts. This was a principal factor in winning the war on the Asiatic front, as was admitted by Lord Allenby.

(d) The Allied war aims were enumerated by President Wilson in his famous Fourteen Points, which were the basis of the armistice between the victors and the defeated.

(e) These same principles were not only ignored in the peace treaty with regard to Egypt, but even the enemy, Turkey, was forced to recognise the British Protectorate over Egypt. This was in direct violation of the 1840 treaty signed between the European powers, Turkey and Mohammed Aly guaranteeing Egypt full autonomy over her territory in all but a few points.[7]

(f) Not only did the peace treaty ignore the international treaties signed in good faith in the past, but it was also incomprehensible that Egypt, who had assumed part of the sacrifices of war on the side of the allies, should not be recompensed by part of the results of victory. Instead she was being treated worse than the liberated provinces of the Turkish Empire who, previous to the war, did not have even a semblance of independence.

(g) The proposed treaty if ratified would force Egypt into the hell of revolution. Saad goes on to enumerate the grievances and conditions in Egypt when she asked for permission to present her case to the Peace Conference, and the consequent attitude taken by Britain towards the delegates of the Egyptian people. The arrest of its leaders and their deportation resulted in a magnificent movement of patriotism in which all classes were united amongst both the Moslems and Christians of the nation.

(h) He appealed to France to stand by Egypt, if not for the sake of right and justice, at least for the ties of friendship, education and culture that have always reigned between Frenchmen and Egyptians. He ended by asking France to raise her voice in favour of Egypt's right to independence.

His appeal was signed

Saad Zaghloul Pasha<br>President of the Egyptian Delegation

*

Zaghloul's appeal in Paris fell on deaf ears. The *coup de grace* was given to it when on April 19th, 1919 the United States of America gave formal recognition to the British Protectorate.

---

[7] If it had not been for the intervention of the allies, Egypt, by its conquests in 1832–1839 would have gobbled up the whole Ottoman Empire.

With international backing for Egypt's case lacking, it now became apparent to the world that the issue of the Protectorate and Egypt's call for independence had to be fought out between Egypt and Britain.

This fact was not lost upon Saad Zaghloul, or the British authorities in Egypt, at the head of which was the newly appointed High Commissioner Lord Allenby. He was supposed to carry out a policy inherited from a series of vacillating politicians, who had lost touch with the realities of the situation in Egypt. As a field commander his natural instinct was to survey his terrain, plan his campaign, and then carry it out. His ensuing actions have been criticised by a series of British politicians, especially his successor Lord Lloyd, who inherited a much easier task in Egypt.

Lord Allenby, on his appointment in 1919 had to face an antagonistic united country clamouring for independence, whereas Lord Lloyd in 1925 took over a bewildered and divided country, in which some of the British headaches had already been alleviated by his predecessor. It is easy to criticise after an event. Lord Lloyd's natural inclination seems to have been to run rough-shod over any opposition, in spite of realising clearly that such a policy could not be defended by moral arguments. He was encouraged in this by the apprehensive vested interests of the foreign community, who rightly saw that a free and independent Egypt would surely at some time jeopardise their privileged position in the country.

In spite of this, Lord Lloyd tried to be objective in his review of the period in question, when he stated:

'The leaders of the Nationalist party were technically quite correct, therefore, in asserting that we had secretly changed our policy, without consulting or giving notice to the Egyptian people. To this assertion there was no answer that we could make, except to reply that the situation was different from what they thought, *and it was so because we wished and intended it to be so.*'

He continued that the Egyptian case was summoned up admirably by Sir Valentine Chirol in his statement that:

'Egypt's case for complete independence was drawn from our repeated promises, that the occupation would be only temporary, and from our more recent declarations during the Great War, that it was being waged to give freedom to small nations, and from our proclaimed adhesion to the doctrine of self determination, and to President Wilson's fourteen points. Nor need I expatiate again on their resentment of the British policy of silence as to the meaning and purpose of the Protectorate, by which during the war, we forcibly modified the status of Egypt, and gave her a new Ruler, without vouchsafing any explanation to the people, or taking into confidence the representative bodies, which we had ourselves endowed her.'[8]

[8] *Egypt since Cromer*, Lord Lloyd, Part 1, Chapter XXII, page 344.

With such a situation facing him Lord Allenby, as early as April 19th, 1919 tried to pressurise Lord Curzon to allow him to announce that a Royal Commission under Lord Milner would be sent out in May of that year, to survey and report on the situation.

London was reluctant to send out a mission immediately, because it did not realise the gravity of the situation. At the same time the Egyptian Government felt that if the mission should come out at all, it should arrive after the signature of the peace with Turkey, in the hope that Egypt might be able to obtain advantage by waiting; especially as Italy had not yet recognised the validity of the Protectorate.

During the following months, between April and November 1919, the political atmosphere in Egypt either waxed hot or cold. Sometimes regrettable incidents committed on both sides were few, whereas at other times it was more agitated, with consequent attacks and reprisals. The atmosphere depended very much on what the news was from Europe.

The Milner mission arrived in Egypt on December 7th, 1919. Its terms of reference were as follows:

'To enquire into the causes of the late disorders in Egypt, and to report on the existing situation in the country and the form of the constitution, which, *under the Protectorate*, will be best calculated to promote its peace and prosperity, the progressive development of self government and institution, and protection of foreign interests.'[9]

The words *under the Protectorate* in its terms of reference did not augur well for Egypt's aspirations.

Saad was still in Europe; the Egyptians felt that Britain in spite of sending out a commission of eminent men still wanted to maintain the Protectorate and the only way to counter such a move was to boycott the commission.

Under the circumstances, the Sultan and the government were the only Egyptians who entered into relations with the mission on their arrival, and even then, there was a marked reserve in their attitude, refusing to express any opinion. The boycott of the mission was adhered to by the country as a whole.

It is interesting to note however, that although the men held themselves entirely aloof from expressing their views to the commission, the women were more positive in their attitude. They addressed an open letter to Lord Milner's commission at a public meeting held in St. Mark's Cathedral (Morkosieh), Cairo on December 12th, 1919 from the women of Egypt,

[9]*Egypt since Cromer*, Lord Lloyd, Part II, page 12.

which put Egypt's case very clearly. (A copy of this letter is among the appendices.)

*

I will now quote from Mme Hoda Chaaraoui's memoirs, on how the Central Wafdist Committee for Women was formed. She says on page 202 of her memoirs published in Arabic by the Dar El Hilal:

'At that time I had left for Luxor, in which the Central Wafdist Committee for Women was formed and it all happened when I was away from Cairo: I was advised of it by a letter from Mme Esther Fahmy Wissa stating that on the 8th of January 1920 a meeting was held at St. Mark's Cathedral (Morkosieh) and that the ensuing ballot had been very successful, with the following results: Mme Chaaraoui Pasha (139 votes), Mme Fahmy Bey Wissa (102 votes), Mme Omar Pasha Sultan (100 votes), Mme Riad Pasha (98 votes) Mme Hegazi Bey (75 votes), Miss Fikria Hosni (68 votes) Mme Ahmed Bey Abusbaa (65 votes), Mme Makkary Bey (63 votes), Mme Elwy Pasha (52 votes), Mme Rafiq Bey Fathi (50 votes), Mme Mugib Bey Fathi (50 votes), Mme Takla Pasha (38 votes), Mme Doctor Ahmed Ezzat (38 votes), Mme Ahmed Eff Ghanem (33 votes), Mme Wissa Wassef Eff (23 votes).'

Mme Chaaraoui continues: 'Madame Esther Fahmy Wissa stated in her letter: "I believe that the majority of these ladies are suitable, and I am sending you herewith, a protest in duplicate, which please sign as President, and return same, which I hope will be received by return of post, as the matter is urgent".'

It is further recounted by Mme Chaaraoui in her memoirs that the Wafdist Central Committee for Women's declared policy was to inform the Wafdist delegation of women's aspirations, and at the same time to help achieve its aim of complete independence *as long as it adhered to its proclaimed principles*. This statement seems to have been an afterthought, to justify future events.

Procedural rules laid down by the Committee at their first meeting stated that all decisions should be carried by a majority vote, and in the case of a split vote, preference would be given to the side on which the President had voted.

It is to be remembered that these memoirs were published thirty years after Mme Chaaraoui's death, and long after she had split with Saad Zaghloul and the Wafd. There are several discrepancies between these published memoirs and other sources of this period. One was the open letter addressed to the Milner Commission by the Women of Egypt from a public meeting held at St. Mark's Cathedral (Morkosieh) on December 12th, 1919, five days after the arrival of the commission, was referred to in the memoirs on page 204 as having been sent by the Wafdist Central Committee for Women on its first official meeting held on January 16th, 1920, over a month after the mission had arrived in Egypt. This fact seems unreasonable both from the content of the open letter and the timing and what was mentioned later in her memoirs on page 209 that:

'The first meeting of the committee was held on January the 16th at Mme Omar Sultan's palace, which I did not attend as I was in Luxor at the time. At this meeting an executive committee was elected, with the following results, Mme Hoda Chaaraoui elected President, Mme Esther Fahmy Wissa, Vice President, Mme Regina Khayatt, treasurer, and Miss Fikria Hosni, Secretary. It was also decided to send a protest to the Milner mission, stating that their last public declaration was full of ambiguity. The question facing them was clear, as both the men and women of Egypt were one in their demand for complete independence, which could not be interpreted except by frankness and justice, and if there should be any discussion on the matter it should be taken up with the Delegation (the Wafd).'

It would seem from this statement that this protest was the one that was sent her by Mme Wissa by post to sign as President, and not the open letter that had been addressed to the Milner Commission from a public meeting held at St. Mark's Cathedral (Morkosieh) on December 8th, 1919, as on that date the Wafdist Central Committee of Women had not been formed, nor had the Executive Committee been elected.

*

But to make a long story short. The mission's task was made much more difficult by the extraordinary silence confronting it. Prominent figures, politicians, government officials and fellaheen all shied away from expressing any opinion at all. They were afraid of being branded as traitors by the students or the local media, which was dominated by the personality of Saad, who had not come back from Europe.

In spite of this situation the commission completed the appraisal of the situation and returned to England in March 1920. They had arrived at the conclusion that the relationship between Egypt and England could not be normalised unless the solution was arrived at by negotiations between two sovereign states, not by a unilateral act of a suzerain dictating terms to a dependent. But it was one thing for the mission to arrive at a conclusion, and another to carry it out to the satisfaction of both parties.

It was then that Adly Pasha Yeghen with the blessing of the British authorities in Egypt, decided to travel to Europe to try to persuade Saad to meet the mission in England, before it finally presented its report. He was able to do this, and Saad arrived in London on June 7th accompanied by several Wafdists, and had a series of conversations with the mission which continued till August of the year. A preliminary understanding was arrived at, known as the Milner–Zaghloul agreement, which was to be submitted to the British government and to Egyptian public opinion for approval. However, it fell short of Egypt's demand for complete independence.

It suggested that the Protectorate should be abolished, and replaced by a treaty of alliance, in which Egypt should be recognised as a constitutional monarchy. At the same time England would retain certain rights in the country, such as a stationary force, which was not to be considered a military occupation, but as a help in defending Egypt's integrity and independence. England was also allowed to retain some advisers for matters which concerned foreign interests in the country. Furthermore, no mention was made of the Sudan.

Saad then sent four members of the Egyptian delegation back to Egypt to test public opinion. They were Mohammed Pasha Mahmoud, Ahmad Lutfi Bey El Said, Abdel Latif Bey El Mekabati, and Aly Bey Maher. At the same time Saad published a manifesto stating that those were the terms offered, neither repudiating them nor endorsing them. This gave a chance to the extreme nationalists, the Hezb El Watan, who had always campaigned for 'no negotiation, before complete evacuation', to state that the terms offered were far short of the complete independence the Wafd had been clamouring for.

The foreigners were aghast when they heard of the concessions proposed by the Milner Commission. But they soon regained their composure when they realised that although a large section of educated opinion might have favoured such a compromise, if it had been endorsed strongly by Saad, there were other vested interests who did not want a solution at the hands of Saad Zaghloul. In many ways he was too avant garde for them, and considered too liberal in his ideas. These interests therefore clamoured for the complete independence of Egypt and the Sudan. A policy of all or nothing.

It is interesting to note that the *Mokattam*, an Arabic newspaper owned by Syrians with European sympathies, voiced an apparently intransigent opposition to any agreement, suggesting that the fellaheen who had not been consulted, would doubtlessly want complete independence. Politics all over the world breed traits of ambition, rivalry, and greed for personal achievements in politicians. These in turn create venom, enmity and calumny towards their political opponents.

In countries which had developed a parliamentary system over many years, there was a certain amount of self-restraint, and responsibility in public expression, in spite of such innate traits being present in its members. In other countries such as Egypt, where general political activity had been forcibly restrained for ages, it was more difficult to hide such feelings, and the natural reaction was to vent them when the opportunity arose.

It was essential after the Milner–Zaghloul report was published, and the lukewarm recommendation given it by Zaghloul, that all political thought and energy should be united, if Egypt was to maximise the bargaining power of its proposed delegation to negotiate with the British Government. But this was not forthcoming.

Britain naturally wished to negotiate with a delegation which could command a cross-section of political consensus in the country. At the same time it did not want to capitulate to what it considered as extremism and chaos, which might potentially jeopardise her vital interests. Sultan Fouad, mindful of the recent revolutions in Russia and Turkey, was loath to enhance the prestige of any political leader who could command the mob. Therefore it became necessary that any negotiations should be headed by a moderate politician who was acceptable to all shades in the country, and especially to Saad Zaghloul. The choice finally fell on Adly Pasha Yeghen who, after much wrangling, was finally accepted by Saad to head a delegation under certain predetermined conditions, to negotiate with Lord Curzon in July 1921.

When Adly returned to Egypt with his proposals he was met by antagonistic crowds, whose slogan was, 'We prefer occupation under Saad, than independence under Adly' (*El Ihtilal taht Saad, Wala El Istiklal taht Adly*). It now became apparent to Allenby that no government would be able to negotiate a settlement unless backed by Saad. But now the politicians who in 1919 had been united in their aims, fell out over the means they were to adopt in attaining them. It was at this time that Madame Hoda Chaaraoui seriously fell out with Saad; she could not accept the way Adly had been treated by the crowds on his return from England. She believed that Saad could have stopped the demonstrations if he had wanted to. She was still rankling over a slight she felt Saad had purposely committed when he cold-shouldered her husband Aly Chaaraoui Pasha, who had criticised the Milner-Zaghloul agreement because all mention of the Sudan had been omitted.

There were other reasons why the situation in the country was getting out of hand, and discontent was felt among the fellaheen. There had been a drop in cotton prices. Landowners who had borrowed money to buy more land when cotton was at 187 dollars[10] a cantar in 1920, were hard pressed to pay their instalments when cotton prices dropped to twenty-one dollars in 1921. Similarly the fellaheen's (the farmer tenants) income had dropped considerably and they were feeling the pinch. It was easy to blame

---

[10]The price of cotton was always referred to in dollars, because its basic rate followed the New York futures market. The dollar in Egypt was calculated as twenty piastres, so there were five dollars in an Egyptian pound. So ten piastres used to be referred to as half a dollar (*nisf riyal*). Similarly five piastres was referred to as a shilling as there were twenty shillings in a pound, at some time a franc must have been worth four piastres as a two-piastre coin was called half a franc (*nisf franc*).

Lord Allenby, 1st Viscount, British High Commissioner 1919–1925

the foreigner who was bent on exploiting them, who wanted cheap cotton for his spinning mills in Lancashire.

With all the unrest in the country it was difficult to persuade anyone to form a government, or to remain long in office. Any decision taken was suspect, all were afraid to be branded as traitors.

Under these circumstances, Allenby the soldier decided to attack. He prohibited a meeting called by Saad Zaghloul for December 22nd, 1921, and when Zaghloul challenged the decision by appealing to the nation, Allenby had him arrested together with a few of his companions, and on December 23rd, 1921, they were taken to Suez and shipped to Aden where they remained till March 31st, 1922 when they were removed to the Seychelles Islands.

By strong military powers Allenby was able to curb a total upheaval, but the antagonism that had appeared between Egyptian politicians in 1921 abated, and they now joined forces. Hatchets were buried for the time being; no minister would take office and government had to be carried out by British under-secretaries of state – a situation that Allenby felt could not be maintained for long and had to be solved.

The whole structure, laid down by Cromer, by which the British ruled through Egyptian ministers, was in a shambles. He could not envisage Britain ruling an antagonistic country for any length of time by military might.

He decided to force the issue. The decision he took has been criticised, misunderstood, and misrepresented. He felt that if moderate Egyptians were helped, a solution could be arrived at. The apparent differences in the British Government's position in the past negotiations, and the intransigent Egyptian position, he felt were not insurmountable. The British were willing to abolish the Protectorate and recognise the independence of Egypt provided that the Egyptians first bound themselves to conditions safeguarding certain British interests, such as their Imperial communications, the protection of foreigners in Egypt, including the minorities, and their position in the Sudan. This the Egyptians had refused to agree to.

Allenby now proposed, 'that the British Government should abolish the Protectorate and grant independence forthwith, but should announce at the same time that Great Britain retained the liberty of action, if her interests demanded it, in certain matters, afterwards known as the "reserved subjects", until such time as an amicable agreement on these subjects could be agreed'. Although a soldier, Allenby proved to be more a statesman than many of those in Whitehall. He argued that British military might was more valid than any pledges squeezed out of Egyptian politicians. In fact by that method of thinking he obtained for England a legal stand in Egypt, which she never had before. He just adjourned the thorny problems, until time itself would solve them.

The British Government were aghast at his proposals, and considered it as an ultimatum. They decided to replace him and his advisers in Egypt. They summoned Allenby and two of his advisers on January 22nd, 1922 for consultation. Before leaving, Allenby drew up a dispatch which he took with him, the last paragraph of which is quoted by General Wavell in his book *Allenby Soldier and Statesmen*, page 95, which demonstrates Allenby's thinking:

'The commission which I hold from His Majesty is to maintain His Majesty's Protectorate over Egypt. I have done so, but I do not think it has elements of durability, and I have now advised its being brought to an end, as it was established by a unilateral declaration. I have laid open to his Majesty's government a course, which in my judgement accords with the general traditions of British Policy and British institutions, and is in the truest interest of the Empire, while it is consistent with that political development of Egypt which His Majesty's government have always desired to encourage, and which has been the goal of labours of my predecessors, men who, in serving their own country, have sought the welfare of the Egyptian people.'

The details of how Allenby prevailed on the British Cabinet to accept his point of view under threat of resignation makes enthralling reading. However it has no place in this book.

On February 28th, 1922 Allenby returned to Egypt and announced:

1) The termination of the Protectorate of Egypt which became an independent sovereign state.
2) Martial law would be withdrawn as soon as the Egyptian government passed an act of indemnity to all inhabitants of Egypt.
3) The following matters were absolutely reserved to His Majesty's government, until such time as it may be possible by free discussion and friendly accommodation on both sides to conclude agreements in regard thereto between His Majesty's government and the government of Egypt:-
   a) The security of the communications of the British Empire in Egypt.
   b) The defence of Egypt against all foreign aggression or interference direct or indirect.
   c) The protection of foreign interests in Egypt, and the protection of minorities.
   d) The Sudan.

Pending the conclusion of such agreements the status quo in all these matters shall remain intact.

*

These matters had to remain till 1936 before a partial agreement was signed, known as the Anglo-Egyptian Treaty 1936, and even then a final agreement on the Anglo-Egyptian question and the Sudan was not achieved until eighteen years later, during the 1952 Revolution in Egypt. The reason for this long delay was due to the disunity of Egyptian politics, which became a power struggle between the Palace allied to what was known as the so called moderate politicians, who had very little popular backing, and the Wafd with its cross-section of the Egyptian people representing the voice of Egypt, but who were considered revolutionary, and the British who backed one side or the other according to circumstances, and who were not in a hurry to change the status quo.

*

But to go back to 1922, Sultan Fouad had been proclaimed King Fouad I of Egypt on March 13th. Egypt was supposed to become a constitutional monarchy. However, a constitution for Egypt had not yet been drawn up, which was one of the tasks facing the country.

King Fouad's intention was to retain as much power as he could for the throne. He wanted to become a real ruler like his father Khedive Ismail, or his great-grandfather Mohammed Aly, the founder of the dynasty. But a lot of water had passed under the bridge since then; monarchs all over the world had lost much of their power and prerogatives.

This was not lost on Fouad, who intended to accomplish his ends by retaining the prerogative of dissolving parliament, giving him the potential of changing a government distasteful to him. This prerogative was used sparingly by a constitutional monarch, who reigned but did not rule. It was used more as a threat than as an instrument of power; a brake, that could be used in an emergency, if it was generally felt that the elected parliament was running away with itself, and had lost the will of the people, and it was necessary to refer back to the nation.

King Fouad used this prerogative to retain personal power by playing off one party against another, but tending to rely on a coalition of minor parties, who were led by what were known as the moderate politicians. These were some of the ablest and best-educated Egyptians, but they did not have much political charisma, having come mainly from the old ruling class who had always kow-towed to the Khedives.

King Fouad had a phobia concerning the Wafd, with their talk about the will of the people. He suspected many of them of having republican tendencies. Had not their leader, Saad Zaghloul, always disapproved of the Khedive Abbas Helmi and his policies?

The King was able, with the help of the British, to use this instrument of power, throughout his reign.

*

Saad Zaghloul was now in exile and Egypt was supposed to have received independence. But it was a qualified independence, subject to certain reservations. To the main body of Egyptian thought, it seemed little more than what had been proposed before. All the thorny problems had still to be solved by negotiation. And who was there to negotiate for them? Their leader in whom they trusted, was in exile, and it was not known if he would ever be allowed to return, or if his health would hold out while he was away.

The fact that the Protectorate had been unilaterally abolished by Britain, and that Sultan Fouad was now King, able to rule by means of a constitution, persuaded some of the politicians that power had returned to the Mohammed Aly dynasty, with whom they should now cooperate. These politicians believed that their nationalism and loyalty could not be doubted, since they had done nothing to bring about the situation that the country was in.

They felt no obligation to clamour for Saad's return, since they were no less nationalist in seeking the country's aspirations, nor were they less able. They felt no guilt in accepting to serve, and take office.

Abdel Khalek Sarwat accepted and was appointed Prime Minister, with the task of forming a commission to draw up a constitution. It took just over thirteen months for the constitution to be enacted on April 19th, 1923. And just over two months later martial law was abolished after the Act of Indemnity became law on July 5th.[11] After a further two months a general election was called by royal decree.

It would seem from the above that all was plain sailing after Allenby's declaration of independence. But the actual fact was that the period between the declaration of independence and the calling of the general election was not without its hiccups.

The difficulties arose mostly in drawing up the constitution. The problems were three points:

a) who should be allowed to vote.
b) what were the King's prerogatives.
c) what title the King should be given.

Educated opinion favoured a limited system of franchise, a sort of plural vote, such as that which had been the basis of the Belgian constitution –

[11]The Act of Indemnity was to provide compensation for those made redundant by the new administation, or those who asked for retirement from public service, whether military or civilian. The eventual cost to the Egyptian Treasury was between seven and eight million pounds. This figure was considered a large price to pay for freedom from the reins of a foreign power, and was so criticised by the Egyptian press.

universal suffrage but conditional both for men and women, as follows:

> One vote for a citizen of a certain age having resided in a constituency for a certain period (a residency qualification). A second vote for capacity (a level of education) and a third vote on the basis of property. It was suggested that a white ticket should be given to the voter with one vote, a green ticket to the voter with two votes, and a red ticket for the voter with three votes. By this procedure it was argued, power would be given to capable people who had a vested interest in the country. It was also argued that such a system would be beneficial to the country, as it would entice people to work hard to improve their education, and harder still to increase their stake in the wealth of the nation. It would also be a brake on the election of any demagogue who could be voted into power by a mass of ignorant people.

These ideas were finally decided against, as no one wanted to be branded as undemocratic. Universal suffrage was decided for men, one man one vote, with the result that the Wafd, who commanded a majority of votes among the ignorant and semi-educated members of the community, obtained 166 seats out of a total of 214 seats in the newly-elected house of deputies.

The result of any free elections in the country for years to come, was a foregone conclusion: any election carried out by a neutral government, without any interference by the authorities, would result in an overwhelming victory for the Wafd.

Under such circumstances, King Fouad felt he could not achieve his ambitions, nor his dreams for Egypt. The constitution was supposed to be drawn up on the Belgian model, the King's position being strictly that of a constitutional monarch. Power was to rest in a parliament of two chambers, a house of deputies, made up of elected members, one man one vote, and a senate partly elected and partly nominated by the King. By procrastination, and playing one side off against the other, the British and the emerging nationalists, King Fouad tried to manoeuvre the drawing up of the constitution in such a way as to give the throne the greatest measure of autocracy. In this way he could fulfil his aspirations, which were to enhance the grandeur of Egypt, and at the same time enhance his own position, and that of his dynasty after him. For in spite of what has been said of King Fouad's dislike of the parliamentary system, because of the constraints a written constitution would have on the power of the throne, at heart his aim was the welfare of his country, *according to his conception.*

He expressed his aspirations and thoughts in a talk he had with Baron Firmin Vander Bosch, a Belgian Honorary Prosecutor – General of the Mixed Courts in Egypt, who recounts in his book *Vingt années d'Egypte*, pages 59–60, the following statement by the King:

> 'What is missing in Egypt is a real governing élite; moulding of character is too hasty; here we have no serious secondary schooling. I want to create an education inspired

by what is happening in Europe. I also want those who are called to guide the destiny of Egypt, to have seriously come into contact with the foreign world. Can you imagine that I have had a Prime Minister who has never crossed the sea? The Egyptians go to Europe for cures or amusement, Vichy and Monumartre. I would like them to go to learn, to gain experience. My aim is to send the greatest number of gifted young people to higher schools in England, France, Italy and Belgium. I have also given thought to specialised schools such as Liège or Gand.

And once the country has had contact with your higher education abroad I want to create a similar education in Egypt. The present university in Cairo is still a shapeless embryo! We have to start from the bottom. If we want to create something complete and coherent we need foreign teachers who would guide the best elements we have. Just let me be, I have my complete plan, studied, and ripe for execution.'

King Fouad's attitude towards the prospective provisions of the constitution were contrary to his way of thought. He genuinely believed that the country was not ripe to rule itself. This was apparent in some words he was supposed to have said at the time of discussing the constitution: 'if you want this Bolshevistic constitution, then I claim all the powers and privileges of Lenin'. To the reply that it was not a Bolshevist constitution, but a democratic one, he recorded, 'Then I claim all powers and privileges of the President of the United States of America'. He ignored the fact that the President was elected by the people, and only for a limited term.

His delaying tactics took the form of trying to gain popularity by impressing on the emerging nationalist feeling in the country that he was the sole power to be counted on to look after the welfare of the nation by insisting that in the preamble of the proposed constitution the King of Egypt should be named King of Egypt and the Sudan. If he could get away with it, well and good. If he could not, it would at least show the nationalists who were clamouring for the unity of the Sudan with Egypt that he was no less patriotic than they were, and he could not but submit to a superior force. He must have known at the time that there was little chance of Britain accepting such a proposal. As a result the British intervened. They could not accept a unilateral alteration of the status of the Sudan Condominium which had been established by a treaty between Britain and Egypt, especially as one of the reserved points to be resolved later, mentioned in the recent declaration of independence of Egypt, was the Sudan.

Lord Allenby gave King Fouad an ultimatum. After exercising every effort to evade the issue for more than twenty-four hours, His Majesty yielded and signed the document Allenby had presented to him.[12]

The years between 1919 and 1922 should be considered as the most important period in Egypt's modern history, as the resultant repercussions marked themselves indelibly on the subconsciousness of the whole area. It showed how a small unarmed country through unity could extract conces-

[12]*Allenby* by Field Marshall Wavell, page 320

225

sions from a much larger force, and at the same time, through disunity could lose much of its potential.

The extraordinary unity found at the beginning of the movement throughout the country, brought out all its latent strength. Although it was unorganised and unaware, it became a sudden awakening, and as a result unleashed all sorts of different forces, which once released were very difficult to control. Once the genie was out of the bottle, it was impossible to put it back.

Although the resultant abolition of the Protectorate and the qualified independence accorded Egypt did not satisfy Egyptian aspirations, as they felt it was not a real independence, yet it heralded in a new era. It showed that the might of nineteenth century imperialism could be shaken, a harbinger of future world events.

However the forces released were very different from what was expected; and the benefits in the long run were as much controversial as unforeseen. The forces released were at the same time political, social, and economic. Politically the forces that should have benefitted the country through its unity, were dissipated through its disunity, emanating from the struggle for power, and party politics, with a result that Egypt was not able to maximise its potential.

However the social effects were far-reaching. The expansionist, monopolistic European society in the country was replaced by a new Egyptian middle class, which tried to do too much and too soon. This resulted in a preponderance of a semi-educated population, looking for office jobs. The majority of these had emigrated from the village to the town, thus turning a large section of producers into consumers. The situation was aggravated by a population explosion, due to the improvement of life expectancy through modern medicine, and the uncontrolled increase in births. There was an increase of forty million in seventy years – fourteen million in 1919 to fifty-four million in 1989, without a corresponding growth in national wealth. Similarly the emancipation of women doubled the work force available, without providing a necessary outlet. *It is interesting to note that the emancipation of women in Egypt, though started by the spark lit by members of the privileged women in Egyptian society, was fuelled by the middle and lower middle class that wanted a higher standard of living earned through going out into the world. Today, after seventy-five years of emancipation, many middle and lower middle class women might prefer a more sedentary and secluded life at home if it could ensure them the amenities they enjoy through working as it would relieve them of the difficulties and chores they face today in confronting the outside world.*

But to get back to the early years of the feminist movement, after the formation of the Central Woman's Committee of the Egyptian Delegation, of which Mme Hoda Chaaraoui was President and Esther was Vice-President. These were the years between 1920 and 1922 before the first cracks

226

started to appear in its unity. The women felt they were fighting for Egypt's independence as they saw fit. They did not draw up policy, as their aim was to help Saad Zaghloul in his mission. However they felt free to state their opinion, even if it was not asked for. They felt they had a right to defend Egypt's point of view in their own way, as long as it did not hamper the men. This can be seen in the articles and replies they made in the press. Those in French were drawn up by Mme Chaaraoui, and those in English by Esther. However they were all submitted to the full committee and agreed upon; all very democratic. But I have found letters written to newspapers by Esther, signed 'Daughter of the Nile'. She was very young and impulsive and had her own logic which was not always that of the majority, and although she never undermined those she was working with, she could never deviate from what she thought was right. She stated her opinion openly, no matter upon whose toes she trod. Sir Valentine Chirol, foreign correspondent of *The Times* newspaper, wrote a series of articles on Egypt and the Egyptian question at the time of the Milner mission in Cairo. One of these articles titled 'Women of Egypt' was published in *The Times* on January 2nd, 1920, which the Egyptian Women's Delegation felt they had to answer, and the following is what they wrote:

'The Egyptian Women'
Answer to Sir Valentine Chirol's article No. 5

As representatives of the Central Women's Committee of the Egyptian Delegation, we feel it our duty to reply to Sir Valentine Chirol's article in the Times of January 2, 1920 on 'The Women of Egypt'.

Sir Valentine says that the 'fellaheen' women are treated by their men merely 'as beasts of burden', a very unfair statement considering that a woman who chooses to share her husband's daily tasks and who 'rules her home', and who develops considerable business capacities, cannot with justice be compared to a 'beast'.

As to the deficiency of education in Egypt respecting both men and women, we can only say that the fault lies chiefly with the government which is under British control, and which has done very little to promote education in our country. And although we have many 'private schools', yet we can only be blamed for not having more, and *Independent Egypt* will see to their increase in the future. Writing under the heading of 'The Political Whirlwind' Sir Valentine forgets that the women of Egypt in spite of those being mostly illiterate, descend from a long line of highly civilised people, and although they have not acquired their social and intellectual upbringing at schools, yet they are born with a good amount of commonsense and instinctive wisdom which qualifies them to fulfil their positions both socially and intellectually in a remarkable way. Their traditions of six thousand years of civilisation have transmitted to them high conceptions of good manners which have become natural characteristics of their race, and we can say that where they excel most, it takes all the effort and life-long teachings of the great masters of Europe to spur their people forwards to develop similar qualities, and all the self-sacrificing elements and strength of will to follow in their wake.

In fact we may go so far as to say that Egyptian women one or two generations ago, always looked with contempt on what they saw of western civilisation and manners, which they considered inferior to their own, and it is only our generation that has erred and tried to do away with the old, and follow blindly in the way of the new. Fortunately for us we have been checked in our lives, and we are pleased to say that we have come of age and have begun to discriminate between the good and the bad, so that we may cling to some of the good, and discard some of the new, forming a social and intellectual standard of our own.

Sir Valentine probably does not know that the 'veiled woman of Egypt' has nearly as much liberty as she would desire, and it does not really need the '*stirring cry*' for '*complete independence*' to '*make an irresistible appeal*' which would '*promote ideas of freedom*' to bring her into the streets to '*break the monotony*' of her life. Neither did she do it to '*ingratiate*' herself with her '*lord and master*', her position in the home was enough to ensure her place in her husband's affections, to whom she was the proper helpmate.

But it needed all the injustice and avarice of British politics, and all the military repressions of the British authorities to drag the veiled women of Egypt out of their homes to protest on behalf of their oppressed brethren, thus following their purpose as the other living half of Egyptian society.

The article speaks of the women taking part with the men in building barricades and '*though they generally dispersed when fighting actually began, some of them returned to gloat over deeds of violence perpetrated by the men*'. What kind of fighting does Sir Valentine refer to? Was it the fight that took place between the unarmed demonstrators and the British machine guns and armed cavalry? The women of Egypt must have shown great cowardice by dispersing '*when fighting actually began*' to escape the treacherous bullets falling in showers around them mixed with the blood of their men and children, the unarmed and pacific demonstrators . . . It must have been a very one sided fight indeed, and we are surprised that an *Englishman forgets himself to revive its memories*.

'Brutal deeds of violence perpetrated by men'?

It would be most unnatural for a woman '*to gloat over brutal deeds of violence*' committed on her own menfolk, for as everyone knows, the British troops do not leave their massacred on the roads for Egyptian women '*to gloat over*'.

It would have been more truthful and more comprehensible to have said that the women of Egypt came back to mourn over '*the brutal deeds of violence*' committed on their men and children.

As to any animosity between Egyptian and English women in particular, we have no reason to think so, as English people in Egypt are on the whole rarely sociable with anyone and we cannot think that an Egyptian lady ever missed Anglo-Egyptian Society. It is true that those of us who have mixed a little with English women in Egypt and have treated them with great kindness and hospitality, have often had good reason to regret our experiences, and we are not keen to renew them.

As to the '*future harvest of social demoralisation*' foreseen by the *writer* there is not the least danger of it ever taking place, and furthermore we are here to see that it never does. We stand at a most interesting page in Egypt's history, and we have all hopes that our women may stand at the forefront of noble womanhood leading the human race to brighter futures, as women did in Ancient Egypt.

on behalf of the Women of Egypt
MEMBERS OF THE CENTRAL WOMEN'S COMMITTEE
OF THE EGYPTIAN DELEGATION
Signature
Hoda Chaaraoui, Esther Fahmy Wissa, Ihsan Ahmed Chaker,

Regina Habib Khayatt, Naima Abusbaa, Ulfat Ratib,
Nemat Ahmed Hegazi, Faika Rafik, C. Riaz, Fikria Hosni, Mounira Eloui,
Farida Sinout Hanna

One can deduce from the above, how up to date and informed were these dedicated Egyptian women in the first quarter of the twentieth century. They followed what was written in the foreign press, and were quick to refute what they felt was a misrepresentation of the Egyptian case.

*

The following is a letter by Esther signing herself 'Daughter of the Nile', which is self explanatory.

Mr. Clemenceau's Visit to Egypt.
Answer to the *Egyptian Gazette* of February 6, 1920.
When it was known in London that President Wilson was going to visit England after the Armistice, the English papers spared no room nor effort to convince the public to meet President Wilson with great enthusiasm.

It is needless to say that the public did not favour Mr. Wilson's views, for he presented to them the bogey who was to deprive them of some of their claimed 'Rights' over the dominion of the seas. But they differed from the Egyptians, in that they were capable of showing the greatest hypocrisy by enthusiastically cheering their unwelcome guest before the gates of Buckingham Palace.

The Egyptians are not going to meet Mr. Clemenceau with as much enthusiasm as the English did Mr. Wilson, because perhaps Egyptians today are conscious neither of any great obligation for favours past, or expectant of favours to come from the man of France, as the English were bound to feel towards the American President. But it neither means that they are going to disapprove of Mr. Clemenceau's visit to Egypt on his honeymoon. They know too well that the great man of France bartered away their rights, simply because he found it in the interests of his country to do so, not because he was averse towards Egypt's aspirations, that he acted as he did. Egypt graciously welcomes Mr. Clemenceau with her sunshine and smiles. She is sure that the great man in his innermost soul will sigh in sympathy, as he watches the glorious Nile, and records the history of its great people. . . . She knows he will sigh because he had to act towards her as he did, although against his conscience, to serve the interests of his country. Egypt will welcome Mr Clemenceau because she knows she has his sympathy, as well as the sympathy of every Frenchman, although they were actually unable to help her.

As to that 'phlegmatic' and capable nation so 'cool in her judgement that she is able to make a right-about turn without much ado with her army tactics'. We are sure she can make very little advance with the Egyptians, as long as she is unconscious of her unfair play towards them. Our rightful claims and her conscience, will block her way at every turn, just as 'The angel's sword did with Baalam's ass.' And if in spite of this, England should still persist in treading on her conscience and other people's rights, perhaps she will one day find her defeat in Egypt, as all other dominating powers have done before, it will be a pity if history has to repeat itself once more in the twentieth century.

229

Egypt will never agree to give up her national rights to England, or any other power, neither can Mr. Clemenceau nor any other man convince her to do so, and if England encouraged by her military strength, refuses to give up what is not hers, time will give every one their dues, and we can abide our time.

As to the threat that 'the easiest thing for England to do, was to retire to the Suez Canal, annex the Sudan, and leave the Egyptians to look after their own affairs'. We cannot understand how she could do it. The Sudan belongs to Egypt and Egypt to the Sudan, since the beginning of history, and it would be strange indeed if England crowned her history by robbing Egypt of the source of her life. The Nile is as necessary to Egypt, as the spinal cord is to the human body, and if the Nile source is separated from Egypt, then we must anticipate to behold the dead corpse of the most ancient and wonderful country in the world, carried before the annals of history as the best example of England's world-famous reforming capacities.

Mr. Clemenceau is welcome but he will not influence our political views, for we are neither prejudiced against the English, nor in particular favoured towards the French. We are fighting for our rights. That's all, and nothing short of realising them will satisfy us. We are ready for all sacrifice and good old Father Time will give us our due.

Daughter of the Nile

I do not know why Esther wrote this letter and sent it in the name of Daughter of the Nile, and not in the name of the Committee. There may have been a controversy at the time as to whether it was diplomatic to antagonise French public opinion then, especially as Saad Zaghloul was trying to rally French opinion in Paris.

The cracks that became apparent in Egyptian political unity during 1921, appeared smoothed over for a time, after Saad and some of his followers had been exiled in December of that year.

During that period the women's committee seemed more or less unified, although a creeping change was taking place. Some of the women were tending to back the point of view of their husbands. But on the whole they were critical of their men's behaviour. A little of the euphoria and enthusiasm seemed to have dwindled. Esther was a little less active after she had lost her son Adly who was run over by a motor car. I had just been born. She became pregnant again with my younger brother whom she called Adly (after her other son Adly who died).

Mme Hoda Chaaraoui the President of the Women's Central Committee had fallen out with Saad Zaghloul, and although she buried the hatchet during his exile, she tended to be more interested in women's liberation than in politics, although she still voiced her views on political matters. In March 1923 she formed the Egyptian Women's Union whose aims were both political and social, and since she was a Moslem, she was able to lay stress on the Egyptian woman's status, the majority of whom were Moslem. One of the first demands the newly formed Egyptian Women's Union made to the government, was to change the law to allow secondary education for girls in government schools, as well as raising the minimum marriage age for girls to sixteen, to allow them to mature, both mentally and physically.

Esther, being a Copt, agreed and encouraged medical and educational reform, but she could not broach any subject which had to do with Islamic tenets. She stayed on in the Central Committee of Wafdist women, and became its spokeswoman, as can be seen by the letters she sent to Lord Allenby as from July 1922. They were mostly defending Saad Zaghloul, and the Zaghloulist point of view, and trying at the same time to better the living conditions of those in prison or exile. (Copy of letter of thanks, and translation from Mme Zaghloul in the Letters.) She still voiced her own opinions and her independence in the way she thought. Her ideas were not always orthodox, a trait which she never relinquished till the day she died.

In March 1923 an invitation was addressed to the women of Egypt from the World Union of Women to attend a conference in Rome. The eventual Egyptian delegation was headed by Mme Hoda Chaaraoui, and included Esther and her maternal aunt (Wissa's daughter) Mme Regina Khayatt, as well as other ladies. The conference lasted from May 12th to 19th, 1923. An incident mentioned in Mme Chaaraoui's memoirs about this conference was that on their arrival in Rome, they found that the thirty-six delegations from different countries had all prepared their National flags to be placed on the podium. The Egyptian delegation had not brought such a flag, so she asked the Egyptian students in Rome to prepare an Egyptian flag to include the Crescent and the Cross. The students made their flag larger than those of the other countries, stating that since Egypt was the most ancient civilisation present, her flag should be larger than the rest. There was no time to make a new flag, so Mme Chaaraoui when presenting the folded flag to the chairwoman of the conference, stated the students' point of view. The chairwoman took the flag and smiled when she heard the reason. But when she opened the flag and found it was made up of the Crescent and the Cross, she was greatly moved, and ordered it to be placed on her left side, the right side being occupied by the flag of the host country, Italy. The delegation met the Pope as well as Mussolini.

*

1923 was the year in which the Egyptian constitution was drawn up. Allenby had to interfere several times to try to persuade the King that he should accept being a constitutional monarch, where he reigned but did not rule, notwithstanding the Royal prerogative of being able to dissolve parliament and hold new elections. The throne abused this power several times between the years 1924 and 1952, whenever it felt threatened. This was made easier by those politicians who curried favour with the Palace, or by pressure from the British, which led eventually to the 1952 revolution.

Saad Zaghloul returned to Egypt in September 1923. In his absence those nationalists who were not in jail could not really assess the situation.

This was neither independence nor interdependence, but a trick being played on them by the British once again. A concealed occupation disguised as a constitution had been introduced using the King as a stooge. Their attitude was *plus royaliste que le roi*; nothing less than the complete independence of Egypt and the Sudan was their cry.

On his return to Egypt, Saad who had been away for two years, had not quite fathomed the situation he tried to play it low. In his first public speech he said:

> 'You are accustomed to obey me, but I am not a prince. I do not descend from any royal family, before whom it is the custom to bend. I am a fellah, the son of fellah, the issue of a very modest family, which my adversaries qualify as even humble. Blessed be such humbleness. I am not rich, so that your support for me, can bring you no financial gain. I have no prestige. Despite that you all rally around me, showing that you court neither riches nor prestige, but rather under certain circumstances, prison.'

This sort of rhetoric appealed to the man in the street. Saad could also be very hard and stinging on those he considered his detractors whom he called bought traitors and enemies of the nation. He used catchy phrases such as 'complete independence or death', 'no ministry to be submitted to a control', meaning British advisers. Such statements raised the passions of the crowd, but were not conducive to stability. He hit out at Egyptians whom he thought were conspiring against him.

During the last few months of 1923 a government under Yehia Pasha Ibrahim was preparing for elections. Saad was never quite sure whether the administration would somehow rig the coming elections against his party. The Wafd had a very good organisation all over the country, in contrast to the rest of the parties. The results of the elections were overwhelmingly in favour of the Wafd.

During Saad's exile, most of the leading members of his party were in prison or in exile with him, and no real policy had been formulated. Many promises had been made, by those on the spot, but nothing concrete had been planned. The four reserved points had still to be negotiated with Britain. He had taken office with the firm hope of being able to successfully negotiate a treaty with the first Labour government in England headed by Mr. MacDonald, who had always voiced sympathy with Egypt's case. But the opening moves by Britain and Egypt were not hopeful.

On March 15th, 1924, the first Egyptian Parliament was opened. A telegram from the Prime Minister of Britain to the 'Newest of Parliaments' was read out: 'I believe that Egypt and Great Britain will be tied by a strong bond of friendship, our desire is to see this bond made stronger, on a permanent basis. For this purpose the government of His Majesty the King is ready now, and at any time to negotiate with the Egyptian government.'

Against this was King Fouad's speech from the throne, stating the opinion and policy of the Egyptian government which said:

> 'You have before you one of the most grave and delicate tasks upon which the future of Egypt depends, the task of realising her complete independence in the true meaning of the word . . . My government is ready to enter into negotiations free of all restrictions, with the British government, so as to realise our national aspirations with regards to Egypt and the Sudan.'

It did not angur well. On one side the British were saying they were willing to talk, but nothing else. And on the other Egypt's statement was a rigid presentation of her position, implying a complete repudiation of all that had been accomplished up till then. (Saad in exile had always criticised the 1922 declaration of qualified independence.)

The Labour government when put to the test, would not yield to Egypt's demands. Saad Zaghloul had been rather naive in his expectations, he had counted on a *volte face* in British foreign policy. He hadn't realised that foreign policy in Britain was drawn up by permanent under-secretaries, who did not change radically with a change of government. It was not likely that they would recommend a change in Lord Curzon's Conservative policy to that of Mr. MacDonald, the first Labour Prime Minister, especially as Saad Zaghloul was simply asking for the abrogation of the 1922 declaration, by the dropping of the reserved clauses, and the evacuation of Egypt and the Sudan, without offering anything in return.

Furthermore, during the preceding months, between the formation of Saad's government in March, and the start of negotiations at the end of September, Egypt was not easy. She had been making difficulties about the amounts to be paid as compensation to British employees leaving Egyptian government service. She also discontinued service of Ottoman loans secured by the Egyptian tribute to Turkey, which had been agreed upon whilst Egypt was a vassal of Turkey. Egypt now argued, and with some logic, that since she was a sovereign state she should not be asked to secure payments of the Ottoman debt, since Egypt did not owe Turkey any tribute. These amounts Egypt had continued to pay, right up to the time of Zaghloul's government. On June 25th, 1925, the Egyptian government refused to pay. It is to be noted that much of this debt was held by Britain or Britons. At the same time the Council of Ministers were proposing to strike out of the Budget the annual subvention to the British army of occupation, which the Egyptian Government had agreed to pay in 1907.

Under these circumstances Ramsay MacDonald refused to countenance a change in policy and when Saad told him that these were not his demands alone but also those of the whole country, as represented by the elected Parliament Ramsay MacDonald is reputed to have answered, 'Your Pashas and your Beys demand complete independence? Tell them, that we will give them complete independence when they will give it to their fellaheen'.

It is to be noted that at the time we are writing about, the Egyptian fellah was free. He may have been exploited at times by domineering landlords. But what is said about Egyptian feudalism is completely erroneous. There was never a feudal system in Egypt, as there was in Europe, where the peasant was tied to the land and his lord. The Islamic laws of inheritance precluded the accumulation and retention of large areas of land for more than one generation. Polygamy and the high birth rate broke up all the large properties. The trouble always was that the demand for cultivatable land was always more than the supply. This pushed up the price of land, and its rentable value. Fellaheen competed to hire land, which did not leave them much profit.

The fellah was not free at the time of state monopolies, during the rule of the Turks, and Mohammed Aly. Then he could do nothing but work on the rulers, or the concessionaires, land. He was even less free when he hired land and did not know his liabilities. But when he started to own land, and knew what his dues and liabilities were, he was free. This was thanks to the system of taxation introduced by Cromer. The fellah became free of the usurer, when the five-acre law was promulgated in 1913 by Kitchener.

Since negotiations had failed with the Labour Government, in whom he had placed so much hope, there was not much hope of successful negotiations with the Conservative Government, under the leadership of Sir Austin Chamberlain, which had succeeded the Labour Government in 1924. At least not in the near future.

In Egypt Saad's opponents were gloating over his failure. He had always criticised and undermined any of their efforts. Now when he had been given the chance, he had not been able to deliver the goods. Saad returned to Egypt empty-handed. He told the people, 'They offered me suicide, and I refused.' The next speech from the throne in early November 1924, was less extreme in tone. He realised that the government and parliament's duty was to solve the country's internal problems, such as the improvement of education and other matters. He could not leave Egypt stagnant and demoralised under the pretext that the British would not offer him complete independence on a silver platter, with no strings attached.

But his political opponents would not now let him off the hook; they stated that he had lost his will to fight, that he was becoming too old for office, that he found it easier to distract the country with internal matters, in order to remain in power.

They clamoured for him to fulfil his promises: to get rid of the occupation forces and obtain the full independence of Egypt and unity with the Sudan. There were rumours that the Khedive Abbas Helmi and the 'Hizb

El Watan' were fomenting troubles in Egypt and the Sudan; and they accused Saad of conspiring with the Khedive. An opposition weekly, the *Kachkoul*, caricatured Saad wickedly. Its clever articles, and brilliant caricatures, drawn by Juan Sintes, so infuriated the young Wafdist students, that they burnt down its premises. Saad was accused by the opposition of having encouraged them, adding that he was trying to stifle any criticism of himself in the country. They reminded everyone of his dictatorial manner in parliament, even towards members of his own party. They nicknamed it 'Saad's Parliament'. They said it was made up of illiterate deputies and that in spite of Egypt being a country of fourteen million Egyptians, a great many Egyptians were highly educated but were ignored. The opposition reminded everyone of Saad's high-handed manner, in which he dictated his decisions to the deputies, accepting no contradictions. He was reputed to have told a deputy who had got up to make certain remarks about the government:

'Under what principle have you been elected?'
'Under your principles,' replied the deputy.
'Therefore there is no reason for this discussion,' replied Saad.

At another time, when he was being badgered in the House about the Sudan, he shouted, 'Have you got an army? If you want me to get you the moon, then provide me with a ladder, so that I will climb up and get it for you'.

He was finding out bitterly that it was easier to criticise when in opposition, than when ruling and being attacked from all sides.

Under these circumstances, depressed, and suspected of trying to overthrow the King, he tendered his resignation to King Fouad, who would not accept it. He felt that if he could not defend himself against his opponents, he would lose his prestige with the people, and would not be of use to the country. He realised that many governments had ruled without being backed by the people, and had not been able to accomplish anything. But those who had been backed by the people were able some way or another to achieve some amelioration of the state of affairs. But all this internal strife did not concern the British. The Egyptians were sorting out their own affairs, and they were quite content with the status quo. They were even becoming reconciled to the idea of cooperating with Saad at least he would be able to keep the King in check. During an audience Saad had with the King, the mob had kept up a continual cry of 'Saad or Revolution'. On leaving the palace Saad openly thanked and dismissed the crowd.

Three days after the audience with the King on November 19th, 1924, at midday Sir Lee Stack Pasha Sirdar (commander-in-chief) of the Egyptian Army, and Governor-General of Sudan, together with his ADC and Australian chauffeur, were shot at and wounded by a group of hotheads who were able to escape in a taxi. The wounded were taken to the Residency, where Saad arrived two hours later, to make enquiries into the crime. Allenby pointed to the wounded ADC and chauffeur and said, 'This is your doing'. He wanted to lead him in to the Sirdar's room, but was advised that this would not be acceptable to Lady Stack. Zaghloul turned with hardly a word and hurried out[13].

Sir Lee Stack died just before midnight the next day. This assassination threw the whole country into consternation. Everyone felt that England now had the opportunity of dealing Egypt a terrible blow. Both among the British and Egyptian community there was a great sense of shock at this senseless crime.

*

Sir Lee Stack was a man of great personal charm. He had been liked and respected by both Egyptians and British. He had served both Egypt and the Sudan for twenty-three years. Feelings in the British community ran high, most of it was directed against Allenby, whom they felt had tolerated extremism, and should have been very much firmer.

Allenby felt very badly. He felt that he had been betrayed by the Egyptians. He had obtained for them a qualified independence, against much opposition from the local British and foreigners, and despite great apprehension in Whitehall. He had put Egypt on the right route to full independence in the future. He never forgave Saad Zaghloul, and spoke of him ever afterwards as 'that wicked old man'[14]. To be fair, Saad Zaghloul and the leading Wafdists had no previous knowledge of the crime, or any inkling of its being prepared. He realised that for Egypt 'it was worse than a crime, it was a blunder'. For his own ambitions it was fatal. He said sadly, shortly afterwards, *'Pour moi c'était un coup mortel'*.

Esther told us of a time, when she was trying to raise his spirits, she found him saying, 'it's over, it's over'. She answered, 'Don't say that Pasha, the country is all behind you. If you have three good men whom you can trust you can win the day'. He answered, 'Name them!' She started naming people but he shook his head at every name. Then he said, patting her on the head, 'You have the right spirit my daughter'.

Sir Lee Stack was given an official funeral. King Fouad was represented by a chamberlain. The Egyptian Ministers, led by Saad Zaghloul, followed the cortège. It was attended by Egyptian princes, senators and deputies. The whole diplomatic corps was present in full dress. The coffin was borne

[13]*Allenby, Soldier and Stateman* by Lord Wavell, page 333
[14]*Allenby, Soldier and Stateman* by Lord Wavell, page 340

236

to the grave by eight British warrant officers, serving with the Egyptian army. It took an hour for the procession to pass a point. It seemed as if all Cairo had turned out to watch the procession.[15]

This senseless assassination placed the Egyptian Government in a dilemma that it was not able to get out of. Allenby had decided to deliver Egypt an ultimatum that same afternoon after the funeral. He had cabled the Foreign Office its proposed terms. At the same time he was afraid that the government might resign before he could deliver it. Parliament was convening at 5 p.m. On realising he was not able to receive Whitehall's reply before that time, he decided to go it alone. Dressed informally in a grey lounge suit and soft hat, accompanied by 400 lancers, he drove to the Prime Minister's office, which was opposite Parliament Building, in sight of the deputies who were starting to assemble. He went straight to the Prime Minister's room and read him the ultimatum, which was as follows:

After a preamble giving Britain's point of view on the happenings, and the reasons leading up to them, he enumerated the requirements of His Majesty's Government:

1) Present an apology for the crime.
2) Prosecute an enquiry and bring the criminals to book.
3) Suppress all future demonstrations.
4) Pay forthwith a fine of £E500,000.
5) Order immediately the withdrawal of all Egyptian officers from the Sudan, together with all purely Egyptian units of the Sudan Army.
6) Notify the competent department that the area to be irrigated at Gezira was to be increased from 300,000 feddans to an unlimited figure as needs may arise.
7) Withdraw all opposition by the Egyptian Government to the reserved point concerning the protection of foreign interests in Egypt.

Failure to comply with all these demands would result in His Majesty's Government taking appropriate action to safeguard her interests in Egypt and the Sudan.

It is to be noted that the reply from the Foreign Office was much less harsh. It felt that the demand for an indemnity tasted of 'blood money' and the words 'unlimited irrigation' should be replaced by 'such extension of Gezira irrigation as may be considered possible without detriment to Egypt, decided by a technical commission containing a member appointed by the Egyptian government.'

However the ultimatum had been presented, and Allenby stuck by it, subject to it being toned down in the future, according to circumstances.

[15]*Allenby, Soldier and Stateman* by Lord Wavell, page 337

Saad's reply was simple. It expressed horror at the crime and promised to pursue the criminals and exact exemplary punishment, but it absolved the Egyptian Government of all responsibility and could not accept any of the demands except that of the indemnity. A cheque for £E500,000 was signed by the Minister of Finance, who had been appointed a day or two before the assassination.

In reply, Allenby again took action without obtaining permission from the British Government. He occupied the customs in Alexandria.

Saad now realised that he could do nothing and he presented his resignation amidst a tumult in the Egyptian Parliament. This time King Fouad accepted the resignation and Ziwar Pasha was asked to form a government. He accepted the conditions of the ultimatum and the customs were evacuated. The British now felt they were able to make concessions to a friendly government. The amount of land to be irrigated in the Gezira was settled by a commission in which Egypt was represented. Ziwar Pasha who was the President of the Senate, formed his government from elements who were not members of Parliament. A decree was issued suspending Parliament, and on its expiry, a new decree was issued dissolving it.

The opposition now attacked Saad without mercy. There is a saying in Arabic, 'When the bull falls, the carving knives increase' (*Lama yogaa el tor, y'iktar el Sakakeen*). Foreign newspapers dragged Saad's name in the mud. Saad at first guarded his silence. He had left office stating that he would support any government that would draw the country out of its delicate situation. Ismail Sidki had been nominated in Ziwar's government as Minister of the Interior. He toured the country stating that Saad had brought the country to a state of chaos. He swore that Saad and his partisans would never again regain power. 'No', he would say, 'the country will never see again, those days of anarchy.'

The result of the elections held in March seemed to be a draw and both sides claimed victory – the government and the opposition (the Zaghloulists).

Parliament was opened formally by the King on March 23, 1925. Zaghloul was elected President of the Chamber by 123 votes to 85. This was a shock for Ziwar's Ministry who had counted on a majority for their candidate. At the opening of the evening session no ministers were present, and work proceeded normally. At 7.45 p.m. the doors opened and the Prime Minister and the rest of the ministers entered. He read a royal decree dissolving Parliament. New elections were promised for autumn after a new electoral law had been passed. Saad Zaghloul now described the dissolution of Parliament as against the constitution, and 'a presumptuous blow to national dignity'. Comments on the period before the election and after the election were made by Esther in her two letters sent to Lord Allenby in March 1925. The period between the dissolution of parliament and the

Reception of Wafdist Youth Committee of the Port area for Mrs Esther Fahmy Wissa, on her arrival from Europe after one of her conferences

A peace rally where Esther was to speak

new elections was very active in Esther's political life, up until the death of Saad Zaghloul.

I only found out by going through her papers after she died that she had formed a political committee of the ladies who remained with Saad called the Saadieh Committee. It was formed to help Saad and his party when they were out in the wilderness, and to instruct the nation in heavenly principles, without which they would never achieve their aims (see Appendix No 6 – Educational Reform – addressed to Mme Sherifa Riad). Many of the women were now fed up with politics. Some sided half-heartedly with their husbands, others became less keen. There was no longer the energy and unity of aims which had been found in 1919. Saad Zaghloul was no longer their unchallenged leader, clamouring for the abolition of the Protectorate. The situation was overshadowed by party politics, in which women felt they were neither wanted nor needed, and should keep out.

Mme Chaaraoui and a few others still had their political views and were willing to state them forcibly. They still wanted to reform the laws governing women's status in society; they still wanted to be accorded the right to vote.

But men had become more selfish, afraid of losing man's prerogative. They did not want to share their political power with women. But they could not push them back into the Harem once they were out, so they encouraged them to become more interested in social affairs. This was taken up by most of the privileged women of society, even by princesses, who became patrons of different charitable works.

New charities sprang up all over the country. Clinics tending to the medical needs in the poorer parts of the towns and villages were opened. Kindergartens for children, where they could learn and be fed were established. They were all carried out meticulously by their founders who sacrificed their money and time.

In 1924 Esther started a charitable society in Alexandria called 'The Work for Egypt Society'. She ran it till 1962 when it was taken over by the Ministry of Social Affairs; but that is another story.

*

The reader by now may have gathered what the political atmosphere in the country was. The newly elected parliament had been postponed and then dissolved by the King at its very first session on the advice of the acting Prime Minister Ziwar Pasha. Such a situation showed that the minority parties, made up of the old politicians, the educated élite, and those who were cooperating with Ziwar Pasha, could not countenance a rule by the so-called majority of the nation, the Zaghloulists, whom they classified as the rabble or the mob.

240

The Zaghloulists on their part were up in arms. They described what had happened as unconstitutional, which strictly speaking it was.

The British could not care less. Their conditions had been stipulated, and it was up to Egypt to solve its own problems. It could stew in its own juice.

Britain's declared attitude was different. She contended that prior to 1922 her policy had been to occupy Egypt, to supervise the administration in the interests of the inhabitants of Egypt both foreigners and nationals, and prepare the Egyptian people for self-government, until such time as they were capable of governing themselves – notwithstanding the fact that Britain had commercial and defence interests in the country, which she felt were vital to her imperial status, which she intended to hold on to. Her present policy, she declared, was to maintain the status quo, while admitting at the same time that Egypt was a sovereign state. However she claimed a special position for herself vis-à-vis all other powers, with regard to her imperial security until she was able to negotiate specific agreements with Egypt, which safeguarded her vital interests. However Egypt was free to develop her national institutions in accordance with her aspirations. Lord Allenby had decided to resign after the assassination of Sir Lee Stack. He had been subject to criticism from the British community and members of the Foreign Office, which culminated in the inconsiderate appointment by Sir Austen Chamberlain of Mr. Neville Henderson as adviser in Cairo. However Allenby would not give anyone the satisfaction of announcing the date of his resignation. He postponed the announcement for six months. He left Egypt on June 14th, 1925 accompanied by a remarkable demonstration of widespread affection, not only from his personal friends and from the inhabitants of Cairo, but from all classes throughout Egypt. The Egyptians felt that it was through Lord Allenby personally that they had been able to obtain the qualified independence that she now enjoyed.

Esther fell ill with typhoid in April of that year, and for a long time it was touch and go. She was in Alexandria at the time, and her sister Gamila, ten years her junior, was helping to look after her. Even on what she thought was her death bed, she tried to arrange things for the welfare of her husband and her family. She now had four children, she made Fahmy and her sister Gamila promise to get married in the case of her death. She thought that Gamila would be the best wife for her husband, and the best mother to her children. She was probably right in her judgement, but she had not taken into consideration the points of view of the beings concerned. A born Pharaoh!

The last letter Esther wrote to Lord Allenby was on June 2nd, 1925. It was sent from Alexandria where she was convalescing after her long illness. As usual Lord Allenby answered her letter in his own handwriting, the next day (see letters).

241

In spite of their difference in opinion over political matters, Esther had great esteem for Lord Allenby. She saw in him the honest, upright and courteous opponent he was, who cared for the underdog, and who was willing to take a risk for a principle he thought right. All these qualities were paramount in her way of thinking. This can be noticed throughout her correspondence with him for three years. It is true that most of his replies to her letters were not much more than acknowledgements to her long letters, but it is noticeable that he thought about what she wrote. She never wished to publish these letters during her lifetime.

Lord Allenby died in 1935. I only publish them now to throw a light on the character of a caring man, who may have been misrepresented by both the British and the Egyptians.

A letter found among Esther's belongings dated November 11th, 1925 acknowledged the receipt of a letter sent by her dated November 1st, 1925 to the new High Commissioner, Lord Lloyd, and was signed by the Oriental Secretary. The contents of Esther's letter is not known, as no copy was found and is irrelevant. It is needless to say that she never wrote to him again as far as I can tell. I mention this to highlight the difference in behaviour of two diplomats holding the same position. The attitude of the new High Commissioner was a far cry from that of his predecessor.

*

During the period between the departure of Lord Allenby on July 25th, 1925, and the arrival of the new British High Commissioner, Lord Lloyd, in October the political scene in the country had become more fluid.

King Fouad had always felt that Saad Zaghloul and the Wafd were a threat to the throne and an obstruction to his rule as an absolute monarch. For in spite of his accepting the 1923 constitution he had never been reconciled to it.

Now that parliament was dissolved and the country was being ruled by what was known as the King's Party (*Hezb El Malik*) under the premiership of Ziwar Pasha, who was reputed to be anti-Wafd, as well as being a staunch Royalist and pro-British. King Fouad felt he would be able to consolidate his power if he could stifle all opposition.

The Premier helped by Hassan Nashaat Pasha the Head of the Royal Cabinet, tried to attract all politicians outside the main parties to join the King's Party. To enhance the chances of success, a draft law on political parties was drawn up, which was designed to give the Palace extensive powers enabling it to suppress all political opposition.

The two main parties, the Wafd and the Liberal Constitutionalists, were apprehensive of such manoeuvring. They felt that the 1923 constitution was

Lord Lloyd, High Commissioner 1925–1929

being jeopardised, and political parties in general were being weakened. This resulted in a *rapprochement* between them.

Saad Zaghloul then published a declaration to the effect that he strongly supported a proposal that had been recently canvassed. This intimated that whether parliament was summoned by the King or not, it should assemble on November 21st, in accordance with the provisions of the constitution. The government answered three days later, on November 18th, prohibiting the assembly of parliament, and banning all demonstrations, with the result that troops and police blocked all approaches to the Houses of Parliament on November 21st: 134 Deputies and 56 Senators then assembled at the Continental Hotel and proceeded to elect Saad Zaghloul as President of the Chamber (Wafd). They also elected Mohammed Mahmoud (Liberal Constitutionalist) as Vice-President and Abdel Hamed Said (Hezb El Watan) Nationalist, as Vice-President. The significance of this meeting lay in the fact that for the first time the Nationalists, Liberal Constitutionalists and the Wafd had publicly associated themselves in a common cause.

In spite of the above on December 8th the government promulgated a new electoral law disenfranchising 10 percent to 15 percent of the existing electorate. This further incensed public opinion. The King was becoming increasingly unpopular, and the government was believed by all and sundry to be subservient to him.

It was in this atmosphere that on December 10th Nashaat Pasha was gazetted as Minister Plenipotentiary to the Court of Madrid, and left the Palace. This may have been due to the influence of the British who were always afraid that the King might get out of hand.

Their policy for the next thirty years was to play off the Palace against the political parties, two sides of a triangle keeping the third side in check.

Esther at this time could only see that the government was trying by all means to keep the legitimate representatives of the country from having their say. She canvassed and wrote articles in the press chastising everyone she felt was not behaving in a correct manner.

The policy of the government led the leaders in opposition to declare that they would boycott any future election carried out under the new electoral law; and at the same time they called for a congress to be held on January 19th to decide on what further action should be taken to remedy the situation. This induced the government to back away from the new electoral law, and substitute it with the electoral law of 1924 that had been ratified at the time by both houses of parliament. A date for the coming elections was consequently fixed for May of the same year. It was a foregone conclusion that under whatever law the elections were held, the Wafd was bound to be returned with an overwhelming majority. (That is, unless the elections were cooked by the government in power.)

Esther's writings before the elections expressed her fear that somehow the elections would be cooked. She appealed to the innate sense of nationalism of the ordinary Egyptian to resist any mischief that was being concocted by the government.

The results of the election were made public on May 25th. Out of a total of 201 seats, the Wafdist party under Zaghloul Pasha had secured 144 seats, the Liberal Constitutionalists 25 seats, the Nationalists (Hezb el Watan) 5 seats, the Independents 17 seats, and the King's party 7 seats.

For a week it was uncertain what Saad as the leader of the majority would demand. The King did not mind leaving the decision to the British. He knew that they would hate to have to deal with a government led by Zaghloul. So he would let someone else pick the chestnuts out of the fire.

Similarly, the Wafdist party, having attained the majority in parliament, did not want to rock the boat. They did not mind having a moderate government led by a politician such as Adly Pasha Yeghen in office, with Saad Pasha Zaghloul holding the real power in parliament. However it was not sure that Saad would accept such a suggestion. The other parties also feared a dissolution to be followed by a further suspension of the constitution, with a subsequent drift towards autocracy of the Palace. So the mood was for compromise and moderation. It was with a great sense of relief when on June 3rd at a banquet given at the Continental Hotel, Cairo to celebrate Saad's victory, a Wafdist Deputy got up and spoke a few words urging Saad not to overstrain his health by undertaking the cares of office, but rather to conserve and cherish it in the interest of the fatherland. The deputies needed no further urging: they cheered their heads off. Saad Pasha Zaghloul turned to Adly Pasha Yeghen who was sitting next to him. He said, 'I am too weak to reply, let someone else speak for me'. No one did. And the meeting broke up after a good lunch. On June 7th the new ministry was formed under the premiership of Adly Pasha Yeghen. It contained seven Wafdists and three Liberal Constitutionalists. Saad Zaghloul Pasha became President of the Chamber of Deputies, which he ruled with an iron hand. If a deputy became over-insistent in a speech, it only needed one word from Zaghloul for that deputy to sit down meekly. If there was no quorum in the house, Zaghloul's method was to suspend the session and walk out into the lobby, where he would lecture the lounging deputies, and returning to the presidential chair, would ring his bell, with a result that the deputies would hasten to their seats like chastened schoolboys.

It must be remembered that parliamentarianism as understood in the West was in its infancy in Egypt at that time. Many of the newly-elected deputies came straight from the country. Parliament became a school for democracy and on the whole it succeeded surprisingly well, notwithstanding the criticism of the foreign press, and in books written by Europeans. Many older parliaments took centuries to develop before they were able to achieve the level of democracy arrived at in the Egyptian Parliament over a couple of decades.

And in spite of all the obstacles that parliamentarianism in Egypt had to surmount due to the manipulations of the different political forces in the country in its short life of twenty-eight years the traditions, regulations, and democratic behaviour that it had developed through its adaption of traditions of older institutions in the West became the norm. It could be favourably compared with any of the parliaments of the time, especially if one took into consideration the upheavals and different political systems and ideas that had emerged in the world between the two world wars and especially after the end of World War II.

We should remember that the principle of consultation (*Shoura*) was an old Arab tradition, and had been the basis of government since the days of Islam, in spite of final decisions being taken by the ruler.

For the next two years the pendulum moved between moderation and conciliation on the one hand and extremism and confrontation on the other. The King always trying to niggle the government and the establishment, the British trying not to impose their will unless they felt their position was threatened. Saad Zaghloul wanted to crown his life's work by coming to a final settlement with Britain; but Saad's task was made more difficult by the views expressed by the more radical members of his party. It was under these circumstances that Adly Pasha Yeghen resigned on April 17th, 1927 on what seemed a curiously trivial matter. A motion had been tabled during the discussion of the Budget in the Chamber. The government should be thanked for the encouragement it had extended to the Bank Misr, whose founders Talaat Harb Pasha and Medhat Yeghen Pasha, had been behind many of the national projects of industrialisation that were taking place in the country. The motion was moved and for some reason rejected by a large majority of the House perhaps because the country was passing through financial difficulties at the time, due to a drop in cotton prices, and the landowners not wishing to reduce rents. Adly Pasha considered this to be a vote of no confidence in the government's policy and resigned. But the reason behind the resignation probably lay much deeper. The government was on a collision course with the British and the Palace. The Minister of War, Khashaba Pasha, was pressing for an increase in the Egyptian army's strength, the creation of an air force, and freedom from the control of British senior officers. He was backed in this by the more radical members of the Wafd, led by Ahmed Maher and Nokrashy, who had just been acquitted of complicity in the murder of Sir Lee Stack the Commander-in-Chief of the Egyptian army. The British and the Palace were reluctant to disturb the status quo, and a greatly increased army, controlled by a government that could become hostile to the British or the Palace, was to be opposed at all costs. The government's view was that

Abdel Sarwat Pasha

Ismail Sidki Pasha

Mahmoud Fahmy el Nokrashi Pasha

Ahmed Maher Pasha

from a legal point of view the army did not fall under any of the reserved points of the 1922 declaration of independence.

With the resignation of Adly Pasha, Sarwat Pasha was prevailed upon to accept office. The Wafd accepted him to head the new Cabinet but not to kow-tow to British demands by retaining their influence over the Egyptian army. The British contemplated getting the King to dissolve parliament and rule by decree, until such time as a more favourable atmosphere should prevail. Lord Lloyd thought of requesting the dispatch of a warship to Alexandria as a show of force. However Sarwat was a diplomat, and although he backed the view that legally the army lay outside the points that had to be negotiated, he agreed that the status quo would be maintained. At the same time Egypt would negotiate with Britain on her right of maintaining a British garrison in the country. The British Foreign Office, although agreeing with Lord Lloyd in principle, was vacillating on what measures should be taken. So the compromise was a relief to all; the crisis had been averted and it was now possible to try to obtain an agreement on the four reserved points, while Saad still had influence. For although it was never sure whether he would wax hot or cold, yet it was felt that he would like to crown his career by obtaining full independence for Egypt, and he was the only person in the country at the time who could control public opinion.

Lord Lloyd preferred waiting, allowing the first move to come from Egypt. But Sir Austen Chamberlain, the Secretary of State, took the opportunity of pressing on Sarwat Pasha the necessity of some permanent agreement between Britain and Egypt. This occurred towards the end of King Fouad's visit to England in July 1927, when Sarwat Pasha accompanied the King. In fact a draft treaty of alliance was produced by Sarwat, and an alternative draft was proposed by the Foreign Office. Sarwat promised to return in October to continue the negotiations. He was counting on Saad to help carry it through.

However fate had its say in the matter. On August 23rd after a short illness Saad died. A central influence in Egypt had disappeared, and it was impossible to foretell what the reaction would be. The country received the news of Saad Pasha Zaghloul's death with consternation. A sense of deep sorrow filled the air. The King, as well as Sarwat Pasha, the Premier, were still in Paris when they were informed. The King ordered that Saad Pasha should be given an official burial with full military honours. The funeral took place the next day at 4 p.m., and all shops and offices were closed as a sign of mourning. An eerie silence interspersed with the sobs of a whole nation overshadowed the country. The funerary procession started at the House of the People (Saad Pasha's residence) which was known by that name because of the many political meetings that had over the years taken place there. People of all walks of life followed the gun carriage, members of all the syndicates, the diplomatic corps, and others. Seventeen cannon shots were fired when the body left the house, and a further seventeen were fired when he was placed to rest; more than 300,000 people followed the burial procession. Similar processions were carried out all over the country. The newspapers in Egypt had black borders for several days, and government offices were closed for three days running. The country was at a standstill. In front of his tomb his worst enemies mourned him, standing side by side with his best friends. The house in which he had lived with his wife was bought by the State to remain, as it always had been in his lifetime, as the House of the Nation. Three statues were erected in his memory in Cairo, Alexandria and Port Said. It was the culminating honour to the son of the fellah, who had so caught the imagination of the country, that they considered him their protector and their father, but reminding them at the same time that he was only a mortal like everyone else.

The description of the funeral and the atmosphere was mentioned by Foulad Yeghen in his book *Saad Zaghloul* published in Paris by Des Cahiers de France in 1927. Foulad Yeghen was a nephew of Adly Pasha Yeghen and for many years was one of Zaghloul's greatest critics. Later he felt that he had been too hard on him, and this book was an apology.

With the death of Saad Pasha Zaghloul, it became apparent to many people that no politician would be able to negotiate and carry through an agreement, without the approbation of the majority party, that is, the Wafd.

Sarwat Pasha had started negotiations with Sir Austen Chamberlain before Saad's death. In fact a draft treaty had been worked out, and was ready to be ratified by the Cabinet and Parliament. Sarwat did not wish to bring matters to a head: he wished to keep negotiations open until he could obtain ratification, whereas the British wanted a clear answer as soon as possible. When Sarwat finally put the proposals to the cabinet it was rejected. The official reply was that 'the draft treaty, by reason both of its basic principles and its actual provisions, was incompatible with the independence and sovereignty of Egypt, and moreover it legalised occupation of the country by British forces'.[16]

Lord Lloyd had tried to get Nahas Pasha to agree before the Cabinet gave its official reply. But he could get nowhere with Nahas. 'Nahas Pasha asserted that it was quite useless to discuss *this or any other treaty* that did not provide for complete evacuation of Egyptian territory by the British Army. He could not agree that one British soldier should remain on Egyptian soil, be it at Suez or Sinai.' He said that England could expect nothing, 'without their removal'. 'But with their removal', he said, 'they would buy Egyptian friendship, which would be an absolute guarantee for all British interests in

[16] *Egypt since Cromer*, Lord Lloyd, Volume II, page 258

Egypt'. Sarwat resigned immediately after the cabinet rejection of this draft.

On March 15th, 1928 Nahas Pasha formed the first Ministry. He was a popular figure with the general public right up to the end of his life, in spite of the ups and downs of his career.

\*

It would seem as if the mass of the people recognised themselves in these two Egyptians of peasant stock. Saad Pasha Zaghloul and Mustapha Pasha el Nahas. And although their personal looks were very different, they both had that charisma that won over the ordinary man-in-the-street.

Saad Pasha was a good-looking, hoary-headed, imposing figure, with a great deal of personal charm, and although he came from peasant stock and poor beginnings, yet he had acquired all the refinements of the Turkish rulers.

Nahas Pasha was a vociferous ex-judge with a pointed skull and a distinct squint. Although of a gruff and imposing nature he remained a peasant through and through. It was this simplicity that many of his followers found so attractive. He was known as *Ragil Tayib*, a good and kind fellow. He was forthright in his speech, he called a spade a spade, was absolutely fearless, and difficult to persuade if suspicious. He would accept no opposition from his colleagues, and was prone to listen to all those who whispered in his ears. Esther thought that the Wafd under Nahas would follow Saad's policy in encouraging the participation of women in the struggle for complete independence. But on the contrary, Nahas did not want women poking their noses into politics, and he told them so clearly. He did not mind them discarding their veils, or improving their education, but he had no intention of helping them to obtain their political rights, which resulted in Esther's active role in Egyptian politics becoming less apparent. She still made speeches and wrote articles, but not as a spokeswoman or as feminist leader for the party, but as a nationalist.

She was still considered a leader amongst the feminist movement, attending feminist congresses all over the world. But the torch of the Egyptian feminist movement that was trying to improve the status of the majority of women in the country (the Moslem woman), was carried and nurtured by Mme Hoda Chaaraoui and her followers, as mentioned before.

Esther concentrated more on the improvement of Egyptian women and their children through social works. She was particularly interested in:

a) The YWCA
b) Work for Egypt Society
c) And other charities.

*Young Women's Christian Association (YWCA)*

Among Esther's many social works was her active involvement from the 1920s till 1983 with the YWCA. Other members of the family were also deeply involved with its work in Egypt.

I will try to relate briefly how this worldwide institution originated, and how it started and developed in Egypt. How through its spirit and activities it was able to nurture in its members a sense of belonging, giving, sharing and cooperating, which helped to build traits of leadership and responsibility. Many of these traits were absorbed from the behaviour of the dedicated professionals who were employed, and the unstinting sacrifice and work of its volunteers.

In spite of its being a Christian association, the YWCA's membership was open to women of any nationality, colour or creed.

It all started in 1855 when two separate movements in England which had practically the same aims amalgamated.

The first movement was led by Miss Emily Cainard who wished to provide spiritual guidance through Christian principles for young girls who had cut away from their mother's apron strings, and had migrated to the big cities to earn their livings.

The second was founded by Miss Emma Roberts who was concerned with providing cheap and clean living quarters, in a Christian atmosphere for the increasing numbers of young women in the big cities, especially London. She felt that when looking for accommodation a young naive woman might easily succumb to the temptations that London provided.

During the Crimean war many young women such as Florence Nightingale volunteered as nurses to serve at the front, and about the same time single women seemed to appear more frequently in different jobs in several parts of the world. The example that London provided caught the imagination of other countries, and soon similar groups were formed in the USA and other European and Scandinavian countries.

In 1898 a world association was formed with its headquarters in London. It took the name of the Young Women's Christian Association. At a later date its headquarters were transferred to Geneva. At first it drew its membership from Europe, England and North America, but soon it spread into other nations, such as India, China, Australia, New Zealand, Egypt, Syria and other countries in South East Asia and Africa. All these associations had the same aims. Their main principle was belief in God the Father, the Son and the Holy Ghost and their motto was, 'By love serve one another'. Their emblem was a blue triangle denoting 'Developing Spirit, Mind and Body'. In 1876 two young English ladies resident in Egypt, who were members of the original movement in England, named Miss Van Sommer and

Miss Golloch, gathered a group of young Englishwomen who had come out to Egypt in different occupations, with a view to meeting regularly in a Christian atmosphere. They rented premises in Sharia Maghrabi, and their annual subscription was ten piastres – less than two shillings. This group grew into the International YWCA in Egypt.

In 1901 the World Association of the YWCA advertised in a London newspaper asking for contributions to establish a centre in Cairo. Egypt had become an important point on the map, the crossroads of three continents – Europe, Africa and Asia. The advertisement asked for a volunteer to come out and administer the new centre.

Miss Rosa Marginson came out to Egypt and rented premises for the Association in Sharia Kasr el Nil. These were inaugurated by the Duchess of Connaught when she was visiting Egypt and were known as Connaught House. This remained the home of the Association for many years. Membership fees at that time were raised to twenty-five piastres per annum – about five shillings. In 1905 there were about forty-five members, mostly British, who were working as nannies, nurses, teachers, missionaries and secretaries.

The Association changed its premises several times after its inauguration in 1905. Its membership was really international in the 1920s and early 1930s, and comprised three separate groups of members who had special days in which their activities were concentrated.

The British gathered on Wednesday of every week. Their members came from the same class as mentioned before. Their activities were supervised and planned by a Miss Brodie. The language spoken was English, and their interests were mostly whist drives, arranged dancing parties, exchanging novels, lectures on the history of Egypt and visiting sites. A yearly excursion was arranged to Luxor and Aswan in winter, and others to Port Said, Suez and Alexandria in summer. A yearly trip to Jerusalem and a visit to the holy places was one of the highlights of their activities. The international group gathered each Thursday. It drew its members from all the different foreign communities in Cairo – Greeks, Italians, Turks, etc. At times its members belonged to over twenty-five nationalities. The language they used was French and their activities were supervised and planned for many years by Miss Altman. The interests of this group differed slightly from the former and tended to be directed more towards table-tennis matches, ballet dancing, concerts and the acting of short plays which the members had written. Singing contests were arranged as well as educational excursions and visits to the important sites in the city. The third group were young Egyptian women who joined in the late twenties. They were drawn from a bevy of intellectual young women who had had post-graduate courses in England where they had been sent by the Ministry of Education to specialise in different subjects before taking up senior government posts. Their special day was Friday and their activities were supervised at the start by Miss Guy and then by Miss Pepler. Amongst its members I mention as an example Mrs. Zahia Marzouk who was at the head of social affairs in Alexandria during the time of President Gamal Abdel Nasser. They gathered to reminisce over a cup of tea in the garden of the Association, discuss and borrow books from the library, or spend part of their Fridays around the swimming pool at the Mena House Hotel.

Members of the three groups tried to spend some of their spare time at the weekends at a tent that had been erected near the Pyramids.

In 1920 Mrs Regina Khayatt (Wissa's daughter) was invited to attend a meeting of the Executive Committee of the World YWCA in Geneva, when she was vacationing in Europe for the summer. She was informed of all the different YWCA activities all over the world, and asked if she would become the first President of an Egyptian Branch of the YWCA, to be known as the National YWCA. This would be part of the World Organization to serve young Egyptian girls and women in the principles and aims of the organization. They asked her because of her social position amongst the Egyptian Christians, because she would be able to induce many of her friends and relations to help in promoting the cause.

Mrs Khayatt accepted and was helped greatly in getting the project off the ground by an American missionary, Mrs Phillips, who chose Miss Zahia Mishriki and sent her to be trained at an institute of Christian studies. On her return she was appointed as supervisor of the new Association. She was helped by many of the Coptic society ladies.

They started their activities with lessons on the Holy Bible, in sewing, cutting, needlework etc., in music, in First Aid, cooking and confectionery, as well as making excursions and playing table-tennis. In 1931 the Wissa and Khayatt families allowed the Association to use a piece of land they had on the beach at Glymenopulo in Alexandria as a summer camp. And in 1932 they donated instead a piece of land at Sidi Bishr to build a permanent summer camp, as the land at Glymenopulo had been expropriated to become part of the Corniche.

Mrs Khayatt died in 1942 and the presidency of the National YWCA evolved on to her daughter-in-law, Mrs Edna Robert Khayatt. Edna was George Pasha Wissa's daughter. She remained President of the National YWCA until it amalgamated with the International YWCA in 1948, and continued as President of the new amalgamated YWCA until the 1960s.

In 1938 the Executive Council of the YWCA in Egypt gave the National YWCA permission to use the emblem of the blue triangle symbolising the 'development of spirit, mind and body'.

In 1943 the National YWCA was represented on the Executive Committee of the YWCA in Egypt which included the Cairo International and the branches at Alexandria, Assiout, Port Said and Minieh.

Esther became a member of the board of the Alexandria branch in the 1920s. She was secretary in 1933 and ex-officio for Alexandria on the General Council from 1933 to 1936. On November 13th, 1937 Esther was elected Chairman of the Executive General Council of the YWCA, a position she kept until she resigned the post in November 1948. She was succeeded as Chairman by Mrs Robert Khayatt who retained the chairmanship until she left Egypt in the 1960s. She was also President of the amalgamated YWCA in Cairo. Esther became Chairman of the Alexandria YWCA in 1942 and remained there until 1983.

Aida Fanous, Esther's sister, was Chairman of the Assiout branch of the YWCA until she came to live in Alexandria in the late fifties.

During all this period whether she was in the chair or not, the two-day summer meeting of the Executive Council of the YWCA in Egypt was held at Esther's residence in Alexandria.

In the meantime the Home International which had its headquarters in Geneva and whose main aim was to provide living quarters for young girls, amalgamated with the YWCA. Their Alexandria hostel did the same, and Esther who had been on the board of the Home International, became the Chairman of the newly amalgamated board known as the Alexandria YWCA. It closed its premises in Rue Nebi Daniel in Alexandria and the premises of the Home International became the premises of the new amalgamation. Among the highlights of the YWCA's activities in Alexandria was the annual bazaar held in the first week in December. It was usually held at the Cecil Hotel where all the ladies interested in the YWCA had their individual stalls. After the hotel was nationalised in the 1960s and most of the foreign ladies had gone, my mother used to give a charity dance and dinner at her residence and a donation to compensate for the loss of revenue.

*Work for Egypt Society*

In 1924 Esther helped to found a charitable society, which was given the name of 'Work for Egypt Society' and intended to open other branches all over the country. Its aims, based on her own principles, were lofty. The society survived in Alexandria until 1962, when it was taken over by the Ministry of Social Affairs, who felt that they could put its large grounds and buildings to a better use. Alexandria was truly a cosmopolitan town for many years. It was the business centre of Egypt, whereas Cairo was the political centre. The different foreign communities all had charities which they financed by contributions. Help was also provided by different business firms. They were administered and run by volunteer workers drawn from society women. The individual charities usually had dedicated and persevering women, who were the driving force, to direct them.

Work for Egypt Society became mother's pet charity. Its aims expressed

Active Social Committee of the Alexandria Red Crescent
Mrs Fahmy Bey Wissa, Mrs E.T. Peel (Treasurer), Mrs Ahmed Pasha Kamel
(Chairman), Mrs D. Gaudi (Assistant Treasurer), Mrs Th. Karam, Mrs P. Griparis,
Count P. de Zogheb, Mr Anthony Carr (Secretary), Mtre Gaston Zananiri

A visit to the Schutz Clinic of the Work for Egypt Society

a strong awareness of the weaknesses in the Egyptian community, and the desire of some individuals to overcome them. Their declared goal was to enhance the moral behaviour of Egyptians as a whole, by raising the ethical standards of Egyptian women and by boosting their capacity to act as social beings, and as useful members of the Egyptian nation.

It must be remembered that Esther was disappointed in the political atmosphere that prevailed in the country at the time. Egyptian women were wavering in their concept of how best to achieve independence. Many of them had forsaken the spirit of independent thought, solidarity and enthusiasm that had characterised the movement towards political and social emancipation in its early years. They had begun to move towards their husband's ideas. In Esther's opinion men had abandoned the principles she thought were right. They were jostling each other for position on the road to personal ambitions. And although she was a leader and fighter with a compassionate heart, Esther was no politician. She saw everything in black and white and could not recognise the grey.

The Society's aims included interesting women in charitable and social works and to teach them to care for others as well as themselves. This work should befit their status in society, as well as being within their capacity to perform. The success of the community should come about through the financial and moral support of the privileged members of society helping poor families, who could prove their need.

This help took the form of care for their sick children, who were treated at an out-patient clinic at Schutz Ramleh, a suburb of Alexandria. The clinic was owned and built on land purchased by the society out of contributions collected by Esther and other philanthropic Alexandrian women.

Patients were treated free and were provided with the prescribed medicines. A general practitioner and nurse were employed on a permanent basis. A visiting oculist and an ear and throat specialist were available three days a week.

I remember the first general practitioner who was employed for years by the Society. He was a white Russian refugee, a certain Dr. Vladimir Bogalanski, whom my mother used to bring home sometimes to lunch.

Amongst its other activities the Society provided pre-school education in the mornings for children of poor families. They were given a glass of milk and a sandwich and an orange. Advice and help were also given to boys concerning their primary education. They were guided into choosing vocations which would give them a better chance of success in life. Mothers were taught how to keep their children clean, and places were provided where working mothers could leave their children.

Since the Society was a corporate body, it was subject to the laws of the land. Politics and religion as subjects of discussion were taboo. However the Society stipulated that it had a duty to provide mothers with advice on the improvement of their moral behaviour, consistent with the religion of the country as laid down in the constitution. The Society drew its revenue from:

a) Subscriptions collected from both active and non-active members. The former paid an annual subscription of one pound and the latter two pounds. These payments could be settled by monthly or quarterly instalments. People who performed exceptional services for the Society, or helped the Society financially by donating not less than five pounds a year, were called Members of Honour.
b) Income came from activities such as annual plays, concerts, fêtes, special cinema shows etc. arranged and carried out by the Society on its own account.
c) Contributions from the public, and other subventions.
d) A monthly lottery controlled by the government.

I remember one play given by the Society either in 1930 or 1931 in the open air at the Antoniades Gardens. These very beautiful gardens together with a palace were donated in 1918 to the Alexandria Municipality by its owner Sir John Antoniades. An amusing story is told about how the donation came about. The Sultan Fouad was visiting the palace and gardens with Sir John Antoniades, and made a complimentary remark about them. Sir John returned the compliment by saying 'Everything in Egypt belongs to you, your Highness'. The next day the Municipality sent for the keys to the property. A rather tall story to believe.

These gardens and palace were founded in the 1870s – the same time as the Alexandria Zoo at Nouzha, and are adjacent to it.

The play given by the Work for Egypt Society was a version of *Singing in the Rain*, and was acted by young cosmopolitan Alexandrian society. It was supposed to have three showings on three consecutive nights, but after the first two nights, which were a great success, the spectators were drenched in a sudden freak rainstorm and the last showing had to be cancelled.

The accounts were kept in the office in the basement of our house by the family accountant and secretary Moussa Effendi, an ex-headmaster who had beautiful handwriting. These accounts were audited each year by one of the auditing firms in Alexandria. Such firms audited the accounts of charitable societies without charge, as part of their civic contribution.

Anyone of any worth in society felt that it was their moral duty to put their weight behind voluntary works for the betterment of the community at large, as well as their own special social projects. In those days there were fewer government regulations and restrictions, and people did not stint either the money they spent or the personal effort they put into whatever they felt was right. But with the increasing interference from less competent

257

officials, together with the intrinsic difficulties of voluntary work, many dedicated people gave up in despair.

I remember the conscientiousness of our accountant every month meticulously going through the thousands of returned lottery tickets to see if the Society had lost the first prize. That is, if the winning ticket had been sold to a lucky member of the public. It was the Society's good fortune if the first prize drawn had not been sold at all.

The Society's articles stated that it could only be liquidated by a decision taken by seventy-five per cent of its members and the choice of another charity to whom the Society's assets were to be donated must be made at the same time as the decision to liquidate.

In 1962 the director of the Ministry of Social Affairs in Alexandria intimated that she needed the Society's premises for an institution to teach young girls handicrafts. She demanded that the Society should go into liquidation, as its aims were too old-fashioned and were irrelevant to the Ministry's plans for the development of social affairs. She asked that the assets should be donated to the above-mentioned project. Esther could not envisage losing the project she had nurtured with all the trouble and effort she had put into the Society for thirty-eight years. The Society's board also wanted to donate the assets to an institution of their own choosing, and not one dictated to by the government. Esther was prepared to go to court about it. However we, her children, persuaded her to give in. This was not the time to be stubborn. She compromised, but the resulting agreement was not put into writing. This was that the Society would donate its assets to the Ministry's project on condition that the new project should retain the name of Work for Egypt Society. However once the Ministry got its hands on the premises, they conveniently forgot all about retaining the name.[17]

Esther was on the boards of many other charitable societies, such as the Red Crescent and the Coptic Ladies' Society, but although she attended their meetings she was not as actively involved with them as she was with the YWCA, the Home International affiliated with La Maison des Jeunes Filles in Geneva, and Work for Egypt Society. However she spent much time at the Red Crescent during the cholera epidemic in Alexandria in 1948, and during the 1967 and 1973 wars.

---

[17]Looking through the balance sheet of the Society for the year 1928 which I found amongst mother's papers, I noticed that subscriptions and donations amounted to £E83 – whereas the gross income from the charity show which was held at the Casino San Stephano was £E1393. And the net income from it after taxes, was £E1031. At the same time it is interesting to note that all expenses of the Society for medicine, salaries etc. amounted to £E863 for the year 1928.

The fate of Egyptian politics between 1928 and 1936 – the date of the signing of the Anglo-Egyptian Treaty of Friendship – was hectic. There was a continual struggle for position and supremacy between the three main protagonists in the country. From the palace King Fouad was always trying to augment royal power at the expense of constitutional government. The Wafd, led by Nahas Pasha, representing a cross-section of the populace, felt that since they represented the majority they should rule. And the British were always afraid of losing their grip on the country, together with their privileged position, in spite of the fact that Egypt was supposed to be a sovereign state, with the exception of the four reserved points that were to be resolved by negotiation.

The 1923 constitution was suspended once again in July 1928. The King had dismissed Nahas's government after a few months in power, under the pretext that whilst he was Vice-President of the Chamber, Nahas considered abolishing the Royal Court Council in favour of Prince Seif el Din, who was trying to re-acquire his property, which was being administered by the Court under the control of the Palace. The implication was not that anything dishonest had actually taken place, but that it was unethical that the question should be discussed by lawyers and members of the House. The result was that Egypt was governed by decree under the premiership of Mohammed Mahmoud Pasha (a Liberal Constitutionalist). The new government tried to come to an agreement with Britain in June 1929, but the Wafdist opposition was difficult to overcome. It should be noted that Nahas Pasha and those accused with him were called before a disciplinary court of the Lawyer's Bar. They were acquitted in February 1929 (see photograph of reception given celebrating the acquittal, published in the *Mussawar* of February 15th, 1929).

New elections were held under the 1923 constitution in December of that year, which the Wafd won with a large majority. Nahas became Premier for the second time and resumed negotiations with Britain, but they broke down over the Sudan, from which the Egyptians had been virtually excluded since the death of Sir Lee Stack in 1924. Nahas Pasha resigned in June 1930, and King Fouad appointed Ismail Pasha Sidki as Premier. The 1923 constitution was abrogated and another was proclaimed by royal decree.

Sidki ruled the country with an iron fist. He did all that was in his power to break the Wafd. But this had the opposite effect; the Wafd boycotted the elections which were held in 1931, and Sidki's strong-arm tactics became an anathema to everyone. The King was becoming more unpopular, as were the British, with the result that the King dismissed the Sidki Government in 1933. After which the King appointed several governments which

259

Celebration of the acquittal of Nahas Pasha

Nahas Pasha
on his right Gharably Pasha, Makram Bey Ebeid, Fakhry Abdel Nour
Bey; on his left Hamad el Bassel Pasha, Gaafar Fakhry Bey, Salama
Mikhail Bey

H.H. Prince Seif el Din

Aly Maher Pasha

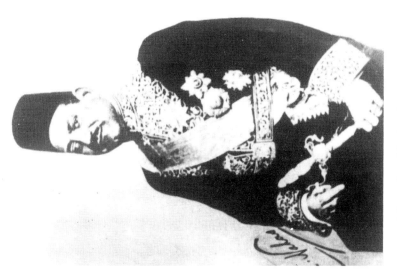

Mustapha el Nahas Pasha

ruled the country by decree. During this period the universities and political parties were clamouring for the return of the 1923 constitution. I remember that Esther made a few speeches at the time demanding the return of the 1923 constitution. One of these speeches was made at the Fouad Ist University in Cairo. The Wafd, under Nahas, in spite of the harrassment they were submitted to by the authorities, were becoming more popular day by day.

By 1934 King Fouad was ailing, and felt he did not have much more time to live. His only son, Farouk, was under age and at school in England. He wanted to make sure that there would be no trouble with the succession if anything should happen to him. At the same time the British were preoccupied with the world situation; they wanted a peaceful Egypt on their side in case of war.

A new High Commissioner, Sir Miles Lampson, was brought out from China, and the 1923 constitution was restored in May 1935. King Fouad died in April 1936 and elections were held in May of the same year. The Wafd won the majority in the general elections and Nahas Pasha became the Prime Minister for the third time. He headed a delegation of seven Wafdists and six prominent politicians from the other parties, and quickly came to an agreement in August 1936. This was known as the Anglo-Egyptian Treaty of Friendship of 1936.

King Fouad had set the machinery working but he died before seeing the result. His arch-enemy, Nahas Pasha, was in the saddle once again, and a friendship had been struck up between Nahas Pasha and the British High Commissioner, Sir Miles Lampson. This was to have such dire affects on the throne during the reign of his son, King Farouk. Details of how the treaty of friendship came about are mentioned in the chapter *The Quiet Diplomat.*

*

During the war years Esther did not travel, but remained in Egypt and concerned herself with looking after her social work. Once the treaty of 1936 had been signed with England, which was hailed by the country as a great victory for the Wafd, Esther did not feel it necessary to concern herself with Egyptian politics. Women were not wanted by the men. In 1937 the Wafd was dismissed by the young King Farouk, the darling of the nation. Nahas Pasha asked Esther to head a party of women to fight for constitutionalism and the return of the Wafd to power by reviving the Wafdist Feminist Committee. She declined, women had been disbanded by Nahas after the death of Saad, and she found no pressing reason to fight for specifically party politics, and not for the country as a whole. She had become less enchanted with Egyptian politics because they seemed to be more concerned with the aggrandisement of their members, instead of the general welfare of the nation. My father, on the other hand, was becoming more involved. He had been elected to the Wafd party executive, and was active in his constituency, the Laban district in Alexandria. He had kept his seat in the Senate since its inception in 1924. Esther helped him in his constituency, keeping an open house for his electors, and giving any help she could with his other projects, whilst working assiduously at things that interested her more.

Nahas Pasha had been dismissed by the young King Farouk, because he felt that Nahas Pasha and the Party were becoming a threat to the throne. He was influenced by the ambitions of Aly Maher Pasha who had become the King's adviser, and whose ambition was to be the power behind the throne.

Farouk was led to believe that Nahas was turning into another Mussolini. He had just formed a Wafdist youth movement known as the Blue Shirts, in opposition to a Fascist youth movement formed by Misr el Fatah, known as the Green Shirts, led by Ahmed Hussein.

*

Although Esther and other members of the family were at the forefront of the 1919 revolution, they were not involved in the 'Economic Nationalism' that was born directly from the Revolution.

Industry and commerce prior to 1919 was practically all in the hands of foreigners. Taxation was non-existent and companies prospered. The Egyptian by nature was a farmer, and excelled in growing cotton, which was exported to spinners abroad and reimported as finished cotton goods. After 1921 we copied India in her fight for independence. She had started a cottage industry to produce cheap cotton cloth for the masses and thus boycott British goods. But we were more ambitious. In 1922 a group of Egyptians led by Talaat Pasha Harb and Midhat Pasha Yeghen founded a purely Egyptian bank which they named 'Bank Misr'. This became the nucleus of the Misr group of companies, which covered a whole range of industries, from producing films to buttons, the most successful project being a group of spinning and weaving mills. And though the national industries passed through certain difficulties at different times, and the Government had to come to the bank's rescue in the early years of World War II, still they weathered all the storms, and became the bulwark of the Egyptian economy prior to 1952.

*

The years between the accession of King Farouk and the 1952 Revolution are referred to when they are relevant throughout the story, but Esther did not concern herself much with Egyptian politics during this period. She felt that with the signing of the Anglo-Egyptian treaty of friendship in 1936, which was endorsed by all the parties and the nation, it was up to the Egyptian politicians to make the best of things. If they did not, it was their lack of moral character that stood in the way.

Father's health was precarious after the end of World War II, and part of her time was taken up looking after him.

With the advent of the 1952 Revolution the old political set-up became obsolete, politicians became onlookers instead of participants. No one really knew what was happening, or who was in charge. A whole new scene was being enacted in front of our eyes, which did not always make sense.

I would like to include in this story an allegory in verse whose author wishes to remain anonymous. It was written by a young person without malice, with a sense of humour describing the play which was being enacted. It read as follows:

### The Ballad of the Jumping Fleas

I'll now begin this anxious tale
   Of Fleas I haven't met,
Who leapt so high into the air,
   They haven't landed yet,
They haven't landed yet because,
   They don't know where to set.

For I've been told by scientists,
   The jumping of a flea,
Considered in the nature world
   Is quite extraordinary.
But even fleas can jump too high,
   To come down comfortably.

These fleas jumped through Ambition's Gate
   Into a garden Power,
Where reigned a myopic butterfly,
   That wiled away the hour,
By gambling recklessly with trees,
   And flirting with each flower.

For flirting with each fickle flower,
   And gambling with the trees,
We'll banish you to far-off lands,
   Or give you DDT's.
Enough corruption evil ways,
   Cried out the righteous fleas.

Before the butterfly set off,
　　He gave the fleas advice,
Through mentioning my flighty ways,
　　You'll promulgate my vice,
Remember please, that also fleas,
　　Are not considered nice.

I've never seen a soul as yet,
　　Applaud or laud a flea.
I've always heard, upon my word,
　　A flea brings anarchy.
So change your ways, if you want praise,
　　And imitate the bee.

We will not only imitate,
　　Announced the leading flea,
We'll pass a law, that all ignore,
　　Our past identity.
And then we'll build a little hive,
　　And live just like the bee.

With unity and discipline,
　　We'll keep the garden clean.
And crown a silly silent sort,
　　A quiet kind of Queen.
A very quiet kind of Queen,
　　Who will not intervene.

We'll gather honey from the flowers,
　　And put it in a cell,
And all who are dissatisfied,
　　Will end up there as well,
We also must uproot the weeds,
　　Who venture to rebel.

And so the fleas began to work,
　　Upon their garden plots,
Collected honey from the flowers,
　　And flowers from their pots.
Forget-me-nots disguised their names,
　　By taking off their 'nots'.

As weeds were hard to recognise,
　　The busy fleas soon found,
It was so much more practical
　　To dig up all the ground.
It really did not matter much,
　　That nothing grew around.

Then unexpectedly the Queen,
    Rebelled against her fate,
Declared she'd always understood,
    Her job was to create.
'I will not sit upon the throne,
    And merely vegetate'.

The fleas cried, 'This will never do,
    We must find out a way,
In which our Queen will find it is
    Impossible to stay.
For she is far too popular
    To poison her away.'

They held flea meetings twice a day,
    And three times every night.
It was becoming difficult
    To somewhat keep polite.
It was so much more logical,
    To end up in a fight.

At last they found a way in which,
    The Queen they could disown,
By making headlines in the press,
    They sadly made it known.
'Her Gracious Majesty the Queen
    Had turned into a Drone.

'We're very sorry to point out',
    They added at this stage,
'That life has changed considerably
    In this atomic age,
And changing of the sexes is
    Becoming quite the rage'.

And when the little Queen had gone,
    Upon her endless ride,
The fleas returned once more to work,
    With energy and pride.
But nothing new would seem to grow,
    Where all the old had died.

The fleas then made another speech,
    'We hope you realise,
We're passing through the winter stage,
    Where every darned thing dies.
But with the coming of the spring,
    We'll spring a big surprise.

And so dear friends upon this note,
   We'll let the present be,
Adieu to all of you for now.
   We can but wait and see.
The winter months are long and drear,
   The spring is yet to be'.

\*

It is too early to comment objectively on Egyptian policy or politics of the last forty years. It needs the next generation to evaluate the pros and the cons of what has happened to and in Egypt. I will only touch on a few things which I either find amusing or interesting in this period.

I was in Austria in the summer of 1952 with my young family when the King abdicated. We had all felt in the few months before July that something was very wrong, but no one imagined what was happening behind the scenes.

On our return to Egypt in the first few days of September, my father was not at all well. There was talk of land reform, and he could not make out how we were going to survive. As mentioned in the chapter *The Quiet Diplomat*, although we were considered rich by most people, the reality was that we had always been in debt to the banks and our land was mortgaged. It was only in the last three years before the Revolution that we finally paid off our mortgages, by selling off our land in the Fayoum. And although we had always lived well and were never deprived of anything, we always knew that we were not rich and would have to work for our living. No absentee landlordship for us.

Similarly my father and mother had always lived on their yearly income from the farms, which were rented out to farmers in Upper Egypt. The income just covered the style of life that they had been used to. It had been a high standard, but there was no liquid cash or savings behind it. All the family's capital was in land, a house in Alexandria, a share in the house in Assiout and our faith in God.

On my return to Alexandria I was told that I had to go to Cairo and represent the Wissa family. There was no other senior member of the family in the country at the time, and a member of a delegation of landowners was required. The delegation was presenting a petition to General Mohammed Naguib, the head of the revolutionary council, suggesting that the proposed Agrarian Reform bill should be turned into an Income Tax bill, and that death duties should be increased. This would level out over a period of time any large holdings of land. At the same time it would allow landowners to sell their land and invest the proceeds. This petition had been suggested by Aly Maher Pasha, the Prime Minister, and all the arrangements for the meeting had been made by him. I left for Cairo and joined the delegation and proceeded to the headquarters of the Revolutionary Council in Heliopolis. We met the legal adviser to the Revolutionary Council, Salah Hafez, and were then taken in to General Mohammed Naguib. We presented the petition, shook hands and were led out of the room. We were a sorry lot; about ten people representing the large land-owning families. I was the only member of that delegation who did *not own one acre*, as my father was alive at the time, and any land we had was in his name. In those days it was not usual for children to get anything from their parents before their death. Parents kept their hands tightly on the purse strings.

Next day our photos came out in the papers, giving our names and the amount of land we were each supposed to own. I was thirty-one at the time and I was said to own *28,000 acres of agricultural land.* The press only made a small mistake. *They mixed me up with the founder of the dynasty Hanna Wissa who with his brother Wissa Wissa owned 28,000 acres in the year 1900.* We all laughed at the time at this mistake. But *what is sad*, is that the security authorities never seemed to realise the mistake, for I read in the memoirs of the Head of Security at the time, that a conspiracy had been concocted by the Prime Minister together with the large landowners. These were all named, me included, with a view to trying to have the Agrarian Reform bill shelved. *There was never any conspiracy: we were all scared stiff*, and poor me, not owning one acre of land.

An amusing story was told at the time, about an Agrarian Reform employee, who arrived in Assiout by train. He gave his bag to the station porter, and asked him his name to make sure he got back his bag. The porter answered 'Wissa'. (The reader realises that the name Wissa could be a Christian name as well as our family name.) To which the Agrarian Reform employee answered, 'Have you presented your declaration of all the land you own?'

*

The Agrarian Reform law came out towards the end of September 1952. It stipulated in Article 4 that every landowner was allowed to retain two hundred acres. He could also dispose of a further 100 acres to his children on condition that the transaction was registered officially.

Father died suddenly on October 5th, 1952 about ten days after the promulgation of the law. He had no time to register the 100 acres in his children's names. It meant that Fahmy Wissa's wife and children would only have 200 acres instead of 300. Most people would have taken this lying down. But not Esther; she went and bearded the Revolutionary Council in their den. She met General Mohammed Naguib, and Colonel Gamal Salem, who was in charge of land reform, and explained how fate had

268

cheated her children out of the 100 acres. Egyptians are compassionate by nature, and the Council felt that she had made her point. So they added a second paragraph to the law in Article 4 which stated that if a person died before he was able to register the 100 acres for his children in their names, it should be considered as if he had registered them.

Many families in the country benefitted from this addition brought about by mother's courage. She visited Mohammed Naguib quite a lot and discussed politics with him. She found him a very reasonable and charming personality. She also visited and wrote to President Nasser several times and she tried to warn him of the dangers of Communism. To which he answered by letter that Egypt was not heading towards the Communism she feared, but was only adapting a very mild Socialist policy that had been worked out by experts (see copy of letter in the Letters).

In 1977 her eldest son Gamil died suddenly with a heart attack. He was the apple of her eye but I did not see her cry once, although she was devastated and became very pensive and silent.

With the death from cancer of her other son Adly in 1984, Esther became more resigned to old age. Till her last days it was only her physical incapacity that stopped her running all over the place. For the last three years she was bed-ridden and in pain, served by a day and night nurse. But one never heard her complain except for an *aille*, an exclamation of pain now and then. She was always young in spirit, game to do anything or go anywhere. She enjoyed being with people and having her mind stimulated. One never really knew what she would come out with, or what she was thinking of, but she had no malice and never said anything nasty about anyone. In 1987 her beloved sister, Gamila, died suddenly and it was a great shock to everyone. We decided not to tell her, and when she asked after Gamila, we told her she had gone to Cairo to look after her sister Marie who was ailing. Every now and then she'd ask 'How is Marie, isn't Gamila coming back?' We would tell her perhaps in a few days. She was capable of dialling the phone which was next to her bed and speaking to them in Cairo, but she never did. She knew in her heart of hearts that Gamila had died, but she did not want to face reality, preferring to remain under the illusion that her sister had not died and would come back some day.

For the last three years of her life I felt she was just waiting to die without complaining.

I was in England in August 1990 when the phone rang and I was told that Esther had passed away. My sister Nadia and my sister-in-law, Nabila, Adly's widow, were staying in the house and had just left the room when the maid came to tell them that Esther had died. We were never the same again. An era had just ended.

269

H.E. Fahmy Bey Wissa (in dress of Bey 1st Class accorded by the Khedive Abbas Helmi II)

# BOOK TWO – THE QUIET DIPLOMAT

*The Quiet Diplomat (1885–1952)*

The quiet diplomat was my father, Fahmy Bey Wissa, and although I have made much of my mother's role in the country, I have said very little about my father.

The two were very different in character, you might even say opposites, although both of them were public figures in their own way and time, and in the limelight. Many people have told me 'I remember your father', and then they'd recount some incident connected with him that happened, to them or a friend or relation. Mother on the other hand, who lived for forty years after his death, and who had not given up public service except during the last ten years of her life, was rarely mentioned, except within her close circle of friends, and contacts. I have often wondered at this anomaly; could it be that father was associated with a different era, thought of nostalgically; an era that had disappeared and would never return.

Mother who lived until very recently, in an era full of difficulties and upheavals, was forgotten by the public, unless she was mentioned by some newspaper recollecting the years when she was active in politics.

Esther was a good speaker. I should think she never felt better than when she was chairing a meeting, or on the platform making a speech, or at home writing an article. She was willing to give her opinion on any subject, not always very diplomatically, and at times controversially.

Fahmy on the other hand was not a good speaker because he lisped. I don't think he wrote an article in all his life; his opinions were always given quietly and in private. Yet he was able to get his way. He was a perfect diplomat to his fingertips, very meticulous in his dress, in fact a dandy. He was at ease in any company, able to mix easily with what is called the old aristocracy, 'The Turco-Egyptians' the powerful, the rulers, whom he would entertain at the house at times. If they brought their wives, mother would attend, otherwise they were stag parties. When the ladies attended, father was a great favourite with them. He was what the French call *sympathique*. But I think in his heart of hearts he preferred the lesser folk, the real Egyptian, whom he liked and understood.

Although a Copt, many of his friends, or at least the people he frequented were mostly Moslems. He was not at all fanatical, and you could not call him religious; he could not stand the humbug of priests. All those who knew him liked him, even loved him.

H.E. Fahmy Bey Wissa – Senator (1924–1952) in Senator's dress

During the month of Ramadan, the holy month of fasting for the Moslems, he gave several *Iftars* (breaking of the fast), after sunset, to which he invited different categories of people, his footballers, young police officers, young army officers, the Municipality, the Governorate, his constituents, and people with whom he came in contact. These were purely men's occasions. They were entertained in the house or in the garden depending on the season and weather. On the day of an Iftar, father used to fast in respect for his Moslem brothers and broke the fast with them. Similarly on the Coptic Good Friday he invited his Moslem friends to participate in the breaking of the Christian fast which terminated when the Church came out at 6 p.m. His Moslem friends also fasted on these occasions.

He encouraged the young and talented in their careers. For example he was able to obtain an audition for a young singer to broadcast on the Alexandria programme, with the result that she became a popular and well-known singer. (She later put herself up for election as a Deputy, was elected and became a very useful member of the Legislative Assembly, and married a Cabinet Minister.)

Although Esther was father's first cousin once removed, and came from the same background, yet they had a very different upbringing and outlook. Maybe it was this difference that made theirs such a successful marriage.

Mother had been brought up by English governesses, and had graduated from the American College at Assiout she had a tendency to argue and discuss everything with her teachers and her lawyer father, whereas Fahmy had been brought up by his doting mother and sisters, before spending five years at the American College in Beyrouth, and subsequently four years at Hertford College, Oxford. He had left home as a boy of thirteen and returned as a young man of twenty-two. He had spent over nine years abroad, free from parental authority, yet tradition and custom were uppermost in his upbringing. He had great respect for, and awe of his father but I don't think there could have been much dialogue between them. The following incident demonstrates the relationship between father and son, as recounted by Fahmy:

> Although Hanna Wissa was a heavy smoker, smoking over a hundred cigarettes a day, his sons out of respect and tradition would never smoke in front of him. One day, after his return from Oxford, Fahmy was smoking his pipe in the hall, when he saw his father coming down the stairs. He quickly put the lit pipe into his pocket, not wanting his father to see him smoking. Hanna stood there purposely talking to him, until Fahmy's pocket caught fire.

Hanna died in 1907 and father found himself heir to a big fortune which consisted mostly of agricultural land, so his natural career should have been as a gentleman farmer, instead of which he opened a bank with his brother Nassif. All the family hangers-on became the staff although they had never had any banking experience. I don't know what induced the brothers to open a bank. Maybe they got the idea because Bushra Pasha Hanna, another rich landowner, owned a bank, with the result that most of Bushra's dud clients became the best clients of the Wissa Bank. This resulted in them being forced to shut down. Father had to mortgage his land to pay off his share of the debts; that was in 1915 after a moratorium had been declared because of the war.

An amusing incident happened in 1937. My elder brother Gamil liked having a flutter at the tables. A casino had just opened at Sidi Bishr in Alexandria called *La Maisonette*, and Gamil who had come out for the summer holidays from University in England, was taken there by some friends. He lost more than he could afford, and signed a promissory note for the rest. The next day the Casino sent a collector to father's office who agreed to pay the debt. But when he was scolding Gamil he asked him in Arabic, 'What made you do such a thing?' Gamil who had a sense of humour, and knew how to get around father answered – also in Arabic – 'You opened a bank when you were twenty-two and lost, and I did the same thing, I opened a bank and lost'. The repartee amused father, and Gamil got off, scot-free. I never had the same relationship with my father. He disapproved of all my escapades, from which he had to retrieve me. I never was able to have that same carefree relationship that Gamil had, except maybe in the last few years of my father's life, after I had married Philae, his cousin Zaki Bey Wissa's daughter, who gave him two grand-daughters. He was getting older, and I was more sure of myself, and we were able to talk and joke more, which brought us nearer together.

I don't know when father became a Freemason. He had belonged to a British Lodge when he was a student in England, and although I have no knowledge of freemasonry, I know he was a '33' and head of an Egyptian Lodge. During the years between his return from Oxford and his marriage in 1913 he spent much of his time in Cairo, and freemasonry took up some of it. He was apparently not actively interested in politics although a member of the Nationalist Party. He was well thought of in Palace circles and was received and liked by the Khedive Abbas Helmi (another Free-mason), who in fact bestowed the title of Bey 1st Class on him and his brothers. It was said that father was expert at the Turkish bow, all through his life, in spite of his gain in weight. This entailed bowing and retreating at the same time when leaving an audience with the monarch.

It is not known how much effort father put into his studies at University, but from the pictures in his album of Oxford, he seemed to be having a jolly good time. He loved and appreciated sport of all kinds. He shot well and was a good rider; and since he was small of build was also useful as a coxswain. He told us of the first time he was being tried out as a cox. He got so excited when his boat pulled ahead that he lost control, and of

# MOHAMMED ALY DYNASTY

King Fouad I. First King of Egypt, brother of Sultan Hussain, Khedive Tewfic, son of Khedive Ismail, uncle of Khedive Abbas Hilml II. 1917-1936

King Farouk I. Son of King Fouad I, deposed by the Revolution of 1952. 1936-1952

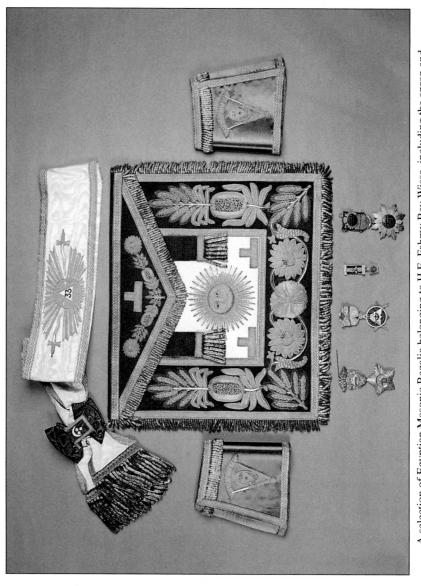

A selection of Egyptian Masonic Regalia belonging to H.E. Fahmy Bey Wissa, including the apron and gauntlets of the Grand Master

Map showing international borders, railways available, and auto routes which were used during the mission

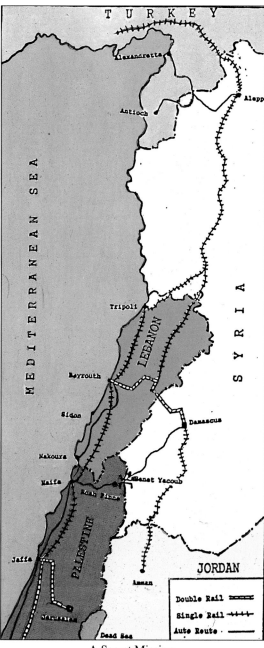

A Secret Mission

THE SPOUTING ROCK

Probably an artificial squared vent made at the time of the Ptolemys

Visitors throwing their coins in the Spouting Rock, making a wish, and watching little boys diving in for a bet

Little boys climbing in and out of the Spouting Rock today for money

Fahmy Wissa, Master of a Masonic Lodge

H.E. Fahmy Bey Wissa (wearing the sash marked '33' of the Freemasons)

course they lost; he was then dropped by his mates in the river.

Khedive Abbas Helmi sent him a Khedivial band and carriage to Assiout, for his wedding, as can be seen in the pictures.

During the war years political activity in Egypt was restricted, and when it resumed after the armistice, most people gravitated towards and supported the Wafdist cause under Zaghloul. Mother at the time was vociferous for Egyptian independence, and defended Saad's ideas, whereas father supported the cause as best he could, but was not particularly active. He was still liked and respected in the new Palace circles.

It was after the 1919 revolution that the family made their headquarters in Cairo though travelling at times to Assiout. By that time they had three children; two boys and a girl. Mother was very proud of her young family. The eldest, Gamil, was more poised, the second, Adly, was a very boisterous boy, and Doussa was a precocious little girl. Mother was very busy with politics, and although she had a British nanny for the children, she took time off to supervise them. On March 22nd, 1921 I was born on the houseboat (*Dahabieh*) called *Queen*. Mother had had a dream that she had given birth to a baby boy, who got up and threw down an older child. She did not take much notice of that dream then, but when I was forty days old and it was the nanny's afternoon off Esther was feeding me when she heard a tremendous commotion and shouts from the road outside. The servants came in screaming. The children had been dressed by the nursemaid to go to the Sporting Club and the car was waiting on the other side of the road. Adly was racing Gamil to get into the seat first by the chauffeur. A lady learning how to drive knocked Adly down and he was killed on the spot. Mother later interpreted her dream as meaning that I had usurped the place of my elder brother, just as Jacob had usurped the place of Esau. This incident devastated mother. It changed the whole course of Fahmy's and her lives. She could not bear to go back to Assiout and live in father's house.

She had always loved ancient Egyptian history, and as a young girl she used to write poems and articles under the name 'Isis, daughter of the Nile'. When she got married she had the entrance halls painted with ancient Egyptian scenes. She now believed that these paintings were unlucky. She abandoned everything as it was, took nothing out of that house and whenever they went back to Assiout on a holiday, or for work, they stayed with her mother, Balsam. She never spent a night in father's house again. The family now made their headquarters in Alexandria. Father and mother went down and bought an acre of land on a hill, one of the highest spots in Alexandria, just after the Casino San Stefano.

They built the house we all lived in, where much has happened, where the walls and rooms could tell many secrets. Before Alexandria was built up with high-rising buildings, from the windows one could see the lights in the

Prince Farouk standing, Ismail Sidki Pasha, Prime Minister, standing to his right, next to him at the back is Said Zuficar Pasha, the Grand Chamberlain, September 1933

H.E. Fahmy Bey Wissa, President of the Union Recreation, presenting the players of both teams to Prince Farouk, September 1933

harbour eight miles away. At that time the sea-front corniche had not been built, and one had only to go down a few steps from the road passing our front gate to be on the beach.

Mother died in her bed on August 28th, 1990, in the house that she and father had supervised in building.

In 1923 the Wafd executive were choosing candidates to represent it in all constituencies in Egypt for election to the Senate. Mother asked Saad Zaghloul to propose her brother Louis Fanous as a candidate for the Senate in one of the Assiout constituencies, and although Saad put the matter up to the Committee three times, the local committee rejected it saying that they could not cooperate with Louis. He was too dogmatic. The Secretary of the Wafd Executive wrote a letter to mother stating how much they and Saad regretted not being able to accord the one favour she had ever asked for (see the letter from the Committee in the appendix)

The Wafd won the elections and when the nominations of the Government came out, father was nominated Senator to the Laban district in Alexandria. He kept this seat until his death in 1952. He became a Senator in the first Parliament in 1924 by nomination, and he kept his seat by election throughout the next twenty-eight years, although he was opposed at times by some very powerful opponents.

The Laban district in Alexandria includes the docks and the denser and poorer quarters of the city. It was in that district that he discovered a small football club, which he turned into the most popular football club in Alexandria, 'The Union Recreation'. They bought land and over the years improved the standard of the grounds. He was the Union Recreation's first President, and remained as such until his death in 1952. He was able to have the Palace accept that the heir apparent should become its patron; and every year the young Prince Farouk used to come to the club and inaugurate the football season. When he became King he was still interested in the Club, and when he did not attend in person he used to send a representative to attend the yearly opening.

In Alexandria there were three main Egyptian football clubs at the time, The Union Recreation presided over by father; the Olympic, whose President was Hussein Sabry Pasha, Queen Nazli's brother, and Governor of Alexandria; and the Tram Football Club presided over by Hussein Bey Said, the Managing Director of the Ramleh Electric Railway.

Football in Egypt was a completely amateur affair, and footballers signed up for two seasons. All the clubs competed for the better players at the time of signing up. The only incentive for the players was a job, where they had nothing better to do than to play football. For the Governor it was easy to keep his players and entice others; he could always offer them a job as a policeman or as a clerk in the governorate. The same thing was easy for the Director of the Ramleh Electric Railway. He had plenty of jobs as con-

H.M. King Farouk watching the inauguration of the 1936 football season at the Union Recreation Club, Alexandria. Standing to his right is Ahmad Pasha Hassanein, and to his left Fahmy Bey Wissa. In the far right, crossing his hands, is Sir Amin Osman Pasha, Cabinet Minister, next to him on the left is Abdel Fatah Pasha el Tawil, Cabinet Minister.

H.M. King Farouk inaugurating 1937 football season.
H.M. King Farouk presenting the cup to a player, standing next to the King, Prince Abbas Halim, and next to the player Fahmy Bey Wissa.

H.H. Prince Omar Pasha Toussun (known as the uncrowned king of Alexandria) and H.E. Fahmy Bey Wissa, founders of the Alexandria Stadium

The Alexandria Stadium
for £3000!

Extracts from the Ahram Sport
Magazine, in honour of the
African Games 1991

استاد الاسكندرية .. بثلاثة آلاف جنيه!

FAHMY BEY WISSA
A founder member

ABDEL KADER MOURSI
Stadium manager, 1991

THE INAUGURATION OF THE ALEXANDRIA STADIUM IN
1929

The Pashas watching the football match between a selection of players from
Cairo teams and those of Alexandria.

The idea of building a stadium goes back to 1924 thanks to
Mr Bolonachi, a Greco-Egyptian, founder of the Olympic Committee of
Egypt. He suggested to H. M. King Fouad to host the first African Games in
Alexandria. King Fouad agreed and donated £3000 towards the project.
This was followed by a campaign for contributions led by H. H. Prince Omar
Toussun, Fahmy Bey Wissa, Abdel Fatah Bey El Tawil, Aly Ghazalat and
Shaheen Effendi, the Palace writer.

The stadium was built and completed in four years, by the
Municipality of Alexandria. Its inauguration in 1929 was celebrated by a
football match between a selection of Cairo players, captained by Mukhtar El
Titch, and those of Alexandria, captained by El Sayed Hooda. The result was
a win for Alexandria, 0 - 1, the winning goal being scored by the Union
Recreation star Mahmoud Houda.

However, the African Games were postponed due to differences
among the powers and the stadium was used until 1951 for local events and
for inter club football matches. The first international event held at the
Alexandria Stadium was that of the 1st Mediterranean Championships of
1991.

A reception at one of the tenants on our farms

Crossing on a barge across the Ibrahamieh Canal

Farmers cheering and dancing. You can see Captain Stanley Cayzer who had just married Doussa standing behind the Parliamentary Secretary.

EDWARD WISSA'S FOOTBALL CLUB, ASSIOUT UPPER EGYPT CLUB (*NADI EL SAID*).

Fahmy Bey Wissa, centre, on his right, Aziz Pasha Abaza, the Governor, then the Commandant of Police on his left. Edward G. Wissa, President of the Club and on the far left Gamil Wissa, watching a match between the local club and players from the Union Recreation in Alexandria.

Fahmy Bey Wissa being received by the Governor of Assiout, Aziz Pasha Abaza. Next to him Esther and next to her Fahmy Bey, the Commandant of Police. Behind Fahmy Bey, Adly Chaker Tadros, his Parliamentary Secretary.

ductors or ticket collectors in the tram company, but it was difficult for father; he had to go round to the different company directors asking them for jobs for his boys.

The Alexandrian public loved the Union Recreation. They considered it the peoples' club, whereas the other clubs were those belonging to the authorities.

One way father tried to hold on to his players when their contracts were up for renewal, was to cart them off to his farm in Assiout for the summer. There they would have plenty of food and rest and recreation and be far away from any influence of those who would try to entice them away. He'd bring them back having signed a new contract to train before the new football season started.

He was sponsor or co-sponsor for the swimming championships and Olympics in Alexandria. In fact he was very keen on all activities to do with sport. He was one of the main founders of the Alexandria Stadium.

Another member of the family who was interested in football, was George Pasha Wissa's eldest son Edward who founded a club known as the Upper Egyptian Club (*Nadi el Said*) which was active until the Revolution. Father used to send down trainers from the Union Recreation in Alexandria to coach the upcoming footballers. (See photo taken in 1943 when father became a Cabinet Minister and the Assioutites wanted to make a fuss of him, and asked him to come down to Assiout, his birthplace. You can see in this photo in the centre, father, on his right, Aziz Pasha Abaza, the Governor of Assiout, then the Commandant of Police, and on his left Edward Wissa the President of the club, and my brother Gamil, the last person on his left.)

This match was between the players of father's club in Alexandria, the Union Recreation, and the Assiout Club founded by Edward (see a couple of further photos taken at the time; the captions will be self-explanatory).

We now arrive at an incident, based on hearsay and circumstantial evidence which I feel is important. I will call this a Secret Mission.


*A Secret Mission*

In July 1935 father told us that he was leaving with Hussein Pasha Sabry, Queen Nazli's brother, and Governor of Alexandria, and a third person on a pilgrimage to Jerusalem. Christians, Moslems and Jews consider Jerusalem as sacred. Although we all knew that father hated travelling, and never left when mother went abroad to feminist and other conferences, we thought nothing of it at the time. He left for Palestine for ten days and when he came back he told us of the wonderful time he spent.

Years later after father had died, my brother Gamil asked me, 'Do you remember that voyage, when father told us he was going to Jerusalem?' I

H.H. Fahmy Bey Wissa in Grand Master's Regalia of an Egyptian Masonic Lodge

answered, 'I do, I was fourteen at the time.'

He said, 'Well, he did not go to Jerusalem, he went to meet the Khedive Abbas Helmi on the borders between Turkey and Syria. This was at the express wish of King Fouad, who was ailing of cancer at the time, in order to arrange with the ex-Khedive, not to contest the accession of Prince Farouk to the throne, in case of his death, before Farouk became of age.' Both Hussein Pasha Sabry and the third person were high-ranking Free-masons, as was the ex-Khedive, Abbas Helmi.

I thought nothing of it at the time. But going through my father's belongings looking for data for this book, I came across an old passport, used for one journey, amongst his Masonic paraphernalia.

I am including photocopies of the different pages of this passport with visas and stampings, denoting that the voyage was certainly not a pilgrimage to Jerusalem, but was something much more important. The following is surmise but is probable, based on fact and circumstantial evidence. I will first quote from a book called *Sultans in Splendour* by Philip Mansel. On page 166 he states that King Fouad strengthened his control over his own dynasty by the following:

'At first Abbas Helmi, "the Khedive over the Water", was as much a problem to him as "the King over the water" had been to the Hanoverians in Great Britain. In 1924 the Khedive is described as "a source of anxiety amounting to obsession". No Egyptian politician who met Abbas Helmi in Europe could expect to hold office under King Fouad in Egypt. The rhyme "Allah Hai, Abbas gai" (As God is alive, so will Abbas come back), was repeated everywhere. However ruined by the crash 1929, the ex-Khedive had to make terms. By a treaty in French and Arabic signed in 1931 he affirmed his loyalty to King Fouad, and renounced his claims for £E30,000 a year.'[18]

As this seemed a temporary settlement, Fouad wanted a permanent settlement of the matter.

I will now return to my story based on hearsay, and the evidence of the visas in my father's passport.

1) On July 27th, 1935 father asked for a passport. It was issued on the same day in Alexandria under the number 18042. It was valid for Syria, Palestine, England, France, Italy, Switzerland, Austria, etc.
2) On the same day, he asked for and obtained a traveller's visa to Palestine. This was issued on July 27th 1935 by the British Consul-General in Alexandria for one single journey to Palestine.
3) On July 29th, 1935 he obtained a visa for one single journey to Syria and Lebanon from the Consul-General of France in Alexandria.

---

[18]To the above Philip Mansell: Pro. Fo. 371/10022/9549 Clerk. Kerr to Macdonald, AH 122/11, treaty of 12 May 1931

4) On July 31st, he left Alexandria by boat to Palestine.
5) On August 1st, 1935 he arrived in Haifa.
6) The next markings in the passport are at a crossing to the north of Lake Tiberias, exit from Palestine at Rosh Pinna and entry into Syria at Benet Yacoub, a mountain pass between Palestine and Syria. These were dated August 4th, 1935. The only way to get to these points was by car on the single route to Damascus.

(The accompanying map shows the routes and railways available at the time.)

For four days there are no markings on the passport.

7) The next marking in the passport was Passport Control at Nakoura, the French frontier point between Lebanon and Palestine. You could only arrive there on the coast road by car from Beyrouth.
8) He was given an *emergency* visa for one single entry into Palestine by the Government of Palestine stamped at Ras el Naqura dated August 8th, 1935.
9) Another marking stated, 'Government of Palestine Entry in direct transit only valid until August 11th 1935 issued on August 8th, 1935.'
10) Another stamp dated August 8th, 1935 was Embarkation from the Port of Haifa.
11) The next stamp was Arrival in Alexandria on August 9th, 1935.

From the above there is no doubt that this was no ordinary trip or pilgrimage. They went nowhere near Jerusalem, in fact they travelled in the opposite direction, like a cloak and dagger story, covering their tracks all the way. Since they crossed into Syria at Benet-Yacoub, the first stop could only have been Damascus. If that had been their publicly declared destination, it would have been easier and quieter to sail to Beyrouth and take a train to Damascus. If, as I heard, a meeting took place somewhere in the north of Syria or near the Turkish border, it could only have been around Aleppo, which was a quick journey by train from Damascus. They probably travelled back from Aleppo to Beyrouth by train, then from Beyrouth to Haifa on the coastal road by car, entering Palestine at the border post at Nakoura, as marked on the passport.

To the world they had left for Haifa, gone to Jerusalem, and come back to Egypt from Haifa. No one would be any the wiser about their secret mission unless you examined their passports.

King Fouad died in April 1936, and King Farouk acceded to the throne without any opposition from any of the Royal Princes.

MISSION ACCOMPLISHED.

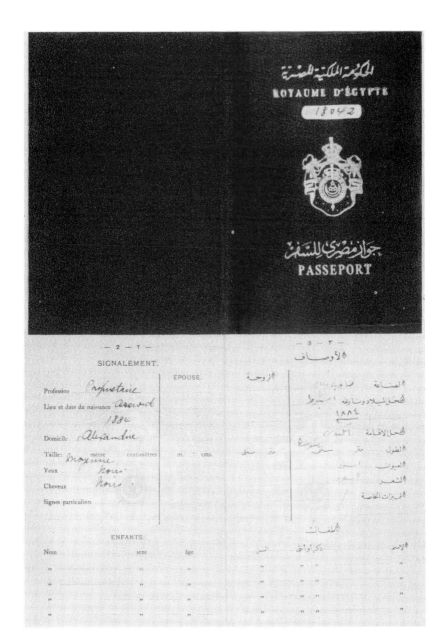

289

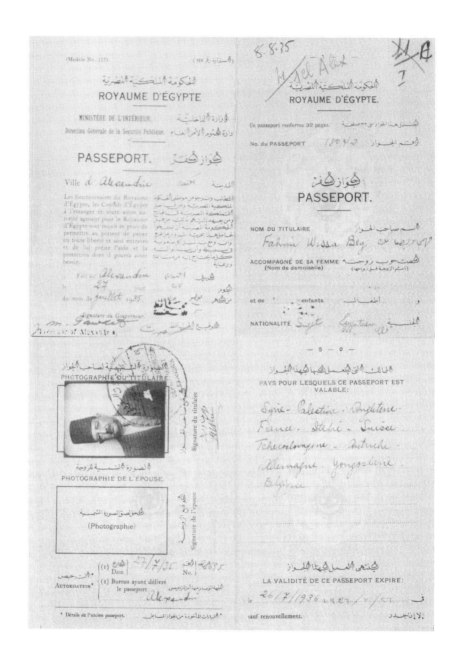

فترة التسجيل

يختص قنصل كل قنصلية مصرية بقيد أسماء المصريين
المقيمين في دائرة اختصاصه ويكون القيد في
سجل علمًا بقدم م من المستندات التي تثبت حسب يتم المصرية
أو القيد معروض على كل مصري مقيم مدة ستة شهور
أواكثر في دائرة القنصلية

أن يكون القنصلية إذا طلب في ميعاد ستة شهور ميتاريخ
حضور الطالب لدائرة القنصلية أما إذا طلب بعد هذا الميعاد
تحصر عنه الرسوم المقررة في التعريفة القنصلية
(المادة ١٥ من المرسوم قانون الصادر في ٥/٨/١٩٢٥ الخاص بالنظام القنصلي)

## REGISTRE D'INSCRIPTION.

Les consuls tiennent un registre dans lequel sont inscrits
les noms des Égyptiens résidant dans leur circonscription.
L'enregistrement est fait sur la production de documents
prouvant la nationalité égyptienne.

L'enregistrement est obligatoire pour les Égyptiens résidant
depuis six mois ou plus dans la circonscription consulaire. Il est
effectué gratuitement s'il est demandé dans les six mois à
compter du jour de l'arrivée dans la circonscription consulaire.

Passé ce délai, les droits prévus par les règlements consu-
laires seront exigés.

(Article 15 du Décret-loi du 5/8/1925 relatif à l'Organisation Consulaire).

ENREGISTREMENT. — القيد

VISAS — إشارات الاعتماد

VISAS — إشارات الاعتماد

### TRAVELLER

No. 1792

Seen good for PALESTINE

visa valid for one single journey only

British Consulate General,

Alexandria 2 7 JUL 1938

J. M. Walsh

H.M. VICE CONSUL

Syrie

1-11-85 un
seul — Syrie et au Liban

495
99.7.95
494
10
PERÇU
P 13½

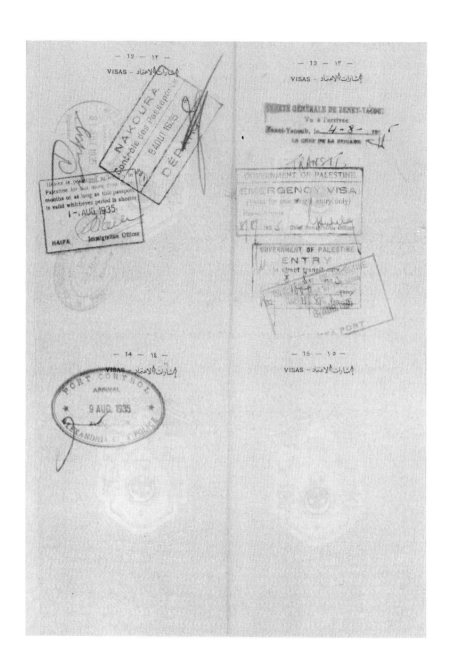

292

After Saad Zaghloul's death in 1927 the power struggle in Egypt was between three main forces:

1) The Palace, backed by the minority parties, which included all the politicians and intellectuals who had split away from Saad and the Wafd.
2) The Wafd, led by Nahas, which included the students in the schools and university, the city mobs, the fellaheen in the country, and the majority of Egyptian landlords, in short the main cross-section of the country.
3) The British, with their senior government officials and their occupying army.

For most of the time the struggle was a combination of three sides of a triangle, the Palace and the British trying to keep the third in place. By 1934 the country was in a turmoil, the University and the people were clamouring for a return to parliamentary rule under the 1923 Constitution abolished by King Fouad; at the same time they were demanding a solution to the Anglo-Egyptian problem.

The rest of the world was in a state of unrest. The rise of dictatorships in Germany and Italy was causing concern, together with the Abyssinian crisis, and the weakness of the League of Nations. These all raised the spectre of war.

In Egypt the ailing King who desired in the event of his death to see a peaceful transfer of the throne to his son, the heir apparent, precluded the use of strong arm tactics. Under all these combined circumstances it was essential for Britain to reappraise the situation.

They arrived at the conclusion that some agreement acceptable to both parties had to be worked out. The result was that King Fouad appointed a new Prime Minister, Tewfik Nessim Pasha who promised to restore the 1923 Constitution after the election of a new parliament. At the same time, King Fouad persuaded the politicians to form a National Front, which included Nahas Pasha, Sidki Pasha and Mohammed Mahmoud Pasha. The idea was to negotiate a treaty of friendship with Britain on the lines of the rejected draft treaty of 1930, acceptable to all the country.

The elections were held in 1936, and, as foreseen, the Wafd won the election. Nahas Pasha became Prime Minister. He headed a delegation of seven Wafdists and six other politicians from the different parties, and successfully negotiated a 'Treaty of Friendship' known as the Anglo-Egyptian Treaty of 1936. The British had come to realise the depth of feeling in the country. Similarly the Wafd had to be reconciled to the idea of patching up old wounds.

The time was ripe for an understanding as clouds of war lingered on the horizon. Reason had to prevail, Egypt needed the help of England as much as England needed the help of Egypt. Sir Miles Lampson, the new ambassador to Egypt, taking the advice of dedicated Britons such as Mr. R.W.G. Reed, headmaster of Victoria College, contacted clear-sighted pragmatic Egyptians such as Amin Osman, later Sir Amin Osman Pasha, and Mohamed Farghaly Pasha, a financier and cotton exporter. Both were old Victorians, capable of contacting the Wafdist leaders to persuade them that Britain was sincere in her desire to come to a fruitful and fair solution, in the interest of both parties. I don't think father or mother had anything to do with the actual negotiations, or details, but a couple of dinner parties were given at our house in Alexandria, to which both the Egyptians and British were invited.

Father at the time, though a member of the party as a Wafdist Senator was not a member of Wafd Executive Committee. It was not until Neguib Iskandar and Nokrashi Pasha split with the Wafd and formed the Saadist party, that father was elected to the Executive Committee of the party in September 1937. For the next few years father was preoccupied with sports and his constituency, the Laban district. But in 1943 after Makram Ebeid split with Nahas and left the Wafd, he was appointed a member of the Cabinet as Minister of Civil Defence. Makram had left, publishing what was called 'The Black Book' enumerating the dark deeds of the Wafdist party. It consisted mostly of favours accorded to friends and to the relations of Nahas's young wife, the most damning of which was that Mme Nahas had brought a fur coat into the country without paying customs dues. These are paltry deeds if one compares them with what is happening in the world today. It had always been the policy of the Wafd to promote their supporters among the Government officials when they came to power in recompense for the years they were forgotten and got no promotion, when the party was in opposition. In fact these forgotten civil servants were called *el Manseyin* or 'the Forgotten Ones'.

When he was appointed Minister he made a statement to the the press: 'I own so many acres, I am telling you this as I do not want anyone to say that I became rich, whilst in the Ministry.' Father who was both a friend of Makram and Nahas, tried to get the old friends and comrades to patch up their differences, but Makram was adamant and left the Wafd. He later formed his own party, the 'Kotla'.

Titles in Egypt were awarded by the King on the advice of the government in power, or for services rendered to the Palace. Such titles were practically automatic when a civil servant, or member of the forces, attained a certain grade. Thus the title of Pasha was awarded to a General, or a Cabinet Minister. These titles were also given to civilians in the private sector, who contributed largely to public works; such as building a hospital, or supplying clean water to a village. In all cases these were the prerogative of the monarch. However the King, according to the Constitution, could not bestow a title on a member of Parliament, whether a deputy or senator

A reception given by Mr R.W.G. Reed, Headmaster of Victoria College, who was the catalyst between the British and Egyptians, resulting in the Anglo-Egyptian Treaty of Friendship in 1936.

Mr Reed can be seen between Mr and Mrs Amin Osman (later Sir Amin and Lady Osman Pasha); Mrs Esther Fahmy Bey Wissa to the left and Mohammed Pasha Farghaly to the extreme right.

King Farouk I
Son of King Fouad I, deposed by the Revolution of 1952

while he held office, except in the case of his being chosen as a Minister. Father had received his title of Bey from the Khedive Abbas Helmi, before he became a senator. And as he was a senator from 1924 to 1952, he was not able to receive the title of Pasha except during the period he was a Cabinet Minister in 1943, but at that time the King was not in the mood to award any titles to any of Nahas's Ministers, the Wafd Government under Nahas having been imposed on him by the British Ambassador at gunpoint. He was however called Pasha by everyone, as being his right. Father was further prevented from receiving the title of Pasha, on resuming his political life as senator after Nahas's resignation in 1944. Similarly the title of Bey was bestowed by the monarch, automatically on the lesser grades in government service, or to those who contributed smaller amounts to public works.

It is amusing to note that practically everyone among the gentry was called 'Bey' within his circle of friends and acquaintances, or by an inferior addressing him as a sign of respect. This Beyship was known derisively as *Bey Ommo*, meaning 'His mother's Bey' – those who were given the title by their mothers, when speaking of their sons or husbands to a servant or inferior.

Similarly a son of a Pasha was always referred to as Bey by everyone, although such titles could not be used officially unless they had been awarded by the monarch.

In 1945 father's seat in the Senate came up for re-election, and although the Wafd boycotted the elections, fearing that the elections would be cooked, father put himself up for re-election; he was opposed by two very influential members of the Alexandria community. In fact on the day of the election, the walls were plastered with posters, put up in the middle of the night stating that father had withdrawn his candidature. It was a long and tiring day, but when the votes were counted at night, father had won a clear majority on the first ballot. This election campaign taxed father's health a lot, and although the whole family helped, he had been going to rallies, and meetings, calling at people's houses, walking around his constituency for two months. With the result that a few months after he was elected he had a heart attack. The Australian heart specialist Doctor Fisher, who had come out to Egypt during the war as an army doctor, but who stayed on for some time after the war as a Professor at the Alexandria University, advised father to rest in bed, otherwise he would not give him six months to live.

One of father's phobias was a bed. He had three bedrooms at home and used to roam from one room to the other, or about the house. He could doze off easily in a chair, or in the car, with the radio blazing away or people chattering around him, but the moment everyone went to bed and the house became silent, he was wide awake. He had been like that during

CROWN PRINCE ASFA WASON OF ETHIOPIA ON AN OFFICIAL VISIT
TO EGYPT

Fahmy Bey Wissa delegated officially to accompany the Prince during his stay,
Ahmed Hussanein Pasha, the head of the King's Royal Cabinet walking behind
the Prince. Senator Louis Fanous can be seen in the background.

Delegation accompanying Crown Prince Asfa Wason of Ethiopia.

all the years I knew him. I could not understand how anyone was able to sleep in a chair, as I used to love my bed and drop off to sleep as soon as my head was on the pillow.

Father received the shock of his life when he heard that he had to stay in bed; he preferred to die first. His reaction was that he would not go to bed at all. The following was his routine for the next five years:

He hired two new chauffeurs and bought himself a Chevrolet station wagon, in which he was persuaded to have a couch installed. During the day he'd come home to lunch, doze for a while in the chair till about five, spend a couple of hours at the Football Club, or at his café where a special corner was reserved for him and his cronies, and have his *Shisha* – hubble-bubble. He would then probably go to the Mohammed Aly Club or Syrian Club for a drink or to dinner somewhere. Then he'd come home, get into a nightgown, get into the station wagon and drive around. He had bought a chalet outside Alexandria at Agami and would go there with anyone who would go with him. He would drive around with friends until all hours of the morning then would call round for mother or any of the family who needed a lift, finally coming home at 6 a.m. He'd get into bed, rest a bit, have his massage, bath, and shave, and then breakfast. He would then get into the car and go to his office till lunch time.

Although he was a Christian he liked listening to the Koran, if it was chanted by a good reader. We now had a new member on our large staff; he hired himself a reader called Sheikh Madian who lived, until his death a few years ago, in our basement on the ground floor. He started reading the Koran for father on his long night journeys, and if father dozed off, the chauffeur would park in the street and Sheikh Madian would stop his chanting. As soon as he woke up the car would move again, and the chanting would resume if requested. Sheikh Madian stayed on as caretaker after father died. Sheikh Madian married the resident washerwoman and chanted at weddings or funerals, to make a little extra money.

In 1947 I went to my father and told him I wanted to marry Philae Wissa, my mother's cousin, and I wanted him to go and ask for her hand from her father Zaki Bey Wissa, his first cousin. Father refused to go. He told me, 'I don't want to be refused; she'll never marry you; her father will never accept.'

However I went and asked Uncle Zaki myself and he answered 'Certainly old boy, if Philae accepts; come and have a drink'. Philae and I had been good friends since childhood, and had both confided in each other about our heart pangs throughout the years. I had asked her to marry me, but she had not quite decided. She was not quite sure that I was really in love with her. When she came into the room while I was having a drink, her father smiled, 'Hanna wants to marry you.' She answered, 'But I haven't made up my mind.' I answered, 'Of course you have.' I then rang

H.H. Prince Omar Toussun, H.E. Mustapha Nahas Pasha, Prime Minister, and H.E. Fahmy Bey Wissa, Minister of Civil Defence. Standing behind Fahmy Bey is Mr Adly Shaker Tadros, his Private and Parliamentary Secretary, 1943

Reception given for Mustapha Nahas Pasha, standing next to him, Fahmy Bey Wissa. Fouad Pasha Serag-el-Din in white behind Nahas Pasha, next to him, Sir Amin Pasha Osman

H.E. Neguib Pasha El Hilali, several times Prime Minister, and Prime Minister at the time of the 1952 Revolution, chatting to H.E. Fahmy Bey Wissa. In the background to the right behind Fahmy Bey is Sir Amin Osman Pasha (old Victorian), and a link between the British and the Wafd in the negotiations of the Anglo Egyptian Treaty of 1936. Sir Amin Osman Pasha was assassinated in 1946, for which the late President Anwar Sadat was accused and acquitted.

H.E. Fahmy Bey Wissa and officers returning from the battle of Falugga in Palestine, at an *Iftar* given for them in the month of Ramadan, at his house in Alexandria.

up mother and father and announced our engagement. They both came to congratulate us, and to ask officially for her hand. I will elaborate later on our wedding, which was a grand affair, and to which both Makram Ebeid and Nahas Pasha attended the reception as can be seen from the photos. There were also other politicians from different parties.

In 1948 father entertained some of the officers who fought at the Battle of Faluga to an *Iftar*, see photos.

In 1949 King Farouk appointed a caretaker government under Hussein Sirry Pasha, to prepare for new elections; he had new palace advisers, who were friendlier to the Wafd. After the Palestine debâcle, and rumours of defective arms, it was thought opportune to have free elections, even if the Wafd should win. It would at least silence many of the tongues in the opposition.

The elections took place in 1950. My brother Gamil put himself up for election as deputy for the Laban district backed by the Wafd. Gamil won his seat in Parliament, which he kept until the parliamentary system was abolished by the 1952 Revolution, in spite of being opposed by a very strong competitor. For two years both seats for the Laban district were held by father and son, as Senator and Deputy

In July 1952 the revolution broke out, and within three days the King had left, parties were told to cleanse themselves, and talk of limiting land-ownership was in the air. Father's whole world was crumbling around him. A week after the promulgation of the 1952 Agrarian Reform law, on October 5th, 1952, whilst he was lunching with the family and some friends at his chalet in Agami, his head just dropped on his shoulder and he died. He lived a *Grand Seigneur* and died in the nick of time.

# BOOK THREE – THE HOUSE ON THE HILL

*Alexandria and the House on the Hill*

The House on the Hill is our house. It reminds one of Alexandria in its heyday, with its sea breezes, its damp July and August, its calm and peaceful October and November, and its predictable storms which follow year in year out on approximately the same date.

Our house was built between the years 1922 and 1924, when my parents decided to live in Alexandria. It was built on a hill on one of its highest spots. At night and until about thirty years ago one could see the lighthouse blink every two seconds from the harbour about ten kilometres away.

It was Esther's house of her dreams; part of it looked from the outside like a castle and it even had a tower. Although she was down to earth and practical in many ways, she was romantic at heart.

The plans were drawn up and executed by Italian architects using Egyptian workmen, with mother supervising. Only the best materials were used for the decorative mouldings on the ceilings which were five and half metres high. The house was cool for most of the year, but could be cold and draughty for a couple of months each winter. We had to keep warm by roasting chestnuts in the grate of the fireplace.

The layout of the buildings and garden were the joint effort of father and mother. It was their work of love. It was an elastic house and accommodated everyone. It was enlarged several times during her lifetime and she used to have a recurring dream that she was continually finding new rooms that she did not know of.

In the foundations of the house she buried a steel box enclosing Psalm 23 of David which starts 'The Lord is my shepherd, I shall not want', together with a few gold pounds and a few grains of wheat. If truth be told it was a blessed house, withstanding the vicissitudes of time. Its gates were never closed; no one was ever turned away during Esther's lifetime if they needed a meal. And in spite of the gates and the back door being always open we never had a burglary. If anything was ever missing from the house, it was an inside affair. Father once said, 'When I built this house, every room had two keys; today, you can't even find the door knobs'. The front door was only closed during the winter months to keep out the wind and rain.

It was our family home where we were all brought up. When we grew older and lived part of the time away from Alexandria, we all kept our

# THE HOUSE ON THE HILL

When it was young

When it grew old

rooms, and returned home when we were in Alexandria. 'The Fahmy Wissa Bastion' was the main residence of my mother for sixty-eight years, and in which she died at the age of ninety-six on August 28th, 1990.

The main building was built in the middle of a three-quarter acre garden on top of a hill which sloped down north and south to the adjacent villas with their gardens which bordered our property.

Our eastern border overlooked the Ramleh Electric Railway tram-lines which passed about twenty metres below our hill. We had built our garden wall about fifteen metres from our borders leaving a strip of land which we used for about forty years as an out-garden which we planted with salads and fruit trees of *guavas* and *gishtas* (custard apples). It was envisaged as potentially part of a planning project of the Alexandria Municipality to build two roads running parallel to both sides of the tram-lines.

In 1963 this strip of land was expropriated and the projected roads were built, which resulted in the municipality constructing a retaining wall covering the side of the hill as a protection to the road beneath. We knew at the time of purchasing the property, that one day we would lose the extra land which induced us to build our garden wall well inside our borders instead of on the edge.

Our house was part of the suburb of Ramleh, whose name was derived from the Arabic word *Ramla* meaning 'sand', since it was mostly rocky sand-hills. In places these hills sloped gently towards the shore, but elsewhere they overlooked the sea with a sheer drop of ten or twelve metres. The terrain was a series of ups and downs, but with a gradual upward tendency as it progressed northwards. The suburb started at Stanley Bay, a popular bathing beach a ten-minute walk from Bulkeley tram station, and proceeded north past Glymenopoulo, another popular beach to Palais (Palace) tram station named after the 'Palace of Sorrows' that dominated the sea front. The Palace of Sorrows or *Saraya el Hazina* was built by the Khedive Tewfik as his summer resort, but he died before he was able to occupy it. It was used by Khedive Abbas Helmi II before work began on Montazah Palace, and later by Sultan Hussein's widow, Sultana Malak, when she came to Alexandria. It was a palace built within large grounds on high rocks overlooking the sea, encompassed by high walls whose ramparts were armed with cannons.

Due to the topography of Alexandria, what became the Ramleh Electric Railway Company was obliged, in the second half of the nineteenth century, to cut through rocky hills and sand in order to lay its lines on level ground. The line ran from Ramleh Station to its terminal at Victoria Station, eight kilometres north, where Victoria College was built in 1909. Ramleh Station was opposite the Eastern harbour built by the Ptolemys in 200 BC.

Our property lay between two tram stations on this line, four hundred and fifty metres apart.

When we bought the land our station was called St George; it was later changed to Sarwat Pasha named after the Egyptian Prime Minister in 1927. The next station further north was named after a Mr Laurens, a large cigarette manufacturer who lived there.

The Ramleh Electric Railway was named so because at one time it was a railway before becoming a tramway. A concession had been given to a British company to build a railway from Ramleh Station into a suburb in the desert known as Ramleh (Sand). This was a favourite residence of the British and other foreigners. The heart of this suburb was at a point in the vicinity of Stanley Bay, which later was called Bulkeley Station.

Mr. Wright in his book *Twentieth Century Impressions of Egypt* on page 430 wrote the following description of Bulkeley. 'Bulkeley where the members of the British colony reside in pretty villas situate in gardens overlooking Stanley Bay'.

E.M. Forster describes it as:

'We are now in the heart of Ramleh ('Sand') the straggling suburb where the British and other foreigners reside. Lovely private gardens, the best in Egypt. Left of the station is Stanley Bay, a fine bit of coast scenery and a favourite bathing place (also the Anglican Church of All Saints).'

The company was inaugurated in January 1863 when the first horse-drawn train began to take passengers from Alexandria to Ramleh, roughly where Bulkeley is located now. The horses were soon replaced by a steam engine (August 1863) which forty years later, more precisely in 1904, gave way to an electric tramway.

The names given to the railway stations (later tram stations) strewn along the line became the names of the Ramleh districts. Initially they were very few in number. One of these stations was named after a Captain Bulkeley who was a member of the board of the railway company, (later the tram company). Mabel Caillard related a charming story about a little drama that was caused by the naming of this station. It brought to an end the friendship of Captain Bulkeley and Mr Fleming, a neighbour and a colleague on the board. The latter was away on holiday when the company decided to name stations after distinguished personalities (preferably its own members) who lived close by.

It would seem that a new junction was being planned where the lines would divide in two directions; the main line was to pass through San Stefano and end in Victoria, running parallel to the coast. The new off-shoot was to serve another part of the suburb, shaped like a half circle and passing through a densely populated area called Bacos, after Mr Bacos who owned most of the property in that area. It was to end at San Stefano. This became known as the Bacos line.

On his return from holiday Mr Fleming found that the new junction had been named after Captain Bulkeley. He was furious because he had wanted it to be called Fleming after himself. He did not accept the explanation that his house was further away than Captain Bulkeley's – which it was. The company, in a truly British fashion, found a compromise. It created a new station duly christened Fleming, five hundred yards away, on the subsidiary line, on its way to Bacos. We are told, however, that the friendship between Fleming and Bulkeley was never restored. Before the drama the two friends used to travel daily together in the same compartment. After the dispute each of them used to walk from their nearby homes in opposite directions towards their respective stations and went to work, probably on the same train (or tram) but in different compartments. The two stations are still known by the same names. (Both the Victoria Line and the Bacos Line pass through Bulkeley.)

*

But to get back to the house on the hill. Both the main gate and the garage gate were on Sarwat Pasha Street that ran along our western border facing the sea. This was a macadamized road with gas lamps all along it. They were lit each evening by a man running along the street with a flame on top of a pole. Both ends of the street turned east to the tram stations. There were only six villas with their large gardens on our street, three on each side. The rest was sandy clay occupied by Bedouin squatters tending their herds of goats and living in tents. They had been living there before any houses had been built, and earned their living by guarding the newly-built villas from any marauders. They were a proud and independent lot and would allow no one to encroach on what they considered their domain. Bedouin families lived all along the coast; they were usually named after the first squatter on that particular spot. So you would have the children of Sheikh Aly, or Sheikh Youssef or Sheikh Saleh. Each family squatted on a piece of land and tended their goats, and guarded the properties of anyone purchasing land in their vicinity. It was a question of family honour for them that no one dared approach their protégés, that is, as long as they were retained to guard them.

You could hear them chanting in the silence of the night, when they were celebrating a wedding, a circumcision or other festivity, beating their lively rhythms interspersed with gunshots fired in the air.

Past the Bedouin camps at the northern end one would turn west over a few mounds of sandy clay on to the golden sand washed by the sea. Before we were of school age we would be taken to the beach by our nannies on most mornings where we tried to catch baby shrimps, either with small fishing nets, or in a jar covered by a bit of cloth with a hole in it. We enticed the shrimps in by having a bit of bread at the bottom of the jar, dangling it in the shallow pools among the rocks. There were very few people on the beach in those days, perhaps just another nanny with her brood. The nannies gossiped and we children played with each other on the rocks.

Early in the morning one might see native women in their long cotton dresses bathing in the sea. Most of them had no idea how to swim they just splashed about in the shallow water; they then left in their clinging wet clothes, wrapped in their long black body shawls, before anyone could see them. These women did not wear bathing costumes as they considered them indecent, although in reality clinging cotton dresses are much more revealing. They were always accompanied by their young sons or brothers, who had not reached the age of puberty.

At the other end of Sarwat Street leading to Sarwat Station was Princess Mahivech's house, known as the Princess's House. I remember it was a pinkish two-storey building, with a cornet-shaped turret coloured grey, as if it was covered in lead. It looked like a house from a fairy-tale book; you would expect a witch to appear at any moment. It was built in the midst of a large garden which led straight on to the beach.

If we wanted to get to the beach on that side, we had to pass the gates of the garden, where two very large wolf-like dogs always seemed to be barking. They were very fine and well-kept dogs, given their daily walk by their grooms. I used to be scared stiff of them if they ever passed our gate, or if I ever passed the princess's gate and they were peering out.

Not far from the open beach under the Princess's House into the sea there projected a sand and rock bank on which was constructed a private beach known as the Ladies' Private Bathing Quarters, *Hammam El Sitat* (The Ladies' Bath). It was enclosed in a wooden building of cabins opening on the inside to an area for bathing, shallow at one end and deeper as you went further in. It was sheltered from outside viewers, and was part of the facilities of the Casino San Stefano Hotel. The ladies who used it had to have a season ticket, be staying at the hotel or buy a daily ticket.

Two hundred metres further up on the beach you came to another wooden building jutting out from the Casino San Stefano built on pylons into the sea. This was the men's private bathing quarters. We were taught how to swim by being dropped into the sea at the deep end. The diver life-guard jumped in after us, swam under the water beneath us, and if we started to splutter or panic, he'd hold us up. There were also lines of rope stretching from the deep to the shallow end on which we could cling.

Father used to take us boys bathing twice a week during the summer months to the Casino bathing building, and after our swim, we would have a thumping good breakfast sent down from the house. He'd probably have one or two of his cronies with him as he rarely moved around without someone tagging along. After the first few lessons we loved it and considered it a great treat. There were no nannies, governesses or women to bother us, it was purely a men's affair. We continued using the Casino San Stefano bathing facilities until the 'Corniche' was built in 1932, which changed the face of Alexandria completely.

## The Casino San Stefano

The Casino San Stefano was built as a first class hotel. It was a landmark in Alexandria, and was built at a point facing the sea, where both the lines of the Ramleh Electric Railway met. It was the station before Sarwat Pasha Station on the Victoria line where we lived. It provided a whole lot of amusements that guaranteed a clientele from all walks of life. During the summer season from May 1st to the end of October it had a firework display every Saturday. As children we were able to watch it from our house as a treat. It also had a cinema show with a new film every night. All sorts of games were concentrated in a corner of its large grounds. Tea dances and dinner dances with first class bands took place in the different ballrooms. Symphony concerts were held during the season. A yearly flower show took place every spring. This was won for many years running by Amin Bey Khayatt, Bistawrous's son; you can see the Sultan Hussein's Cup for first prize in one photo and H.H. Prince Omar Toussum standing with Amin Bey Khayatt discussing Amin's marvellous ferns in the other. Both photos were taken at the Casino San Stefano Annual Flower Show. There was a stage on which plays were performed and a gambling casino. It was frequented by people of all ages. Most people had season tickets to get in, but their profits came from different paying attractions once visitors were in. Its popularity dwindled after 1932 and with the building of the Corniche it lost its beach front and much of its land, which was taken up by the new road. It also lost much of its charm, and became steadily noisier because of traffic on its sea border. In 1940 it was rented to Victoria College as the school premises, as Victoria College itself had become the sixty-fourth General Hospital attached to the British war effort.

I was too young to go regularly to the Casino San Stefano in its heyday. We were taken occasionally as a great treat. When we were old enough to go out on our own, there were many more amusing places which had sprouted up with the enlarged suburb which developed after the building of the Corniche which ran along the sea front between the King's two palaces. The older one was at Ras el Tin overlooking the harbour, and the other at Montazah. My elder brother and sister went regularly with their cousins to the Casino San Stefano in the time of its greatest success.

A bed of plants in flower for which Amin Bey Khayatt won first prize: The Sultan Hussein Cup

Photo of Amin Bey Khayatt with H.H. Prince Omar Toussoun, discussing Amin Bey's magnificent ferns

Further up the tram-line, in fact at its terminal, lay Victoria College – a large British school with large playing fields run on British public school lines to educate future Middle Eastern leaders in British thought and principles. Both King Hussein of Jordan and Crown Prince Abdel Illah of Iraq were old Victorians, as well as many other leaders, notables and princes from Abyssinia and other Middle Eastern countries. It was a great school for cosmopolitanism. Religion and politics were taboo subjects. Being a boarding school as well as a day school, many boys joined the kindergarten and left after they got their Oxford and Cambridge Higher Certificate, before proceeding to universities mainly in England.

About fifty percent of students were day-boys. They were of all nationalities and religions, those who could afford the fees. There were British, Greek, Armenians, White Russians, Italians, Belgians, Egyptians, Moslems, Jews and Christians in all their denominations. There were hardly any French or Germans, they went to their own respective schools. Many of the day-boys joined Victoria College when they were twelve or over, having been to Greek, Armenian or Italian schools, before coming to finish at Victoria College. There was no fanaticism or favouritism. All students were treated the same by teachers or staff, and it was due to this mixture of races, nationalities and creeds, working, playing and quarrelling together, having to accept, understand and compromise with each other that made most of the pre-1952 graduates of Victoria able to get on successfully in most parts of the world.

\*

When writing about a house or a town you have lived in, it becomes in a way your story, as it encapsulates your perceptions and feelings about things.

The House on the Hill and Alexandria in spite of them being entities in their own right, became my own story, as I can only describe my feelings, thoughts and deeds in relation to their existence.

As a child and a growing boy I was always hungry and interested in food, so many of my memories have to do with food and the kitchen. I even became an amateur cook. I always feel that food tasted a lot better when I was a boy, than it does today.

For many years we had a chef, who in his youth had been taught his art by French chefs who had come out to Egypt for a season or two at the big hotels. He became as good as any of them. I call cooking an art because good cooking is an art. Our chef, together with other chefs employed by the big families, wrote a book in Arabic comparable to Mrs Beeton's. Perhaps some of it was taken from it. Egyptian cooking was good cooking; it was known as Franco-Turkish cooking – a mixture of the best in both kitchens. We prided ourselves on having a good kitchen at home. Many a good cook was trained first as a kitchen boy (*marmiton*) then as assistant chef in our house. The promising ones were sent by my father to the Mohammed Aly Club in Alexandria to work in their reputable kitchens, for the summer for nothing, just to learn the art of French cooking from French chefs who were brought out from France during the summer months. Our present cook although now getting long in the tooth and not in very good health, was originally one of the promising lads who went on these training bouts.

Our chef, till I was about eighteen, was named Osta Hassan Naama. He was a first-class pastry and sweet maker, making wonderful creations out of coloured sugars and almond croquants.

I used to arrive home from school hungry and go straight into the kitchen, watching him making things and tasting them especially if the grown-ups were having a party that day. In those days children never appeared at adults' parties.

Osta Hassan was my best friend among the staff, he always gave me tit-bits, and he was my banker for many years. He died whilst he was still with us. He was the only person who always had ready cash in the house. I remember when I was about twelve borrowing ten piastres from him. I used to get ten piastres a week as pocket-money from my mother. Our governess was away at the time and mother was looking after us.

Freda our English governess was a beautiful and versatile English trained midwife, originally brought out to Egypt from Manchester by my mother to help her have her seventh child whom she did not really want. She became nanny to the two younger children and governess to my younger brother and myself, who were at school. When we misbehaved Freda punished us by making us write lines; fifty lines, a hundred lines at most.

I went to mother and asked her for my pocket-money. Maybe it was a day or two early, and she said I had to wait. I said I couldn't as I had borrowed ten piastres from the cook.

'You borrowed money from the cook?' said mother in a shocked voice.

'Yes mother,' I replied.

'It is absolutely wrong to borrow money,' she said. 'I won't give it to you unless you write out 1000 times 'I will not borrow.'

'But mother,' I protested, 'No one in the world gives anyone 1000 lines.'

'Well I do,' she answered, 'You won't get the ten piastres unless you write those 1000 lines.'

I filled up a few pages of lines and gave them to her. I was sure she wouldn't bother to count them, and I was right, she didn't. I paid back my debt to the cook. I always used to tease her by saying, 'You remember those 1000 lines you gave me for borrowing when I was young? Well I've never stopped borrowing since, I had to get my 'efforts' worth.'

Alexandria in the twenties was very different to it in the thirties and forties after the Corniche was built and still more different after the early sixties and the subsequent population explosion.

There were about four hundred thousand people in Alexandria and its suburbs in 1920 and about eight hundred thousand in 1950, and it is estimated today that Alexandria and its outskirts has a population of over four million.

One of my recollections of the house was when the young family moved into part of the house before it was completely finished, and I was bundled into a blanket and carried out of it into the garden next door belonging to Sarwat Pasha.

A fire had broken out under the balcony of the first floor, where the carpenters were melting glue for some of the panelling. I remember the erupting orange flames, and black smoke, father shouting and giving orders, and then the big red fire-engine arriving. It seems there was not much damage done, but I don't remember being taken back into the house.

I remember mother in a big straw hat going round with the gardener Osta Ibrahim, discussing the layout of the individual flower beds, and at times digging and raking the beds herself.

I remember playing marbles with the kitchen boys and gardener boys when I could get away from the nursery. We were not supposed to, but we did, when we could it was such an escapade. We learnt all sorts of dirty words from them, and my first erroneous ideas about sex were learnt from what I heard from the servants as a child, which were all wrong, as they were using slang words which I interpreted incorrectly. Grown-ups never spoke to children about the birds and the bees, and a lot of what they knew was hearsay. I wish I knew when I was young what little children know today!

My memories of the House on the Hill and Alexandria can be divided into periods: pre-school days till 1929, school days till 1939, days before my marriage, in 1947 and days since.

As this is not an autobiography, I will try and confine the tale to the happenings in the House as seen by me, and what I remember of Alexandria, in its different periods, and anything that I have heard amusing or quaint about it.

My remembrance of pre-school days in Alexandria, was that the suburb Ramleh was all sand, at least the part we lived in. It was interspersed with roads leading to houses in their gardens, and the sea.

As children our morning was breakfast, lessons and then the beach if there was time. After lunch we rested lying on our beds for an hour pretending to sleep, then going either to ballet classes, playing in the garden, or attending Sunday School at the CSSM (Children's Sunday School Mission) where we would be taken somewhere on the beach to sing hymns, listen to Bible stories, have our sandwiches and lemonade provided by the parents, or went on picnics usually with other children of the family.

There were two favourite spots for picnics, the sand hills and the Spouting Rock. To get to the sand-hills you had to go for about three kilometres along the road known as *Route d'Abu Kir*, or the Rosetta Road. Abu Kir was a little fishing village on Abu Kir Bay where Nelson had sunk the French Fleet in 1798. It was twelve kilometres away from Victoria tram station. However, before you reached the Bay at Abu Kir train station the road forked off to Rosetta so it had both names, the part to Abu Kir Station was usually called the Abu Kir Road and the prong going off to Rosetta was called the Rosetta Road. At the time I am writing about, the Abu Kir area was occupied as an RAF Station.

We named the spot off the road where we picnicked as the sand-hills, because of its sand-dunes stretching for two or three kilometres to the sea-shore, though we never explored it. Parts of it were planted with date palms, otherwise it was just pure golden sand. These hills were situated south of the King's domains, and his palace at Montazah. This was before the Corniche was built. The access to the palace was either by Royal train into the King's private station or by a private causeway leading off the road to Abu Kir.

These hills have now disappeared and have been replaced by miles of built-up area right up to the sea front. The sand itself has been sold as building material for the ever expanding city.

Whilst writing this chapter I thought I would go and explore the district I am writing about, to see if I could make out what had actually happened.

My recollections though vivid in parts about the sand-hills were a bit vague as to their exact location, I knew we came to them before passing the King's private causeway, but how much before I could not tell due to the built-up area on the present inside road. I am glad I bothered to do so, and I was surprised at what I found. I knew there was a road that led through the King's domain of farm land, fruit and other gardens on to the old road to Abu Kir. I remember its entrance being protected by Palace guards, and as children we knew it was the road to the King's palace. Later on it never crossed one's mind to explore it. It was easier to get to Abu Kir for a good fish lunch by taking the Corniche then skirting outside the Palace walls on the new road, until it joined the old Abu Kir a couple of kilometres north of the Palace.

I started looking for the causeway outside the King's Palace. It was not apparent where it had been, or where it started. Eventually I found it about 300 metres south of the Palace, its entrance concealed by recently built buildings, but once on it one realised it was a royal road. It was about fif-

The Avenue of Palms as it is today, being the causeway used by King Fouad. This section leads from the vicinity of the Palace to the main road (see photo below).

This section of the Inside Road to Abu Kir is the continuation of the Avenue of Palms used by King Fouad on his trip from Montazah to Ras el Tin before the building of the Corniche as it is today.

teen metres wide, an asphalted road at a higher level than the agricultural fields and gardens on each side. It was still in good condition as there was very little traffic on it, beautiful palms were planted on both sides of what I could call an avenue. I drove up it, exhilarated, no noise, little traffic, I could not believe my eyes. The only people who used it were probably people going to their fields or trying to get to the Corniche by a backway. There did not seem to be anyone about. After about three kilometres it turned onto the old Abu Kir road at about two hundred metres north of the Fire Brigade Station. I followed this road back to Victoria. I noticed for the first time that this part of the road to Abu Kir was much wider than the part to the north of the causeway, and it was also planted on both sides with the same type of palms. But now they were dilapidated and not looked after, the road was in a worse condition due to the considerable traffic of lorries, some of the palms had been cut down to make way for factory entrances, built right up to the edge of the road. But if you start from Montazah on the causeway, with a bit of imagination you could see that this was an avenue built for a King, and used by a King, King Fouad, when moving between the royal palaces at Montazah and Ras el Tin.

*

The other favourite spot for our picnics was in the vicinity of the Spouting Rocks. It was part of high-up rocks that jutted into the sea, mostly covered in sand far from the waves. To get to it you had to trudge for miles on the seashore, or that's what it felt like, or go by donkey which was much more fun. It was a wild and weird place far away from nowhere, you climbed up rocks and looked into holes that led through the rock into the sea below, which penetrated beneath us and spouted out through the blow holes and cracks. Some of these vents had been artificially squared by the ancient Alexandrians, who loved scientific toys and fitted them with musical horns and mechanical mills.

We used to look down one special large squared hole, which led into the sea beneath the rocks. Every few seconds you'd hear a frightening noise, and a spout of water would come belching out of the hole. It was called 'The Spouting Rock', the French called it *Le Trou du Diable* and in Arabic it was called *Bir Massoud*, or 'Massoud's Well'. The phenomenon was caused by the crash of the waves against the rocks rushing through a passage in the rock beneath the hole and then receding.

It can be found today very near where the Automobile Club is situated. Cabins and other amusements have been built in the vicinity, the hole itself was a favourite spot, and still is, for lovers who throw their coins into the hole and make a wish. The habit had as its origin the wiles of Sheikh Massoud, a squatter on the spot in ancient times, who induced gullible lovers to throw their coins in the hole and make a wish. He would then retrieve them when they left. When we were children a Greek had built a little hut nearby on the sand and sold refreshments. Little boys still risk their lives by diving in for coins and either climbing out or reappearing in the sea when the water rushes back.

*

Most of these memories were of the younger members of the family. Gamil was six years older and my sister Doussa was three years older. They rarely accompanied us. While we had nannies, they had governesses.

But I remember in 1926 mother employed a new governess for all of us before leaving on one of her trips abroad to a feminist or peace conference. She was a Russian refugee from Bolshevism, and she arrived with her son Alexander who was Gamil's age. I remember mother and son very well. I was a bit jealous of Alexander; he had come with all sorts of toys, much better than we ever had. I remember a collection of steamboats; I never saw any of them perform but they were very imposing. Alexander used to take fencing lessons with my brother Gamil in the schoolroom; we were too small to participate, and so just looked on.

I mention this story because of what follows. When mother came back from her trip, Adly my younger brother, who was about four at the time, asked her:

'When are you going to die Mamma?'

She asked him, 'Why?'

He answered, 'So that Papa can marry Mrs F.' As you can imagine the result was that Mrs F was packed off the same day with her son and his toys. I don't know why Adly should have asked such a question. Mrs F may have told him, 'If your mother should die, I'll marry your father.'

I never remember father having taken any notice of her. Anyway my grandmother Teta Balsam was staying with us at the time, and I don't think she would have stood any nonsense. She spent every summer with us till about 1934, when she built her chalet on land bought by her husband in 1900; eighteen acres of beach land, which only became accessible after the building of the Corniche. Teta Balsam used to sit on our veranda on the first floor leading to the garden, facing the gate, buying fruit, or quails, or any other goodies from the itinerant vendors, who carried their goods on their heads, stopping at each gate crying out their wares. They always carried a sort of weighing device with them. She'd beckon to them, they'd come up the drive and on to the veranda, and they'd have a little haggle, and she'd always buy off them. We loved having Teta come for the summer, she was always generous, and gave us piastres or shillings which

Mohammed Aly Square showing statue of Mohammed Aly on his horse, as in the 1920s

Mohammed Aly Square as it is today seventy years later

Corner of Rue Cherif, and side street leading to the Union Restaurant as seen in the 1920s

'Bourse' replaced by car park, same corner of Rue Cherif which became Salah Salem Street, and side street leading to the Union Restaurant as it is today.

Rue Saad Zaghloul showing trams in the 1920s, no cars apparent, only horse and carriages

Rue Saad Zaghloul as it is today, 70 years later

we put in our money-boxes. These were black and coloured cast iron figures of a head and torso of a negro with bright black eyes and white eyeballs, cast curly black hair, a big wide mouth with red lips, and an arm stretched across its chest with an open palm. You put your coin in the palm, pressed a lever on its back and the arm was raised towards the head and the coin would slip into the open red lips and drop into the body. You could not retrieve the money by shaking or any other way, unless you unscrewed the bottom.

We had all mother's family, brothers, sisters staying with us in the summer, but they were all very stingy. None of them ever gave us a nickel.

Another of my recollections during this period was when Adly was given a morphine injection instead of an injection for his asthma. It seems that mother asked to see the children as usual when she was at home in the evening, she was told by the nurse that Adly was asleep and she had not been able to wake him up since the doctor gave him the injection. Mother rang up the doctor and the mistake was discovered. It was decided that they had to wake him up if they wanted to save his life. Once awake he had to be kept awake at all costs, until the effect of the drug wore off, which took all night. I was sleeping in the same room and could see what was going on. Baby chicks had been brought and placed on his bed for him to play with, father gave him a whole lot of gold pounds to interest him. He was talked to and sung to. The long and short of it was that he pulled through. All through his life Adly was accident-prone.

## The Lights

An annual event that interested the whole of Alexandria was the celebration of the King's birthday. We called it 'The Lights' when the whole town came to see the sea front and all the city lit up.

All government buildings, shops and companies decorated their premises with thousands of lights, as did private individuals who wanted to show their allegiance to the throne and lit up their villas in Ramleh. The whole town was ablaze with electric bulbs, as were the ships in the harbour and Ras el Tin Palace.

The king's procession of red Rolls Royces with black tops whizzed past the cheering crowds standing on the footpaths, and the parked motor cars with their occupants. The king's procession started from Montazah, past some houses and government buildings which were illuminated. But the real illuminations started just before Mazarita, at the northern point of the Eastern harbour, where the Corniche commenced. Once the king's procession had passed on its way to Ras el Tin Palace, the traffic was allowed to move, and everyone drove around town gazing with open mouths at the magnificent illuminations. This was always followed by a fireworks display.

The illuminations always attracted the man in the street who looked forward to this yearly outing; they even put words to the first few bars of the National Anthem, which was supposed to have been written by Verdi for Khedive Ismail. These words were:

*Salam Salam ya Affandina*
*Kol Sanna Taamil Zina*

which could be translated roughly into:

*We salute, we salute our Royal Highness*
*May you bring us each year your decorations*

It is noted that motor cars painted the bright royal colour red with black tops were always palace cars. No other motor car was allowed to use those colours.

*

Much has been written about Alexandria and its cosmopolitan society, during the period between the two world wars, so I will not try to describe it, but it suffices to say that Alexandria before the building of the Corniche was not able to maximize its potential as a bathing resort, considering it had seventeen kilometres of sea front from Ras el Tin to Montazah.

This front was made up of several small bays which could protect bathers from the treacherous currents of the open sea. All these bays had wide stretches of sand, perfect for sunbathing and beach sports and safe swimming, but most of them were inaccessible except for two, Stanley Bay and Glymenopulo, as peoples' properties until the building of the Corniche had been extended haphazardly right up to the sea-shore.

Most Alexandrians liked spending some of their time on the beach if they could. They usually had some bathing facility arranged between friends and family and since the most accessible were at the two spots mentioned above they became popular beaches. The rest were too difficult to get to and only someone who lived in the vicinity was able to get to them and use them. A third accessible beach was Anfouchy, an area that was frequented by all those who lived round the docks and harbour area. It was purely a native beach frequented by very few people of other nationalities.

All the good bathing beaches or bays were linked by narrow stretches of beach facing the open sea which constituted dangerous bathing. The whole coast line was patrolled by coastguards belonging to the frontier police, and before roads were built, when it was only sand, it was guarded by the Camel Corps. Wherever one was able to bathe you'd find a life-guard, they watched the bathers and put up flags denoting the weather; a black flag

323

Before the building of the Corniche, showing the huts with straw sides and raisable flaps.

After the building of the Corniche and the building of cabins by the Municipality on three levels

324

meant that it was forbidden to bathe, a red one that you bathed at your own risk, and a white one that it was safe.

Stanley Bay and Glymenopulo were developed as bathing centres by the Municipality by allowing individuals to put up their wooden shacks or huts and charging them ground rent for the space they occupied. Most of these huts had one thing in common: a raised platform, part of it forming a closed area for changing and an outside veranda whose sides and front were made up of wooden framed straw matting. The front was a flap with a padlock at the bottom. Once you raised the flap and propped it up with a wooden pole you had an extra shady area for your hut. Some people had been able to have raisable flaps on three sides of the hut. When the Corniche was built, the Municipality built cabins on several levels at Stanley Bay for rent. (See photos of Stanley Bay before and after the building of the Corniche).

After the Corniche the seafront was slowly developed, Sidi Bishr No. one then two then three, and after 1952 Montazah Palace was given as a concession to an Italian company who built cabins all along its numerous bays. A whole new summer resort was built at Maamoura from land expropriated from the royal family or undeveloped beaches.

Due to the population explosion in the last forty years together with the emergence of a new middle class much of Egypt's coast from Alexandria to Mersa Matrouh 291 kilometres west of Alexandria has been developed as a summer resort.

One of the inaccessible or difficult beaches to get to was where my father-in-law Zaki Bey Wissa and his sister Regina Habib Khayatt (Wissa's daughter) built their summer houses, which were each built on two acres of land right off the beach at Palais Tram Station but at a much lower level than the Palace of Sorrows which overlooked the area about 300 metres away. These gardens extended right onto the beach where they had rented a spot from the Municipality and built their huts. It was not one of the best bathing spots as it was not protected by a bay but faced the open sea. My wife Philae remembers after passing through a little wood in the garden, they used to open a little door in the wall like Alice in *Alice in Wonderland* and walk on to the beach in the early mornings, have their morning bathe and after changing, have breakfast on the beach brought down from the house in large trays by suffragies in their white *kuftans* (robes) and red sashes supervised by Zaki Bey's majordomo Abdu in his black tie and trousers and white jacket.

Two of Wissa's other children had bought land in Ramleh and had built villas opposite each other as summer resorts on the outskirts of Alexandria. They were George Pasha Wissa and his sister Farouza, Mrs Alexan Pasha Abiskharoun. George Pasha's villa adjoined the Second Eleven playing fields of Victoria College, where both families had boys as boarders.

ZAKI BEY WISSA'S FAMILY

Zaki Bey Wissa centre, to his right Shafiga his wife, Toutou and Victor, to his left Gertie, her arm around Philae and Ernest

The family also built a Protestant Church at Palais which was opened when all the family came down in the summer and closed when they went back to Assiout. But today it is open all the year, serving their large congregation, doing good work and looked after by a resident clergyman, Rev. Guindi Ibrahim.

There were other places of relaxation in Alexandria other than the beaches, the Alexandria Sporting Club with its eighteen-hole golf-course and other sports used exclusively by members or their guests although its race-course and stands were open to the public when the races came to Alexandria for the summer. Most of the club's income which maintained their grounds kitchens and playing fields was derived from the *pari-mutuel* of the races.

In 1925 an English Jew named Mr Joseph Smouha arrived in Alexandria supposedly with a million pounds to build a spinning factory, this figure told me I feel may be exaggerated, but instead of a spinning factory he was able to buy a large part of the marshes that extended between the Mahmoudieh Canal and the route d'Abu Kir from the domains of Prince Omar Toussoun. He succeeded, in spite of earlier trials and failures by other people, in reclaiming this area. The plans were presented at a World Exposition in Geneva in 1927 at *L'Exposition d'Hurbanism Sociale*. First prize was won by its designer Mr Closier. The executive engineer was named Mr Naglowsky.

He started by building another sporting club with an eighteen-hole golf course, together with other sport facilities and a second race-course allowing the race goers in Alexandria to go one week to the Sporting Club and the next to the Smouha Racing Club. (Many preferred Smouha Golf Course to the Alexandria Sporting Club Course.) Mr Smouha then divided the land into building plots. At first he thought he'd build villas and sell them on credit, but he found that people preferred buying the land on credit and building their own villas. The only drawback with Smouha City was that the level of the land was lower than most of the adjoining city and the streets became waterlogged in winter before a good drainage system was introduced. Smouha City was sold off in plots since the mid-thirties, a new entrance to the zoo and the gardens at Nouzha were opened up on to Smouha City, whereas previously the main entrance and exit was from the road along the Mahmoudieh Canal, which at one time was an outing for the Alexandrian who wanted to go for a carriage drive along the canal, where little restaurants and cafes were built.

Today the Mahmoudieh Canal area is purely an industrial zone.

*

The House on the Hill has been called several names at different times:

327

some called it *La Maison du Bon Dieu*, others *Liberty Home*; I have even heard it called *A Mad House*. It was different in my opinion to many houses. It had a carefree atmosphere, and it always felt to me as if it was alive and moving, and had a life of its own, resembling a chameleon changing with the moods and needs of its occupants.

Although each one of us felt it was his personal home, to live and entertain in as he saw fit, yet it only had one real boss when my father was alive, and mother was supervising it. In many ways it ran itself, the staff were of the best and well-trained, so we were able to give our orders without stepping on each other's toes. Mother and father did not cramp our style, and it was large enough to accommodate most of our whims. But it was different after father's death, the atmosphere and conditions had changed as I will recount later.

As children, teenagers, or married until father's death in 1952 we were carefree as regards the house. We each had our private quarters which we occupied when in Alexandria, and in spite of some of us earning our livings, everything was laid on free, staff, food, repairs etc. My wife and I since our marriage in 1947 lived in Minieh a quaint little town on the Nile in Upper Egypt where I worked with an English cotton firm until 1957 after which we came back to Alexandria to live permanently.

During this period we only stayed in the house every alternate summer, and we never considered this as living in Alexandria. In Minieh our main preoccupation was my work in the factory, keeping the children's nannies happy, worrying about their health, or who we were going to invite to play bridge or to go out shooting duck with on the Nile in the afternoon, and in our spare time planning our summer holidays every alternate year in Europe.

As children, teenagers and until married we had always been encouraged by our parents to have our friends come to us at home, we never thought of sleeping out, although some of our friends used to spend weekends with us, and at times months during the summer holidays. We never thought of sleeping elsewhere. This behaviour was never spelt out to us, but we felt it wasn't done to do otherwise. It was not difficult to behave in this manner, we could entertain royally; anyway not many people were willing or had the accommodation to invite one to spend the night.

When we lived in Alexandria permanently we instilled the same behaviour in our daughters, always encouraging them to entertain at home, and have their friends to stay if their parents allowed it. But it was more difficult to convince our daughters that we were not being old fashioned and pig-headed when we refused to let them spend a night at some girl friend's. Happily they weren't really inclined to, habits and mores had changed since we were young and they must have thought our ideas unreasonable, although I always considered myself very avant garde!

With father's death on October 5th, 1952 and the decision of the Agrarian Reform Board to leave a total of 300 acres to the Fahmy Wissa family, 200 acres for the original owner and 100 acres for his children, it was not possible to hold on to the house and our way of living if each of us wanted to inherit or go on his own. The Fahmy Wissas had always been a united family and we wanted mother to live the life she had always been used to. We left decisions, the work and trouble to mother and the eldest male amongst us, which was my brother Gamil. He was a senior partner in an Egyptian joint stock company that owned rice mills, so he had all the necessary staff to fill in forms and do all the other paperwork. We discussed matters as a family between the heirs and decided that we would keep the house open, and live in it, for whomsoever of the family wanted to. All the income from the 300 acres would go towards the house's expenses, we would have to reduce the staff from twenty-four to eight, a cook, two suffraggis, a chauffeur for mother, a gardener and a maid, a washerwoman and porter who would also wash our cars. Those of us who wished to grow the land themselves, could do so but would pay its rental value to the house. My younger brother Adly wanted to farm the land he inherited, and had built a flour mill on part of the property. He was not married and it was decided he'd go on as usual. My sister Doussa was married and lived in England, another sister Nadia was married and living with her husband, I was married and living in Minieh. It was also decided that if anyone of us wished to sell his share of the land inherited, it had to be land rented to small farmers, and in that case he could do so, but would compensate the family with its rental value each year, which would go towards the house's expenses. In that way the house wouldn't be the loser and it would give each one of us the chance of trying to maximize his income. I was one of the heirs who decided against keeping any agricultural land for myself. I was more interested in the cotton business. I had become a junior partner in the firm I worked for, and was ambitious and wished to grow. It was decided at the time that if the expenses of the house were more than its income the working members of the family who were not planting land themselves and who had jobs would make up any deficit if they were living permanently in the house. Mother would also help if need be from her own small private income.

We decided that each individual family living in the house would look after their own breakfasts and dinners in their own apartments. Lunch would be provided for any one who wanted to come down to lunch in the dining-room downstairs. The staff had all their meals out of the general expenses. If we needed extra staff each family would provide its own, so I had a nanny for my children, and a private suffraggi who would cook our breakfasts and dinners and look after our flat in the house. The main cook could also help out, for individual needs, but each family would foot the bill for its requirements.

As I was the first in the family to have had any children, father and mother decided in 1950 that the two rooms we occupied after we got married were too cramped and did not provide enough space to bring up a family, so they decided to build us another floor. We came back the next year from Minieh to find that we had a flat to ourselves, furnished down to the cutlery marked with an 'N' to denote it was the nursery cutlery as it was of the same pattern as some of the house cutlery.

In this way the Fahmy Wissas were able to keep up appearances. People could not understand how we were able to do it.

*

To go back to my childhood, it must have been in 1926 that we had a convertible maroon Panhard. It was driven by our English chauffeur called Dory. I remember him in his white chauffeur's coat with blue cuffs and collar and chauffeur's cap, taking us out on our picnics or to the English Church at Mustafa Barracks by our nannies. I also remember a year or two later another Panhard a black hard-top, driven by a Sudanese very good looking chauffeur in blue livery called Abbas who stayed with us until World War II when he got a much better paid job with the Americans in Cairo. He always used to come and see us when he came down to Alexandria. This Panhard could hardly pull itself up our hill, it spluttered and coughed and stalled, and father soon got rid of it and bought us a light blue Nash which lasted us from 1930 to 1936 when he bought a beige Desoto. I remember the streets were patrolled in those days by British constables on their motor bikes, who would chase after us, and stop the car if we ever exceeded the speed limit. I remember hearing about Abbas standing under Gamil's window imitating Dracula and scaring the wits out of him having brought him back from the late show at the cinema.

I have an old photograph of Mme Saad Zaghloul Pasha and other ladies taken after a lunch she had had at the house standing on our front steps. You can see me in the photo holding a little flag in one hand and clinging on to mother with the other. Gamil and Doussa were also in the foreground holding little flags; this must have been in the summer of 1926.

I remember Miss Agnes Slack in 1929 when she came and stayed with us for a month or so, and the parties and reunions mother gave to make her friends sign the pledge (a promise not to drink). Father refused to attend these meetings and slipped out of the house and had his drink at the club or elsewhere, he would not sign the pledge, nor would my brother Gamil and Doussa. Doussa told Miss Slack that she couldn't sign as she was in the habit of having wine at dinner when she dined with father, which was probably not true, because we never served wine at lunch or dinner except at formal dinner parties given by the parents to which none

H.H. Prince Omar Toussoun seated centre right opposite Esther, centre left, and Fahmy Bey Wissa at the far end on the right

Maybe at the same reception, except that the Governor of Alexandria, H.E. Hussein Sabry Pasha, brother of Queen Nazli, is seen at the bottom of the stairs

of the children were ever invited. I don't know if mother ever signed the pledge, but it was not difficult for her because she did not like drink anyway, except maybe for a small cognac at times which she said was for medicinal purposes.

*

### The Aborted Feud

Assiout in the first half of the twentieth century was very different to what it is today, the Assiout University had not been built, and in spite of it being the capital of Upper Egypt, most of the inhabitants were local except for certain foreigners such as the American missionaries, the remnants of the Riverboat Evangelists, and other Americans working in their hospitals and their girls' and boys' schools. There was a large Coptic Orthodox community. Their clergy were now more enlightened and educated, having had to compete for their flock with the Coptic Protestants led by Egyptian Pastors. The weakness of the Protestant movement emanated mainly because of the many different denominations found within it.

The gentry consisted of large well-known landed families both Moslem and Christian, those in politics and government came mainly from the Moslem community. In spite of this Assiout had two mayors, a Moslem mayor (*Omda*) usually a member from the well known family, the Sabits, and a Christian mayor, who in the 1920s was Habib Pasha Shenouda who married Hanna Wissa's daughter Louisa. Habib Pasha was wealthy in his own right, a descendant of an old family of merchants. The Shenoudas always used to boast that they were from an older family than the Wissas. They had made their fortune in trading with the Sudan, including the trade of slaves, that is before slavery was abolished in Egypt in the 1870s by Khedive Ismail.

In 1934, Habib Pasha having died several years earlier, his son Samuel was mayor (*Omda*) of Assiout. His youngest brother Youssef turned up on our doorstep in Alexandria. He had always been known as a daredevil getting into all sorts of scrapes. He wanted to see his uncle Fahmy. It seems that he had had a fight with someone from the House of Sabit, and he drew a gun on him. I don't think anyone was hurt but it was an insult that had to be settled as it could turn into a blood feud. The first time I saw my cousin Youssef was when he turned up that day. I was in the garden riding my bicycle. He took it from me and started riding it up and down the veranda stairs. He was a good-looking young man of twenty-two bubbling over with fun. I later knew he was a great one with the girls. He had a terrific sense of humor always exaggerating any story he told.

He told my father that he had run away from Assiout as he was going to

332

be shot. He stayed with us for a few days and father got him a job on one of the boats of the Khedivial Mail Line as a trainee and then as a junior officer. He travelled on their boats as an officer for five or six years, and dared not go back to Assiout, or leave Alexandria when he was in Egypt. The two families became reconciled after a time through the intercession of father, who was considered the head of our clan he was for many years a director of the Khedivial Mail Line.

*

There were several good restaurants in Alexandria. The best was The Union in a little road opposite the stock market at Mohammed Aly Square. It was owned by two Greeks, a first class cook and his butler brother. They had the best food, service and cellar in Alexandria. It had a little bar at the back of the restaurant and a porch or a patio where you could sit on the sidewalk and eat oysters sold by a little old fisherman and have a *mezze* with your drinks. It was one of father's favourite spots with particular friends such as Neguib el Helali Pasha last Prime Minister before the Revolution, and Dr Abdel Said Pasha the well-known Alexandrian physician who regularly had his 'one whisky' there every night.

*

The Union had a Greek waiter called Christo, who had a bee in his bonnet. He believed he knew the spot where Alexander the Great's tomb was situated. Alexander's magnificent tomb with all its riches, was mentioned by several ancient writers and was supposed to be situated in Alexandria within an area of about one square mile of the middle of the city not far from the Eastern harbour. Christo was able to persuade several of the patrons of the Union to back him financially, he also attracted the attention of Hussein Pasha Sobhi head of the Municipality, who believed in his theories. Every now and then one of the roads would be cordoned off, because Christo decided that this was the spot that had to be excavated. Modern Alexandria probably covers the ancient. Every now and then a road collapses into part of the ancient city.

*

Pastroudis, the well-known restaurant started as a bakery. It was enlarged to a teashop with an adjoining bar with very good *mezzes* and finally into a restaurant/night club. It was frequented by the Assioutites when they came to Alexandria in the Summer. Part of it resembled a French café with tables on the wide sidewalk opposite the car park. Since it was on Rue Fouad, it was in easy reach of the best cinemas. It was run by its charming

333

owner Mr Pastroudis. I knew him in the 30s and 40s as a very good looking tall Greek with silver hair. He was helped by his very good looking wife, who carried on alone after he died. It was very popular with racegoers and Cairoites who liked sitting out after the races, discussing what had happened to which horse, or those who wanted a drink before lunch, or have a light meal before going to the cinema. One of its attractions was that there was no difficulty in finding a place to park.

It should be noted that the present car park has been enlarged due to the removal of a huge sand mound called Kom el Dik. This mound covered a large part of ancient Alexandria which was buried under it. It was decided to remove it, and a concession was given to a Polish mission in the 1960s to excavate it. The mission was able to uncover the ancient amphitheatre, which faces Pastroudis today and is one of the sites of Alexandria.

*

Many people, who came out of the cinema and felt hungry and did not want to spend much, could get a delicious *fool* sandwich at a *fool* shop owned by a Mr Benjamin, for one piastre. This was situated just opposite the Majestic Cinema on Saad Zaghloul Street. (*Fool* are cooked fava beans that can be eaten as a meal with little extras, or in a sandwich.) It is said that the Pasha has fool for breakfast, the labourer for lunch, and the donkey at dinner. I am mentioning this as I would like to tell you an amusing story I heard about Mr Benjamin. It seems that when he started on the road to making a fortune, he sold fool sandwiches off a wheelbarrow outside the National Bank of Egypt. He made a roaring trade as all the bank employees had a sandwich for breakfast before going into work, and maybe another coming out at lunch time. A friend of his who saw he was making pots of money, thought that he'd touch him for a loan. So he went up to him and said:

'God has helped you Benjamin and I would like you to help me in return.'

'How can I do that?' asked Benjamin.

'By lending me five pounds,' said his friend.

Benjamin answered, 'I'd love to but I can't.'

'But why not?' asked his friend.

'Because I have an agreement with the National Bank,' answered Benjamin.

'What sort of an agreement could you have with the National Bank?' asked his friend.

'I agreed that I would not lend anyone money, and the Bank agreed not to sell fool sandwiches,' answered Benjamin.

*

I started to learn to drive a car when I was about ten. Our chauffeur Abbas taught me, and when I was about thirteen I was quite proficient. I asked father if he could get me a driving licence. He refused, and in fact he asked them at the Alexandria Governorate not to issue one to me. They were not so strict in those days, there were not many cars on the streets, and although officially you had to be eighteen before you could get a driving licence, it was always possible to wangle one. I was determined to get a driving licence by hook or by crook, I must have had a crooked gene in me, which I probably would have called *shatara* today.

I don't know how I scraped enough money for a train fare, and instead of going to school one day I took the first train to Cairo, and went straight to the Traffic Department by taxi. I asked to be issued with a driving licence. The Egyptian officer in charge said I was not eighteen. I said I was, so he took me to the Traffic Inspector, a British officer named Mr Jones, who asked me my age. I answered him in English that I was eighteen. He said I didn't look eighteen. I said, 'But you can't condemn me on my looks.' Mr Jones asked for my birth certificate. I told him I didn't have it with me as I was born in Paris and it was with father who was travelling. A whole pack of lies.

'Well can't you get me a member of your family who could vouch for you?'

'Yes I can,' I answered. So off I went in a taxi to the Ramsis Club where I knew a distant cousin of father's would be playing cards. His name was Kamel Raffael, and he used to spend the summer with us. I found him and asked him to come and vouch that I was eighteen. He came along with me, and I was able to get the licence. I went back to Alexandria the same afternoon and no one was the wiser of my escapade.

I am telling this story because of accidents I had two years running on the same date, February 17th. That was when I was fifteen and sixteen which would have been more serious if I had had no licence as it would have invalidated our insurance policy.

Father never trusted me; I suppose he was right. He always had to rescue me from my escapades. Everyone seemed to know or find out if ever I did anything wrong. Whereas maybe it was more hush hush with my elder brother.

In 1936, when my mother was in America lecturing, she came back with a 1937 Buick Roadmaster, and in the meantime father had replaced the Nash with the Desoto. My brother Gamil was away at a university in England, and Doussa was at Cheltenham Ladies' College. We now had two cars and one chauffeur so there was always a car in the garage; all I needed were the keys. All our lives anyone of us children could sign for petrol when we were in the cars, we always took our petrol from Sheikh Aly at Glymenopulo. Sheikh Aly was a concessioner of Shell.

Mother knew I drove well, and she liked going some Sundays to Church, but she did not always have a car; it probably was with father driven by the chauffeur. So I always volunteered to drive her. At that age I had no governess, but a tutor in summer, an Egyptian missionary type, but I could get away from him whenever I wanted. Mother always had the keys, so I'd ask for them whilst she was dressing, supposedly to bring the car out of the garage and round to the front door. Once I got my hands on the keys, I'd take the car and quickly have duplicates cut at a shop a couple of tram stations away. Once back from church, I'd give her back her keys. No one ever realised that I was continually using the other car. Of course in summer when my brother came back from England he used the spare car, and I had to go by tram, or hire a little Fiat Balila for 50 piastres a day when I could afford it.

The first time I was caught out was on February 17th, 1937. Mother and father had gone down in the Buick in the afternoon when I decided I'd take the Desoto and go to the skating-rink at Sporting. I proceeded by the road adjoining the tram-lines to Sporting. I was not going fast. I could see two men standing on the footpath. Just as I came up to them, one of them decided to cross the road. I had no time to stop. I saw him fly up in the air and come down on the other side of the road. I got out of the car, saw that I could do nothing. He was not dead, but bleeding at the head, I dashed into the grocery that was just by the scene of the accident. People had started crowding round the car and I knew if I went out I'd be lynched. So I rang up the Sidi Gaber police station and told them that I was so and so's son, and that I'd had an accident and would they send a couple of policemen to accompany me to the police station, and an ambulance for the injured man.

I knew where I would probably find father at that time. He usually had his hubble-bubble with his cronies in the reserved corner they kept for him at the café on the Corniche, the Tougariah.

I rang the café up and asked for anyone that was with Fahmy Bey. When one of his friends came to the phone I told him what had happened, and asked that father should come and get me out of the police station.

Within a quarter of an hour, an ambulance arrived, took away my injured victim, and a police car arrived with two policemen. I asked them to get into the car with me and we drove to the police station, where I was met by father.

He shouted at me, 'Instead of doing your lessons, you are rushing round town trying to kill people.' After having taken down all the details, I was allowed to go home. Father came to some agreement with the man when he got out of hospital a week later, it was not serious. I had to go to court and was fined £E5. I don't know why. I had a valid driving licence, was insured, and I didn't think it was my fault. The man just walked off the path right under the wheels. The impact was hard as it had dented the mudguard, which was pretty tough in those days, so they probably assumed I was going above the speed limit for that area. Of course they took away my keys, but I had another set, anyway. I was in disgrace and had to lie low for some time.

The next year, on February 17th, father and mother had both gone to Assiout, taking the chauffeur Abbas and the Buick, and we were left at home. I was too old to have anyone look after me, and my younger brother Adly mixed with my younger sisters who had a Spanish governess Mme. Bordon.

I thought I'd take my girl-friend out for a drive. She was an English girl, her father was an officer in the RAF at Abu Kir and she lived with her mother in a flat next to Victoria College.

I got the Desoto out of the garage, called for her and was crossing the tram-lines at Bulkeley junction, I had the radio on, and as it made an awful crackling sound going over the tram-lines I bent down to turn off the radio. A tram had just started from Bulkeley Station on to the Bacos line. You could not see it because there was a café on the corner of the crossing, and I did not see the crossing guard waving his red light as I bent down. I was just able to catch a glimpse of the tram as it appeared. It would have hit us amidship and would have cut the car in half. I quickly swung the steering wheel round turning the car on to the tram-line in the same direction as the tram was moving, and the car was pushed by the tram up the line for a few metres. Of course the car had to have major repairs, and I had to go to the police station. I pushed my friend into a taxi and told her to go home. I rang up a retired senior officer in the police force, a relation of ours, and asked him to meet me at Fleming police station as I had had an accident. I was met at the police station by our relation, and was questioned by the police officer. They asked me if I had anyone in the car with me. I said I didn't, but on asking the traffic policeman he said he thought he saw a lady get out of the car. When asked if she was an Egyptian or foreigner, he answered, 'I couldn't really tell. They all wear the same clothes nowadays.' The car was looked after by the insurance, I was fined £E10, when the case came up in court. For the next three years it was difficult for me to get at the cars though I did at times. I had more money and I preferred hiring a car at 50 piastres a day on the weekends. There was also a lady who owned a little Austin staying with us, a friend of mother's, and she used to lend me her car when she wasn't using it.

*

It was probably in 1938 that the ex-Prime Minister Nahas Pasha came to lunch, and mother asked me to read his palm. I had been studying palmistry for a few years, according to 'Cheiro'.

337

I was interested in my own fate, and loved holding girls' hands, looking into their eyes and reading their fortunes. I have never been able to make out if there is any truth in palmistry. You can probably tell a person's character and how it is developing, and I am not sure if the same line on two different people's hands means the same thing. Over the years I have watched the lines on my hand change and tried to follow the change with what was happening to me. I think lines must be interpreted, especially the sun line or line of success, on what the person feels inside him, if he is satisfied or not. You could possibly see a very good sun line on a politician's hand which would mean brilliant success in a career in which he was satisfied. The same line on a poor fisherman's or gardener's hand would not mean that they were going to be politicians with brilliant careers, but that they felt that they were a success in their vocations. It is all relevant to the person and his concepts of life and his ambitions. Lines change throughout one's life and in a general way you can interpret them, but they should be taken in context with each individual person.

Nahas Pasha was very interested in having his hand read and mother was proud in showing off her supposedly intelligent progeny. He had an interesting hand, with definite signs of successes and failures. He wanted to know if he was going to become Prime Minister again. Nahas Pasha was a likeable, simple and gullible person in many ways.

*

### Pistol Packing Mama

I will now tell you a little story that happened in Alexandria. It concerns my aunt Zakia, father's sister, the widow of Chaker Tadros Khayatt. Her husband had died young and she was left to look after four daughters. Winnie the eldest married Albert Khayatt. Albert was the son of George Khayatt, a prominent Wafdist in the 1919 revolution who was imprisoned by the British. Winnie was having her second child in 1932. She was being delivered at home as most people did in those days. She was attended by a well-known Alexandrian gynaecologist. It seems that she was having a difficult labour, she had developed eclampsia, and the doctor feared she might not pull through. He told my aunt that he wanted to go down and get some medicines. My aunt Zakia, fearing that he would not return, pulled out a pistol and stood over him. 'You get on with your job. You stay and deliver my daughter of her child, and if she dies you die too.' The poor doctor was forced to stay, and Winnie was delivered of a baby boy, which they called Chaker, after his grandfather.

Chaker Khayatt lives in Connecticut in the USA. He married a lovely American girl named Edith Yuengling whom we all know as Cricket. They have four grown-up children, three girls and a boy. Chaker is quite a business tycoon, very attached to and proud of his Egyptian lineage.

*

Until 1933, our house in summer was fully occupied, and we played musical beds or musical rooms, between summer and winter. My grandmother and my aunt Aida and her two children used the two bedrooms and bathroom on the ground floor when they came to Alexandria in the summer; mother and father had a room on the next floor up with a private bathroom, and the next four rooms and a bathroom were occupied by Gamila and Marie, Esther's two sisters whilst they were at school in Alexandria. (They got married in 1932.) My sister Doussa and brother Gamil used the next two rooms and there was a spare room used for guests and when father wanted to change beds. In the wing there were two rooms and a bathroom which were the children's rooms. The governess and my two small sisters used the inner room, my brother Adly and I used the outer room, and we had a bathroom to ourselves above the wing on the ground floor.

On the roof there was a big room eight metres by five metres with its private bathroom where there were six or eight beds for the boys, unmarried uncles and friends that came down from Assiout for the summer. There were two rooms over the childrens' rooms with a bathroom used by the maids. In winter of course the house was practically empty and we could spread out. It was in 1928 or 1929 that Victor Wissa, Zaki Wissa's son, came back from Oxford to stay with us in winter, when his parents had closed their house and gone back to Assiout. He was being trained at one of the cotton brokers at Minet el Bassal, as he was going to help run his father's ginning factory at Beni Korra in Upper Egypt. He used to go down at seven a.m. before mother was up, and come back in the afternoon at about four, go to sleep and then go out and paint the town red at about eight in the evening. He used to say that the Italian maid Giovanna used to sing under his window, and when he complained to her she said she had to sing when she was sad. He wondered what he could do to make her happy and shut her up.

One day he met mother as he was going out. She said, 'Victor, your mother and father are away, you must come and stay with us.'

He answered her, 'Cousin Esther I've been staying in your house for the past six months.'

Another of Esther's cousins, Edward Wissa, son of George Pasha Wissa, who married my aunt Marie Fanous in 1932, used to call Esther, 'our sister who art in heaven.'

When we all went to the cinema at night, we used to take two rows, as there were so many of us because, during the summer, friends and relations would come round in the evening, have a spot of dinner and then we'd all go to the cinema. On one of these occasions, during the interval mother turned round and spotted my brother Adly, who had not been able to get a seat in the row behind and had taken one further back. She looked at him and said to us, 'I seem to have seen that face before.' I don't know if she was being funny or it was just absent-mindedness. Mother's sense of humour was peculiar. She'd laugh at the wrong point in a joke, and sometimes she would say things that she thought funny, but no one else did.

*

### The Night I Knocked his Head off

It was in 1943 that this remarkable incident happened to me.

Many young men residents of Alexandria, who wanted to help in the war effort formed an ambulance unit attached to the British Red Cross and St John's Association. It was known as the Alexandria Volunteer Ambulance Unit. We wore uniforms and had as our commanding officer Dory Sevastopoulo, a Greco-Egyptian whose father was the President of the Board of the National Insurance Company of Egypt. Our headquarters were adjoining the building occupied by the ATS at the beginning of Rue Fouad. We had a joint car park with the girl ambulance drivers who had come out to Egypt as volunteers bringing their privately donated ambulances with them. Their unit was called the MTC short for Motor Transport Corps. We had been provided with ambulances by the British Red Cross, and their care and maintenance was the responsibility of the British army.

Individually we were on duty on certain days a week and on call during air raids or emergencies. We were given a pass enabling us to move about in an air raid, and a little red circle in the middle of the blue painted car lamps denoted that we could circulate freely at all times.

I was called out one evening during an air raid. It was a full moon, and though there was a full blackout at that time it was possible to drive easily and make out things clearly. I was not driving very fast and just before the Ibrahimieh Police Station on the Route d'Abu Kir, I suddenly saw a man in front of the car. I slammed on my brakes but I touched him. He fell in front of the car. I got out and put my hand on the mudguard. It was covered with hot sticky blood. The body was lying in front of the wheels, but the head was about a yard away from it! I couldn't believe my eyes. I had knocked his head off his body. People started gathering as if from nowhere. I walked towards the police station, where an officer had come out and was walking towards me. I told him who I was, and that my father was a cabinet minister in Cairo and that I'd knocked a man's head off. He came up to the car, looked down at the man, and shouted at him, 'Get up you son of a bitch.' The man got up. He continued 'Don't you know that this gentleman can have you arrested for walking around in an air raid. What were you doing roaming the streets?' The man answered, 'I went out to get some dinner for me and my children and was coming back with a bowl of lentil soup for them.' I realized then that the blood on the mudguard was lentil soup, all hot and sticky, and the head that I could see in the moonlight was an upside-down bowl. I breathed a sign of relief and gave the man a pound which would have bought him twenty bowls of lentils in those days. He left, blessing me, going back to get more lentils for his supper, and I continued my drive to the ambulance unit.

Another tale which happened to one of the drivers in our unit, who did not know much English, but who was proficient in French, goes something like this:

He was driving his ambulance transporting four wounded Indians who had been taken off one of the warships in the harbour. He was to drive them slowly in convoy with the other ambulances to a hospital at Busseli, a little fishing village between Abu Kir and Rosetta, where he would deposit his patients. When they were about seven or eight kilometres from their destination, the bell rang in his cabin denoting that one of the patients wanted something. He stopped the car, opened the back of the ambulance and asked if anyone needed anything. One of the Indians cried out: 'I want peess, I want peess.' The driver answered: 'we all want peace' and slammed the door and drove off. You can imagine what happened to the poor Indian.

\*

## The Night he Spent in a 'Mad House'

It was in the summer of 1941 and we had a full house, not a spare bed for anyone. We called it musical beds. My aunt Gamila and her husband Philip, her two children, Farid and Ragia, and their English nanny, a Miss Buchanan were staying with us. My sister Doussa had come down from Cairo with a friend called Yvonne Townley to spend a few weeks holiday at our house.

I had a friend, the son of Princess Abbas Halim from her first husband who was staying with me for the summer whilst his mother was away in Europe. Father was leaving next morning for Cairo on the first train, as he had to attend an important session in the Senate. Philip and my brother Gamil were dining out.

Yvonne arrived home about midnight, accompanied by a British officer, a war correspondent. As soon as they arrived the air raid siren wailed, there was no circulation. The trams had stopped, there were no taxis, so Yvonne went up to Doussa and asked if it was possible to provide her with a couple of cushions and a blanket for the young officer as he was forced to spend the night in the hall below.

As I have mentioned before, father hardly slept and he usually roamed the house all night. He always stayed downstairs during an air raid, and sat under the roofed part of the veranda facing the main garden gate. He hated being cooped up in the house during a raid, and preferred watching the searchlights and tracer bullets that could be seen twelve kilometres away in the harbour.

When Yvonne came into the house with her officer friend, father thought she'd brought him home for some hanky panky. He shouted up in Arabic to mother, 'Esther, Esther what are you turning this house into? I can't have strange men sleeping here!'

Esther answered, 'Don't worry Fahmy, the poor fellow will only be sleeping in the hall downstairs.' She brought him down a couple of cushions and a blanket. Our war correspondent understood Arabic.

The air raid was over at about half past four and Gamil came home first. He came in by the front door which was open, going past father on the veranda. The officer got up and introduced himself and told him the story of why he was there. He got up again and repeated his story about fifteen minutes later when Philip came home. Father, as usual, had been roaming around the house at night in and out from the veranda. He was probably very suspicious and was making sure that the officer was still there and had not slipped upstairs. At about five father went upstairs to have his shave, bathe, and get dressed. His private valet had arrived to help, and the servants started arriving to prepare breakfast for father who left a little later at six-fifteen feeling reassured that morality in the house had been maintained.

I came down at seven-thirty to have breakfast and get to work by eight-thirty. Coming down the stairs, I saw someone sitting in an armchair in the hall. I thought it was my friend Midhat, but I couldn't understand how he was there, I had left him asleep. As I approached him the gentleman got up and introduced himself reciting his story of why he was there. He asked me doesn't anyone sleep in this house? I led him into the dining-room, gave him a good breakfast and took him downtown with me. Next day the story was all over town, of how our officer had spent a night in a 'Mad House'.

## When the Germans took over Alexandria

One night in May 1942 father got a telephone call from the ministry in Cairo telling him that all the family should leave immediately for Cairo.

# THE HOUSE ON THE HILL

A reception for Abdel Khalek Hassouna Pasha, Governor of Alexandria

At the bottom of the steps you can see Fahmy Bey Wissa; Abdel Khalek Hassouna Pasha is in the light grey suit on the step above. Standing behind the Governor, Jayes Bey, Head of the Political Police and Investigations; and Shaheen Effendi propping himself on the pillar at the top of the stairs, and Omar Bey Hamada, Head of the Traffic Department, standing in front of Shaheen.

Abdel Khalek Pasha Hassouna, Governor of Alexandria, chatting to Fahmy Bey Wissa

Hassouna Pasha was later Secretary-General of the Arab League for many years.

Alexandria would have to be evacuated, as they were considering blowing up the bridges in the Delta to stop any German advance. The Germans had by that time almost reached Alamein, and it did not look as if anything could stop them.

Mother and father packed the family into two cars and decided to leave that night for Cairo. I was working at the time in a British cotton firm in Alexandria, as well as driving ambulances when needed. I said I did not believe the Germans would break through, and that our firm didn't intend closing and I didn't intend leaving. I suggested father could get me a permit for four new tyres, as mine were practically worn out, which would enable me to escape if Alexandria really was evacuated. They promised to send me a permit to purchase tyres as soon as they got to Cairo.

They kissed me goodbye and wished me luck, they said, 'We are leaving you with Shaheen Effendi who has a shotgun, the assistant cook, one of the house servants (suffragies), the gardener, gatekeeper, washerwoman and other staff.'

Shaheen Effendi was a friend of father's who had turned up about three years earlier, and had been given a room in the basement. He had his meals with us, played *tric trac* and dozed in the garden. He never went outside the garden gate although I'd asked him several times to come with us to the cinema. He was an amiable old man, who looked a little like one of the Seven Dwarfs. He stayed with us for about seven years and then left as suddenly as he came, in order to open a cigar and pipe shop in one of the main streets in Cairo.

I never knew for what reason he was staying with us and why he left, we never questioned or thought about our parent's actions; children in those days were supposed to be seen and not heard.

I was later told by my brother that Shaheen Effendi was a Freemason, who had got into some trouble and could have been arrested if he had been found. However since father was a Senator and had parliamentary immunity and his house could not be searched, and in spite of the authorities knowing his whereabouts, they did not bother to do anything about it. Seven years later whatever misdemeanour he had committed had been sorted out and, as no punishment was due, he left the house.

But to get back to the days of the flap. Alexandria was empty, the streets, shops and restaurants were empty, and where once Alexandria had been teeming with troops and officers it was now deserted. One could choose any of the beautiful girls in Alexandria, that had not left, and they would be falling all over themselves for you to take them out to dinner, whereas before the flap there was fierce competition with us poor civilians who had no chance of success.

One day I was summoned by my ambulance unit and asked to deliver an ambulance to the British Embassy in Cairo. Many of the members of the unit had left for the Sudan because they feared Alexandria would be overrun any day by the Germans. I took delivery of the ambulance and proceeded by the agricultural road to Cairo. I left at about five a.m. and arrived in Cairo about·ten a.m. Once the ambulance was delivered, I thought I would go and see my parents.

Father and mother were living on a houseboat on the Nile. I found mother at home, and she greeted me and anxiously said, 'How did you get here?'

I replied, 'By the agricultural road.'

'But how did you get past the Germans?' she asked.

'What Germans?'

'The Germans that took over Alexandria yesterday,' she said.

'No Germans took over Alexandria.'

'But they did,' she insisted.

'Abdel Fatah Pasha Yehia rang up his house in Ramleh and was answered by a German. You can't go back to Alexandria.'

I assured her that there were no Germans in Alexandria. The only troops that were in Alexandria for twelve hours had been the Australians that came off the ship and went straight up to the front with their armour.

The Egyptians were all very excited when they saw the Australians and were saying: 'Now that the Australians have come it will be all right, they know how to fight.'

Mother was still very insistent that I should not return to Alexandria, for she was sure the rumour was true that the Germans were there.

However, I went back by train, which took me twenty-four hours. When I finally got there, I found no Germans.

The rumour had started when Abdel Fatah Pasha Yehia had rung up his house in Alexandria and was answered by a German. It came about because Abdel Fatah Pasha Yehia had a bungalow at Mersa Matruh or some other place near the border, and since he had been a minister of communications he had a telephone line connected between his house in Alexandria and his bungalow which now was behind the German lines. Somehow the telephone line had been left connected to the bungalow instead of Alexandria, and when the Pasha rang up his home in Alexandria, a German answered him from his bungalow.

*

We were staying at my sister Doussa's in London in 1989 when she said she was having Ena Nelson Ryan in for a drink. I had heard of Ena, she was a good friend of the family and I had always wanted to meet her. Doussa asked us to stay and not to go out that evening.

When I was introduced she said, 'I know a friend of yours who knew you when you were about ten.'

I immediately replied 'Dick Candlish'. I don't know how the name, or person came to my mind. I hadn't seen him since 1929, when he used to come home from school with us and play in the garden, and I hadn't thought of him since. But now I remembered his face, and that he was very good at climbing drain-pipes and getting into the house through the windows. The servants nicknamed him *Harami Ingilisi* which meant 'English thief'. We were never able to achieve such exploits, although we would have loved to do so.

I asked her to ring him up and we took them all out to dinner.

Dick reminded me of the House on the Hill. He said he could never forget it, it made such an impression on him. He remembered every detail of it, how he used to run up and down the back stairs, and try to explore every nook and cranny – he said it reminded him of a castle. He told me a story that I had never heard before, of how one day he climbed through the window while we were doing something else, and went exploring in the house. He came to the main dining-room and opened the door. Father was having a men's party, and the guests saw a little fair-haired English boy standing at the door, and were intrigued. They called him in and started talking to him, asking him all sorts of questions, and his answers greatly amused them. He was very proud as a child that he had met all these important people.

Dick had left Egypt soon after and had never come back. He had served most of his life in the Middle East in the army, with General Glubb Pasha in Jordan, in the Yemen, and elsewhere. But the house had made such an impression on him that he could never forget it. I always try to meet him whenever I am in England.

\*

*Entertainment*

As children our birthday parties were attended mostly by cousins in Alexandria. The games and food were arranged by our nannies, and the only other guests were children being looked after by other nannies who were friends of ours. My cousin Philae, who later became my wife, attended all our parties whenever she was in Alexandria.

As young schoolboys we invited our boy friends from school, but that was only on our birthdays or some special occasion. These were also attended by our governesses. Philae also came to these all-boy parties, joined in our games, she could run, ride a bicycle or jump down three or four steps at a time. She also used to play the piano for us.

When we became teenagers, our parties were mixed, we had no nannies or governesses and arranged them ourselves. We danced, played games like murder, sardines and postman's knock, drank lemonade, and if we could, beer as well. During the winter months we tried to have parties every week. Sometimes they were surprise parties, especially when we went to other boys' houses, but I preferred preparing everything myself if it was at our house. We got all the cakes from Delice, a teashop in Alexandria, as the family had an account there and I only had to ring them up and buy what we needed and put it on the account. Sandwiches were made by the Suffragies and if ever we needed anything more substantial we'd just ask the cook, and he would prepare it.

When I left school and started work we did not have the same sort of parties. During the war I started dating girls and entertained outside, and of course my interests had changed. I liked mixing with a different crowd, going to play bridge at the Sporting Club after lunch, went back to work in the afternoon till six-thirty then either went back to the club to play more bridge, or study the form for the races next week. I loved the races which I followed until about 1970. I still played bridge at the club until 1979 when I had a car accident.

Another of our activities, especially after I got married, was to go fishing when in Alexandria. We fished off a bridge at Edco about half-way to Rosetta. This was a small tributary of the Nile which flowed into the Mediterranean Sea, and as long as the entrance on the seashore was not clogged and the sea was able to flow in, there were plenty of fish to be had, especially sea trout. There were also migratory species of fish like the eel which came each year to breed in the murky waters.

We were surprised at one time to see Dutchmen in their clogs walking up the road. On asking what it was all about we were told it was a Dutch company that had come to catch eels, smoke them in Egypt and then export them to Holland.

We also fished in the evening at the Fishing and Shooting Club at Silsileh before the Russians occupied the vicinity to put up their Radar Station. We'd sit and fish till midnight, and have our drinks and light meals served to us by the club as we fished. On Saturdays and Sundays during the summer there was clay pigeon shooting at the club out over the sea. We called it the Tiro with a *pari-mutuel*. It was very pleasant having your dinner and having a punt.

As we grew older and our children grew up the dancing parties became our children's dancing parties. At the beginning we tried to be in the vicinity when all these strange boys and girls came to the house. I forgot what it was like to be young, and I felt that the young people of the seventies were not the same as the young people of the thirties.

Remembering my own youthful antics, I hated the thought of anyone flirting with our daughters. They did not always appreciate my attitude. My younger daughter got married in the United States in 1976 and my elder daughter in Alexandria in 1978.

*

It is not possible to write about the House on the Hill and not mention the wedding receptions that were held there.

As children, Doussa, my sister, and Toutou, Philae's sister, decided to play at having a wedding. Philae and I were chosen as the bride and groom (Philae had to be bribed with a tea-set to accept). They dressed us up. The bride's train was made up of mosquito netting. Doussa was the priest, Toutou was the bride's mother and Adly was the best man. We had a reception in the garden with some cousins as guests, sandwiches, lemon-ade and a fruit cake made by the cook. We were supposed to live happily ever after.

Later on, five wedding receptions took place in the house and garden. My sister Doussa's in 1943, our marriage in 1947, my sister Sadette in 1957, my brother Adly in 1962 and our daughter Shahira in 1978.

They all took place in the garden at night, which was very conducive to a successful wedding reception. A dance floor was always laid out in the garden, which at one time we rented from the British Boat Club situated in the harbour. Later and when we were not able to rent the floor, I had one made. It was a sixteen-square metre parquet dance floor, made up into eight sections, two square metres each. So it could be laid down as one large dance floor or several small ones in different parts of the garden.

At all of these receptions the garden was decorated with coloured lights in the shrubbery and trees which gave it a fairy-like look. All the food was cooked by family chefs. It was the habit of all good chefs in Egypt to help one another with the preparation of their buffets at a wedding or a similar occasion. They would be generously tipped by the master of the house, but they considered that they were lending a helpful hand to the host-chef. Even if the visiting chef was better, he was always considered a helping guest. It was a sort of chef's etiquette between themselves. We only ordered the wedding cake from a well-known teashop. It was always a rich fruit cake with almond paste and royal icing.

Doussa's was the first wedding reception held in the garden on August 8th, 1943. I know the date because a friend rang me up today, August 8th, 1993 and told me that Doussa's wedding was mentioned in an Arabic weekly called *October* which has an article each week on what happened on that day fifty years ago The title of the small block written in Arabic read:

349

Part of the reception in the garden on August 8th, 1943. At one table Esther, Lady Killearn, Lady Peel, ADC, Mrs Nahed Sirry – wife of Hussein Sirry Pasha several times, Prime Minister – Stanley Cayzer, Winnie Khayatt, next table Gertie Wissa and others.

The minister of Civil Defense Fahmy Bey Wissa celebrated the marriage of his daughter Fardous (Doussa) to captain Stanley Cayzer, an officer in the British Army who emanates from a well-known British family. The ceremony was restricted to both families as Mrs Fahmy Wissa's maternal aunt (Mrs Regina Habib Khayatt) had passed away a short time before. In the evening a reception to dinner was given in Fahmy Wissa Bey's garden for friends and colleagues of the bridegroom, where they ate, drank and danced in the moonlight, listening at times to soft music. Lady Killearn the British Ambassador's wife, opened the buffet with the bride and bridegroom. The bride is the eldest daughter of Fahmy Bey, she went to school for several years in England. She met her bridegroom in Cairo two years ago. Part of the reception can be seen in the photo where both Lady Killearn and mother are turning and looking probably towards the photographer, with Lady Nora Peel next to her, officers and other people at the same table, and friends at other tables.

In order not to be repetitive I will only describe *our* wedding in detail.

Philae and I got married on July 7th, 1947. We married in a hurry as we wanted to get to Europe before July 15th, 1947, as on that date Egypt was leaving the sterling area. A new finance minister called Darwish felt it would be better for Egypt if she went it alone. We did not know exactly what money we would be allowed under the new regulations, whereas before that date we were able to obtain a letter of credit for all our needs.

Our wedding was a grand affair. I was father's first son to be getting married, and though he was always doubtful that I'd make a good husband, the family went out of their way to make it a splendid wedding. Father invited all his political friends, mother all her friends, and each member of both families had their list of invitations; over 500 guests attended.

Both Nahas Pasha and Makram Ebeid Pasha were there, despite the fact that they were bitter political opponents, whereas at one time they had been bosom friends. Yet the atmosphere was pleasant all round, and the garden itself was large enough to ensure that no one trod on one another's toes.

Philae and I left the reception about 11.30 p.m., before all sorts of professional singers and dancers arrived who put on a show which lasted till the early hours of the morning. We had opened the buffet and cut the cake, danced briefly for a while and then left. Those who liked dancing continued to do so to the sounds of the jazz band on a part of the dance floor in a corner of the garden away from the main reception area on the lawn, where a stage had been erected with the rest of the floor.

I think the success of a good party is to be liberal with your drinks from the start and get people into a good mood, talking to each other, breaking the ice. The Wissas were proficient at giving good parties.

Tradition obligated the bride to turn only right on the route to the

# A WEDDING AT THE HOUSE ON THE HILL

On July 7th, 1947 the wedding of Hanna Wissa to Miss Philae Zaki Wissa was celebrated.

Bride and Bridegroom in the drawing-room of the house

Mustapha Nahas Pasha, to his right bride and groom, Louis A. Fanous, Senator, standing, to his left Fahmy Bey Wissa and Zaki Bey Wissa fathers of the bride and groom

Political rivals in different parts of the garden. Both Mustapha Nahas Pasha and Makram Ebeid were political buddies. They became political rivals.

Mrs. Zaki Bey Wissa (mother of the bride), bridegroom, bride, Mustapha Nahas Pasha, Senator Louis Fanous at back, Esther, Fahmy Bey, and Zaki Bey

Fahmy Bey seated, Adib Tewfick, Dr. Amin Boctor, Dr. Labib Boulos. At the back Samuel Shenouda (Mayor of Assiout), Elia Shenouda brother of Mayor, Louis Fanous at back, Makram Ebeid Pasha in the dark dinner jacket

353

Shahira and Nicholas listening intently to the good advice being given

# UN GRAND MARIAGE

JEUDI soir à huit heures a été célébré en l'Eglise St Marc de la Communauté Anglicane, le mariage de la toute gracieuse Shahira, fille de M. et Mme Hanna Wissa (petite fille de feu Fahmy H. Wissa et de Madame Esther Wissa) avec M. Nicolas E. Fielding "Chartered accountant" et avocat de Londres, actuellement en mission en Egypte.

Les jeunes époux ont reçu la bénédiction nuptiale en présence d'une grande affluence de parents et d'amis.

Le cadre fleuri de la chapelle, l'éloquence souriante du jeune officiant, les hymnes nuptiaux brillamment exécutés sur l'orgue par le bienheureux Violet Sensun, la voix émouvante de Mme Iris Madkalin à la tribune, ont ajouté à la cérémonie autant de touches d'art et de goût.

La mariée ravissante dans sa robe d'une discrète élégance a fait son entrée au bras de son père M. Hanna Fahmy Wissa notre sympathique concitoyen. Suivaient Mme Hanna Wissa mère de la mariée M. et Mme Ernest Fielding, parents du marié, les membres de la famille, les demoiselles d'honneur et un essaim de chérubins qui semaient de fleurs le chemin du cortège nuptial, jusqu'au Maitre autel où attendaient le jeune marié et le témoins.

Après la cérémonie religieuse un fastueux souper a réuni les invités dans les jardins illuminés de la villa Fahmy Wissa à Ramleh. Là, durant une ambiance de joie et d'amitié, parmi les chansons, les flûtes, et les tambourins, le couple a été salué par les ovations de plusieurs centaines de convives. Ceux-ci, servis par un immense flexiphone de buffets et de buvettes, dignes des contes orientaux, ont défilé devant le couple et les parents, souhaitant de longs jours de bonheur et de prospérité à la belle Leyonum, descendante d'un grand lignée et au raffinement raviseur ne sur le bords des mers bordeles.

Entourée de ses charmants enfants, Madame Esther Fahmy Wissa dont la vénérable demeure voyait fleurir un nouveau rameau, accueillait heureuse et souriante les hommages de ses nombreux hôtes et amis.

C.S.

church but it was difficult at times not to do so and one had to work out beforehand the exact route to take. It was a superstition denoting the hope that everything would go right for the newly-weds all through their lives. Philae's procession took time in finding the right roads to church whilst I was waiting with Gamil, my best man, in church, biting my finger nails.

I will only mention my daughter Shahira's wedding as I found a press cutting describing it, written by the editor of one of the French daily papers in French and a photo of part of the ceremony in church.

I tried to give her as grand a wedding as was given to me by my parents. It was more difficult in 1978 as the lights were continually going out, which threatened to spoil the ceremony at church or at the reception in the garden. I overcame this problem by having a special generator brought to the church, and another for the garden, manned by electricians seconded officially by the Electricity Company. The wedding went off without a hitch, and the guests danced till the early hours of the morning. Everyone tried to make it a great success, and it reminded them of days gone by. The difference between Shahira's wedding and ours was that we left early at our wedding but remained to the bitter end at hers.

*

So far I have mentioned quite a lot about the upstairs of the house, but little about its downstairs.

It was called a Mad House because of what happened upstairs, but 'Liberty Home' and *La Maison du Bon Dieu* were names given by governesses because of what they saw happening downstairs.

I would like to mention a little bit of what was happening downstairs, which was ostensibly under control in the days of father, but became less so as time went on.

I will concentrate on two characters: Fatma the washerwoman, and Sheikh Madian, a Koran reader employed by father in 1947 when he decided he wanted to roam all night in his car.

Fatma came to us in 1938, under the following circumstances: Miss Potter who liaised between the Home International branch of *La Maison des Jeunes Filles* in Geneva and the YWCA in Alexandria rang up mother one night and told her that the police had just brought in a young woman whom they had picked up and who seemed rather retarded, and had nowhere to go. Miss Potter was wondering whether mother could find her some job in our house. She would not require much pay but only a roof, clothing and food. She could probably be taught how to wash clothes, or perhaps clean the bathrooms.

Mother who was always game for a good cause said she would take her and find something for her to do in the basement helping the washerwoman who slept out and only came three times a week. (There were no washing machines in those days.)

The family heard nothing more about Fatma, and we only knew the following story years later.

Mother's maid came to her one day and told her that Fatma was in the family way. The girl had not been put near the menservants' quarters in the garden, but had been given the use of a room that was our old school and fencing room in the basement. It was a very large room forty metres square with wood block floors, in one corner of which we stored old tyres, brooms and other household effects. Fatma was young and as mother did not want such pregnancies recurring, she wanted to know which one of the servants was responsible for seducing this simple girl. She asked Fatma directly if she was visited by anyone at night.

'No one,' answered Fatma.

'Someone must come to see you.'

'No one,' she repeated.

'Who keeps you company in your room? Who sleeps with you in your room?'

'No one, no one,' answered Fatma. 'I only sleep with tyres and brooms.' No one ever found out who the culprit was, nor which broom or tyre was guilty. Mother suspected one of the kitchen boys. Mother took her down to the hospital and got her aborted. Fatma never got pregnant again, but she was able to improve her status downstairs.

Sheikh Madian was father's private Koran reader during the last years of his life, and although a Christian father liked listening to the Koran if it was read well.

When he died we decided to keep Sheikh Madian on. We did not need a Koran reader, but we needed a gatekeeper and someone to wash the cars. Sheikh Madian said he was willing to do both jobs, for small pay, and he would live in the little lodge at the gate – we would provide him with food and a couple of *galabias* (robes) a year and he would be quite happy. He only stipulated that he should be allowed to read the Koran at weddings and funerals by which he could earn a little more money. At such a time we were not to worry as he would get his brother the street barber to look after the gate. Mother agreed.

During the week Sheikh Madian would be wearing his ordinary galabias but when he went out on official duty he would wear a woollen cloak, a silk robe and sash under it and a turban. He looked quite a dandy.

His brother the street barber was also quite a character. He had a square white beard with drooping mustaches, an old hat perched askew on his head. He would sit on the footpath outside our house and shave any passer-by who wished it for a piastre or two. He was probably provided with food from the house and shared Sheikh Madian's room at the gate at night, with no one the wiser, and mother who ran the house didn't care. She couldn't be bothered with trifles.

One day Sheikh Madian announced that he wanted to marry Fatma. Mother was delighted. I don't think Madian really cared about women, but he wanted someone to wash his clothes, cook him titbits and look after him, and it was more comfortable for him to move into the schoolroom with his wife. They occupied this room until well into the 1980s, when they both died.

Madian still was our official gate-keeper but the room at the gate now was used unofficially by his brother, whom we could see at times peering out of the little window. He was never employed by us, but he guarded the gate as if it was his own until his death.

Sheikh Madian extended his influence with the outside world as time went on. He started making talismans, and many a time we'd see a strange person coming into the basement of the house, and if we asked who they were we'd be answered they have come to see Sheikh Madian to attend a wedding or funeral, though we knew it was to get a talisman. We sometimes felt that we should not be there, or ask such a question.

My brother Gamil always thought he was crooked, but I tolerated him. I always believe that it is better to deal with people you know, than people you don't. Once you classify a person right, you won't get any surprises.

Sheikh Madian was very good with me after I had my car accident in 1979, and had to sit for six months in a chair. He slept outside my bedroom door during that time helping me every time I needed to move. He was the only one able to do that as he was very strong, and he never once complained.

Fatma became a very good wife to him. She looked after him well, feeling she had gone up in the world, as she was now the wife of a respectable Sheikh. She always called him *Am El Sheikh*, which meant 'my uncle the sheikh,' a sign of respect.

At some time in the 1960s the staff downstairs felt that they needed a television. The only person who had any spare cash was Fatma, as mother had been saving her salary for her since 1938.

The staff influenced her and Madian to ask for her money and buy a television. When mother was told about Fatma's wish she said it was a lot of nonsense, she did not need a television, it was a waste of money. Fatma became so insistent and the servants were telling her that mother was never going to give her her dues, so we decided to induce mother to give her the money she needed. The school room now became the salon where Fatma entertained. She'd make the staff tea and they would all watch the television together.

The closed area in the garden where we kept and grew plants now became the head gardener's domain. He was allowed to garden for other

A reception given for Esther Fahmy Wissa at the Alexandria Sporting, when she was made an Honorary Life Member, on the occasion of her and of four other ladies being given the *Wissam el Kamal* (The Order of Perfection) by the late President Gamal Abdel Nasser in 1969, being the 50th anniversary of the 1919 Revolution.

Congratulating her

358

people, and both his son and grandson helped for free when needed. They were fed with everyone else, and did a roaring trade in plants exchanging and selling. If we dared ask anyone why a stranger was walking round the garden, the answer we'd get was, 'He has come to see Salem the gardener.'

*

At one time mother used to go to the Sporting Club each afternoon, have tea and play her game of bridge. She would call for her bridge partners, and drop them at their houses on her way back.

She had been made an honorary member of the club in 1969 when President Gamal Abdel Nasser awarded her the decoration of *Wissam el Kamal* for her work in the 1919 Revolution. Her bridge in the afternoon was a daily routine, and she was a well-known, liked and respected member.

After her illness in 1981 she stopped going to the club. She had always to be accompanied, which she felt was degrading. She had been a very independent and active person all through her life and could not bear being restrained. She told my wife one afternoon on the steps of the house before she got ill, 'You know it is terrible to get old.'

When she became bed-ridden and had to be attended to by maids day and night, the house became less controllable. With my brother dead I was having to look after everything.

The servants were becoming intolerable, and I would have kicked them all out, except that I did not want to disturb the status quo, or upset mother in any way. So I closed my eyes to many things that I would not have stood for under other circumstances. I felt that it was a 'Liberty Home' that had too much liberty.

The rest of my family criticised me, and said I had let things slip and should have put my foot down. But I had not the heart to upset mother in any way.

One thing one must admit, even at its direst moments the House on the Hill had its own charm which emanated from the personalities of those who built it and put their love in it, and lived in it.

Now that all its old occupants are either dead or scattered all over the globe, it still stands dignified, although lonely, on the hill.

Every story has an end, but this story has no end, as long as the River Nile rises in the south, passes through this land of Egypt and flows into the Mediterranean Sea. Actors will take their final bows, to be replaced by others on the scene, whose actions will seem as déja vu, a repetition of what has happened before confirming once more the adage that 'nothing is new' and that 'history shows that man never learns from history.'

# BOOK FOUR – LETTERS

Saba Pasha, Ramleh,
July   , 1922

To    His Excellency
      The Field Marshal, Lord Allenby,
      Bacos

Excellency,

The Women's Committee of the Egyptian Delegation begs to bring before your Excellency the following:

The Egyptian nation has received another great blow by the arrest of the members of the Delegation who are accused of circulating a seditious circular.

We do not quite understand how agitating you deem the circular, but one thing we know and are sure of, that we are living in a time of great suppression of liberty and terrorization. Considering the actual conditions of Egypt today under martial law, the strong censorship of the papers, the espionage on individuals, and the absolute fettering of liberty, we are at a loss what to make of the situation.

We only regret that it should be your Excellency who is made responsible for such a position. Being a great soldier, and used to conquer in a fair fight, we can fully understand how you must feel the onesidedness of our fight today.

The Egyptian nation on one side, headed by a few faithful and zealous leaders, absolutely armless, claiming her rights, is met by strong martial measures; her leaders are exiled on untried accusations, her protests are ignored, her liberty fettered, and when her faithful sons call upon her children to raise their voice, they are imprisoned and accused of sedition. And more than that, criminal actions are taken against them. Where does justice come in, your Excellency?

If the aim is terrorizing the people, which is most inconsistent with British traditions, we beg to inform your Excellency that we will not be terrorized. We are naturally a pacific nation and we are doing lawfully, and will do in the same way all we can to see that justice is done to us, and in so doing, we may have to die for our claims. But we are not criminals, and we shall never justify crime. If some irresponsible person commits these crimes, it is for the authorities to catch him, and punish him, but it is not for the authorities to visit his sins on the nation. And if your Excellency chooses to look at matters in the right light, you will see how unjust and unbased is the accusation that has been leveled at the members of the Delegation, who are standing up for the rights of the people.

Being an Englishman and having had all the advantages of highly moral political upbringing, we can only beg of you to let your better self dominate, and use your traditional instincts of freedom and liberty towards poor struggling Egypt, and try to bring out the better element in the moral standard of the country.

You know that the means which are being carried out now only work to crush all noble and patriotic sentiments in the people, and only serve to give power to the servile, self-interested, flattering type of men.

Is it meet for England of all countries, to fight the moral standard of a people and to breed these contemptible traits in the nation? We are sure that looking at it from that point of view, you will shrink from standing in such a position, and although you are a soldier and are used to fighting, yet we believe that you will always fight for a good and worthy cause.

We are also certain that you fully realize that after all, brutal power does not count, and some day in the long run, justice and truth must come out topmost, and in hoping that you will always stand for justice and truth, we are

Yours faithfully,
(For the Committee)
**Esther Fahmy Wissa**
Vice President

Note: No answer was found to this letter among Esther's papers. Although an empty envelope dated 31st July, 1922 in Lord Allenby's handwriting was found.

To His Excellency
   The Field Marshal, Lord Allenby,
   Bacos

Excellency,

Madame Zaghlul Pasha has quite recently received a letter from the Seychelles to say that her husband is ill, and that probably a change of climate would save him.

Remembering your promise to us to remove Zaghlul Pasha from the Seychelles if his health needed it, we would beg, under the present circumstances to remind you of your promise. We hope it will not be too late. It would indeed be a great calamity if Zaghlul Pasha dies in those islands. The country then would feel justified in thinking that he was sent there to die, and it would be such a terrible idea, so difficult to uproot if once it takes seed in the minds of the people. Besides, your Excellency knows that it always serves to keep good relations between one country and another, especially between our country and yours, and although we are comparatively a small country to yours, yet the mouse may help the lion some day.

As to Madam Zaghlul going to the Seychelles, we hope your Excellency would see the difficulties of a lady of her class would undergo in travelling there, and we pray that you will arrange for Zaghlul Pasha and his party to be removed to some place nearer Egypt, where his health would improve and where his wife could rejoin him if need be.

We regret very much that you have such a mistaken opinion about him, for we thoroughly believe that he is the man whom Egypt needs to carry her on towards emancipation.

It is a pity that instead of making him and Egypt your friend, you have shown towards him such a perverse spirit, and so naturally have lost the sympathy of the nation.

He remains the national hero always, and if anything befalls him, he will be the saint and martyr. Morally your country will be the loser, although you are so strong and powerful, and we would so loathe that this will be the final end.

However, you are experimenting, and you may think it forward of me to give advice.

Anyhow please don't kill the old man; we shall never forgive you, neither will history.

We beg that you will let us know as soon as possible that you have taken the necessary measures for releasing them from the Seychelles.

In awaiting your reply with good news,
We are
yours faithfully,
(For the Committee)


**Esther Fahmy Wissa**
Vice President

Note: No answer was found to this letter among Esther's papers.

**A letter found among Esther's papers from Field Marshal Lord Allenby dated 30th of August 1922 in reply to a letter from Esther of the same date copy of which was not found among her papers.**

Ramleh,<br>
30th August, 1922

Dear Madame,

The prisoners to whom you refer, in your letter of today's date, are only allowed to see their own relations, at fixed times by permission of the military authorities. I regret, therefore, that I cannot grant your request that you and Madame Riaz Pasha shall visit them. I am today ordering an officer to visit them, and to give me an exact report as to how they are being treated and under what conditions they are living. I assure you that I have every intention that they shall be well treated. I quite understand, and I sympathise with, your good intentions; but it is impossible for me to accept you as my envoys in the matter of deciding on the suitability of their surroundings or of the building to which they will be removed.

Yours sincerely,
**Allenby**

Saba Pasha, Ramleh,
Sept. 1, 1922

To His Excellency
  The Field Marshal, Lord Allenby,
  Bacos

Excellency,

Since yesterday, I have had the occasion to communicate with Madame Wassef Bey Ghali, who has been to visit her husband in prison. She has written me a letter which I enclose the details of the life our prisoners are leading. Her husband was three days in his cell, after which he was removed to hospital on account of failure of health. Thinking perhaps, that the conditions of the prisoners was altered since then, I also met Mr Albert Khayatt, who has been to see his father, George Bey Khayatt, and he seconded Mme. Ghali's report.

I am sure your Excellency can imagine the condition of these gentlemen, locked up during 22 hours of the day in a two meter cell in the Cairo hot weather, in light and darkness, undergoing all sorts of discomfort, ennui and indignity, sharing the private life, and being in daily contact with criminals of the worst character.

Your Excellency can also value their morale in seeming cheerful, in spite of all those sufferings and horrors. For although unfortunate circumstances have stood against them and they have been condemned to taste of this life, yet they are innocent both in the sight of God and in the sight of man, and it is their suffering that is going to be the salvation of our country.

As I have said before, we only regret that it is your Excellency who has taken this responsibility on his shoulders. Fourteen million people in Egypt, and all Englishmen and women and the world over are weighing your actions, and although you may have strong reasons and feelings of outrage because of those unfortunate crimes committed against the English, yet it does not justify punishing innocent people for the crimes of malefactors.

The Nationalists, and the members of the Delegation who are working for Egypt's rights are handicapped on every side. They are not allowed to speak up or to act, and when they call on the nation to protest against these suppressive measures, and to raise their voice by all possible means, they are sentenced to death, and then to seven years penal service and £5,000 fine.

They are thrown into ordinary prison cells to suffer all kinds of indignities and horrors, of which certainly your Excellency is not aware. I cannot think that you could have imagined anything so horrible. Probably you are not acquainted with the conditions in Egyptian prisons.

Could I still hope to convince your Excellency on the futility of the present policy. You have declared Egypt's independence, and your statement to us is that you are preparing Egypt for self government and giving it a parliament.

Do you therefore intend, to give us a fair chance, or are you delivering us to the mercy of a party, to a despotic rule?

Our best men, our independent self-sacrificing free minded men, the brave struggling element of the country are in prison, or exile, anyone who dares remonstrate, shares the same fate; who are we going to vote for in the elections?

Under such conditions, we will refuse the elections. We cannot anticipate an Egyptian parliament composed of the party to whom you are delivering us, and who are likely to hold full sway in the time of the elections. And this parliament will be called that of independent Egypt! No, Lord Allenby, we do not want such affairs as the Assiut events of the reception of Zaghlul Pasha repeated. If you are sincere in your promises and political declarations, you must give us a fair chance. As I told your Excellency in the past; your present policy is fighting the noble element of the country, practically putting it out of the way, if you don't succeed in crushing its spirit altogether, it is opening the way for the despicable natures to come forth.

I am sure you understand my point of view. If one is brave enough to stand up against you for his principles which he considers right, you cannot fail to value him more than another who will cower before you and fall back on his principles, or will flatter you for his own ends. He may help you to carry out your policy; but can you trust the welfare of a country whom you are befriending, and whom you declare you are leading to a good democratic government, to that person?

An honest independent Egypt, as an ally will be more serviceable to you than an unprincipled dependency. Those men who are betraying their country to you will betray your confidence one day.

In pressing times (and many of them are sure to come) you will never be able to count on them. You Englishmen, ought well to understand this point of view, and I am sure you would prefer having a faithful enemy than a faithless friend. Am I not right in my surmise?

Remember that I am not self-interested in any way. My aim in life is to see my country on her feet, holding her own among the nations of the world, standing on good solid foundations, supported by true honest citizens. To me the moral conditions of my countrymen, matter more than anything else, and that is why we are struggling today. It is through suffering and tribulation that the best is created in man, and our cross will be purified by the fire of these adversities.

Although we are suffering and most of us unjustly, yet we are glad of it for the sake of the country. I fear that there is more suffering to come but Egypt shall be saved and this shall be through suffering.

We are going to stand one day as one of the few blessed nations of the earth. We are certain of this, and although our curse now is our disunity, and our misery is caused by the help of our own people, yet the fire to which you are exposing us will purify us and in time will unite us.

If I cannot convince you of this, go ahead Lord Allenby. The pains and groans of our innocent sufferers will reach a higher court some day and will have justice. I only regret it for your own sake and that is why I still come to you.

However, if you still want to follow your experiment till the end, please don't expose our prisoners to discomforts; we have your promise that they will be well treated; also to see to the Seychelles exiles that they are removed to a more habitable region, and go ahead. Our principals and just aims will stand for us in the long run and we are ready to wait.

We have had no news of Zaghlul Pasha whatsoever for some time, although we have heard from the others. Would your Excellency kindly tell us how he fares and the probable reasons which may account for lack of news?

Yours sincerely,

**Esther Fahmy Wissa**

Saba Pasha, Ramleh

**Text of letter received from Field Marshal Lord Allenby dated 1st September, 1922 in reply to Esther's letter of the same date.**

Ramleh
1st September, 1922

Dear Madame,

I have received your letter of today's date and its enclosure from Madame Wassef Bey Ghali. I have also had a report from one of my officers, and I am taking steps to improve the conditions under which the prisoners are living. As regards Zaghlul Pasha, I have no reason to believe that his health is otherwise than normal; but I hope to be able to give you news of him in a few days time.

Yours sincerely,
**Allenby**

Ramleh.

1st September.

Dear Madame,

I have received your letter of today's date and its enclosure for Madame Hanife Bey Ghali. I have also had a report from one of my officers, and I am taking steps to improve the conditions under which the prisoners are living. As regards Zeghlul Pasha, I have no reason to believe that his health is otherwise than normal; but I hope to be able to give you news of him in a few days time.

Yours sincerely,

Allenby.

Saba Pasha, Ramleh
Sept. 5, 1922

To His Excellency
The Field Marshal, Lord Allenby
Bacos

Excellency,

We beg to thank your Excellency for the measures you have taken for bettering the conditions of the prisoners, especially your decision for their removal for better quarters soon.

We hear also that Zaghlul Pasha is now at Gibraltar, which climate is better than that of the Seychelles. But what about his companions? They have not been removed. Is it because there was no room on board ship for them, and you are removing them to join Zaghlul Pasha on the next boat, or ... but we dare not think it? Surely you don't mean to keep them in the Seychelles, separated from the old man? It will be just like dropping out of the frying pan into the fire. To be with one's companions in exile is the only consolation they have, and besides from the 15th of September the Seychelles' climate begins to be unbearable. As Mrs Fanous related to your Excellency, when the ladies' delegation visited you, the weather is unbearable during eight months of the year. Would it not be the completion of your kindness to remove them all to Gibraltar, to be together in an acceptable climate? I am sure it is not the nature of the conqueror of Palestine to mend matters in little bits. A big soul will award his opponents a fair fight, all comfort, and will feel kindly towards them in goodwill.

I do hope matters will mend soon. I wish you would save the country all these trials of the coming months, and go at it in the only right way. Nevertheless, I hope that when the present policy is carried through and fails, your Excellency will just fall back on the other method, and see how it will work. I sincerely hope it will be your Excellency who will carry the latter through. You know that only just, frank, straightforward, and free methods succeed in the end, and to get at the right people facilitates and strengthens future relations between countries.

I have a lot that I could tell you, but of course knowing that your Excellency is busy and perhaps cannot afford to give us some of your time, I do not venture to ask it of you. However, I count on your

374

goodwill and I hope to hear from your Excellency that the rest of the Seychelles exiles will be removed to join their leader.

Yours sincerely,

**Esther Fahmy Wissa**

Note: No answer was found to this letter among Esther's papers.

Shepheard's Hotel, Cairo
The 18th September, 1922

To His Excellency,
The Field Marshal, Lord Allenby
Ramleh

Excellency,

Many thanks for allowing me to visit my cousin George Bey Khayatt. Unfortunately I found him in a very bad state of health. He is diabetic and at present is suffering from boils, which in a case of that sort may become very serious. I was shocked at the change in him, but of course it is what might be expected in the case of a diabetic man leading a prison life. I very much fear that if he remains a few days more where he is, it will be the end of him.

Hamed Pasha El Bassel has bronchitis and fever, and the doctor is afraid that it might lead to tuberculosis.

Wassef Bey Ghali is weak and he has been in the hospital during most of his confinement. Morcos Bey Hanna is also being seen by the doctor.

Although the condition of the prisoners has been improved, thanks to your orders, yet their present state of living has been far from satisfactory.

The cells where they are enclosed are swarming with bugs, because George Bey Khayatt has told me he caught about a hundred one night. Their beds and coverings are those used in prison, naturally, and so they prefer sleeping uncovered although it is damp and sometimes cold at night.

On one occasion one of them had severe colic during the night, and it was quite three quarters of an hour before he could get help. They are under lock and key from six p.m. until the morning.

Naturally they can't take any supper as they lose their appetite enclosed in those tiny cells.

Now although they are allowed much more than at the beginning yet their remaining in the prison house cannot improve matters much. It is quite obvious that every exception made in their favour deranges the whole prison system, and it can neither be satisfactory to them nor convenient for the prison authorities. The only solution for them is to be removed at once so that things may be made normal in the prison and bearable for our political prisoners.

I cannot understand why your Excellency's decision for removing them to better quarters has not been carried out. It seems that the delay is made here, and deliberately. Would it be opportune of me to ask your Excellency to issue a telegraphic order tomorrow to have them removed at once. I assure you, Lord Allenby, that their condition is pitiful. They try to be brave before visitors but I was able to probe their real state of mind and body. I think the bugs are enough to make life unbearable at night in a tiny cell where you can't even run away from them.

If the house at Meadi is not quite ready for them we can fix it up for the present. We are ready to supply the necessary furniture, and the electric light can be fixed in a day or two, if proper means are taken, in the meantime it can be replaced by lamps.

If, on the other hand, you do not think the house at Meadi suitable then you might send them to the Kasr-el-Nil Barracks. They will be far better there than in that prison. The main thing is to remove them at once as I am afraid their state of health may become quite serious. I know that in cases of diabetes a boil may cause death any time and George Bey Khayatt looks nearer death than life.

As I am not closely acquainted with the others I cannot judge the great change in their appearance as others have done.

For humanity's sake and justice issue your orders tomorrow and please send me a wire as to your decision at my address in Cairo.

I assure you that I mean well and all my hope is that your country and mine can come to a full understanding.

Awaiting your answer I am

Yours sincerely,

**Esther Fahmy Wissa**

Answer - Egyptian State Telegraphs.

**Office of origin:** Bacos
**Receieved:** Ezbekia Office 19th September, 11.50 a.m.

Madame Fahmy Wissa, Shepheards Hotel, Cairo

It is hoped that arrangements will shortly be completed for transfer to other quarters meanwhile more suitable accommodation will be provided at present place.

**Allenby**

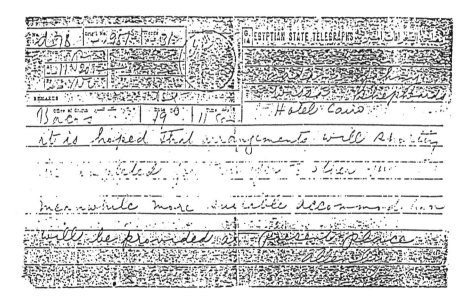

To His Excellency
The Field Marshal, Lord Allenby
Bacos

Excellency,

I heard lately that Madame Zaghlul Pasha has asked to join her husband as she received news from him that he was ill. I hope his illness is nothing serious, as anything that may happen to him may be attributed to his exile, and may cause a great bitterness of feeling in the country which would implicate any future relations. I myself who am the least "rancorous" of all my countrymen, may feel most bitter against the present policy, if Zaghlul Pasha were to die in exile.

I feel it my duty to convince your Excellency that the return of Zaghlul Pasha is absolutely necessary for the welfare of the country and the interests of Britain, at the present moment. In the case of any coming war it will be in the interest of both our countries to have some satisfactory agreement that will award us our claims of independence and on the other hand protect your vital interests in this country.

Zaghlul's influence, when once you settle matters fairly with him, will keep the country from any pro-Turkish movement and will facilitate matters for you.

On the other hand, if there is no war the present regime will not serve Great Britain. We believe, the idea of the present regime is to get rid of the influence of the Zaghlulists and thus obtain a majority in the coming elections, they would then succumb to England's terms for Egypt's independence by sanctioning it in the coming parliament. Now what you call the moderate party, are by far the great minority. They are mostly all opportunists who care nothing either for the English or for the real welfare of the country, or on the other hand, they are people who have no grit for fighting, and they believe in taking what they can until another war or chance may drive you out of Egypt.

The real Egyptian is not with them, and their parliamentary elections will not succeed, although Zaghlul and his party may be away, and the members of the Wafd are imprisoned. Yet there are many more Zaghlulists in the country and they are only restricted by the great suppression that is now being used. They will fight for liberty in the elections; even though the cabinet officials may try to use the Omdahs and officials to influence the people by threats and promises as they are wont to do.

Now for a good straightforward man like your Excellency this policy will not do. It will be more in your line to follow your own noble instincts and to allow the country full freedom, so that whatever treaty is enacted by the two governments, may be sound and firm, and may work out for the good of both parties.

Now Zaghlul's life is very precious to both you and us and we must do our best to protect it. Will it not be the most humane act and the most compatible with your nature to bring back the old man and his party and to free the political prisoners, and to allow full freedom in the country, and to see the result?

I assure you that the latter policy will be the safest. It is enough that it would take place under true and just principles, and can we ever be afraid ofo that?

Enough for man to do what is right and the rest may be left to God. As to the other method we will leave it to the intriguing mischevious souls who will reap the fruit of their actions one day, and may their consciences, if they have any, be their judges.

This is my true advice to you, Lord Allenby, because I am convinced that you are a good man, and although you felt justified in the measures you have taken lately because of the crimes committed against the English, yet I am certain you must feel the whip has fallen on the wrong people. It will be fairer to catch the real criminals and pubish them.

As to the Seychelles prisoners I hope your Excellency has already taken measures to remove them from that awful climate, which is starting to become unbearable and allow the country to have a real glimpse of your good heart, which is today screened behind the shadows of that awful Saroit regime.

Would your excellency kindly tell me now, if any such steps will be taken soon and if any hope may be envisaged by us of enjoying a reali liberal, democratic atmosphere during the elections?

I sincerely hope that a decision may already have been made and that I will have the first advantage of having the good news.

Yours sincerely,

**Esther Fahmy Wissa**

**Text of letter dated 25th of September, 1922, from Lord Allenby in reply to Esther Fahmy Wissa's letter of the same date.**

The Residency
Ramleh
25th Sept. 1922

Dear Madame Wissa,

In reply to your letter of today:- I have no reason to suppose that the health of Zaghlul Pasha is any worse; but I am glad that Madame Zaghlul is going to join him. I thank you for the advice you give me in your letter, and I am sure that you mean all you say; but I regret I cannot do as you wish.

Yours sincerely,
**Allenby**

380

Oct 18th 1922

To His Excellency
The Field Marshal, Lord Allenby
Ramleh

Excellency,

A letter has just reached me from members of the family of William Effendi Makram, with a copy of the report of his health, sent to your Excellency today, made by a consultation of four medical men, one of whom was his private doctor before his exile.

From that report and Makram Effendi's telegram to Dr Sobhy, it seems that his health is far from satisfactory; in fact his case seems serious, and worthy of immediate consideration.

Would it be inappropriate of me to trouble your Excellency another time to look into the matter?

It seems that the Seychelles' climate is unsuitable to the health of these Egyptian gentlemen, and as individuals they seem to be sufferers from some complaint or other. Now under these circumstances, I am sure your Excellency will not hesitate to put in a word for their immediate removal from the Seychelles. It is quite obvious that no great political advantage will be gained in keeping them in a place which threatens their health every moment. Political reasons may tend to keep them away from their country, but no reason can justify exposing them to any sort of discomfort or conditions that may undermine their health.

The case seems to be very serious and I am certain that your Excellency does not need persuasion for their immediate removal.

Makram Effendi's family have sent your Excellency the report of his health through your secretary. They are very anxious that it reaches you at once, as they are greatly worried about his health. Would your Excellency kindly let me know that it has reached you, and that you are taking steps for removing these exiles from the Seychelles to a place where their health will not suffer.

I am certain that your Excellency is not the man to neglect looking at once into a humane act, and I have not yet lost hope that you will soon turn the wheel towards a different policy which will be more consistent with the nature of a man like your Excellency, and which will tend to strengthen relations between your country and ours, through the right people.

381

Hoping to have the pleasure of hearing good news from you.
I am
Yours sincerely
**Esther Fahmy Wissa**

**Letter dated October 20th, 1922, from the First Secretary at the Residency in reply to a letter dated October 18th, 1922, to Lord Allenby from Esther Fahmy Wissa.**

No.16017/18

THE RESIDENCY,

RAMLEH.

October 20th, 1922.

Madam,

I am directed by His Excellency the High Commissioner to acknowledge the receipt of your letter of October 18th concerning the health of William Makram effendi.

I am to inform you that Lord Allenby has telegraphed to the Governor of the Seychelles acquainting him with the opinion of the four medical men to whom you allude, and asking him to have Makram effendi medically examined and to report the result.

I am, Madam,

Your Obedient Servant,

FIRST SECRETARY.

Mrs.Fahmi Wissa Bey,
 Saba Pasha,
  Ramleh.

Dahabieh Queen
Kasr-el-Debarah, Cairo
April 19, 1923

To His Excellency,
   The Field Marshal, Lord Allenby,
   Cairo

Excellency,
   I should like to have an interview with your Excellency before I leave for Alexandria on Saturday. Would it be convenient for you to give me an appointment?
   We appreciate the first good step you have taken on behalf of Zaghlul Pasha, and we hope this will be the beginning of a new and more effective policy for establishing good relations between our two countries.
   Yours sincerely,
   **Esther Fahmy Wissa**

**Text of letter from the Private Secretary of Lord Allenby dated April 19th, 1923, in reply to a letter by Esther Fahmy Wissa of the same date.**

The Residency
Cairo

April 19th, 1923

Madame,

With reference to your letter of today. I am to say that Lord Allenby
will be glad to see you tomorrow, Friday, at 11 a.m.
If this hour is <u>not</u> convenient to you, would you be so kind as to telephone to me?

Your Obedient Servant
**signature**
Private Secretary

**Copy of letter found among Esther Fahmy Wissa's papers from the Private Secretary of Lord Allenby dated May 29th, 1923 in reply to a letter from Esther dated May 23th of which no copy was found.**

No.14083/·y

THE RESIDENCY,

C A I R O.

May 29th, 1923.

Madam,

      I am directed by Lord Allenby to acknowledge the receipt of your letter of May 23rd, on the subject of the release of certain prisoners now interned.

I am, Madam,

Your Obedient Servant,

*Cratwell.*

PRIVATE SECRETARY.

Mme.Esther Fahmy Wissa,
    Saba Pasha,
      Ramleh,
        Alexandria.

The Residency,
Ramleh.

27th July, 1923

Dear Madame Wissa,

In reply to your letter of today's date:-
I regret that my time is so fully occupied that I cannot have  the pleasure of seeing you before I leave.  I go early on the 29th.
You may rest assured, however, that you have my sympathy and I am keenly anxious that Saad Pasha Zaghlul may come to an agreement with the British Government.

    Yours sincerely,
    **Allenby**

Note: No letter was found among Esther's papers to her letter of the same date referred to by Lord Allenby.

27th July.

Dear Madame Nina,

In reply to your letter
of today's date :—

I regret that my time
is so fully occupied that I
cannot have the pleasure of
seeing you before I leave.
I go away on the 29th —

You may rest assured, however,
that you have my sympathy;
and I am keenly anxious that
Saad Pasha Zaghloul may
come to an agreement with
the British Government.

Yours sincerely

Allenby.

388

The Residency,
Ramleh
Egypt

October 8, 1924

Dear Madame Fahmy Wissa,

I shall be delighted to go to tea with you on Saturday.  My many
thanks.

Alas!  I have no wife, but I will bring the young man you scolded
so severely about that admirable Sudan irrigation scheme.

Yours sincerely,
**A. C. Kerr**

Ramleh
October 16, 1924

Dear Madame Fahmy Wissa,

I was so very sorry not to be able to accept your kind invitation to dinner. It was charming of you to have thought of it and I hope that you will think of it again some time.

Unhappily I have some Zionists from Jerusalem dining with me tonight and on Saturday I am engaged to dine in your own Zaghlulist circles.

My many thanks all the same.

We all enjoyed your tea party very much.

Yours sincerely,

*[handwritten reproduction of the same letter follows]*

The Residency
Cairo

2nd November, 1924

Dear Madame Wissa,

Many thanks for your letter of 29th Oct. My wife and I are both well; and have had a pleasant voyage and a good holiday. I, too, am sorry that there have been no fruitful negotiations between our two governments; as we are all anxious for a satisfactory agreement. I am interested in all you say; but you make a mistake in regarding me as a politician or a partisan, nor am I - as you seem to think - afraid of doing right:- though I thank you for your advice.

If you will lend me your "Vision on the Ideal Commonwealth", I shall be very pleased and grateful.

Yours sincerely,
**Allenby**

Note: No letter to Lord Allenby dated 29th October, 1924, was found among Esther's letters to which he refers in his letter dated 2nd November, 1924.

**THE RESIDENCY,
CAIRO.**

HIGH COMMISSIONER
FOR EGYPT.

Dear Madame Nina,

Many thanks for your letter of 29th Oct. My Wife & I are both well; and have had a pleasant voyage & a good holiday. I, too, am sorry that there has been no fruitful negotiation between our two Governments; &c. We are all anxious for a satisfactory agreement. I am interested in all you say; but you make a mistake in regarding me as a politician or a partisan, nor am I, as you seem to think, afraid of doing right:— though I thank you for your advice.

If you will lend me your "Vision on Indeed Commonwealth," I shall be very pleased & grateful.

Yrs sincerely

Allenby

392

The Residency
Cairo

9th November, 1924

Dear Madame Wissa,

I thank you for your letter of 7th instant, and for the "Vision of the Ideal Commonwealth", which I return herewith. I have read it with great interest. It is a high ideal; and I wish I could think it practical, but I cannot, I am not therefore, able to advise you as to whether or where you should publish it.

Sincerely yours,
**Allenby**

Note: No letter to Lord Allenby dated 7th November, 1924, was found among Esther's letters to which he refers in his letter dated

9th Nov! /24 -

THE RESIDENCY,
CAIRO

Dear Madame Weisa,

I thank you for your
letter of 7. inst. and for the
"Vision of the Ideal Commonwealth"
etc. I return herewith.
I have read it with great
interest. It is a high ideal,
& I wish I could think it prac-
-tical, but I cannot.
I am not, therefore, able to
advise you as to whether or
where you should publish
it. Sincerely yours -

Allenby

394

The Continental-Savoy
Cairo
Nov. 24, 1924

To His Excellency
  The Field Marshal, Lord Allenby
  Cairo

Excellency,

Sir Lee Stack Pasha has died, and his death was a great blow to the Egyptian nation, not because of the political outcome, but because it was a dastardly crime, and a plot meant to hit the nation in its most vital spot. We mourn the man personally as he was good and gentle, and it is a pity that righteous men have to suffer for the unrighteous. However I sincerely hope that the crime will be brought home to its originator, and that the criminals will receive due punishment.

But be sure that no man who is working for the country, has had anything to do with it. This crime has been instigated for self-interest only, and at the expense of the country.

But what I cannot measure, fathom, or understand, is the last action of the British Government. What political result are you going to gain from it? The idea of casting terror in the hearts of the people is too old-fashioned and most gainless. We are not afraid, and we're never going to be afraid. Our belongings and our lives are at your disposal and you can go right ahead. A man who "loves father, mother, son or daughter, more than his principles, is not worthy of them, and he who puts his hand on the plough does not look backwards."

Of course Sir Lee Stack's murder is only an excuse for a policy that has been coveted and desired from the beginning, and all the world knows that. We know that all this has to happen. It has been foreseen and foretold. "It is impossible but that offenses will come; but woe unto him, through whom they come."

Personally, I think that all clever British politicians are dead and your people are making a mess of everything. The present policy is not our loss, although we may lose money, life and other things but it is for your detriment. "You", of course, does not apply personally, it is British policy.

I believe that you are the "rod of God's indignation" against the peoples whom He wants to bless, Egypt, Assyria and Israel.

He has delivered them up into your hands, so that through your oppression and the fire of your affliction, they may come to understand the secret of living and the will of God; but their salvation is sure and the day is drawing nigh. Do read Isaiah, 10 and 19 and note that although Chapter 10 has been once fulfilled, yet it is linked with the millennium and that has not yet come. Then read Daniel 11:40.

The old Imperialistic system of Government is too antique for the present generation, and it is now reeling like a drunkard. People are revolting, and this system is avenging itself. It shall have a last fight, but a terrible one, and those who are standing for liberty, righteousness and truth are going to suffer. Greed, covetousness and the love of gain are at the bottom of it all, and nations are showing their true colours. Clever politicians shielded those colours from people's eyesight in the past, but in this last fight, they cannot do it any more.

Go ahead, British policy, but go home, Lord Allenby. This situation is not for you. I should not like the man I have honoured and respected and known as genuinely good, to carry on the coming policy. Let a wicked man come, and hurry up with it. And if you and I live in some future years we may talk the past over again.

I may not see your Excellency again, so I wish you goodbye, and good wishes.

Yours sincerely,
**Esther Fahmy Wissa**

The Residency,
Cairo

24th Nov, 1924

Dear Madame Wissa,

Many thanks for your letter of today; and I greatly appreciate the kind references to Sir Lee Stack.

As you know, I am not a politician; so I will not discuss controversial points with you. I have read the chapters in Isaiah and Daniel, of which you speak; but I confess that I have never been able to understand prophecy. Again I thank you for your words of friendship towards myself; and I am with sincere good wishes.

Yours truly,
**Allenby**

28th Feb., 1925

To His Excellency
    The Field Marshal, Lord Allenby
    Cairo

Excellency,

I wonder if it pays for people to continue misunderstanding. After all, it seems to me that all great calamities the world has known have accrued out of misunderstanding, or the refusal of some to understand the real situation.

I am afraid that the present policy in Egypt will only end in disaster. It is apparent that England has not yet taken in, the real nature of the Egyptian political movement. She thinks that in destroying Zaghlul's position in Egypt, she will be able to settle the question, but this is far from right.

Believe me, Lord Allenby that what I am telling you is sincere, because I cannot be otherwise, and it is only the desire to save you, and us, so much unnecessary trouble that pushes me in spite of everything to plead with you.

If Zaghlul is broken, the Egyptian movement will still continue. We are determined that even at the cost of our life, our country is going to be saved. That does not mean saved from English Occupation only, but saved from itself. We want to teach our people real democratic government based on true foundations of justice and liberty. We want to make of this people an honest, straightforward living nation that is worthy to carry the name of this ancient and wonderful land.

I think you can sympathise with our aspirations, and in spite of the great odds that are against us in every way, I am sure your Excellency can appreciate the sentiments that spur us on to fight, never giving up hope, never relenting, until Egypt realises her true claims for independence.

Believe me that it is not England's hate that actuates our feelings, but Egypt's love, and we wish that England had tried to make of us a real honest people. We reproach British policy in Egypt for ignoring this fact, and now, after all we read in your papers and the statements in your parliament, we do not really know how we stand with each other. To thwart our hopes and induce us to give up our national rights is an impossibility. To make us believe that the crumbs of independence which you are willing to throw us are a boon is unthinkable. Our full rights are sacred, and our minds are made up to realise them if not today, then tomorrow.

We regret the principles on which the Egyptian administration is working today, for which we blame England. If she had not wished to back these treacherous doings, we would have been able to regulate matters between us according to Constitutional Law. But the purpose for which British policy aims is not going to succeed. The only efficacious methods England could ever use with Egyptians were the honest, straightforward ones. We gave you no trouble in the past, because we believed that you were capable of all good, but now, that the Englishman is not true to himself, he has become of no value in our eyes.

Do not forget that Egyptians are not an ordinary Oriental race. They are the remains of an ancient and highly civilised people, and although they have been buffeted by every political wind, yet the nucleus of ancient civilisation is in them and they are a problem.

I am an Egyptian, brought up in Western ways and I can thoroughly understand our point of view and yours.

It would have been only consistent with our aspirations that relations would have been linked by a friendly treaty between us both, and I daresay if the conditions were favourable to our complete rights we would have been true to any enacted agreement recognised by our own people; but England's material ambitions and her Imperialistic requirements, seem to have blindfolded her to right, therefore we are at a sword's end today.

An Empire is alright, when it is carried on old honest methods with an older fashioned mentality, but today an Empire can only be the human bond, and spirit of cooperation that ties people together, in love of some universal interest and good. England had a chance of carrying out that policy, but now that every one suspects her, I do not know if she will be able to regain confidence.

The position all over the world is bad today and I do not know if we can hope for peace. I am afraid great world trouble is at the door, and what will England's position be? Her salvation only can come through her renunciation of selfish ambitions, and realisation of all human hopes, both internal and external and this reminds me of the wisdom of the saying, "Agree with thy adversary quickly, whilst thou art in the way with him; lest at any time the adversary deliver thee to the judge and the judge deliver thee to the officer and thou be cast into prison. Verily I say unto thee, Thou shalt by no means come out thence, till thou hast paid the uttermost farthing."

And after all the higher Judge is above, and He must regulate the accounts of the oppressed and the oppressor, so will England still tread on other people's rights?

I leave it to your Excellency to hold up the cause of right, and this is a far more superior cause to fight for than the invasion of any land.

The service that will be done to your country, will even be greater than the service done to our people. So won't England's famous soldier act?

Yours sincerely,
**Esther Fahmy Wissa**


Cairo
28th Feb, 1925

Dear Madame Wissa,

I thank you for your letter of today's date containing your views on the present situation. I can but hope that the future is not so gloomy as you fear.

Yours sincerely,
**Allenby**

Cairo
28th Feb?

Dear Madame Wissa,
I thank you for your letter
of today's date — containing
your views on the present
situation — . I can but
hope that the future is not
so gloomy as you fear.

Yrs sincerely

Allenby

401

St. George, Ramleh
March 5, 1925

To His Excellency
The Field Marshal, Lord Allenby
Cairo

Excellency,

You may remember that soon after your return last Autumn, I told you in one of my letters "Never to be afraid of doing right. Right will always right itself," and you answered that you were never afraid of doing right.

I should like to ask your Excellency if you really think that the British policy that you are carrying out today is right?

For one thing you are indignant at that terrible murder of the Sirdar, and we are more indignant than you. How could it ever have occurred to you that Zaghlul's party should have had a hand in it? Some murderous designers in this country are exploiting you, they count on your hatred of the nationalist movement, and your mistrust of the Zaghlulists believing them to be able of committing crimes, these they commit and try to lay the blame on the Zaghlulists. If you fail to find out who these murderous hands, are and apply justice to them, then you are falling short of doing right. All the wickedness in Egypt is exploiting you, and still British policy in Egypt favours it. The terrible breaches of the Constitution which are carried out in Egypt today by the treacherous hands that you are always falling back on, to carry out your policy, can only be attributed to the British authorities. The blame does not really fall on them as we know them as genuinely bad, but all the blame falls on the authorities that put them in power, and of course in the end your policy will be the sufferer.

England reached her wonderful world position on the shoulders of those honest pious Englanders, who always stood up for justice and truth, but when her men now fail to carry on this sound and moral policy England's position will greatly suffer. The brave Englishman's wonderful pledge to "Ride abroad redressing human wrongs," cannot be changed today to "Ride abroad exploiting human wrongs," and succeed.

No one can understand your position, Lord Allenby, and can sympathise with you as well as myself, but because you think our

402

interests clash, you abandon the honest people of Egypt, and back the dishonest ones. What a mess this policy is making! An honest man like you, is made to carry out a false policy and is blamed because it fails! I should like one of your wonderful British Conservative ministers that are in power today, to try this position and see how they could unravel it. But this is always the way, and England always uses her men as tools.

Tell them Lord Allenby, that an Egyptian lady says that British policy is like a wheel whose central axis is all wrong, but whose spokes are honest, and it is only through the sincere convictions of these honest spokes that she is able to move; and tell them that the day these honest spokes find her out, England will fail. So her salvation can only be when these honourable spokes insist on changing the axis to righteous ends.

All the world is moving onwards today, thoughts are changing, ideas are developing, a great evolution of thought is racing upwards, and England is standing still. And when things are not moving on as she wants them, she is losing her head, and is falling back on old blunted tools.

An Englishman can only move straight, because he is not treacherously clever and wily enough to move on crooked paths, so the day he misses the main road and tries the winding paths, he will lose his way, and this is what British policy is doing today.

My heart is sore over my country and yours, but I see more light for my country than for yours. We are moving upwards, because there is an honest voice heard here; you are moving downwards because you have missed the way. Tell your politicians that, and tell them that an Egyptian lady says it. And believe me that it is only my great conviction and desire that a just and sound basis of government may be established all over the world for the good of mankind; and an honest sympathetic alliance may be enacted by our two governments for the welfare of my people, and the satisfaction of yours that make me come to you, and I often wonder if you are not the man who is going to help Egypt.

Egypt is very dear to me, and the poorest little fellah is like my own child, and I am going to work for him, even if it costs my life. But of course, only on the highway of equity and righteousness. So will your Excellency not join hands with me in the creation of a new wonderful Egypt? It is not futile, it must come to pass, so we are on a sure path, and I should like your name to come down in history as a real great man.  Do you think it is worthwhile?

Yours sincerely,

**Esther Fahmy Wissa**

**Copy of letter from Private Secretary, dated 10th March 1925**

THE RESIDENCY,

CAIRO,

10th March, 1925.

Madam,

   — I am directed by the High Commissioner to acknowledge the receipt of your letter to His Excellency of March 5th.

I have the honour to be,

Madam,

Your obedient Servant,

*a. ƎH wiqq m*

PRIVATE SECRETARY.

Madam Esther Fahmy Wissa,
   St. George,
    Ramleh,
     Alexandria.

To His Excellency
The Field Marshal, Lord Allenby
Cairo

Excellency,

Now that the elections have again resulted in a majority of Zaghlulists in spite of all the atrocious pressure of the administration, your Excellency can understand how strong the nationalist movement is in the country. Egypt has changed, a new spirit reigns today; we are all ready for sacrifice where before we fled from sacrificing the least thing.

Believe me it is futile to crush nationalism in Egypt, so the only thing England can do with impunity is to encourage the rights of the people, the fellah, and to see that in no way their rights can be tampered with by that levantine mixture of Pashas. They are the real danger to the country, and they will be the biggest menace to British interests in the future if they are not kept within Constitutional laws which must be strictly applied. It is quite plausible, that influential men that are willing to crush the country's aspirations so unscrupulously today violating all laws to please a foreign power, can only betray the country, and you yourselves will always run the risk of being betrayed, too.

Believe me that he who is honest against you will be honest with you, and vice versa, and these men are not even honest to themselves. I know that they are thinking of changing the electoral laws and limiting them to the tax payers and the literate, leaving out the poor fellah who is really the honest element in the country. The danger of this is unlimited.

For God's sake, stand up for the fellah as your country has always professed doing, and believe me these people have no real influence in the country now. They are corrupting it. But I hope you will not encourage that any longer. There are honest people in Egypt today who are going to stand up for the people, but I should like you to prove to my countrymen that the British really are not as bad as they think, and the only way you could do this is to encourage a sound democratic government, in spite of these unscrupulous men.

This is the only sound advice I can give you, because I know that real independence will never be given us; we will have to get it and the only way to it is the way of self-sacrifice and righteousness and it is really in your interest that we should move on this road. "An honest independent Egypt as an ally will be more serviceable to you than an unprincipled dependency." Therefore, I hope that in defending the rights of the mass of Egyptians, you will, help us to make real honest men in this country who will be a help to humanity instead of a hindrance.

I wonder if these suggestions I have given you will be acceptable. I do not know, but be sure that our ways are not really so far apart. My country and yours cannot really do without each other; we produce raw material, you manufacture same and we must work together on a basis of voluntary cooperation. But my people must be raised up morally and it will take some effort to do it.

Will your Excellency help, or must I have another futher obstacles to fight against? I leave it to your big soldier spirit and your honest, upright character.

Yours sincerely,
**Esther Fahmy Wissa**


Note: No reply has been found among Esther's papers to this letter.

To His Excellency
   The Field Marshal, Lord Allenby
   Cairo

Excellency,

If I have delayed in expressing my heartfelt regrets for your departure, it is because I have been ill. I was down with Typhoid Fever for two months, and have just recently come down to my home in Ramleh for convalescence. In fact this is the first time I have taken up a pen to write.

We do, regret your departure, although my advice to your Excellency was to resign your post, and I think you can now infer that it was my friendly regard for your person that made me tell you so, and that at the risk of our own peace and temporary welfare. For we believe that Egypt's great tribulation has begun, and I did not care for my esteemed friend, and the real good man you are, to stand up as God's ordained whip for my country. Yes, Egypt is going to suffer, and greatly, but it is for my people's final welfare. Through suffering, they shall know the real things that matter in life and their morals shall be raised higher.

For what purpose was I spared in this long illness, I do not know? I hope for honest and loyal service of my country, which I think will need a great deal, and I still have hopes that in you, one of England's great men, Egypt may find a friend and an advocate who will plead for this poor country, fallen prey to political intrigue, with no one to hold it up, not even some of its own men.

And can I rightly say that although your Excellency, in following British policy, has had to stand on the adverse side of the political view, I have adopted in my country's interest, yet I can say that I always felt that the gulf of difference between us could be bridged, and we have been able to meet across it and shake hands above it as friends.

We are living in a wonderful historical time, and the pangs and travails that the world is undergoing will only be the birth pains of a new era, where all egoism and strife will be removed, and when humanity will only recognise itself, and then perhaps individuals like you and I can talk the past over again, as a horrible nightmare that should never have taken place.

I would have liked to have said "Goodbye" to your Excellency and to Lady Allenby, but I shall not be able to go to Cairo and I do not know if your Excellency will be in Alexandria.

However, I should be delighted and greatly honoured to receive you in my home, so if you could possibly spare the time to pay me a little visit, I should count it a great favour.

You may rest assured however, of my good wishes to you and my sincere friendship as well as my great estimation of your high qualities; and in spite of the differences that exist between our two nations today, I hope you and I may do each other a good turn, for who knows what the future may hold for us. Of course, it can only be based on absolute confidence we can have in one another, and I think we cannot doubt the integrity of our dispositions.

May God bless you and yours, and may He provide for us a happy, worthy future and a good recompense for all our aspirations.

And in wishing you happy and prosperous days, I beg to convey my kindest regards and best wishes to Lady Allenby, whom I have not had the pleasure of knowing better.

Yours sincerely,
**Esther Fahmy Wissa**

The Residency
Cairo

3rd June, 1925

Dear Madame Wissa,

I thank you for your letter of yesterday's date, and am grateful for your kind words about myself. I regret to hear that you have been so ill, but hope that you are making good progress towards complete recovery.

It is with great sorrow that I leave Egypt; but I shall always take a keen interest in Egyptian affairs, and I hope to revisit Egypt in the near future.

My wife joins me in kindest remembrance and best wishes.

Yours sincerely,
**Allenby**

Dear Madame Wissa,

I thank you for your letter of yesterday's
date, and am grateful for your kind words
about myself. I regret to hear that you
have been so ill, but hope that you are
making good progress towards complete
recovery. It is with sorrow that I
leave Egypt; but I shall always take
a keen interest in Egyptian affairs, and
hope to revisit Egypt in the near future

My Wife joins me in kindest remembrances
and best wishes.

Yours sincerely,

Allenby.

410

The Residency,

Cairo.

June 7th, 1925.

Dear Madame Wissa,

I have shown your letter to the High
Commissioner, who is very sorry that your invitation
should have reached you too late.     From our
records it seems to have been despatched in time.

Viscount Allenby warmly reciprocates your kind
wishes, and much regrets that he cannot visit
Alexandria and avail himself himself of your hospitality
before his departure for England on June 14th.  He
assumes that you will have by now received your letter
from him in reply to your's of a few days ago.

With kindest regards,

Believe me yours sincerely

*Arthur Wiggin*

411

**Copy letter from Oriental Secretary**

No.14083/25.

THE RESIDENCY,

CAIRO.

November 11th, 1925.

Madam,

      I am directed by His Excellency the High Commissioner to acknowledge with thanks the receipt of your letter dated November 1st.

      I am,

        Madam,

          Your obedient servant,

          ORIENTAL SECRETARY.

Mme. E. Fahmy Wissa,

    St. George,

        Ramleh.

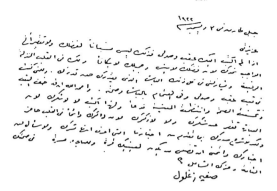

**Translation of a letter sent to Esther Fahmy Wissa from Safia Hanem Zaghloul wife of Saad Pasha Zaghloul. It was sent from Gibralter dated 3rd December 1922. They had been transferred to Gibraltar from the Seychelles where Saad had been exiled by the British who now felt that the weather in the Seychelles might be bad for his health.**

Gibraltar          3rd December 1922

My dearest,

If I have not written to you as soon as I arrived, it was not because I forgot your kindness, nor was it for want of performing my duty towards you, because your services cannot be forgotten nor your favours ignored. You have a special exalted place in my heart. The Pasha feels the same way towards you, and he has the highest appreciation for your virtues. But I was very tired on our arrival and preoccupied with the Pasha's health, but thank God that we are less tired, and our health is improving slowly, and our life is becoming more normal, and that is why I am able to write to you to thank you, but words are not able to express our thanks, or to forget you, for your memory is always present in our hearts. I know that you will feel happy to receive our news, we also ask how are you keeping? We wish that your eye should shed no tear, nor a hurt enter your life, and may you have perfect health and prosperity throughout.

Safia Zaghloul

413

دار الكتب الجمهورية العربية

مكتب الرئيس

السيد، استر فهمى وصــــا

تحية طيبة    وبعد

نقد وانني رسالتك ا وانى اذ اشكر لك تهنئتك الطيبة

برئاستى للجمهورية المصرية .

ولعلك قرأت نصوص الدستور ووقفت منها على اتجاهاتنـا

الاقتصادية والاجتماعية والسياسية المبينة فى كـــــتـاب

" روح الدستور " وهى اتجاهات قريب من الاشتراكية المعتدلة

لا الاشتراكية التى خشيتها فى كتابك .

وانى أن هذا الاتجاه هو الذى يخفف من وطأة التطرف

والحركات اليسارية الهدمة .

وثق أن كل مشروع وكل تخطيط اقتصادى انما يقوم على

دراسة ذوى الخبرة والجدين والخبراء العالميين .

وبالله أمــــال التوفيــق والسـدبـــد .

والله اكبر والعزة لمصــر .

القاهرة فى ٥ / ٨ / ١٩٥٦

رئيـــس الجمهوريـــة

---

## Translation of letter addressed to Mrs. Esther Fahmy Wissa by the late President Gamal Abdel Nasser dated 5/8/56

Mrs. Esther Fahmy Wissa,

After ....... our best regards.

I received your letter in which you expressed your heartiest congratulations for my election as President of the Republic.

You will be aware of the articles of the constitution, and will have realised our trend of thought, in Economic, Social, and Political matters as laid down in the book "The Spirit of the Constitution" which is oriented towards a balanced Socialism, not the type of Socialism that you were afraid of.

I think that such a program will lessen the possibility of political extremism, and destructive left wing movements.

Please believe me that any Economic project or plan envisaged by us is based on a comprehensive study by dedicated specialists proficient in their field and the expertise of World Wide Authorities.

I pray to the Almighty for concord.

God is Great and Prosperity to Egypt.

President of the Republic
Signed Gamal Abdel Nasser

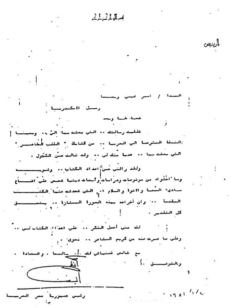

## Translation of letter from President Anwar el Saddat to Mrs. Esther Fahmy Wissa dated 20th January 1981.

## IN THE NAME OF GOD THE ALL MERCIFUL AND COMPASSIONATE
### The President

Mrs. Esther Fahmy Wissa,

Heartiest Greetings.

I received your letter sent me, and with it your translated book into Arabic "The Virgin Heart" which you sent me as a present, and which I appreciate and accept with pleasure.

I noticed its exceptional structure and the different religious subjects and studies it contained which advocate principles such as love, brotherhood and peace. All of which have been related in the Holy Books, I congratulate you on its presentation in this excellent manner, which deserves full appreciation.

I thank you once again, for dedicating this book to me, and to the good feelings you express towards me.

With my best wishes to you for health happiness and success.

Anwar El Saddat
President of the Egyptian Arab Republic

# Appendix 1

Translation of a letter sent to George Bey Khayatt member of a prominent Coptic family, from Saad Zaghloul dated the 24th November 1918, barely a few days after Saad Zaghloul had made his momentous demand that he should head a delegation to the Peace Conference at Versaille to ask for the abolition of the Protectorate and granting Egypt complete independence. The significance of this letter demonstrates the unity of thought between Copts and Moslems vis-a-vis Egypt's national aspirations. And the concern by the majority of informing the minority that there would be complete equality in an Independent Egypt.

=========================================

His Excellency George Bey Khayatt member of the Egyptian Delegation (the Wafd) On the occasion of new members joining the delegation (Wafd) I made the following statement: "I thank all newly joined members for cooperating with us, and especially their Excellencies George Bey Khayatt and Sinut Bey Hanna, for in doing so, they revealed their belief in the honour of our aims and the worthiness of our cause; and in their joining hands with us in the struggle for the welfare of the Egyptian nation, it reveals that there is no difference in its components or creeds.

Such sentiments cannot be received except with honour and estimation, for it reflects a reality and a comprehension of all we stand for and our firm intentions, to make no distinction between the majority and the minority, as we consider we are all members of one nation who have equal rights both in civic and political domains, each according to his own ability. For without such interpretation there is no true independence which should appear as clear as light. This statement was approved unanimously.

As you were not present at this meeting I wished to inform you of the above.'

Saad Zaghloul:   Head of the Egyptian Delegation (Wafd)
24th November 1918

# Appendix 2

*An open letter to Lord Milner's Commission*

Gentlemen,

Egypt has finally decided not to interview your honourable commission as long as it comes under the name of the British Protectorate in Egypt. Representing the women of Egypt, we are also definitely agreed on that point. However, we would like to give you a fair idea of the present situation of Egypt, as it really is. Many have given their opinions on the 'why and what' of the Egyptian Movement, but though some have slightly touched on the truth, yet the whole is far from the truth.

The Egyptian Movement is wholly and thoroughly a patriotic movement, void of all religious, or Turkish influence. It has absolutely nothing to do with Bolshevism, and it is not an indirect outcome of the high cost of living, as some have declared. The country is in an excellent financial condition, and with a 'good deal of charity' and generosity our poor are provided for, as his Lordship is aware.

The Egyptian Movement is purely patriotic. Lord Milner in his book 'England in Egypt' spoke of the improbability of a revolution in Egypt. He considers the Arabi Revolution as the *strongest proof of the intensity of old misgovernment*, and he may be right. We may take it then that to-day's revolution is the *strongest proof of British misgovernment in Egypt*. Truthfully speaking, we can say that misgovernment was not the immediate cause of the present movement, but we cannot deny, that it had its part in arousing the dormant qualities of our ancient race. Egypt is the land of *paradox* as Lord Milner says, and it is not strange to see unexpected things suddenly happen. The spark of patriotic greatness, smothered for so many centuries, by the ashes of numerous invasions, and subdued by the influence of a darker civilization, than that which it enjoyed, in its own times, has existed all along.

British influence, though indirectly, and twentieth century civilisation directly, have helped, no doubt, to clear away these aches, and the late British misgovernment, and wrongful policy, have supplied the fuel for the present flame in Egypt. (We thank Great Britain, for so doing).

England has boasted of well governing Egypt for the past years. WE THANK ENGLAND. Prestige had a great deal to do with England's success through as Lord Milner says 'There is no such thing as prestige'. It was not the prestige of military power that preserved the docility and pacific disposition of the race, during British rule (Egyptians do not fear guns); it was the prestige of England's good reputation. The Egyptian honoured the

418

Englishman in former times because he lived under the delusion that the Englishman never commits anything dishonourable or dishonest.

He ranked the Englishman as the embodiment of truthfulness, honesty, justice, and other good qualities. He considered him as the man of fair play, who always keeps his word. His defects of course, he also knew extreme egoism and pride. The Egyptian looked up to the Englishman along with the well-known courtesy of the East, which perhaps accounted for the *hasty buttoning up of the jacket to the chin*, of the small 'effendi' when approached by a superior official, and which was mistakenly taken as a token of servility, which made a *most unfavourable impression on the typical Briton*. Nevertheless admiration leads to imitation, and imitation in time leads to acquirement, and even a delusionary reputation has its good effect on the admirer, and as even the small 'effendi' has gradually grown these qualities, whose roots have always existed in his heart, and it is all thanks to the British Occupation.

England has declared time after time, that her occupation in Egypt was temporary, and, of a philanthropic nature. Lord Milner has confirmed this view of the occupation when he said, that it is *exact opposite of the truth that the power of England is used without regard for the feelings and welfare of the people, and, with the sole object of furthering her own commercial interests, and paving the way to annexation*. Other English politicians have repeatedly declared their policy in the same tone, and we cannot understand why England has failed to stand by her word.

Imagine, Honourable Gentlemen the impression that England's policy has left on our minds. Her actions of late justify the conclusion we arrived at, and will you excuse us for putting it bluntly into words.

England *must* have come with the *sole object of furthering her own commercial interests, and, paving the way to annexation.*

England's ambition *was* to annex Egypt. It must have been only the fear of clashing with the interests of other great powers, that made her pretend otherwise, at that time, England entered Egypt on false pretexts.

She did not enter as a conqueror which would have been frank and more honourable; she seems to have preferred carrying out her policy by false declaration, she deprived all Egyptians of their arms; then under Martial Law, declared her protectorate, over Egypt. We were simply stolen in the dead of night, from our place with other powers. If England sees this as it really is, we still hope that she will not tread on her spirit of manliness and bravery and accept this abominable position. Furthermore, England cannot still the voice of our just protestations. From henceforth, we can only be governed by military force, and by that alone, and that is what British protection is amount to.

Egypt on the other hand, living under delusion believed England, she counted on her word of honour. She never suspected. She gave England every help. She furnished all requirements of the army in Palestine. She gave her men, her beasts, and her corps. She became the military centre of the British army in the East, and all in goodwill, in confidence counting on England's honour and England's sense of justice.

She found out, but only too late alas: that in helping to crush imperialism in Germany, she had fallen into the jaws of a greater imperialism, and this was the nation on whom she lavished her confidence and affection.

Do you wonder then, most Honourable Gentlemen; that Egypt protests, that Egypt now suspects and distrusts, that Egypt cannot and will not parley with you; your sense of British traditions alone can answer you and we hope they will.

Representing Egypt's mothers, sisters and daughters, we would inform you that there are only two alternatives to the EGYPTIAN QUESTION: England must either keep up to her reputation and reconquer our respect and friendship, or in other words, stand by her word, a word she signed, and endorsed. England should abolish immediately the Protectorate, and should give Egypt her just claim of INDEPENDENCE. If so, England shall be our friend, our benefactor and everything that is desirable and compatible with our complete independence. She will still have a hand, as the promoter of the welfare of Egypt, thus helping the children of the Pharaohs to live to the virtues and traditions of their great fathers. Are we not worth the trial.

The other alternative, and it will be a sad one, will be, – England blinded by greed and love of material gain, will crush the sense of honour and will take Egypt first stealthily, and then by force.

Our protests will be met by firearms as we have already witnessed England has enough power to do so with her army, navy, and aerodromes. But we shall protest, and protest. We shall fight armless; our blood shall soak the soil of our fathers, and we shall die happy.

Perhaps our history in the time of the Romans and afterwards endorses these last words. Do not forget Honourable Gentlemen, the one hundred thousand martyrs, at the time of Diocletian, and please note that these Egyptians that left their mark on history, are the fathers of these, who will seal present history, and their blood is the same.

We beg you to excuse our frankness, but perhaps it is better to be frank, especially in a time when all the world is sick of hypocrisy, and the old system, and, nothing can remain after the great conflict of the world of to-day, but LIBERTY, JUSTICE and TRUTH. Virtues will come up topmost in the long run, and we hope that Great Britain will not fail to be its champion.

THE WOMEN OF EGYPT
Public meeting of Egyptian Women
St. Mark's Cathedral
Cairo, December 12th, 1919

420

# Appendix 3

Translation of a letter sent by Hamed Pasha El Bassel Secretary General of the Wafd to Esther Fahmy Wissa on October 27th, 1923 requesting that her brother Louis should be nominated by the Wafd to a seat in Parliament.

Respected Lady,

I received your letter related to the question of your brother Louis. I would like to inform you that this matter has taken up much time in the affairs of the Wafd during several meetings, and that is because the Assiout local committee which is responsible for recommending nominations decided unanimously that they would not agree to the nomination of Louis because of personal traits which negated his nomination to Parliament.

When the Wafd went over the matter they decided unanimously at a meeting not attended by the President that they would not nominate Louis. However, the President asked us to reconsider the matter, which we did on two occasions on his insistence and at both meetings the members reiterated their decision.

Dear Respected Lady, I assure you that I and all my colleagues to whom you lent a helping hand, when we were exiled, or in prison, find it very difficult to refuse the first request that you have put before us, which we are unable to fulfil.

But if you only knew what his Excellency the President did with the whole Wafdist Committee, when he demanded that the matter of your brother Louis should be settled in a manner satisfactory to you, so much so that the discussion became very heated, especially when he heard of the erroneous ideas that were passing through your mind, which made you wish to review the whole position in detail by yourself and your family.

I assure you that all the members of the Wafd bear the greatest respect to you due to your comprehension, manners and patriotism.

I am writing to you this letter to let you know, however, that the Wafd still refuse to nominate Louis, and we hope that you will appreciate the reasons for our decision, and will be able to accept them, and not allow your thoughts to roam far away from reality and misjudge us.

To end, I would like to present to you my greatest respect and my heartiest salutations.

Hamed El Bassel

Le Caire, le      192      مصر في ٧ كانون سنة ١٩٢٢

حضرة السيد المحترم

وصلني خطابه الذي من مسألة أن حضرة لويس ينبه على أفندك أنه لفت المسألة حينئذٍ زنا لويس من أعمال الوفد وحيدة مجلات وذلك لأنه أسرورا إلى أن حول على على ويراسل الرئيس كتبت للوفد بأنهما على أنظار لا تفضل مطلقا تشبيه لويس على ما من صفحات كثيرة وذكر من شأنه أنه لا يمكنه أن يرشح عصرا للبرلمان

ولما نظر الوفد ذلك قرر بالإجماع وحبته لم يمكنها لم يكونه معالي الرئيس وعز تشبيه وقد طلب معالي الرئيس إعادة نظر اللجنة والوفد ذلك مرتبة فأن مرحب للكشف وذلك وذلك وذلك من ذلك

أن بتم السيد المحترم ـ أؤكد لك أني وحبير أخوان الأندية كما كان السيد الطيار أربعتنا بتأ نهم جميعا بالسيد عن عمله حبه إلى أن أول مسألة الوفد من عندنا من مخول لا تقضي، ولكن لو علمت أن معالي الرئيس وصل بنر الوفد بأجمعه نبتأ به طلبك وأزمانك أن أحد كان هذه المادة فد شبتم حبا لما من ذلك أن لفت المادة تستدعي الموسع فيط من خول أنت وعا تلتك أن أحد ما أشرت أليه من سور اللجنة

وأؤكد لك أيضا أنه وجميع أعضاء الوفد ليقدرون لك الاحترام العظيم السائق بفضلك وأدبك وطنيتك

فلذا أن حبطك على أنه أن حضرتك لا يمكنك أن بعملنا الوفد عز تشبيه ولك نية الغيرة ذا رجاء من مداركك أن تقدر رفضت الظروف وأن لا تذهب بعيدا أسور الظنه

وذا الختام أقدم لحضرتك مزيد احترامي وعظيم ...

# Appendix 4

Paris, February 1925

Madame Chairman, ladies,

I am delighted with this opportunity of meeting again with some of the members of the Paris Congress, which has left a very favourable impression on our minds.

Suffragettes have, in the past, been painted by men as presumptuous women who want to step out of their dominion to trespass on that of man.

In our case it has not been so, we stepped out of the very narrow field that was allotted to us and to help man in his political aspirations, and seeing his shortcomings and his failings, we undertook to share the greater part of the responsibility and we are pointing out to our people the very narrow way of right that will lead them to freedom and emancipation.

As for you, I have noticed that there has not been a pioneer in a hard struggle who has not had a worthy idealistic purpose to spur him onwards, and it is only the great faith in one's cause and the conviction of his ideas that give him strength and courage to fight the hard fight of right against might, and it is really only after success is achieved that the weaker, drifting element joins in. Therefore no selfish presumptuous purpose could have kept up the efforts of these wonderful women pioneers, who stood in cold and darkness, in derision and ridicule, holding the banner of equal rights until the slow imagination of man comprehended that woman was the helpmate for him, and he had to accept her as such.

Now I am certain that woman did not take this initiative, leaving the warm shelter of the home, with its delightful treasures – the children – for the sake, merely, of having the vote. The vote was only the reason, but not the end. Women's end was the bettering of the conditions under which the happiness of the home depended. She hated poverty, ignorance, squalor, which led to disease, crime, and unrest.

She looked towards the suffering masses, and she felt that it was not a case of the survival of the fittest, but it was a case of raising up humanity out of the dustheap on which it was thrown. She realised that nationally as internationally, any sick part of the community rendered pain unto the whole, and it was for the health and welfare of the whole that the part was to be healed.

Now who can fight the battle of the oppressed. It is the oppressed themselves who are crushed under the heavy weight of their deficient circumstances and who have never enjoyed the benefit of a high education and upbringing, who are not able to use the weapons of argument as skilfully as their more fortunate opponents, who have had the best that life could award them? If we leave them to fight their own battle they will never be able to hold their own, and their defeat and the weight of their miserable circumstances will only push them to desperate measures which often result in revolution and bloodshed, and this can only mean the overturning of the tables.

No ladies, someone else must fight their battle, someone who has had the best of life, education, culture and favourable circumstances. We do not want to hear the cantankerous, shrill protests of the oppressed, but we want to hear the generous strong voice of the happy and prosperous defending the cause of the weak. And it is not a matter of satisfying the mouth of the hungry, or throwing a mouthful of bread to stop their pressing needs, but it is an efficacious method we want, that will guarantee a healthy system of co-operation providing for the needs of all human beings, and the responsibility falls heavily on the shoulders of we women.

The world has reached a stage nowadays when Mammon and the God of Force are both seated on the throne of worship, and the turmoil and chaos that exist in the world to-day bode of explosion. We will try to avoid this explosion by taking the side of right against might, and if in spite of the great efforts, might will not heed, then perhaps, out of the explosion that shall surely ensue, a clear definite road cut out by woman, may remain among the debris of the old system as a pathway to better things. But woman must be convinced of her mission and must see that she does not serve either right or left out of the very narrow path of right, and then perhaps the right of peace, born of the efforts of women, may prevail and a new and happy era may be the lot of mankind.

I say narrow path because the line of right is very narrow, and so narrow that sometimes even so called righteousness becomes a tyranny, and it is for us to see that real freedom and goodwill, and the spirit of love, may be the dominating factors in all our actions, and in a spirit of humility and kindness, a new standard of leadership may be introduced into the world where he, who would be the greatest, must be the servant of all.

# Appendix 5

Article published in *La Française* (Journal de progrés féminin, Paris Samedi 14 Fevrier, 1925) under the heading *L'émancipation des Egyptiennes*.

La Française a signalé, il y a quelques semaines, l'appel addressé par les femmes Égyptiennes à l'opinion publique, sur l'initiative de Mme Charaouy Pacha.

Les Egyptiennes se mêlent actuellement de façon trés active à la politique. Par amour pour leur pays, dont elles voudraient l'indépendence, elles ont osé se livrer à des démonstrations publiques dans les rues du Caire et exercent un véritable apostolat.

Une lettre écrite par l'une d'elles, Mme Fahmy bey Wissa, nous donne quelques détails fort intéressants.

'En poursuivant cette lutte pour la liberté de leur pays, dit-elle notamment, les Egyptiennes sont arrivées à conquérir leur propre liberté, et la femme voilée jouit adjourd'hui d'autant de liberté qu'elle se désire.'

Un comité de plus de mille femmes, réuni dans une église, a donné naissance à la délégation a fortement contribué à la libération des chefs Zagloulistes exilés aux Seychelles et prisonniers au Caire, quelques-uns de ses membres ayant très éloquemment plaidé auprés de la Résidence, en faveur des condamnés.

Au Parlement, les Egyptiennes ont, aujourd'hui des logues réservées d'où elles assistent fréquemment aux débats parlementaires qu'elles suivent avec grand interérêt.

Les Egyptiennes, d'ailleurs, ont l'impression de se trouver en face d'une tâche ardue mais inéluctable.

'C'est elles seules, écrit Mme Fahmy bey Wissa, qui peuvent sauver l'Egypte de cette malheureuse situation. Elles brûlent pour leur pays d'un amour infatigable, elles sont prêtes à tout sacrifier pour le faire sortir se son effroyable condition morale . . . elles ont la claire vision d'un avenir admirable: l'Egypte encore une fois mère de la véritable civilisation. . .'

# Appendix 6

*Education Reform*

To my dear friend Sherifa Riad

I read with interest the interview you gave to the *Daily Telegraph*. I agree with your concern about a reform of education especially in schools for girls. I have frequently thought about it, and wish it could be realised.

I also agree with your statement that Egyptian ladies have rushed too quickly into party politics. But there is one point that you have missed, and that is, that when we entered the political field, there were no women parties in Egypt, we were all solidly behind the principles of the Egyptian Delegation (Wafd) calling for complete independence of Egypt and the Sudan.

But when some members split from the Wafd, we did not follow suit as they did, but stood steadfast. So I don't think that this could be called partisanship. If we had maintained our original stand, supporting our original cause, and rejecting any deviation or incursion by external influences, our first women's society would have remained above party politics. These differences started before Saad Zaghloul returned from exile, and long before he formed a government, with the result that our efforts stagnated and our society slept for two years, during which time we did very little work.

But when negotiations failed, due to the British discouragement of our aspirations, and after the shameful assassination of the Sirdar, which the British exploited to smother our national movement we formed the Saadeya Society for Women, to resist the danger that was meant to eliminate our national identity through the weakening of our wills to struggle.

So you see my lady, there is no place for party politics in our society, we support all those who call for the complete independence of Egypt and the Sudan, and on such a basis I'm willing to work with you, on condition that we are not subject to outside influences, and that men will leave us alone, to work with clear consciences, for the good of this country, whom we vowed to support with all our strength, and to sacrifice all that is dear to us.

The reason for Egypt's slavery, my lady, is the decline in our morals. Before the Egyptian can be free in this country, he must realise the meaning of freedom, sacrifice and courage; he must learn to support right, no matter what it costs him; and walk in the path of righteousness caring for public welfare, before his own well-being, and expecting no recompense or personal benefit for his public efforts. For it must be realised that man is mortal, whereas principles are immortal.

Unless the Egyptian is armed with a strong faith in the righteousness of his cause, believing completely in victory, there is no hope for independence. For the road to independence is straight and narrow. If one is able to overcome difficulties at every step, and remove the obstacles encountered, he will achieve his aim, as long as he remains faithful to his cause.

However if one exaggerates the problem due to the difficulties encountered, losing heart and stopping in one's tracks, entreating to be given what is superfluous to your opponent's need, you will be given the scraps, while they eat the meat.

These are my principles for independence. However I have not lost hope in my country men, in spite of the weakness of character noticeable in some of them. My feelings have not changed towards them, and I still believe they can be reformed, so I am willing to shoulder their weaknesses and support them, and heal them with the spirit of love, reconciliation and sacrifice.

It should be remembered that the Heavenly principles and Wisdom which were laid down in God's laws, of yore, were not accepted by my people, who considered them theoretical and far from natural, or human desires, and therefore they discarded them and gave them no heed. It is the same Godly principles that make me patient with them, like a mother's patience with her son. Because I know that my people will stumble at every step on the road to independence, until such time as they learn that they cannot move forward unless they are manned by righteous principles. So what we reject now, because we do not understand, will be understood, through our experiments and crises. So patience my lady with these people, patience. For they will survive, honoured and free; for if we have to lose men, money, life, or peace of mind, to attain this goal, the sight of our beloved people as models of perfection, and goodness, bearing the light of knowledge and real culture, will suffice as our recompense. These are our principles so I am willing to work with you and any of the ladies who wish to join us in trying to improve political, social, and psychological behaviour.

I am proud, after I have known you personally, and felt the magnanimity of your character and your humility, to work with you, subject to the motto: 'Humility and no Pride'.

For Glory and all praise is to God, and it is up to man to work with sincerity, stability and faith.

I share with you your complete belief that in the person of our beloved King, we will find the best support and greatest encouragement for our work.

With my best wishes and respect to your person, I remain,

**Esther Fahmy Wissa**

# Appendix 7

Translation of a cutting from an Arabic newspaper (name unknown), date early 1925.

*A Protest Of The Saadia Party Women's Committee*

The Saadia Party Women's Committee strongly protests against the seizure of its last election pamphlets which were in no way illegal.

If the present government's fear of people's criticism concerning its manipulation of the constitution and the violation of the freedom to vote made it resort to the confiscation of their pamphlets, then it would be better for it to amend these illegalities.

If the government's passion for power and the desire to foil Saad and the Saadists have driven it to such illegal means, then the people will not trust the government of those who have violated the constitution.

If, on the other hand, the government did so to comply with England's policy, then we must hold the government responsible for agreeing to the dictum that there is danger in an Egyptian being governed by an Egyptian as he never respects the constitution nor freedom but will gratify his desires and self-interest.

Nowadays people are watchful and will not allow anyone to violate their constitutional rights.

The other thought which grieves us is that the government might be taking these illegal steps, in such an obvious manner, to anger the people who will retaliate by what could disturb the security of the nation, thus giving England the opportunity to grip the country in an iron fist. Such is the perspicacity of British policy; to incite the Egyptian against the Egyptian so as to lose none of their colonial interests. The moral and material losses would revert on the Egyptian himself, turning him into a pawn in British hands and a victim of his compatriot's corruption.

Can any of the cases, previously mentioned, be applied to you as Ministers? If proven so, the people will hold you responsible.

Countrymen, this government's actions are obvious to you. if you really want freedom, humble them in the elections so as to be taken into consideration in the future. Watch those who tamper with your rights and this will lead you to complete independence in spite of any resistance and you will gain the freedom for which you have sacrificed your most dear.

Members of the Wafd, you have before you the most disgusting image of an illegal and greedy government and must feel the degree of anger burning in people's hearts from the illegal actions that thwart the rights of Egyptians.

However if you come to power one day, and allow yourselves to comply with this spirit, then the people will vent on you their actual resentment and also judge you for the violation of their rights.

You, their supporters, if you think you have succeeded with your abetment of their offenses then you must know that he who accepts the undermining of an Egyptian's rights and the violation of the constitution cannot be trusted with the reins of government.

If you defend the country's constitution just to gain personal benefits then you are done for and your consciences are dead. Shame on you, to back injustice and to be silent over the rights of the Egyptians. Fear God, so as not to be among the losers.

Members of the National Party and followers of the hero Moustapha Kamel, whose main concern and desperate struggle was to gain Egyptian independence and repossess all its rights, where are you? Why are you silent? Has the spirit of Moustapha Kamel died with his death? Have you become corpses?

Our only hope lies in preserving the rights and freedom of the Egyptian and consolidating the constitution. If you disregard it for personal reasons then you will have strayed from the path of freedom.

Egyptians, you all know that corruption is the only obstacle in your way towards independence. If your morals are dead then your hope of independence is also dead even if the forces of occupation leave the country today. Know that a free nation, vigilant over its rights, cannot be enslaved. An independent nation if it ever neglects to defend its rights will be robbed of its independence. So, can't you understand?

Many of you fear the independence of Egypt because you fear the morals of your compatriots and believe your rights will be lost because of their despotic greed. Now will you not defend the rights of the Egyptians, so that freedom may prevail and each Egyptian feel his rights secure?

Signed:
Olfat Rateb, Ilham El Masry, Mrs Morcos Pasha Hanna, Mrs Mohammad Bey Moussa, Mrs Fahmy Bey Wissa, Regina Khayat, Tomader Sabry, Hedayat Barakat, Wagida Thabet, Wahiba Niazy, Faika Zakaniya, Soad Fahmy El Khalfawy, Mrs Aly Bey Refaat, Saniya Dowidar, Neamat Hassanein, Dawlat El Shamsy, Amina El Shamsy, Faika Zaghloul, Amina Thabet, Fahima Thabet, Mrs Osman Bey Youssef, Mrs Taher Bey El Lozy, Mrs Abd El Salam Bey Fahmy, Aliya Saad El Din, Soraya Hafez El Gammal, Fahima Soliman, Mrs Hafez Bey Madkour, Amna Nada, Wafika Zakariya, Mrs Mohammed Bey Sadek Ammar, Mrs Naguib Iskandar, Mrs Dr. Hamdy, Mrs Said Bey Taher, Mrs Said Bey Madkour, Mrs Amin Bey Youssef, Mrs Mohammad Bey Yousef, Mrs Mohammad Bey Mansour, Mrs Abbas Bey Mansour.

احتجاج

# Appendix 8

*In Love Not in Hatred We Work for Egypt*

Sons of Egypt,

Colonial politics have shaken your nationalism and weakened your hopes of independence, dissolving your unity and depleting you of your capacities. It grieves us that those who implement this policy are among the sons of Egypt and knowingly stab at her heart. It is the hatred and bitterness embedded in their own hearts that blinds them from realising the country's best interests. If ever their conscience pricks them they resist it, for the drive of hatred is uppermost in their hearts, prodding them on, to carry out deeds that they would have censured in others for committing the same.

What we see is a weakened and defenceless Egypt, instead of a glorious Egypt, eager to learn the principles of freedom and independence so as to raise her head high among civilised nations. We find, that some of her sons crush freedom and liberty of individuals with the excuse that they are trying to shield people from being misled, once more, by electing others than themselves.

Do you think that you can transfer the trust people have in others to yourselves?

If what you said and are saying about your opponents is true can you by your actions convince people to trust you and find in you the haven of their expectations? You stop at nothing to reach your aims. What do you guarantee us, faithful citizens, that will ensure us truth and justice? Do you want to deprive us of our rights by such means knowing full well that you are backed by a foreign power and that whatever power you hold is used only to humiliate and stifle our freedom?

Fellow citizens, no, certainly not. We would have followed you if we had found in you constructiveness instead of destruction, honesty instead of lies. Justice instead of injustice, probity instead of crooked ways, integrity instead of the persuance of personal interest, love instead of hatred, a commitment to our aspirations instead of negligence and courage in place of cowardliness.

Do you believe that if you win the elections by such means and form a parliament based on such deeds, that this nation, deprived of its rights, whose freedom you have usurped in order to gain ground for yourselves, will endorse these actions and accept you? We did not ask for total independence just to undergo your despotism nor did we seek our complete

431

freedom just to suffer your tyranny. Colonial policy has encouraged your illegal actions, so as to dampen our hopes in an Egyptian government so that we would ask for their continued presence to protect us from you. We realise that you are but tools, in their hands, to be used to fight against your country's aspirations while you are oblivious of it. In any case, may our true nationalism protect us from our anger against you which is only directed against colonialism, a power which tries in vain, to dispossess us of our innate character.

However, we will censure you, resist you and settle accounts with you as brothers whom we cannot but love. We will demand from you truth, force you to respect liberty, compel you to probity and only accept from you honesty and justice.

Fellow countrymen, remember that the Egyptians are a people, alive and aware, not blind to your deceptions and misdeeds. If you do not respect them and afford them consideration they will neither respect your nor acknowledge you, nor will they trust or give you their affection. Know that only the nation is eternal, because individuals die but principles remain. What you sow today, your children and grandchildren will reap tomorrow; for they are of your flesh and blood. Egypt will claim its usurped freedom and history will record your actions whether to your credit or not, as friends or enemies of Egypt. So for Egypt's sake won't you change for the better?

Esther Fahmy Wissa

بالحكمة لا بالكرامة

دليل لمصر

ايها مصر :

قامت السياسة الاستعمارية ان تهزم قوميتكم ، ان نضعف آمالكم في الاستقلال ، وان نفرق ملككم ، ونقصم عراكم ، وبسومها ان يكون من ناء مصر من يفقدون هذه السياسة ويطعنون عبر في قلبها وهم يدرون ، ولكن الكرامة الحق المتدلل في صدورهم تيام عن تقدير صلاحة الوطن فنظلوا ومدارك الوانفلون فاذا وخزم ضميرهم قاوموه ، لان دوام الكرامة اقوى من ، هو يدفعهم رغم ارادتهم الى ارتكاب ما كارا زبون غيرهم لو ارتكبوه

، هذه مصر الضعيفة ، مقبر المسكينة ، مصر لجبانة التي ترد ان ... تنهل مبادىء الحرية الاستقلال ، مصر التي تريد ان ترفع رأسها بن الامم المتمدينة ، نرى من ابنائها من يدوسون ل الحرية ويقتلون استقلال الافراد دعوى هم لا يريدون ان ينخدع الشعب فينتخب برهم مرة اخرى !!

اجل . فهل بمثل هذه الطرق يمكن ان ننقذ ة الشعب من غير كم اليكم ؟

وهل انزا صح ما تقلنوه او تقولونه عن تقدومكم يمكنكم بهذه الاعمال ان تجعلوا الامة ن اتقة لكم وتثق ان عدبكم ملحا ابنا على ناكا ، الم لا تستكينون من شيء في سبيل يكم؟ فو هيان نزدام لما ان الشعب المخص مجس نا اتقة اماني والعداله ؟ وانيف نريدون بعارة احتمرنا بهذه الطرق وانتم علمتنا ان ساطة الاحبة مستمدة لكون الثروة تجاوكم ؟ بودون مبا ان عنايتيكم ونبين نرده ما اعطيناه كامر يطا ان انتب ؟

ولكنا نادبكم ، وقناومكم ، ونسوى حسابنا معكم وانتم اخوتنا ولا يمكننا الا ان معكم ومع دام دامت خزعكم على احترام الحرية ، رتطاليكم بالمانى وكرمكم على الاستقامة ولا قبل منكم الا الازمهة والعداله .

رجل نكون اذا هم م في الانتخابات بهذه نفترق ونزنمع كـ ... اما قلنا قلع حذه الاعمال ، ارهدت الأمر المسلوت حنبرا التي فنام حريتها لنقدموا لكم جنيبا ، نسبم لكم وناوى عنكم او خيب : ايها بنات الاستقلال التام لنستطع علينا وانا نشد ا حر ما الكبلة لمستمدوا فيا ددا نتحكم سياست الاستعمار على هذه الاعمال عبر الناهوبة لباس من حكم المصري وسلب شاهما لتبنا بكم ، فما ملم انكم لتم الا آلات في بدنا مخارب كم امال امتكم وانتم لا تدرون ، وفي اي حال لهباذ مصر بنا ان ننخب علبكم . وبني اما نخضب على النوة الاستعمارية وحدنها ؟ ذلك النوة التي ماول عينا ان نخرجها من قدرتنا التي نترها عليها .

وقالبرا ايها المواطنون ، كرة ، نا مامل لو بأتم ... نكم ما دا، اذ... دل... نقل لو راببا ، كم و نقصم عراكم دل نخبب وعدد دل انخور ، واستدام هدا، ادا، شجاح ... راجه بدل الفرض ، وصـكا ملمابنا بدل ال... ادا، دما وشبعابة دال الاستمى

وقالبرا ايها المواطنون ان انشعب المصري حب وهو قد مى عن اغنل السوء والباطل ، دنا، نخله وره ولم نعبوره له حسابا ، فهو لا نخرمكم ولا مب لكم حساب، ولا يوليكم تنته ولا ننخخ عبه ونقا كم لصارنا وكماية منكم استهدادا ، واعلموا انكم لستم بافين حل انشعدر الناي لاردالافراد فانون،اما المبادى، بابة واعلموا ان الزمان رعو ءاليوم ستحصدون او يبعده بوكا او احقادكم حد عد وهم من بنكم وحبكم وان الناريخ سيبيخل عليكم؟ او لكم كل اعمالكم وسيبكتكم اما من اصدقاء مصر واما من اعدائها . فبل في حب مصر لا نستم المصريون ؟

استر فهمي وبيصا

# Appendix 9

*Kawkab El Shark March 7 1925*

## A Protest Of The Women's Committee

Today's constitutional government of Egypt, is following policies which are completely incompatible with freedom and justice. It has the temerity to deport a famous Egyptianised member of the press, Emil Effendi Khoury, an editor of the esteemed newspaper *Al Ahram*. His only crime was that he defended the country's constitution and the freedom of Egypt.

The Saadia Women's Committee strongly protests such despotism and announces to the public that people, such as Emil Effendi, who defend the rights of Egyptians should not be considered foreigners but as one of her own sons. A foreigner to Egypt is the traitorous nationalist who does not stop tampering with the rights of Egyptians, treading them beneath his feet and violating the sanctity of the constitution.

The Committee requests all members of the Egyptian press to protest strongly against these endless actions, unlike any which happen in no other free country. They should all stand united to support truth and to promote freedom. Otherwise those who abstain should be considered as having ignored the rights of the Egyptian Press and should not deserve a share in its honour.

Signatures:
Olfat Rateb, Ehsan El Masry, Mrs Morcos Pasha Hanna, Mrs Mohammad Bey Moussa, Mrs Fahmy Bey Wissa, Regina Khayat, Tomader Sabry, Hedeyat Barakat, Wagida Sabet, Wahiba Niazy, Faika Zakariya, Soad Fahmy El Khalfawy, Mrs Aly Bey Refaat, Saniya El Dowedar, Neamat Hassanein, Bamba Morcos Louka, Tawhida El Messeiry, Mrs Amin Bey Youssef, Aliya Saad El Deen Neamat El Shamsy, Dawlat El Shamsy, Amina El Shamsy, Faika Zaghloul, Amina Sabet, Fahima Sabet, Mrs Osman Bey Youssef, Mrs Taher Bey El Lozy, Mrs Abed El Salam Bey Fahmy, Soraya Hafez El Guindy, Mrs Aly Amer, Mrs Mahmoud Bey El Gammal, Fahima Awad Soliman, Fatma Awad Soliman, Mrs Hafez Bey Madkour, Amna Nada, Wafika Zakariya, Mrs Mohammad Bey Sadek Ammar, Mrs Naguib Iskandar, Mrs Said Bey Taher, Mrs Dr. Hamdy Bey, Mrs Said Bey Madkour, Mrs Amin Bey Youssef, Mrs Mohammad Bey Youssef, Mrs Mohammad Bey Mansour, Mrs Abbas Bey Mansour.

كوكب الشرق

٢٣٤٢ = ٧ مارس سنة ١٩٢٥

## احتجاج لجنة السيدات
### في جلستها الدورية

تدير حكومة مصر الدستورية اليوم على خطاط ذاتي ثبتتا كل حرية وعدل وقد تجرأت على ... الصحافة المتأخرين يتهزؤون الاستاذ أنبل أندي نوري أحمد المحرري جريدة الاهرام الغراء ولا جرم عليه ولاذنب اقترف الى انه دافع عن دستور البلاد وحرية الفرد المصري .

فلجنة السعدية للسيدات تحتج أشد الاحتجاج على هذه الاعمال الاستبدادية وتعلن ملأ أن امثال أنبل انتدى المدافعين عن حقوق المصرين لا يمحسون أجانب عن البلاد بل هم من أبناء وطنها الاجنبي عن مصر هو الوطني ... المصري ... يستك عن المس بحقوق الشعب المصري في دفاعه على حريته وبنتزك حرمة دستوره . واللجنة تطالب رجال الصحافة المصرية أن يحتجوا شديد الاحتجاج على هذه التصرفات التي لا أحد لما ولا مثيل في بلاد حرة وان يتخذوا جميعهم أعوانا للحق وانصارآ للحرية والا نكل من يتخلى من ذلك بحسب مفرطا في حقوق الصحافة المصرية ورجلا لا نصيب لهمن كرامتها

---

ألفت راتب و احسان المصري . مدام مرتضى باشا حرم محمد بك موسى . مدام فهمي بك وبعثرا جونا خياط . نصر صبري . هدية بركات . وجيده ثابت . وهبه نيازي . فائقة ذكريه . سعاد فهمي الجلناوي . حرم على بك رفعت . منيه الدودار . نعمت حجين . عبه مرأص لوقا . توحيده المصيري . حرم أمين بك يوسف . على سعد الدين . نعمت ... . دولت الشعبي . امينه الشعبي . عائشة زغلول . أمينه ثابت . نبيهه ثابت . حرم عثمان بك يوسف . حرم طاهر بك الفوزي . حرم عبد السلام بك فهمي نخري . ... حرم ... البزل . نبيهه عرض سليمان . قائمه ... مذكور ... . آمنه ... وكريمة . حرم محمد بك صادق هزار . مدام نجيب اسكندر . حرم سعيد بك طاهر . ... كور حدي بك . حرم سعيد بك مذكور . حرم أمين بك يوسف . حرم محمد بك يوسف . حرم محمد بك منصور . حرم عباس بك منصور .

# Appendix 10

(An interview published in *The Manchester Guardian* Wednesday June 30th, 1926.)

*The Women's Movement in Egypt,* Fleet Street, Tuesday.

Mme Fahmy Wissa Bey, who came to London from the Conference of the International Woman Suffrage Alliance in Paris, is a leader of the women's movement in Egypt. Today she gave a *Manchester Guardian* representative an interesting account of its origin and its aims. It is a recent development, and like all the other movements in Egypt it has grown out of the National movement. 'We had first to have a Parliament,' she explained, 'before we began to talk about votes for women.' Long before the war, she said, an Egyptian woman writer worked for the emancipation of women. She was a Mohammedan, and her hope was to free them from the veil, but she died without accomplishing this. This new movement had its real beginning in March, 1919, with a demonstration made by a thousand veiled women in the streets of Cairo. This was after the military had been called out to suppress a demonstration by the Nationalists against the refusal to let Zaghlul Pasha leave Egypt with a delegation for England. The women, full of indignation, said they would also demonstrate, and there followed the extraordinary scene of these secluded women wrapped in their veils attempting to march through the streets. The soldiers barred their way and made them disperse. They returned to their homes, but have never gone back to the old way of thinking that was symbolized by the veil, nor do they wear the veil except occasionally and for its beauty.

A number of these women had been interested in social and patriotic work, and now they were fired with the belief that they could help their country in many practical ways. They had not been organised, and most of them had not known each other before that day, which not only introduced but united them. They at once organised several societies, each of which carries on its own special work.

## A School for Girls

The new Women's Society is engaged in educational and philanthropic work. We all came together and said, 'Now what can we do for Egypt?' and we started a school for girls which has two hundred pupils. They receive an elementary education and training in a great variety of industries, machine-knitting, dressmaking, carpet-making, and so on. They are doing well, for the Egyptians are very industrious and efficient.'

Another society whose members have been elected by Egyptian women is political and aims at Egyptian independence. Mme. Wissa is its president. The Feminist Union is a suffrage society whose President is Mme Hoda Chaaraoui, and in 1923 it was affiliated to the International Woman Suffrage Society at the International Conference in Rome. It aims at securing complete political equality, and at changing the laws relating to marriage at sixteen years for a girl and eighteen years for a youth. It is now working to abolish polygamy. Polygamy is now practised by the upper classes, but it is by no means uncommon for a peasant to have two or even three wives.

'We want our girls to have equal chances of education, for the building up of the home depends on the women, and the home means the coming generation. It means Egypt. This demand for the education of girls is widely supported by the parents who understand its importance. There are now two women's clubs in Egypt, one of which is a Christian training centre, a purely Egyptian enterprise.'

Mme Wissa said the number of men and of women in Egypt was almost equal. Organised women are trying to uplift their nation in every way. One way is by raising the moral standard in all political and social dealings. The ideal they upheld was that of moral integrity.

## The Drug Traffic

As social reformers the Mohammedan women are trying to get rid of many traditions that do not belong to Mohammedanism but have grown around it. 'We want,' said Mme. Wissa, 'to fight the drug traffic and to improve the conditions of the fellaheen who are the backbone of the nation. With regard to education and hygiene, we hope to have in every town branches for these purposes. And we are now organising a campaign to sent young men and women all over the country to preach against the use of drugs.

'We know that our country can never reach the standard we are aiming at unless it has a system of compulsory education, but we realise that in present conditions this would mean that the fellaheen would leave their fields and crowd into the cities. So we want to improve the conditions of life in the villages, first of all by introducing a supply of fresh water. The scanty water they get is not clean, and we shall not get rid of the diseases that are causing great havoc until we get good fresh water. We also want sanitation, for at present there is none in the villages, and better homes built for the workers. We suggest that the landowners should spend a few months every year among their tenants in order to understand how they live. Instead of that they are accustomed to spend their lives in the city enjoying the luxuries provided by the fellaheen's hard toil.'

The fellaheen, who work tirelessly and make the wealth of Egypt, pay heavy taxes. Mme. Wissa said she thought there was more public spirit among the rich men than there used to be, and still more among the wealthy women. There are several industrial schools for girls, a very good child welfare centre in Cairo, and dispensaries in different parts of the country.

Mme. Wissa herself belongs to a Coptic family, and she explains that, while Egypt has assimilated other races who have come with successive invasions, the Copts, who are Christians, are the descendants of the Egyptians of Pharaonic times. She has a tremendous pride in her country, in its ancient history, its industry, efficiency, and high moral standard, and a profound belief in its great future. It was interesting to hear from her that about forty Egyptian girls are now studying in London and preparing to serve their country.

# Appendix 11

*The Egyptian Woman of Today*

A speech delivered by Madame Esther Fahmy Bey Wissa at the Egyptian Club in England on Saturday, July 3rd, 1926

Ladies and Gentlemen,

It is indeed a great pleasure for me to address the young men and women of my country who are here in this land acquiring an education that will enable them to give their best to the country we all love so much, and if I do not address you in your own language it is only out of courtesy to our English friends, present, whom we cordially invite to hear something about the Egyptian woman of today.

I do not need to say that the Egyptian woman of ancient times was advanced and emancipated, enjoying equal rights with man.

History reveals the fact, and the greatness of the ancient Egyptian nation itself denotes that woman was the equal of man, consequently the country was renowned and prosperous. We then passed through a period in our history of invasion and subjection, the moral standard of the people gradually grew less, until woman completely lost her rights and became a victim of man's desire and caprice.

Here we have a picture of degeneration, ignorance, and political subjection. Once woman's standard was lowered, the nation followed suit, and this wonderful land of great renown and ancient prosperity became the prey of every imperialistic policy that has swept through the ages. Demoralisation and subjection moved in a vicious circle until it became a very hard task indeed to free the nation from the state in which it has fallen.

And here woman steps in again. It is only through her education and training that a remedy can be applied. For when once she rises up to her responsibilities and undertakes to fulfil her mission in building up a model generation on sound principles, the tentacles of subjection can then be broken; and freedom, morality and prosperity could be able to step in, and a new healthy circle is started.

The woman of Egypt today is fully aware of her responsibilities. She knows what is required of her, and she is waiting to fulfil her duty. She has even shifted the responsibility of the country's demoralisation on to her own shoulders, and she is undertaking to mend the past.

439

She does not stand as an onlooker criticising and rebuking, but she has plunged into the mire where an aspiring generation is struggling to rise above the demoralised traditions and ignorance of the past, and she is toiling to clear the way before her people.

The woman of Egypt fully realises that the greatness of a nation can only be built on sound moral foundations, therefore she has taken the lead in pointing out to her people how their liberty can be attained.

And it is in this particular moment of our history, and in this great struggle for freedom that we come across the great truths that lie behind principle which cannot be overlooked, but, unfortunately, it is only by stumbling against them that we come to recognise them.

But the woman of Egypt does not mind the fall. She is sympathetically watching and guarding that the spirits of her people are not broken, and that is all that matters. The falls and shocks through which they learn are not to be feared, they are for the building up of the new Egypt.

The efforts of the Egyptian woman today tend to move in three directions, educational, social and political.

We have free schools, entirely run by women societies, where elementary and industrial education can be had. The girls are taught, besides reading, writing, arithmetic; sewing, dressmaking, embroidery, machine knitting, carpet making and other industries.

Our efforts tend towards acquiring for our people compulsory education as in all civilised countries, but the danger alleged to threaten the country by educating the fellah could be easily avoided. It is feared that if the Egyptian peasants are educated, they will leave the villages and overcrowd the towns, and as our country is not industrial the danger of unemployment will be very great.

This is so, especially as the conditions of the villages are so bad that no educated man could put up with that life. There is no water system, a fellah woman has still to walk some good distance to fill a jar with muddy water from the Nile, and that even is not fit for use. It is infested with microbes and the result is filth, squalor and disease.

Bilharziasis and Ancilostoma are the greatest menace to the lives of our people. Thousands and millions of our fine well-built men fall under the curse of these two diseases, and within a few months of sickness nothing but skeletons remain to testify how Egypt looks after her sons. Because of bad sanitation we have typhoid epidemics, which are disastrous, and all this can be avoided if a clean water system is available, and if the simplest rules of hygiene are carried out.

She should make village life comfortable enough to satisfy the demands of an educated community, and to arrive to this. She should suggest that every landowner spends a few months of the year in his village among his tenants, where he should provide free private schooling for the education of boys and girls, and where the influence of his educated womenkind can be felt, so that a new conception of life may be introduced into the peasant lives, and, by imitation, a new standard of living can be acquired.

Another danger that threatens our people is the traffic in drugs, and because of the Capitulations under whose shelter this trade is carried out without risk of detection, the Government's endeavours in combating same is inefficacious. Our plan is to raise a campaign by which our young men and women would go into the villages and warn the people of the danger of this deadly poison.

We need great social reforms. Our country under the different invasions has adopted laws and traditions which are not compatible with the civilisation of the present age, and we have to sort out these traditions, to do away with the bad and to retain the good. Our first duty is to establish the family laws on good, sound, just bases, doing away with polygamy and restricting divorce laws. By so doing we give woman her rights, and when once they are insured, and when once she feels her responsibility towards her race, she will rise up to her calling and upbringing of the future generation will receive due attention.

There can be no oppression or violation of right if a satisfactory result can be acquired, and as long as the powerful are almighty, right can have no sway, and the result is demoralisation, disorder and dispute.

We even need a religious reform. I am not a Moslem, but I have studied Islam as it is given in the Koran. I find that all our traditions are anti-Islamic and if the spirit of real Islam was carried out, the Islam of Abraham, Jacob and his sons, of Issa (Jesus) and the Apostles (hawarien) then Islam would have a different history altogether, and I would beseech the intelligent element in my country to study their religion thoroughly and interpret it in the highest ideal sense and give its message to the people who are religious, and who need the right spiritual food. The Egyptians have always been religious, it is better to give them a good sound religion than to deprive them of it.

We have dispensaries in different parts of the country, where the peasant women are taught simple rules of hygiene for the children. We have child welfare centres, and we have clubs where our girls meet to carry out the work they are interested in. This is all a beginning of greater things, and as long as the spirit is the right one a great deal can be achieved.

We have a feminist movement tending to equality of rights, social, educational and political. We aspire to women suffrage, when once our independence is attained. We can meet every objection that is raised in that quarter with a good sound argument, and I think the country will benefit from our services.

And now we come to the political movement in our country. The Egyptian woman is taking an active part in the national movement. We are not actuated by hatred of the British who happen to be the rulers of our country today, but we are actuated by a great love for our country, and we realise that no great progress can be made for our welfare unless we Egyptians hold ourselves responsible for the state of our country, and can govern it in the right way. It was the National Movement that awoke the Egyptian woman to realise what was needed for the emancipation of her country, and it is through her efforts in that direction that she detected the moral drawbacks of the nation and that she is trying to remedy.

The Egyptian woman cannot be thwarted in her efforts for the freedom of her industry. She knows the obstacles that confront her, it is not so much the Imperialistic power with all its militarism and diplomacy – that need be conquered – but it is the weakness and demoralised state of the people which she is fighting against and that is the greater obstacle. But she knows that the fight and conflict which they have to go through is the only purifying remedy that can clear away the dross that has mixed itself with the pure gold of the ancient civilisation, therefore she does not lose heart. She is aware that when her people can stand on their feet and defy wrong, and never lend themselves to wrong, the independence of their country will be acquired, and instead of patron and patronized, we would have developed into a trustworthy nation, fit to hold its own with any other power, and a friendly co-operative alliance can be enacted.

Independence has to start in the heart of the individual before it can be in possession of the nation. Liberty has to be the liberty of soul before it can be the liberty of a country, and when men lend themselves to corruption, bribery and lust, no hope of liberty can be entertained.

I do not blame the various foreign countries exploiting our failings, but I blame my own people for allowing themselves to be exploited. We have a wonderful Arabic colloquial saying, which is very true: 'Walk straight, your enemy will not know where to attack you'. How true is that saying. We want straightforward, honest, true men, and our country will attain her end.

The women of Egypt have implicit faith in their cause. They believe that their country is going to be one of the moral, leading powers of the world, and although they know the sacrifice that has to be offered, and the affliction that their country has to pass through, yet they are willing to advance, and they know that they will arrive. They, like Abraham, have accepted to offer Isaac on the alter of sacrifice, but they are also certain that when this obedient spirit to duty is conceived, the redeeming ram will be forthcoming, and their hopes for their country are very great.

And as a last word to this interesting gathering who represent a privileged set of my countrymen and women, I say, every one of you is responsible for the welfare of Egypt. You have a chance of acquiring education on the best lines. Put it to advantage, make the best of your chances, and offer it in the service of your country. Never think but that each one of you is responsible for the moral upbuilding of your country, and each one of you has to be a detectless foundation stone in this building, for if any structure is feeble, the fault lies in the individual stone, so your responsibility is very great. And it is only when we awaken to a keen sense of responsibility that any sound construction can be erected, and Egypt, rising Egypt, has every hope in you.

We do not want to hear your criticisms of your countrymen. We want to hear you individually acknowledging your own faults, and making up your minds to do away with them. We want to feel that you are wide awake to the needs of your country, and that you are ready to sacrifice every self interest to the honest upright service of the great cause. We want you to be true to yourselves, so that you can be true to others. We want to know that your own self-respect is attained, and the respect of others will be your reward.

We want above all solidarity, a firm, loving, wise solidarity, which can never be broken, a solidarity which overlooks any self-interest, which forgives all personal wrongs, but which never forgets the interests of the community, and which strikes hard on every wrong that affects its principles.

We want you young men and women here in this country to remember that you represent Egypt, that every slackness on your part reflects on the country, which is so much in need of those who support her. One generation has to lay itself down to found the great structure that will be the future Egypt. We women have decided to sacrifice ourselves to this end, and we have every hope that you will join hands with us in this great effort which will mark the date of the new birth of Egypt the blessed.

Esther Fahmy Wissa.

# Appendix 12

*Coptic Women Combat Illiteracy*

(*The Christian Science Monitor*, Boston, Tuesday, July 23, 1929)

'To fight illiteracy and foster the arts' is the aim of Mme. Esther Fahmy Wissa Bey, the distinguished Egyptian feminist. She is a Copt, that is to say, an Egyptian Christian, of aristocratic lineage and great wealth, who helped start the womens' movement in 1918. Since then she has divided her time between encouraging the Nationalists in their struggle for independence and in organizing social welfare work among the women.

'I foresee the day when Egypt will be free to work out her own destiny,' Mme. Wissa declares, 'And when that day comes our women must be ready to share fully in the advancement of our country.'

Few women of contemporary Egypt are so well equipped as Mme. Wissa to lead the cultivated minority of women in the vital work of social betterment. As a student of the civilization of ancient Egypt, she knows what Egyptian women achieved in the past. And as a friend of Saad Zaghlul Pasha, as well as of those patriots who now strive to carry on his policies, she has secured a thorough grasp of the problems of the present era. It is her conviction that the progress of Egypt depends chiefly on the moral fiber of her people which must be strengthened by educating the masses.

'We need a Moses to lead us and through uplifting our women we will develop one,' Mme. Wissa told me recently.

## Societies for Women's Advancement

To open doors of educational opportunities for women she employs her brilliant gifts as journalist, polemic speaker and organizer. Not content with the opening of training schools for girls, which alone was a great victory for women, she enlisted the support of many of the wealthiest women of Egypt to form the New Woman Society. Together they raised sufficient funds to start a school for orphans, where in addition to elementary training, girls are taught rug-making and fine needle work. Formerly orphans were fortunate in securing employment as inexperienced servants but today they go forth equipped to earn the wages of skilled artisans.

Encouraged by the success of this effort, Mme. Wissa determined to dig still deeper at the roots of ignorance. For years she has befriended the wives of the fellahin, Egypt's vast army of illiterate peasants, who toil on the cotton lands of the Nile Valley, and she has given aid to the desperately poor of Cairo and of Alexandria. From this intimate study she was convinced that to reach bedrock in social betterment, a way must be devised to instruct mothers. With this purpose in view she organized the Work for Egypt Society which opened child welfare units in Cairo and Alexandria. Just as this movement was being launched, cotton, which is the backbone of Egypt's prosperity, declined in value and the political situation grew steadily more involved. All of her resourcefulness was taxed to the utmost to keep her colleagues united and enthusiastic in the arduous task of its maintenance. Last year Mme. Wissa organized an education fête at Alexandria which was such excellent entertainment that donations from the men equalled those of the women. Eighty boys and girls took part in this historical pageant built around the picturesque personality of King Tut-ankh-Amen. In the background this great king was shown reviewing the glories of his day revealed to him in dance and song. Then the climax came with his vision of Egypt's destiny in a far-off day – a virile, free country working independently to promote peace among nations.

## Working Through an Interim

After such an enterprise, it is scarcely surprising that the Minister of Education yielded to the plea of the society to add a course in child welfare to the curriculum of the training school for girls.

Soon after, and while other important measures were pending, the Cabinet fell and parliament was suspended for three years. This political crisis is a severe limitation on all programs for social betterment, but the women are accustomed to waiting, watching and working. Every reform to date has been achieved under difficulties. The Coptic women are thoroughly aware of the needs of their country, and are determined that education work shall proceed. 'If it is necessary, we shall go back into the political arena, where we started our work of freedom for ourselves and for Egypt,' declares Esther Fahmy Wissa, the intrepid leader of the Christian women.

# Bibliography

Dr. Andrew Watson, *The American Missions in Egypt 1854–1896* Presbyterian Board of Publication Pittsburg U.S.A.

Field Marshal Wavell, *Allenby* George G. Harrap & Co. Ltd., London, Sydney, Toronto and Bombay

Jasper Yeates Brinton, *The American Effort in Egypt* Alexandria 1972

Walter A. Fairservio Junior, *The Ancient Kingdom, of the Nile* Mentor Books U.S.A. October 1962

John Russell Young, *Around the World with General Grant*

Alfred Tillyard, *Agnes E. Slack* Heffer Sons Ltd. Cambridge England 1926

Juliette Adam, *L'Angleterre en Egypte* Imprimerie de Centre 1922 Paris

Kyriakos Mikhail, *Copts and Moslems under British Control (Egypt)* Published by Smith Elder & Co. 1911 London

Gardner Wilkinson, *The Customs and Manners of the Ancient Egyptians* Pub. John Murray 1878

Artemis Cooper, *Cairo* Hamish Hamilton Ltd. London

Dr. Riad Sorial, *The Coptic Community in Egypt in the Nineteenth Century* Cairo

Georges Posener with the assistance of Serge Sauneron & Jean Yoyotte, *A Dictionary of Egyptian Civilisation* Methuen & Co. Ltd – London WC2

Cyril Aldred, *The Egyptians* Thames & Hudson Ltd. 1962

Frederic W. Fuller, *Egypt and the Hinterland* Longmans Green & Co., London, New York & Bombay 1903

Jean & Simone Lacouture, *Egypt in Transition* Methuen & Co. Ltd. London

Lord Lloyd, *Egypt Since Cromer* Vol 1 & 2 Macmillan & Co. Ltd. London 1932

Dr. Ibrahim Noshi, *Egypt in the Days of the Ptolemies* Cairo

Veronica Ions, *Egyptian Mythology* Hamlyn Publishing Group Ltd. Middlesex

Amal Kamel Bayoumi el-Soubky, *The Feminist Movement in Egypt Between Two Revolutions 1919–1952* Published Cairo 1986

Librairie Hachette, *Les Guides Bleus – Egypte* Paris 1956

Manfred Lurkes, *The Gods and Symbols of Ancient Egypt* Fakenhan Press Ltd. Fakenham Norfolk

Robert A Armour, *Gods and Myths of Ancient Egypt* Printed by the American University, Cairo

Darl el Hilal, *Hoda Chaarawi's Memoires* Published in Arabic ISBN-977-7031-97-2

Daniele Ragheb, *Hoda Chaarawi* Cairo

Sylvester Chaleur, *Histore des Coptes d'Egypte*

Amin Youssef Bey, *Independent Egypt* Pub. John Murray, Albermarle St. London

Trevor E. Evans, *Killearn Diaries 1934–1936* Pub. Sidgwick & Jackson – London

Beth Prim Howell, *The Lady on the Donkey* Pub. E.P. Doulton & Co. New York

Gordon Waterfield, *Lucie Duff Gordon* Pub. John Murray, Albermarle St. London

Renah Hogg, *A Master Builder on the Nile*

Adam George Benis, *Une Mission Militaire Polonaise en Egypte* Cairo 1938

Cairo, *Memoirs of Fakhry Abdel Nour on the 1919 Revolution*

Cairo, *Memoirs of Salib Sami 1891–1952*

Otto F.A. Meinardus, *Monks and Monasteries of the Egyptian Deserts* The American University, Cairo Press, Cairo

St. Mary's Monastery Al-Muharrag, *Mount Qousqam* Assiout, Egypt

Earl of Cromer, *Modern Egypt Vol. 1 & 2* Macmillan & Co. Ltd. London 1908

Tom Little, *Modern Egypt* Ernest Benn Ltd. London

S.H Leader, *Modern Sons of the Pharoahs* Hodder & Stoughton, London, New York, Toronto

Raymond Flower, *Napoleon to Nasser* Printed by Compton Press, Wilts, G.B.

Ramses and Roly, *Oriental Spotlight* Printed in Great Britain by Butler & Tanner Ltd. Frome and London

Edouard Driault, *Précis de l'Histoire d'Egypte*

Angelo San Marco, *Précis de l'Histoire d'Egypte*

Emile Selim Amad, *La Question d'Egypte 1841 – 1938* Les Editions Internationales, Paris 1938

Brian M. Fagan, *The Rape of the Nile* Macdonald & James Pub. London

Gallini Pasha Fahmy, *Souvenirs* Cairo

Mohsen Mohammed, *Saad Zaghloul* Cairo

Foulad Yeghen, *Saad Zaghloul* Les Cahiers de France 1927

E.L. Butcher, *The Story of the Church of Egypt – two vols.* Smith Eldes & Co. 1897 London

Earl E. Elder, *Vindicating a Vision*

Baron Firmin Van Den Bosche, *Vingt Années d'Egypte* Lib. Academique Perrin Paris 1932

Mrs. Phoebe Choucri, *Y.W.C.A.* Cairo

# INDEX

448

Cyril the Reformer 90, 109

disease 440
Doss, Habib Bey 178
drug traffic 438
drugs 441
Dual Control by France and Britain 66, 79, 141, 144

Ebeid, Makram 129, 190, 294, 303
  at wedding 351; *353*
education 121, 154, 440; *see also* schools
Edward VII 109
Egypt 202; *see also* Ancient Egypt; British in Egypt
  1919 Revolution 190, 201, 202, 206
  1952 Revolution 30, 58, 121, 201
  agriculture policy 56, 58, 148, 160
  Arab rule 25–33
  British and French influence 141, 144–5
  character of people 170
  Christianity 24–7, 68, 107, 141
  constitution (1923) 162, 223–5, 231, 244, 259, 262, 293
  courts 65
  currency 218 n
  debts 63, 66, 78, 142, 144
  Dual Control 65, 79, 141, 144
  economy 263
  elections 232, 238, 244, 259, 279, 303
  feminist movement 190, 192, 194, 196–7, 226
  French invasion 42; *43*
  Islamic conquest 28–42
  land ownership 39, 58, 76–7, 81–3
  language 17
  Memlukes rule 35–6, 38
  Moslem religion adopted 28–9
  nationalism 143, 148, 198–203, 213, 226, 406
  parliament 245–6
  politics (1923–5) 231–40; (1925–8) 242–50; (1928–36) 259, 262
  Protectorate (1914) 55, 161–65,

  198–9, 212–21, 418–20
  religions 141, 143, 442
  social welfare 194
  struggle for independence 148, 190, 198–203, 226
  and the Sudan 68–73; map 69
  taxation 78–80, 146, 234
  titles 294, 297
  tolerance of religions 55, 56
  Turks rule 38–42, 143–5
  universal suffrage 224
  writing 17
Egyptian Feminist Union 194, 197
Egyptian Movement 418
Egyptian Museum, Cairo 63
Egyptian Revolution (1952) 30, 58, 121
Egyptian Women's Union 230
El Nil, Dada Bahr 170
emancipation of Egyptian women 190, 192, 194, 196–7, 226–30, 426–46
Europeans 61, 65

Fahmy, Gallini Pasha 105; *142*
Fanous, Aida 186, 254
Fanous, Akhnoukh 28, 130, 135, 170, 173
  death 197
  marriage 102–4
Fanous, Balsam 103–105, 130, 170, 174, 318
Fanous, Esther Akhnoukh *see* Wissa, Esther
Fanous, Gamila 186, 241, 269
Fanous, Louis Akhnoukh 170, 279, 420; *352–3*
  at Oxford University 122, 128
  in the Senate 128; *298*
Fanous, Mingida 102–3, 170
Fanous, Raphael 102, 170
Fanous, Riad 170
Fanous, Sami 170
Fanous family *171, 172*
Farid, Mohammed 148
Farouk, King 175, 262; *278, 280, 296*
  influenced by Maher 263
  patron of football club 279; *278*

452

453